German for Reading

German for Reading

A Programmed Approach

Second Edition

Karl C. Sandberg
MACALESTER COLLEGE

John R. Wendel
UNIVERSITY OF ARIZONA

Focus *an imprint of*
Hackett Publishing Company, Inc.
Indianapolis/Cambridge

A Focus book

Focus *an imprint of*
Hackett Publishing Company

Printed in the United States of America

18 17 16 15 1 2 3 4 5 6 7

For further information, please address
Hackett Publishing Company, Inc.
P.O. Box 44937
Indianapolis, Indiana 46244-0937

www.hackettpublishing.com

Cover design by Brian Rak
Composition by Integrated Composition Systems, Spokane, Washington

Library of Congress Cataloging-in-Publication Data

Sandberg, Karl C., author.
German for reading: a programmed approach / Karl C. Sandberg, Macalester College;
John R. Wendel, University of Arizona. — Second Edition.
pages cm
Includes index.
ISBN 978-1-58510-745-2 (pbk.)
1. German language—Programmed instruction. I. Wendel, John R., author II. Title.
PF3112.5.S2 2015
438.2'421—dc23 2015006317

The paper used in this publication meets the minimum requirements of American National Standard for Information Sciences—Permanence of Paper for Printed Library Materials, ANSI Z39.48–1984.

Contents

Chapter Six

Chapter Seven

Chapter Eight

Chapter Nine

Chapter Ten

Chapter Eleven

To the Student

You may find it helpful at the outset to know the assumptions of the authors. We gladly state them: language is the most significant and fascinating of human phenomena; serious scholars read other languages than their own; for everyone it is interesting and enlightening to see how another culture expresses its perception of reality through its language; everyone can learn language; everyone who can learn his own language can learn a new language; the principles and techniques of programmed learning can significantly increase the efficiency and decrease the frustrations of language study.

We have also assumed that your study time is valuable and that if you have been introduced to this text it is because sometime you seriously wanted to learn to read German. We have therefore made use of new approaches and developments in programmed learning in order to provide you with the most systematic and direct means possible of doing so.

German for Reading presupposes no previous acquaintance with German and can be used with equal effectiveness by graduate students in the arts and sciences who are preparing to pass a reading knowledge examination, or by undergraduates who are beginning to deal seriously with the problems of reading. It may be used before, simultaneously with, or after an aural-oral introduction to German. Its programmed format permits it to be used either as a classroom text or by individuals working on their own.

In a course emphasizing oral proficiency, *German for Reading* can be used as a complement to the principal text; in a course oriented toward reading, it can be used as the primary text, with the course moving at a proportionately more rapid rate.

Although the primary aim of *German for Reading* is to give you, the student, the foundation for beginning to read in many specialized fields, it is also a cultural reader. Reading passages have been chosen to acquaint you with significant figures, for good or ill we might add, in the broad range of German culture: history, literature, philosophy, politics, psychology, sociology, and theology.

What you may expect to get out of the course

When you finish *German for Reading* you should be able to recognize the meanings signaled by all the basic grammatical patterns of German, plus the meanings of about twelve hundred content words. You will also have developed numerous techniques of reading in a foreign language which will enable you to learn new vocabulary and derive meanings from context without depending totally on a dictionary. With some additional work to build vocabulary in special fields, you will be able to start using German as an academic tool in research or in coursework in some field. You should be able, for example, to read a German newspaper or journal with fair to good comprehension or to begin the serious study of German literary texts.

What you should expect to put into the course

The above results are predictable on the basis of classroom testing and depend on your fulfilling the following conditions:

1. That you spend the 80–120 hours of study time that it has taken other students to complete the course.
2. That you study and review *consistently.*
3. That you familiarize yourself with the theoretical base of the book and follow the instructions.

Format of the text

One of the basic assumptions of *German for Reading* is that among the 10,000–20,000 words that one must be able to recognize in order to read German easily (estimates differ), the first priority in order of presentation should go to the function words (those that do not have a meaning in and of themselves, e.g., **wo**, *where* or **denn**, *for*) and grammatical signals (e.g., verb endings) as opposed to the content words (the words that do express a meaning by themselves, e.g., **vergessen**, *to forget* or **Pferd**, *horse*). It is the function words and grammar structures of the language which provide the framework of context. Accordingly, this text is so organized as to make a systematic presentation of the patterns and function words of German while helping you to develop reading skills and to build a basic recognition vocabulary of content words.

Each chapter is thus composed of several sets of grammar explanations with accompanying exercises and a short reading passage. As you do these exercises, you will find that they introduce the vocabulary and structures of the reading passage while also reviewing pertinent material from previous chapters. Each exercise calls for some kind of response from you and is programmed through the left-hand column to provide you with an immediate verification of the accuracy of your response. At the end of each chapter is a progress test which enables you to determine for yourself how well you have learned the material.

The advantages of this format are numerous—you spend all of your time in active reading instead of in the mechanical process of thumbing to the end vocabulary; you are not dependent on the classroom or professor in order to establish meaning; you can thus proceed as rapidly as you want to or as slowly as you need to; and at the same time you are learning to read eminent German writers in their own words almost at the outset.

How to use the text

1. Begin each section by reading the explanations of the grammar. If the terminology used is unfamiliar to you, consult the definitions of grammatical terms in the appendices.
2. Proceed then to do the exercises following each section. They ask for some kind of response from you, such as supplying the missing words, choosing the correct alternative, or simply stating the meaning of the German sentence. *Cover the left-hand verification column with a card until you have made the response asked for.*
3. After you have made an active response to the German sentence, slide your card down on the left-hand column and verify your answer. When the instructions ask you to translate the German to English, remember that there are often several ways of translating to achieve the same meaning. Your version does not need to coincide exactly with the version in the text so long as the general meaning is the same.

   The success or failure of your efforts depends to a large extent on how well you follow this procedure. If you do not make a real effort to read the German before looking at the

English, you will probably not be able to read the German passage at the end of the section.

4. Each time you meet a word that you do not recognize immediately, underline it. After you learn its meaning put a circle around it (but *do not* write the English equivalent between the lines). After you have finished the set of exercises, review the circled words, and associate them with their context.
5. Then take the progress test and see which points you need to review. Learn each block of material thoroughly before going on.
6. Study in short blocks of time. If you were to allot two hours a day to the study of German, it would be better to divide them into four periods of thirty minutes each than to spend the two hours consecutively.
7. *Review frequently!* Before each new chapter, spend five minutes or so reviewing the words you have circled in the previous chapter.

A note regarding German spellings

German spellings in this book are not in accordance with the reforms in force since August 1998. As the first edition was put together in the early 1970s, using original German texts predating this period, it has not been thought necessary to update this current edition with changes in usage currently in vogue. In fact, it should be to the student's advantage to see how the way the language was before current usage.

Acknowledgments to the First Edition

The authors are indebted to many colleagues and students for advice and helpful criticism in the preparation of this text. Special thanks are due to Professor Richard Clark of Macalester College for help in conducting a testing program of a preliminary version, to Professor Otto Sorenson of Macalester for a critical reading of the manuscript, to Mrs. Barbara Heather of the University of Arizona for much help and valued assistance in the preparation of the manuscript, and to students at Macalester and the University of Arizona who generously shared their responses and offered suggestions for the revision of the preliminary text.

K.S.
J.W.

Acknowledgments to the Second Edition

This edition of *German For Reading* would not have seen the light of day had it not been for an inquiry from Brian Rak, editorial director of Hackett Publishing Company, regarding a possible second edition of this book.

My thanks go to him for his support; to Liz Wilson, production director at Hackett Publishing; Lori Rider, copyeditor; Suzanne Harris, composition and page-layout manager; Laura Clark and Jill Cooley, production coordinators; Marie Deer, proofreader; and unknown others who have contributed to making this edition possible.

The current revision has been significantly enhanced by the helpful suggestions and critiques of three anonymous readers. Wherever possible, I've endeavored to incorporate their suggestions into the materials of the book.

I regret to say that since the first edition of *German For Reading*, my colleague and the inspiration behind this book is no longer with us. His knowledge, wit, and insights are sorely missed.

J.R.W.

Chapter One

1. *Cognates—definition*
2. *Nouns—recognition, gender, and cognate patterns*
3. *Nouns—formation of the plural forms*
4. *Compound nouns*
5. *Cognates—partially similar meanings*
6. *False cognates*

1. *Cognates—definition*

1. The task of learning German vocabulary is simplified by *true cognates*, i.e., words which have similar spellings and identical or similar meanings. From common Germanic roots come cognates such as **Sommer** and *summer*, **Wolf** and *wolf.* From other common roots come cognates such as **Echo** and *echo*, **Sphäre** and *sphere.*

2. The task is sometimes hindered by *partial cognates* (words which look alike but have both similar and divergent meanings) and *false cognates* (words with similar spellings but no related meanings).

Partial cognates:

Existenz = *existence* but also *subsistence*
Fleisch = *flesh* but also *meat* or *pulp*

False cognates:

Rock = *coat, skirt*
Kind = *child*

3. A logical first step in learning to read German is to learn how to recognize the true cognates and to become aware of the partial or false cognates.

2. *Nouns—recognition, gender, and cognate patterns*

1. All nouns in German are capitalized:

Der Mann trinkt ein Glas Bier. *The man drinks a glass of beer.*

2. German nouns, unlike English nouns, are one of three genders: masculine, feminine, or neuter. Masculine nouns are often preceded by a form of **der** (*the*) or **ein** (*a* or *an*), feminine nouns by a form of **die** or **eine**, and neuter nouns by a form of **das** or **ein**. (The case of these articles will be explained in chapter 4.)

3. A knowledge of the following consonant relationships which exist between German and English will help you to recognize or remember German-English cognates more readily:

	GERMAN	ENGLISH
f, ff (medial or final)	usually corresponds to	*p*
	ein Schiff	*a ship*
	die Hilfe	*the help*
pf (initial, medial, or final)	usually corresponds to	*p, pp*
	der Pfeffer	*the pepper*
	ein Apfel	*an apple*
	der Trumpf	*the trump*
b (medial or final)	usually corresponds to	*v* or *f*
	das Silber	*the silver*
	taub	*deaf*
d	usually corresponds to	*th*
	die Erde	*the earth*
	ein Bruder	*a brother*
ch	usually corresponds to	*k*
	die Milch	*the milk*
	der Mönch	*the monk*
cht	usually corresponds to	*ght*
	die Macht	*the might*
	ein Licht	*a light*
g	usually corresponds to	*y* or *i*
	der Weg	*the way*
	eine Magd	*a maid*
k	usually corresponds to	*ch* or *c*
	der Käse	*the cheese*
	die Klasse	*the class*
s, ss, ß (medial or final)	usually corresponds to	*t*
	eine Straße	*a street*
	das Wasser	*the water*
	das Los	*the lot (fate)*
tz, z	usually corresponds to	*t*
	eine Katze	*a cat*
	das Salz	*the salt*
t	usually corresponds to	*d*
	das Wort	*the word*
	der Traum	*the dream*

What are the English cognates of the following German words?

	1. ein Affe
1. *an ape*	**2.** der Pfeffer
2. *the pepper*	**3.** ein Pfund
3. *a pound*	**4.** die Pflaume
4. *the plum*	**5.** ein Tropfen
5. *a drop*	**6.** der Dieb
6. *the thief*	**7.** die Leber
7. *the liver*	**8.** eine Öffnung
8. *an opening*	**9.** die Pfeife
9. *the pipe*	**10.** ein Ding
10. *a thing*	**11.** eine Feder
11. *a feather*	**12.** der Schmied
12. *the smith*	**13.** die Milch
13. *the milk*	**14.** der Storch
14. *the stork*	**15.** ein Kuchen
15. *a cake*	**16.** die Leuchte
16. *the light*	**17.** die Nacht
17. *the night*	**18.** das Recht
18. *the right*	**19.** das Leder
19. *leather*	**20.** eine Tochter

20. *a daughter*	**21.** der Pfennig
21. *the penny*	**22.** ein Auge
22. *an eye*	**23.** der Nagel
23. *the nail*	**24.** eine Kirche
24. *a church*	**25.** das Kinn
25. *the chin*	**26.** ein Kamerad
26. *a comrade*	**27.** der Schweiß
27. *the sweat*	**28.** der Regen
28. *the rain*	**29.** eine Kammer
29. *a chamber*	**30.** die Hitze
30. *the heat*	**31.** das Zinn
31. *tin*	**32.** das Herz
32. *the heart*	**33.** der Tag
33. *the day*	**34.** das Blut
34. *the blood*	**35.** ein Netz
35. *a net*	**36.** die Zunge
36. *the tongue*	**37.** eine Tür
37. *a door*	

PROGRESS TEST

Give the English cognate of the following German words.

	1. eine Pfeife
1. *a pipe*	**2.** die Leber
2. *the liver*	**3.** das Ding
3. *the thing*	**4.** ein Kuchen
4. *a cake*	**5.** die Nacht
5. *the night*	**6.** ein Auge
6. *an eye*	**7.** ein Kamerad
7. *a comrade*	**8.** das Kinn
8. *the chin*	**9.** die Hitze
9. *the heat*	**10.** das Herz
10. *the heart*	**11.** der Tag
11. *the day*	

When you can recognize all of the above consonant shifts, go on to the next section.

3. *Nouns—formation of the plural forms*

1. Written English usually signals the plural by means of a final *-s* (table, table*s*), a vowel change (m*a*n, m*e*n), or by a quantity word + *-s* or a vowel change (*some* chair*s*, *some* m*e*n). Written German usually signals the plural of nouns by the use of the definite article **die** (or a quantity word) plus

(a) the noun endings **-e, -er, -n, -en:**

der Arm	*the arm*	**die Arm*e***	*the arms*
das Kind	*the child*	**die Kind*er***	*the children*

der Staat	*the state*	**die Staat*en***	*the states*
die Frau	*the woman*	**die Frau*en***	*the women*
der Bauer	*the farmer*	**die Bauer*n***	*the farmers*

(b) an umlaut added to a medial vowel:

der Vater	*the father*	**die V*ä*ter**	*the fathers*
die Tochter	*the daughter*	**die T*ö*chter**	*the daughters*

(c) the noun endings and an umlaut:

die Hand	*the hand*	**die H*ä*nd*e***	*the hands*
der Fuß	*the foot*	**die F*ü*ß*e***	*the feet*
der Mann	*the man*	**die M*ä*nn*er***	*the men*
das Buch	*the book*	**die B*ü*ch*er***	*the books*

Notice that you must look for a *combination* of **die** (or various plural markers to be discussed later, e.g., **diese**, *these*) and one of the above:

das Mädchen	*the girl*	***die* Mädchen**	*the girls*
die Mutter	*the mother*	**die M*ü*tter**	*the mothers*

Since **Mädchen** carries an umlaut in the singular, the only way to tell the plural is by the addition of **die. Mutter,** being feminine, takes **die** as the definite article in both the singular and the plural, and the plural is therefore recognized only by the addition of the umlaut.

2. There are a few words ending in **-el** or **-en** that add neither an ending nor an umlaut. The plural of these words is signaled only by the definite article **die:**

der Onkel	*the uncle*	***die* Onkel**	*the uncles*
der Wagen	*the car*	***die* Wagen**	*the cars*

3. Some nouns taken from modern foreign languages form their plural by adding **-s:**

das Auto	**die Auto*s***
das Restaurant	**die Restaurant*s***
das Hotel	**die Hotel*s***
das Radio	**die Radio*s***

4. The ending **-(e)s** is usually the sign of the genitive (possessive) case of masculine and neuter nouns in the singular, which will be explained later.

Which of the following is the plural form? What distinguishes it from the singular?

	1. der Garten die Gärten
1. **die Gärten:** the umlaut and **die** (*gardens*)	2. die Töchter die Tochter
2. **die Töchter:** the umlaut (*daughters*)	3. der Finger die Finger
3. **die Finger: die** (*fingers*)	4. die Maus die Mäuse
4. **die Mäuse: -e** and umlaut (*mice*)	5. der Arm die Arme
5. **die Arme: -e** and **die** (*arms*)	6. der Fuß die Füße
6. **die Füße: -e**, umlaut, and **die** (*feet*)	7. die Haare das Haar
7. **die Haare: -e** and **die** (*hair*)	8. das Buch die Bücher
8. **die Bücher: -er**, umlaut, and **die** (*books*)	9. die Männer der Mann
9. **die Männer: -er**, umlaut, and **die** (*men*)	10. die Felder das Feld
10. **die Felder: -er** and **die** (*fields*)	11. der Onkel die Onkel
11. **die Onkel: die** (*uncles*)	12. das Haus die Häuser
12. **die Häuser: -er**, umlaut, and **die** (*houses*)	13. die Lippe die Lippen
13. **die Lippen: -n** (*lips*)	14. die Klassen die Klasse
14. **die Klassen: -n** (*classes*)	15. die Familien die Familie
15. **die Familien: -n** (*families*)	16. die Türen die Tür
16. **die Türen: -en** (*doors*)	17. die Radios das Radio
17. **die Radios: -s** and **die** (*radios*)	18. das Café die Cafés
18. **die Cafés: -s** and **die** (*cafés*)	19. die Minute die Minuten

19. die Minuten: -n (*minutes*)	**20.** der Satellit die Satelliten
20. die Satelliten: -en and **die** (*satellites*)	**21.** die Nacht die Nächte
21. die Nächte: -e and umlaut (*nights*)	**22.** die Schulen die Schule
22. die Schulen: -n (*schools*)	**23.** die Sofas das Sofa
23. die Sofas: -s and **die** (*sofas*)	**24.** das Licht die Lichter
24. die Lichter: -er and **die** (*lights*)	**25.** die Sonne die Sonnen
25. die Sonnen: -n (*suns*)	

PROGRESS TEST

Which of the following forms is the plural?

	1. die Töchter die Tochter
1. die Töchter	**2.** die Onkel der Onkel
2. die Onkel	**3.** die Füße der Fuß
3. die Füße	**4.** das Buch die Bücher
4. die Bücher	**5.** die Lippen die Lippe
5. die Lippen	**6.** die Studenten der Student
6. die Studenten	**7.** das Hotel die Hotels
7. die Hotels	

When you can recognize the plural forms of the above nouns, go on to the next section.

4. *Compound nouns*

1. Characteristic of German is the coining of new words by combining simpler German words:

krank (*sick*) + **das Haus** (*house*) = **das Krankenhaus** (*hospital*)
die Hand (*hand*) + **der Schuh** (*shoe*) = **der Handschuh** (*glove*)
das Wasser (*water*) + **der Stoff** (*stuff*) = **der Wasserstoff** (*hydrogen*)
das Volk (*people*) + **der Wagen** (*car*) = **der Volkswagen**

As in the first and last example above, there is often a connective (**-(e)s-** or **-(e)n-**) between the two elements, but this will not hinder your comprehension of the word.

2. The gender of the noun is determined by the last component.

3. The plural of a compound noun is determined by the plural of the last component:

das Krankenhaus	*the hospital*
die Krankenhäuser	*the hospitals*
die Wasserstoffbombe	*the hydrogen bomb*
die Wasserstoffbomben	*the hydrogen bombs*

Guess the meanings of the following compound nouns.

	1. **der Zahn** = *tooth* **der Arzt** = *doctor* **der Zahnarzt** = __________
1. *dentist*	2. **das Jahr** = *year* **die Zeit** = *time* **die Jahreszeit** = __________
2. *season*	3. **der Flug** = *flight* **der Hafen** = *harbor, port* **der Flughafen** = __________
3. *airport*	4. **das Schwein** = *pig, swine* **das Fleisch** = *meat* **das Schweinefleisch** = __________
4. *pork*	5. **die Bürger** = *townspeople, citizens* **der Meister** = *master* **der Bürgermeister** = __________
5. *mayor*	6. **sich rasieren** = *to shave* **der Apparat** = *apparatus* **der Rasierapparat** = __________
6. *razor*	7. **das Leben** = *life* **das Mittel** = *means* **das Geschäft** = *business, shop* **das Lebensmittelgeschäft** = __________

7. *grocery store*	8. **unter** = *under* **der Grund** = *ground* **die Bahn** = *railroad, railway* **die Untergrundbahn** = __________
8. *subway*	9. **das Leder** = *leather* **die Ware** = *goods* **die Produktion** = *production* **die Lederwarenproduktion** = __________
9. *production of leather goods* *Note the reversal of the two parts and the added "of".	10. **die Sonne** = *sun* **das System** = *system* **das Sonnensystem** = __________
10. *solar system*	11. **das Silber** = *silver* **der Berg** = *mountain* **das Werk** = *work(s)* **das Silberbergwerk** = __________
11. *silver mine*	12. **der Friede** = *peace* **der Hof** = *yard, court* **der Friedhof** = __________
12. *cemetery*	

5. *Cognates—partially similar meanings*

1. A German cognate may have meanings additional to its English counterpart:

die Seite	*side*	but also	*page* (of a book)
die Macht	*might*		*authority*
der Hund	*hound*		*dog*

2. The meanings of partial cognates must be determined from the context or from a dictionary:

	1. **Der Vater sitzt mit der kleinen Tochter auf der Bank.** = *The father is sitting on the* __________ *with his small daughter.* The German **Bank** suggests the English *bank* which normally would not make sense in this context. Remember in German the letter **k** may often be equivalent to the English *ch*. The word is __________.
1. *bench*	2. **Es gibt Eis zum Nachtisch.** = *There is* __________ *for dessert.* The reference to dessert suggests that **Eis** would not be translated by *ice* but by __________.

2. *ice cream*	3. **Darf man den Brief mit einer Feder schreiben?** = *Is it all right to (can you) write the letter with a ___________?* Here the context suggests that the translation of **Feder** is not *feather* but __________
3. *pen*	

6. *False cognates*

1. Many false cognates exist between German and English. Since the meaning will not always be discernible from the context, you will have to establish the meaning by means of a dictionary:

das Tier	*the animal* (not *deer*)
der Tisch	*the table* (not *dish*)
das Gift	*the poison* (not *gift*)

What is the English meaning of the italicized words?

	1. Der Mensch ist ein *Tier.* Man is an ___________.
1. *animal*	2. Nimm die Ellbogen vom *Tisch*! Take your elbows off the ___________!
2. *table*	3. Der Löwe ist der König der *Tiere.* The lion is the king of ___________.
3. *beasts*	4. Arsen ist ein gefährliches *Gift.* Arsenic is a dangerous ___________.
4. *poison*	5. Er sitzt am *Tisch* und liest die Zeitung. He is sitting at the ___________ reading the paper.
5. *table*	6. *Gift* ist kein schönes Geschenk. ___________ is not a nice gift.
6. *Poison*	

Chapter Two

7. *Verbs—cognates*
8. *Verbs—partial and false cognates*
9. *Present tense verb endings; personal pronouns*
10. Es gibt, es ist, es sind

Reading: Die Geographie Deutschlands

7. *Verbs—cognates*

1. All German verbs in their infinitive form end in **-en** or sometimes simply **-n:**

beginn*en*	*to begin*
wander*n*	*to hike, to walk, to wander*

There are many cognate verbs in German and English which will facilitate your learning to read.

2. Remember that infinitives may also be used as nouns simply by capitalizing the verb. The gender will always be neuter. To translate an infinitive used as a noun into English add *-ing* to the English infinitive:

beginnen	*to begin*
das Beginnen	*the beginning*
trinken	*to drink*
das Trinken	*the drinking*

(If any of the grammatical terms in these explanations is unfamiliar, please consult the glossary of grammatical terms in the Appendices.)

Cover the left-hand column with your card. Give the meaning of the German words. Move your card down to verify your rendering

	1. bringen
1. *to bring*	**2.** denken
2. *to think*	**3.** finden
3. *to find*	**4.** hindern

4. *to hinder*	**5.** sinken
5. *to sink*	**6.** das Sinken
6. *(the) sinking*	**7.** schlummern
7. *to slumber*	**8.** kämmen
8. *to comb*	**9.** kommen
9. *to come*	**10.** das Kommen
10. *(the) coming*	**11.** das Marschieren
11. *(the) marching*	**12.** marschieren
12. *to march*	**13.** suchen
13. *to seek, to look for, to search for*	

8. *Verbs—partial and false cognates*

1. Some partial German-English cognates are as follows:

liegen	*to lie, to be situated*
lernen	*to learn, to study*
sagen	*to say, to tell*
scheinen	*to shine, to seem, to appear*
tun	*to do, to make, to put*

2. False cognates, such as the following, need to be memorized:

bilden	*to form, to educate*
bekommen	*to receive, to get*
handeln	*to act, to trade, to bargain*
mangeln	*to lack, to be wanting*

The following exercises prepare you to read the passage at the end of the chapter on the geography of Germany.

	1. In the verb **schieben**, you might expect the **b** to become ___________ in English.
1. **v**: *to shove (to push)*	2. den Mann schieben
2. *to push the man* (The use of **den**, accusative case, is discussed in section 15.)	3. **die Grenzen** = *the borders* die Grenzen verschieben
3. *to shift the borders*	4. **mehrfach** = *repeatedly* die Grenzen mehrfach verschieben
4. *to shift the borders repeatedly*	5. **versuchen** = *to try, to attempt* Sie versuchen, Land zu gewinnen.
5. *They try to obtain land.*	6. **größten** = *largest* den größten Staat bilden
6. *to form the largest state*	7. **spielen eine Rolle** (In English one would say to ___________ a role.)
7. *play*	8. **zusammen** = *together* eine Rolle zusammen spielen
8. *to play a role together*	

PROGRESS TEST

Choose the answer which expresses the meaning of the indicated German word.

1. **versuchen,** Land zu gewinnen
   (a) to forsake (b) to forgive (c) to try
2. den größten Staat **bilden**
   (a) to educate (b) to form (c) to construct
3. die Grenzen **verschieben**
   (a) to forsake (b) to shovel (c) to shift

Answer key: **1.** (c); **2.** (b); **3.** (c).

9. *Present tense verb endings; personal pronouns*

1. The stem of a verb is found by dropping the final **-en** or **-n** of the infinitive:

sing*en*: sing-; **wander*n*: wander-.**

2. The present tense of most German verbs is recognized by one of the following endings attached to the stem:

ich sing*e*	*I am singing, I sing. I do not sing, do you?*
du sing*st*	*you are singing, you sing. You do not sing, do you?*
er, sie, es sing*t*	*he, she, it is singing, sings. He does not sing, does he?*
wir sing*en*	*we are singing, we sing. We do not sing, do we?*
ihr sing*t*	*you are singing, you sing. You do not sing, do you?*
sie sing*en*	*they are singing, they sing. They do not sing, do they?*
Sie sing*en*	*you are singing, you sing. You do not sing, do you?*

Note that one German form expresses all three forms of the English present. There is no progressive form (*I am singing*). Nor is there a German equivalent of "do" to form questions, or statements with a negative. (Do you sing? No, I do not sing, but I do play the piano.)

3. **Sie** capitalized can only be translated *you*, unless it begins a sentence. To differentiate between **sie** (*she*) and **sie** (*they*) you must look to the verb ending. To differentiate between **Sie** (*you*), **sie** (*they*), and **sie** (*she*) at the beginning of a sentence, you must look at the verb ending or the context in which **Sie** is used.

4. **Du** and **ihr** are used when addressing family, close friends, children, animals, God, and other deities. For polite and formal relationships **Sie** is used.

Notice that **er** and **sie** may refer either to persons or to things.

(The word **ihr** has other meanings; *her, to her, their*; and when capitalized *your.*)

5. The conjugations of **sein** (*to be*), **haben** (*to have*), and **werden** (*to get, to become, will, be going to*) are irregular:

	sein		**haben**		**werden**	
ich	**bin**	*I am*	**habe**	*have*	**werde**	*become*
du	**bist**	*you are*	**hast**	*have*	**wirst**	*become*
er, sie, es	**ist**	*he, she, it is*	**hat**	*has*	**wird**	*becomes*
wir	**sind**	*we are*	**haben**	*have*	**werden**	*become*
ihr	**seid**	*you are*	**habt**	*have*	**werdet**	*become*
sie	**sind**	*they are*	**haben**	*have*	**werden**	*become*
Sie	**sind**	*you are*	**haben**	*have*	**werden**	*become*

Werden itself means *will* or *be going to* only when combined with the infinitive to form the future. This point will be taken up later.

Select the correct answer. Be sure to cover the left-hand column with a card. Circle any words that you do not immediately recognize.

	1. **er singt** (*he/they*)
1. *he*	2. **sie singt** (*she/they*)
2. *she*—the third-person singular verb ending tells you	3. **Singen Sie?** (*they/you*)
3. *you*—the capitalized S tells you	4. **ich singe** (*I/you*)
4. *I*	5. **ihr singt** (*you/we*)
5. *you*	6. **es singt** (*it/we*)
6. *it*	7. **du singst** (*you/he*)
7. *you*	8. **sie singen** (*she/they*)
8. *they*—the third-person plural verb ending tells you	9. **wir singen** (*we/it*)
9. *we*	

Which pronoun goes with the following verbs?

	10. _____findet (**ich/er**)
10. **er**	11. _____findet (**sie/du**)
11. **sie**	12. _____finden (**Sie/ihr**)
12. **Sie**	13. _____findet (**ihr/ich**)
13. **ihr**	14. _____finde (**ich/sie**)
14. **ich**	15. _____findet (**sie/wir**)
15. **sie**	16. _____finden (**ich/sie**)
16. **sie**	17. _____findet (**du/es**)
17. **es**	18. _____findest (**du/sie**)

18. du	**19.** _____finden (**er/wir**)
19. wir	

Now select the best translation according to the context.

	20. schon = *already* Das Wasser kocht schon. (**kocht** = *boils/is boiling*)
20. *is boiling*	**21.** Sie geht schon nach Hause. (**geht** = *goes/is going*)
21. *is going*	**22. heute** = *today* **wieder** = *again* Heute fliegt sie wieder nach Italien. (**fliegt** = *is flying/flies*)
22. *is flying*	**23. auch** = *too, also* Lernt er auch Deutsch? (**lernt** = *learns/is learning*)
23. *is learning*	**24. oft** = *often* Wir gehen oft ins Theater. (**gehen** = *go/are going*)
24. *go*	**25. nur** = *only* Paul tanzt nur mit Margarete. (**tanzt** = *dances/is dancing*)
25. *dances*	**26. wo** = *where* Wo wohnen Sie? (**wohnen** = *live/do . . . live*)
26. *do . . . live?*	**27. die Zeit** = *time* Hat er heute Zeit zu studieren? (**hat** = *have/does . . . have*)
27. *Does* he *have* time to study today?	

Select the correct pronoun to go with the verb.

	28. _____bin (**ich/er**)
28. ich	**29.** _____werdet (**er/ihr**)
29. ihr	**30.** _____habt (**sie/ihr**)
30. ihr	**31.** _____wirst (**du/sie**)

31. du	32. _____ist (**ich/es**)
32. es	33. _____hat (**sie/ich**)
33. sie	34. _____seid (**ihr/er**)
34. ihr	35. _____werden (**sie/du**)
35. sie	

Select the correct translation.

	36. **Ich bin** hier. (*I am/you are*)
36. *I am* here.	37. **Wir haben** einen Hund. (*we have/they have*)
37. *We have* a dog.	38. **Ihr seid** dumm! (*she is/you are*)
38. *You are* stupid!	39. **Er hat** Hunger. (*you have/he has*)
39. *He is* hungry. (Lit.: *He has* hunger.)	40. **Ihr werdet** älter. (*I am getting/you are getting*)
40. *You are getting* older.	41. **Es wird** kalt. (*it is getting/they are getting*)
41. *It is getting* cold.	42. **Sie sind** in dem Hause. (*they are/she is*)
42. *They are* in the house.	

PROGRESS TEST

Choose either the appropriate pronoun or the correct form of the verb.

1. __________ findet
(a) du (b) Sie (c) wir (d) ihr

2. __________ lernst
(a) du (b) er (c) ich (d) ihr

3. ich __________
(a) kocht (b) koche (c) kochen (d) kochst

4. er __________
(a) werdet (b) werden (c) wird (d) wirst

5. ihr __________
(a) sind (b) sein (c) bin (d) seid

Answer key: **1.** (d); **2.** (a); **3.** (b); **4.** (c); **5.** (d).

Now read the following phrases and vocabulary drawn from the reading passage.

	1. **liegen** = *to lie, be located, to be (when giving location)* Deutschland **liegt** in Europa.
1. Germany *is located* in Europe.	**2.** **wohnen** = *to live* Die Deutschen **wohnen** in Deutschland.
2. The Germans *live* in Germany.	**3.** **dieser, diese, dieses** = *this* Dieses Land, in dem die Deutschen wohnen, ist . . . (**in dem** here probably means—*in which/in the*)
3. This country *in which* the Germans live is . . .	**4.** **zwischen** = *between* Der Rio Grande ist die Grenze zwischen den USA und Mexiko. (**Grenze** = __________)
4. *border, boundary* The Rio Grande is the border between the United States and Mexico.	**5.** Deutschland hat **keine** natürlichen Grenzen. (**keine** = *some/no*)
5. Germany has *no* natural borders.	**6.** **fast** = *almost* Deutschland hat **fast** keine natürlichen Grenzen.
6. Germany has *almost* no natural borders. (The context tells us that the German word **fast** is not the equivalent to our English *fast*.)	**7.** **verschieden** = *different* Verschiedene Lander **grenzen an** Deutschland. (**grenzen an** probably means __________)
7. Different countries *border on* Germany.	**8.** **umgrenzen** = *to enclose, to surround* Deutschland ist von verschiedenen Ländern **umgrenzt**. (**umgrenzt** probably means __________)
8. *enclosed, surrounded* Germany is *surrounded* by different countries.	**9.** Deutschland liegt zwischen Holland und Polen, zwischen Dänemark und der Schweiz.

9. Germany lies between Holland and Poland, between Denmark and Switzerland.	**10.** Deutschland liegt nicht in Amerika. (**Nicht** probably means—*definitely/ not*)
10. Germany is *not* in America.	**11.** **verstehen** = *to understand* Verstehen wir Deutschland als ein Land? (**als** probably means—*as/than*)
11. Do we understand Germany *as* a country?	**12.** **schwer** = *difficult, heavy* Ist es schwer, dieses Land zu verstehen? (**schwer** in this sentence means ______)
12. Is it *difficult* to understand this country?	**13.** Warum verstehen wir die europäischen Länder nicht? (**Warum** is a question word which probably means—*where/why*)
13. *Why* don't we understand the European countries?	**14.** Deutschland liegt fast inmitten aller europäischen Länder. (**inmitten** probably means—*in the middle of/ outside of*)
14. Germany is almost *in the middle of* all European countries.	**15.** **stehen** = *to stand, to be* Warum steht Deutschland inmitten aller großen Konflikte? (This question presupposes that Germany has been in a large number of major wars: *true/false*)
15. True—Why is Germany in the midst of all big conflicts?	**16.** **Geschichte** = *history, story* Die Geschichte Deutschlands ist interessant. (**Deutschlands** means __________)
16. The history *of Germany* is interesting.	**17.** **A Volkswagen** is a car for all __________
17. people	**18.** **Völker**, the plural of **Volk**, means __________.
18. *peoples, nations*	**19.** Alle Völker Europas spielen eine Rolle in der Geschichte dieses Landes. (a) **Europas** means __________. (b) **dieses Landes** means __________.
19. (a) *of Europe* (b) *of this country*	**20.** **viele** = *many* Viele verschiedene Nationen spielen eine Rolle in der Geschichte dieses Landes.

20. Many different nations play a role in the history of this country.	**21.** **wollen** = *to want* Wir wollen die Deutschen als ein Volk verstehen. (**wollen verstehen** means __________)
21. *want to understand* We want to understand the Germans as a people.	**22.** **das Land** = *country* **die Karte** = *map, chart, card* **die Landkarte** = __________
22. *map*	**23.** **anschauen** = *to look at* Wir wollen eine Landkarte anschauen.
23. We want to look at a map.	**24.** **wenn** = *when, if* Wenn wir Deutschland verstehen wollen . . . (**wenn** means here—*if/when*)
24. *If* we want to understand Germany . . .	**25.** **müssen** = *must, to have to* . . . müssen wir nicht nur Geschichte lernen . . .
25. . . . we must not only learn history . . .	**26.** **sondern** = *but* (*rather*) **auch** = *also* . . . sondern auch eine Landkarte anschauen.
26. . . . but also look at a map.	**27.** Rom ist eine Stadt in Italien. (**Stadt** means—*city/building*)
27. Rome is a *city* in Italy.	**28.** Römer wohnen in der Stadt Rom. (**Römer** means __________)
28. *Romans* Romans live in the city of Rome.	**29.** **seit** = *since* **Seit der Römerzeit** probably means __________ (*Since the Romans came/Since the time of the Romans*)
29. *Since the time of the Romans*	**30.** **Durchgang** = *thoroughfare* (literally *"through passage"*) Deutschland ist **ein Durchgangsland.**
30. Germany is a *country through which others travel* (or: a *transit country*).	**31.** Seit der Römerzeit **ist** Deutschland ein Durchgangsland.
31. Since the time of the Romans Germany *has been* a land through which others travel. (Note change of tense.)	**32.** Deutschland ist heute die größte Nation Europas, **außer** Rußland, natürlich. (*outer/except*)
32. Today Germany is the largest nation in Europe, *except* Russia, of course.	**33.** **vereinigen** = *to unite* Die **Vereinigung** Deutschlands war ein großes Problem.

33. The *unification* of Germany was a big problem.	**34.** **die Frage** = *the question* **ganz** = *all, entire* Die **Vereinigungsfrage** steht hinter der ganzen Politik Europas.
34. The *question of unification* lies behind all European politics.	**35.** Die **Außenpolitik** der Bundesrepublik . . . (If **Innenpolitik** means *domestic policy,* **Außenpolitik** probably means __________.)
35. The *foreign policy* of the Federal Republic . . .	**36.** Das **Vereinigungsproblem** steht hinter der ganzen Außenpolitik Europas.
36. The *problem of unification* lies behind all European foreign policy.	**37.** Kanada ist ein Nachbarland der Vereinigten Staaten. (**Nachbarland** means __________)
37. *neighboring country* Canada is a neighboring country of the United States.	**38.** **der Raum** = *room, space, area* Deutschland ist ein umgrenzter Raum. (**umgrenzt** = *enclosed/open*)
38. Germany is an *enclosed* area.	**39.** **fest** = *firmly, solidly, permanently* Dieses Land ist kein fest umgrenzter Raum.
39. This land is not a permanently enclosed space.	

Before you go on to the next section, review all of the words you have circled.

10. Es gibt, es ist, es sind

1. Geben means *to give* but **es gibt** is used as an idiom to indicate existence. It is translated *there is* or *there are* depending on the context:

***Es gibt* eine Universität in Hamburg.**	*There is a university in Hamburg.*
***Gibt es* viele Studenten auf der Universität?**	*Are there a lot of students at the university?*

2. **Es ist** (*there is*) and **es sind** (*there are*) express existence in a definite place of limited extent:

***Es ist* nur ein Mensch in diesem Haus.**	*There is only one person in this house.*
***Es sind* drei Menschen in dem Volkswagen.**	*There are three people in the Volkswagen.*

3. The past of these expressions is:

es gab	*there was, there were*
es war	*there was*
es waren	*there were*

Give the meanings of the indicated phrases.

	1. **sehr** = *very* Sehr viele Länder umgeben Deutschland. (**umgeben** probably means __________)
1. Very many countries *surround* Germany.	**2.** **die** = *which* **Es gibt** neun Länder, die Deutschland umgeben.(*there is/there are*)
2. *There are* nine countries which surround Germany. (As you see, **die** can be used as a relative pronoun meaning *who* or *which,* as well as an article meaning *the.*)	**3.** **die Mitte** = *middle, center* **Es liegt** in der geographischen Mitte Europas.(*there is/it is*)
3. *It is* in the geographical center of Europe.	**4.** **einmal** = *once* Einmal **gab es** viele Deutsche in der Tschechoslowakei.(*it gave/there were*)
4. *There were* once many Germans in Czechoslovakia.	**5.** Warum **ist es** ein Durchgangsland? (*is there/is it*)
5. Why *is it* a country through which others travel?	**6.** **da** = *since* (when the verb is at the end of the clause). . . da **es** fast keine natürlichen Grenzen **gibt**.(*it gives/there are*)
6. . . . since *there are* almost no (hardly any) natural borders.	**7.** **eigentlich** = *really, actually* Gab es eigentlich **ein** Deutschland? (*a/one*)
7. Was there really *one* Germany?	**8.** **Es war** sehr schwer, diese Frage zu verstehen. (*there was/it was*)
8. *It was* very hard to understand this question.	**9.** Es gibt wieder e i n Deutschland, das heute der größte Staat Europas bildet.
9. There is once again *one* Germany, which today forms the largest state in Europe. (Note: written German may give added emphasis to a word by spreading the letters apart; English would italicize the word.)	**10.** **das Gebiet** = *the area, region* **Es waren** auch romanische, slawische und magyarische Völker auf diesem Gebiet.(*there were/they were*)
10. *There were* also Romanic, Slavic, and Magyar peoples in this region.	**11.** **also** = *therefore, so* Also **gibt es** seit der Römerzeit romanische, slawische und magyarische Völker auf diesem Gebiet.(*there were/there have been*)

11. So *there have been* Romanic, Slavic, and Magyar peoples in this area since the time of the Romans.	**12.** Er hat nur eine **Landkarte** Europas. **Landkarte** probably means________.
12. *map* He has only one map of Europe.	**13.** Vier (4) verschiedene Länder waren **auf** der Landkarte.(*on/to*)
13. Four different countries were *on* the map.	**14.** **Es waren** nur vier Länder auf der Landkarte.(*they were/there were*)
14. *There were* only four countries on the map.	**15.** **Es gibt** viele Völker, die in Europa wohnen.(*there is/there are*)
15. *There are* many peoples which live in Europe.	**16.** **Es sind** viele Länder, die in diesem Gebiet liegen.(*there is/there are*)
16. *There are* many countries which lie (with)in this region.	**17.** Die Russen wohnen in Rußland. (**Rußland** means __________)
17. *Russia* The Russians live in Russia.	**18.** Also **war es und ist es** das größte Problem der Politik Europas.(*he was and is/it was and is*)
18. So *it was and is* the biggest problem of European politics.	**19.** **nennen** = *to call* Wir nennen diesen Teil Europas Mitteleuropa.
19. We call this part of Europe central Europe.	**20.** In der geographischen Mitte Europas, **die** wir Mitteleuropa nennen, findet man Deutschland.(*which/the*)
20. In the geographical center of Europe, *which* we call Central Europe, we find (one finds) Germany.	

PROGRESS TEST

Mark the phrases which you do not identify correctly, and then review them before going on.

1. **Es sind** nur vier Länder auf dieser Landkarte.
   (a) *they are* (b) *there are* (c) *there were*

2. **Es war** nur eine Landkarte an der Wand.
   (a) *there was* (b) *it was* (c) *it is*

3. **Gab es** eigentlich ein Deutschland?
   (a) *is there* (b) *was there* (c) *did he give*

4. **Es waren** nur vier Länder auf der Landkarte.
   (a) *they were* (b) *there were* (c) *there are*

5. **Es ist** nur eine Person in dem Volkswagen.
   (a) *it is* (b) *there is* (c) *he is*

Answer key: **1.** (b); **2.** (a); **3.** (b); **4.** (b); **5.** (b).

Die Geographie Deutschlands

Wenn wir Deutschland als ein Land verstehen wollen, müssen wir nicht nur seine Geschichte lernen, sondern auch eine Landkarte anschauen. Die Geographie Deutschlands kann uns sehr viel sagen. Deutschland liegt in der geographischen Mitte Europas, in dem Teil Europas, den wir Mitteleuropa nennen. Natürlich liegt nicht nur Deutschland in diesem Gebiet, sondern auch andere Länder. Hier wohnen germanische, slawische, romanische und magyarische Völker. Außer Rußland ist Deutschland der größte Staat Europas, nicht nur in Bevölkerung,[1] sondern auch in Industrie und Bruttosozialprodukt.[2] Man kann verstehen, warum die Vereinigung Deutschlands schon lange hinter der ganzen Politik Europas steht.

Dieses Land, in dem die Deutschen wohnen, ist kein fest umgrenzter Raum, da es fast keine natürlichen Grenzen gibt. Wenn wir die Landkarte wieder anschauen, finden wir nur im Norden und im Süden „natürliche Grenzen". Im Norden gibt es die Nord- und die Ostsee,[3] im Süden die Bayrischen Alpen,[4] den Bodensee[5] und den Rhein. Nach Westen und Osten liegt Deutschland offen.

Neun verschiedene Länder umgeben Deutschland: Dänemark, die Niederlande, Belgien, Luxemburg, Frankreich, die Schweiz, Österreich, die Tschechrepublik und Polen. Es ist nicht schwer zu verstehen, warum dieses Land seit der Römerzeit inmitten aller großen Konflikte steht, warum es ein Durchgangsland ist. Die Grenzen im Osten und im Westen verschieben sich,[6] wenn Deutschland oder seine Nachbarländer versuchen, mehr Land oder Lebensraum[7] zu gewinnen. Skandinavier vom Norden, Römer vom Süden, Slawen vom Osten, Romanen[8] vom Westen und Nomadenvölker aus dem Südosten, alle diese Völker spielen eine Rolle in der Geschichte dieses Landes.

---

1 *population*
2 *gross national product*
3 *North Sea and Baltic Sea*
4 *the Bavarian Alps*
5 *Lake Constance*
6 *change*
7 *living space*
8 *Neo-Latin peoples*

Chapter Three

11. *Word order—the basic structure of German sentences*

1. The task of reading German is greatly facilitated if you know how to locate the verb. Generally speaking, the personal form of the verb is found in one of three places in German:

(a) immediately after the subject (normal word order)
(b) immediately preceding the subject (inverted word order)
(c) at the end of the sentence or clause (dependent word order)

2. These three basic forms of German word order are as follows:

(a) *Normal word order*
Subject and its modifiers + verb + verbal modifiers

Der alte Mann / *geht* / langsam in das Haus.
*The old man **goes** into the house slowly.*

(b) *Inverted word order*
Any word or phrase except an interjection + verb + subject and its modifiers + other modifiers

Wann / *kommt* / Karl / nach Hause?
*When **is** Karl **coming** home?*
***Gehen* / Sie / bitte nach Hause!**
*Please **go** home!*
Den Hund / *sehe* / ich / auf der Straße.
*I **see** the dog in the street.*

(c) *Dependent* (*or transposed*) *word order*
Subordinating conjunction or words functioning as such + subject and its modifiers + other modifiers + verb

Ich weiß, / daß / der alte Mann / in das Haus / ***geht.***
I know that the old man ***is going*** *into the house.*
Der alte Mann, / der / in das Haus / ***geht,*** **/ ist mein Vater.**
The old man ***going*** *into the house is my father.*
Paul weiß, / warum / ich / Deutsch / ***studiere.***
Paul knows why I ***am studying*** *German.*

Notice that in English the regular word order is retained in dependent clauses. In German any dependent clause calls for dependent word order, i.e., for the inflected verb to be last.

The following exercises introduce new vocabulary for the reading passage and give you practice in recognizing the basic patterns of German word order. Continue to circle any words which you do not immediately recognize, and identify the subject and verb of each clause, before translating.

	1. **besprechen** = *to discuss* In diesem Kapitel besprechen wir andere Länder, **wo** man Deutsch spricht. (*who/where*)
1. In this chapter we discuss other countries *where* German is spoken. (or: where they speak German)	**2.** **Außer** Deutschland gibt es andere Länder . . . (*in/besides*)
2. *Besides* Germany there are other countries . . .	**3.** Außer Deutschland gibt es andere Länder, wo man die deutsche Sprache spricht.
3. Besides Germany there are other countries where they speak the German language.	**4.** **selbst** = *self* **stehen** = *to stand* **stand** = *stood* (past tense of **stehen**) ein **selbständiges** Land = __________
4. an *independent* country	**5.** Österreich ist heute ein selbständiger und neutraler Staat.
5. Today Austria is an independent and neutral state.	**6.** **Jeder** weiß, daß Österreich heute ein selbständiger und neutraler Staat ist. (*everyone/no one*)
6. *Everyone* knows that today Austria is an independent and neutral state.	**7.** **obwohl** = *although* Obwohl Österreich heute ein selbständiger und neutraler Staat ist . . .
7. Although today Austria is an independent and neutral state . . .	**8.** **hängen** = *to hang* **zusammen** = *together* **zusammenhängen** = __________

8. *to be connected* (lit.: to hang together)	**9. eng** = *closely* . . . hängt Österreichs Geschichte sehr eng mit der deutschen Geschichte zusammen.
9. . . . Austria's history is very closely connected with German history. (Note that the prefix **zusammen** is separable and comes at the end of the sentence.)	**10. sein** = *its* (*his, her*) Seine Geschichte hängt sehr eng mit der deutschen Geschichte zusammen.
10. Its history is very closely connected with German history.	**11. umgeben** = *surrounded* Österreich ist **nur** von acht Ländern umgeben. (*now/only*)
11. Austria is surrounded by *only* eight countries.	**12. gemeinsam** = *common* Österreich hat gemeinsame Grenzen mit nur acht Ländern.
12. Austria has boundaries in common with only eight countries.	**13. der Gegensatz** = *contrast* Im Gegensatz zu Deutschland ist Österreich nicht von so vielen Ländern umgeben.
13. In contrast to Germany Austria is not surrounded by so many countries.	**14.** Obwohl Österreich nur von acht Ländern umgeben ist . . .
14. Although Austria is surrounded by only eight countries . . .	**15.** Im westlichen und im südlichen Teil des Landes sind Berge und Täler. (If **Berge** means *mountains,* **Täler** probably means __________)
15. *valleys* In the western and southern part of the country there are mountains and valleys.	**16. berühmt** = *famous* Diese Berge und Täler sind sehr berühmt.
16. These mountains and valleys are very famous.	**17.** Da diese Berge und Täler so berühmt sind . . .
17. Since these mountains and valleys are so famous . . .	**18. besuchen** = *to visit* . . . besuchen Millionen von Menschen dieses Alpenland.
18. . . . millions of people visit this alpine country.	**19. bedecken** = *to cover* Da Berge und Täler Österreich bedecken . . .
19. Since mountains and valleys cover Austria . . .	**20.** . . . gibt es viele Touristen, **die** das Land besuchen. (*who/the*)

20. . . . there are many tourists *who* visit the country. (Remember that **die, der, das**, etc., can be used both as articles and as relative pronouns, i.e., "the" and "who" or "which." They are relative pronouns when the verb is last.)	**21.** **ungefähr** = *approximately* Berge und Täler bedecken ungefähr 60% der **Oberfläche** Österreichs. (*tourist industry/surface*)
21. Mountains and valleys cover approximately 60% of the *surface* of Austria.	**22.** Ungefähr 60% der Oberfläche Österreichs ist von den berühmten Bergen und Tälern bedeckt.
22. Approximately 60% of the surface of Austria is covered by its (the) famous mountains and valleys.	**23.** **die Donau** = *the Danube* Der andere Teil ist Donauland.
23. The other part is Danube country.	**24.** In dem Donauland liegt **Wien**. (*wine/Vienna*)
24. *Vienna* is (lies) in the Danube country.	**25.** Wien, die **Hauptstadt** Österreichs . . . (If **Haupt** means *main* or *principal,* **Hauptstadt** must mean ________)
25. *capital* Vienna, the *capital* of Austria . . .	**26.** **die Gesamtbevölkerung** = *the entire population* **Ein Fünftel** der Gesamtbevölkerung Österreichs wohnt in Wien. (*a fourth/a fifth*)
26. *A fifth* of the entire population of Austria lives in Vienna.	**27.** Hier liegt Wien, in **dem** heute ein Fünftel der Gesamtbevölkerung wohnt. (*the/which*)
27. Here is Vienna, in *which* a fifth of the entire population lives today.	

PROGRESS TEST

The following sentences are intended to test your recognition of grammatical forms. Therefore, some of the vocabulary is new. Simply respond to the sentences by choosing the correct answer.

1. Seit Jahrhunderten erlebt die Schweiz auf ihrem Boden keinen Krieg mehr.
   The subject of **erlebt** *is*
   (a) Krieg (b) Boden (c) Jahrhunderten (d) Schweiz

2. Wir wissen, daß die Schweiz die Achtung und das Vertrauen der Welt genießt.
   Schweiz *is the subject of*
   (a) wissen (b) Vertrauen (c) genießt (d) Achtung

3. Ungefähr 60% der Oberfläche Österreichs ist von den berühmten Bergen und Tälern bedeckt.
   The subject of **ist** *is*
   (a) Bergen und Tälern (b) 60% der Oberfläche Österreichs (c) ungefähr (d) Österreichs

4. Zweimal bedrohten die Türken Zentraleuropa.
The subject of **bedrohten** *is*
(a) die Türken (b) Zentraleuropa (c) zweimal

5. Hitler und der Anschluß vereinigten Deutschland und Österreich.
The subject of **vereinigten** *is*
(a) Hitler (b) Anschluß (c) Hitler und der Anschluß (d) Deutschland und Österreich

6. Wenn Deutschland versucht, mehr Lebensraum in Polen zu gewinnen, dann gibt es Krieg.
The subject of **gibt** *is*
(a) dann (b) Polen (c) es (d) Krieg

Answer key: **1.** (d); **2.** (c); **3.** (b); **4.** (a); **5.** (c); **6.** (c).

Review the words you circled in the frames as well as any points missed on this test. Then go on to the next section.

12. *Future tense*—werden

1. **Werden** + infinitive tells you that the reference is to future *time*:

Viele Menschen *werden* das Gebirgsland *besuchen.*	*Many people* ***will visit*** *the mountainous country.*
Wann *wird* er nach Österreich *fliegen?*	*When* ***is*** *he* ***going to fly*** *to Austria?*

2. In normal and inverted word order the infinitive is generally at the end of the clause. In dependent word order the infinitive precedes **werden**:

Du *wirst* doch den Brief bald *bekommen.*	*You* ***will*** *surely* ***get*** *the letter soon.*
Aber vielleicht *wirst* du den Brief morgen *bekommen*.	*But maybe you* ***will get*** *the letter tomorrow.*
Ich weiß, daß du niemals einen Brief *bekommen wirst.*	*I know that you* ***will*** *never* ***receive*** *a letter.*

The subject of word order with modal verbs will be taken up in greater detail in other sections.

3. Remember that **werden** without the infinitive expresses the meaning *to get, to become:*

Der Mann *wird* alt.	*The man* ***is getting*** *(is becoming) old.*

Give the tense and meaning of the verbs in the following sentences.

	1. **die Sprache** = *language* **deutschsprachig** = *German speaking* Sie **werden** noch mehr von den deutschsprachigen Ländern **lesen**.
1. You *will read* even more about German-speaking countries.	2. Wir **lernen** noch mehr über den Einfluß der deutschen Kultur.
2. We *are learning* even more about the influence of German culture.	3. Vielleicht **werden** wir mehr über die deutsche Kultur **lernen**.
3. Maybe we *will learn* more about German culture.	4. **etwas** = *something* Wir **werden** auch etwas über die Schweiz **sagen**.
4. We *will* also *say* something about Switzerland.	5. **möglich** = *possible* Es ist möglich, daß Sie etwas von der Habsburger Monarchie **lesen werden**.
5. It is possible that you *will read* something about the Hapsburg monarchy.	6. Der Großvater **wird** alt.
6. Grandfather *is getting* old.	

13. *Adjectives—cognates, agreement, comparison*

1. An adjective limits, qualifies, or describes a noun. As with verbs and nouns, there are a number of cognate adjectives which will facilitate your reading knowledge of German:

alt	*old*
jung	*young*
grün	*green*
dumm	*stupid, dumb*

2. For the purposes of reading it is important to be able to identify gender, number, and case. Some of the grammatical signals which help you to do so are the adjective endings, which are either *strong* or *weak*.

3. Strong adjective endings show gender, number, and case of the noun, when no preceding word gives this information. With the exception of masculine and neuter genitive, these endings are readily associated with the forms of the definite article (see chapter 4, §15, no. 3).

	MASCULINE	FEMININE	NEUTER	PLURAL
Nominative	**-er**	**-e**	**-es**	**-e**
Genitive	**-en**	**-er**	**-en**	**-er**
Dative	**-em**	**-er**	**-em**	**-en**
Accusative	**-en**	**-e**	**-es**	**-e**

The concept of case will be discussed in chapter 4.

Gut*en* Wein kann man nicht überall finden. (masc. acc.) — *You cannot find good wine everywhere.*

Alt*e* Männer sitzen auf der Treppe. (nom. pl.) — *Old men are sitting on the steps.*

Ein dumm*es* Kind hört nicht auf seine Eltern. (neuter nom.) — *A stupid child does not listen to his parents.*

Ein gut*er* Ruf ist köstlicher als groß*er* Reichtum. (masc. nom.) — *A good reputation is more precious than great riches.*

Note that the **-er** of **köstlicher** (*more precious*) is not a strong adjective ending but indicates the comparative form of **köstlich** (*precious*). See no. 6 below.

4. An adjective takes a weak ending if it is preceded by any limiting article which indicates gender, number, and case. The weak endings are:

	MASCULINE	FEMININE	NEUTER	PLURAL
Nominative	**-e**	**-e**	**-e**	**-en**
Genitive	**-en**	**-en**	**-en**	**-en**
Dative	**-en**	**-en**	**-en**	**-en**
Accusative	**-en**	**-e**	**-e**	**-en**

It is not necessary to learn the weak endings in order to be able to read German, however.

Der alt*e* Mann und seine schöne Frau wohnen in diesem alt*en* grau*en* Haus. — *The old man and his beautiful wife live in this old gray house.*

5. The majority of adjective endings in German will be weak.

6. Adjectives which do not appear before the noun they modify have no ending:

Der Mensch wird *alt*, aber bleibt doch *dumm*. — *Man grows old, but yet (he) remains stupid.*
Klaus ist ein Jahr *älter* als seine Schwester. — *Klaus is one year older than his sister.*

As you respond to the following exercises, pay special attention to adjective and noun endings as indicators of number.

	1. Es gibt andere Länder Europas, wo man Deutsch spricht. (**andere Länder** = *another country/other countries*)
1. There are *other countries* in Europe where German is spoken (lit.: where one speaks German). (*man* = one, they, you)	**2.** You can tell that **andere Länder** is plural because of ___________.
2. the umlaut and the endings (i.e., das Land vs. andere Länder)	**3.** Deutschland hat eine gemeinsame Grenze mit Österreich.
3. Germany has a border in common with Austria.	**4.** Österreich hat gemeinsame Grenzen mit acht verschiedenen Ländern. (**gemeinsame Grenzen** = *common border/common borders*)
4. Austria has *borders in common* with eight different countries.	**5.** You can tell that **gemeinsame Grenzen** is plural because __________.
5. **ein** is missing and because of the ending added to **Grenze**	**6.** Die Schweiz ist ein neutrales Land.
6. Switzerland is a neutral country.	**7.** **wirklich** = *really* Gibt es wirklich neutrale Länder? (**neutrale Länder** = *neutral country/neutral countries*)
7. Are there really (such things as) *neutral countries?*	

PROGRESS TEST

Tell whether the italicized nouns are singular or plural. If you miss any of the following, review the preceding exercises before continuing.

1. Alle guten *Pläne* scheitern. (**scheitern** = *to fail*)

2. *Kriege* sind nicht neutral.

3. *Die Schweiz* ist ein europäisches Paradies.

Answer key: **1.** plural: plans; **2.** plural: wars; **3.** singular: Switzerland.

14. *Adverbs*

An adverb describes or gives more information about an adjective, a verb, or another adverb. Adverbs in German do not differ as words from their adjectival counterparts, whereas they do in English.

Er läuft *schnell*.	*He runs **quickly**.*
Er spricht *langsam*.	*He speaks **slowly**.*
Sie machen das *gut*!	*You do that **well**.*

This section will introduce you to ten common adverbs. Continue to circle words which you do not immediately recognize.

	1. Wir wollen **noch** Frankreich besuchen. (*still/never*)
1. We *still* want to visit France.	**2.** Im Sommer bedeckt der Schnee **noch** die Alpen. (*never/still*)
2. The snow *still* covers the Alps in the summer.	**3.** **Vielleicht** schaut er die Landkarte an. (*maybe/not*)
3. *Maybe* he is looking at the map.	**4.** Die Landkarte hängt **noch** an der Wand. (*still/never*)
4. The map is *still* hanging on the wall.	**5.** **Heute** lesen wir, daß die Schweiz ein europäisches Paradies ist. (*yesterday/today*)
5. *Today* we read that Switzerland is a European paradise.	**6.** **Vielleicht** ist es auf der Landkarte. (*perhaps/not*)
6. *Perhaps* it is on the map.	**7.** Heute ist Deutschland **wieder** vereinigt. (*again/still*)
7. Today Germany is united *again*.	**8.** Kann uns die Geographie Deutschlands **sehr** viel sagen? (*little/very*)
8. Can Germany's geography tell us *very* much?	**9.** Hier leben **auch** viele Völker. (*therefore/also*)
9. Many nations live here *also*.	**10.** Ich habe Ungarn **nie** besucht. (*never/still*)
10. I have *never* visited Hungary. (**habe besucht** = present perfect tense)	**11.** Nicht **sehr** viele Länder umschließen die Schweiz. (*little/very*)
11. Not *very* many countries surround Switzerland.	**12.** Du kennst das Land **also** nicht. (*so/also*)

12. *So* you don't know that country.	**13.** **Heute** ist Deutschland eine große Macht. (*today/tomorrow*)
13. *Today* Germany is a great power.	**14.** Ist Frankreich **auch** eine große Macht? (*also/still*)
14. Is France *also* a major power?	**15.** **Nur** Rußland hat eine größere Bevölkerungszahl. (*still/only*)
15. *Only* Russia has a larger population.	**16.** **Schon** im Jahre 955 beginnt Österreich . . . (*not yet/already*)
16. *Already* in the year 955 Austria begins . . .	**17.** **die Uhr** = *watch* Schweizer Uhren kennt **heute** jeder. (*tomorrow/today*)
17. *Today* everyone has heard of Swiss watches.	**18.** Schweizer Käse kennt man **auch**. (*therefore/also*)
18. We *also* know about Swiss cheese.	**19.** Karl weiß **schon**, daß Deutschland eine große Macht ist. (*therefore/already*)
19. Karl *already* knows that Germany is a great power.	**20.** Maria kommt **nie wieder** nach Österreich. (*again and again/never again*)
20. Maria will *never again* come to Austria. (**kommt** here has future meaning)	

PROGRESS TEST

Give the correct meaning of the italicized words. Mark those which you do not give correctly the first time, and review them before continuing.

1. Bedeckt der Schnee im Sommer *noch* die Alpen?

2. Hier leben *auch* viele Völker.

3. *Nur* Hitler vereinigte Deutschland und Österreich.

Answer key: **1.** still **2.** also **3.** only

READING PREPARATION

This section reviews structures already studied and introduces vocabulary necessary for the reading passage. Continue to circle new or unfamiliar words.

	1. Jetzt werden wir etwas sagen über Österreichs Einfluß **auf** das politische Leben Europas. (*on/of*)
1. Now we will say something about Austria's influence *on* the political life of Europe.	**2.** Schon im Jahre 955, dem **Geburtsjahr** Österreichs . . . (*birthday/year of the birth*)
2. Already in the year 955, the *year of the birth* of Austria . . .	**3.** **ausüben** = *to exert* **auszuüben** = *to exert* . . . **beginnt** dieses Land einen großen Einfluß auf Europa auszuüben.
3. . . . this country *begins* to exert a great influence on Europe. (Notice the use of the present tense for historical present.)	**4.** . . . beginnt dieses Land einen großen Einfluß auf das kulturelle und politische Leben Europas auszuüben.
4. . . . this country begins to exert a great influence on the cultural and political life of Europe.	**5.** **bleiben** = *to remain* Die Habsburger bleiben fast 650 Jahre an der Macht.
5. The Hapsburgs remain in power almost 650 years.	**6.** **spielen** = *to play* Die Habsburger Familie spielt eine politisch aktive Rolle in der Geschichte Österreichs.
6. The Habsburg family plays a politically active role in Austria's history.	**7.** **bis zum** = *until the . . .* Bis zum Jahre 1918 bleibt die Habsburger Monarchie Österreich-Ungarn an der Macht.
7. Until the year 1918 the Hapsburg monarchy of Austria-Hungary remains in power.	**8.** **und zwar** = *namely* Nur einmal sind Deutschland und Österreich vereinigt, und zwar unter Hitler (1938–45).
8. Only once are (were) Germany and Austria united, namely under Hitler (1938–45). (Note German present tense referring to a historical past event.)	**9.** **die Beziehung** = *relation* Österreichs **Beziehungen** zu den ost- und südeuropäischen Ländern . . . (*singular/plural*)
9. Austria's *relations* with the East European and South European countries . . .	**10.** **einstige** = *former* Österreichs einstige **wertvolle** Beziehungen . . . (*valuable/unimportant*)

10. Austria's former *valuable* relations . . .	**11.** **wichtig** = *important* Österreichs einstige wertvolle Beziehungen zu den ost- und süd-europäischen Ländern sind **auch heute noch** wichtig.
11. Austria's former valuable relations with the East European and South European countries are *also* important *still today*.	**12.** Der Eiserne Vorhang hängt nicht mehr zwischen Österreich und den osteuropäischen Ländern. (If **Eiserne** is *iron*, then **Vorhang** is ______)
12. *curtain* The Iron Curtain no longer hangs between Austria and the East European countries.	**13.** Der Eiserne Vorhang existiert also nicht mehr?
13. So the Iron Curtain no longer exists?	**14.** **sollten** = *ought* Vielleicht sollten wir etwas über die Schweiz sagen.
14. Maybe we ought to say something about Switzerland.	**15.** Vielleicht werden wir wieder etwas über Österreich sagen.
15. Maybe we will say something about Austria again.	**16.** Da die Schweiz ein neutrales Land ist, erlebt **sie** keinen Krieg.
16. Since Switzerland is a neutral country, *it* does not experience any war. (**Sie** refers here to the feminine noun **die Schweiz**.)	**17.** **der Boden** = *territory* (*floor, ground*) **auf seinem Boden** = *on its territory* Seit Jahrhunderten erlebt dieses neutrale Land keinen Krieg auf seinem Boden.
17. For centuries this neutral country has not experienced any war on its territory.	**18.** **vertrauen** = *to trust* Die Welt vertraut diesem kleinen Land.
18. The world trusts this little country.	**19.** **genießen** = *to enjoy* Dieses Land genießt das Vertrauen der Welt.
19. This country enjoys the trust of the world.	**20.** **die Achtung** = *respect* Als neutrales Land genießt die Schweiz **nicht nur** die Achtung, **sondern auch** das Vertrauen der Welt.
20. As a neutral country Switzerland enjoys *not only* the respect *but also* the trust of the world. *nicht nur . . . sondern auch* (idiom)	**21.** Dieses klassische Gebirgsland ist berühmt für seine **wunderschöne Landschaft**. (**Wunderschöne Landschaft** must mean *extremely beautiful* __________.)

21. *landscape* This classic mountain country is famous for its *extremely beautiful landscape.*	**22.** **ansehen** = *to consider, respect* (also: *to look at*) **das Ansehen** = *esteem* Das klassische Gebirgsland, welches viele Menschen jedes Jahr besuchen, genießt internationales Ansehen.
22. The classic mountain country, which many people visit every year, enjoys international esteem.	**23.** **die Währung** = *currency* **das Bankwesen** = *banking institutions, banking system* Nicht nur ist die schweizerische Landschaft berühmt, sondern auch die Schweizer Währung und das Schweizer Bankwesen.
23. Not only is Swiss scenery famous but also Swiss currency and Swiss banking institutions.	**24.** Die Schweizer Währung und das Schweizer Bankwesen genießen internationales Ansehen.
24. Swiss currency and Swiss banking institutions enjoy international esteem.	**25.** Jeder kennt doch auch Schweizer Schokolade, Schweizer Uhren und Schweizer Käse. (**Käse** probably means __________.)
25. *cheese* Surely everyone has also heard (knows) of Swiss chocolate, Swiss watches, and Swiss cheese.	**26.** **vieles** = *much* **tun** = *to do* Wir können noch vieles über die Schweiz sagen, aber wir werden es nicht tun.
26. We can still say much about Switzerland, but we will not (literally: do it).	

Andere deutschsprachige Länder

Außer Deutschland gibt es andere Länder Europas, wo man die deutsche Sprache spricht, z.B[1]., Österreich und die Schweiz. Österreich ist heute ein selbständiger und neutraler Staat, aber seine Geschichte hängt sehr eng mit der deutschen Geschichte zusammen. Im Gegensatz zu Deutschland hat Österreich gemeinsame Grenzen mit acht verschiedenen Ländern: Deutschland, die Schweiz, Liechtenstein, Italien, Slowenien, Ungarn, die Slowakei und die Tschechrepublik. Im westlichen und im südlichen Teil des Landes sind die berühmten Berge und Täler, das Alpenland, das ungefähr 60% der Oberfläche Österreichs bedeckt. Das andere ist Donauland. Hier liegt Wien, Hauptstadt des Landes, in dem heute ein Fünftel der Gesamtbevölkerung wohnt.

Schon im Jahre 955, dem Geburtsjahr des Habsburger Österreichs, beginnt dieses Land, einen großen Einfluß auf das kulturelle und politische Leben Europas auszuüben. Am Ende des 13. Jahrhunderts beginnt die Habsburger Familie eine politisch aktive Rolle in der Geschichte Österreichs zu spielen. Bis zum Jahre 1918 bleibt die Habsburger Monarchie Österreich-Ungarn an der Macht. Nur einmal sind Deutschland und Österreich vereinigt, und zwar unter Hitler (1938–45).

Heute sind Österreichs einstige wertvolle Beziehungen zu den ost- und südeuropäischen Ländern wieder sehr wichtig, da der Eiserne Vorhang zwischen Osten und Westen nicht mehr existiert.

Über die Schweiz können wir vieles sagen. In diesem Land spricht man nicht nur Deutsch, sondern auch Französisch, Italienisch und Romaunsch, einen romanischen Dialekt. Nur fünf Länder umschließen dieses Land: Deutschland, Frankreich, Italien, Liechtenstein und Österreich. Seit Jahrhunderten erlebt dieses Land keinen Krieg mehr auf seinem Boden. Als neutrales Land genießt es die Achtung und das Vertrauen der Welt. Die Schweiz ist berühmt für ihre wunderschöne Landschaft. Hier ist das klassische Gebirgsland, welches viele Menschen jedes Jahr besuchen. Schweizer Schokolade, Schweizer Uhren und Schweizer Käse kennt doch jeder. Die Schweizer Währung und das Schweizer Bankwesen genießen auch internationales Ansehen. Wenn es ein europäisches Paradies gibt, dann ist es die Schweiz.

---

1 zum Beispiel: *for example*

Chapter Four

15. *Case of the noun*

1. There are four different cases in German: the nominative, the genitive, the dative, and the accusative.

(a) The nominative case is used for the subject and for a predicate noun when the predicate noun is a repeat of the subject:

***Der Wagen* fährt sehr schnell.**	***The car*** *goes very fast.*
Walter ist *der Mann*.	*Walter is* ***the man***.

(b) The genitive expresses possession or relationship. It also is used with certain prepositions and verbs, and is often translated by *of the,* by an adjective, or by *'s* (plural *s'*):

Ich höre die Stimme *der Frau*.	*I hear the voice* ***of the woman****, the* ***woman's*** *voice.*
Gert arbeitet trotz *der Hitze*.	*Gert works (is working) in spite* ***of the heat.***
Was halten Sie von der Zivilisation *des Westens*?	*What do you think about Western civilization (the civilization* ***of the West****)?*
***Vaters* Freund wohnt in München.**	***Father's*** *friend lives in Munich.*
Er schämt sich *seiner Armut*.	*He is ashamed* ***of his*** *poverty.*

(c) The dative is the case of the indirect object. Certain verbs and prepositions also call for this case:

Ich gebe *meinem Freund* das Buch.	*I am giving the book* ***to my friend***.
Peter antwortet *dem Lehrer* nicht.	*Peter does not answer* ***the teacher***.
***Auf dem Haus* sitzt ein Storch.**	*A stork is sitting* ***on top of the house***.

(d) The accusative is the case of the direct object; it is also used with certain prepositions:

Hans findet *das Hotel*.	*Hans finds* **the hotel**.
Er fährt *durch die Stadt*.	*He drives* **through the city**.

2. Case is shown by the endings of the article or adjectives preceding the noun, or, less frequently, by the noun itself. Familiarity with the cases of German will help you to identify the role of the noun in the sentence. Context will also give a clue as to what role a noun plays in a sentence. A knowledge of the position of the verb relative to the subject will give additional help. But the case endings are still the most direct way of identifying the role a noun plays, especially when a direct or indirect object introduces the sentence:

Wolfgang schreibt sein*em* Freund ein*en* Brief. *Wolfgang is writing his friend a letter.*
Sein*em* Freund schreibt Wolfgang ein*en* Brief.
Ein*en* Brief schreibt Wolfgang sein*em* Freund.

3. The following tables show the forms of the definite and indefinite article of the various cases:

	MASCULINE	FEMININE	NEUTER	PLURAL
Nominative	**der**	**die**	**das**	**die**
Genitive	**des**	**der**	**des**	**der**
Dative	**dem**	**der**	**dem**	**den**
Accusative	**den**	**die**	**das**	**die**
Nominative	**ein**	**eine**	**ein**	**keine** (*not any*, or *no*)
Genitive	**eines**	**einer**	**eines**	**keiner**
Dative	**einem**	**einer**	**einem**	**keinen**
Accusative	**einen**	**eine**	**ein**	**keine**

There is no plural of **ein,** but the case endings are added to possessive adjectives (see chapter 16, § 56) as well as to **kein.**

State whether the indicated nouns are used as subjects (nominative), objects (dative or accusative), or in an expression of possession or relation (genitive).

	1. **der Wissenschaftler** = *scientist* **Die** deutschen **Wissenschaftler** sind weltbekannt.
1. subject (nominative plural): German *scientists* are world famous.	**2.** **der Dichter** = *the poet* Wir sprechen jetzt von **den** deutschen **Dichtern** und **Wissenschaftlern.**
2. object (dative plural: **von** always takes the dative, and moreover, the noun ending "n" shows dative plural): We are now talking about German *poets* and *scientists.*	**3.** **Das Universum** ist groß.

3. subject (nominative): *The universe* is large.	**4.** **die Vorstellung** = *conception* Die Vorstellung **des Universums** war im 19. Jahrhundert ganz anders als heute.
4. genitive: In the 19th century the conception *of the universe* was completely different from what it is today.	**5.** **hat geändert** = (*has*) *changed* Einsteins Relativitätstheorie hat unsere Vorstellung **des Universums** geändert.
5. genitive: Einstein's theory of relativity has changed our conception *of the universe.*	**6.** **unwiderruflich** = *irrevocably* Einstein hat unsere Vorstellung **des Universums** unwiderruflich geändert.
6. genitive: Einstein irrevocably changed our conception *of the universe.*	**7.** **der Bereich** = *sphere* **der Kulturbereich** = *cultural sphere* In **dem** deutschen **Kulturbereich** sind viele Länder.
7. object (dative singular): Many countries fall within *the* German *cultural sphere.*	**8.** **stammen aus** = *to come from* Aus **dem** deutschen **Kulturbereich** stammt auch der jüdische Religionsphilosoph Martin Buber.
8. object (**aus** always takes the dative): The Jewish religious philosopher Martin Buber also comes from *the* German *cultural sphere.*	**9.** **die Bewegung** = *movement* Der Expressionismus ist **eine** literarische **Bewegung**.
9. subject (predicate nominative): Expressionism is *a* literary *movement.* (The Latin *-us* of Expressionismus is dropped in English.)	**10.** **sowie** = *as well as* **zugleich** = *at the same time* **zugleich . . . sowie** = *both . . . and* **Der Expressionismus** ist zugleich eine künstlerische sowie eine literarische Bewegung.
10. subject (nominative): *Expressionism* is both an artistic and a literary movement.	**11.** **mit** = *with* Die Mona Lisa hat nichts mit **dem Expressionismus** zu tun.
11. object (**mit** always takes the dative): The Mona Lisa has nothing to do with *Expressionism.*	**12.** In **der** deutschen **Geschichte** ist Martin Luther zugleich Politiker sowie Theologe.
12. object (dative singular): In German *history* Martin Luther is both a politician and a theologian.	**13.** **verheerend** = *devastating* **verheerendster** = *most devastating* **Der Dreißigjährige Krieg** (30 Years War) war Deutschlands verheerendster Krieg.
13. subject (nominative singular): *The Thirty Years War* was Germany's most devastating war.	**14.** **führen** = *to lead* Luthers 95 Thesen führen zu **dem** verheerendsten **Kriege** Deutschlands. (**dem** = dative/accusative)

14. dative (**zu** always requires the dative): Luther's 95 theses lead to Germany's most devastating *war.*	**15.** **ihre Märchen** = *their fairy tales* **Die Brüder Grimm** sind berühmt für ihre Märchen.
15. subject (nominative plural): *The Grimm brothers* are famous for their fairy tales.	**16.** **unterhalten** = *to entertain* Die Brüder Grimm und ihre Märchen unterhalten Kinder und Erwachsene noch heute. (If **Kinder** means *children*. **Erwachsene** probably means ___________.)
16. *adults* The Grimm brothers and their fairy tales entertain children and adults even today.	**17.** **leisten** = *to achieve* **Die** deutsche **Kultur** leistet sehr viel auf **dem Gebiet der Wissenschaft.**
17. (Note the three different cases: nominative, dative, and genitive.) German *culture* achieves a great deal *in the field of science.*	**18.** **gab** = *gave* **Die Bibelübersetzung** gab **den Deutschen** eine gemeinsame Sprache.
18. **die** = nominative; **den** = dative plural: *The translation of the Bible* gave *the Germans* a common language.	**19.** **vergessen** = *to forget* **Den größten** von allen vergessen wir aber nicht: Mozart.
19. object (accusative): But let us not forget *the greatest* of all: Mozart. (**Aber** in the middle of a phrase means *but* or *however.*)	**20.** Thomas Mann und Bertolt Brecht spielen **eine** große **Rolle** in **der Weltliteratur.**
20. **eine** = accusative; ***Rolle*** is the direct object. **der** = dative; it is governed by the preposition **in**: Thomas Mann and Bertolt Brecht play *a* large *role* in *world literature.*	**21.** **rein** = *pure* Die deutsche Kultur gibt uns auch ein Beispiel **der** reinen **Humanität.**
21. genitive: German culture also gives us an example *of* pure *humanity.*	**22.** Albert Schweitzer stammt aus **dem Elsaß.**
22. object (**aus** always takes the dative): Albert Schweitzer comes from *Alsace.*	**23.** In der Zivilisation **des Westens** gibt es keine andere Kultur . . .
23. **des** is always genitive: In *western* civilization there is no other culture . . .	**24.** **hat beigetragen** = *has contributed* Es gibt keine andere Kultur, die **zur** (**zu der**) **Geschichte der Musik** soviel beigetragen hat wie die deutsche.
24. object (dative singular); genitive singular: There is no other culture which has contributed as much *to the history of music* as German culture.	**25.** **der Komponist** = *the composer* Wie heißt **der** größte deutsche **Komponist?**

25. subject (nominative): What is the name *of the* greatest German *composer?*	**26.** Abraham Lincoln wurde am (an dem) 12. Februar geboren. (**wurde geboren** = __________)
26. Abraham Lincoln *was born* on the twelfth of February.	**27.** Er ist im (in dem) Jahre 1865 gestorben. (**ist gestorben** = __________)
27. He *died* in the year 1865.	**28.** Können Sie mir den Namen **eines Dichters** nennen, der 1749 geboren wurde und 1832 gestorben ist?
28. **eines** = genitive: Can you tell me the name *of a poet* who was born in 1749 and who died in 1832?	

PROGRESS TEST

What is the case of the indicated phrases?

1. Der Sohn **der Frau** hat keine Schokolade mehr.
   (genitive/nominative)
2. Für Amerika begann **der zweite Weltkrieg** am 7. Dezember 1941.
   (nominative/genitive)
3. **der Löwe** = *lion*
   Er gibt jetzt dem Löwen **den unschuldigen Christen.**
   (dative plural/accusative singular)
4. **Den Christen** gibt er die Löwen.
   (dative plural/accusative singular)
5. Die Geschichte **des Landes** ist schon alt.
   (nominative/genitive)
6. Siehst du **das junge Mädchen** da drüben?
   (nominative/genitive/accusative)
7. **Die Frau** gibt Paul ein Stück Schokolade.
   (nominative/accusative)
8. Versteht sie **die deutsche Kultur?**
   (nominative/accusative)

Answer key: **1.** genitive; **2.** nominative; **3.** accusative singular: He is now giving the innocent Christian to the lion. 4. dative plural: He gives the lions to the Christians. **5.** genitive; **6.** accusative; **7.** nominative: The woman is giving Paul a piece of chocolate. **8.** accusative: Does she understand German culture?

When you can easily recognize all of the above vocabulary, go on to the next section.

16. *Past tense of weak verbs*

1. There are two kinds of verbs in German: strong and weak. A weak verb does not change its stem vowel in any of its past forms, whereas a strong verb does. Most German verbs are weak.

Weak: **glauben** (*to believe*) — **ich glaubte** (*I believed*)
Strong: **singen** (*to sing*) — **ich sang** (*I sang*)

2. The sign of the past tense of weak verbs is a **-t-** added to the stem:

	leben (*to live*)	**antworten** (*to answer*)	**reden** (*to speak*)	**öffnen** (*to open*)
ich	**lebte**	**antwortete**	**redete**	**öffnete**
du	**lebtest**	**antwortetest**	**redetest**	**öffnetest**
er, sie, es	**lebte**	**antwortete**	**redete**	**öffnete**
wir	**lebten**	**antworteten**	**redeten**	**öffneten**
ihr	**lebtet**	**antwortetet**	**redetet**	**öffnetet**
sie	**lebten**	**antworteten**	**redeten**	**öffneten**
Sie	**lebten**	**antworteten**	**redeten**	**öffneten**

You will notice that an **e** is inserted before the **-t-** when the stem ends in **-t, -d,** or a succession of dissimilar consonants. Do not confuse the **-t-** of the past tense with the **-t** which is part of the stem:

Ihr arbeit*et* zu schnell. — *You work too fast.*
Ihr arbeit*etet* zu schnell. — *You work**ed** too fast.*

3. Both the first and third person singular of the weak verb in the past tense end in **-e:**

ich sagte — *I said*
er sagte — *he said*

4. The German **-t-** added to the stem corresponds to the English **-d** in designating the past:

ich lache — *I laugh*
ich lachte — *I laughed*

5. German past tense is used primarily for literary narration and description and is translated by the English past or past progressive, depending on the context.

Als sie *kamen*, *arbeiteten* wir. — *When they **came**, we **were working.***
Als wir in der Schule *waren*, *arbeiteten* wir immer schwer. — *When we **were** in school, we always **worked** hard.*
***Arbeitete* er schwer, als er in der Schule *war*?** — ***Did** he **work** hard when he **was** in school?*

The purpose of this section is to enable you to distinguish the past from the present of weak verbs and to familiarize you further with the vocabulary of the reading passage. Respond to the sentences by giving the correct meaning of the indicated verbs.

	1. Ins 20. Jahrhundert **gehören** Komponisten wie Mahler und Hindemith. (*belong/belonged*)
1. Composers such as Mahler and Hindemith *belong* to the twentieth century.	**2.** Beethoven **gehörte** ins 19. Jahrhundert. (*belongs/belonged*)
2. Beethoven *belonged* to the nineteenth century.	**3.** **das Beispiel** = *the example* Wir **erinnerten** uns an Beispiele wie die Brüder Grimm und ihre Märchen. (*remember/remembered*)
3. We *remembered* examples such as the Grimm brothers and their fairy tales.	**4.** **manchmal** = *sometimes* Manchmal **erinnern** wir uns auch an Kaiser, Diktatoren, Könige und Politiker. (*remember/remembered*)
4. Sometimes we also *remember* emperors, dictators, kings, and politicians.	**5.** **das Gebot** = *the commandment* Schweitzer **verkörpert** das Gebot: „Du sollst deinen Nächsten lieben wie dich selbst.“ (*embodies/embodied*)
5. Schweitzer *embodies* the commandment: "Thou shalt love thy neighbor as thyself."	**6.** **glauben** = *to believe* Manche Menschen glauben. daß auch Gandhi dieses Gebot **verkörperte.** (*embodies/embodied*)
6. Some people believe that Gandhi also *embodied* this commandment.	**7.** **was für ein** = *what kind of* Was für eine Macht haben die Ideen von Marx und Engels über die heutige Welt?
7. What kind of power do the ideas of Marx and Engels have over today's world?	**8.** Wir wissen schon, was für eine Macht die Ideen von Marx und Engels auf unsere heutige Welt **ausübten.** (*exert/exerted*)
8. We already know what kind of power the ideas of Marx and Engels *exerted* over today's world.	**9.** **Spielen** Bonhoeffer und Bultmann eine führende Rolle in der heutigen Theologie? (*do . . . play/did. . . play*)
9. *Do* Bonhoeffer and Bultmann *play* a leading role in today's theology?	**10.** Er **sagte** uns, daß Barth und Tillich schon damals eine große Rolle in der protestantischen Theologie **spielten.** (*tells/told*) (*play/played*)
10. He *told* us that Barth and Tillich already *played* a great role in Protestant theology at that time.	**11.** **trauen** = *to trust* **das Mißtrauen** = __________

11. *distrust, mistrust, suspicion*	**12.** **gegenseitig** = *mutual, reciprocal* Grenzen sind ein Symbol des gegenseitigen Mißtrauens.
12. Boundaries are a symbol of mutual distrust.	**13.** Die Grenzen, die uns Menschen zu oft **trennen**, sind ein Symbol des gegenseitigen Mißtrauens. (*separate/separated*)
13. The boundaries which too often *separate* us as human beings (lit: us humans) are a symbol of mutual distrust.	**14.** **der Haß** = *hate* Nicht nur die Grenzen des Mißtrauens, sondern auch die Grenzen des Hasses **trennten** die europäischen Nationen. (*separate/separated*)
14. Not only the boundaries of mistrust but also the boundaries of hate *separated* the European nations.	**15.** **Feiert** man Wunderkinder wie Mozart nicht mehr, nur Athleten? (*celebrates/celebrated*)
15. Do we not *celebrate* (lit.: Does one not celebrate . . .) child prodigies like Mozart anymore, just athletes?	**16.** **welch** = *which* Welche Dichter **meinen** sie? (*do . . . mean/did . . . mean*)
16. Which poets *do* they *mean?*	**17.** **wissen** = *to know* **ich weiß** = *I know* Ich weiß, welche Philosophen ihr **meintet.** (*mean/meant*)
17. I know which philosophers you *meant*. (The verb **wissen** has irregular forms. See chap. 6, §26.)	**18.** **schließlich** = *finally* Eine gemeinsame Sprache **führte** schließlich zu einer politischen Einheit. (*leads/led*)
18. A common language finally *led* to political unity.	**19.** **leisten** = *to produce, accomplish* Ein großes Gebiet, wo die deutsche Kultur sehr viel **leistet**, ist die Wissenschaft. (*produces/produced*)
19. A large area in which (where) German culture *produces* a great deal is science.	**20.** Einstein **leistete** sehr viel auf dem Gebiet der Physik. (*accomplishes/accomplished*)
20. Einstein *accomplished* a great deal in the field of physics.	**21.** **sich verbreiten** = *to spread* Der Einfluß des deutschen Expressionismus **verbreitete sich** noch weiter. (*spreads/spread*)
21. The influence of German Expressionism *spread* still further.	**22.** **abbauen** = *to dismantle, to do away with* Das Vertrauen zueinander: dadurch bauen wir die Grenzen ab? (*do do away with/did do away with*)

22. Trusting in one another: by doing this *do* we *do away with* the boundaries?	**23.** Wissen Sie, ob Napoleon die Grenzen zwischen den Ländern **abbaute,** als er Kaiser war? (*do away with/did away with*)
23. Do you know if Napoleon *did away with* the borders between countries when he was emperor?	**24.** **wenig** = *little* Ich **brauchte** wenig über diese berühmten Künstler zu sagen. (*need/needed*)
24. I *did* not *need* to say much (*needed* to say little) about these famous artists.	**25.** Diese Komponisten sind so berühmt, daß ich wenig über sie zu sagen **brauche**. (*need/needed*)
25. These composers are so famous that I *do* not *need* to say much about them.	**26.** **der Anfang** = *the beginning* Man **findet** die expressionistische Bewegung in Deutschland am (an dem) Anfang des 20. Jahrhunderts. (*present/past*)
26. present: You *find* the Expressionist movement in Germany at the beginning of the twentieth century.	**27.** **Unterhalten** Grimms Märchen Kinder und Erwachsene noch heute? (*present/past*)
27. present: Do Grimms' fairy tales still *entertain* children and adults today?	**28.** Wie lange **arbeitete** Einstein an der Formel $E = mc^2$? (*present/past*)
28. past: How long *did* Einstein *work* on the formula $E = mc^2$?	**29.** **gründen** = *to base* Worauf **gründete** er seine Theorie? (*present/past*)
29. past: What did he base his theory on?	**30.** **zeigen** = *to point out* Was **zeigen** uns Jung und Freud heute? (*do show/are showing*)
30. What *do* Jung and Freud *show* us today?	**31.** Wissen Sie, daß damals ganz Europa Mozart als Wunderkind **feierte**? (*celebrates/celebrated*)
31. Do you know that at that time all of Europe *celebrated* (*was celebrating*) Mozart as a child prodigy?	**32.** **glauben** = *to believe* **unglaublich** = __________
32. *unbelievably, unbelievable*	**33.** Unglaublich primitive Instinkte **schlummern** in uns. (*are slumbering/slumber/do slumber*)
33. Unbelievably primitive instincts *slumber* (*are slumbering*) within us.	**34.** **die Seele** = *the soul* Schlummerten viele primitive Instinkte auch in der griechischen Seele zur Zeit Platons? (*slumbered/were slumbering*)

34. Were there also many primitive instincts *slumbering* in the Greek soul at the time of Plato?	**35.** **was für** = *what* Freud und Jung zeigen uns, was für unglaublich primitive Instinkte in uns schlummern.
35. Freud and Jung show us what unbelievably primitive instincts slumber within us.	**36.** Wer spielte eine **führende** Rolle in der Musikgeschichte? (*leading/driving*)
36. Who played a *leading* role in the history of music?	

PROGRESS TEST

Tell whether the indicated verbs are in the past or present.

1. Der Architekt Gropius **verbreitet** seinen Einfluß weiter auf andere Architekten.
2. Wissen Sie, ob auch Gandhi dieses Gebot **verkörperte?**
3. Sie **beurteilte** uns nicht.
4. Ich weiß, welche Philosophen ihr **meintet.**
5. Dadurch **bauen** wir die Grenzen **ab**.
6. Obwohl manche sich über Schweitzers ärztliche Methoden Gedanken **machen . . .**
7. Was **zeigten** uns Planck und Hahn?

Answer key: **1.** present; **2.** past; **3.** past; **4.** past; **5.** present; **6.** present; **7.** past.

When you can easily distinguish the present from the past tense of weak verbs, go on to the next section.

17. *Past tense of* haben, sein, *and* werden

The past tense forms of **haben, sein,** and **werden** are as follows:

	haben	**sein**	**werden**
ich	**hatte** (*had*)	**war** (*was*)	**wurde** (*became*)
du	**hattest**	**warst** (*were*)	**wurdest**
er (sie, es, man)	**hatte**	**war** (*was*)	**wurde**
wir	**hatten**	**waren** (*were*)	**wurden**
ihr	**hattet**	**wart** (*were*)	**wurdet**
sie	**hatten**	**waren** (*were*)	**wurden**
Sie	**hatten**	**waren** (*were*)	**wurden**

Give the meaning of the following bolded items.

	1. Ich **habe** eine Theorie über den Einfluß von der Politik auf Künstler. (*have/had*)
1. I *have* a theory about the influence of politics on artists.	2. **darüber** = *about that* Ich **hatte** eine Theorie darüber. (*have had/had*)
2. I *had* a theory about that.	3. **der Ursprung** = *the origin* Die Astronomen **haben** zwei verschiedene Vorstellungen von dem Ursprung des Weltalls (des Universums). (*have/had*)
3. Astronomers *have* two different ideas (conceptions) of the origin of the universe.	4. **Hatte Hitler** viel Macht am Anfang der dreißiger Jahre? (*Does Hitler have/Did Hitler have*)
4. *Did Hitler have* much power at the beginning of the thirties?	5. **Wir hatten** keinen Einfluß auf ihn. (*we have/we had*)
5. *We had* no influence on him.	6. **Hattest du** einen Bruder? (*Do you have/Did you have*)
6. *Did you have* a brother?	7. **Hast** du eine Schwester? (*do . . . have/did . . . have*)
7. *Do* you *have* a sister?	8. Ich weiß, daß ihr keine Zeit **habt.** (*do . . . have/did . . . have*)
8. I know that you *do* not *have* any time.	9. **eigentlich** = *actually, really* Eigentlich **hattet ihr** keine Zeit. (*you don't have/you didn't have*)
9. Actually *you didn't have* time.	10. **der Arzt** = *the doctor* **seit wann** = *since when, how long* Seit wann **ist** der Arzt hier? (*is/has been*)
10. How long *has* the doctor *been* here? (Lit.: Since when *is* the doctor here?) (Also notice how **seit** and the present is expressed by the present perfect in English.)	11. **das Geld** = *the money* Seit wann **hat** er das Geld? (*has/had/has had*)
11. How long *has* he *had* the money? (Lit.: Since when *has* he the money?	12. **Stammte** Schweitzer **aus** dem Elsaß? (*does come from/did come from*)
12. *Did* Schweitzer *come from* Alsace?	13. **Wer war** der Arzt aus dem Elsaß? (*who is/who was*)
13. *Who was* the doctor who came from Alsace?	14. **arm** = *poor* **die Armut** = __________

14. *poverty*	**15.** **vergessen** = *to forget* **die Vergessenheit** = __________
15. *oblivion* (the condition of being forgotten)	**16.** **das Los** = *the lot (fate)* **Sind Armut und Vergessenheit** das Los vieler Künstler? (*are poverty and oblivion/were poverty and oblivion*)
16. *Are poverty and oblivion* the lot (fate) of many artists?	**17.** **Es waren** eigentlich viele, die gegen Hitler waren. (*there is/there were*)
17. Actually, *there were* many who were against Hitler.	**18.** **Ihr seid** alle Politiker! (*you are/you were*)
18. *You are* all politicians!	**19.** **der Monat** = *the month* **Sie ist** schon seit zwei Monaten in Deutschland. (*she is/she has been*)
19. *She has* already *been* in Germany for two months.	**20.** **gestern** = *yesterday* **Warst du** gestern in Salzburg? (*are you/were you*)
20. *Were you* in Salzburg yesterday?	**21.** **Bist du** ein Fan von Elvis? (*are you/were you*)
21. *Are you* a fan of Elvis?	**22.** **Ich werde** alt. (*I am getting/I was getting*)
22. *I am getting* old.	**23.** **dick** = *fat* **Ich wurde** dick. (*I am getting/I got*)
23. *I got* fat.	**24.** **Du wirst** groß. (*you are getting/you were getting*)
24. *You are getting* big.	**25.** **Du wurdest** Arzt. (*you are becoming/you became*)
25. *You became* a doctor.	**26.** **Sie wird** nicht dick, sondern dünn. (*she is getting/she got*)
26. *She is getting* thin, not fat. (Lit.: *She is* not *becoming* fat but thin.)	**27.** **fahren** = *to travel* **Wird sie** nach Salzburg **fahren**? (*will they travel/will she travel*)
27. *Is* she *going to go* to Salzburg? (Lit.: *Will she travel* to Salzburg?) (Remember **werden** + infinitive denotes future time.)	**28.** **nie** = *never* Die Franzosen **werden** Napoleon nie **vergessen**. (*will forget/become forgotten*)

28. The French *will* never *forget* Napoleon.	**29. Wurde Schweitzer** Theologe? (*does Schweitzer become/did Schweitzer become*)
29. *Did Schweitzer become* a theologian?	**30. Wir werden** Physiker und Politiker. (*we are becoming/we were becoming*)
30. *We are becoming* physicists and politicians.	**31.** Freud und Jung **wurden** Psychiater und Psychologen. (*become/became*)
31. Freud and Jung *became* psychiatrists and psychologists.	**32. Ihr werdet** Musiker. (*you are becoming/you were becoming*)
32. *You are becoming* musicians.	**33. Wurdet ihr** Künstler? (*are you becoming/did you become*)
33. *Did you become* artists?	**34. Werden sie** Wissenschaftler? (*are they becoming/were they becoming*)
34. *Are they becoming* scientists?	

PROGRESS TEST

Give the meaning of the sentence and the tense of the indicated verbs.

1. **Hatte** Hitler viel Macht am Anfang der dreißiger Jahre?
2. **Ihr wurdet** Künstler.
3. **Warst** du gestern in Salzburg?
4. **Du wurdest** Arzt.
5. **Hattest** du einen Bruder?

Now give the meaning of the indicated words.

6. Wie können wir zum Teil die Grenzen **abbauen,** die uns Menschen zu oft trennen?
   (a) to forget (b) for nothing (c) to do away with (d) to enjoy
7. Gibt es eine andere Kultur, die zur Geschichte der Musik soviel **beigetragen hat** wie die deutsche?
   (a) has contributed (b) has harmed (c) has defamed (d) has made famous
8. Auf dem wissenschaftlichen Gebiet **leistet** sie auch sehr viel.
   (a) lasts (b) accomplishes (c) is striving (d) loses
9. Aus dem deutschen Kulturbereich **stammt** auch der jüdische Religionsphilosoph Martin Buber.
   (a) criticizes (b) praises (c) remained (d) comes
10. **Eigentlich** gibt es sehr wenige große deutsche Künstler.
    (a) at the present time (b) actually (c) formerly (d) however
11. Die einzige große künstlerische **Bewegung** ist der Expressionismus.
    (a) movement (b) figure (c) idea (d) technique

12. Luthers 95 Thesen führten zu dem **verheerendsten** Kriege Deutschlands.
(a) most unusual (b) most devastating (c) most remembered (d) most ludicrous

13. Luthers Bibelübersetzung führte **schließlich** zu einer gemeinsamen Sprache und zu einer politischen Einheit.
(a) originally (b) unknowingly (c) tumultuously (d) finally

Answer key: **1.** Did Hitler have much power at the beginning of the thirties? (past) **2.** You became artists. (past) **3.** Were you in Salzburg yesterday? (past) **4.** You became a doctor. (past) **5.** Did you have a brother? (past) **6.** (c); **7.** (a); **8.** (b); **9.** (d); **10.** (b); **11.** (a); **12.** (b); **13.** (d).

Before going on to the reading passage, review all of the words you have circled.

Deutsche Kultur

Wenn wir von deutschen Dichtern, Künstlern, Philosophen, Wissenschaftlern, Komponisten und Theologen sprechen, meinen wir nicht nur die, die aus Deutschland stammen, sondern auch die, die Deutsch als Muttersprache sprechen. Dadurch bauen wir zum Teil die Grenzen ab, die uns Menschen allzuoft trennen. Wie heißen diese Menschen, die nicht nur in der deutschen Kultur, sondern oft auch in der Welt eine führende Rolle spielen?

Wenn wir von Philosophen sprechen, so erinnern wir us an Namen wie Kant, Hegel, Marx, Engels, Schopenhauer, Nietzsche, Spengler, Heidegger und Karl Jaspers. Wir wissen schon, was für eine Macht die Ideen von Marx und Engels auf unsere heutige Welt ausübten.

Deutsche Dichter wie Goethe, Schiller, Kafka, Brecht und Thomas Mann spielen eine große Rolle in der Weltliteratur. Die Brüder Grimm und ihre Märchen unterhalten Kinder und Erwachsene heute immer noch.

In der Zivilisation des Westens gibt es keine andere Kultur, die soviel zur Geschichte der Musik beigetragen hat wie die deutsche. Also braucht man wenig über Namen wie Bach, Haydn, Beethoven, Schubert, Schumann, Brahms und Wagner zu sagen. Zu dem 20. Jahrhundert gehören Richard Strauss, Mahler, Schönberg, Anton Webern, Hindemith, Alban Berg und Carl Orff. Vergessen wir aber nicht den Komponisten, in Salzburg geboren, als Wunderkind von ganz Europa gefeiert und in Armut und Vergessenheit gestorben: Mozart.

Auch ein großes Gebiet, wo die deutsche Kultur sehr viel leistet, ist die Wissenschaft. Astronomen. Mathematiker. Physiker und Chemiker, wie Kepler, Leibniz, Bunsen und Kirchhoff, Röntgen, Planck, Hahn, Heisenberg und Einstein, haben unsere Vorstellung des Universums und des Atoms unwiderruflich geändert. Psychologen und Psychiater, wie Freud und Adler aus Österreich und Jung aus der Schweiz, zeigen uns, was für unglaublich primitive Instinkte in uns schlummern oder wie die Erfahrungen[1] unserer Kindheit uns als Erwachsene beeinflussen.[2]

Auch ein Beispiel der reinen Humanität gibt uns die deutsche Kultur, wenn auch[3] aus dem Elsaß stammend[4] Albert Schweitzer: Theologe, Musiker, und Arzt von Beruf, aber auch Philosoph,

1 *experiences*
2 *influence*
3 *even though*
4 aus . . . stammend = *coming from*

Humanist und Christ. Protestantische Theologen wie Paul Tillich, Karl Barth und Rudolf Bultmann und der Katholische Theologe Hans Küng sind bekannte und wichtige Namen für die Geschichte der Religion. Der große judische Religionsphilosoph Martin Buber stammt auch aus dem deutschen Kulturbereich.

Manchmal erinnern wir uns an Kaiser, Könige, Diktatoren und Politiker. Hier sollen wir den Einfluß von Friedrich Barbarossa, Friedrich dem Großen und Maria Theresia, Bismarck, Hitler und Adenauer nicht vergessen. Und obwohl[5] Martin Luther Theologe war, dürfen wir seine Rolle in der Politik nicht übersehen. Seine 95 Thesen beginnen die Reformation, die zu dem verheerendsten Kriege Deutschlands führt, dem Dreißigjährigen Kriege. Seine Bibelübersetzung, die den Deutschen eine Bibel gibt, gibt ihnen auch eine gemeinsame Sprache, die schließlich zu einer politischen Einheit führt.

---

5 *although, (even) though*

Chapter Five

18. *Prepositions—genitive case*

1. The case of the noun changes according to the preposition which precedes it. Some prepositions govern the genitive case, some the dative, and some the accusative:

Trotz **des schlechten Wetters bleibt er draußen.** (genitive)	***In spite of*** *the bad weather he remains outside.*
Er wohnt *bei* seiner Tante. (*dative*)	*He lives* ***with*** *his aunt.*
Sie läuft *durch* das Haus. (*accusative*)	*She runs* ***through*** *the house.*

2. The more commonly used prepositions followed by the genitive case are:

(an)statt	*instead of*
Anstatt **des Bruders kommt die Schwester.**	*The sister is coming* ***instead of*** *the brother.*
trotz	*in spite of, despite*
Trotz **des schlechten Wetters fliegt er morgen nach New York.**	***In spite of*** *the bad weather he is flying to New York tomorrow.*
während	*during*
Während **des Tages schläft er.**	*He sleeps* ***during*** *the day.*
wegen	*on account of, because of*
Wegen **meiner Freunde bleibe ich hier.** **Meiner Freunde *wegen* bleibe ich hier.**	*I am staying here* ***on account of*** *my friends.*
außerhalb	*outside (of)*
Er wohnte *außerhalb* der Stadt.	*He lived* ***outside*** (***of***) *the city.*

innerhalb — *inside (of), within*

Innerhalb **eines Tages wird er diese Aufgabe vergessen.** — ***Within*** *a day he will forget this lesson.*

diesseits — *(on) this side of*

Diesseits **des Flusses liegt eine Fabrik.** — ***On this side of*** *the river is a factory.*

jenseits — *(on) that side of*

Jenseits **des Flusses ist Luftverpestung.** — ***On the other side of*** *the river is air pollution.*

oberhalb — *above*

Oberhalb **des Dorfes steht eine einsame Kirche.** — ***Above*** *the village is (stands) a lonely church.*

unterhalb — *below, beneath*

Unterhalb **der Kirche liegt ein verlassener Friedhof.** — ***Below*** *the church lies a deserted cemetery.*

um . . . willen — *for the sake of*

Um **seines Vaters** ***willen*** **ging er nicht ins Kino.** — ***For*** *his father's* ***sake*** *he did not go to the movies.*

The following exercises give you practice in recognizing the meaning of prepositions. Choose the correct meaning of the indicated words. Remember to keep the left-hand column covered until you have made a real effort to read the German.

	1. **Anstatt** eines Kanzlers hatten die Deutschen einen Diktatoren. (*because of/instead of*)
1. *Instead of* a chancellor the Germans had a dictator.	**2.** **Statt** eines Königs haben wir in den Vereinigten Staaten einen Präsidenten.
2. *Instead of* a king we in the United States have a president.	**3.** **die Angst** = *anxiety* **Trotz** der Psychologie haben wir immer noch Angst. (*in spite of/because of*)
3. *In spite of* psychology, we are still filled with anxieties.	**4.** **Trotz** unserer Humanität gibt es viel Haß auf dieser Welt.
4. *In spite of* our humanity, there is a lot of hate in this world.	**5.** **Während** des Krieges waren wir in Berlin. (*during/moreover*)
5. *During* the war we were in Berlin.	**6.** **wird verpestet** = *is becoming polluted* **Wegen** der vielen Autos wird die Luft verpestet. (**die Luft** probably means __________)

6. *the air* *Because of* the many cars the air is becoming polluted.	**7.** **Während** dieses Jahrhunderts wird die Luft immer mehr verpestet?
7. *During* this century is the air becoming more and more polluted? (The verb is in the present passive voice; see §64.)	**8.** Sprechen die Deutschen **wegen** der Bibelübersetzung eine gemeinsame Sprache? (*in spite of/because of*)
8. Do the Germans speak a common language *because of* the translation of the Bible?	**9.** **geteilt** = *divided* Gab es **wegen** Hitler nach dem Krieg ein geteiltes Deutschland?
9. Was there a divided Germany after the war *because of* Hitler?	**10.** **Trotz** unserer Vorstellungen des Universums verstehen wir immer noch nicht das Warum.
10. *In spite of* our conceptions of the universe, we still do not understand the "*why of it.*" (Notice that **Warum** is here used as a noun.)	**11.** **Statt** einer neuen Vorstellung des Universums hatten sie wieder ein Nichts.
11. *Instead of* a new conception of the universe they again had nothing (i.e., their ideas again did not conform to their observations).	**12.** Das Land liegt **außerhalb** seines Einflusses. (*within/outside of*)
12. That country lies *outside of* his influence. (**das** can have the meaning "that" when stressed)	**13.** Peter wohnt **außerhalb** der Stadt.
13. Peter lives *outside of* the city.	**14.** **die Ruhe** = *peace* **Innerhalb** der Städte gibt es keine Ruhe mehr. (Being the opposite of **außerhalb, innerhalb** must mean __________)
14. *within* *Within* the cities there is no longer any peace. (**der Staat** = *state;* **die Stadt** = *city*)	**15.** **Innerhalb** eines Jahres müssen wir diese Arbeit zu Ende bringen.
15. *Within* a year we must bring this work to an end.	**16.** **die Kirche** = *the church* **Oberhalb** der Kirche sieht man einen Weinberg.
16. *Above* the church you see a vineyard.	**17.** **das Tal** = *valley* **Unterhalb** des Dorfes liegt das Tal.
17. *Below* the village lies the valley.	**18.** Liegt ein Wald **außerhalb** des Dorfes?
18. Is there a forest *outside of* the village?	**19.** ***der* See** = *the lake* **Unterhalb** des Dorfes liegt ein See.

19. *Below* the village lies a lake. (cf. ***die* See** = *the sea, the ocean*)	**20. Jenseits** des Atlantischen Ozeans liegt Europa.
20. Europe lies *on the other side of* the Atlantic Ocean.	**21.** Europa liegt **diesseits** des heutigen Rußlands.
21. Europe is located *this side of* present-day Russia.	**22.** Wollen die Menschen **diesseits** des Meeres in Ruhe und Frieden leben?
22. Do the people *on this side of* the ocean want to live in peace and quiet?	**23. aufhören** = *to stop, desist* **Um** Himmels **willen**, hören Sie auf! (*because of/for the sake of*)
23. *For* heaven's *sake*, stop it!	**24. Um** Ingrids **willen** will er nicht mehr kommen.
24. *For* Ingrid's *sake* he is not going to come anymore. (Here **will nicht** expresses resolution, intention)	**25. Um** Pauls **willen** brauchen Sie nicht mehr zu kommen.
25. You do not need to come *for* Paul's *sake* anymore.	**26.** Gibt es ein **Jenseits**? Viele wissen das nicht, aber alle wissen, daß es ein **Dies-seits** gibt. (In a discussion of religion **Jenseits** and **Diesseits** probably refer to __________)
26. Is there a *next world?* Many people don't know, but everyone knows that there is a *present world* (*a this side*).	

PROGRESS TEST

Choose the correct meaning of the indicated words.

1. **verfolgen** = to persecute
   Wurde Kopernikus von der Kirche verfolgt **wegen** der neuen Vorstellung des Weltalls?
   (a) in spite of (b) during (c) because of (d) instead of
2. **Trotz** des schlechten Wetters werden wir nach Salzburg fahren.
   (a) beneath (b) in spite of (c) because of (d) on the other side of
3. **Anstatt** des Friedens werden wir nur Krieg haben.
   (a) instead of (b) during (c) in spite of (d) because of
4. **Außerhalb** der Stadt finden Sie einen kleinen See.
   (a) in addition to (b) because of (c) in spite of (d) outside of
5. **fliegen** = *to fly*
   Während des Sommers müssen wir nach Österreich fliegen.
   (a) ago (b) on account of (c) before (d) during
6. **der Wachtturm** = *watch tower*
   Jenseits der Grenze steht ein großer Wachtturm.
   (a) because of (b) on that side of (c) on this side of (d) in spite of

Answer key: **1.** (c); **2.** (b); **3.** (a); **4.** (d); **5.** (d); **6.** (b).

19. *Prepositions—dative case*

1. The dative case is used with the following prepositions:

aus	*out of, (made) of, from (cities or countries)*
Er geht *aus* dem Hause.	*He goes **out of** the house.*
Die Vase ist *aus* Glas.	*The vase is **made of** glass.*
Ich komme *aus* Hamburg.	*I come **from** Hamburg.*
außer	*except, besides*
***Außer* ihm ist niemand da.**	*No one is there **except** him.*
bei	*near, at, in or at the house of, with*
Das Restaurant liegt *beim* (*bei dem*) Bahnhof.	*The restaurant is **near the** railway station.*
Er ist *beim* Arzt.	*He's **at the** doctor's.*
Er ist *bei* seinem Freund.	*He is (over) **at** his friend's (house).*
Hast du den Brief *bei* dir?	*Do you have the letter **with** you?*
gegenüber	*opposite, across from*
Der Lehrer sitzt mir *gegenüber*.	*The teacher is sitting **opposite** me.*
mit	*with*
Sie schreibt *mit* einem Bleistift.	*She is writing **with** a pencil.*
nach	*after, to (cities and countries)*
Wir fahren nächstes Jahr *nach* Deutschland.	*We're going to go **to** Germany next year.*
***Nach* dem Zweiten Weltkrieg gab es ein geteiltes Deutschland.**	***After** World War II there was a divided Germany.*
seit	*since, for (duration of time)*
***Seit* der Zeit spricht er nicht mehr mit mir.**	***Since** that time he has not spoken with me (anymore).*
Wir wohnen *seit* einem Jahr in Bonn.	*We have been living in Bonn **for** a year.*
von	*from, of, by (authorship), about*
Der Brief kommt *von* meinem Freund.	*The letter comes **from** my friend.*
Sie sprechen *vom* Wetter.	*They're talking **of** (**about**) **the** weather.*
Diese Symphonie ist nicht *von* Brahms.	*This symphony is not **by** Brahms.*
zu	*to*
Was sagte er *zu* Ihnen?	*What did he say **to** you?*

2. As you have no doubt noticed previously, several of these prepositions may be contracted with the definite article:

beim = **bei dem**
vom = **von dem**
zum = **zu dem**
zur = **zu der**

Hans wohnt *beim* Onkel.	*Hans lives* **with his** *uncle.*
Paula geht *zur* Universität.	*Paula goes* **to the** *university.*

Choose the best meaning for the indicated words. Continue to circle unfamiliar words for review.

	1. Der Präsident kommt **aus** dem Hotel. (*of/out of*)
1. The president is coming *out of* the hotel.	**2.** **steigen** = *to climb* Hans steigt **aus** dem Auto. (*out of/away from/into*)
2. Hans is getting *out of* the automobile.	**3.** Friedrich ist **aus** Berlin. (*of/out of/from*)
3. Friedrich is *from* Berlin.	**4.** Jörg wohnt **bei** seinem Onkel. (*away from/with*)
4. Jörg lives *with* his uncle (*at* his uncle's).	**5.** Emil war gestern **bei** seiner Tante. (*by/at the home of*)
5. Emil was *at* his aunt's yesterday.	**6.** Inge wohnt **bei** der Kirche. (*near/at*)
6. Inge lives *near* the church.	**7.** Potsdam liegt **bei** Berlin. (*with/at/near*)
7. Potsdam is *near* Berlin.	**8.** **dir** = *you* Hast du kein Geld **bei** dir? (*near/with/at*)
8. Don't you have any money *with* you?	**9.** **sich** = *you* Haben Sie das Buch **bei** sich? (*with/near*)
9. Do you have the book *with* you?	**10.** Fahren Sie morgen **nach** München? (*after/to*)
10. Are you going to go *to* Munich tomorrow?	**11.** **das Essen** = *eating, the meal* **Nach** dem Essen trinken wir eine Tasse Kaffee. (*after/to*)
11. *After* eating (the meal) we drink a cup of coffee.	**12.** Was **wird aus** Deutschland? (If **wird** means *will become,* **aus** must mean: *of/out of/from*)

12. What will become *of* Germany?	**13.** Heute besteht Irland **aus** zwei Teilen. (*from/of/out of*)
13. Today Ireland consists *of* two parts.	**14.** **gesehen** = *seen* **geteilt** = *separated, divided* **Vom** (von dem) kirchlichen Standpunkt aus gesehen, ist Deutschland geteilt? (*from the/outside of the*)
14. Seen *from the* standpoint of the church, is Germany divided?	**15.** Deutschland war **von** 1871 bis 1945 ein Staat. (*of/by/from*)
15. Germany was a single state *from* 1871 to 1945.	**16.** **Seit** dem 3. Oktober 1990 ist es wieder ein Staat. (*in spite of/since*)
16. *Since* October 3, 1990, it is again a single state.	**17.** **ganz** = *entirely, wholly* **das Ganze** = __________
17. *the whole, the entirety*	**18.** **wurde vereinigt** = *was united* Deutschland wurde **von** Bismarck zu einem Ganzen vereinigt. (*of/by/from*)
18. Germany was united into a whole *by* Bismarck.	**19.** **die Gegenüberstellung** = *the confrontation* War Deutschland einmal ein Symbol für die Gegenüberstellung **von** Osten und Westen? (*by/from/of*)
19. Was Germany once a symbol of the confrontation *of* East and West?	**20.** **vorwiegend** = *predominantly, mainly, chiefly* Zeigt Deutschland eine Gegenüberstellung **zwischen** dem vorwiegend protestantischen Norden und dem hauptsächlich katholischen Süden? (*between/by/from*)
20. Does Germany exhibit (lit.: show) a confrontation *between* the predominantly Protestant North and the predominantly Catholic South?	**21.** **Außer** Deutschland waren auch andere Länder geteilt, zum Beispiel Irland, Vietnam und Korea. (*except/besides*)
21. *Besides* Germany other countries were also divided, for example, Ireland, Vietnam, and Korea.	**22.** **der Schwerpunkt** = *focal point* Geographisch und historisch gesehen, ist Deutschland ein Land **mit** vielen Schwerpunkten, Ländern und Dialekten.

22. From a geographical and historical point of view, Germany is a country *with* many focal points, states, and dialects.	**23.** **mannigfaltig** = *diverse, varied* Die Landschaft Deutschlands ist auch mannigfaltig.
23. Germany's scenery is also varied. (**Landschaft** = landscape, countryside)	**24.** **Seit** Luther hat Deutschland eine gemeinsame Sprache. (*for/since*)
24. *Since* Luther Germany has had a common language.	**25.** **beim** is the contraction of __________
25. **bei dem**	**26.** **vom** is the contraction of __________
26. **von dem**	**27.** **zum** is the contraction of __________
27. **zu dem**	**28.** **zur** is the contraction of __________
28. **zu der**	

PROGRESS TEST

Give the meanings of the indicated words. If you miss any of them, review them before continuing to the next section.

1. **bestehen aus** = *to consist of*
   Heute besteht Irland **aus** zwei Teilen.
2. Herbert wohnt **bei** seiner Tante.
3. Deutschland war einmal ein Symbol für die Gegenüberstellung **von** Osten und Westen.
4. **Außer** Deutschland waren auch andere Länder geteilt, zum Beispiel Irland, Vietnam und Korea.
5. Geographisch und historisch gesehen, ist Deutschland ein Land **mit** vielen Schwerpunkten, Bundesländern und Dialekten.
6. **Nach** dem Essen trinken wir eine Tasse Kaffee.
7. **Seit** Luther hat Deutschland eine gemeinsame Sprache.
8. Was sagte der deutsche Dramatiker Bertolt Brecht **zur** Wiedervereinigungsfrage?

Answer key: **1.** of; **2.** with (at the home of); **3.** of; **4.** besides; **5.** with; **6.** after; **7.** since; **8.** about.

20. *Prepositions—accusative case*

1. The accusative case follows these prepositions:

bis	*until, to, as far as*
Wir bleiben *bis* vier Uhr.	*We're staying* ***until*** *four.*
Er fährt nur *bis* München.	*He is only traveling* ***as far as*** *Munich.*
durch	*through, by means of*
Reist du nicht *durch* Italien?	*Aren't you going to travel* ***through*** *Italy?*
Das Haus wurde *durch* den Wind geschädigt.	*The house was damaged* ***by*** *the wind.*
für	*for*
Der Vater kaufte einen Ball *für* seinen Sohn.	*The father bought a ball* ***for*** *his son.*
gegen	*against, around or about (time), toward (direction)*
Ich habe nichts *gegen* ihn.	*I have nothing* ***against*** *him.*
Erika kommt *gegen* sechs Uhr nach Hause.	*Erika will come home* ***about*** *six o'clock.*
ohne	*without*
***Ohne* Wasser kann man nicht leben.**	*One cannot live* ***without*** *water.*
um	*around, at (time)*
Der Bus fährt *um* die Ecke.	*The bus goes (is going)* ***around*** *the corner.*
Kommt Anja *um* sechs?	*Is Anja coming* ***at*** *six?*
wider	*against*
Das ist *wider* meine Natur.	*That is* ***against*** *my nature.*

2. Two accusative prepositions usually follow their objects, similar to English: I saw him two years *ago*.

entlang	*along*
Den Fluß *entlang* stehen hohe Bäume.	*Tall trees stand* ***along*** *the river.*
lang	*for*
Viele Jahre *lang* war er ein armer Mensch.	***For*** *many years he was a poor man.*

3. Several of these prepositions may be contracted with the definite article:

durchs = **durch das**
fürs = **für das**
ums = **um das**

Michael läuft *durchs* Haus. — *Michael is running **through the** house.*

Select the meaning of the indicated prepositions which is suggested by the context.

	1. **bleiben** = *to stay* Zwei Monate **lang** blieb Margarete auf dem Lande. (*along/for*)
1. *For* two months Margarete stayed in the country. (For past tense of strong verbs see §35.)	**2.** Die ganze Familie sitzt wieder **um** e i n e n Tisch. (*around/for*)
2. Once again the whole family is sitting *around* a single table.	**3.** **die Ecke** = *the corner* Alois geht **um** die Ecke zum Postamt. (*at/for/around*)
3. Alois goes *around* the corner to the post office.	**4.** **Um** drei Uhr komme ich wieder nach Hause. (*at/for*)
4. *At* three o'clock I will come home again.	**5.** **bitten** = *to ask* **höflich** = *courteous, polite* Der Räuber bat mich höflichst **um** mein Geld. (*for/at/around*)
5. The robber asked me most courteously *for* my money.	**6.** **wer** = *whoever, who* Wer nicht mit mir ist, ist **wider** mich. (Bibel) (*for/against*)
6. Whoever is not with me is *against* me.	**7.** **mag** = *can, may* Ist Gott für uns, wer mag **wider** uns sein? (Bibel) (*for/against*)
7. If God is for us, who can be *against* us?	**8.** **Graz:** a city in Austria Kommen Sie bald **wieder** nach Graz! (*against/again*)
8. Come back to Graz *again* soon! (Note: **wieder** is an adverb, not a preposition.)	**9.** Wann werden wir Sie **wieder** sehen?
9. When will we see you *again*?	**10.** **die Niederlage** = *the defeat* die Niederlage des Dritten Reiches

10. the defeat of the Third Reich	**11.** Deutschland war im Jahre 1945 e i n Staat **bis** die Niederlage des Dritten Reiches. (*after/until/before*)
11. Germany was a united state *until* the defeat of the Third Reich in 1945.	**12.** **beide** = *both* **getrennt** = *separated* Die beiden deutschen Staaten, die Bundesrepublik Deutschlands (BRD) und die Deutsche Demokratische Republik (DDR), blieben **bis** 1990 getrennt. (*to/as far as/until*)
12. The two German states, the Federal Republic of Germany and the German Democratic Republic, remained separated *until* 1990.	**13.** **Bayern** = *Bavaria* Fahren Sie nur **bis** München, die Hauptstadt Bayerns! (*until/as far as*)
13. Go only *as far as* Munich, the capital of Bavaria!	**14.** **reisen** = *to travel* Darf man eigentlich **durch** die ganzen Vereinigten Staaten ohne Paß reisen? (*throughout/by means of*)
14. Can one really travel *throughout* the whole United States without a passport?	**15.** Wurde Deutschland sprachlich **durch** Luther zu einem Ganzen vereinigt? (*through/by*)
15. Was Germany linguistically united into a whole *by* Luther?	**16.** **voraussehen** = *to foresee* Ist es wahr, daß **gegen** 1945 die Niederlage des Dritten Reiches klar vorauszusehen war? (*towards/against*)
16. Is it true that *towards* 1945 the defeat of the Third Reich was clearly foreseen (to be seen)?	**17.** **die Gnade** = *mercy* **Gegen** seine Feinde zeigte er keine Gnade. (*against/towards*)
17. He showed no mercy *towards* his enemies.	**18.** Im Zweiten Weltkrieg kämpften Engländer, Russen, Amerikaner, Franzosen und noch andere Nationen **gegen** die Deutschen. (*against/towards*)
18. In the Second World War the English, Russians, Americans, French, as well as other nations fought *against* the Germans.	**19.** Das Los der Hitler-Politik: Deutsche **gegen** Deutsche. (*towards/against*)
19. The fate (lot) of Hitler's policies: Germans *against* Germans.	**20.** **das Gefängnis** = *the prison* Die Mauer in Berlin war eine Barrikade **für** Westberliner und ein Gefängnis **für** Ostberliner.

20. The Berlin Wall was a barrier *for* West Berliners and a prison *for* East Berliners.	**21.** **schön** = *beautiful* **die Schönheit** = __________
21. *beauty*	**22.** **einmalig** = *unique* Dresden war berühmt **für** seine einmalige Schönheit.
22. Dresden was famous *for* its unique beauty.	**23.** **sichern** = *to safeguard, protect* **Ohne** die Mauer in Berlin konnte die DDR die ökonomische Stabilität nicht sichern. (*without/with*)
23. *Without* the Berlin Wall the German Democratic Republic could not safeguard its economic stability.	**24.** **nachts** = *in the night* Nachts **um** zwölf werden wir den Film sehen.
24. *At* twelve midnight we will see the film.	**25.** **stattfinden** = *to take place* **Ohne** Konzessionen konnte die Wiedervereinigung Deutschlands nicht stattfinden. (*because of/without*)
25. The reunification of Germany could not take place *without* concessions (**konnte** = past tense of **können**).	**26.** Die **Mauer entlang** gab es viele Wachttürme.
26. *Along the Wall* there were many watchtowers.	**27.** Wien, heute die Hauptstadt Österreichs, war fast fünf Jahrhunderte **lang** deutsche Hauptstadt. (*for/long*)
27. Vienna, today the capital of Austria, was the German capital *for* almost five centuries.	**28.** **Durchs** is the contraction of __________
28. **durch das**	**29.** **Fürs** is naturally the contraction of __________
29. **für das**	**30.** And **ums** can only be the contraction of __________
30. **um das**	

PROGRESS TEST

Choose the correct meaning for the indicated words.

1. **Bis** die Bundesrepublik und die DDR die notwendigen Konzessionen machten . . .
   (a) after (b) until (c) before (d) while
2. Wurde Deutschland sprachlich **durch** Luther zu einem Ganzen vereinigt?
   (a) in spite of (b) during (c) against (d) by

3. Ist es wahr, daß **gegen** 1945 die Niederlage des Dritten Reiches klar vorauszusehen war?
   (a) towards (b) away from (c) against (d) for
4. Der Räuber bat mich höflichst **um** mein Geld.
   (a) until (b) towards (c) around (d) for
5. Die Mauer in Berlin war ein Gefängnis **für** Ostdeutsche und eine Barrikade **für** Westberliner.
   (a) until (b) with (c) for (d) toward
6. Konnte eine Wiedervereinigung je stattfinden **ohne** Konzessionen?
   (a) with (b) through (c) although (d) without
7. Wer nicht mit mir ist, ist **wider** mich.
   (a) against (b) in favor of (c) with (d) without
8. Die Mauer **entlang** gab es viele Wachttürme.
   (a) through (b) along (c) because of (d) in spite of
9. Zwei Monate **lang** blieb Margarete auf dem Land.
   (a) languishingly (b) through (c) for (d) after

Answer key: **1.** (b); **2.** (d); **3.** (a); **4.** (d); **5.** (c); **6.** (d); **7.** (a); **8.** (b); **9.** (c).

21. *Prepositions—dative/accusative*

1. Some prepositions may be followed either by the dative or by the accusative case.

2. The dative case designates confinement to a particular *location*. The accusative indicates motion towards a specific *destination*. The translation of the preposition varies according to the English verb upon which it depends.

3. The prepositions are listed along with specific examples in both cases, first in the dative, then in the accusative:

an	*at, on, to*
Ich sitze *an* dem Fenster.	*I sit **at** the window.*
Ich gehe *an* das Fenster.	*I go **to** the window.*
Das Photo hängt *an* der Wand.	*The picture is **on** the wall.*
Hängt Wilhelm auch etwas *an* die Wand?	*Is Wilhelm going to hang something **on** the wall, too?*
auf	*on, upon, on top of, in, into, onto*
Wir sitzen *auf* dem Sofa.	*We are sitting **on** the sofa.*
Wir setzen uns *auf* das Sofa.	*We sit down **on** the sofa.*
Mein Großvater wohnt *auf* dem Lande.	*My grandfather lives **in** the country.*
Das Kind rannte *auf* die Straße.	*The child ran **into** (**onto**) the street.*

hinter	*behind*
Das Kind steht *hinter* dem Tisch.	*The child is standing* ***behind*** *the table.*
Das Kind geht *hinter* den Tisch.	*The child is going* ***behind*** *the table.*
in	*in, into, to*
Sie bleibt *in* der Kirche.	*She is staying* ***in*** *the church.*
Sie geht *in* die Kirche.	*She is going* ***into*** *the church.* *She goes* ***to*** *church.*
neben	*beside, next to*
Ihr sitzt *neben* dem neuen Studenten.	*You are sitting* ***next to*** *the new student.*
Setzt euch *neben* den neuen Studenten!	*Sit down* ***next to*** *the new student!*
über	*above, over, about, across*
Wir fliegen *über* den Bergen.	*We are flying* ***above*** *(**over**) the mountains.*
Wir fliegen *über* die Berge.	*We are flying* ***over*** *(**across**) the mountains (from one side to another).*
unter	*under, beneath, below, among*
Der Teufel ist *unter* den Menschen.	*The devil is* ***among*** *the people.*
Eine Katze schleicht *unter* das Haus.	*A cat slinks* ***under*** *the house.*
vor	*before, in front of, ago (time)*
Du stehst *vor* dem Haus.	*You are standing* ***in front of*** *the house.*
Du gehst *vor* das Haus.	*You are going* ***to the front*** *of the house.*
***Vor* fünf Jahren lernte ich schwimmen.**	*I learned how to swim five years* ***ago****.*
zwischen	*between*
Sie sitzt *zwischen* den zwei großen Bäumen.	*She is sitting* ***between*** *the two big trees.*
Sie setzt sich *zwischen* die zwei großen Bäume.	*She sits down (is sitting down)* ***between*** *the two big trees.*

4. Several of these prepositions may be contracted with the definite article:

an dem	=	**am**
an das	=	**ans**
auf das	=	**aufs**
hinter das	=	**hinters**
in dem	=	**im**
in das	=	**ins**
über das	=	**übers**
unter dem	=	**unterm**
unter das	=	**unters**
vor das	=	**vors**

Er geht *vors* Haus. *He goes **to the front of the** house.*
Wir werden den Ball *übers* Haus werfen. *We are going to throw the ball **over the** house.*
Der faule Mensch liegt *im* Bett. *The lazy man lies **in** bed.*
Eleanor Rigby sitzt *am* Fenster. *Eleanor Rigby sits **at the** window.*

Give the meaning of the indicated prepositions as well as of the entire sentences.

	1. Hofften die Deutschen **in** der DDR mehr auf eine Wiedervereinigung als die **in** der Bundesrepublik?
1. Did the Germans *in* the German Democratic Republic hope more for a reunification than those *in* the Federal Republic?	**2.** Deutschland ist immer noch geteilt, **in** den hauptsächlich protestantischen Norden und den vorwiegend katholischen Süden.
2. Germany is still separated *into* the largely Protestant North and the largely Catholic South.	**3.** Berlin ist wieder die Hauptstadt Deutschlands und liegt nicht mehr getrennt.
3. Berlin is again the capital of Germany and is no longer divided.	**4.** Er kaufte ein Haus **neben** dem Haus seines Vaters.
4. He bought a house *next to* his father's house.	**5.** **die Jungen** = *the boys* Die Jungen gehen **hinter** den Kuhstall.
5. The boys are going *behind* the barn (cow shed).	**6.** **Hinter** dem Kuhstall finden Sie die Jungen.
6. You will find the boys *behind* the barn.	**7.** **mir** = *me* Meine Freunde helfen mir **über** die Straße.
7. My friends help me *across* the street.	**8.** **erst** = *only* (*for the first time, not until*) Erst **unter** Bismarck wurde die preußische Hauptstadt Berlin die Hauptstadt Deutschlands.
8. Only *under* Bismarck did the Prussian capital Berlin become the capital of Germany.	**9.** **mich** = *me* Diese Klasse wird mich **unter** die Erde bringen.
9. This class will be the death of me. (Lit.: will bring me *under* the earth.)	**10.** **das Bild** = *picture* **die Wand** = *wall* Das Bild hängt **an** der Wand.
10. The picture hangs *on* the wall.	**11.** Niemand klopft **an** die Tür.
11. No one is knocking *on* (*at*) the door.	**12.** **die Arbeit** = *work* Gehen Sie **an** die Arbeit? (*at/on/to*)
12. Are you going *to* work?	**13.** Er ist jung **an** Jahren. (*on/to/in*)

13. He is young *in* years.	**14.** **klein** = *little* Stellen Sie die Lampe **auf** den kleinen Tisch! (*in/to/on*)
14. Put the lamp *on* the little table.	**15.** **wiederholen** = *to repeat* Können Sie das **auf** deutsch wiederholen? (*on top of/in/at*)
15. Can you repeat that *in* German?	**16.** Wir alle gehen **auf** die Universität. (*at/on/to/in*)
16. We all go *to* the university.	**17.** **Vor** dem Haus steht ein schöner Mercedes. (*before/in front of/ago*)
17. *In front of* the house is a beautiful Mercedes.	**18.** Some of the more common contractions of this group of prepositions are: **am** = __________
18. **an dem**	**19.** **Ans** is the contraction of __________
19. **an das**	**20.** Similarly **aufs** is the contraction of __________
20. **auf das**	**21.** **Ins** can only be a contraction of __________
21. **in das**	**22.** **Im** is no doubt a contraction of __________
22. **in dem**	**23.** Occasionally one sees **hinterm,** a contraction of __________
23. **hinter dem**	**24.** or **unterm**, a contraction of __________
24. **unter dem**	**25.** Keep in mind that it is always a (*definite/indefinite*) article which is contracted.
25. definite	

22. *Infinitival phrases*

The prepositions (**an**)**statt**, **ohne**, and **um** may introduce infinitival phrases having the following meanings:

(an)statt . . . zu	*instead of*
ohne . . . zu	*without*
um . . . zu	*(in order) to*

Anstatt **in die Bibliothek *zu gehen*, geht er ins Kino.**	***Instead of going*** *to the library he goes to the movies.*
Ohne **ein Wort *zu sagen*, starb er.**	***Without saying*** *a word, he died.*
Um **Deutsch *zu lernen*, muß man viel arbeiten.**	(***In order***) ***to learn*** *German you have to study a lot.*

(Notice the form and position of the verb in each of the above examples.)

Choose the correct phrase or meaning as called for, and then give the English meaning of the sentence. (Notice the position of ***zu*** *in the infinitival phrase in relation to the infinitive.)*

	1. **Anstatt** nur eine Hauptstadt **zu haben** wie England und Frankreich, hat Deutschland mehrere gehabt. (*in order to have/instead of having*)
1. *Instead of having* only one capital, as England and France (do), Germany has had several.	**2.** **die Gesellschaft** = *society* **einheitlich** = *uniform* **Statt** eine einheitliche Gesellschaft und e i n e n Staat **zu haben** wie Groß-britannien und Frankreich . . . (*in order to have/instead of having*)
2. *statt . . . zu* *Instead of having* a uniform society and *one* state as (do) Great Britain and France . . . (The separation of the letters of a word as here with **e i n e n** indicates the word is stressed. Here it also changes the meaning of the word from *a* to *one*.)	**3.** **die Lage** = *the situation* **Ohne zu verstehen,** was Deutschland damals war, können wir Deutschlands heutige Lage nicht verstehen. (*without understanding/in order to understand*)
3. *Without understanding* what Germany was then, we cannot understand Germany's current situation.	**4.** **hinzufügen** = *to add to* **Ohne hinzuzufügen,** daß die Deutschen keine einheitliche Gesellschaft hatten wie die Engländer und Franzosen . . .
4. *Without adding* that the Germans did not have a uniform society as the English and the French did . . .	**5.** **wahrscheinlich** = *probably* **Um** die heutige Lage Deutschlands besser **zu verstehen,** müssen wir wahrschein-lich wissen, was Deutschland einmal war. (*in order to understand /instead of understanding*)
5. *In order to understand* Germany's present situation we probably need to know what Germany once was.	**6.** **kennenlernen** = *to become acquainted with, to get (learn) to know* Robert wird nach Deutschland fahren, **um** die verschiedenen Stämme und Dialekte **kennenzulernen.**

6. Robert will go to Germany *in order to get to know* the different tribes and dialects.	**7. umgekehrt** = *vice versa* **Ohne** die Mundart (den Dialekt) **zu können,** kann der Bayer den Friesen nicht verstehen und umgekehrt.
7. *Without knowing* the dialect the Bavarian cannot understand the Frisian, and vice versa.	**8. das Vertrauen** = *trust* Vielleicht haben wir Menschen, als Bürger verschiedener Nationen, nicht das Vertrauen zueinander . . .
8. As citizens of different countries maybe we do not have the trust towards one another . . .	**9. die Not** = *need, necessity* **notwendig** = __________
9. *necessary*	**10. aufbauen** = *to build* . . . das notwendig ist, **um** eine Welt des Friedens **aufzubauen**.
10. . . . that is necessary *in order to build* a world of peace.	**11. Um** eine Welt des Friedens **aufzubauen,** müssen wir als Bürger Vertrauen zueinander haben.
11. We must trust one another as citizens *in order to build* a world of peace. (Lit.: *In order to build* a world of peace, we as citizens must have trust in one another.)	**12. hat verdorben** = *has corrupted* **Anstatt** eine neue Welt **aufzubauen**, haben wir die alte verdorben.
12. *Instead of building* a new world we have corrupted the old one.	

READING PREPARATION

The following exercises introduce and review vocabulary for the reading passage. Continue to circle new or unfamiliar words.

	1. wurde vereinigt = *was united* Deutschland wurde durch Luther und Bismarck zu einem Ganzen vereinigt.
1. Germany was united into a whole (a nation) by Luther and Bismarck. (**Wurde** plus past participle forms the passive voice.)	**2.** Nach Hitlers Sturz wurde Deutschland geteilt.
2. After Hitler's fall, Germany was divided.	**3.** Deutschland, das sprachlich durch Luther und und viel später politisch von Bismarck zu einem Ganzen vereinigt wurde, wurde nach Hitlers Sturz wieder geteilt.

3. Germany, which was united into a whole by Luther linguistically and much later by Bismarck politically, was again divided after Hitler's fall.	**4.** Großbritannien und Frankreich haben praktisch nur eine Hauptstadt.
4. Practically speaking, Great Britain and France have only one capital.	**5.** **im Vergleich zu** = *in comparison to* **mehrere** = *several* Im Vergleich zu Großbritannien und Frankreich hat Deutschland mehrere Städte . . .
5. In comparison to Great Britain and France, Germany has several cities . . .	**6.** **galten** = past tense of **gelten** (*to serve*) Im Vergleich zu Großbritannien und Frankreich hat Deutschland mehrere Städte, die als historische Zentren der verschiedenen Länder Deutschlands galten.
6. In comparison to Great Britain and France, Germany has several cities which served as historical centers of the different regions of Germany.	**7.** Heute haben die Deutschen wahrscheinlich immer noch nicht eine gemeinsame Tradition, eine einheitliche Gesellschaft und e i n e n Staat wie die Engländer und Franzosen.
7. Today the Germans probably still do not have a common tradition, a uniform society, and *one* state the way the English and French do.	**8.** Leipzig und Dresden sind Städte, die früher in der Ostzone waren.
8. Leipzig and Dresden are cities which were formerly in the East Zone. (The term East Zone was used before the official forming of the German Democratic Republic, i.e., GDR.)	**9.** **die Messe** = *the fair* **damals** = *at the time* Leipzig, die älteste Messestadt Europas, und Dresden, die Hauptstadt des Landes Sachsen, waren in der Ostzone.
9. Leipzig, the European city with the oldest trade fair, and Dresden, the capital of the state of Saxony, were in the East Zone.	**10.** **wohnen** = *to live in* Germanische Völker wohnen in Deutschland.
10. Germanic peoples live in Germany.	**11.** **bewohnt** = *inhabited* Deutschland ist ein Land, von germanischen Völkern bewohnt.
11. Germany is a country inhabited by Germanic peoples.	**12.** **zum Teil** = *in part* Deutschland ist ein Land, von germanischen Völkern bewohnt und zum Teil von einer gemeinsamen Sprache vereint.
12. Germany is a country inhabited by Germanic peoples and united in part by a common language.	**13.** Wegen der Berliner **Mauer** . . .

13. Because of the Berlin *Wall* . . .	**14.** **schneiden** = *to cut* **zerschneiden** = *to cut into pieces . . .* wurde Berlin in zwei Teile zerschnitten.
14. . . . Berlin was cut into two parts.	**15.** **lag** = *lay* Berlin, die Hauptstadt Deutschlands, lag in zwei Teile zerschnitten.
15. Berlin, the capital of Germany, lay cut into two parts.	**16.** **trennen** = *to divide, to separate* Die Mauer trennte die Bürger Berlins.
16. The Wall separated the citizens of Berlin.	**17.** **gegenüber** = *opposite* **stellen** = *to put, to place* **gegenüberstellen** = *to confront* **die Gegenüberstellung** = *confrontation* Die Gegenüberstellung von Osten und Westen . . .
17. The confrontation of East and West . . .	**18.** **zeigen** = *to show* Was zeigt uns die Berliner Mauer?
18. What does the Berlin Wall show us?	**19.** **der Vorhang** = curtain der **Eiserne Vorhang** = _______
19. the *Iron Curtain*	**20.** Was **zeigte** uns der Eiserne Vorhang? (*does show/ did show*)
20. What *did* the Iron Curtain *show* us?	**21.** **früh** = *early* **früher** = *earlier* In Deutschland war die christliche Welt früher **einig**?
21. Was the Christian world in Germany *united* earlier?	**22.** **die Wirtschaft** = *the economy* **wirtschaftlich** = *economic* **Werden** heute politische und wirtschaftliche Probleme **diskutiert**?
22. *Are* political and economic problems *being discussed* today? (cf. ch. 20: present passive verb form)	**23.** **suchen** = *to search for, to look for, to seek* **Werden** Wege **gesucht** . . .
23. *Are* ways *being sought* . . .	**24.** **zusammen arbeiten** = *to work together* . . . **wie** die Menschen zusammen Leben und arbeiten können?
24. *as to how* people can live and work together?	**25.** Wie können wir Menschen **verschiedener** Konfessionen, Religionen und Nationalitäten zusammen leben und arbeiten?

25. How can we people *of different* confessions, religions, and nationalities live and work together?	**26.** **sicher** = *sure, certain, safe, secure* **sichern** = *to secure, to guarantee, to fortify, to steady* Was **sollte** die Berliner Mauer **sichern**?
26. What *was* the Berlin Wall *supposed to guarantee*?	**27.** **die Zukunft** = *future* **spielen** = to play Welche Rolle **wird** Deutschland in der Zukunft Europas **spielen**?
27. What role *will* Germany *play* in the future of Europe? (**Werden** + infinitive = future tense)	**28.** **bleiben** = *to remain, to stay* Diese Frage bleibt **noch** offen.
28. This is *still* an open question. (Lit.: This question *still* remains open.)	**29.** **besprechen** = *to discuss* Heute nach der Mauer **werden** nicht nur die Probleme Deutschlands **besprochen** . . . (*are being discussed/were being discussed*)
29. Today after the Wall not only *are* Germany's problems *being discussed* . . .	**30.** . . . sondern auch die Probleme Europas.
30. . . . but also the problems of Europe.	**31.** „Wenn Deutschland einmal vereint sein wird—jeder weiß, das wird kommen, niemand weiß, wann—wird es nicht sein durch Krieg." (Bertolt Brecht, ca. 1950)
31. "When Germany is once again united—everyone knows that will come, no one knows when—it will not be through war."	

Review the words you have circled throughout this chapter and then go on to the reading passage.

The following has been criticized as an oversimplification of historical data, but then the purpose of the passage is to introduce the student to accessible German vocabulary, not to be the last word on German history.

Deutschland gestern, heute und morgen

Obgleich Deutschland sprachlich durch Luther vereinigt wurde, war es fast nie e i n Reich. Nur von 1871 unter Bismarck bis 1945 war Deutschland wirklich ein Staat. Deutschland ist seit Luther von einer gemeinsamen Sprache vereinigt, aber vom kirchlichen Standpunkt gesehen, ist es immer noch geteilt: in den vorwiegend protestantischen Norden und den vorwiegend katholischen Süden. Noch etwas teilt dieses Land: die verschiedenen Stämme und Dialekte, die heute noch existieren. Diese Dialekte sind die wahre Sprache der Germanen. Noch heute kann ein Bayer die Mundart (den Dialekt) der Friesen nicht verstehen und umgekehrt.

Hinzuzufügen ist, daß die Deutschen keine gemeinsame Tradition, keine einheitliche Gesellschaft, keinen Staat hatten, wie die Engländer oder die Franzosen. Im Vergleich zu Großbritannien und Frankreich, welche praktisch nur eine Hauptstadt besitzen, London und Paris, hat Deutschland mehrere Städte, die als historische Zentren der verschiedenen Länder Deutschlands galten, zum Beispiel: die alte Kaiserstadt Frankfurt; die preußische Hauptstadt Berlin, die erst unter Bismarck die Hauptstadt Deutschlands wurde; München, die Hauptstadt Bayerns; die alte Hansestadt Hamburg; Leipzig, die älteste Messestadt Europas; und Dresden, berühmt für seine einmalige Schönheit und als Hauptstadt des Königreichs Sachsen. Wien, heute die Hauptstadt Österreichs, war fast fünf Jahrhunderte lang deutsche Hauptstadt.

Das alles hilft uns vielleicht, die heutige Lage Deutschlands besser zu verstehen: ein Land, von germanischen Völkern bewohnt und zum Teil von einer gemeinsamen Sprache vereint. Geographisch und historisch gesehen, ist es ein Land mit vielen Schwerpunkten, Ländern und Dialekten.

Nach dem Zweiten Weltkrieg war dieses Land im Kleinen ein Symbol für ganz Europa: nämlich für die Gegenüberstellung von Osten und Westen, Norden und Süden. Der Eiserne Vorhang zeigte, daß wir Menschen als Bürger verschiedener Nationen nicht das Vertrauen zueinander hatten, das notwendig ist, um eine Welt des Friedens aufzubauen.

Die Berliner Mauer zeigte im Kleinen die Gegenüberstellung von Osten und Westen. Der protestantische Norden und der katholische Süden in Deutschland zeigten, daß früher die christliche Welt nicht einig war. Aber heute werden nicht nur die politischen und wirtschaftlichen Probleme Europas diskutiert, sondern auch Wege werden gesucht, wie die Menschen verschiedener Konfessionen, Religionen und Nationalitäten zusammen leben und arbeiten konnen.

Der Eiserne Vorhang ist weg. Die Mauer, die der DDR die ökonomische und politische Stabilität sichern sollte ist auch weg. Berlin, die lange Jahre in zwei Teilen zerschnitten war, ist wieder vereinigt.

Welche Rolle werden Deutschland and die Deutschen in der Zukunft Europas spielen? Diese Frage bleibt noch offen.

Chapter Six

23. *Personal pronouns—declension*
24. *Modal auxiliary verbs—present tense*
25. *Modals—idiomatic meanings*
26. Wissen, kennen

Reading: From Franz Kafka:
Hochzeitsvorbereitungen auf dem Lande
From Friedrich Nietzsche: Der Antichrist

Review! Before beginning chapter 6, take a few minutes to review the words and phrases you circled in the previous chapters.

23. *Personal pronouns—declension*

1. The personal pronouns introduced in chapter 2 have the following case forms:

1st PERSON	**SINGULAR**		**PLURAL**		**SING. & PLURAL**	
Nominative	**ich**	*I*	**wir**	*we*		
Genitive	**meiner**	*(of) me*	**unser**	*(of) us*		
Dative	**mir**	*(to) me*	**uns**	*(to) us*		
Accusative	**mich**	*me*	**uns**	*us*		
2nd PERSON						
Nominative	**du**	*you*	**ihr**	*you*	**Sie**	*you*
Genitive	**deiner**	*(of) you*	**euer**	*(of) you*	**Ihrer**	*(of) you*
Dative	**dir**	*(to) you*	**euch**	*(to) you*	**Ihnen**	*(to) you*
Accusative	**dich**	*you*	**euch**	*you*	**Sie**	*you*

3rd PERSON					
Nominative	**er**	*he*	*it*	**sie**	*they*
Genitive	**seiner**	*(of) him*		**ihrer**	*(of) them*
Dative	**ihm**	*(to) him*	*(to) it*	**ihnen**	*(to) them*
Accusative	**ihn**	*him*	*it*	**sie**	*them*

SINGULAR

Nominative	**sie**	*she*	*it*	
Genitive	**ihrer**	*(of) her*		
Dative	**ihr**	*(to) her*	*(to) it*	
Accusative	**sie**	*her*	*it*	
Nominative	**es**	*it*	*he*	*she*
Genitive	**seiner**	*(of) it*	*(an archaic form)*	
Dative	**ihm**	*(to) it*	*(to) him*	*(to) her*
Accusative	**es**	*it*	*him*	*her*

2. Notice that in German **er, sie,** and their inflected forms may be translated into English with *it.*

Der Motor läuft nicht.	*The motor doesn't run.*
***Er* läuft nicht.**	***It** doesn't run.*
Die Maschine ist kaputt.	*The machine is broken.*
***Sie* ist kaputt.**	***It** is broken.*

3. Likewise **es** and its inflected forms may be translated with *he, she, him, her.*

Das Männlein sagte nichts.	*The little man said nothing.*
***Es* sagte nichts.**	***He** said nothing.*
Das Mädchen ist schön.	*The girl is beautiful.*
***Es* ist schön.**	***She** is beautiful.*

In recent usage, **sie** *may be used to refer to the nouns* **Mädchen** *and* **Fräulein**.

This set of exercises is intended to familiarize you with the declension of the personal pronouns. Select the correct meaning and give the case of the indicated pronouns.

	1. **denken** = *to think* **gedenken** = *to remember* Gedenken Sie **meiner** nicht mehr!
1. Remember *me* no more! (genitive) (Think *of me* no more.)	2. Der Dramatiker gibt **mir** ganz neue Gedanken. (*of me/me*)
2. The playwright gives *me* completely new ideas. (dative)	3. Für **mich** kaufst du den neuen Wagen? (*me/I*)
3. Are you buying the new car for *me*? (accusative)	4. **sich schämen** = *to be ashamed of* Schämt er sich **deiner?** (*of you/of her*)
4. Is he ashamed *of you*? (genitive) (Note that **sich schämen** is a reflexive verb. See §50.)	5. Rudi erklärt **dir,** wie er die Barrikade stürmte. (*to you/yours*)
5. Rudi is explaining *to you* how he stormed the barricade. (dative)	6. Besucht er **dich** morgen? (*you/me*)

6. Is he going to visit *you* tomorrow? (accusative)	**7. harren** = *to wait for, expect* Karl ist in München. Karin harrt **seiner.** (*for him/for her*)
7. Karl is in Munich. Karin is waiting *for him*. (genitive)	**8. leisten** = *to perform, achieve, make, do* **Hilfe leisten** = *to help* Ich leiste **ihm** keine Hilfe mehr. (*her*/(*to*) *him*)
8. I do not help *him* anymore. (dative)	**9.** Wir leisten **ihr** keine Hilfe mehr. (*her/him/you*)
9. We do not help *her* anymore. (dative)	**10.** Erst müssen wir **ihn** umringen. (*them/him*)
10. First we have to surround *him*. (accusative)	**11.** Jetzt erinnere ich mich **ihrer**. (*you/her*)
11. Now I remember *her.* (genitive) (Note: Depending on the context **ihrer** could also mean *them*.)	**12.** Jetzt erinnere ich mich **Ihrer**. (*you/her*)
12. Now I remember *you*. (genitive)	**13. wußte** = *past of* **wissen**, *to know* Ich wußte nicht, daß es **euch** gehörte. (*to you/to us/to her*)
13. I did not know that it belonged *to you*. (dative)	**14.** Ich wußte nicht, daß das Stück Käse **ihr** gehörte. (*to you/to her*)
14. I did not know that the piece of cheese belonged *to her.* (dative)	**15. rasend** = *furious* Der Gedanke, daß er ihr untreu ist, macht **sie** rasend. (*she/her*)
15. The thought that he is unfaithful to her makes *her* furious. (accusative) (Note: Depending on the context **sie** could also mean *them*.)	**16.** Der Gedanke, daß sie **ihm** untreu ist, macht ihn rasend. (*to her/to him/to you*)
16. The thought that she is unfaithful *to him* makes him furious. (dative)	**17. der Stoß** = *an abrupt shove with force* **schieben** = *push* Das Auto läuft nicht. Geben Sie **ihm** aber keinen Stoß. Schieben Sie nur, bitte. (*him/it/them*)
17. The car does not run. Don't give *it* a shove. Please, just push. (dative)	**18.** Ich kann **es** nicht finden. (*he/it*)
18. I cannot find *it*. (accusative)	**19.** Es waren **unser** fünf. (*of us/of them/of you*)

19. There were five *of us.* (genitive)	**20.** **fremd** = *foreign* Diese Mundart ist **uns** fremd. (*to you/to us/to them*)
20. This dialect is foreign *to us.* (dative)	**21.** Dieses Gefängnis kann **uns** nicht halten. (*of us/us*)
21. This prison cannot hold *us.* (accusative)	**22.** Der Gedanke, daß er **ihr** untreu ist, macht sie rasend. (*to her/to you*)
22. The thought that he is unfaithful *to her* makes her furious. (dative) (Remember that **ihr** means *you* only in the nominative.)	**23.** Der Gedanke, daß er **ihnen** untreu ist, macht sie rasend. (*to him/to them*)
23. The thought that he is unfaithful *to them* makes them furious. (dative)	**24.** **sich erbarmen** = *to have pity* Er erbarmt sich **euer**. (*on you/on us/on her*)
24. He has pity *on you.* (genitive)	**25.** **versprechen** = *to promise* Wir versprechen **euch**, nicht mehr zu kommen. (*you/her*)
25. We promise *you* not to come anymore. (dative)	**26.** Sie versucht nicht mehr, **euch** zu sehen. (*you/us*)
26. She is not trying to see *you* anymore. (accusative)	**27.** Wir versprechen **ihr**, nicht mehr zu kommen. (*her/you*)
27. We promise *her* not to come anymore. (dative)	**28.** Ihr versprecht **ihm**, nicht mehr zu kommen! (*you/him*)
28. You promise *him* not to come anymore! (dative)	**29.** **Ihr** seid alle Dummköpfe! (*her/you*)
29. *You* are all blockheads! (nominative)	**30.** **ist bewußt** = *is aware* Obwohl sie vor ihm stehen, ist er **ihrer** nicht bewußt. (*of them/of her*)
30. Although they are standing in front of him, he is not aware *of them.* (genitive) (**stehen** indicates the plural.)	**31.** Obwohl sie vor ihm steht, ist er **ihrer** nicht bewußt. (*of them/of her*)
31. Although she is standing in front of him, he is not aware *of her.* (**steht** indicates the singular.)	**32.** Die gesamte Bevölkerung wird **Ihnen** folgen. (*you/them*)

32. The entire population will follow *you.* (dative) (Notice the capital letter—**Ihnen**—which distinguishes the 2nd person pronoun from the 3rd person plural pronoun.)	**33. dürfen** = *to be permitted, may* Ich darf mit **ihnen** sprechen. (*you/them*)
33. I may speak with *them.* (dative)	**34.** Wir verstehen **sie** schon nicht mehr. (*they/he/them*)
34. We already do not understand *them* anymore. (accusative)	**35.** Uns verstehen **sie** nicht mehr. (*they/her/you*)
35. *They* do not understand us anymore. (Nominative)	**36.** Es sind **Ihrer** drei. (*of her/of them/of you*)
36. There are three *of you.* (genitive) (**Ihrer** = *of you;* **ihrer** = *of them* or *of her.*)	**37.** Maria spricht nur Französisch. Wir verstehen **sie** nicht. (*them/her*)
37. Maria speaks only French. We don't understand *her.* (accusative)	**38. Sie** versteht uns nicht. (*they/she*)
38. *She* doesn't understand us. (nominative) (The verb ending tells you the number.)	**39.** Ich kann **Sie** nicht verstehen! (*you/her/them*)
39. I cannot understand *you!* (accusative)	

PROGRESS TEST

Choose the correct answer. Review any points you miss before going on.

1. Jetzt erinnere ich mich *ihrer.*
Depending on the context, *ihrer* could be translated:
(a) her, them (b) her, you (c) them, you (d) us, them

2. Der Gedanke, daß er *Ihnen* untreu ist, macht mich rasend.
(a) him (b) her (c) you (d) them

3. Ich wußte nicht, daß es *euch* gehörte.
(a) us (b) you (c) them (d) me

4. Karin harrt *unser.*
(a) us (b) you (c) him (d) them

5. Erst müssen wir *sie* umringen.
sie can be translated as:
(a) you, them (b) they, us (c) she, they (d) them, her

Answer key: **1.** (a); **2.** (c); **3.** (b); **4.** (a); **5.** (d).

24. *Modal auxiliary verbs—present tense*

1. The modals and their approximate meanings are:

permission:	**dürfen**	*to be permitted* or *allowed to, may*
ability:	**können**	*to be able to, can*
possibility:	**mögen**	*to like (to), may, to care for*
necessity:	**müssen**	*to have to, to have got to, must*
obligation:	**sollen**	*to be obliged* or *supposed to, are to, shall*
intention:	**wollen**	*to want to, intend to*

2. Notice that the present-tense endings of the modals follow the weak and strong verb patterns for the plural but not for the singular:

ich darf *I may*
du darfst
er, sie, es darf
wir dürfen
ihr dürft
sie dürfen
Sie dürfen

ich kann *I can*
du kannst
er, sie, es kann
wir können
ihr könnt
sie können
Sie können

ich mag *I like*
du magst
er, sie, es mag
wir mögen
ihr mögt
sie mögen
Sie mögen

ich muß *I must*
du mußt
er, sie, es muß
wir müssen
ihr müßt
sie müssen
Sie müssen

ich soll *I am to, I am supposed to*
du sollst
er, sie, es soll
wir sollen
ihr sollt
sie sollen
Sie sollen

ich will *I want to*
du willst
er, sie, es will
wir wollen
ihr wollt
sie wollen
Sie wollen

3. Modal verbs are auxiliary or "helping" verbs. They are usually accompanied, as in English, by the infinitive form of the verb. In German, this dependent infinitive will generally be found at the end of the clause, or in dependent word order as the next to the last word:

Heinz *will* nächstes Jahr nach Deutschland *fliegen*. — *Heinz* ***wants to fly*** *to Germany next year.*

Will **Heinz nächstes Jahr nach Deutschland *fliegen*?**	***Does*** *Heinz* ***want to fly*** *to Germany next year?*
Ich weiß, daß Heinz nächstes Jahr nach Deutschland *fliegen will*.	*I know that Heinz* ***wants to fly*** *to Germany next year.*

4. Remember that **werden** (**er wird**), not **wollen** (**er will**), is used in forming the future tense:

Heinz *wird* nächstes Jahr nach Deutschland *fliegen*.	*Heinz* ***is going to*** *(**will**)* ***fly*** *to Germany next year.*

This set of exercises reviews vocabulary from previous chapters and asks you to differentiate between the various modals. Select the correct meaning of the indicated verbs.

	1. **anbieten** = *to offer* **Darf** ich dir ein Stück Schweizer Schokolade anbieten? (*dare/may*)
1. *May* I offer you a piece of Swiss chocolate?	2. **Dürfen** wir sagen, daß die Teilung Deutschlands ein Symbol für die Teilung Europas war? (*may/must*)
2. *May* we say that the division of Germany was a symbol for the division of Europe?	3. **Kann** er historisch und sehr einfach erklären, was Deutschland eigentlich war? (*is able to/does intend to*)
3. *Is* he *able to* explain historically and very simply what Germany really was?	4. **das Mittelalter** = *the Middle Ages* **Können** Sie mir vier Künstler des deutschen Mittelalters nennen?
4. *Can* you name me four artists of the German Middle Ages?	5. **Darf** man sagen, daß Luther sprachlich und Bismarck politisch Deutschland zu einem Ganzen vereinigten? (*must/may*)
5. *May* one say that Germany was united into a whole by Luther linguistically and by Bismarck politically?	6. Er **mag** weltbekannt sein, aber ich werde trotzdem seine Bücher nicht lesen. (*may/must*)
6. He *may* be world famous, but I will still (in spite of it) not read his books.	7. Seines Stils wegen **will** ich seine Bücher lesen. (*will/want to*)
7. I *want* to read his books because of his style.	8. Den Kaffee **mögen** wir nicht. (*may/do . . . like*)
8. We *do* not *like* the coffee.	9. Heute **kann** ein Bayer nicht die Mundart des Friesen verstehen und umgekehrt. (*is . . . able to/may*)

9. Today a Bavarian *is* not *able to* understand the dialect of a Frisian, and vice versa.	**10.** **Müssen** alle, die Deutsch lernen, sehr intelligent sein? (*must/may*)
10. *Must* everyone who studies German be very intelligent?	**11.** **Muß** er wissen, welche Rolle Adenauer in der deutschen Geschichte spielte? (*does . . . have to/may*)
11. *Does* he *have to* know what role Adenauer played in German history?	**12.** Nietzsche **mag** ein großer Philosoph sein, aber . . . (*must/may*)
12. Nietzsche *may* be a great philosopher, but . . .	**13.** . . . **muß** ich seine Werke lesen? (*do . . . have to/am . . . to*)
13. . . . *do* I *have to* read his works?	**14.** **unsere Feinde** = *our enemies* **Sollen** wir unsere Feinde lieben? (*are . . . supposed to/are . . . allowed to*)
14. *Are* we *supposed to* love our enemies?	**15.** **Müssen** Sie erklären, was dieses Land teilt? (*do . . . have to/are . . . able to*)
15. *Do* you *have to* explain what divides this country?	**16.** **Wollen** die beiden Staaten die notwendigen Konzessionen machen? (*do . . . want to/are . . . obliged to*)
16. *Do* both nations *want to* make the necessary concessions?	**17.** **Will** er die Grenze zwischen Polen und Deutschland vernichten? (*may/does . . . intend to*)
17. *Does* he *intend to* do away with the border between Poland and Germany?	**18.** Du **sollst** deinen Nächsten lieben wie dich selbst. (*shalt/may*)
18. Thou *shalt* love thy neighbor as thyself.	**19.** Sie **wollen** nicht die Mona Lisa wieder anschauen? (*may/do . . . want to*)
19. You (they) *do* not *want* to look at the Mona Lisa again?	**20.** **Will** Luther eine neue Kirche gründen? (*will/does . . . want to*)
20. *Does* Luther *want to* found a new church?	**21.** **je wieder** = *ever again* **Wird** es je wieder ein geteiltes Deutschland geben? (*will/become*)
21. *Will* there ever again be a divided Germany?	**22.** **Wird** die christliche Welt je einig sein? (*will/does . . . want to*)
22. *Will* the Christian world ever be united?	**23.** **Will** die christliche Welt je einig sein? (*will/does . . . want to*)

23. *Does* the Christian world ever *want to* be united?	**24.** **verschieben** = *to shift* Er **will** die Grenzen zwischen Polen und Deutschland nicht vernichten, nur verschieben. (*does . . . want to/will*)
24. He *does* not *want to* destroy the borders between Poland and Germany, only to shift them.	**25.** Lehrt uns die Geschichte, daß wir je eine Welt des Friedens aufbauen **werden?** (*will/become*)
25. Does history teach us that we *will* ever build a world of peace?	

PROGRESS TEST

Choose the correct meaning of the indicated verbs.

1. *Willst du* Deutsch lernen?
(a) Can you (b) Will you (c) Should you (d) Do you want to

2. *Darf* man sagen, daß seine Bücher weltbekannt sind?
(a) May (b) Must (c) Ought (d) Will

3. Seine Bücher *mögen* weltbekannt sein, aber ich will sie nicht lesen.
(a) must (b) should (c) may (d) like to

4. Seine Bücher *werden* weltbekannt.
(a) are worth (b) will (c) are becoming (d) intend to

5. Sie *wird* seine Bücher nicht lesen.
(a) is becoming (b) wants to (c) may (d) will

Answer key: **1.** (d); **2.** (a); **3.** (c); **4.** (c); **5.** (d).

25. *Modals—idiomatic meanings*

1. The dependent infinitive may be omitted if it is clear what the omitted verb is:

Darf man hier Fußball spielen? Ja, das darf man.	*May one play soccer here? Yes, one may (play).*

2. It is common practice to omit the verbs **gehen** (*to go*), **tun** (*to do*), or any other verb of motion or doing, especially if motion is already indicated by the accusative case or an adverb:

Er will hinaus.	*He wants to go out.*
Darfst du das?	*May you do that? (Are you allowed to?)*

3. Idiomatic meanings must be learned by observation and practice. Here are some of the more common idiomatic usages:

The affirmative of **dürfen** denotes permission; the negative **nicht dürfen** denotes lack of permission and is translated *must not:*

Er darf hier bleiben.	*He can (is allowed to, may) stay here.*
Sie dürfen hier nicht rauchen.	*You must not smoke here.*

Können implies ability, possibility, permission:

Er kann gut lesen.	*He can (is able to) read well.*
Ich kann schwimmen.	*I know how to swim.*
Das kann wahr sein.	*That may be true. (It is possible that that is true.)*
Sie können heute ins Kino gehen.	*You can go to the movies today.*

Mögen expresses inclination, liking, possibility:

Ich mag das nicht tun.	*I don't care (like) to do that.*
Er mag dieses Buch nicht.	*He doesn't like (doesn't care for) this book.*
Das mag sein.	*That may be (so).*

Müssen expresses necessity or obligation and is usually translated by *must, have to,* or *have got to:*

Sie müssen jetzt nach Hause gehen.	*You have got to (have to) go home now.*
Ihr müßt das tun.	*You must do that. (You have to do that. You've got to do that.)*

Sollen implies an obligation or a conjecture (rumor):

Du sollst nicht stehlen.	*Thou shalt not steal.*
Sie soll um neun Uhr zu Hause sein.	*She is expected (supposed) to be home at nine o'clock.*
Herr Richter soll sehr reich sein.	*Mr. Richter is said to be very rich.*

Wollen expresses volition, intention, determination; it also translates *to claim to* and *to be about to:*

Ich will morgen sehr früh aufstehen.	*I want (intend, am determined) to get up very early tomorrow.*
Ich wollte eben gehen.	*I was just on the point of going (I was just about to go).*
Er will reich sein.	*He claims to be rich.*
Er will reich werden.	*He wants to become rich.*

The following exercises introduce new vocabulary for the reading passage and give you practice in recognizing the modal verbs. Give the best meaning for the indicated word.

	1. Wir **wollen** eine Diskussion von Nietzsches und Kafkas Ideen über Macht beginnen. (*want/will*)
1. We *want* to begin a discussion of Nietzsche's and Kafka's ideas on power.	**2. die Gewalt** = *force, power* Wir **werden** eine Anekdote von der Gewalt des Militärs lesen. (*will/want to*)
2. We *will* read an anecdote about the power of the military.	**3. erzählen** = *to tell (a story)* Kafka **erzählt uns eine Anekdote** von der Gewalt des Militärs.
3. Kafka *tells us an anecdote* about the power of the military.	**4. ergreifen** = *to seize* In dieser Anekdote kommen zwei Soldaten und **ergreifen** einen Zivilisten.
4. In this anecdote two soldiers come and *seize* a civilian.	**5.** Es **kamen** zwei Soldaten und **ergriffen** mich. (*Are the verbs in the present or the past?*)
5. Two soldiers *came* and *seized* me. (**Es** is a dummy subject.)	**6. zu jeder Zeit** = *at any time, always* Die zwei Soldaten **können** ihn zu jeder Zeit ergreifen. (**können** expresses—*ability/desire*)
6. ability: The two soldiers *can* seize him at any time.	**7. sich wehren** = *to defend oneself* Er **kann** sich nicht wehren, denn sie halten ihn fest. (**kann** here expresses—*possibility/ability/permission*)
7. ability: He *can*not defend himself, for they are holding onto him tightly.	**8. führen** = *to take, to lead* Die Soldaten führen ihn vor **ihren** Kapitän. (*her/their*)
8. The soldiers take him to *their* captain.	**9. der Herr** = *the superior* Die Soldaten führen **den Zivilisten** vor ihren Herrn. (*civilian/civilians*)
9. The soldiers take the *civilian* to their superior.	**10.** Die Soldaten **sollen** den Zivilisten vor ihren Herrn, einen Offizier, führen. (*may/are to*)
10. The soldiers *are to* take the civilian to their superior, an officer.	**11. bunt** =*bright, colorful* **Wie** bunt ist seine Uniform! (*why/how*)
11. *How* colorful his uniform is!	**12.** Er **mag** seine bunte Uniform. (*may/likes*)

12. He *likes* his colorful uniform.	**13.** **fragen** = *to ask* Der Zivilist fragt: „Was **wollt** ihr denn von mir, ich bin ein Zivilist." (*will/want*)
13. The civilian asks, "What do you *want* of me—I am a civilian." (**Denn** here serves merely as an intensifier due to its position, i.e., not the first word in the sentence.)	**14.** Der Zivilist **will** sich gegen den Offizier wehren. (*will/wants to*)
14. The civilian *wants to* defend himself against the officer.	**15.** Es **mag** sein, daß du ein Zivilist bist. (**mag** expresses—*possibility/inclination*)
15. possibility: It *may* be that you are a civilian.	**16.** **fassen** = *to seize* Das **hindert** uns nicht, dich zu fassen. (*prevent/help*)
16. That does not *prevent* us from seizing you.	**17.** **lächeln** = *to smile* Der Offizier lächelte und sagte: „Das **wird** uns nicht hindern, dich zu fassen." (*wants to/is . . . going to*)
17. The officer smiled and said, "That *is* not *going to* prevent us from seizing you."	**18.** **denn** = *for* Wir **können** dich fassen, denn das Militär hat Gewalt über alles. (*may/can*)
18. We *can* seize you, for the military has power over everything.	**19.** **nach** = *according to* Das Militär **mag** Gewalt über alles haben, aber **es soll nicht**, Kafka nach.
19. The military *may* have power over everything, but *it shouldn't have*, according to Kafka.	**20.** Kafka nach **können** Zivilisten sich nicht gegen die Gewalt des Militärs wehren. (*may/can*)
20. According to Kafka, civilians *can*not defend themselves against the power of the military.	**21.** **betreffs** = *concerning* Nietzsche ist berühmt für seine Ideen betreffs des „Übermenschen".
21. Nietzsche is famous for his ideas concerning the "overman" (or "superman"). (**Betreffs** takes the genitive case.)	**22.** **hat gemacht** = *did* Um die deutsche Geschichte besser zu verstehen, müssen wir wissen, was der Nationalsozialismus mit Nietzsches Ideen gemacht hat.
22. In order to increase our understanding of German history, we must know what National Socialism did with Nietzsche's ideas.	**23.** **die Macht** = *power* **das Glück** = *happiness* Das Gefühl der Macht **kennen,** das ist Glück! (*to know/to be able to*)

23. *To know* the feeling of power, that is happiness!	**24.** **erhöhen** = *to increase* Nietzsche nach **soll** alles, was das Gefühl der Macht im Menschen erhöht, gut sein. (*is supposed to/might be*)
24. According to Nietzsche, everything which heightens the feeling of power in a person *is supposed to* be good.	**25.** **die Zufriedenheit** = *contentment, satisfaction* Nietzsche **will**, daß der Mensch nicht Zufriedenheit, sondern mehr Macht sucht. (*will/wants*)
25. Nietzsche *wants* people to seek more power, not contentment.	**26.** **der Widerstand** = *obstacle* Um Glück zu kennen, **muß** man nicht nur gegen Widerstände kämpfen . . . (*must/may*)
26. In order to know happiness one *must* not only fight against obstacles . . .	**27.** **überwinden** = *to overcome* . . . sondern man **muß** diese Widerstände auch überwinden.
27. . . . but one *must* also overcome these obstacles.	**28.** **wird überwunden** = *is being overcome* Glück ist ein Gefühl davon, daß ein Widerstand überwunden wird.
28. Happiness is a feeling that an obstacle is being overcome. (Note that **davon** is not translated here.)	**29.** Was ist **schlecht?** (**Schlecht,** the opposite of **gut,** means ___________)
29. *bad* What is *bad*?	**30.** **schwach** = *weak* **die Schwäche** = *weakness* Was **stammt aus** der Schwäche? Alles was schlecht ist. (*leads to/stems from*)
30. What *stems* from weakness? Everything that is bad.	**31.** **Kann** alles, was aus der Schwäche stammt, schlecht sein? (*does . . . know/can*)
31. *Can* everything which stems from weakness be bad?	**32.** **die Mißratenen** = *misfits* **die Schwachen** = *weaklings* Nietzsche hat auch etwas über den Mißratenen und Schwachen zu sagen.
32. Nietzsche also has something to say about misfits and weaklings.	**33.** **zugrunde gehen** = *to perish* Nietzsche nach **sollen** die Schwachen und Mißratenen zugrunde gehen. (*should/are expected to*)
33. According to Nietzsche, the weak and the misfits *should* perish.	**34.** **noch dazu** = *moreover* Man **soll** ihnen noch dazu helfen. (*should/is said to*)

34. Moreover, one *should* even help them (in this).	**35.** **schädlich** = *damaging, dangerous, pernicious* **das Laster** = *vice, depravity* Das Christentum **soll** schädlicher als irgendein Laster **sein**. (*ought to be/is said to be*)
35. Christianity *is said to be* more damaging than any vice.	**36.** Ich kann diesen deutschen **Satz** nicht lesen. (*sentence/principle*)
36. I cannot read this German *sentence.*	**37.** Kann der erste **Satz** unsrer Menschenliebe sein: Zugrunde mit den Schwachen und Mißratenen? (*principle/sentence*)
37. Can the first *principle* of our love of mankind be: Down with the weaklings and the misfits?	**38.** **die Tüchtigkeit** = *efficiency* **die Tugend** = *virtue* Tüchtigkeit, nicht Tugend, **will** der Grund des Glückes sein. (*wants to/claims to/will*)
38. Efficiency, not virtue, *claims to* be the foundation of happiness.	**39.** **hinführen** = *to lead to* Wo **wird** der Wille zur Macht diese Welt hinführen? (*will/becomes*)
39. Where (to what) *will* the will to power lead the world?	**40.** **der Rand** = *edge, brink, verge* **das Verderben** = *ruin* **Wird** der Wille zur Macht diese Welt an den Rand des Verderbens führen?
40. *Is* the will to power *going to* lead this world to the brink of ruin (or: bring this world to the verge of ruin)?	

PROGRESS TEST

Choose the correct meaning for the indicated words.

1. Die Soldaten **mögen** den Zivilisten nicht vor ihren Herrn, einen Offizier, führen.
   (a) may not (b) do not care to (c) should not (d) will not
2. Ich **kann** mich nicht wehren, denn sie halten mich fest.
   (a) will (b) can (c) must (d) am to
3. Das Militär **mag** Gewalt über alles haben, aber es soll nicht!
   (a) may (b) will (c) must (d) is thought to have
4. Das Christentum **soll** schädlicher sein als irgendein Laster.
   (a) ought to be (b) desires to be (c) may be (d) is said to be

5. Die Schwachen und die Mißratenen **sollen** zugrunde gehen.
(a) must (b) may (c) should (d) want to

6. Wenn man Deutsch sprechen **will**, so **wird** man nach Deutschland gehen müssen.
(a) will . . . will (b) wants . . . becomes (c) will . . . becomes (d) wants . . . will

7. Was man will, ist nicht immer was man **soll**.
(a) shall (b) should (c) is said to be (d) claims to be

8. Was man **mag,** ist nicht immer was man **darf.**
(a) wants . . . can (b) may . . . can (c) likes . . . may do (d) cares . . . wants

Answer key: **1.** (b); **2.** (b); **3.** (a); **4.** (d); **5.** (c); **6.** (d); **7.** (b); **8.** (c).

26. *Wissen, kennen*

1. The verb **wissen** (*to know*), in the present tense, follows the conjugation pattern of the modals:

ich weiß		***wir wissen***
du weißt	***Sie wissen***	***ihr wißt***
er, sie, es weiß		***sie wissen***

Note: Do not confuse the first and third person form **weiß** with **weiß** meaning white.

Kennen (*to be acquainted or familiar with, to know*) takes the regular present-tense verb endings:

ich kenne		***wir kennen***
du kennst	***Sie kennen***	***ihr kennt***
er, sie, es kennt		***sie kennen***

2. **Wissen** means *to know a fact* (either you know it, or you don't):

***Weißt* du, wann er kommt?**	***Do** you **know** when he is coming?*
Ich *weiß*, wie spat es ist.	*I **know** what time it is.*

3. **Kennen** means *to be acquainted with, to be familiar with:*

***Kennen* Sie Herrn Braun?**	***Do** you **know** Mr. Braun?*
***Kennt* ihr Kafkas Werke?**	***Are** you **familiar with** Kafka's works?*

Remember that **können** may also be translated *to know* (*a language*):

Ich *kann* Deutsch.	*I **know** German.*

The verbs *to speak, read*, and *write* are here understood to be included in **kann.**

The purpose of the following exercises and review sentences is to point out the differences between **wissen**, **kennen**, *and* **können**. *Give the correct meaning of the indicated words.*

	1. **nennen** = *to call* **Weißt** du, was Nietzsche gut nennt?
1. *Do* you *know* what Nietzsche calls good?	**2.** Natürlich **wißt** ihr, was schlecht ist.
2. Of course you *know* what is bad.	**3.** **Wissen** Sie, was schädlicher ist als irgendein Laster?
3. *Do* you *know* what is more dangerous than any vice?	**4.** **Kennen** Sie Nietzsches Werk *Zarathustra?*
4. *Are* you *acquainted with* Nietzsche's work *Zarathustra*?	**5.** Er **kann** sich überhaupt **nicht** gegen die Soldaten wehren.
5. He *cannot* defend himself against the soldiers at all.	**6.** Die Soldaten **kennen** mich nicht.
6. The soldiers *do* not *know* me (*are* not *acquainted* with me).	**7.** Das **kann** uns überhaupt nicht hindern, dich zu fassen.
7. That *can*not prevent us from seizing you at all.	**8.** Das Gefühl der Macht **kennen,** das ist Glück!
8. *To know* the feeling of power, that is happiness!	**9.** Wer **kann** das denn glauben?
9. Who *can* (*is able to*) believe that?	**10.** **Kennst** du den alten Herrn?
10. *Do* you *know* the old gentleman?	**11.** Das **können** sie nicht.
11. They *can*not *do* that. Or: They *do* not *know* how to do that.	**12.** Ich **weiß** schon, wie weiß das Stück Papier ist.
12. I already *know* how white that piece of paper is.	

READING PREPARATION

The following is further preparation for the reading passage from Nietzsche's Der Antichrist *as well as practice with German word order. Express in English the meaning of the German sentences.*

	1. Alles erhöht die Macht.
1. Everything increases power.	**2.** Alles, was im Menschen die Macht erhöht, . . .
2. Everything which increases power in people . . .	**3.** Alles, was das Gefühl der Macht im Menschen erhöht, . . .

3. Everything which increases the feeling of power in people . . .	**4.** **der Wille** = *the desire* Alles, was das Gefühl der Macht, den Willen zur Macht im Menschen erhöht, . . .
4. Everything which increases the feeling of power, the desire for power (the will to power) in people . . .	**5.** Alles, was das Gefühl der Macht, den Willen zur Macht, die Macht selbst im Menschen erhöht, ist gut.
5. Everything which increases the feeling of power, the desire for power, power itself in people, is (morally) good.	**6.** Glück ist ein Gefühl.
6. Happiness is a feeling.	**7.** Ist Glück ein Gefühl, daß die Macht wächst?
7. Is happiness a feeling that power is growing?	**8.** Ist Glück ein Gefühl, daß die Macht wächst, daß ein Widerstand überwunden wird?
8. Is happiness a feeling that power is growing, that an obstacle is being overcome?	**9.** Was ist Glück?—Das Gefühl davon, daß die Macht wächst,—daß ein Widerstand überwunden wird.
9. What is happiness?—the feeling that power is growing,—that an obstacle is being overcome.	**10.** Tüchtigkeit ist eine Tugend.
10. Efficiency is a virtue.	**11.** Tüchtigkeit ist für Nietzsche eine Tugend.
11. For Nietzsche efficiency is virtue.	**12.** Für Nietzsche ist Tüchtigkeit Tugend im Renaissance-Stile, *virtu*, moralinfreie Tugend.
12. For Nietzsche efficiency is virtue in the Renaissance style, *virtu**, virtue free of moral hypocrisy. (* *Virtu* may mean here any or all of the following: manliness, bravery; ability, fitness, soundness, excellence, proficiency; virtue.)	**13.** **das Mitleiden** = *pity, sympathy, compassion (literally: suffering with)* Das Mitleiden ist schädlicher als irgendein Laster.
13. Compassion is more damaging than any vice.	**14.** **die Tat** = *the deed* **das Mitleiden der Tat** = *the active compassion* Das Mitleiden der Tat ist schädlicher als irgendein Laster.
14. Active compassion is more harmful than any vice.	**15.** Ist das Mitleiden der Tat mit allen Mißratenen und Schwachen schädlicher als irgendein Laster?
15. Is active compassion for all misfits and weaklings more damaging than any vice?	

PROGRESS TEST

A. Choose the correct meaning for the indicated words.

1. Ist es *schädlich* für die Gesundheit, wenn man raucht und trinkt?
(a) beneficial (b) damaging (c) healthy (d) indifferent

2. Er *wehrte sich* vergebens gegen die Macht der Liebe.
(a) forced himself (b) fought himself (c) defended himself (d) submitted himself

3. „Im Anfang war die *Tat!*" (Goethe)
(a) deed (b) death (c) test (d) chaos

4. „Ach!"—spricht er—„die größte Freud' ist doch die *Zufriedenheit!*" (Wilhelm Busch)
(a) contentment (b) joy (c) dismay (d) despair

B. Choose the approximate meaning for the following.

1. Tugend, nicht Krieg, ist, was den Menschen erhöht.
(a) War is beneficial to man.
(b) Virtue, not war, is what makes the man.
(c) Peace, not vice, is what man should exalt.
(d) Peace, not war, is what enhances man.

2. Das Gefühl der Macht ist erster Satz unserer Menschenliebe.
(a) The desire for power is the first principle of mankind.
(b) The first sentence we read is that the feeling of authority is part of our love for mankind.
(c) The feeling of power is the first principle of our love for our fellow human beings.
(d) The principle of love is the first step on the road to power.

Answer key: A. **1.** (b); **2.** (c); **3.** (a); **4.** (a).
B. **1.** (b); **2.** (c).

Review all of the words you have circled in this chapter. Then go on to the reading passage.

Franz Kafka: Hochzeitsvorbereitungen auf dem Lande

Es kamen zwei Soldaten und ergriffen mich. Ich wehrte mich, aber sie hielten fest. Sie führten mich vor ihren Herrn, einen Offizier. Wie bunt war seine Uniform! Ich sagte: „Was wollt ihr denn von mir, ich bin ein Zivilist." Der Offizier lächelte und sagte: „Du bist ein Zivilist, doch hindert uns das nicht, dich zu fassen. Das Militär hat Gewalt über alles."

Friedrich Nietzsche: Der Antichrist

Was ist gut?—Alles, was das Gefühl der Macht, den Willen zur Macht, die Macht selbst im Menschen erhöht.

Was ist schlecht?—Alles, was aus der Schwäche stammt.

Was ist Glück?—Das Gefühl davon, daß die Macht wächst,—daß ein Widerstand überwunden wird.

N i c h t Zufriedenheit, sondern mehr M a c h t; n i c h t Friede überhaupt, sondern Krieg; n i c h t Tugend, sondern Tüchtigkeit (Tugend im Renaissance-Stile, *virtu*, moralinfreie Tugend).

Die Schwachen und Mißratenen sollen zugrunde gehen: erster Satz unsrer Menschenliebe. Und man soll ihnen noch dazu helfen.

Was ist schädlicher als irgendein Laster?—Das Mitleiden der Tat mit allen Mißratenen und Schwachen—das Christentum . . .

Chapter Seven

Reading: From Dietrich Bonhoeffer: Widerstand und Ergebung

27. *Comparison of adjectives*

1. There are three basic forms of the adjective, both in German and in English:

Positive	**alt**	*old*
Comparative	**älter**	*older*
Superlative	**ältest-**	*oldest*

2. The comparative form in German is recognized by the **-er** ending, the superlative by the **-(e)st-** attached to the positive form. **Mehr** (*more*) and **meist** (*most*) are not used in forming the comparative forms in German: **interessant, interessanter, interessantest-.**

3. The following adjectives have irregular forms:

groß, größer, größt-	*big*
gut, besser, best-	*good*
hoch, höher, höchst-	*high*
nah(e), näher, nächst-	*near*
viel, mehr, meist-	*much, a lot*

4. Monosyllabic adjectives with stem vowels of **a, o,** or **u** generally add an umlaut for the comparative and superlative forms. Generally polysyllabic adjectives do not:

warm, wärmer, wärmst-	*warm, warmer, warmest*
einfach, einfacher, einfachst-	*simple, simpler, simplest*

But:

gesund, gesünder, gesündest-	*healthy, healthier, healthiest*

5. In addition to the comparative endings, adjectives have the case endings explained earlier. Do not confuse the normal adjective ending with the comparative form:

der alte Mann	*the old man*
ein alter Mann	*an old man*
etwas älter	*somewhat older*
der ältere Mann	*the older man*
ein älterer Mann	*an older man*
alle älteren Männer	*all older men*
der älteste Mann	*the oldest man*
Der Mann ist am ältesten.	*The man is oldest.*

Note that there are two forms of the superlative in German: **der älteste, die älteste, das älteste**, etc., and **am ältesten,** which occurs only after the noun.

6. Common adjective formulas are:

(nicht) so . . . wie: (nicht) so alt wie	*(not) as old as*
. . . als: älter als	*older than*
je . . . desto . . .: je älter, desto besser	*the older, the better*
immer . . .: immer älter	*older and older*
Gretel ist nicht so alt wie Sonja.	*Gretel is not as old as Sonja.*
Gertraud ist älter als du.	*Gertraud is older than you.*
Je älter der Wein, desto besser schmeckt er.	*The older the wine, the better it tastes.*
Wir werden alle immer älter.	*We are all getting older and older.*

The reading passage for this chapter is from one of Dietrich Bonhoeffer's letters from prison. In the next set of exercises you will practice recognition of the comparative forms of adjectives, review old vocabulary, and learn new vocabulary for this reading passage. Remember to circle unfamiliar words for review.

	1. Im letzten Kapitel mußten Sie einen Abschnitt (Paragraphen) aus Nietzsches *Der Antichrist* lesen.
1. In the last chapter you had to read a paragraph out of Nietzsche's *The Antichrist*.	**2.** Nietzsche wurde 1844 geboren und starb im Jahre 1900.
2. Nietzsche was born in 1844 and died in (the year) 1900.	**3.** Nietzsche nach gibt es zwei Sorten Menschen: die Starken und die Schwachen und Mißratenen.
3. According to Nietzsche there are two kinds of people: the strong and the weaklings and misfits.	**4.** Um **stärker** zu werden, muß man Widerstände überwinden.

4. In order to become *stronger,* one must overcome obstacles.	**5. der Durchschnittsmensch** = *the average person* War Nietzsche körperlich **stärker** oder **schwächer** als der Durchschnittsmensch?
5. Was Nietzsche physically *stronger* or *weaker* than the average person?	**6.** Was ist **schädlicher** als irgendein Laster?
6. What is *more harmful* than any vice?	**7.** Das Christentum ist **am schädlichsten.**
7. Christianity is *the most harmful.*	**8.** Das **schönste** Gefühl im Leben ist, daß die Macht in einem wächst.
8. The *most beautiful* feeling in life is that power is growing within you (in oneself).	**9. Das Schönste** im Leben ist das Gefühl, daß die Macht in einem wächst.
9. *The most beautiful thing* in life is the feeling that power is growing within you. (Notice how the adjective is used as a neuter noun.)	**10.** Sprechen wir jetzt von Dietrich Bonhoeffer.
10. Let us now talk of Dietrich Bonhoeffer.	**11.** Bonhoeffer war Christ.
11. Bonhoeffer was a Christian.	**12.** Bonhoeffer wurde am 4. Februar 1906 geboren.
12. Bonhoeffer was born on the 4th of February, 1906.	**13. verhaften** = *to arrest* **wurde verhaftet** = *was arrested* Im Jahre 1943 wurde er von den Nazis verhaftet.
13. In the year 1943 he was arrested by the Nazis.	**14. wider** = *against* **der Stand** = *standing position* **der Widerstand** = *resistance* **der Kampf** = *fight* **der Widerstandskämpfer** = ________________.
14. *the resistance fighter*	**15. hinrichten** = *to execute* **wurde hingerichtet** = *was executed* Er wurde am 4. Februar 1906 geboren, im Jahre 1943 verhaftet und schließlich am 9. April 1945 als **Widerstandskämpfer** hingerichtet.
15. He was born on the 4th of February, 1906, arrested in 1943, and finally executed as a *resistance fighter* on April 9, 1945.	**16.** Nietzsches Werk *Der Antichrist* ist gegen das Christentum.

16. Nietzsche's work *The Antichrist* is against Christianity.	**17.** **der Brief** = *letter* Als Bonhoeffer im Gefängnis war, **schrieb** er viele Briefe über das Christentum. (*writes/wrote*)
17. When Bonhoeffer was in prison he *wrote* lots of letters about Christianity.	**18.** **ja** = *yes* **bejahen** = *to affirm* Bonhoeffer bejaht in seinen Briefen das Christentum.
18. Bonhoeffer affirms Christianity in his letters.	**19.** Nietzsche meint, **das Beste,** was ein Mensch tun kann, ist die Macht in sich selbst erhöhen.
19. Nietzsche feels (that) *the best thing* a person can do is to increase power within oneself.	**20.** **verzichten auf** (**etwas**) = *to renounce, abandon* (*something*) Bonhoeffer meint, **das Beste,** was man tun kann, ist völlig darauf verzichten, aus sich selbst etwas zu machen.
20. Bonhoeffer feels *the best thing* a person can do is to fully abandon making something (out) of oneself (. . . is to give up totally the idea of making anything of himself/herself).	**21.** **möglich** = *possible* **die Möglichkeit** = *possibility* Welche Meinung finden Sie **besser**? Gibt es **bessere** Möglichkeiten?
21. Which opinion do you find *better?* Are there *better* possibilities?	**22.** **das Verhältnis** = *the relation* Welcher, Nietzsche oder Bonhoeffer, ist **einsamer** in seinem Verhältnis zum Weltall?
22. Which one, Nietzsche or Bonhoeffer, is *more lonely* in his relation to the universe?	**23.** **in dem** = *in which, in whom* Der **gute** Mensch ist der Mensch, in dem die Macht wächst, Nietzsche nach.
23. The *good* person is the individual in whom power is growing, according to Nietzsche.	**24.** Das Christentum ist **das schädlichste** Laster.
24. Christianity is *the most harmful* vice.	**25.** **werfen** = *to throw* Bonhoeffer will, daß der Mensch sich **ganz** in die Arme Gottes wirft.
25. Bonhoeffer wants people to throw themselves *completely* into the arms of God (to rely *totally* on God).	**26.** **so etwas** = *something like that* Nietzsche sagt, nur **ein Schwacher** tut so etwas. (*a weak person/a weaker person*)
26. Nietzsche says, only *a weak person* does a thing like that.	**27.** Wer ist **schwächer?** Ein Mensch, der sich in die Arme Gottes wirft, oder ein Mensch, der das nicht tut?

27. Who is *weaker*? Someone who relies on God, or someone who does not? (Lit.: A person who throws himself into the arms of God . . .)	**28.** **sprechen** = *to speak* **besprechen** = *to discuss* **Was für** Themen bespricht Bonhoeffer in seinen Briefen?
28. *What kind of* topics does Bonhoeffer discuss in his letters?	**29.** **die Diesseitigkeit** = *this-worldliness, secular life, preoccupation with things of this world* In seinem Brief vom 21.7.1944 bespricht Bonhoeffer das Thema der Diesseitigkeit.
29. In his letter of July 21, 1944, Bonhoeffer discusses the topic of the secular life. (cf. **diesseits** = *this side*)	**30.** **bequem** = *comfortable, easygoing* Bonhoeffer meint, der bequeme Mensch lebt in platter und banaler Diesseitigkeit.
30. Bonhoeffer feels that the comfortable individual lives a shallow and banal secular life (cf. English *flat*).	**31.** **die Aufgeklärten** = *the enlightened (persons)* **die Betriebsamen** = *the busy (persons)* Aber auch die Aufgeklärten und Betriebsamen leben in platter und banaler Diesseitigkeit.
31. But enlightened and busy people also live a shallow and banal life of preoccupation with things of this world.	**32.** **tief** = *profound (deep)* **die Zucht** = *discipline* Tiefe Diesseitigkeit ist für Bonhoeffer **voller** Zucht. (*fuller/full of*)
32. For Bonhoeffer a profound secular life is *full of* discipline (i.e., is characterized by discipline). (**Voller** is a genitive form.)	**33.** **der Tod** = *death* In seinen Briefen spricht er von dem Tod und der **Auferstehung**. (After speaking of the death of the body one may speak of the ______ of the body.)
33. *resurrection* In his letters he speaks of death and the *resurrection*.	**34.** **die Erkenntnis** = *knowledge* **gegenwärtig** = *present* Die Erkenntnis des Todes und der Auferstehung ist **immer** gegenwärtig in der tiefen Diesseitigkeit.
34. Knowledge of death and the resurrection is *always* (i.e., *constantly*) present in the profound secular life.	**35.** Johannes der **Täufer** und Jesus Christus waren **große** und **tiefe** Menschen. (From the context, you may guess that he is talking about John the __________.)
35. John the *Baptist* and Jesus Christ were *great* and *profound* individuals.	**36.** Wer war der **größere, tiefere** Mensch: Johannes der Täufer oder Jesus Christus?

36.	Who was the *greater* and *more profound* individual: John the Baptist or Jesus Christ?	**37.**	Christus war nicht **so alt wie** Johannes, aber er war doch der **größere, tiefere** von den beiden.
37.	Christ was not *as old as* John, but he was nevertheless the *greater, more profound* of the two.	**38.**	Hier kann man nicht sagen, **je älter, desto besser.**
38.	Here one cannot say *the older the better.*	**39.**	**sterben**= *to die* **starb** = *died* Als er starb, war Bonhoeffer nicht **so alt wie** Nietzsche.
39.	When Bonhoeffer died, he was not *as old as* Nietzsche.	**40.**	Bonhoeffer war **jünger** als Nietzsche, als er starb.
40.	Bonhoeffer was *younger than* Nietzsche when he died.	**41.**	Nietzsche nach ist Krieg **besser** als Friede.
41.	According to Nietzsche war is *better* than peace.	**42.**	**Je stärker** der Mensch, **desto besser** ist er; **je schwächer, desto schlechter.**
42.	*The stronger* the person, *the better* he is; *the weaker* he is, *the worse* he is.	**43.**	Das Gefühl der Macht in einem Menschen wird **immer stärker, je mehr** er Widerstände überwindet.
43.	The feeling of power in a person becomes *stronger and stronger, the more* he overcomes obstacles.	**44.**	**wirken** = *to cause, to produce* **Immer schädlicher** wirkt das Christentum, je mehr es Mitleiden der Tat mit allen Mißratenen und Schwachen hat.
44.	Christianity produces *more and more harm the more* it has active compassion for all misfits and weaklings.	**45.**	Mit den Jahren lernt Bonhoeffer **immer mehr** die tiefe Diesseitigkeit des Christentums kennen und verstehen.
45.	As the years go by, Bonhoeffer comes to know and understand *more and more* the profound preoccupation with the things of this world that is characteristic of Christianity.	**46.**	**Je mehr** man völlig darauf verzichtet, aus sich etwas zu machen, **desto mehr** wirft man sich Gott ganz in die Arme.
46.	*The more* completely you give up the idea of making anything of yourself, *the more* completely you rely on God.	**47.**	Darf man sagen, daß Nietzsche das Christentum **nicht so gut** versteht **wie** Bonhoeffer?
47.	Can one say that Nietzsche does *not* understand Christianity *as well as* Bonhoeffer?	**48.**	Für Bonhoeffer ist der wahre Mensch ein Christ. Und für Nietzsche?
48.	For Bonhoeffer the true individual is a Christian. And what about for Nietzsche?	**49.**	Das Christentum ist eine alte Religion.

49. Christianity is an old religion.	**50.** Das Christentum ist **älter als** der Islam aber nicht **so alt wie** das Judentum.
50. Christianity is *older than* Islam but not *as old as* Judaism.	**51.** Das Judentum ist **die älteste** von den drei Religionen.
51. Judaism is *the oldest* of the three religions.	

PROGRESS TEST

Choose the correct answer for the italicized words.

1. Das *schönste* Gefühl im Leben ist, daß die Macht in einem wächst.
(a) beautiful (b) most beautiful (c) more beautiful (d) beautifully

2. *Je schwächer* man ist, *desto mehr* Schwierigkeiten wird man haben.
(a) the more . . . the merrier (b) the weaker . . . the better (c) the stronger . . . the more (d) the weaker . . . the more

3. Bonhoeffer war *nicht so alt wie* Nietzsche als er starb.
(a) not as old as (b) not so much older than

4. Er war ein *einfacher* Mann.
(a) more ordinary (b) ordinary (c) very ordinary (d) most ordinary

5. Ist das Christentum *genau so schädlich wie* Nietzsches Ideen?
(a) not as harmful as (b) just as harmful as (c) more harmful than (d) none

Answer key: **1.** (b); **2.** (d); **3.** (a); **4.** (b); **5.** (b).

28. *Comparison of adverbs*

1. The forms of the German adverb in the comparative and superlative do not differ essentially from those of the predicate adjective:

Die Frau singt schön.	*The woman sings beautifully.*
Die Frau singt schöner.	*The woman sings more beautifully.*
Die Frau singt am schönsten.	*The woman sings the most beautifully.*

The **am** __________ **-en** form is the only superlative of the adverb.

2. The same adjective formulas mentioned above apply to the adverb as well:

Der Franzose spricht *schneller* als der Deutsche.	*The Frenchman speaks* **more rapidly** *than the German.*

Wido singt *nicht so laut* wie du.	*Wido does* **not** *sing* **as loudly** *as you.*
***Je schöner* sie singt, *desto mehr* schwärme ich für sie.**	***The more beautifully*** *she sings,* ***the more*** *I am enraptured with her.*
Er spricht *immer langsamer*.	*He speaks* **more and more slowly.**

3. The following adverbs are irregular:

bald, eher, am ehesten	*soon, sooner, soonest*
gern, lieber, am liebsten	*like (to do something or to do something gladly or with pleasure)*

Gern and its comparative forms are translated as follows:

Ich trinke *gern* Wasser.	*I* **like** *to drink (or drinking) water.*
Ich trinke *lieber* Milch.	*I* **prefer** *to drink milk.*
Ich trinke *am liebsten* Bier.	*I* **like** *to drink (like drinking) beer* **most of all**.

This section continues to introduce vocabulary for the reading passage and gives you practice in recognizing the adverb forms. Give the meaning of the indicated words.

	1. **antworten** = *to answer, reply* **die Antwort** = *the answer, reply* Er **beantwortet** die Frage.
1. He *answers* (*is answering*) the question. Cf. **Er antwortet auf** die Frage: He *answers* (*is answering*) the question.	**2.** **eine Frage stellen** = *to ask a question* **Am liebsten** stellt er ganz einfache Fragen, die schwer zu beantworten sind.
2. He *likes best* to ask very simple questions which are hard to answer.	**3.** **heilig** = *holy, saintly* Bonhoeffer will **lieber** glauben als ein Heiliger werden.
3. Bonhoeffer would *rather* believe (have faith) than become a saint.	**4.** **mögen** = *to like* **mochte** = *liked* **möchte** = *would like* Bonhoeffer will **lieber** sagen: er möchte glauben lernen.
4. Bonhoeffer *prefers* to say (wants *rather* to say), he would like to learn to have faith.	**5.** Er möchte **am liebsten** ein ganz einfacher Mensch sein, **der** glauben kann. (**der** = *the/who*)
5. *Most of all* he would like to be a very simple person *who* is able to believe (have faith). (Notice that **der** is here used as a pronoun.)	**6.** **gelebt hat** = *lived* Bonhoeffer glaubt **gern,** daß Luther in der tiefen Diesseitigkeit gelebt hat.
6. Bonhoeffer *likes to* believe that Luther lived a life of profound worldliness.	**7.** **widersprechen** = *to contradict* (+ dative object) Warum widersprechen sie ihm so **gern**?

7. Why do they *like* to contradict him so much?	**8.** **im allgemeinen** = *generally* Im allgemeinen möchte man **am lieb-sten** alles wissen: da man nicht kann, so glaubt man.
8. In general what people would like *best* is to know everything: since they cannot, they have faith.	**9.** **der Pfarrer** = *the pastor* **das Gespräch** = *the conversation* Er erinnert sich **gern** an das Gespräch, das er vor 13 (dreizehn) Jahren mit einem jungen französischen Pfarrer hatte.
9. He *likes* to recall the conversation which he had 13 years ago with a young French minister.	**10.** Im allgemeinen wirft man sich **gern** Gott ganz in die Arme?
10. In general, does one *like* to rely completely on God?	**11.** **das Erlebnis** = *experience* **erleben** = __________
11. *to experience*	**12.** **die Lasziven** = *the sensualists* Die Aufgeklärten, die Betriebsamen, die Bequemen und die Lasziven **werden** die tiefe Diesseitigkeit des Lebens nicht bald erleben. (**werden** = *will/are becoming*)
12. The enlightened, the busy, the comfortable, and the sensualists *will* not soon experience a life of profound worldliness.	**13.** **leer** = *empty* Sie werden **eher** das leere Nichts erleben.
13. They will *be more likely to* (*sooner*) experience empty nothingness.	**14.** **Eher** will Bonhoeffer sich in die Arme Gottes werfen als ein Heiliger werden.
14. Bonhoeffer would *rather* (*sooner*) rely on God than become a saint.	**15.** Bonhoeffer meint **am ehesten** zu glauben, wenn er darauf verzichtet, etwas aus sich selbst zu machen.
15. Bonhoeffer feels that he *is most likely to* believe when he gives up trying to make something of himself. (**Darauf** refers to the idea in the following phrase.)	**16.** **Eher** wird der Pfarrer ein Heiliger als ein Gläubiger.
16. The minister is *more likely* to become a saint than a believer.	**17.** Das Gespräch wird **bald** zu Ende sein.
17. The conversation will *soon* be at an end.	**18.** **erst** = *not until, only* (*first*) **Am ehesten** können wir uns erst nächstes Jahr wiedersehen.
18. *At the earliest* we cannot see each other again until next year.	**19.** **leiden** = *to suffer, bear* **das Leiden** = __________

19. *suffering*	**20.** **nimmt** = *present of* **nehmen,** *to take* Nimmt man das Leiden Gottes in der Welt **ernst**?
20. Do people take *seriously* the suffering of God in the world?	**21.** **Ernster** kann er das Leiden Gottes in der Welt nicht nehmen.
21. He cannot take the suffering of God in the world *more seriously* (than he already does).	**22.** **Immer mehr** versteht Bonhoeffer die tiefe Diesseitigkeit des Christentums.
22. Bonhoeffer comes to understand the profound worldliness of Christianity *more and more.*	**23.** Wir stellen uns **ganz einfach** die Frage, was wir mit unserem Leben eigentlich wollen.
23. We *very simply* ask ourselves the question, what do we really want from our life.	**24.** Er war ein **einfacher** Mann. (*simple/simpler*)
24. He was a *simple* man.	**25.** Er war ein **einfacherer** Mann als sein Sohn.
25. He was a *simpler* man than his son.	**26.** **wer** = *who* Wer kann **es einfacher** machen?
26. Who can do it *more simply*?	**27.** Man lernt glauben **erst** in der vollen Diesseitigkeit des Lebens.
27. Not until one lives completely in this world does one learn to believe (have faith). (Or: One learns to believe *only* by living completely in this world.)	

PROGRESS TEST

Choose the correct answer.

1. Bonhoeffer will *lieber* glauben als Heiliger werden.
(a) love (b) live (c) rather (d) sooner

2. Warum widerspricht er ihm so *gern?*
(a) love (b) like (c) endearingly (d) lovely

3. Er kommt *eher* als ich.
(a) later (b) more slowly (c) faster (d) sooner

4. *Einfacher* kann er es nicht erklären.
(a) more simply (b) simply (c) most simply (d) simple

5. Er singt *am liebsten* ein altes Volkslied.
(a) preferably (b) endearingly (c) most sweetly (d) most likes

Answer key: **1.** (c); **2.** (b); **3.** (d); **4.** (a); **5.** (d).

29. *Adjectives used as nouns*

1. Adjectives used as nouns are capitalized, but they retain their adjective endings:

Der *blinde* Mann ist nicht hier.	*The* **blind** *man is not here.*
Der *Blinde* sitzt in der Ecke.	*The* **blind man** *sits (is sitting) in the corner.*

2. Adjectival nouns may be masculine, feminine, neuter, or plural. If masculine or feminine, singular or plural, they refer to persons:

der Alte	*the old man*
die Alte	*the old woman*
ein Armer	*a poor man*
eine Arme	*a poor woman*
die Alten	*the old people*
die Armen	*the poor people*

If neuter, they refer to an abstract quality or a thing:

***Das Rote* will ich.**	*I want* **the red one.**
Das ist *das Schöne* daran.	*That is* **the beautiful thing** *about it.*

3. Neuter adjectival nouns are commonly found after indefinite pronouns such as:

allerlei	*all kinds of, all sorts of*
Sagt er *allerlei Dummes?*	*Does he say* **all sorts of stupid things?**
alles	*all, everything*
Wir wünschen Ihnen *alles Gute!*	*We wish you* **all the best!**
etwas	*something*
***Etwas Neues* wissen Sie doch!**	*You must know* **something new!**
nichts	*nothing*
Sie hat *nichts Neues* gesagt.	*She said* **nothing new.**
viel	*much*
Er hat *viel Gutes* getan.	*He did a* **lot of good.**
wenig	*little*
Sie hat nur *wenig Gutes* über ihn zu sagen.	*She has* **little** *to say about him that is* **good**.

In three instances the adjective will not be capitalized:

alles andere	*all else*
alles mögliche	*everything possible*
alles übrige	*all the rest*

Give the meaning of the indicated words.

	1. Ein **aufgeklärter** Mensch ist er nicht.
1. He is not an *enlightened* human being.	**2.** Ein **Aufgeklärter** ist er nicht.
2. He is not *an enlightened human being (man, person).*	**3.** Es gibt keinen **aufgeklärteren** Menschen auf der Welt.
3. There is no person (one) in the world who is *more enlightened* (. . . *more enlightened* person in the world).	**4.** Er glaubt, daß er **der aufgeklärteste** Mensch auf der Welt ist.
4. He believes that he is *the most enlightened* person in the world.	**5.** In einem **betriebsamen** Menschen findet man die tiefe Diesseitigkeit nicht.
5. In a *busy* individual one does not find profound acceptance of the worldly life.	**6.** In einem **Betriebsamen** findet man die tiefe Diesseitigkeit nicht.
6. One does not find in a *busy individual* a profound acceptance of the worldly life.	**7.** Auch nicht in einem **bequemen** oder **lasziven** Menschen.
7. Not in a *comfortable* or *lascivious* person either.	**8.** Auch nicht in einem **Bequemen** oder **Lasziven.**
8. Not in a *comfortable* or *lascivious person* either.	**9.** Der Pfarrer sagte, er möchte ein **heiliger** Mann werden.
9. The pastor said he would like to become a *holy* man.	**10.** Der Pfarrer sagte, er möchte ein **Heiliger** werden.
10. The pastor said he would like to become a *saint.*	**11.** . . . einen Gerechten oder einen Ungerechten . . . (If **einen Gerechten** means *a just person,* **einen Ungerechten** must mean ________.)
11. *an unjust person*	**12.** . . . einen Kranken oder einen Gesunden (If **einen Kranken** means *a sick person,* **einen Gesunden** must mean ________.)
12. *a healthy person*	**13.** Kranke und gesunde, gerechte und ungerechte Menschen gibt es überall.
13. There are sick and healthy people, just and unjust people everywhere.	**14.** Überall sieht man die **Kranken** und die **Gesunden**, die **Gerechten** und die **Ungerechten.**
14. You see the *sick* and the *healthy*, the *just* and the *unjust* everywhere (the *righteous* and the *unrighteous*).	**15.** **Etwas anderes** als ein **Heiliger** will Bonhoeffer werden.

15. Bonhoeffer wants to become *something other* than a *saint.*	**16.** **Nichts Plattes** und **Banales** darf in dem wahren Christ sein.
16. There must be *nothing shallow* and *banal* in the true Christian.	**17.** If **Brief** is *a letter* and **Wechsel** is *exchange,* **der Briefwechsel** must mean ________.
17. *correspondence*	**18.** **enthalten** = *to contain* Enthält Bonhoeffers Briefwechsel **viel Ernstes?**
18. Does Bonhoeffer's correspondence contain *much that is serious?*	**19.** **die Zukunft** = *the future* **die Gegenwart** = *the present* **die Vergangenheit** = ________
19. *the past*	**20.** Denken Sie an **etwas Vergangenes** oder an **etwas Gegenwärtiges**?
20. Are you thinking of *something in the past* or of *something in the present?*	**21.** Der Gedanke, daß Gott tot ist, ist **nichts Neues.**
21. The thought that God is dead is *nothing new.*	**22.** Nietzsche hat **wenig Gutes** über das Christentum zu sagen.
22. Nietzsche has *little* to say about Christianity that is *good.*	**23.** **darüber** = *about it* Er hat **viel Schlechtes** darüber zu sagen.
23. He has *much* to say about it *that is bad.*	**24.** **Allerlei Neues** erfährt man, wenn man sich Gott ganz in die Arme wirft.
24. One experiences *all kinds of new things* when one relies on God completely.	**25.** **die Ergebung** = *submission* **sich ergeben** = ________
25. *to submit*	**26.** **heißen** = *to mean, to be called* Sich Gott ergeben heißt, sich Gott ganz in die Arme werfen.
26. To submit to God means to rely on God completely.	**27.** **vergänglich** = *transitory, fleeting* **Alles Schöne** auf der Welt ist vergänglich.
27. *All that is beautiful* in the world is transitory.	**28.** **lehren** = *to teach* **die Lehre** = *teachings* Kommt **wenig Gutes** aus Bonhoeffers Lehre?
28. Is there *little* that is *good* that comes from Bonhoeffer's teachings?	**29.** Findet man **allerlei Gesundes** in Nietzsches Werken?
29. Does one find *all kinds of wholesome things* in Nietzsche's works?	**30.** **Alles mögliche** finden Sie in Nietzsches Werken.
30. You find *just about everything you can imagine* (lit.: *every possible thing*) in Nietzsche's works.	

PROGRESS TEST

Find the approximate meaning of the italicized words.

1. Was ist denn überhaupt *das Schönste* im Leben?
(a) beautiful (b) most beautiful (c) the most beautiful thing (d) most beautifully

2. Tut *ein Schwacher* so etwas?
(a) a weak (b) a weaker (c) a weaker person (d) a weak person

3. *Die Arme* sitzt da drüben, ganz allein und einsam.
(a) the poor woman (b) the arm (c) poor women (d) arms

4. Denken sie an *etwas Gegenwärtiges?*
(a) nothing in the past (b) something in the future (c) much in the present (d) something in the present

5. *Alles Vergangene* kommt nie wieder.
(a) all gone (b) all that has passed (c) everything goes (d) everything passes

6. *Allerlei Neues* erfährt man.
(a) all new things (b) everything is new (c) all kinds of new things (d) every new thing

Answer key: **1.** (c); **2.** (d); **3.** (a); **4.** (d); **5.** (b); **6.** (c).

30. *Uses of* man

1. The indefinite pronoun **man** may be translated by

(a) *one:*

Man* liest in der Bibel, daß** . . . ***One *reads in the Bible that . . .*

(b) *people, you, we, they, anyone,* or *any of the persons,* depending on the context:

Hier spricht *man* kein Deutsch.	***People*** (***they***) *don't speak German here.*
***Man* kann sie überhaupt nicht verstehen.**	***We*** *cannot understand them at all.*

(c) *the passive:*

Man tut* das nicht.** *That* ***is *not* ***done****.*

2. Do not confuse **man** with the noun **der Mann** which is translated as *the man:*

***Der Mann* kommt nicht wieder.**	***The man*** *will not come back.*
Wird *man* geboren, so wird *man* sterben.	*If* ***we*** *are born,* ***we*** *will die.*

3. **Man** is declined as follows:

N	**man**	*one*
G	**eines**	*of one*
D	**einem**	*(to) one*
A	**einen**	*one*

Do not confuse **ein-** forms of **man** with the indefinite article, but note also that occasionally **einer** is used instead of **man** in the nominative:

Wenn *einer* etwas sagt, dann müssen wir aufhören.	*If **anyone** says anything, we (will) have to stop.*

These exercises continue the discussion of Bonhoeffer. Give the English meaning of the following.

	1. **schlechthin** = *simply* Man sieht, daß der Christ nicht ein *homo religiosus,* sondern ein Mensch schlechthin ist.
1. One sees that the Christian is not a *homo religiosus* but simply a human being.	2. **der Unterschied** = *contrast, difference* Der Unterschied zwischen Jesus und Johannes dem Täufer ist groß.
2. The difference between Jesus and John the Baptist is great.	3. **ist geworden** = *has become* Hält der **Mann** es für möglich, daß er ein Heiliger geworden ist?
3. Does the *man* consider it possible that he has become a saint?	4. **der Eindruck** = *impression* **beeindrucken** = *to impress* Der Pfarrer beeindruckte Bonhoeffer sehr.
4. The minister impressed Bonhoeffer a lot. (Or: The minister really impressed Bonhoeffer.)	5. **obwohl** = *although* Bonhoeffer widersprach dem Pfarrer, obwohl der Pfarrer ihn damals sehr beeindruckte.
5. Bonhoeffer disagreed with the pastor although the pastor really impressed him at the time.	6. **der Gegensatz** = *contrast* Man liest, daß Bonhoeffer lange Zeit die Tiefe dieses Gegensatzes nicht verstanden hat.
6. One reads that for a long time Bonhoeffer did not understand the depth of this contrast. (**verstanden** = past participle of **verstehen**)	7. **dachte** = *thought* **könnte** = *could* Bonhoeffer dachte, ein Mensch könnte glauben lernen.
7. Bonhoeffer thought a person could learn to have faith.	8. Viele Christen wollen ein heiliges Leben führen.
8. Lots of Christians want to lead a holy life.	9. **indem er selbst versucht** = *by (himself) trying* Man könnte glauben lernen, indem man selbst so etwas wie ein heiliges Leben zu führen versuchte.

9. One could learn to have faith by trying to lead something of a holy life.	**10.** **später** = *later* **erfahren** = *to discover, experience* Was erfuhr Bonhoeffer später und was erfährt er jetzt? (The context shows that **erfuhr** is _____ *past/present*)
10. *past* What did Bonhoeffer find out later and what is he finding out now?	**11.** **die Stunde** = *hour* Was **erfährt** er bis zur Stunde?
11. What *has* he *found out* up to now (up to this hour)? (English uses the present perfect to express an action beginning in the past and continuing into the present. German uses the present tense.)	**12.** Bonhoeffer dachte, er könnte glauben lernen . . .
12. Bonhoeffer thought he could learn to have faith . . .	**13.** **da** = *since* (when the verb is at the end of the phrase or sentence) . . . da er ein heiliges Leben zu führen versuchte.
13. . . . since he was trying to lead a holy life.	**14.** **bekehren** = *to convert* **ein bekehrter Sünder** = *a converted* _______
14. *sinner*	**15.** **sei es** = *be it* (subjunctive) Man soll völlig darauf verzichten, aus sich etwas zu machen, sei es einen Heiligen, einen bekehrten Sünder oder einen Kirchenmann.
15. One must totally give up trying to make something of oneself, be it a saint, a converted sinner, or a man of the church.	**16.** **nennen** = *to call* **sogenannt** = *so-called* **die Gestalt** = *figure, type* Ein Kirchenmann ist eine sogenannte priesterliche Gestalt.
16. A man of the church is a so-called priestly type.	**17.** Er dachte, er könnte glauben lernen, **indem er selbst** ein heiliges Leben zu führen versuchte.
17. He thought he could learn to have faith by trying to lead a holy life. (Lit.: . . . *in that he himself* would try to lead . . .)	**18.** Er dachte, er könnte glauben lernen, indem er selbst **so etwas wie** ein heiliges Leben zu führen versuchte.
18. He thought he could learn to have faith by trying to lead *something like* a holy life.	**19.** **ratlos** = *perplexed* **die Ratlosigkeit** = __________

19. *perplexity*	**20.** **der Erfolg** = *success* **der Mißerfolg** = __________
20. *failure*	**21.** **die Aufgabe** = *assignment, duty* Bonhoeffer nennt dies Diesseitigkeit, nämlich in der Fülle der Aufgaben, Fragen, Erfolge und Mißerfolge, Erfahrungen und Ratlosigkeiten leben.
21. By worldly life ("this-worldliness") Bonhoeffer means living in the fullness of life's duties, questions, successes and failures, experiences, and perplexities. (Lit.: Bonhoeffer calls this this-worldliness, namely to live in the fullness . . .)	**22.** **übermütig werden** = *to become proud, arrogant* Oft kann man **bei** Erfolgen übermütig werden. (*with/by*)
22. Often one can become arrogant *with* success.	**23.** **irre werden** = *to become confused* Oft kann man **an** Mißerfolgen irre werden. (*at/by*)
23. One can often become confused *by* failures.	**24.** **sollte** = *should, could* Wie **sollte** man bei Erfolgen übermutig oder an Mißerfolgen irre werden . . .
24. How *could* one become arrogant with successes or confused by failures . . .	**25.** **mitleiden** = *to suffer with* . . . wenn man im diesseitigen Leben Gottes **Leiden** mitleidet? (*sufferings/joys*)
25. . . . if one shares God's *sufferings* in the worldly life?	

PROGRESS TEST

Choose the answer which most closely approximates the indicated statement.

1. *Man sagt,* daß alles möglich ist.
(a) the man says (b) man says (c) one says

2. Die Betriebsamen, die Aufgeklärten, die Bequemen und die Lasziven wissen genau, daß die tiefe Diesseitigkeit voller Zucht ist.
(a) The busy, the enlightened, the comfortable, and the lascivious appreciate the secular life.
(b) They know that the profound secular life has many restrictions.
(c) The profound secular life embraces only those who know discipline.
(d) The busy, the enlightened, comfortable, and lascivious can never know the profound secular life.

3. Bonhoeffer beeindruckte den Pfarrer, obwohl der Pfarrer ihm damals widersprach.
(a) Bonhoeffer made an impression on the minister even though the minister contradicted him.
(b) Bonhoeffer impressed the minister because Bonhoeffer contradicted him.
(c) Bonhoeffer contradicted the minister even though the minister impressed him very much.

4. Nietzsche nach gibt es zwei Sorten Menschen: die Starken und die Schwachen und Mißratenen.
(a) According to Nietzsche it is better to be strong than weak.
(b) After Nietzsche come two groups of people, the old, and the misfits.
(c) According to Nietzsche there are two groups of human beings, those who are strong and those who are weak and misfits.

5. Wenn man völlig darauf verzichtet, in der Fülle der Aufgaben, Fragen, Erfolge und Mißerfolge, Erfahrungen und Ratlosigkeiten zu leben, dann wird man ein Heiliger, ein Gerechter, ein bekehrter Sünder.
(a) One becomes a saint by renouncing all of life's experiences.
(b) Only by living a full life can one become a righteous person.
(c) To fully live one must experience all things.

Answer key: **1.** (c); **2.** (b); **3.** (a); **4.** (c); **5.** (a).

Briefe und Aufzeichnungen aus der Haft
Neuausgabe 1970, Seite 401–402. Chr. Kaiser Verlag, München.

Dietrich Bonhoeffer: Widerstand und Ergebung

Ich habe in den letzten Jahren mehr und mehr die tiefe Diesseitigkeit des Christentums kennen und verstehen gelernt. Nicht ein *homo religiosus,* sondern ein Mensch schlechthin ist der Christ, wie Jesus—im Unterschied wohl zu Johannes dem Täufer—Mensch war. Nicht die platte und banale Diesseitigkeit der Aufgeklärten, der Betriebsamen, der Bequemen oder der Lasziven, sondern die tiefe Diesseitigkeit, die voller Zucht ist, und in der die Erkenntnis des Todes und der Auferstehung immer gegenwärtig ist, meine ich. Ich glaube, daß Luther in dieser Diesseitigkeit gelebt hat.

Ich erinnere mich eines Gespräches, das ich vor 13 Jahren in Amerika mit einem französischen jungen Pfarrer hatte. Wir hatten uns ganz einfach die Frage gestellt, was wir mit unserem Leben eigentlich wollten. Da sagte er: ich möchte ein Heiliger werden (—und ich halte für möglich, daß er es geworden ist—): das beeindruckte mich damals sehr. Trotzdem widersprach ich ihm und sagte ungefähr: ich möchte glauben lernen. Lange Zeit habe ich die Tiefe dieses Gegensatzes nicht verstanden. Ich dachte, ich könnte glauben lernen, indem ich selbst so etwas wie ein heiliges Leben zu führen versuchte . . .

Später erfuhr ich und erfahre es bis zur Stunde, daß man erst in der vollen Diesseitigkeit des Lebens glauben lernt. Wenn man völlig darauf verzichtet hat, aus sich selbst etwas zu machen—sei es einen Heiligen oder einen bekehrten Sünder oder einen Kirchenmann (eine sogenannte priesterliche Gestalt!), einen Gerechten oder einen Ungerechten, einen Kranken oder einen Gesunden—und dies nenne ich Diesseitigkeit, nämlich in der Fülle der Aufgaben, Fragen, Erfolge und Mißerfolge, Erfahrungen und Ratlosigkeiten leben—, dann wirft man sich Gott ganz in die Arme, dann nimmt man nicht mehr die eigenen Leiden, sondern das Leiden Gottes in der Welt ernst, dann wacht man mit Christus in Gethsemane, und ich denke, das ist Glaube, das ist „Metanoia"[1], und so wird man ein Mensch, ein Christ (vgl.[2] Jerem.[3] 45!). Wie sollte man bei Erfolgen übermütig oder an Mißerfolgen irre werden, wenn man im diesseitigen Leben Gottes Leiden mitleidet?

---

1 *metanoia—a Greek word meaning "repentance"*
2 vgl. (vergleiche) = *cf. (compare)*
3 *Jeremiah*

Chapter Eight

31. *Interrogative and relative pronouns* wer *and* was

1. Wer may be used as an interrogative pronoun (to ask questions) or as a relative pronoun (to join two clauses). It refers only to persons and is declined and translated as follows:

Nominative	**wer**	*who*
Genitive	**wessen**	*whose*
Dative	**wem**	*(to) whom*
Accusative	**wen**	*whom*

***Wer* ist dein Freund?**	***Who*** *is your friend?*
***Wessen* Buch ist das?**	***Whose*** *book is that?*
***Wem* geben Sie die Schokolade?**	***To whom*** *are you giving the chocolate?*
***Wen* sieht Jürgen?**	***Whom*** *does Jürgen see?*
***Wer* sieht Jürgen?**	***Who*** *sees Jürgen?*

Note: "who" is used as the objective form in English by the vast majority of American English speakers:

Who are you giving the chocolate to?
Who does Jürgen see?

2. When **wer** is not used in a question, it is translated as "*he who,*" or "*whoever,*" or "*those who.*"

***Wer* das sagt, ist kein Freund von mir.**	***He who*** (***whoever***) *says that is no friend of mine.*
	Those who *say that are no friends of mine.*

3. **Was** may also be used as an interrogative or relative pronoun. It is not declined and refers only to things. It may be translated as *what, whatever, that, which:*

Was **ist das?**	***What*** *is that?*
Was **sieht Jürgen?**	***What*** *does Jürgen see?*
Ich weiß, ***was*** **er sagt.**	*I know* ***what*** *he is saying.*
Alles, ***was*** **er sagt, ist die Wahrheit.**	*Everything* (***that***) *he says is the truth.*
Das, ***was*** **sie sagen, ist falsch.**	***What*** (***that which***) *they are saying is false.*
Was **ich sehe, (das) weiß ich.**	***Whatever*** *I see, (that) I know.*

4. When a form of **wer** or **was** is used in a dependent clause (a relative pronoun clause), the verb will be at the end of the clause:

Ich weiß, wer da ***ist.***	*I know who* ***is*** *there.*
Helmut weiß, mit wem Sie nach Deutschland ***fahren.***	*Helmut knows who you* ***are traveling*** *to Germany with.* *Helmut knows with whom you* ***are traveling*** *to Germany.*

This section contains vocabulary and phrases drawn from the previous two chapters. Give the meanings of the indicated words.

	1. **Wer** ergreift den Zivilisten?
1. *Who* is apprehending the civilian?	2. **Wer** spricht gegen das Christentum?
2. *Who* is speaking against Christianity?	3. **Wessen** Wort sollen wir ernst nehmen?
3. *Whose* word are we to take seriously?	4. **Wessen** Idee ist das?
4. *Whose* idea is that?	5. **Wem** sollen wir helfen?
5. *Who* (*Whom*) are we supposed to help?	6. **Wem** wirft man sich ganz in die Arme?
6. *Upon whom* does one rely completely?	7. **Wen** ergreifen die Soldaten?
7. *Who* are the soldiers seizing? (Whom do the soldiers seize?)	8. **Wen** führen die Soldaten vor ihren Herrn?
8. *Who* (whom) do the soldiers take to their superior? (Lit.: . . . lead before their superior)	9. **Mit wem** spricht der Pfarrer?
9. *With whom* is the minister speaking?	10. **Wer** soll zugrunde gehen?
10. *Who* is supposed to perish?	11. **Was** soll zugrunde gehen?

11. *What* is supposed to perish?	**12.** In **wessen** Arme soll man sich ganz werfen?
12. Upon *whom* should one rely completely? (Lit.: Into *whose* arms should one throw himself completely?)	**13.** **Wer** möchte glauben lernen?
13. *Who* would like to learn to have faith?	**14.** **Was** muß man glauben lernen?
14. *What* must one learn to believe?	**15.** **Wo** ist heute ein wahrer Mensch?
15. *Where* is a true human being today?	**16.** **Wo** sollen die Schwachen und Mißratenen hingehen?
16. *Where* are the weaklings and misfits to go?	**17.** **Wer** die Leiden Gottes in der Welt ernst nimmt, wird ein Mensch, ein Christ.
17. *Whoever* takes the sufferings of God in the world seriously will become a human being, a Christian.	**18.** **Was** aus der Schwäche stammt, ist schlecht.
18. *Whatever* stems from weakness is bad.	**19.** **Was** ist schädlicher als irgendein Laster?
19. *What* is more harmful than any vice?	**20.** Alles, **was** aus der Schwäche stammt, ist schlecht.
20. Everything *which* stems from weakness is bad.	**21.** **Wer** hält mich fest?
21. *Who* is holding me tight?	**22.** Ich weiß nicht, **was** ihr von ihr wollt.
22. I do not know *what* you want of her.	

PROGRESS TEST

Select the correct translation for the indicated words.

1. Er kann sich nicht erinnern, *wer* das Gespräch begonnen hat.
(a) where (b) whose (c) what (d) who

2. *Was* aus der Schwäche stammt, ist schlecht.
(a) whatever (b) whose (c) whoever (d) where

3. *Wo* ist heute ein wahrer Mensch?
(a) who (b) where (c) what (d) to whom

4. *Wessen* Leiden sollen wir ernst nehmen?
(a) who (b) where (c) whose (d) what

5. *Wem* sollen wir helfen?
(a) when (b) whom (c) what (d) whose

6. *Wen* führen die Soldaten vor ihren Herrn?
(a) whom (b) from whom (c) when (d) what

Answer key: **1.** (d); **2.** (a); **3.** (b); **4.** (c); **5.** (b); **6.** (a).

32. *The interrogatives* wann, warum, wie, wo, welch-, *and* was für ein

1. The interrogatives below are translated as follows:

wann	*when*
warum	*why*
wie	*how*
wo	*where*
welch-	*which, what*
was für ein	*what kind of (a)*

2. None of these interrogatives except **welch-** and **was für ein** are declined (none have case endings):

***Wo* ist der Mann?**	***Where*** *is the man?*
***Warum* kommt er nicht?**	***Why*** *does he not come? (**Why** doesn't he come?)*

3. Welch- acts as a limiting adjective and thus will take an ending which indicates the gender, number, and case of the noun it precedes:

In *welchem* Haus wohnt Norman?	*In **which** house does Norman live?*
***Welche* Frau hat sieben Kinder?**	***Which*** *woman has seven children?*

4. Ein of **was für ein** (plural **was für**) is declined as the indefinite article **ein. Für** does not function as a preposition in this expression:

***Was für eine* Frau ist sie?**	***What kind of a*** *woman is she?*
***Was für* Frauen sind sie?**	***What kind of*** *women are they?*

Was für ein (**was für**) used in exclamations are translated *what a* or *what:*

***Was für ein* Auto!**	***What a*** *car!*
***Was für* Leute!**	***What*** *people!*

This section contains vocabulary and phrases from previous chapters. Give the meanings of the indicated words.

	1. **Wann** war Deutschland erst vereinigt?
1. *When* was Germany first united?	2. **Warum** sind Wien und die Donau das Tor Mitteleuropas?
2. *Why* are Vienna and the Danube the gateway to Central Europe?	3. **Warum** sind Österreichs einstige wertvolle Beziehungen zu ost- und sudeuropäischen Ländern zum Teil abgeschnitten?
3. *Why* are Austria's former valuable relations with eastern and southern European countries partially cut off?	4. **blieben** = *past of* **bleiben** **Wie lange** blieben die Habsburger an der Macht?
4. *How long* did the Hapsburgs remain in power?	5. **Wo** spricht man die deutsche Sprache?
5. *Where* is the German language spoken? (*Where* do people speak the German language?)	6. **Wo** liegt jetzt die Grenze zwischen Deutschland und Polen?
6. *Where* is the border between Germany and Poland now?	7. **der Schweizerbund** = *the Swiss Confederation* **Wie alt** ist der Schweizerbund?
7. *How old* is the Swiss Confederation?	8. **gelten** = *to pass for, are considered* **Warum** hat Deutschland mehrere Städte, die als historische Zentren gelten?
8. *Why* does Germany have several cities which are considered to be historical centers? (Notice that **die** is here used as a relative pronoun and requires the verb **gelten** to be last.)	9. **Wann** hat die Wiedervereinigung Deutschlands stattgefunden?
9. *When* did the reunification of Germany take place? (**hat . . . stattgefunden** = present perfect of **stattfinden**, §46)	10. **Wer** vereinigte Deutschland und Österreich zum ersten und einzigen Male?
10. *Who* united Germany and Austria for the first and only time?	11. **Wo** ist der Bodensee?
11. *Where* is Lake Constance?	12. **Welche** neun Länder umringen Deutschland?
12. *Which* nine countries surround Germany?	13. Dürer und Grünewald sind Maler **welches** Landes?
13. Dürer and Grünewald are painters *from which* country?	14. **Welchen** Dialekt sprechen Sie?

14. Which (what) dialect do you speak?	**15.** **Was für ein** Mann war Bismarck?
15. *What kind of a* man was Bismarck?	**16.** **herrlich** = *wonderful* **Was für** herrliche Schokolade!
16. *What* wonderful chocolate!	**17.** **der Esel** = *donkey* **Was für** dumme Esel!
17. *What* stupid fools (asses, donkeys)!	**18.** Es gibt andere Länder, **wo** man die deutsche Sprache spricht.
18. There are other countries *where* the German language is spoken.	**19.** **Wie** hat die Wiedervereinigung Deutschlands je stattgefunden?
19. *How* did the reunification of Germany ever take place?	**20.** **Wo** ist die Schweiz?
20. *Where* is Switzerland?	**21.** Hier ist das klassische Gebirgsland, **welches** Millionen von Menschen jedes Jahr besuchen.
21. Here is the classic mountain country *which* millions of people visit every year.	**22.** **Wie** schmeckt der Schweizer Käse?
22. *How* does the Swiss cheese taste?	

PROGRESS TEST

Choose the correct translation for the indicated words.

1. *Warum* sind Österreichs einstige wertvolle Beziehungen zu ost- und südeuropäischen Ländern zum Teil abgeschnitten?
   (a) when (b) how (c) why (d) where
2. *Wie* ist es möglich, daß Hitler immer noch großen Einfluß auf Europa ausüben kann?
   (a) how (b) when (c) where (d) who
3. *Wo* ist Karl Marx geboren?
   (a) who (b) where (c) when (d) why
4. In *welcher* deutschen Stadt Europas findet man das Brandenburger Tor?
   (a) that (b) why (c) when (d) which (what)
5. *Was für* Pläne hatten die Türken?
   (a) why (b) what kind of (c) when (d) who

Answer key: **1.** (c); **2.** (a); **3.** (b); **4.** (d); **5.** (b).

33. *Separable verb prefixes*

1. In German, as in English, it is possible to form new verbs and meanings by adding a prefix:

stehen	*to stand*
***be*stehen**	*to exist, to pass* (a test)
***ge*stehen**	*to confess*
***ver*stehen**	*to understand*
***auf*stehen**	*to get up*
***bei*stehen**	*to aid, to stand by*
***vor*stehen**	*to stand before, to preside over*

2. Verb prefixes are either separable or inseparable. Prefixes such as **be-**, **ge-**, and **ver-** in our above examples are inseparable prefixes, i.e., they are never separated from the stem. Few in number, the other common inseparable prefixes are **emp-, ent-, er-**, and **zer-.**

3. Separable prefixes, however, are numerous. Primarily, they are either adverbs or prepositions, and the meaning of the prefix is generally added to the verb. **Auf-**, **bei-**, and **vor-** in the above are examples of prepositions used as separable prefixes.

4. The separable prefix will always be at the end of the clause, where it may or may not be attached to the verb, depending on the word order of the clause or on the verb tense:

Normal word order, present:
Ich stehe um acht Uhr *auf.* — *I get up at 8 o'clock.*

Inverted word order, past:
Stand er um acht Uhr *auf?* — *Did he get up at 8 o'clock?*

Dependent word order, present (past):
Ich weiß, daß er um acht Uhr *auf*steht(*auf*stand). — *I know that he gets up (got up) at 8 o'clock.*

Inverted word order, imperative:
Stehen Sie um acht Uhr *auf!* — *Get up at 8 o'clock!*

In the present and simple past tenses, in normal or inverted word order, and also in the imperative, the prefix is separated from the rest of the verb.

5. A separable prefix verb used with a modal is found at the end of a clause and is joined with its prefix:

Darf* ich mit Ihnen zum Bahnhof *mitfahren? — ***May** I **ride along** with you to the railroad station?*

Ich weiß, daß er mich nicht *ansehen will.* — *I know that he does not **want to look at** me.*

6. As has been mentioned, prepositions used as separable verb prefixes will be found at the end of the clause. Used simply as prepositions, they precede their objects:

Der Professor *sieht* die Studenten scharf *an*.	*The professor* ***looks at*** *the students sharply.*
Der Professor geht *an* die Tafel.	*The professor goes* ***to*** *the board.*

7. Two common adverbial prefixes are **hin** and **her**. **Hin** denotes motion away from; **her** denotes motion toward the speaker or observer. They are often used in conjunction with other prefixes:

Dieser Kurs *wächst* mir zum Halse *heraus*.	*I've had enough of this course (lit.: This course* ***grows up*** *to my throat* ***and out****.)*
Das Ewig-Weibliche *zieht* uns *hinan*. (Goethe)	*The eternal feminine* ***draws*** *us* ***upward****.*

Her, with an adverb or phrase of time, may indicate past time and is then translated *ago:*

Es ist schon lange *her*, daß ich Geld hatte.	*It was a long time* ***ago*** *that I had money.*

Give the infinitive form of the verbs in the following sentences.

	1. Schauen wir die Landkarte an!
1. anschauen—Let us look at the map.	**2.** Wie leidet man im diesseitigen Leben Gottes Leiden mit?
2. mitleiden—How does one suffer with God's suffering in this earthly life (how does one share in God's sufferings in this life here on earth)?	**3.** Wann löste sich die Habsburger Monarchie auf?
3. auflösen—When did the Hapsburg monarchy break up?	**4. fand** = *past of* **finden** Vor dreizehn (13) Jahren fand ein Gespräch zwischen Bonhoeffer und einem jungen französischen Pfarrer statt.
4. stattfinden—Thirteen years ago a conversation took place between Bonhoeffer and a young French pastor.	**5.** Die Geschichte Österreichs hängt sehr eng mit der deutschen Geschichte zusammen.
5. zusammenhängen—The history of Austria is very closely connected to German history.	**6.** Bauen wir eine Welt des Friedens oder des Krieges auf?
6. aufbauen—Are we building a world of peace or war?	**7.** Die Soldaten hielten den Zivilisten fest.
7. festhalten—The soldiers held the civilian fast (tight).	

What are the meanings of the following sentences?

	8. einflußreich = *influential* **der Schriftsteller** = *writer* Sigmund Freud ist ein einflußreicher Schriftsteller.
8. Sigmund Freud is an influential writer.	**9. einer** = *one* Er ist einer **der** einflußreichsten Schriftstellern **der** modernen Zeit.
9. He is one *of the* most influential writers *of* modern times.	**10.** Wie Sie schon wissen, ist er der Vater **der** Psychologie und **der** Psychoanalyse.
10. As you already know, he is the father *of* psychology and *of* psychoanalysis.	**11. dieses Kapitels** = *of this chapter* **seiner** = *of his* Am Ende dieses Kapitels **werden** Sie einen seiner Gedanken über die Liebe lesen. (*will/become*)
11. At the end of this chapter you *will* read one of his ideas about love.	**12. der Nächste** = *neighbor* Freud schreibt, daß er es sehr schwer findet, seinen Nächsten zu lieben.
12. Freud writes that he finds it very difficult to love his neighbor.	**13.** Heinrich Heine ist ein berühmter deutscher Dichter des 19. Jahrhunderts.
13. Heinrich Heine is a famous German poet of the 19th century.	**14.** Auch er findet es sehr schwer, seinen Nächsten zu lieben.
14. He too finds it very difficult to love his neighbor.	**15.** Sie werden auch lesen, was Heine über dieses Problem zu sagen hat.
15. You will also read what Heine has to say about this problem.	**16. folgendes** = *the following* Die Bibel sagt uns folgendes über das Problem der Nächstenliebe.
16. The Bible tells us the following about the problem of loving one's neighbor.	**17.** Du sollst den Nächsten lieben wie dich selbst.
17. Thou shalt love thy neighbor as thyself.	**18.** Ist es möglich, den Nächsten zu lieben, wenn man sich selbst nicht liebt?
18. Is it possible to love one's neighbor, if one does not love oneself?	**19. fordern** = *to demand* **die Forderung** = *challenge, demand, standard* Die Nächstenliebe ist eine sehr ideale Forderung.
19. Loving one's neighbor is a very ideal demand (challenge).	**20. stolz** = *proud* **der Anspruch** = *claim* Das Christentum ist sehr stolz auf diesen Anspruch der Nächstenliebe.

20. Christianity is very proud of this claim of loving one's neighbor.	**21.** **vorweisen** = *to show, to display* Das Christentum weist diese sogenannte Idealforderung als seinen stolzesten Anspruch vor.
21. Christianity displays this so-called ideal standard as its proudest claim.	**22.** **gewiß** = *certainly* Diese sogenannte Idealforderung ist gewiß älter als das Christentum, **das** sie als seinen stolzesten Anspruch vorweist. (*which/the*)
22. This so-called ideal standard is certainly older than Christianity, *which* displays it as its proudest claim.	**23.** **zustande bringen** = *to bring about, to accomplish* Wie bringen wir die Nächstenliebe zustande?
23. How are we to accomplish (bring about) loving our neighbor?	**24.** Wissen Sie, wie man **das** zustande bringen kann? (*which/that/the*)
24. Do you know how one can accomplish *that?*	**25.** **fremd** = *strange, foreign* Wie wird es uns möglich, einen **Fremden** zu lieben?
25. How does it become possible for us to love a *stranger?*	**26.** **gleichstellen** = *to put on an equal footing* Freud stellt den Fremden seinen Freunden nicht gleich.
26. Freud does not put a stranger on an equal footing with his friends.	**27.** Er glaubt, daß es gewiß ein Unrecht an seinen Freunden ist, wenn er den Fremden ihnen gleichstellt.
27. He believes it is certainly an injustice to his friends, if he puts a stranger on the same level with them.	**28.** **nah** = *near* **zusehen** = *to look on, to take care* Wenn er näher zusieht. . . .
28. If he looks more closely . . .	**29.** **schwierig** = *difficult* **die Schwierigkeit** = *difficulty* Wenn er näher zusieht, findet er noch mehr Schwierigkeiten.
29. If he looks more closely he finds even more difficulties.	**30.** **das Gebot** = *commandment* Ein zweites Gebot heißt: Liebe deine Feinde!
30. A second commandment is: Love thine enemies!	**31.** **weisen** = *to show, to point* **abweisen** = *to turn away, to reject* Freud weist es ab, seine Feinde zu lieben.
31. Freud rejects the idea of loving his enemies. (**Es** anticipates the following phrase.)	**32.** **wahr** = *true* **der Schein** = *appearance* **wahrscheinlich** = *likely, probable* Es ist wahrscheinlich, daß der Feind das Gebot auch abweisen wird.

32. It is likely that the enemy will also reject the commandment.	**33.** **fordern** = *to demand, to exact* **auffordern** = *to ask* (*to challenge*) Fordere den Nächsten auf, dich zu lieben wie sich selbst!
33. Ask your neighbor to love you as he loves himself!	**34.** Wenn wir den Nächsten auffordern, uns zu lieben wie sich selbst, wird er es tun?
34. If we ask our neighbor to love us as he loves himself, will he do it?	

PROGRESS TEST

Choose the correct infinitive form of the verb in the following sentences.

1. Legt uns Liebe Pflichten auf?
(a) liegen (b) auflegen (c) legen

2. Ein Leid stößt meinem Freund zu.
(a) stoßen (b) einstoßen (c) zustoßen

3. Kommen Sie doch mit mir!
(a) kommen (b) mitkommen

4. Ich weiß, daß er mich durch keinen eigenen Wert anzieht.
(a) anziehen (b) durchanziehen (c) anziehtwissen

Now give the meaning of the indicated words.

5. Das ist ja schon eine Woche *her.*
(a) here (b) her (c) ago (d) toward the speaker

6. Er sieht *zum Fenster hinaus.*
(a) into the window (b) by the window (c) out of the window (d) toward the window

Answer key: **1.** (b); **2.** (c); **3.** (a); **4.** (a); **5.** (c); **6.** (c).

34. *Inseparable verb prefixes—meanings*

Inseparable verbal prefixes originally had certain fundamental meanings which may or may not have been retained when used with individual verbs. This section introduces you to these prefixes.

1. **be-** changes intransitive verbs to transitive (i.e., lets the verb take a direct object):

kommen *to come*
bekommen *to receive* (direct object: *something*)

wohnen	*to live*
bewohnen	*to inhabit* (direct object: *a place*)
antworten	*to answer*
beantworten	*to answer* (direct object: *a question*)

2. ent- (*or* **emp-** *before* **f**) *denotes:*

(a) the beginning of an action:

stehen	*to stand*
entstehen	*to come into existence*

(b) the meaning of opposite:

wickeln	*to wind up, to wrap up*
entwickeln	*to develop, to unwind, to evolve*
fangen	*to catch*
empfangen	*to receive*

(c) the meaning of separation:

gehen	*to go*
entgehen	*to escape*
laufen	*to run*
entlaufen	*to run away*

(d) lost meaning:

finden	*to find*
empfinden	*to feel*

3. er- denotes successful completion of an action or origin:

leben	*to live*
erleben	*to experience*
reichen	*to reach*
erreichen	*to attain*
raten	*to guess*
erraten	*to guess correctly*

4. ge-:

(a) shows result or completeness as shown in the past participle:

machen	*to make*
gemacht	*made*

(b) may also denote successful action:

gewinnen	*to gain, to win*

5. miß- (generally an inseparable prefix) usually corresponds to English *mis-* or *dis-*. It denotes that something is amiss, false, wrong, or bad:

verstehen	*to understand*
mißverstehen	*to misunderstand*
trauen	*to trust*
mißtrauen	*to distrust*
handeln	*to act, to behave*
mißhandeln	*to abuse, to ill-treat*

6. ver- has several meanings:

(a) it may denote that the action of the verb miscarried:

kennen	*to know*
verkennen	*to fail to recognize*
spielen	*to play*
verspielen	*to lose money in playing*

(b) it is sometimes the equivalent of *for-*:

vergessen	*to forget*
vergeben	*to forgive*

(c) it may denote an action carried out to its logical conclusion:

hungern	*to hunger*
verhungern	*to die of hunger*

7. zer- denotes the destruction or damage resulting from the original verb and has the meaning of *to pieces, in pieces:*

brechen	*to break*
zerbrechen	*to break to pieces*
stören	*to disturb*
zerstören	*to destroy*

The following exercises combine practice in recognizing prefixes with introduction of more vocabulary for the reading passages. Give the meanings of the entire sentences. Remember to circle new words for review.

	1. **kennen** = *to know* **bekennen** = *to confess* **ehrlich** = *honest, honestly* Was muß Freud ehrlich bekennen?
1. What must Freud honestly confess?	**2.** **die Feindseligkeit** = *hostility* Freud muß ehrlich bekennen, der Fremde hat mehr **Anspruch** auf seine Feindseligkeit, sogar auf seinen Haß.
2. Freud must honestly confess that the stranger has more *claim* to his hostility, even to his hatred.	**3.** **zeigen** = *to point out, to show* **bezeigen** = *to show, to express* **die Rücksicht** = *consideration* Freuds Feinde bezeigen ihm keine Rücksicht.
3. Freud's enemies don't show him any consideration.	**4.** **gering** = *slight, small, inferior* Der Feind bezeigt ihm nicht die **geringste** Rücksicht.
4. The enemy does not show him the *slightest* consideration.	**5.** **gewinnen** = *to gain, to win* **davon** = *therefrom* Was gewinnt man davon, daß man nur seine Freunde liebt?
5. What does one gain from loving only one's friends?	**6.** **horchen** = *to listen, to overhear* **gehorchen** = *to obey* Es scheint, daß Freud **dem Gebot** der Nächstenliebe nicht gehorchen kann oder will.
6. It appears that Freud cannot or will not obey *the commandment* to love one's neighbor. (Note that **gehorchen** calls for a dative object.)	**7.** **trauen** = *to trust, to dare* **mißtrauen** = *to mistrust, to suspect* Scheint es Ihnen, daß Freud **dem Gebot** der Nächstenliebe mißtraut?
7. Does it appear to you that Freud mistrusts *the commandment* to love one's neighbor? (Note that **mißtrauen** calls for a dative object.)	**8.** **brauchen** = *to use, to need* **mißbrauchen** = *to misuse, to abuse* Man kann und **will** sogar das Gebot der Nächstenliebe mißbrauchen.
8. One can and even *wants* to abuse the commandment to love one's neighbor.	**9.** **dienen** = *to serve* **verdienen** = *to earn, to deserve* Wenn ich **einen anderen** liebe, muß er es auf irgendeine Art verdienen.
9. If I love *someone,* he must deserve it (be worthy of it) in one way or another.	**10.** **die Kultur** = *culture, civilization* **die Gesellschaft** = *society* **die Kulturgesellschaft** = ____________

10. *civilized society*	**11.** **lauten** = *to read, to be as follows* **Eine der** sogenannten Idealforderungen der Kulturgesellschaft lautet: Du sollst den Nächsten lieben wie dich selbst. (*the one/one of the*)
11. *One of the* so-called ideal standards of civilized society reads: Thou shalt love thy neighbor as thyself.	**12.** Diese Idealforderung ist weltberühmt und gewiß **älter als** das Christentum. (*as old as/older than*)
12. This ideal standard is world famous and certainly *older than* Christianity.	**13.** Das Christentum aber **weist** diese Idealforderung als seinen stolzesten Anspruch **vor**.
13. Christianity, however, *displays* this ideal standard as its proudest claim.	**14.** **sicherlich** = *surely* Das Gebot ist gewiß älter als das Christentum, aber es ist sicherlich nicht sehr alt.
14. The commandment is certainly older than Christianity, but it is surely not very old.	**15.** **fremd** = *foreign, strange* In historischen Zeiten war das Gebot **den Menschen** noch fremd. (acc. sing./dat. plural)
15. dative plural: the adjective **fremd** requires a dative object. In historical times the commandment was still foreign *to people* (people still knew nothing of it).	**16.** Freud fragt: „Warum **sollen** wir das? Was **soll** es uns helfen?"
16. Freud asks, "Why *should* we *do* that? How *is* it *going to* help us?"	**17.** **Vor allem** aber, wie bringen wir das zustande? (*for everyone/above all*)
17. *Above all,* however, how do we accomplish this?	**18.** Wie verdient man die Liebe **eines anderen** Menschen? (genitive/nominative)
18. genitive: **ein anderer Mensch** would be nominative. How does one earn the love *of another* person?	**19.** Freud meint, daß ein Fremder seine Liebe **auf irgendeine Art** verdienen muß. (*artfully/in some way*)
19. Freud feels that a stranger must *in some way* merit his love.	**20.** **ähnlich** = *similar to, like* Wenn unser Nächster **uns ähnlich ist,** so können wir ihn lieben, sagt Freud.
20. Freud says, if our neighbor *is similar to us,* then we can love him.	**21.** **wichtig** = *important* **das Stück** = *piece, bit;* here: *aspect, respect* Freud meint, man verdient seine Liebe, wenn man **ihm** in wichtigen Stücken ähnlich ist. (*him/to him*)

21. Freud feels one earns his love when one is similar *to him* in important respects. (Note that **ähnlich** requires a dative object.)	**22.** **in dem einen** = *in the other* Freud meint, man verdient seine Liebe, wenn wenn man ihm in wichtigen Stücken, so ähnlich ist, daß er in dem einen sich selbst lieben kann.
22. Freud feels a person is worthy of his love when that person is so similar to him in important respects that he can love himself in that other person.	**23.** **vollkommen** = *perfect* Freud sagt, ich kann den anderen lieben, wenn er **soviel vollkommener** ist als ich, daß ich mein Ideal von meiner eigenen Person in ihm lieben kann.
23. Freud says, I can love another if he is *so much more perfect* than I that I can love my ideal of myself (of my own person) in him.	**24.** Wir müssen den Nächsten lieben, wenn er der Sohn **unseres** Freundes ist. (*of your/of our*)
24. We must love our neighbor if he is the son *of our* friend.	**25.** Wenn er mir fremd ist, sagt Freud, wird es **mir schwer**, ihn zu lieben. (*hard for me/hard for him*)
25. If he is a stranger to me, says Freud, it is (becomes) *hard for me* to love him. (Note that **schwer** calls for a dative object hence "for.")	**26.** **ziehen** = *to pull* **anziehen** = *to attract* Wenn er mich durch keinen **eigenen Wert** anziehen kann, wird es mir schwer, ihn zu lieben. (*own worth/one word*)
26. If he cannot attract me by his *own worth* it will be (becomes) difficult for me to love him. (Note: The context suggests a future result based on a present condition.)	**27.** Dieser Fremde ist nicht nur **im allgemeinen** nicht liebenswert . . . (*in general/not at all*)
27. *In general,* this stranger is not only not worthy of love . . .	**28.** . . . sondern er hat auch im allgemeinen mehr Anspruch auf meine **Feindseligkeit**. (*friendship/hostility*)
28. . . . but in general he also has more claim to my *hostility.*	**29.** **mindest**: irregular superlative form of **wenig** = *less* **wenig, weniger, wenigst-** or **wenig, minder, mindest-** Der Fremde scheint nicht die **mindeste** Liebe für mich zu haben.
29. The stranger does not seem to have the *slightest bit of* (*least bit of*) love for me.	**30.** **das Bedenken** = *hesitation, reflection* **schädigen** = *to injure* Ein Fremder **hat keine Bedenken,** mich zu schädigen.

30. A stranger *does not hesitate* to injure me.	**31.** **der Nutzen** = *advantage, use* Wenn es ihm einen Nutzen bringt, hat der Fremde keine Bedenken, mich zu schädigen.
31. If it brings him an advantage, the stranger does not hesitate to injure me.	**32.** **groß** = *large, great* **die Art** = *manner* **großartig** = *magnificent, wonderful, splendid* Das ist ein großartiges Gebot.
32. That is a magnificent commandment.	**33.** **lauten** = *to sound, to read* Wie lautet jenes großartige Gebot wieder?
33. How does that magnificent commandment read again?	**34.** **ja** = *indeed* **würde** = *would, were to* Ja, wenn jenes großartige Gebot lauten würde . . .
34. Indeed, if that magnificent commandment were to read . . .	**35.** **widersprechen** = *to contradict, to object* Ja, wenn jenes großartige Gebot lauten würde: Liebe deinen Nächsten wie dein Nächster dich liebt, dann würde ich nicht widersprechen.
35. Indeed, if that magnificent commandment were to read: Love thy neighbor as thy neighbor loves thee, then I would not object (to it).	**36.** **fassen** = *to grasp, to take hold of* **faßbar** = *tangible, concrete* **unfaßbar** = *incomprehensible, unintelligible* Es gibt ein zweites Gebot, das mir noch unfaßbarer scheint. **Es heißt**: Liebe deine Feinde. (*it is/it calls*)
36. There is a second commandment which appears even more incomprehensible to me. *It is:* Love thine enemies.	**37.** **eher:** from **bald, eher, ehest-** **Weil** der Nächste eher dein Feind ist, sollst du ihn lieben wie dich selbst. (*while/because*)
37. *Because* your neighbor is more apt to be your enemy, you should love him as yourself.	**38.** **der Fall** = *case, situation* Das ist ein ähnlicher Fall wie das *Credo quia absurdum,* **das** unfaßbar ist. (*which/the*)
38. That is a case similar to that of *Credo quia absurdum* (I believe it, because it is absurd), *which* is incomprehensible.	**39.** **die Begründung** = *reason* Mit welchen Begründungen **wird** mein Nächster mich abweisen? (*become/will*)
39. For what reasons *will* my neighbor reject me?	**40.** **nämlich** (adj.) = *same* Wird der Nächste **genau** so antworten wie ich und mich mit den nämlichen Begründungen abweisen? (*exactly as/probably*)

40. Will my neighbor answer *exactly as* I do and reject me for the same reasons?	**41.** **derselbe, dieselbe, dasselbe** = *the same* **das Recht** = *right;* here: *grounds* Ich hoffe, nicht mit demselben objektiven Recht, aber dasselbe wird **auch** er meinen. (*you/also*)
41. I hope not with the same objective grounds, but he will *also* hold the same opinion.	**42.** **denn** = *for* **der Lohn** = *reward* **der Zöllner** = *publican* Denn so ihr liebet, die euch lieben, was werdet ihr für Lohn haben? Tun nicht dasselbe auch die Zöllner? (Bibel)
42. For if ye love them which love you, what reward will ye have? Do not even the publicans do the same?	**43.** Was **halten** Sie davon? (*hold/do . . . think*)
43. What *do* you *think* about that?	**44.** **die Gesinnung** = *disposition, belief* **Was für eine** Gesinnung hat der Dichter Heinrich Heine? (*what for a/what kind of a*)
44. *What kind of a* disposition does the poet Heinrich Heine have?	**45.** **friedlich** = *peaceable* Der Dichter Heine hat die **friedlichste** Gesinnung. (*peaceable/most peaceable*)
45. The poet Heine has the *most peaceable* disposition.	**46.** **bescheiden** = *modest* Der Dichter hat nur bescheidene **Wünsche**. (*wishes/wounds*)
46. The poet has only modest *wishes.*	**47.** **die Hütte** = *cottage, hut* **das Strohdach** = *thatched roof, straw roof* Er will eine bescheidene Hütte mit einem Strohdach.
47. He wants a modest cottage with a thatched roof.	**48.** **die Blume** = *flower* **das Fenster** = *window* **die Tür** = *door* **der Baum** = *tree* Seine Wünsche sind: eine bescheidene Hütte, ein Strohdach, Blumen **vor** dem Fenster, einige schöne Bäume **vor** der Tür. (*for/in front of*)
48. His wishes are a modest cottage, a straw roof, flowers *in front of* the window, some beautiful trees *in front of* the door.	**49.** **der Feind** = *enemy* Heine will seine Feinde an den Bäumen **aufgehängt** sehen. (*hang/hung*)

49. Heine wants to see his enemies *hung* from the trees.	**50.** **etwa** = *some* Heine will etwa sechs bis sieben **seiner** Feinde an diesen Bäumen aufhängen. (*of his/his*)
50. Heine wants to hang some six or seven *of his* enemies from these trees.	**51.** **das Glück** = *fortune, happiness, (good) luck* **glücklich** = *fortunate, happy* Wenn etwa sechs bis sieben seiner Feinde an diesen Bäumen hängen, dann **ist** er glücklich.
51. When some six or seven of his enemies are hanging from these trees, then he *will be* happy. (Lit.: *is*)	**52.** **zufügen** = *to add to, to cause, to do to* **die Unbill** = *injustice* Seine Feinde fügten **ihm** allerlei Unbill im Leben zu.
52. His enemies did all kinds of wrong *to him* in their lifetime. (Note use of dative case with **zufügen**.)	**53.** **verzeihen** = *to forgive* Heine kann **seinen Feinden** nicht verzeihen . . .
53. Heine cannot forgive *his enemies* . . . (Note **verzeihen** takes a dative object.)	**54.** . . . bis er sie aufgehängt sieht.
54. . . . until he sees them hanged.	**55.** **der Tod** = *death* Vor ihrem Tode wird er ihnen die Unbill nicht verzeihen, die sie ihm im Leben zugefügt haben.
55. Before their death he will not forgive them the wrong they have done to him in their lifetime.	**56.** **die Freude** = *joy* Welche Freude will Heine erleben?
56. What joy does Heine want to experience?	**57.** **lassen** = *to let, to cause* **aufhängen lassen** = *to cause to be hanged* **Etwa** sechs bis sieben seiner Feinde will er an den Bäumen aufhängen lassen. (*some/something*)
57. He wants *some* six or seven of his enemies hanged from the trees.	**58.** Laß mich die Freude erleben, daß an diesen Bäumen etwa sechs bis sieben meiner Feinde **aufgehängt werden.** (*will hang/are hanged*)
58. Let me experience the joy that comes from seeing some six or seven of my enemies *hanging* from these trees. (Lit.: let me experience the joy that some six or seven of my enemies *are hanged* from these trees.)	**59.** **rühren** = *to touch, to stir up, to move* **gerührt** = *full of emotion* Mit gerührtem Herzen werde ich ihnen alle Unbill verzeihen.

59. With a heart full of emotion I will forgive them all their wrongdoing.	**60.** **gehenkt worden sind** (passive) = *have been hanged* **früh** = *early* Ja, man muß seinen Feinden verzeihen, aber nicht früher, als bis sie gehenkt worden sind.
60. Yes, one must forgive one's enemies, but not before they have been hanged.	

PROGRESS TEST

Choose the correct meaning of the indicated inseparable prefix verbs. Note that the inseparable prefix may radically change the meaning of the primary verb.

1. Freud kann nicht der Idee entfliehen, daß er seine Feinde hassen soll.
If **fliehen** means *to flee,* then **entfliehen** must mean __________.
(a) to flee toward (b) to flee from (c) to flee with

2. Ich erwarte meinen Freund um sechs.
If **warten** means *to wait,* then **erwarten** must mean __________.
(a) to expect (b) to wait (c) to wait on

3. Wollen wir Freuds Argument zergliedern?
If **gliedern** means *to organize, to arrange,* then **zergliedern** must mean __________
(a) to disorganize (b) to forget to organize (c) to analyze

4. Ich darf sein Argument nicht verwerfen.
If **werfen** means *to throw,* then **verwerfen** must mean: __________.
(a) to throw up (b) to approve (c) to condemn

And now choose the approximate meaning of the following sentences.

5. Wenn wir den Nächsten auffordern, uns zu lieben wie er sich selbst liebt, wird er es tun?
(a) Whenever we command our neighbor to love us as we love ourselves, will he do it?
(b) When we further ourselves by loving our neighbor as he himself does, won't he challenge us?
(c) If we command our neighbor to love us as he loves himself, will he do it?
(d) none

6. Mein Feind braucht nicht einmal einen Nutzen davon zu haben, um mich zu zerschlagen.
(a) My friend doesn't need an excuse to condemn me.
(b) The fiend really does not need to injure me.
(c) My enemy is nuts to attack me.
(d) My enemy does not need to gain a benefit by smashing me to pieces.

7. Wenn ich es recht überlege, habe ich unrecht.
(a) Whenever I truly lay it on him, I am uneasy.
(b) It is not right for me to give it to him.
(c) If I were truly mean, I would be wrong.
(d) I am wrong, if I truly think it over.

8. Ja, man muß seinen Feinden verzeihen, aber nicht früher als bis sie gehenkt worden sind.
(a) Yes, one must forgive one's friends, but not until they have been hanged.
(b) Yes, one must forgive one's enemies, but only after they have been hanged.
(c) Yes, one's enemies must be hanged, if they are not to be forgiven.
(d) Yes, one must forgive one's enemies, even if they are not hanged.

Answer key: **1.** (b); **2.** (a); **3.** (c); **4.** (c); **5.** (c); **6.** (d); **7.** (d); **8.** (b).

Sigmund Freud: Das Unbehagen in der Kultur

Eine der sogenannten Idealforderungen der Kulturgesellschaft . . . lautet: Du sollst den Nächsten lieben wie dich selbst; sie ist weltberühmt, gewiß älter als das Christentum, das sie als seinen stolzesten Anspruch vorweist, aber [sie ist] sicherlich nicht sehr alt; in historischen Zeiten war sie den Menschen noch fremd . . . Warum sollen wir das? Was soll es uns helfen? Vor allem aber, wie bringen wir das zustande? Wie wird es uns möglich? . . . Wenn ich einen anderen liebe, muß er es auf irgendeine Art verdienen . . . Er verdient es, wenn er mir in wichtigen Stücken so ähnlich ist, daß ich in ihm mich selbst lieben kann; er verdient es, wenn er soviel vollkommener ist als ich, daß ich mein Ideal von meiner eigenen Person in ihm lieben kann: ich muß ihn lieben, wenn er der Sohn meines Freundes ist . . . Aber wenn er mir fremd ist und mich durch keinen eigenen Wert . . . anziehen kann, wird es mir schwer, ihn zu lieben . . . Es ist ein Unrecht an [meinen Freunden], wenn ich den Fremden ihnen gleichstelle . . .

Wenn ich näher zusehe, finde ich noch mehr Schwierigkeiten. Dieser Fremde ist nicht nur im allgemeinen nicht liebenswert, ich muß ehrlich bekennen, er hat mehr Anspruch auf meine Feindseligkeit, sogar auf meinen Haß. Er scheint nicht die mindeste Liebe für mich zu haben, bezeigt mir nicht die geringste Rücksicht. Wenn es ihm einen Nutzen bringt, hat er kein Bedenken, mich zu schädigen . . . Ja, wenn jenes großartige Gebot lauten würde: Liebe deinen Nächsten wie dein Nächster dich liebt, dann würde ich nicht widersprechen. Es gibt ein zweites Gebot, das mir noch unfaßbarer scheint . . . Es heißt: Liebe deine Feinde . . .

Weil der Nächste nicht liebenswert und eher dein Feind ist, sollst du ihn lieben wie dich selbst. Ich verstehe dann, das ist ein ähnlicher Fall wie das *Credo quia absurdum*.

Es ist nun sehr wahrscheinlich, daß der Nächste, wenn er aufgefordert wird, mich so zu lieben wie sich selbst, genau so antworten wird wie ich und mich mit den nämlichen Begrüdungen abweisen wird. Ich hoffe, nicht mit demselben objektiven Recht, aber dasselbe wird auch er meinen.

Heinrich Heine: Gedanken und Einfälle

„Ich habe die friedlichste Gesinnung. Meine Wünsche sind: eine bescheidene Hütte, ein Strohdach, aber ein gutes Bett, gutes Essen. Milch und Butter, sehr frisch, vor dem Fenster Blumen, vor der Tür einige schöne Bäume, und wenn der liebe Gott mich ganz glücklich machen will, läßt er mich die Freude erleben, daß an diesen Bäumen etwa sechs bis sieben meiner Feinde aufgehängt werden. Mit gerührtem Herzen werde ich ihnen vor ihrem Tode alle Unbill verzeihen, die sie mir im Leben zugefügt.[1] Ja, man muß seinen Feinden verzeihen, aber nicht früher, als bis sie gehenkt worden."[2]

---

1 A past participle needs a helping verb. In this case the understood helping verb is **haben**, i.e., **zugefügt haben.**

2 The verb **gehenkt worden** needs the helping verb **sind,** i.e., **gehenkt worden sind.** Authors may sometimes leave out the helping verbs as in these two instances.

Chapter Nine

35. *Past tense of strong verbs and* werden
36. *Past tense of modals and* wissen

Reading: From Karl Marx: Das Kapital

35. *Past tense of strong verbs and* werden

1. Similar to English, the past tense of a German strong verb is recognized by a vowel change in the stem:

ich singe	*I sing*	**ich sang**	*I sang*
du singst	*you sing*	**du sangst**	*you sang*
er, sie, es singt	*he sings*	**er sang**	*he sang*
wir singen	*we sing*	**wir sangen**	*we sang*
ihr singt	*you sing*	**ihr sangt**	*you sang*
sie singen	*they sing*	**sie sangen**	*they sang*
Sie singen	*you sing*	**Sie sangen**	*you sang*

2. The following endings added to the stem indicate person and number:

(**ich**)	-	(**wir**)	**-en**
(**du**)	**-(e)st** (**Sie**) **-en**	(**ihr**)	**-(e)t**
(**er, sie, es**)	-	(**sie**)	**-en**

With the exception of the first and third person singular, the endings are the same as the present tense endings. Thus it is important to recognize the vowel shift:

Du *verlierst* das Buch.	*You **lose** the book.*
Du *verlorst* das Buch.	*You **lost** the book.*
Wir *sehen* den Mann.	*We **see** the man.*
Wir *sahen* den Mann.	*We **saw** the man.*

3. The verb **werden** is irregular in the past tense:

ich wurde	(**ward**)	*I became, got*
du wurdest	(**wardst**)	*etc.*
er, sie, es wurde	(**ward**)	
wir wurden		
ihr wurdet		
sie wurden		
Sie wurden		

The above alternatives in parenthesis are old or literary forms and far less common.

4. In a few cases not only the vowel changes but the following consonant as well. Below are some of the more common examples:

schneiden	(*to cut*)	**ich schneide**	**ich schnitt**
greifen	(*to grab*)	**du greifst**	**du griffst**
treffen	(*to meet, hit*)	**er trifft**	**er traf**
fallen	(*to fall*)	**sie fällt**	**sie fiel**
leiden	(*to suffer*)	**wir leiden**	**wir litten**
sitzen	(*to sit*)	**ihr sitzt**	**ihr saßt**
ziehen	(*to pull*)	**sie ziehen**	**sie zogen**
gehen	(*to go*)	**Sie gehen**	**Sie gingen**
kommen	(*to come*)	**ich komme**	**ich kam**
stehen	(*to stand*)	**du stehst**	**du standst**

5. Dictionaries and glossaries often indicate this vowel change by listing the principal parts of the verb:

singen, (singt), sang, gesungen
to sing, (sings), sang, sung

or by giving only the vowel change:

singen, (i), a, u

6. To determine the infinitive of an unknown strong verb, observe the consonants of the stem. Then go either to a list of strong verbs to find the corresponding form or to a dictionary to find the proper vowel.

The following exercises introduce the vocabulary of the reading passage, drawn from Marx's Das Kapital, *and give you practice in recognizing the past tense of strong verbs. Distinguish between the present and past tenses in the following sentences.*

	1. **die Nachbarin** = *lady next door* „Karl Marx schreibt wieder ein Buch," sagte die alte Nachbarin.
1. "Karl Marx is writing a book again," said the old lady next door.	**2.** Es heißt *Das Kapital.*
2. It is called *Capital.*	**3.** Verstehen Sie, warum er das Buch **schrieb**? (The present tense of **er schrieb** is ___________.)
3. **er schreibt** Do you understand why he *wrote* the book?	**4.** Wie **hieß** das Buch wieder? (*past/present*)

4. past What *was the name* of the book again?	**5.** **besonders** = *especially* Wissen Sie, was Marx und besonders Engels **sahen**, als sie in England wohnten? (The present of **sahen** is ________.)
5. **sehen** Do you know what Marx and especially Engels *saw* when they lived in England?	**6.** Was sieht man heute in den amerikanischen Großstädten?
6. What does one see today in large American cities?	**7.** Wir alle wissen, **wer** Karl Marx ist. (*where/who*)
7. We all know *who* Karl Marx is.	**8.** Sie wissen auch, daß Marx Deutscher **war.** (*is/was*)
8. You also know that Marx *was* (a) German.	**9.** **die Zusammenfassung** = *summary* Sie **werden** jetzt eine Zusammenfassung von ein paar Seiten aus Marxens *Das Kapital* lesen. (**werden** = *will/become*)
9. You *will* now read a summary of several pages from Marx's *Capital.* (**Marxens** is an older genitive form.)	**10.** **die Arbeit** = *work* **die Bedingung** = *condition* Diese Zusammenfassung **spricht** von den Arbeitsbedingungen in den damaligen englischen Fabriken. (**spricht** = *talks of/talked of*)
10. This summary *talks of* working conditions in English factories of the time.	**11.** **gießen** = *to pour, to cast* **die Gießerei** = *foundry* **das Eisen** = *iron* **die Eisengießerei** = ________
11. *iron foundry*	**12.** **neunjährig** = *nine years old* **morgens** = *in the morning* George Allinsworth, neunjährig, **fängt** um 3 Uhr morgens **an,** in einer Eisengießerei zu arbeiten. (*present/past*)
12. present of **anfangen** Nine-year-old George Allinsworth *begins* work at 3 a.m. in an iron foundry.	**13.** **abends** = *in the evening* **u.s.w.** = **und so weiter** = *and so forth, etc.* Am anderen Tag **fing** er 6 Uhr morgens **an** und **endete** 6 oder 7 Uhr abends u.s.w. (*present/past*)

13. past The next day he *began* work at 6 in the morning and *finished* at 6 or 7 in the evening, etc.	**14.** **daher** = *therefore, hence* Daher **blieb** er die ganze Nacht. (The infinitive of **blieb** is __________.)
14. **bleiben** Hence he *remained* the whole night.	**15.** Er **bleibt** die ganze Nacht in der Eisengießerei. (*present/past*)
15. He *stays* at the iron foundry all night long. (Or: He *spends* the whole night at the iron foundry.)	**16.** **der Schurz** = *apron* **das Fell** = *skin, hide, fur* **das Schurzfell** = ____________
16. *leather apron*	**17.** **die Flur** = *field(s), meadow(s)* Ich **schlafe** auf der Flur mit einem Schurzfell unter mir. (*present/past*)
17. I *sleep* in the fields with a leather apron under me.	**18.** Ich **schlief** mit einer kleinen Jacke über mir. (*present/past*)
18. I *slept* with a little jacket over me.	**19.** **bitte** = *please* **Kommen** Sie bitte **her**! (The infinitive is __________.)
19. **herkommen** *Come here,* please.	**20.** **ebenfalls** = *likewise* **der Hochofen** = *blast furnace* Bevor ich **herkam, arbeitete** ich ebenfalls in einem Hochofen. (*present/past*)
20. Before I *came* here I likewise *worked* at a blast furnace.	**21.** Ich **begann** ebenfalls samstags morgens um 3 Uhr zu arbeiten. (*present/past*)
21. I likewise *began* to work Saturdays at three o'clock in the morning.	**22.** **Beginnt** er auch um 3 Uhr?
22. *Does* he *begin* at 3 o'clock, too?	**23.** Er **geht** schlafen.
23. He *is going* to sleep (to bed).	**24.** **wenigstens** = *at least* **Ging** er wenigstens um 12 Uhr nachts nach Hause? (The infinitive of **ging** is __________.)
24. **gehen** *Did* he at least *go* home at midnight?	**25.** **lassen** = *to let* Er **ließ** das Kind ebenfalls auf der Flur schlafen.

25. He likewise *let* the child sleep in the field.	**26.** **auffassen** = *to understand, to regard* **Laßt** uns nun hören, wie das Kapital selbst dieses Vierundzwanzig-Stundensystem **auffaßt.** (*present/past*)
26. *Let* us now hear how capital itself *regards* this twenty-four-hour system.	**27.** **treiben** = *to drive, to carry on* **übertreiben** = *to exaggerate* **die Übertreibung** = __________
27. *exaggeration, excess*	**28.** **übergehen** = *to ignore, to overlook* Das Kapital **übergeht** die Übertreibungen des Systems.
28. Capital *ignores* the excesses of the system.	**29.** Wie **faßt** das Kapital dieses Vierundzwanzig-Stundensystem **auf**?
29. How does capital *regard* this twenty-four-hour system?	**30.** **brauchen** = *to use, to need* **mißbrauchen** = *to misuse, abuse* **der Mißbrauch** = __________
30. *misuse, abuse*	**31.** **schweigen** = *to be silent, to stop (speaking)* **das Schweigen** = *silence* **das Stillschweigen** = __________
31. *silence*	**32.** Das Kapital **überging** den Mißbrauch des Systems natürlich mit Stillschweigen.
32. Naturally, capital *overlooked* the abuse of the system in silence.	**33.** **die Tagarbeit** = *day work* **die Nachtarbeit** = __________
33. *night work*	**34.** **der Unterschied** = *difference* Wir finden nicht, daß Tag- oder Nachtarbeit irgendeinen Unterschied in der Gesundheit der Herren Naylor und Vickers **macht.**
34. We do not find that work by day or by night *makes* any difference in the health of Mr. Naylor and Mr. Vickers.	**35.** Wir **fanden** keinen Unterschied in der Gesundheit der beiden Herren. (*present/past*)
35. We *found* no difference in the health of the two gentlemen.	**36.** **die Ruhe** = *rest, quiet, peace* **die Ruheperiode** = __________
36. *period of rest*	**37.** **genießen** = *to enjoy* **wechseln** = *to change, to exchange* Wahrscheinlich schlafen Leute besser, wenn sie dieselbe Ruheperiode **genießen**, als wenn sie **wechselt**. (*present/past*)

37. People probably sleep better if they *enjoy* the same period of rest than if it *varies*.	**38.** **Genossen** sie immer dieselbe Ruheperiode? (The infinitive of **genossen** is ___________.)
38. **genießen** *Did* they always *enjoy* the same period of rest?	**39.** Das Kapital **spricht** nur von dem System in seiner „normalen" Form. (*present/past of* ___________)
39. present of **sprechen** Capital only *speaks* of the system in its "normal" form.	**40.** Es **sprach** nur von dem System in seiner „normalen" Form.
40. It only *spoke* of the system in its "normal" form.	**41.** **die Hitze** = *heat* Welch eine Hitze!
41. It is so hot! (Lit.: What a heat!)	**42.** **der Knabe** = *boy* Die Knaben **leiden unter** der Hitze.
42. The boys *are suffering from* the heat.	**43.** **durchaus** = *absolutely, completely* **durchaus nicht** = *not at all, by no means* Die Knaben **leiden** durchaus nicht unter der Hitze.
43. The boys *do* not *suffer* at all from the heat.	**44.** **Litt** der Knabe nicht **von** der Hitze? (*present/past*)
44. *Did*n't the boy *suffer from* the heat? (Or: Did the boy not suffer. . .? **leiden unter** is the norm, not **leiden von** as found in Marx's text.)	**45.** **die Zeitung** = *newspaper* Was **lasen** sie gestern in der Zeitung? (*present/past of* ___________)
45. past of **lesen** What *did* they *read* in the paper yesterday?	**46.** **die Schmiede** = *smithy, forge* In Marxens Buch lesen wir, daß man in der Schmiede von 12 Uhr bis 12 Uhr arbeitet.
46. In Marx's book we read that they work from 12 to 12 in the forge.	**47.** **das Hammerwerk** = *foundry, iron works* **das Walzwerk** = *rolling mill* In den Hammer- und Walzwerken **arbeitete** man oft sechzehn Stunden am Tag.
47. They often *worked* sixteen hours a day in the iron foundries and rolling mills.	**48.** **einzeln** = *individual* In einem Walzwerk ist der nominelle Arbeitstag für den einzelnen Arbeiter 11½ Stunden.
48. In a rolling mill the nominal work day for the individual worker *is* 11½ hours.	**49.** **jung** = *young* **der Junge** = ___________

49. *the boy* (modern German)	**50.** **mindestens** = *at least* Ein Junge **arbeitet** 4 Nächte jede Woche bis mindestens 8½ Uhr abends des nächsten Tages. (*present/past*)
50. A boy *works* four nights every week until at least 8:30 in the evening of the next day.	**51.** **ablösen** = *to relieve* **die Ablösung** = __________
51. *the relief*	**52.** **der Ablösungstermin** = (*work*) *shift* **manchmal** = *sometimes* Drei zwölfstündige Ablösungstermine nacheinander **arbeitete** manchmal ein Junge im Alter von 9 Jahren. (*present/past*)
52. Sometimes a nine-year-old boy *worked* three twelve-hour shifts in a row. (Lit.: one after another)	**53.** Er **tut** es nicht mehr lange. (*present/past*)
53. present tense but with future meaning He *will* not *be doing* it much longer.	**54.** **sterben** = *to die* Er **tat** es so lange bis er **starb**. (*present/past*)
54. He *did* it until he *died*.	**55.** Am nächsten Tag **hatten** wir um 3 Uhr morgens anzufangen. (*present/past*)
55. The next day we *had* (*needed*) to begin at three o'clock in the morning.	**56.** Ich **wohne** fünf Meilen von hier. (*present/past*)
56. I *live* five miles from here.	**57.** Wo **wohntet** ihr, als ihr im Walzwerk **arbeitetet?** (*present/past*)
57. Where *did* you *live* when you *worked* in the rolling mill?	**58.** Die Arbeit **beginnt** 6 Uhr morgens und **endet** 6 oder 7 Uhr abends. (*present/past*)
58. Work *begins* at 6 a.m. and *ends* at 6 or 7 p.m.	**59.** **zwanzig** = *twenty* Wie **faßte** das Kapital selbst dieses Vierundzwanzig-Stundensystem **auf**? (*present/past*)
59. How *did* capital itself *regard* this twenty-four-hour system?	**60.** Wie **faßt** das Kapital selbst die Arbeitsbedingungen **auf**? (*present/past*)

60. How *does* capital itself *regard* the working conditions?	**61.** **die Länge** = *length* **lang** = *long* **länger** = *longer* **verlängern** = *to lengthen, to prolong, to extend* **die Verlängerung** = __________
61. *the lengthening, prolongation, extension*	**62.** **grausam** = *cruel* **unglaublich** = *incredible* Das Kapital **mißbraucht** das System zur grausamen und unglaublichen Verlängerung des Arbeitstages. (*present/past*)
62. Capital *abuses* the system by a cruel and incredible extension of the working day.	**63.** Es **mißbrauchte** das System zur grausamen und unglaublichen Verlängerung des Arbeitstages. (*present/past*)
63. It *abused* the system by a cruel and incredible extension of the working day.	**64.** Es **überging** diese Verlängerung ebenfalls mit Stillschweigen. (*present/past*)
64. It likewise *passed over* this extension in silence.	**65.** Es **sprach** nur von dem System in seiner „normalen" Form. (*present/past*)
65. It *spoke* of the system only in its "normal" form.	**66.** **die Fabrik** = *the factory* **das Fabrikat** = *the (manufactured) product* **die Fabrikation** = *the manufacture* **der Fabrikant** = __________
66. *the manufacturer*	**67.** **der Stahl** = *steel* **der Stahlfabrikant** = __________
67. *the steel manufacturer*	**68.** **die Anwendung** = *application* **anwenden** = __________
68. *to use, to employ something* (not usually people)	**69.** Wieviele Personen **wenden** eigentlich die Stahlfabrikanten **an**? (*present/past*)
69. How many persons *do* the steel manufacturers actually *employ?*	**70.** Die Herren Naylor und Vickers, Stahlfabrikanten, **wendeten** manchmal zwischen 600 und 700 Personen **an.** (*present/past*)

70. Mr. Naylor and Mr. Vickers, steel manufacturers, sometimes *employed* between 600 and 700 persons.	**71.** **äußern** = *to express, to utter* **das Personal** = *staff, personnel* Die 20 Knaben, die zum Nachtpersonal **gehören, äußern** sich wie folgt. (*present/past*)
71. The 20 boys who *belong to* (are part of) the night crew *express* themselves as follows. (Notice the use of **die** as a relative pronoun meaning *who.*)	**72.** Was **folgte**, nachdem sie sich **äußerten?** (*present/past*)
72. What *happened* (*followed*) after they *expressed* themselves?	**73.** Wir **fanden** fast keinen Unterschied in der Gesundheit der Knaben. (*present/past*)
73. We *found* hardly any difference in the health of the boys.	**74.** Was **macht** keinen Unterschied? (*present/past*)
74. What *does* not *make* any difference?	**75.** **ob** = *whether, if* Ob sie wirklich dieselbe Ruheperiode **haben**? (*present/past*)
75. (I wonder) whether they really *have* the same rest period?	**76.** Wahrscheinlich **schliefen** die Leute besser, wenn sie immer dieselbe Ruheperiode **genossen,** als wenn sie **wechselte.** (*present/past*)
76. People probably *slept* better if they always *enjoyed* the same period of rest than if it *varied*.	**77.** **Litten** sie unter der Hitze? **Leiden** sie immer noch?
77. *Did* they *suffer* from the heat? *Do* they still *suffer?*	**78.** **kriegen** = *to get* **Kriegt** man Jungen so viel man **will** für die Arbeit in den Fabriken? (*present/past*)
78. *Do* they *get* as many boys as they *want* for the work in the factories?	**79.** **verwenden** = *to use, to employ* **gering** = *small* **Verwendeten** sie eine geringere Proportion von Jungen? (*present/past*)
79. *Did* they *employ* a smaller proportion of boys?	**80.** **beschränken** = *to limit, to restrict* **die Beschränkung** = __________
80. *the limitation, restriction*	**81.** **wichtig** = *important* **die Wichtigkeit** = _________

81. *the importance*	**82.** Beschränkungen der Nachtarbeit **waren** von wenig Wichtigkeit oder Interesse für uns. (*present/past*)
82. Restrictions on night work *were* of little importance or interest to us.	**83.** Die Jungen **werden** immer größer. (*present/past*)
83. The boys *are getting* taller and taller.	**84.** Die Arbeit **wird** immer geringer. (*present/past*)
84. There *is getting to be* less and less work.	**85.** Die Temperatur **wurde** immer heißer. (*present/past*)
85. The temperature *became* hotter and hotter.	**86.** Es **wurde** auch Arbeit, jeden Morgen um 5 Uhr **aufzustehen**. (*present/past*)
86. It also *became* work *to get up* every morning at five o'clock.	**87.** Die Produktionskosten **werden** dasselbe **bleiben.** (*present/future*)
87. The production costs *will remain* the same.	**88.** **fähig** = *capable* **unfähig** = *incapable* Morgen **wirst** du unfähig, es länger zu tun.
88. Tomorrow you *will become* incapable of doing it any longer.	**89.** Ihr **wurdet** größer als wir. (*present/past*)
89. You *became* taller than we.	**90.** Ihr **werdet** manchmal drei Ablösungstermine nacheinander **arbeiten**, von Montag morgen bis Dienstag nacht. (*present/future*)
90. Sometimes you *will work* three shifts in a row from Monday morning until Tuesday night.	**91.** **geschickt** = *skilled, capable* **das Haupt** = *head* Es **wird** immer schwerer, geschickte Hände und Häupter für jede Abteilung zu finden. (*present/future*)
91 It *is becoming* more and more difficult to find skilled hands and heads for every department.	

Be aware of the passive voice (to be discussed in section 64). Note the following sentence from the reading passage, first given in the present passive, then the past passive: the present or simple past tense of ***werden*** *+ the past participle of a transitive verb.*

	92. In der Schmiede **wird** von 12 Uhr bis 12 Uhr **gearbeitet.**
92. In the forge they *work* from 12 to 12 (it *is worked*).	**93.** **Wurde** in der Schmiede von 12 Uhr bis 12 Uhr **gearbeitet**?
93. *Were* the hours in the forge from 12 to 12 (it *was worked*)?	

PROGRESS TEST

A. Choose the correct infinitive of the following verbs:

1. *Genossen* sie immer dieselbe Ruheperiode?
(a) genossen (b) genießen (c) genesen (d) niesen

2. *Litt* der Junge nicht unter der Hitze?
(a) leiten (b) laden (c) leiden (d) lauten

3. Er *tat* es nur bis sechs.
(a) tuten (b) tun (c) tönen (d) töten

B. Choose the correct past tense verb form of:

1. gehen: Ich__________ . . .
(a) gehe (b) ginge (c) ging (d) gähnte

2. stehen: Du__________ . . .
(a) standst (b) stehst (c) stahlst (d) stankst

3. sehen: und __________ zur Erde.
(a) siehst (b) sagst (c) sehnte (d) sahst

C. Choose the correct equivalent of the indicated word.

1. Sie *kam* Freitag hierher.
(a) is coming (b) came (c) comes

2. Er *erwies* mir jede Rücksicht und Schonung.
(a) showed (b) shows (c) is going to show

3. Er *blieb* die ganze Nacht zu Hause.
(a) stayed (b) stays (c) will stay

4. Morgen *fange* ich zu arbeiten *an*.
(a) am going to begin (b) began (c) begun

5. Das Kapital *überging* die Übertreibungen des Systems.
(a) overlooks (b) overlooked (c) will overlook

6. Sie *verwendeten* einige Jungen in der Fabrik.
   (a) employ (b) employed (c) will employ
7. Die Jungen *wurden* immer größer.
   (a) would (b) become (c) will become (d) became
8. Die Produktionskosten *werden* immer wichtiger sein.
   (a) are becoming (b) were (c) will (d) became

Answer key: A. **1.** (b); **2.** (c); **3.** (b).
B. **1.** (c); **2.** (a); **3.** (d).
C. **1.** (b); **2.** (a); **3.** (a); **4.** (a); **5.** (b); **6.** (b); **7.** (d); **8.** (c).

36. *Past tense of modals and* wissen

1. The modals are conjugated as follows in the past tense:

ich durfte (*I was permitted, allowed to*)
du durftest
er, sie, es durfte
wir durften
ihr durftet
sie durften
Sie durften

ich konnte (*I could, I was able to*)
du konntest
er, sie, es konnte
wir konnten
ihr konntet
sie konnten
Sie konnten

mögen
ich mochte (*I liked to*)
du mochtest
er, sie, es mochte
wir mochten
ihr mochtet
sie mochten
Sie mochten

müssen
ich mußte (*I had to*)
du mußtest
er, sie, es mußte
wir mußten
ihr mußtet
sie mußten
Sie mußten

sollen
ich sollte (*I was supposed to*)
du solltest
er, sie, es sollte
wir sollten
ihr solltet
sie sollten
Sie sollten

wollen
ich wollte (*I wanted to*)
du wolltest
er, sie, es wollte
wir wollten
ihr wolltet
sie wollten
Sie wollten

2. Modals in the past add the weak verb endings to the stem. Note also that the umlaut in the verbs **dürfen, können, mögen,** and **müssen** is dropped.

3. The past tense of **wissen** follows the pattern of the modals:

ich wußte (*I knew*)	**wir wußten**	
du wußtest	**ihr wußtet**	**Sie wußten**
er, sie, es wußte	**sie wußten**	

The first fourteen sentences review the meanings of the modal verbs. Give their meanings and circle any unfamiliar words. The vocabulary is from Das Kapital.

	1. Während der sechs Monate, wo er engagiert ist, **muß** er vier Nächte jede Woche arbeiten.
1. During the six months he is employed he *must* work four nights a week.	**2.** **Muß** man manchmal drei zwölfstündige Ablösungstermine nacheinander arbeiten?
2. Do they sometimes *have to* work three twelve-hour shifts in a row?	**3.** **im Alter von** = *at the age of* **Soll** ein Junge im Alter von zehn Jahren zwei Tage und zwei Nächte nacheinander arbeiten?
3. *Is* a ten-year-old boy *supposed to* work two days and two nights in a row?	**4.** Ihr **sollt** nicht von 6 Uhr nachmittags bis den anderen Tag 12 Uhr während einer ganzen Woche arbeiten.
4. You *are* not *to* work from six in the afternoon until twelve noon of the next day for a whole week.	**5.** Ja, dies ist ein heißer Platz! Ich **mag** ihn nicht.
5. Yes, this is a hot place. I *do* not *like* it.	**6.** Wir **mögen** nicht hören, wie *Das Kapital* dieses Vierundzwanzigstundensystem auffaßt.
6. We *do* not *like* to hear how *Capital* regards this twenty-four-hour system.	**7.** Ich **kann** wenigstens nach Hause schlafen gehen.
7. I *can* at least go home to sleep.	**8.** Wir **können** es nicht recht tun ohne die Nachtarbeit von Jungen unter achtzehn Jahren.
8. We *can*not do it right without boys under eighteen working at night.	**9.** Jungen kriegt man so viel man **will.**
9. We can get as many boys as we *want.* (We can get any number of boys.)	**10.** **einige** = *some* **fortwährend** = *always, incessantly* **Wollen** einige Hände nachts fortwährend arbeiten?

10. *Do* some hands *want to* work continually at night?	**11.** **der Wechsel** = *alternation* **Wollen** einige Hände nachts fortwährend arbeiten ohne Wechsel zwischen Tag- und Nachtzeit?
11. *Do* some hands *want to* work continually at night without alternation between day and night work?	**12.** Die Beschränkungen der Nachtarbeit **dürfen** von wenig Wichtigkeit oder Interesse für uns sein.
12. The restrictions on night work *can* be of little importance or interest to us.	**13.** **die Vermehrung** = *increase* **auf alle Fälle** = *in any case* Die Vermehrung der Produktionskosten **darf** auf alle Fälle **nicht** daraus resultieren.
13. In any case there *must be no* increase in production costs as a result of this.	**14.** Hier **dürfen** sie arbeiten.
14. They can (are allowed to) work here.	

Now distinguish between the present and past of the modals in the following sentences.

	15. Was **soll** ein nomineller Arbeitstag sein?
15. What *is* a nominal working day *supposed to* be?	**16.** Er **sollte** arbeiten, aber er schlief lieber.
16. He *was supposed to* work, but he preferred to sleep.	**17.** Ich weiß nicht, wann ihr anfangen **sollt**.
17. I do not know when you *are supposed to* begin.	**18.** Ihr **solltet** in einem Hochofen arbeiten, ihr tatet es aber nicht.
18. You *were to* work at a blast furnace, however, you did not do it.	**19.** **ein Dritter** = *a third* Ein Dritter, jetzt zehn Jahre, **kann** von morgens 6 Uhr bis 12 Uhr in die Nacht drei Nächte durch arbeiten.
19. A third one, now ten years old, *is able to* work from six in the morning until twelve at night for three nights in a row.	**20.** Wie er arbeiten **konnte**, ohne zu schlafen, verstand er selbst nicht.
20. He himself did not understand how he *was able to* work without sleeping.	**21.** Ihr **konntet** wenigstens nach Hause gehen, weil es nah war.
21. You *could* at least go home because it was near.	**22.** Er sagt, daß sie von 6 Uhr morgens bis 12 Uhr nachts während 14 Tage arbeiten **können**.

22. He says that they *can* work from six a.m. to midnight for fourteen days.	**23.** **da** = *since* Wir **mußten** viele Jungens kriegen, da wir die Produktionskosten nicht vermehren **wollten.**
23. We *had to* get lots of boys since we *did* not *want* to increase the costs of production.	**24.** **ungefähr** = *approximately* Ungefähr zwanzig Knaben unter achtzehn Jahren **müssen** mit der Nachtmannschaft arbeiten.
24. Approximately twenty boys under eighteen years of age *have to* work with the night crew.	**25.** Er fragt, ob wir geschickte Hände und Häupter von Departments haben **müssen.**
25. He asks if we *have to* have skilled hands and heads of departments.	**26.** **der Einwurf** = *objection* Wir **mußten** unseren Einwurf äußern.
26. We *had to* express our objection.	**27.** Er **mochte** nicht jeden Tag siebzehn Stunden arbeiten.
27. He *did* not *like* working seventeen hours every day.	**28.** Er **mag** nicht jeden Tag siebzehn Stunden arbeiten.
28. He *does* not *like* working seventeen hours every day.	**29.** **dagegen** = *on the other hand, against that* Sie **mochten** nicht fortwährend arbeiten, aber was **konnten** sie dagegen tun?
29. They *did* not *like* working continuously but what *could* they do about it? (Lit.: against that)	**30.** Wissen Sie, ob er das überhaupt **mag**?
30. Do you know whether he even *likes* that?	**31.** **der Vierte** = *the fourth* Ein Vierter **wollte** nicht drei Ablösungstermine nacheinander arbeiten.
31. A fourth *did* not *want* to work three shifts in a row.	**32.** **der Fünfte** = *the fifth* **der Chef** = *boss* Weiß der Chef, daß der Fünfte das auch nicht **will**?
32. Does the boss know that the fifth one *does* not *want* (to do) that either?	**33.** Wir **wollen** unseren Einwurf jetzt äußern.
33. We *want to* express our objection now.	**34.** **in Anbetracht** = *considering* In Anbetracht der geringen Proportion von Jungen, die sie verwenden **wollten** . . .
34. Considering the small proportion of boys which they *wanted* to employ . . . (Note that **in Anbetracht** requires a genitive object.)	**35.** Die Übertreibungen dieses Systems **darf** man **nicht** mit Stillschweigen übergehen.

35. One *must not* overlook the excesses of this system in silence.	**36.** In Anbetracht der Vermehrung der Produktionskosten **dürfen** wir **nicht** eine geringere Proportion von Jungen verwenden.
36. Considering the increase in costs of production, we *must not* employ a smaller proportion of boys.	**37.** **die Ablösung** = *removal, relief, relief guard* **die Weise** = *manner, method, way* **ablösungsweise** = __________
37. *in the manner of relief, in successive relief, in relays*	**38.** In den Walzwerken **durften** die Hände Tag und Nacht ablösungsweise arbeiten.
38. In the rolling mills the hands *were permitted* to work day and night in relays.	**39.** **dahingegen** = *on the contrary, on the other hand* Dahingegen **durfte** alles andere Werk Tagwerk sein.
39. On the other hand, all other work *could* be day work.	

PROGRESS TEST

A. Choose the most nearly correct equivalent of the indicated words.

1. Ich *konnte* seine Idee nicht leicht verstehen.
(a) can (b) could (c) had been able to (d) will be able to

2. Er *muß* das Buch bald zu Ende schreiben.
(a) has to (b) had to (c) would have to (d) should

3. Sie *will* unser Problem überhaupt nicht verstehen.
(a) will (b) wanted (c) did . . . want (d) does . . . want

4. Er *mochte* nicht jeden Tag arbeiten.
(a) does . . . like (b) does . . . wish (c) did . . . like (d) was . . . permitted

5. Er *sollte* heute nicht zu arbeiten brauchen.
(a) was . . . supposed to (b) is . . . supposed to (c) shall (d) ought to

6. Ihr *dürft* heute in die Stadt gehen.
(a) will be able to (b) can (c) were permitted to (d) must

B. Choose the most nearly correct equivalent of the following sentences or italicized words.

1. *Er schlief auf der Flur* mit einem Schurzfell unter ihm und einer kleinen Jacke über ihm.
(a) He slipped and fell on the floor.
(b) He slipped out to the field.
(c) He slept in the field.
(d) Sleeping in the field . . .

2. In Anbetracht der geringen Proportion von Jungen, die sie verwenden wollen . . .
(a) Considering the large proportion of girls she wishes to fail . . .
(b) Considering the small proportion of boys they want to employ . . .
(c) One wants to employ as few boys as possible . . .
(d) They want to use as many boys as possible considering the circumstances . . .

3. In den Walzwerken wollten die Hände Tag und Nacht ohne Ablösung arbeiten.
(a) Most hands like to work day and night.
(b) In the rolling mills the hands wished to work day and night without relief.
(c) Not all hands who work day and night wish to work in the rolling mills.
(d) They were not permitted to work in relays.

4. *Ungefähr* zwanzig Knaben unter 18 Jahren müssen arbeiten.
(a) dangerous
(b) not dangerous
(c) approximately
(d) exactly

5. Die Übertreibungen dieses Systems übergeht man mit Stillschweigen.
(a) These systems let everything pass by quietly.
(b) If one overlooks the extreme forms of this system, all is lost.
(c) One helplessly permits these extreme forms to exist.
(d) They pass over the extreme forms of this system in silence.

Answer key: A. **1.** (b); **2.** (a); **3.** (d); **4.** (c); **5.** (a); **6.** (b).
B. **1.** (c); **2.** (b); **3.** (b); **4.** (c); **5.** (d).

Karl Marx: Das Kapital

„In einem Walzwerke, wo der nominelle Arbeitstag für den einzelnen Arbeiter 11½ Stunden war, arbeitete ein Junge 4 Nächte jede Woche bis mindestens 8½ Uhr abends des nächsten Tags und dies während der 6 Monate, wo er engagiert war.“ „Ein andrer arbeitete im Alter von 9 Jahren manchmal drei zwölfstündige Ablösungstermine nacheinander und im Alter von 10 Jahren zwei Tage und zwei Nächte nacheinander.“ „Ein Dritter, jetzt 10 Jahre, arbeitete von morgens 6 Uhr bis 12 Uhr in die Nacht drei Nächte durch und bis 9 Uhr abends während der andren Nächte.“ „Ein Vierter, jetzt 13 Jahre, arbeitete von 6 Uhr nachmittags bis den andren Tag 12 Uhr mittags während einer ganzen Woche, und manchmal drei Ablösungstermine nacheinander, von Montag Morgen bis Dienstag Nacht.“ „Ein Fünfter, jetzt 12 Jahre, arbeitete in einer Eisengießerei zu Stavely[1] von 6 Uhr morgens bis 12 Uhr nachts während 14 Tage, ist unfähig es länger zu tun.“ „George Allinsworth, neunjährig: „Ich kam hierhin letzten Freitag. Nächsten Tag hatten wir um 3 Uhr morgens anzufangen. Ich blieb daher die ganze Nacht hier. Wohne 5 Meilen von hier. Schlief auf der Flur mit einem Schurzfell unter mir und einer kleinen Jacke über mir. Die zwei andren Tage war ich hier um 6 Uhr morgens. Ja! dies ist ein heißer Platz! Bevor ich herkam, arbeitete ich ebenfalls während eines ganzen Jahres in einem Hochofen. Es war ein sehr großes Werk, auf dem Lande. Begann auch samstags morgens um 3 Uhr, aber ich konnte wenigstens nach Hause schlafen

---

1 *Name of a town in England*

gehen, weil es nah war. Am andren Tage fing ich 6 Uhr morgens an und endete 6 oder 7 Uhr abends u.s.w."

Laßst uns nun hören, wie das Kapital selbst dies Vierundzwanzig-Stundensystem auffaßt. Die Übertreibungen des Systems, seinen Mißbrauch zur „grausamen und unglaublichen" Verlängerung des Arbeitstags, übergeht es natürlich mit Stillschweigen. Es spricht nur von dem System in seiner „normalen" Form.

„Die Herren Naylor und Vickers, Stahlfabrikanten, die zwischen 600 und 700 Personen anwenden, und darunter nur 10% unter 18 Jahren, und hiervon wieder nur 20 Knaben zum Nachtpersonal, äußern sich wie folgt: „Die Knaben leiden durchaus nicht von der Hitze. Die Temperatur ist wahrscheinlich 86° bis 90° . . . In den Hammer- und Walzwerken arbeiten die Hände Tag und Nacht ablösungsweise, aber dahingegen ist auch alles andre Werk Tagwerk, von 6 Uhr morgens bis 6 Uhr abends. In der Schmiede wird von 12 Uhr bis 12 Uhr gearbeitet. Einige Hände arbeiten fortwährend des Nachts ohne Wechsel zwischen Tag- und Nachtzeit . . . Wir finden nicht, daß Tag- oder Nachtarbeit irgendeinen Unterschied in der Gesundheit [der Herren Naylor and Vickers?] macht, und wahrscheinlich schlafen Leute besser, wenn sie dieselbe Ruheperiode genießen, als wenn sie wechselt . . . Ungefähr zwanzig Knaben unter 18 Jahren arbeiten mit der Nachtmannschaft . . . Wir könnten's nicht recht tun ohne die Nachtarbeit von Jungen unter 18 Jahren. Unser Einwurf ist—die Vermehrung der Produktionskosten . . . Geschickte Hände und Häupter von Departements sind schwer zu haben, aber Jungens kriegt man so viel man will . . . Natürlich, in Anbetracht der geringen Proportion von Jungen, die wir verwenden, wären[2] Beschränkungen der Nachtarbeit von wenig Wichtigkeit oder Interesse für uns."

---

2 wären = *would be* (subjunctive form of the verb **sein**. See §71.)

Chapter Ten

37. *Coordinating conjunctions*

1. The following words are used as coordinating conjunctions:

aber	*but, however*
denn	*for, because*
oder	*or*
sondern	*but, but rather, but on the contrary* (*or omitted in translation*)
und	*and*

Stefan ging nicht, *sondern* er blieb hier.	*Stefan did not go,* ***but rather*** *he remained here.*
Er wollte es tun, *aber* er konnte es nicht.	*He wanted to do it,* ***but*** *he could not.*

2. The verb in the clauses which these conjunctions link or introduce will be found either immediately after the subject (normal word order) or immediately before the subject (inverted word order):

Normal:

Das Flugzeug *fliegt* nach Deutschland, und wir *bleiben* zurück.	*The plane* ***is flying*** *to Germany, and we* ***are staying*** *behind.*

Inverted:

Kommt **Angelika zu uns, oder *bleibt* sie bei Sabine?**	***Is*** *Angelika* ***coming*** *to your place, or* ***is*** *she* ***staying*** *at Sabine's?*

3. Do not confuse **denn** (*for*), which takes normal word order, with **dann** (*then*), which takes inverted word order:

Sie begannen zu essen, denn sie waren hungrig.	*They began to eat, for they were hungry.*
Florian schrieb den Brief, dann ging er zu Bett.	*Florian wrote the letter, then he went to bed.*

In questions, **denn** may be used in the middle of the clause as an intensifier. Used thus it has a general meaning of *really* or *actually;* often it is untranslatable but shows interest, impatience, or exasperation:

Will er denn das sagen?	*Does he really want to say that?*
Wer ist denn da?	*Who is there?*

Denn is also used in questions for a friendly tone, and is not translated when so used.

Wie heißen Sie denn?	*What's your name?*

4. Several combinations of words function as conjunctions:

sowohl . . . als auch	*both . . . and* or *both. . . as well as*
entweder . . . oder	*either . . . or*
weder . . . noch	*neither . . . nor*
nicht nur . . . sondern auch	*not only . . . but also*

***Sowohl* die Jungen *als auch* die Alten glauben an ihn.**	***Both** young **and** old believe in him.* (Or: ***Both** the young **as well as** the old believe in him.*)
***Entweder* du *oder* Max muß das tun.**	***Either** you **or** Max must do it.*
***Weder* sie *noch* ihre Kinder konnten Deutsch.**	***Neither** they **nor** their children knew German.* (Or: ***Neither** she **nor** her children knew German.*)
Du siehst *nicht nur* den Mond, *sondern auch* die Sterne.	*You see **not only** the moon **but also** the stars.*

Give the correct meanings of the following coordinating conjunctions.

	1. der Fabrikant = *the manufacturer, industrialist* Friedrich Engels ist am 28. November 1820 als Sohn eines Fabrikanten in Barmen (Deutschland) geboren.
1. Friedrich Engels was born in Barmen (Germany) on November 28, 1820, as the son of an industrialist.	**2. das Zweiggeschäft** = *branch store* In Manchester arbeitete Engels als junger Mann für ein Zweiggeschäft seines Vaters.
2. As a young man he worked for a branch of his father's business in Manchester.	**3. kennen** = *to be acquainted with, to know* **lernen** = *to learn* **kennenlernen** = __________
3. *to become familiar with, to get to know*	**4. der Arbeiter** = *worker* **die Frage** = *question* **die Arbeiterfrage** = *question of the working classes, labor question* In England lernt Engels die Arbeiterfrage kennen.

4. In England Engels becomes familiar with the question of the working classes.	**5.** **das Verhältnis** = *condition* In England lernte er die Arbeiterfrage und die sozialen Verhältnisse Englands kennen.
5. In England he became familiar with the problems of the working classes and the social conditions in England.	**6.** **worüber** = *about which* Hier lernte er die Arbeiterfrage und sozialen Verhältnisse in England kennen, worüber er später schrieb.
6. Here he became familiar with the problems of labor and the social conditions in England, about which he later wrote.	**7.** **begegnen** = *to meet* 1842 begegnete er Karl Marx zum erstenmal.
7. In 1842 he met Karl Marx for the first time.	**8.** **die Lage** = *condition, situation* Sein Buch *Die Lage der arbeitenden Klasse in England* erschien zum erstenmal im Jahre 1845.
8. His book *The Condition of the Working Class in England* appeared in 1845 for the first time.	**9.** Lesen wir jetzt, was Engels über die Arbeiterfamilien schrieb.
9. Let us read now what Engels wrote about the workers' families.	**10.** **wohnen** = *to live, to dwell* **die Wohnverhältnisse** = *living conditions* Wir lesen jetzt, in was für Wohnverhältnissen sie damals lebten.
10. We (will) now read what kind of conditions they lived in at the time.	**11.** **folgendes** = *the following* Die Journale erzählen folgendes.
11. The newspapers tell us the following.	**12.** **die Wohnung** = *flat, apartment* Eine Frau lebte in einer Wohnung.
12. A woman lived in an apartment.	**13.** **sterben** = *to die* **die Verstorbene** = *the deceased* (*female*) Dann erzählten die Journale folgendes von der Wohnung der Verstorbenen.
13. Then the newspapers told the following about the flat of the deceased (woman). Note: **der Verstorbene** = *the deceased* (*male*)	**14.** **der Körper** = *body* Ein nackter Körper lag in dem Zimmer.
14. A naked body lay in the room.	**15.** **streuen** = *to strew, to spread* Die Federn waren über den **fast** nackten Körper gestreut. (*fast*/*almost*)
15. The feathers were strewn over the *almost* naked body.	**16.** **die Decke** = *cover* Die Federn waren ihre einzige Decke.

16. The feathers were her only cover.	**17.** **vorhanden** = *at hand* **mager** = *thin, skinny* Die Federn waren über ihren fast nackten Körper gestreut, **denn** es war keine Decke vorhanden. (*for/then*)
17. The feathers were strewn over her almost naked body, *for* there was no cover at hand.	**18.** **zerbeißen** = *to chew up* **das Ungeziefer** = *vermin* Ungeziefer zerbissen den Körper.
18. Vermin were chewing up the body.	**19.** **abgemagert** = *emaciated* **Dann** fand er sie ganz abgemagert und von Ungeziefer zerbissen. (*then/for*)
19. *Then* he found her very emaciated and chewed up by vermin.	**20.** **der Fuß** = *foot* **der Boden** = *ground, floor* **der Fußboden** = __________
20. *the floor*	**21.** **das Loch** = *hole* Ein Loch ist im Fußboden.
21. There is a hole in the floor.	**22.** **aufreißen** = *to tear open* Man reißt ein Loch im Fußboden auf.
22. A hole is torn open in the floor.	**23.** **benutzen** = *to use, to utilize* Man benutzt das Loch im Fußboden . . .
23. The hole in the floor is used . . .	**24.** **der Abtritt** = *privy, toilet* Man reißt einen Teil des Fußbodens auf **und** benutzt das Loch als Abtritt.
24. Part of the floor is torn up *and* the hole is used as a toilet.	**25.** **war aufgerissen** = *was torn up* **wurde benutzt** = *was used* Ein Teil des Fußbodens war aufgerissen. **und** das Loch wurde als Abtritt benutzt.
25. A part of the floor was torn up, *and* the hole was used as a toilet.	**26.** **hatte . . . gewohnt** = *had lived* Sie hatte mit ihrem Mann und ihrem 19-jährigen Sohne in einem kleinen Zimmer gewohnt.
26. She had lived in a small room with her husband and her 19-year-old son.	**27.** **sich befinden** = *to be* Was befindet sich in dem Zimmer?
27. What is in the room?	**28.** **die Bettstelle** = *bedstead* Befand sich eine Bettstelle **darin**?
28. Was there a bedstead *in it?*	**29.** **das Möbel** = (*piece of*) *furniture* **Weder** Bettstelle **noch** Möbel waren in dem Zimmer. (*either . . . or/neither . . . nor*)

29. There was *neither* a bedstead *nor* furniture in the room.	**30.** **sonstig** = *other* Es befanden sich darin **weder** Bettstelle **noch** sonstige Möbel.
30. There was *neither* a bedstead *nor* other furniture in it.	**31.** **der Haufen** = *pile, heap* Der Zeitung nach lag sie tot neben ihrem Sohn auf einem Haufen Federn.
31. According to the newspaper, she lay dead next to her son on a pile of feathers.	**32.** **das Bettzeug** = *bedding* **das Bett(t)uch** = *sheet* Es war **weder** Decke **noch** Bettzeug **noch** Bettuch vorhanden. (*neither . . . nor/either . . . or*)
32. There was *neither* a blanket, *nor* bedding, *nor* a sheet at hand.	**33.** **Dann** erzählte Engels eine andere Geschichte. (*then/for*)
33. *Then* Engels told another story.	**34.** **das Polizeigericht** = *police court* Zwei Knaben **werden** vor das Polizeigericht **gebracht**. (*are brought/were brought*)
34. Two boys *are brought* before the police court.	**35.** **verzehren** = *to consume* Zwei Knaben wurden vor das Polizeigericht gebracht, **denn** sie hatten einen halbgekochten Kuhfuß gestohlen und verzehrt. (*then/for*)
35. Two boys were brought before the police court, *for* stealing and consuming a half-cooked cow's foot. (Lit.: they had stolen and consumed)	**36.** **der Polizeirichter** = *police magistrate* Was tat der Polizeirichter?
36. What did the police magistrate do?	**37.** **nachforschen** = *to inquire, to investigate* Der Polizeirichter mußte alles nachforschen.
37. The police magistrate had to investigate everything.	**38.** **sich veranlaßt sehen** = *to feel obliged* Der Polizeirichter sah sich veranlaßt, weiter nachzuforschen.
38. The police magistrate felt obliged to make further inquiry.	**39.** Wer, was und wo war **denn** die Mutter dieser Knaben? (*than/for/intensifier*)
39. intensifier Who, what, and where was the mother of these boys anyway?	**40.** **die Witwe** = *widow* Sie war die Witwe eines alten Soldaten.

40. She was the widow of an old soldier.	**41.** **ergehen** = *to go, to fare* **war ergangen** = *had fared* Wie war es ihr **denn** überhaupt ergangen seit dem Tode ihres Mannes? (*for/then/intensifier*)
41. intensifier How had she really fared since the death of her husband?	**42.** **reich** = *rich* **die Reichen** = *the rich* **arm** = *poor* **die Armen** = ________
42. *the poor*	**43.** **das Schicksal** = *fate* Das Schicksal **trifft** die Reichen und die Armen. (*strikes/meets*)
43. Fate *strikes* rich and poor (alike).	**44.** **gleich** = *same* **getroffen werden** = *to be struck, meet* **Sowohl** die Reichen **als auch** die Armen können von gleichem Schicksal getroffen werden. (*not only . . . but/both . . . and*)
44. *Both* the rich *and* the poor can meet the same fate.	**45.** **Nicht nur** die Armen, **sondern auch** die Reichen werden von dem gleichen Schicksal getroffen, nämlich dem Tod. (*both . . . and/not only . . . but also*)
45. *Not only* the poor *but also* the rich are met by the same fate, that is, death. (Notice the present passive verb form: **werden getroffen**.)	

PROGRESS TEST

When you correct this test, circle the phrases you miss and review them before continuing.

1. Die Familie wohnte in einem kleinen Zimmer, *aber* sie hatte kein Geld.
(a) and (b) because (c) but (d) but rather

2. **hat verkaufen müssen** = *had to sell, did have to sell*
Hat sie *denn* alles verkaufen müssen, um nur Brot zu bekommen?
(a) for (b) or (c) but rather (d) used as an intensifier

3. **das Elend** = *misery*
Wohnen alle Londoner Arbeiter in einem solchen Elend *oder* nur wenige?
(a) and (b) or (c) but (d) for

4. **der Lumpen** = *rag*
   die Ecke = *corner*
   Sie schliefen nicht auf einem Bett wie wir, *sondern* auf einigen Lumpen, die in einer Ecke lagen.
   (a) but rather (b) or (c) for (d) however

5. *Entweder* lag sie tot neben ihrem Sohn auf einem Haufen Federn, *oder* wir haben es nur geträumt.
   (a) both . . . and (b) either . . . or (c) neither . . . nor (d) not only. . . but also

6. *Sowohl* die Witwe *als auch* ihre kranke Tochter wohnten in dem kleinen Zimmer.
   (a) either . . . or (b) not only . . . but also (c) both . . . and (d) neither . . . nor

7. Es befanden sich darin *weder* Bettstelle *noch* sonstige Möbel.
   (a) both . . . and (b) either . . . or (c) neither . . . nor (d) not only . . . but also

8. *Nicht nur* die Armen, *sondern auch* die Reichen werden von dem gleichen Schicksal getroffen, nämlich vom Tod.
   (a) both . . . and (b) either . . . or (c) neither . . . nor (d) not only . . . but also

Answer key: **1.** (c); **2.** (d); **3.** (b); **4.** (a); **5.** (b); **6.** (c); **7.** (c); **8.** (d).

38. *Subordinating conjunctions*

1. The following words are subordinating conjunctions which have already been used or will be introduced in this chapter:

als	*when*
bevor	*before*
bis	*until*
da	*since, because*
damit	*so that*
daß	*that*
nachdem	*after*
ob	*whether, if*
obgleich, obschon, obwohl	*although*
seit(dem)	*since (the time of)*
weil	*because*
wenn	*if, when, whenever*

2. Subordinating conjunctions introduce dependent clauses, in which the verb is the last element (dependent word order):

Kurt sprach Russisch, *damit* ich ihn nicht verstehen konnte.	*Kurt spoke Russian,* ***so that*** *I could not understand him.*
***Da* Norbert kein Geld hat, kann er nicht ins Kino gehen.**	***Since*** *Norbert has no money, he can't go to the movies.*

3. Wenn is translated *whenever* when referring to customary or habitual action in the past or the present:

***Wenn* Dieter kommt, gehen wir immer spazieren.**	***Whenever*** *Dieter comes, we always go for a walk.*
***Wenn* Lina ging, war es immer dunkel.**	***Whenever*** *Lina went, it was always dark.*

Do not confuse the conjunction **wenn** (*if, whenever*) with the interrogative **wann** (*when*):

***Wann* kommt Judith zu uns?**	***When*** *is Judith coming to visit us?*
Ich weiß, *wann* er zu uns kommt.	*I know* ***when*** *he is coming to visit us.*
Otto weiß es, *wenn* sein Sohn die Wahrheit sagt.	***Whenever*** *his son tells the truth, Otto knows it.*

4. Remember that as a subordinating conjunction **da** means *since, because,* and that as an adverb it means *there* or *then*. It means *there* or *then* in a clause with normal (or inverted) word order.

***Da* die Professorin es tut, dürfen wir es auch.**	***Since*** *the professor* (f.) *does it, we can too.*
***Da* sitzt der arme Mensch.**	***There*** *sits the poor man.*

5. When **ob** is used without an antecedent it is translated *I* (*we*) *wonder whether* or *if:*

***Ob* er heute singt?**	*I* ***wonder if*** (***whether***) *he will sing today?*

6. Do not confuse the subordinating conjunction **als** with the **als** used in comparisons or **als** meaning *as:*

Er ist *größer als* ich.	*He is* ***taller than*** *I.*
Sigrid will *als* Prinzessin zum Ball hin.	*Sigrid wants to go to the ball* ***as*** *a princess.*
Du kamst, *als* ich fort ging.	*You came* ***when*** *I was leaving.*

Give the correct meaning of the following subordinating conjunctions.

	1. **fortsetzen** = *to continue* Wir wollen das Gespräch über Engels Werk fortsetzen.
1. Let us (we want to) continue the discussion of Engels's work.	**2.** Zwei Knaben haben einen halbgekochten Kuhfuß aus dem Laden gestohlen und verzehrt.
2. Two boys stole a half-cooked cow's foot from the store and consumed it.	**3.** **sogleich** = *immediately* Die zwei Knaben wurden vor das Polizeigericht gebracht, **weil** sie aus Hunger einen halbgekochten Kuhfuß von einem Laden gestohlen und sogleich verzehrt hatten.
3. The two boys were brought before the police court, *because* out of hunger they had stolen a half-cooked cow's foot from a shop and immediately consumed it.	**4.** **der Polizeidiener** = *policeman* Der Polizeidiener kam zu der Frau.
4. The policeman came to the woman's house (or: to visit the woman).	**5.** **erhalten** = *to receive* Was **erhielt** der Polizeirichter von den Polizeidienern? (*present/past*)
5. What *did* the police magistrate *receive* from the policemen?	**6.** **klar** = *clear* **klären** = *to clarify* **die Aufklärung** = *clarification, explanation* Der Polizeirichter **erhielt** folgende Aufklärung.
6. The police magistrate *received* the following clarification.	**7.** **hatten . . . besucht** = *had visited* Der Polizeirichter erhielt von den Polizeidienern folgende Aufklärung, **nachdem** sie die Mutter der zwei Knaben besucht hatten.
7. The police magistrate received the following clarification from the policemen *after* they had visited the mother of the two boys.	**8.** **das Hinterstübchen** = *small back room* Der Polizeidiener fand die Frau mit sechs **ihrer** Kinder in einem kleinen Hinterstübchen. (*of her/of their*)
8. The policeman found the woman with six *of her* children in a small back room.	**9.** **das Elend** = *misery* Die Witwe wohnte zusammen mit ihren neun Kindern im größten Elend, **bis** sie es nicht mehr konnte.

9. The widow lived with all of her nine children in greatest misery *until* she was no longer able to.	**10.** **zusammengedrängt** = *crowded together* **Als** der Polizeidiener zu ihr kam, fand er sie mit sechs ihrer Kinder in einem kleinen Hinterstübchen zusammengedrängt, wo sie im Elend lebten.
10. *When* the policeman came to visit her, he found her with six of her children crowded together in a little back room, where they lived in misery.	**11.** **gleich** = *directly* In einer Ecke lagen einige Lumpen, **damit** sie nicht gleich auf dem Boden schlafen mußten.
11. In a corner lay some rags *so that* they did not have to sleep on the bare floor. (Lit.: to sleep directly on the floor.)	**12.** **die Schürze** = *apron* In der Ecke lagen **so viel** alte Lumpen, **als** eine Frau in ihre Schürze nehmen konnte.
12. In the corner there were *as many* old rags *as* a woman could carry in her apron (lit.: could take into her apron).	**13.** **Da** aber die Lumpen der ganzen Familie zum Bette dienten, brauchte keiner gleich auf dem Boden zu schlafen.
13. *Since* the rags served the whole family as a bed, no one needed to sleep on the floor.	**14.** **schlecht** = *bad, poor* **Nachdem** der alte Soldat und spätere Polizeidiener starb, ist es seiner Frau und seinen neun Kindern sehr schlecht ergangen.
14. *After* the old soldier who later became a policeman died, his wife and nine children fared very poorly.	**15.** **Seitdem** sie eine Witwe war, war es ihr sehr schlecht ergangen.
15. *Since* she had been a widow, she had fared very poorly.	**16.** **der Herd** = *stove, hearth* Auf dem **Herde** war ein Feuer.
16. In the *hearth* there was a fire.	**17.** **der Funke(n)** = *spark* Auf dem Herde war **kaum** ein Funken Feuer. (*scarcely/always*)
17. There was *scarcely* a spark of fire in the hearth.	**18.** Immer **wenn** er kam, war auf dem Herde kaum ein Funken Feuer.
18. *Whenever* he came, there was scarcely a spark of fire in the hearth.	**19.** **das Kleid** = *dress* **die Kleidung** = ________
19. *clothing*	**20.** **arm** = *poor* **ärmlich** = *shabby* Zur Decke hatten sie **nichts als** ihre ärmliche Kleidung.
20. For a cover they had *nothing but* their shabby clothing.	**21.** **die Nahrung** = *food, nourishment* Die Witwe und ihre neun Kinder hatten keine Nahrung.

21. The widow and her nine children had no food.	**22.** **erhalten** = *to receive, to get* Um Nahrung zu erhalten, **hatte** sie alles **verkauft.** (*has sold/had sold*)
22. In order to get food she *had sold* everything.	**23.** **hat verkaufen müssen** = *had to sell* **überhaupt** = *absolutely* Sie hat überhaupt alles verkaufen müssen, **damit** ihre Familie etwas zu essen bekam.
23. She had to sell absolutely everything *so that* her family got something to eat.	**24.** **voriges** = *previous* Die arme Frau erzählte ihm, **daß** sie voriges Jahr ihr Bett habe verkaufen müssen, um Nahrung zu erhalten.
24. The poor woman told him *that* she had had to sell her bed the previous year in order to get food. (**Habe** is subjunctive here. Its position with the double infinitive will be explained in chapter 14.)	**25.** **dalassen** = *to leave* (*behind*) **hat dagelassen** = __________
25. *has left, left*	**26.** **das Unterpfand** = *pledge* **Wenn** sie dem Viktualienhändler ihre Bettücher als Unterpfand für einige Lebensmittel daläßt, wird sie nur Lumpen haben, die zum Bette dienen.
26. *If* she leaves her sheets with the food merchant as a pledge for some food, she will only have rags, to serve as a bed.	**27.** Die Witwe hat dem Viktualienhändler ihre Bettücher als Unterpfand dagelassen.
27. The widow left her sheets with the food merchant as a pledge.	**28.** Um Nahrung zu erhalten, hatte sie alles verkauft, **bis** sie nichts mehr hatte.
28. In order to get food she had sold everything *until* she had nothing left.	**29.** **Da** sie ihre Bettücher dem Viktualienhändler als Unterpfand für einige Lebensmittel dagelassen hat, hat sie nur Lumpen, die zum Bette dienen.
29. *Since* she left her sheets with the food merchant as a pledge for some food, she has only rags to serve as a bed. (Lit.: which serve)	**30.** **der Vorschuß** = *advance* (*cash*) Der Polizeirichter gab der Frau einen großen Vorschuß.
30. The police magistrate gave the woman a large cash advance.	**31.** **beträchtlich** = *considerable* Der Polizeirichter gibt der Frau einen beträchtlichen Vorschuß.

31. The police magistrate gives the woman a considerable cash advance.	**32.** **die Armenbüchse** = *poor box, relief fund* Der Polizeirichter gibt der Frau einen beträchtlichen Vorschuß aus der Armenbüchse.
32. The police magistrate gives the woman a considerable cash advance from the poor box.	**33.** **Als** der Polizeirichter der Frau einen beträchtlichen Vorschuß aus der Armenbüchse gab . . .
33. *When* the police magistrate gave the woman a considerable advance from the poor box . . .	

PROGRESS TEST

What are the meanings of the indicated words? Review the ones you miss before going on.

1. *Als* der Polizeirichter der Frau einen beträchtlichen Vorschuß aus der Armenbüchse gab . . .
(a) although (b) after (c) because (d) when

2. Sie hatten nichts, *bis* der Polizeirichter ihnen ein Pfund aus der Armenbüchse zukommen ließ.
(a) until (b) whether (c) if (d) because

3. *Da* sie dem Viktualienhändler ihre Bettücher als Unterpfand für einige Lebensmittel dagelassen hat . . .
(a) so that (b) since (c) although (d) after

4. Sie hatte allmählich alles verkauft oder versetzt, *damit* sie noch essen konnte.
(a) when (b) so that (c) if (d) because

5. *Nachdem* Herr Carter eine Totenschau über die Leiche der 45 jährigen Ann Galway abhielt . . .
(a) if (b) because (c) after (d) although

6. Wissen Sie, *ob* Engels die Londoner Arbeiter viel braver, viel ehrenwerter als sämtliche Reichen von London findet?
(a) until (b) although (c) because (d) whether

7. *Obwohl* die obigen drei Familien in solchem Elend leben . . .
(a) because (b) since (c) although (d) that

8. *Seitdem* die Witwe kein Geld mehr hat, muß sie in einem kleinen Hinterzimmer wohnen, worin kein einziges Stück Möbel ist.
(a) since (b) before (c) whether (d) whenever

9. Zwei Knaben wurden vor das Polizeigericht gebracht, *weil* sie aus Hunger einen halbgekochten Kuhfuß von einem Laden gestohlen und sogleich verzehrt hatten.
(a) while (b) because (c) although (d) if

10. Was sollen wir tun, *wenn* jeder Proletarier von gleichem Schicksal getroffen werden kann?
(a) if (b) although (c) so that (d) until

Answer key: **1.** (d); **2.** (a); **3.** (b); **4.** (b); **5.** (c); **6.** (d); **7.** (c); **8.** (a); **9.** (b); **10.** (a).

READING PREPARATION

These exercises finish introducing the vocabulary and structures necessary to read the passage from Engels. Be sure to review new vocabulary several times before going on.

	1. tot = *dead* **die Toten** = *the dead* **schauen** = *to look* **die Schau** = *show, review, parade, exhibition* **die Totenschau** = __________
1. *inquest*	**2. abhalten** = *to hold* Der Coroner hält eine Totenschau über die abgemagerte **Leiche** der 45-jährigen Ann Galway ab.
2. The coroner is holding an inquest on the emaciated *corpse* of the 45-year-old Ann Galway.	**3. Nachdem** Herr Carter, Coroner für Surrey, eine Totenschau über die abgemagerte Leiche der 45-jährigen Ann Galway abhielt . . .
3. *After* Mr. Carter, coroner for Surrey, held an inquest on the emaciated corpse of the 45-year-old Ann Galway . . .	**4.** Was für eine Aufklärung erhält der Polizeirichter von den Polizeidienern?
4. What sort of clarification does the police magistrate get from the policemen?	**5. rein** = *clean, pure* **reinigen** = *to cleanse, to purify, to clean* Man reinigt den Fußboden.
5. They clean the floor.	**6.** Man reinigte die Leiche.
6. They cleansed the corpse.	**7. unter** = *under* **suchen** = *to seek* **untersuchen** = __________
7. *to examine, to investigate*	**8. der Arzt** = *doctor* Der Arzt konnte die Leiche nicht untersuchen.
8. The doctor could not examine the corpse.	**9. der Buchstabe** = *letter (of the alphabet)* **buchstäblich** = *literally* **Bevor** der Arzt die Leiche untersuchen konnte, mußte man buchstäblich die Federn von ihr reinigen.
9. *Before* the doctor could examine the corpse, it literally had to be cleansed of the feathers.	**10.** Der Arzt konnte die abgemagerte Leiche nicht untersuchen, **bevor** sie gereinigt war.

10. The doctor could not examine the emaciated corpse *before* it was cleaned up.	**11.** **fest** = *tight* **kleben** = *to stick* **Weil** die Federn so fest an ihr klebten, konnte der Arzt die Leiche nicht sogleich untersuchen.
11. *Because* the feathers were stuck so tightly to it, the doctor could not immediately examine the corpse.	**12.** Wissen Sie, **ob** Engels behauptet, alle Londoner Arbeiter lebten büchstäblich in einem solchen Elend?
12. Do you know *if* Engels claims that all London's working class literally lived in such misery?	**13.** **die Ehre** = *honor* **der Wert** = *worth* **ehrenwert** = __________
13. *honorable*	**14.** Ist er ein ehrenwerter Mensch?
14. Is he an honorable person?	**15.** **sämtlich** = *all, entire* **brav** = *good* Wissen Sie, **ob** er die Londoner Arbeiter viel braver, viel ehrenwerter als sämtliche Reichen von London findet?
15. Do you know *whether* he finds London's workers much better, much more honorable than all the rich people of London?	**16.** **die obigen** = *the above* **Obwohl** die obigen Familien in solchem Elend leben, kann man sagen, daß sämtliche Londoner Arbeiter in solchen Verhältnissen leben?
16. *Although* the above families live in such misery, can one say that all London's workers live in such circumstances?	**17.** **einfallen** = *to come to mind, to occur (to someone)* **behaupten**= *to maintain, to hold* **Obgleich** es Engels nicht einfällt, das zu behaupten, will er doch sagen, daß es den Arbeitern nicht gut geht.
17. *Although* it does not occur to Engels to claim that, he still maintains that things do not go well for the workers.	**18.** **leben** = *to live* **hatten . . . gelebt** = *had lived* In welchem Zustand hatten die obigen gelebt?
18. What sorts of conditions had the people mentioned above lived in?	**19.** **Ob** sie in diesem Zustand gelebt hatten?
19. I wonder *whether* they had lived in this condition?	**20.** **Obschon** sie kein Geld hatten, mußten sie doch essen.
20. *Although* they had no money, they still had to eat.	**21.** **werden mit Füßen getreten** = *are trampled* Sie werden mit Füßen getreten.

21. They are trampled upon.	**22.** **ganz und gar** = *completely* Sie wird ganz und gar von der Gesellschaft mit Füßen getreten.
22. She is completely trampled upon by society.	**23.** Ich weiß wohl, **daß** zehn es besser haben, wo einer so ganz und gar von der Gesellschaft mit Füßen getreten wird.
23. I am well aware *that* for every one who is so completely trampled upon by society, ten (people) have a better life.	**24.** **die Schuld** = *guilt, fault* **Kann** jeder Proletarier, ohne seine Schuld, von gleichem Schicksal **getroffen werden?** (*can meet/will meet*)
24. *Can* every proletarian *meet* with the same fate through no fault of his own? (Lit.: *Can* every proletarian *be met by* the same fate without being at fault?)	**25.** **die Anstrengung** = *effort, exertion, strain* Kann jeder Proletarier, trotz allen seinen Anstrengungen, von gleichem Schicksal getroffen werden?
25. Can every proletarian, meet with the same fate no matter how hard he tries (in spite of all his efforts)?	**26.** Was sollen wir tun, **wenn** jeder Proletarier, ohne seine Schuld und trotz allen seinen Anstrengungen, von gleichem Schicksal getroffen werden kann?
26. What are we to do, *if* every proletarian can meet the same fate through no fault of his own, and no matter how hard he tries?	**27.** **die Lage** = *situation, position, condition* In was für einer Lage befinden sich die **braven** Familien?
27. What kind of a situation do the *good* families find themselves in?	**28.** Was **hat** Engels **behauptet**?
28. What *did* Engels *maintain*?	**29.** **fleißig** = *industrious* Aber Engels behauptet, daß Tausende von fleißigen und braven Familien sich in dieser **eines Menschen unwürdigen** Lage befinden. (*unworthy for many men/unworthy of a human being*)
29. But Engels maintains that thousands of industrious and good families find themselves in this situation which is *unworthy of a human being.* (Note that the adjective **unwürdig** takes a genitive object, which precedes the adjective.)	**30.** **die Ausnahme** = *exception* **Da** jeder Proletarier, jeder ohne Ausnahme, vom gleichen Schicksal getroffen werden kann.
30. *Since* every proletarian, every one without exception, can meet with the same fate.	

PROGRESS TEST

Choose the sentence which most closely corresponds to the given sentence.

1. Die arme Frau erzählte ihm, daß sie voriges Jahr ihr Bett habe verkaufen müssen, um Nahrung zu erhalten.
(a) The woman had no money to buy a bed.
(b) Last year she had money to buy a bed.
(c) In order to buy a bed she had to sell her dishes.
(d) She sold her bed to buy food.

2. Die Polizeidiener sahen sich veranlaßt, weiter nachzuforschen, denn sie wollten selber den halbgekochten Kuhfuß stehlen.
(a) The policemen feel the boys stole the cow's foot.
(b) The policemen wanted to steal the cow's foot themselves.
(c) The policemen wanted to do away with the investigation of the cow's foot.
(d) The policemen wanted the investigation of the stolen cow's foot under their jurisdiction.

3. Sämtliche Reichen von London befinden sich in derselben Lage wie die braven, fleißigen Proletarier.
(a) All proletarians are brave and flighty.
(b) Brave and industrious proletarians find the rich very haughty.
(c) The proletarians and the rich share a common fate.
(d) Rich and poor alike are good and industrious.

4. In dem kleinen Hinterzimmer fand man weder Bettstelle noch sonstige Möbel, aber doch einen mit Federn bedeckten Körper.
(a) Feathers were all over the room but not on the furniture.
(b) If one had a bedstead and other furniture they would not need a feather bed.
(c) Feather covered bodies are not much good for furniture.
(d) A feather-covered body was the only object in the room.

Answer key: **1.** (d); **2.** (b); **3.** (c); **4.** (d).

Friedrich Engels: Die Lage der arbeitenden Klasse in England

Bei Gelegenheit einer Totenschau, die Hr. Carter, Coroner für Surrey, über die Leiche der 45- jährigen Ann Galway am 16. Nov. 1843 abhielt, erzählen die Journale folgendes von der Wohnung der Verstorbenen: Sie hatte in Nr. 3, White-Lion-Court, Bermondsey-Street, London, mit ihrem Mann und ihrem 19 jährigen Sohne in einem kleinen Zimmer gewohnt, worin sich weder Bettstelle oder Bettzeug, noch sonstige Möbel befanden. Sie lag tot neben ihrem Sohn auf einem Haufen Federn, die über ihren fast nackten Körper gestreut waren, denn es war weder Decke noch Bettuch vorhanden. Die Federn klebten so fest an ihr über den ganzen Körper, daß der Arzt die Leiche nicht untersuchen konnte, bevor sie gereinigt war, und dann fand er sie ganz abgemagert und über und über von Ungeziefer zerbissen. Ein Teil des Fußbodens im Zimmer war aufgerissen, und das Loch wurde von der Familie als Abtritt benutzt.

Montag den 15. Januar 1844 wurden zwei Knaben vor das Polizeigericht von Worship-Street, London, gebracht, weil sie aus Hunger einen halbgekochten Kuhfuß von einem Laden gestohlen und sogleich verzehrt hatten. Der Polizeirichter sah sich veranlaßt, weiter nachzuforschen, und erhielt von den Polizeidienern bald folgende Aufklärung: Die Mutter dieser Knaben war die Witwe eines alten Soldaten und späteren Polizeidieners, der es seit dem Tode ihres Mannes mit ihren neun Kindern sehr schlecht ergangen war. Sie wohnte Nr. 2, Pool's Place, Quaker-Street, Spitalfields, im größten Elende. Als der Polizeidiener zu ihr kam, fand er sie mit sechs ihrer Kinder in einem kleinen Hinterstübchen buchstäblich zusammengedrängt, ohne Möbel . . . Auf dem Herde kaum ein Funken Feuer, und in der Ecke so viel alte Lumpen, als eine Frau in ihre Schürze nehmen konnte, die aber der ganzen Familie zum Bette dienten. Zur Decke hatten sie nichts als ihre ärmliche Kleidung. Die arme Frau erzählte ihm, daß sie voriges Jahr ihr Bett habe verkaufen müssen, um Nahrung zu erhalten; ihre Bettücher habe sie dem Viktualienhändler als Unterpfand für einige Lebensmittel dagelassen, und sie habe überhaupt alles verkaufen müssen, um nur Brot zu bekommen.—Der Polizeirichter gab der Frau einen beträchtlichen Vorschuß aus der Armenbüchse . . .

Es fällt mir nicht ein, zu behaupten, alle Londoner Arbeiter lebten in einem solchen Elend, wie die obigen drei Familien: ich weiß wohl, daß Zehn es besser haben, wo Einer so ganz und gar von der Gesellschaft mit Füßen getreten wird—aber ich behaupte, daß Tausende von fleißigen und braven Familien, viel braver, viel ehrenwerter als sämtliche Reichen von London, in dieser eines Menschen unwürdigen Lage sich befinden, und daß jeder Proletarier, jeder ohne Ausnahme, ohne seine Schuld und trotz allen seinen Anstrengungen, von gleichem Schicksal getroffen werden kann.

Chapter Eleven

39. *Past tense of irregular weak verbs—conjugation*

1. The following endings and vowel changes signal the past tense of irregular weak verbs:

brennen	*to burn*	**er brannte**	*he burned*
kennen	*to know*	**er kannte**	*he knew*
nennen	*to name*	**er nannte**	*he named*
rennen	*to run*	**er rannte**	*he ran*
senden	*to send*	**er sandte,** (**sendete**)	*he sent*
wenden	*to turn*	**er wandte,** (**wendete**)	*he turned*
bringen	*to bring*	**er brachte**	*he brought*
denken	*to think*	**er dachte**	*he thought*

(In present day usage the above forms in parentheses are primarily subjunctive forms—see chapter 21.)

2. The stem vowel changes from **e** (or **i**) to **a** in every case.

3. The verbs **bringen** and **denken** undergo a consonant change as well as a vowel change.

4. The irregular weak verbs follow this pattern in the past tense:

kennen (*to know, to be acquainted with*)
ich kannte *I knew*
du kanntest
er, sie, es kannte

wir kannten
ihr kanntet
sie kannten

Sie kannten

5. **Senden** and **wenden** may take one of two patterns:

senden (*to send*)		
ich sandte	or	**sendete**
du sandtest		**sendetest**
er, sie, es sandte		**sendete**
wir sandten		**sendeten**
ihr sandtet		**sendetet**
sie sandten		**sendeten**
Sie sandten		**sendeten**

6. The past tense indicative of **senden** has two meanings.

sendete = *sent by radio or TV*
sandte = *sent by mail, courier, person*

7. Do not confuse **konnte** (past tense form of the verb **können** = *can, to be able to*) with **kannte** (**kennen** = *to know, to be acquainted with*).
Do not confuse **brach** (**brechen** = *to break*) with **brachte** (**bringen** = *to bring*).
Do not confuse **er kann** (*he can*) with **er kannte** (*he knew*).

The purpose of the following exercises is to help you distinguish between the present and past tense and to introduce vocabulary from the reading passage. Give the tense and meaning of the indicated verbs.

	1. Wir **brennen** nur Kohle in unserem Ofen. (*present/past*)
1. present We *burn* only coal in our stove.	**2.** Sie **brannten** nur Kohle in ihrem Ofen. (*present/past*)
2. past They *burned* only coal in their stove.	**3.** Er **rennt** schnell. (*present/past*)
3. present He *runs* fast.	**4.** Er **rannte** schnell. (*present/past*)
4. past He *ran* fast.	**5.** **vorig** = *previous, last* Im vorigen Kapitel **sprachen** wir von Engels.
5. In the last chapter we *spoke* of Engels.	**6.** In diesem Kapitel **sprechen** wir über Bismarck.
6. In this chapter we *are going to talk* about Bismarck.	**7.** Bismarck **ist** 1815 **geboren** und 1898 **gestorben**.
7. Bismarck *was born* in 1815 and *died* in 1898.	**8.** Er **lebte** in einer Zeit der Demokratie und der deutschen Macht.
8. He *lived* in a time of democracy and of German power.	**9.** Als eine große historische Persönlichkeit **lebt** er immer noch.

9. He still *lives* as a great historical figure.	**10.** Er **formulierte** viele Reformen für die damaligen sozialen Verhältnisse Deutschlands.
10. He *formulated* many reforms for the social conditions that existed in Germany at the time.	**11.** **ja** = *yes* **bejahen** = *to approve* Die Konservativen **bejahten** seinen damaligen Einfluß auf Deutschland und **bejahen** ihn heute immer noch.
11. Conservatives *approved* the influence which he had on Germany at that time and still *approve* it today.	**12.** **nicht** = *not* **vernichten** = *to destroy* Heute **betrachten** die Liberalen Bismarck als einen Vernichter ihres Landes.
12. Today the liberals *view* Bismarck as a destroyer of their country.	**13.** Wie **betrachteten** die Liberalen Bismarck damals?
13. How *did* the liberals *view* Bismarck then?	**14.** **der Schaden** = *harm* Er **bringt** dem Land nur Schaden.
14. He *does* only harm to his country.	**15.** **unwiederbringlich** = *irreparable, irretrievable* Sie sagen, daß er dem Land unwiederbringlichen Schaden **brachte.**
15. They say that he *did* (lit.: *brought*) the country irreparable harm.	**16.** **vorbereiten** = *to prepare* Sie sagen, daß er dem Land unwiederbringlichen Schaden brachte und das Land auf die Hitlerzeit **vorbereitete.**
16. They say that he did the country irreparable harm and *prepared* the country for the Hitler period.	**17.** **Kennt** man den wahren Bismarck heute?
17. *Do* we *know* the real Bismarck today?	**18.** **Kann** man den wahren Bismarck **kennen?**
18. *Can* we *know* the real Bismarck?	**19.** **Konnte** man damals den wahren Bismarck **kennen?**
19. *Could* they (or: people) *know* the real Bismarck then?	**20.** If **amtlich** means *official* and **das Postamt** means *the post office,* then **das Amt** must mean __________
20. *the office*	**21.** **nennen** = *to call, to name* **ernennen** = *to appoint* Oft **ernennt** ein König den politisch stärksten Mann zu einem Amt.
21. Often a king *appoints* the man who is the strongest politically (lit.: the politically strongest man) to an office.	**22.** **die Meisterschaft** = *eminent skill, mastery* Trotz Bismarcks diplomatischer Meisterschaft . . .

22. In spite of Bismarck's diplomatic skill . . .	**23.** **rufen** = *to call* **berufen** = *to appoint, to send for* Trotz Bismarcks diplomatischer Meisterschaft **berief** man ihn im Jahre 1859 nicht ins Kabinett.
23. In spite of his diplomatic skill, Bismarck *was* not *appointed* to the cabinet in 1859.	**24.** **senden** = *to send* **hat gesandt** = *sent* (*has sent*) **der Gesandte** = *ambassador* Bismarck **als Gesandter** . . .
24. Bismarck *as an ambassador* . . .	**25.** Stattdessen **sandte** man ihn als Gesandten nach St. Petersburg.
25. Instead, he *was sent* to St. Petersburg as ambassador.	**26.** Damals **kannte** man den wahren Bismarck nicht.
26. At that time people *did* not *know* the real Bismarck.	**27.** Am 23. September 1862 **ernannte** Wilhelm I. Bismarck zum Ministerpräsidenten.
27. On September 23, 1862, Wilhelm I *appointed* Bismarck prime minister.	**28.** **eine Rede halten** = *to give a speech* Eine Woche nach seiner Ernennung zum Ministerpräsidenten **hielt** er seine berühmte „Blood and Iron" Rede.
28. One week after his appointment to (the post of) prime minister he *gave* his famous "Blood and Iron" speech.	**29.** Wer heute an Bismarck **denkt,** erinnert sich an seine „Eisen und Blut" Rede.
29. Whoever *thinks* of Bismarck nowadays remembers his "Iron and Blood" speech.	**30.** Damals **dachten** viele, daß Bismarck ein großer Ministerpräsident war.
30. At that time a lot of people *thought* that Bismarck was a great prime minister.	**31.** **sich zuwenden** = *to turn to* **Wenden** wir **uns** heute zu oft starken Politikern **zu,** wenn wir ein Problem haben?
31. *Do* we *turn* to strong politicians too often nowadays when we have a problem? (Note that **zuwenden** governs the dative case.)	**32.** **sich wenden an** = *to turn to* **Wandte sich** das deutsche Volk damals **an** einen starken Politiker, um Deutschlands Probleme zu lösen?
32. *Did* the German people at that time *turn to* a strong politician in order to solve Germany's problems? (Note that the verb + **an** calls for an accusative object.)	

PROGRESS TEST

Choose the correct answer.

1. Wilhelm I. ________ Bismarck zum Ministerpräsidenten.
(a) ernennen (b) ernannte (c) ernannt (d) ernennst

2. Den wirklichen Bismarck ______ man nicht kennen.
(a) kann (b) kannte (c) kennt (d) könnt

3. Elke ________ ihm seinen alten Hut.
(a) brachtest (b) bringst (c) bricht (d) brachte

4. Er ______ sich um und ging zurück.
(a) wandte (b) ranntest (c) sendet (d) kannte

5. Das Haus _____ zusammen.
(a) brachte (b) brauchte (c) brach (d) brecht

Answer key: **1.** (b); **2.** (a); **3.** (d); **4.** (a); **5.** (c).

40. *The genitive case—review*

1. As has been noted, possession and relation are most often expressed in German by the genitive case.

2. The genitive singular of masculine and neuter nouns is recognized by the endings **-(e)s, -en**, or **-(e)ns.** (Nouns ending in **-mus** add nothing, however.) Remember that the preceding article, limiting adjective, or possessive adjective will end in **-es**:

Der Freund mein*es* Mann*es* wohnt in Ungarn.	***My husband's*** *friend lives in Hungary.*
Der Wagen d*es* Student*en* ist schon sehr alt.	*The* ***student's*** *car is already very old.*
Der Grund sein*es* Glauben*s* ist die Liebe.	*The foundation* ***of his faith*** *is love.*

3. Since feminine nouns take no special endings in the genitive singular, the reader must look to the ending of the preceding article, limiting adjective, or possessive adjective to determine the case of the noun. The genitive ending will be **-er**:

Der Sohn dies*er* Frau ist wirklich sehr schlau.	***This woman's*** *son is truly very sly.*

4. The genitive plural of all genders is revealed by the **-er** of the preceding article, limiting adjective, or possessive adjective:

Freunde solch*er* Männer sollte man meiden.	*One should avoid the friends* ***of such*** *men.*

5. The genitive feminine (1) ending of articles, limiting adjectives, or possessive adjectives is the same as the dative feminine (2) and genitive plural (3). To avoid confusing them, consult the context:

(1) **Das Haus d*er* Tante ist nicht weit von hier.**	*Our aunt's house (the house **of the** aunt) is not far from here.*
(2) **Er bringt sein*er* Freundin Blumen.**	*He brings flowers **to his** girlfriend.*
(3) **Die Geschichte d*er* Musikinstrumente ist wirklich sehr interessant.**	*The history **of** musical instruments is really very interesting.*

The following frames contain a review of the genitive case and other grammar points. Give the meanings of the indicated words.

	1. sollten = *should, ought to* Um den Mann Bismarck besser zu verstehen, **sollten** wir seine Ideen kennen.
1. In order to understand (the man) Bismarck better, we *should* be acquainted with his ideas. (Note: **sollten** is here a subjunctive form. See chapter 23.)	**2. darum** = *for that reason* Darum **müssen** wir seine eigenen Reden lesen.
2. For that reason, we *must* read his own speeches.	**3.** Die Reden und Gespräche **des** Ministerpräsidenten helfen uns, seine Gedanken, Philosophie und Persönlichkeit zu verstehen.
3. The speeches and conversations *of the* prime minister help us to understand his ideas, philosophy, and personality.	**4. vorschlagen** = *to suggest* Wenn man seine „Eisen und Blut" Rede liest, dann kann man sehen, welche Rolle er für Preußen damals **vorschlug**.
4. When you read his "Iron and Blood" speech, then you can see what role he *suggested* for Prussia at that time.	**5.** Bismarck nach darf Deutschland nicht auf Preußens Liberalismus sehen.
5. According to Bismarck, Germany must not look to Prussia's liberalism.	**6.** Sondern Deutschland sollte auf die Macht Preußens sehen.
6. Rather, Germany should look to Prussia's power.	**7. die Rüstung** = *arms, armor, armament, weapons* Preußen muß seine Rüstung utilisieren.
7. Prussia must utilize its weapons.	**8. Nur sollte Preußen** seine Rüstung auch utilisieren. (*Only Prussia ought to/Prussia just ought to*)
8. *Prussia just ought to* utilize its armament as well.	**9. die Liebe** = *love* **die Vorliebe** = *predilection* Preußen hat die Vorliebe, **eine zu große Rüstung** zu tragen.

9. Prussia has a predilection for bearing *too many arms.*	**10.** **der Leib** = *body* Ein **schmaler** Leib kann weniger Rüstung tragen. (*fat/slender*)
10. A *slender* body can carry less armor. (or . . . cannot carry as much armor)	**11.** Wir haben die Vorliebe, eine zu große Rüstung für unseren schmalen **Leib** zu tragen. (*body/bodies*)
11. We have a predilection for carrying too much armor for our slender *bodies*. (Note: Were **Leib** plural, a German would consider this frame to mean that each of us has more than one body.)	**12.** Die Vorliebe **der Preußen,** eine zu große Rüstung für ihren schmalen Leib zu tragen . . .
12. The predilection *of the Prussians* for carrying armor too large for their slender bodies . . .	**13.** Bayern, Württemberg, Baden mögen **dem** Liberalismus indulgieren.
13. Bavaria, Württemberg, Baden may cater *to* (*in*) liberalism.	**14.** **anweisen** = *to assign to* Keiner kann ihnen **Preußens** Rolle anweisen.
14. No one can assign them *Prussia's* role.	**15.** Keiner **wird** ihnen Preußens Rolle anweisen.
15. No one *will* assign Prussia's role to them.	**16.** Bayern, Württemberg, Baden mögen dem Liberalismus indulgieren, darum wird ihnen doch keiner Preußens Rolle anweisen.
16. Bavaria, Württemberg, Baden may cater to liberalism, which is why no one will assign Prussia's role to them.	**17.** **zusammen** = *together* **zusammenfassen** = *to gather together, to concentrate* Preußen muß seine Kraft zusammenfassen.
17. Prussia must concentrate its power.	**18.** **zusammenhalten** = *to hold together* Preußen muß seine Kraft zusammenhalten.
18. Prussia must conserve (hold together) its power.	**19.** **nachdem** = *after* Nachdem Preußen seine Kraft zusammenfaßt und zusammenhält . . .
19. After Prussia gathers together and conserves its power . . .	**20.** **das Auge** = *eye* **der Blick** = *glance, glimpse* **der Augenblick** = *moment* **Auf** welchen Augenblick muß Preußen seine Macht zusammenhalten? (*for/on top of*)

20. *For* what moment must Prussia conserve its power?	**21.** **günstig** = *favorable* Nachdem Preußen seine Macht zusammenfaßt, muß es sie **auf** den günstigen Augenblick zusammenhalten.
21. After Prussia concentrates its power, it must conserve it *until* the favorable moment.	**22.** **anwenden** = *to use* Wann muß Preußen seine Macht anwenden?
22. When must Prussia use its power?	**23.** **wird verpaßt** = *is missed* Bevor ein günstiger Augenblick **noch einmal** verpaßt wird, muß Preußen seine Macht anwenden.
23. Before a favorable moment is missed *again*, Prussia must use its power.	**24.** **worden** = *been* Der günstige Augenblick **ist** schon einige Male **verpaßt worden.** (*has been missed/is being missed*)
24. The favorable moment *has* already *been missed* several times. (Present perfect of the passive voice will be discussed in chapter 20.)	**25.** **entscheiden** = *to decide, to determine, to resolve* **der Vertag** = *treaty* Die **Wiener Verträge** entscheiden die Grenzen des damaligen Preußens.
25. The *treaties of Vienna* determine the borders of the Prussia of that time.	**26.** Oft **entschieden** Verträge die Grenzen eines Staates.
26. Treaties often *determined* the borders of a nation.	**27.** **werden entschieden** = *are determined* Preußens Grenzen werden nicht durch Verträge entschieden.
27. Prussia's borders are not determined by treaties. (**Werden entschieden** is in the passive voice.)	**28.** **der Beschluß** = *decision* Preußens Grenzen werden nicht durch Reden und **Majoritätsbeschlüsse** entschieden.
28. Prussia's boundaries will not be determined by speeches and *majority decisions*. (Notice that the German passive present has future meaning in this context.)	**29.** Trotz der Reden und Majoritätsbeschlüsse **werden** die großen Fragen der Zeit nur durch Eisen und Blut **entschieden**.
29. In spite of the speeches and majority decisions, the great problems (questions) of the time *will* only *be resolved* by iron and blood.	**30.** **der Fehler** = *mistake* Das **ist** der große Fehler von 1848 bis 1849 **gewesen.** (*has been/was*)

30. That *was* the great mistake of 1848/1849.	**31.** **das Staatsleben** = *political life* Die Grenzen, notwendig zu einem **gesunden** Staatsleben, werden nicht durch Reden und Majoritätsbeschlüsse entschieden. (*unhealthy/healthy*)
31. The boundaries necessary for a *healthy* political life are not decided by speeches and majority decisions.	**32.** Preußens Grenzen sind zu einem gesunden Staatsleben **nicht günstig**. (*not clear/not favorable*)
32. Prussia's borders are *not favorable* for a healthy political life.	**33.** Preußens Grenzen nach den Wiener Verträgen waren zu einem gesunden Staatsleben nicht günstig.
33. After the treaties of Vienna Prussia's borders were not favorable for a healthy political life.	**34.** Nicht durch Reden und Majoritätsbeschlüsse werden die großen Fragen der Zeit entschieden, sondern durch Eisen und Blut.
34. The great problems of the time are not resolved by speeches and majority decisions but by iron and blood.	**35.** **die Maßregel** = *measure* Wir müssen viele Maßregeln **treffen**. (*hit/take*)
35. We must *take* many measures.	**36.** **haben getroffen** = *have taken* Wir haben viele Maßregeln getroffen.
36. We have taken many measures.	**37.** **das Heil** = *good* Sozialistisch sind viele Maßregeln, **die** wir zum großen Heil des Landes getroffen haben. (*the/which*)
37. Many measures *which* we have taken for the great good of the country are socialistic.	**38.** **sich angewöhnen** = *to become accustomed to, to get in the habit of* Der Staat gewöhnt sich **den Sozialismus** an.
38. The state is becoming accustomed to *socialism*. (**sich angewöhnen** takes an accusative object.)	**39.** Der Staat muß sich **etwas mehr** Sozialismus angewöhnen.
39. The state must become accustomed to *a little more* socialism.	**40.** Etwas mehr Sozialismus wird sich der Staat bei unserem Reiche **überhaupt** angewöhnen müssen. (*really/overhead*)
40. The state will *really* have to become accustomed to a little more socialism in our empire.	**41.** **wiederherstellen** = *to restore* Man stellt die Freiheit wieder her.
41. Freedom is restored.	**42.** **der Bauernstand** = *the peasant class* Man stellt **dem** Bauernstande die Freiheit wieder her.

42. Freedom is restored *to the* peasant class.	**43.** Sozialistisch war Herstellung **der** Freiheit **des** Bauernstandes.
43. The restoration *of the* freedom *of the* peasant class was socialistic.	**44.** **das Eisen** = *iron* **die Bahn** = *path, road* **die Eisenbahn** = __________
44. *the railroad*	**45.** **zugunsten** = *in favor of* Wird jede Expropriation zugunsten **der** Eisenbahn gemacht?
45. Is every expropriation made in favor *of the* railroad?	**46.** Sozialistisch ist jede Expropriation zugunsten **der** Eisenbahn.
46. Every expropriation in favor *of the* railroad is socialistic.	**47.** **zusammenlegen** = *to put or place together* **die Zusammenlegung** = ___________
47. *the consolidation*	**48.** **der Grund** = *land* **das Stück** = *piece* **Stücke** = pl. **die Grundstücke** = _______
48. *plots of land, real estate*	**49.** **die Kommassation** = *consolidation of plots of land;* strictly speaking; reallocation of land (to the peasants) Die Kommassation ist die **Zusammenlegung der Grundstücke.**
49. Kommassation is the *consolidation of plots of land.*	**50.** **der Grad** = *degree, grade, rank* Sozialistisch **im höchsten Grade** ist zum Beispiel die Kommassation.
50. Kommassation, for example, is socialistic *in the highest degree.*	**51.** In vielen Provinzen ist die Kommassation **Gesetz**.
51. In many provinces Kommassation is the *law.*	**52.** Der Sozialismus will Grundstücke **dem** einen nehmen und **dem** anderen geben.
52. Socialism wants to take land *from* one person and give it *to the* other.	**53.** Sozialistisch ist die Zusammenlegung der Grundstücke, **die** dem einen genommen werden und dem anderen gegeben.
53. The consolidation of plots of land *which* are taken from one person and given to the other is socialistic. (Note: . . . *genommen werden* . . . *gegeben werden* = present passive)	**54.** **bewirtschaften** = *to manage* (a farm) Der andere kann das Land besser bewirtschaften.
54. The other person can manage the land better.	**55.** **bequem** = *easy, comfortable* **bloß** = *merely* Der Sozialismus gibt **dem anderen** das Land, bloß weil **der andere** es bequemer bewirtschaften kann.

55. Socialism gives the land *to another* merely because *the other* (person) can manage it more easily.	**56.** Bloß weil **ein anderer** das Land bequemer bewirtschaften kann, gibt der Sozialismus **einem anderen** das Land.
56. Socialism gives the land *to another person* merely because *that person* is able to manage the land more easily.	**57.** **vollständig** = *complete* **vervollständigen** = ________
57. *to complete, to add to*	**58.** Ich **könnte** das Register noch weiter vervollständigen. (Does the context suggest that **könnte** means *could* or *was able to*?)
58. I *could* add to the list still further. (**könnte** is a subjunctive form of **können**)	**59.** **erschrecken** = *to frighten* Viele wollen manche mit dem Wort „Sozialismus" erschrecken. (The subject is: **viele/manche**)
59. **viele** Many (people) want to frighten some (people) with the word "socialism."	**60.** **jemand** = *someone* **Will** man jemand mit dem Wort „Sozialismus" erschrecken?
60. *Do* people *want* to frighten someone with the word "socialism"?	**61.** **fließen** = *to flow* **einfließen** = *to run in, to pour in* **einflößen** = *to instill something* Kann man **jemand** Schrecken einflößen mit dem Wort „Sozialismus"?
61. Is it possible to frighten *anyone* (lit.: to instill fright) with the word "socialism"?	**62.** **das Gespenst** = *specter, ghost, something to fear* Ist für **manche** das Wort „Sozialismus" ein Gespenst?
62. Is the word "socialism" something to fear for *some people*?	**63.** **zitieren** = *to call up* (also *to quote*) Zitiert man Gespenster, wenn man das Wort „Sozialismus" **benützt**? (*uses/used*)
63. Does a person call up ghosts *by using* the word "socialism"? (lit.: if/whenever one *uses*)	**64.** Bismarck **könnte** das Register noch weiter vervollständigen.
64. Bismarck *could* add to the list still further.	**65.** Aber wenn man glaubt, mit dem Worte „Sozialismus" jemand **Schrecken einflößen zu können** oder Gespenster zu zitieren . . .
65. But if you believe you *can frighten* someone or call up ghosts with the word "socialism" . . . (lit.: *can/are able to instill fear*)	**66.** **überwinden** = *to overcome, to surmount* **habe überwunden** = ________

66. *have overcome*	**67.** **längst** = *long ago* Ich habe diesen **Standpunkt** längst überwunden.
67. I overcame this *point of view* long ago.	**68.** **die Wassergesetzgebung** = *the laws governing the use of water* **die Reichsgesetzgebung** = __________
68. *legislation governing the German Reich*	**69.** **durchaus** = *completely* Diese **Überwindung** ist für die Reichsgesetzgebung durchaus notwendig.
69. This *surmounting* is absolutely necessary for legislation governing the Reich.	**70.** So stehen Sie auf einem Standpunkt, den ich längst ganz überwunden habe.
70. Thus you hold a point of view which I overcame completely long ago.	**71.** Sie stehen auf einem Standpunkt, **dessen** Überwindung für die ganze Reichsgesetzgebung durchaus notwendig ist.
71. You hold a point of view, the surmounting *of which* is absolutely necessary for legislation governing the Reich.	**72.** **fähig** = *capable, able* Er ist nicht mehr fähig, das Land zu regieren.
72. He is no longer capable of ruling the country.	**73.** **leider** = *unfortunately* Leider **bringt** ein politisch starker Mann keinen fähigen Nachfolger in das Amt.
73. Unfortunately a politically strong man *does* not *bring* an able successor into office.	**74.** Leider **brachte** Bismarck keinen fähigen Menschen in das Amt.
74. Unfortunately Bismarck *did* not *bring* an able man into office.	**75.** **niederschlagen** = *to strike down* Diktatoren und Tyrannen schlagen alle Opposition nieder.
75. Dictators and tyrants strike down all opposition.	**76.** **der Erfolg** = *success* **zusammenbrechen** = *to break down* (intransitive) Die Opposition gegen Diktatoren, Tyrannen und erfolgreiche Politiker **bricht** fast immer schnell **zusammen.**
76. The opposition against dictators, tyrants, and successful politicians almost always *collapses.*	**77.** **zum Teil** = *to a degree* Die Opposition gegen Bismarck **brach** zum Teil **zusammen.**
77. To a degree, the opposition against Bismarck *collapsed.*	**78.** Aber Bismarck **konnte** die Macht der katholischen Kirche und der Sozialisten nicht brechen.
78. But Bismarck *could* not break the power of the Catholic Church and the socialists.	

PROGRESS TEST

Items 1–10 require recognizing the correct case. Items 11–13 require choosing the correct case. Items 14 and 15 test sentence comprehension. Review any points that you miss before going on.

1. Das Auto **meiner Tante** ist toll.
(a) genitive singular (b) genitive plural

2. Das Auto **meiner Tanten** ist kaputt.
(a) genitive singular (b) genitive plural

3. Er ist am Ende **seiner Kraft**.
(a) genitive (b) dative

4. Keiner wird **der alten Frau** die Wahrheit sagen.
(a) nominative (b) genitive singular (c) genitive plural (d) dative

5. Was war **der große Fehler** der Zeit?
(a) nominative singular (b) genitive singular (c) genitive plural (d) accusative singular

6. Sozialistisch ist jede Expropriation zugunsten **der Eisenbahnen.**
(a) nominative singular (b) genitive singular (c) genitive plural (d) dative plural

7. Die Grundstücke werden **den anderen** gegeben.
(a) accusative singular (b) dative plural

8. Bismarck hat **den Standpunkt** längst überwunden.
(a) accusative singular (b) dative plural

9. Der Soldat **der Arbeit** kann nicht mehr.
(a) genitive singular (b) dative singular (c) genitive plural (d) nominative singular

10. Den guten Willen **der Arbeiter** soll man nicht verachten.
(a) genitive singular (b) dative singular (c) nominative plural (d) genitive plural

11. Was ist die Rolle ____ für Bismarck?
(a) der Sozialismus (b) dem Sozialismus (c) des Sozialismus (d) die Sozialisten

12. Sozialistisch war Herstellung ____ des Bauernstandes.
(a) des Freiheit (b) der Freiheit (c) die Freiheit (d) den Freiheit

13. Der Sozialismus gibt ____ das Land.
(a) die anderen (b) der andere (c) den anderen (d) des anderen

14. Ganz Deutschland sieht auf Preußens Liberalismus, nicht auf seine Kraft.
(a) All of Germany likes Prussia's power, and its liberalism.
(b) Part of Germany likes Prussia's liberalism, but not its power.
(c) All of Germany looks to Prussia's liberalism but not its power.
(d) Prussia's liberalism and its power are dangerous for Germany.

15. Sozialistisch ist, wenn dem einen sein Grundstück genommen werden kann, weil es ein anderer besser bewirtschaften kann.

(a) Socialism means to give land to those who do not deserve it.
(b) Socialism gives land to those who do not know how to run a good farm.
(c) Socialism takes land from one individual and gives it to another because another can better farm it.
(d) Under socialism it does not matter if a person is a good or a poor farmer. Each gets an equal share.

Answer key: **1.** (a); **2.** (b); **3.** (a); **4.** (d); **5.** (a); **6.** (c); **7.** (b); **8.** (a); **9.** (a); **10.** (d); **11.** (c); **12.** (b); **13.** (c); **14.** (c); **15.** (c).

Otto von Bismarck: Aus Erklärungen in der Budgetkommission

Wir haben zu heißes Blut, wir haben die Vorliebe, eine zu große Rüstung für unsern schmalen Leib zu tragen; nur sollen wir sie auch utilisieren. Nicht auf Preußens Liberalismus sieht Deutschland, sondern auf seine Macht; Bayern, Württemberg, Baden mögen dem Liberalismus indulgieren, darum wird ihnen doch keiner Preußens Rolle anweisen: Preußen muß seine Kraft zusammenfassen und zusammenhalten auf den günstigen Augenblick, der schon einige Male verpaßt ist; Preußens Grenzen nach den Wiener Verträgen sind zu einem gesunden Staatsleben nicht günstig; nicht durch Reden und Majoritätsbeschlüsse werden die großen Fragen der Zeit entschieden—das ist der große Fehler von 1848 bis 1849 gewesen—sondern durch Eisen und Blut . . .

Berlin, 30. September 1862

Aus einer Reichstagsrede

. . . Sozialistisch sind viele Maßregeln, die wir getroffen haben, die wir zum großen Heile des Landes getroffen haben, und etwas mehr Sozialismus wird sich der Staat bei unserem Reiche überhaupt angewöhnen müssen. . . . Sozialistisch war Herstellung der Freiheit des Bauernstandes; sozialistisch ist jede Expropriation zugunsten der Eisenbahnen; sozialistisch im höchsten Grade ist zum Beispiel die Kommassation, die Zusammenlegung der Grundstücke, die dem einen genommen werden—in vielen Provinzen ist das Gesetz—und dem anderen gegeben, bloß weil der andere sie bequemer bewirtschaften kann. . . . Das ist alles sozialistisch. Ich könnte das Register noch weiter vervollständigen; aber wenn Sie glauben, mit dem Worte „Sozialismus" jemand Schrecken einflößen zu können oder Gespenster zu zitieren, so stehen Sie auf einem Standpunkte, den ich längst überwunden habe und dessen Überwindung für die ganze Reichsgesetzgebung durchaus notwendig ist . . .

Berlin, 12. Juni 1882

Chapter Twelve

Reading: From Max Weber: Die Erbschaft Bismarcks

41. *Relative pronouns* der *and* welcher*—declension and usage*

1. The relative pronouns **der, die, das** are declined as follows:

	M	F	N	Pl	
N	**der**	**die**	**das**	**die**	*who, which, that*
G	**dessen**	**deren**	**dessen**	**deren**	*whose*
D	**dem**	**der**	**dem**	**denen**	*(to) whom, which, that*
A	**den**	**die**	**das**	**die**	*whom, which, that*

2. Dessen, deren, and **denen** are used as relative pronouns or demonstratives. **Der, die, das, den, dem** can be used as relative pronouns, definite articles, or demonstratives. (For demonstratives, see chapter 15.)

3. The relative pronouns **der, die, das** are quite easy to distinguish from the definite article because they introduce a clause which is set off by commas and has the verb *last*. Definite articles are always followed by the noun or an adjective plus noun, in this case **Mann**:

***Der* Mann, *der* gestern hier war, ist mein Vater.**	***The*** *man* ***who*** *was here yesterday is my father.*

(Article **der** refers forward to **Mann,** relative **der** back to **Mann**.)

4. A relative pronoun agrees in gender and number with the noun to which it refers: however, its case is dependent upon its use in the clause:

Der Hund, *den* ich sehe, sitzt auf einem Stuhl.	*The dog* ***which*** *I see is sitting on a chair.*
Ich sehe den Hund, *der* auf einem Stuhl sitzt.	*I see the dog* ***which*** *is sitting on a chair.*

5. Relative clauses are dependent and therefore show dependent word order, i.e., the verb is to be found at the end of the clause:

Die Frau, mit *der* ich vor zwei Tagen in die Stadt *ging*, ist meine Mutter.	*The woman with* **whom I went** *to town two days ago is my mother.*

The reading passage for this chapter is typical of a kind of scholarly German prose and its long and involved sentences. The following exercises give you practice in identifying the relative clauses. Give the correct meaning of the indicated words.

	1. Der Mann, **dem** er hilft, ist sein alter Vater. (*whom/the*)
1. The man *whom* he is helping is his old father.	**2.** Der Mann, **den** er vorige Woche sah, ist mein Bruder. (*the/whom/him*)
2. The man *whom* he saw last week is my brother.	**3.** Siehst du das Mädchen, mit **dem** er ins Kino geht? (*the/whom/it*)
3. Do you see the girl with *whom* he is going to the movies?	**4.** Das Mädchen, **das** jetzt ins Kino geht, ist ihre Schwester. (*the/who*)
4. The girl *who* is now going to the movies is her sister.	**5.** Das Mädchen, mit **dessen** Vater er ins Kino ging, ist eine gute Freundin von mir. (*those/whose*)
5. The girl with *whose* father he went to the movies is a good friend of mine.	**6.** Die Frau, zu **der** der alte Mann geht, ist unsere Tante. (*whom/of the/the*)
6. The woman *whom* the old man is going to visit (lit.: *to whom* the old man is going) is our aunt.	**7.** **die Eltern** = *the parents* Eure Eltern, mit **denen** ihr immer ins Kino geht, sind nicht mehr so jung. (*those/whom/the*)
7. Your parents, with *whom* you always go to the movies, are not so young anymore.	**8.** Er sieht ihre Eltern, **deren** Auto der Mercedes ist. (*whose/their*)
8. He sees her (their) parents, who own the Mercedes (*whose* car the Mercedes is).	**9.** **haben gelesen** = *have read* Wir haben einige Gedanken aus Bismarcks Reden und Gesprächen gelesen.
9. We have read a few thoughts from Bismarck's speeches and conversations.	**10.** **haben besprochen** = *have discussed* Bismarcks Ideen, **die** wir besprochen haben, handeln von der Außen- und Innenpolitik. (*the/who/which*)
10. Bismarck's ideas *which* we have discussed deal with foreign and domestic affairs.	**11.** Wir wissen, **daß** viele Bismarck als Politiker kritisiert haben. (*the/that/which*)

11.	We know *that* many (people) have criticized Bismarck as a politician.	**12.**	**das Erbe** = *legacy* Was war Bismarcks politisches Erbe?
12.	What was Bismarck's political legacy? (cf. ***das* Erbe** vs. ***der* Erbe** = *heir*)	**13.**	**beurteilen** = *to evaluate* Max Weber, **der** als Sozialökonom und Soziologe weltbekannt ist, hat einmal Bismarcks politisches Erbe beurteilt.
13.	Max Weber, *who* is world-famous as a social economist and sociologist, once evaluated Bismarck's political legacy.	**14.**	**erziehen** = *to educate* ohne eine politische Erziehung = ___________
14.	*without a political education*	**15.**	**alle und jede** = *any kind of, all and every* **Die** Nation war ohne alle und jede politische Erziehung. (*the/who/which*)
15.	*The* nation had absolutely no political education (was without any kind of political education).	**16.**	Die Nation, **die** er hinterließ, war ohne alle und jede politische Erziehung. (*which/who*)
16.	The nation *which* he left behind had absolutely no political education.	**17.**	**erreichen** = *to achieve, to attain* **hatte erreicht** = *had achieved, had attained* Die Nation hatte ein hohes Niveau **der** politischen Erziehung erreicht. (*of/whose*)
17.	The nation had attained a high level *of* political education. (**Der** is here used as a genitive definite article.)	**18.**	**vorher** = *previously* Die Nation hatte **zwanzig Jahre vorher** ein hohes Niveau der politischen Erziehung erreicht.
18.	*Twenty years previously,* the nation had attained a high level of political education.	**19.**	**die Hinsicht** = *respect, regard* In dieser Hinsicht hatte **die** Nation vorher ein hohes Niveau erreicht. (*which/the/who*)
19.	In this respect *the* nation had previously attained a high level.	**20.**	**bereits** = *already* Die Nation stand tief unter dem Niveau, **das** sie in dieser Hinsicht zwanzig Jahre vorher bereits erreicht hatte. (*who/which*)
20.	The nation stood far below the level *which* it had attained in this respect twenty years previously.	**21.**	**sorgen** = *to be anxious, to take care* **besorgen** = *to take care of, to manage, to conduct* **Der** große Staatsmann besorgte für sie die Politik. (*who/which/the*)
21.	*The* great statesman managed the political affairs for it.	**22.**	**gewohnt** = *accustomed* Und vor allem **war** die Nation **gewohnt** . . . (*was accustomed/had accustomed*)

22.	And above all, the nation *was accustomed . . .*	**23.**	**werde besorgen** = *would manage* Und vor allem war die Nation gewohnt, **daß** der große Staatsmann für sie die Politik schon besorgen werde. (*that/which/who*)
23.	And above all, the nation was accustomed to the great statesman's managing its political affairs. (Lit.: And above all, the nation was accustomed *that* the great statesman would no doubt manage the political affairs for it.) (**Werde** is a subjunctive form of the verb **werden**.)	**24.**	**gefährlich** = *dangerous* Der große Staatsmann, **dessen** Politik so gefährlich ist für eine demokratische Nation . . . (*whose/of/that*)
24.	The great statesman, *whose* political ideas are so dangerous for a democratic nation . . .	**25.**	**die Spitze** = *top, point* Die Nation, an **deren** Spitze ein großer Staatsmann steht . . .
25.	The nation at *whose* head a great statesman stands . . .	**26.**	An **ihrer** Spitze wird der große Staatsmann für sie die Politik schon besorgen. (*its/yours*)
26.	At *its* head the great statesman will, no doubt, manage its political affairs. (Lit.: manage the political affairs for it.)	**27.**	**die Zügel** = *reins* Nach Bismarck nahmen Politiker ohne alle und jede Qualification die Zügel **der** Regierung in die Hand. (*of/whose/that*)
27.	After Bismarck politicians without the slightest qualifications took the reins *of* government into their hands.	**28.**	**ergehen** = *to happen, to befall* **etwas über sich ergehen lassen** = *to bear something patiently* Die Nation läßt alles über sich ergehen.
28.	The nation bears everything patiently (accepts patiently everything that happens to it).	**29.**	Die Nation **ließ** fatalistisch **alles über sich ergehen.**
29.	The nation fatalistically *bore everything patiently.*	**30.**	**sich gewöhnen** = *to accustom oneself* **hatte sich gewöhnt** = *had accustomed itself* Die Nation, **die** sich daran gewöhnt hatte, alles über sich ergehen zu lassen . . .
30.	The nation *that* had accustomed itself to bearing everything patiently . . .	**31.**	**das Gefühl** = *state of mind* (also: *feeling, sentiment*) das monarchische Gefühl
31.	the monarchical state of mind, sentiment in favor of the monarchy	**32.**	**nutzen** = *to be of use* **benutzen** = *to use, to utilize* **die Benutzung** = _______

32. *use, utilization*	**33.** **mißbrauchen** = *to misuse* **mißbräuchlich** = *improper, wrong* **die mißbräuchliche Benutzung** des monarchischen Gefühls
33. *the improper use* of the monarchical state of mind	**34.** **die Folge** = *result, consequence* **als Folge** = *as a consequence* Als Folge **der** mißbräuchlichen Benutzung **des** monarchischen Gefühls, ließ die Nation alles über sich ergehen. (*of the/whose/which*)
34. As a consequence *of the* improper use *of the* monarchical state of mind, the nation put up with everything.	**35.** **der Sessel** = *armchair, seat* Was für einen Sessel hat er?
35. What kind of a chair does he have?	**36.** **sich niederlassen** = *to settle down* Sie ließen sich auf Bismarcks Sessel nieder.
36. They settled down in Bismarck's seat.	**37.** **diejenigen** = *those* Diejenigen, **die** sich auf Bismarcks Sessel niederließen, nahmen die Zügel der Regierung in die Hand. (*those/who/they*)
37. Those *who* settled down in Bismarck's seat took the reins of government in hand.	**38.** **leer** = *empty* **leerlassen** = *to leave empty* **leergelassen** = *vacated* Die Qualifikationen **derjenigen,** die sich auf Bismarcks leergelassenen Sessel niederließen . . . (*of those/to those*)
38. The qualifications *of those* who settled down in Bismarck's vacated seat . . .	**39.** **befangen** = *self-conscious, awkward* **unbefangen** = *without inhibition, naturally* **die Unbefangenheit** = *ease* . . . und mit Unbefangenheit die Zügel der Regierung in die Hand nahmen . . .
39. . . . and took the reins of government into their hands with ease . . .	**40.** **nunmehr** = *now* Die Unbefangenheit, mit **der** sie nunmehr die Zügel der Regierung in die Hand nahmen . . . (*who/which/the*)
40. The ease with *which* they now took the reins of government into their hands . . .	**41.** **schwer** = *hard, heavy, great* **schwerst-** = ________
41. *hardest, heaviest, greatest*	**42.** **der Schaden** = *harm, damage* Wo liegt der schwerste Schaden?

42.	Where does the greatest harm lie?	**43.**	**an diesem Punkt** = *at this point, here* Der schwerste Schaden liegt an diesem Punkt.
43.	The greatest harm is at this point.	**44.**	**bei weitem** = *by far* An diesem Punkt lag **der** bei weitem schwerste Schaden. (*the/whose/it*)
44.	Here lay by far *the* greatest harm.	**45.**	Die Tradition, **die** Bismarck hinterließ, war überhaupt keine politische Tradition. (*the/which/it*)
45.	The tradition *which* Bismarck left behind was not a political tradition at all.	**46.**	**selbst** = *self* **stehen** = *to stand* **selbständig** = ________
46.	*independent*	**47.**	**innerlich** = *within* **innerlich selbständig** = ________
47.	*independent from within,* i.e., *independent*	**48.**	**der Kopf** = *head* Ein Diktator wünscht keine innerlich selbständigen Köpfe um sich zu haben.
48.	A dictator does not wish to have independent minds (lit.: independent heads) around him.	**49.**	**tragen** = *to carry, to wear* **ertragen** = *to suffer, to tolerate* Ein Diktator erträgt keine innerlich selbständigen Köpfe.
49.	A dictator does not put up with independent minds.	**50.**	**ziehen** = *to pull* **heranziehen** = *to draw upon, to enlist, to bring in* Er zieht auch keine innerlich selbständigen Köpfe heran.
50.	Neither does he draw upon independent minds.	**51.**	**hatte herangezogen** = *had drawn upon* **hatte ertragen** = *had tolerated* Der Diktator, **dem** die eigenen Ideen heilig waren, hatte innerlich selbständige Köpfe weder herangezogen noch ertragen. (*its/the/to whom*)
51.	The dictator, *to whom* his own ideas were sacred, had neither drawn upon nor tolerated independent minds.	**52.**	**vollends** = *entirely, in every way* Innerlich selbständige Köpfe und vollends Charaktere hatte er weder herangezogen, noch auch nur ertragen.
52.	People with independent minds and strong character he had neither drawn upon nor even tolerated.	**53.**	**schätzen** = *to esteem, to value* Selbständige Köpfe und vollends Charaktere, **deren** innerliche Qualitäten Bismarck nicht schätzte . . . (*its/of the/whose*)

53. People of independent minds and strong character *whose* spiritual qualities Bismarck did not value . . .	**54.** **der Stern** = *star* **der Unstern** = *unlucky star* or *evil star* der Unstern **der** Nation (*the/of the/whose*)
54. the unlucky star *of the* nation	**55.** **wollen** = *to want, to will* **hatte gewollt** = *had wanted, had willed* Der Unstern der Nation hatte dies gewollt.
55. The unlucky star of the nation had willed this.	**56.** **bescheiden** = *modest, moderate* Bismarcks Sohn hatte **wahrlich** bescheidene staatsmännische Qualitäten. (*wrongly/truly*)
56. Bismarck's son had *truly* modest qualities of statesmanship.	**57.** **überschätzen** = *to overestimate* Bismarck überschätzte die wahrlich bescheidenen staatsmännischen Qualitäten **des** eigenen Sohnes. (*of his/whose/that*)
57. Bismarck overestimated the truly modest qualities of statesmanship *of his* own son.	**58.** **erstaunen** = *to be astonished* **erstaunlich** = ________
58. *astonishing, amazing, marvelous*	**59.** Bismarck überschätzte **erstaunlich** die wahrlich bescheidenen staatsmännischen Qualitäten des eigenen Sohnes.
59. Bismarck overestimated *to a surprising degree* the truly modest qualities of statesmanship of his own son.	**60.** **besitzen** = *to have, to own* **besaß** = *had* Bismarck besaß einen Sohn, **dessen** wahrlich bescheidene staatsmännische Qualitäten er erstaunlich überschätzte. (*whose/its/of the*)
60. Bismarck had a son *whose* truly modest qualities of statesmanship he overestimated to a surprising degree.	**61.** **rasend** = *mad, furious, out of control* Ist er **denn** rasend? (intensifier/*for*)
61. intensifier Is he mad?	**62.** **der Argwohn** = *suspicion* Bismarck hatte einen rasenden Argwohn auf alle Persönlichkeiten.
62. Bismarck had an uncontrollable suspicion of all individuals.	**63.** **denken** = *to think* **denkbar** = *thinkable, possible* Das ist **überhaupt** nicht denkbar!
63. That is not *at all* possible!	**64.** **folgen** = *to follow, to obey* **nachfolgen** = *to follow, to succeed* **der Nachfolger** = ________

64. *successor*	**65.** **der Verdacht** = *suspicion* Bismarck hatte alle denkbaren Nachfolger in Verdacht.
65. Bismarck was suspicious of all possible successors.	**66.** Denkbare Nachfolger waren Bismarck **verdächtig**.
66. Possible successors were *suspect* to Bismarck.	**67.** **irgendwie** = *in any way* Der rasende Argwohn auf alle Persönlichkeiten, **die** Bismarck irgendwie als denkbare Nachfolger verdächtig waren . . . (*the/they/who*)
67. The uncontrollable suspicion of all individuals *who* were in any way suspect to Bismarck as possible successors . . .	**68.** **überdies** = *besides* Und der Unstern der Nation hatte überdies gewollt . . .
68. And the unlucky star of the nation had wished besides . . .	**69.** **neben** = *in addition, besides* . . . daß Bismarck neben seinem rasenden Argwohn auf alle Persönlichkeiten . . .
69. . . . that Bismarck in addition to his uncontrollable suspicion of all individuals . . .	**70.** . . . **die** ihm irgendwie als denkbare Nachfolger verdächtig waren . . . (*what/that/who*)
70. . . . *who* were in any way suspect to him as possible successors . . .	**71.** . . . **auch noch** einen Sohn besaß . . .
71. . . . *also* had a son . . .	**72** . . . **dessen** wahrlich bescheidene staatsmännische Qualitäten er erstaunlich überschätzte. (*of his/whose/of that*)
72. . . . *whose* truly modest qualities of statesmanship he overestimated to a surprising degree.	

Since there is much new vocabulary in this section, review and learn the new words carefully before continuing.

PROGRESS TEST

Choose the answers that describe the italicized word. There are two correct answers for each question.

1. Bismarck hinterließ eine Nation, *die* ohne alle und jede politische Erziehung war.
   (a) singular (b) plural (c) nominative (d) accusative
2. Der Unstern der Nation, *der* dies gewollt hat . . .
   (a) nominative (b) genitive (c) singular (d) plural

3. Die staatsmännischen Qualitäten des eigenen Sohnes, *die* Bismarck überschätzte . . .
(a) singular (b) plural (c) nominative (d) accusative

4. Die Spitze der Nation, an *der* der große Staatsmann für sie die Politik schon besorgen werde . . .
(a) nominative (b) genitive (c) dative (d) singular (e) plural

5. Er hinterließ eine Nation, *deren* Parlament völlig machtlos war.
(a) singular (b) plural (c) dative (d) genitive

6. Er hinterließ Probleme, *deren* Lösung nicht so einfach war.
(a) singular (b) plural (c) genitive (d) nominative (e) dative

7. Bismarcks Sessel, auf *den* sie sich niederließen . . .
(a) singular (b) plural (c) dative (d) accusative

8. Das monarchische Gefühl, *dem* man alles verdanken kann . . .
(a) singular (b) plural (c) dative (d) accusative (e) genitive

Answer key: **1.** (a, c); **2.** (a, c); **3.** (b, d); **4.** (c, d); **5.** (a, d); **6.** (b, c); **7.** (a, d); **8.** (a, c).

42. Welcher, welche, welches *as relative pronouns*

1. Welcher, welche, and **welches** may be used as relative pronouns. Each may variously mean *who, which,* or *that.* They are declined as follows:

	M	F	N	Pl
N	**welcher**	**welche**	**welches**	**welche**
G	**dessen**	**deren**	**dessen**	**deren**
D	**welchem**	**welcher**	**welchem**	**welchen**
A	**welchen**	**welche**	**welches**	**welche**

2. There is no genitive form of the relatives **welcher, welche, welches.** Therefore, the genitive forms of the relative **der** are used.

3. The meanings and usage of **welcher, welche,** and **welches** as relative pronouns are the same as for the relatives **der, die, das.** They may refer either to persons or things:

Der Mann, *welcher* eben hier war . . .	*The man* ***who*** *was just here . . .*
Das Auto, *welches* wir gesehen haben . . .	*The car* (***which***) *we saw . . .*

4. You have already encountered forms of **welch-** (*which/what*) in previous chapters. The interrogative **welch-**, commonly called a **der** word, will be explained in chapter 15. It acts as an adjective and precedes the noun it modifies:

Welches **Haus ist es?**	***Which*** *house is it?*
Welcher **Bruder wohnt da?**	***Which*** *brother lives there?*

The following sentences include vocabulary and phrases you have already encountered. Give the meanings of the indicated words as you read them.

	1. Max Weber, **welcher** als Soziologe und Sozialökonom weltbekannt ist . . . (*which/who*)
1. Max Weber, *who* is world-famous as a sociologist and social economist . . .	**2.** **herrschen** = *to rule, to govern* **beherrschen** = *to rule, to govern* Das monarchische Gefühl, mit **welchem** ein starker Staatsmann eine Nation beherrschen kann . . . (*whom/which*)
2. The monarchical state of mind with *which* a strong statesman is able to rule a nation . . .	**3.** Diejenigen, **welche** sich nunmehr auf Bismarcks leergelassenen Sessel niederließen . . . (*which/who*)
3. Those *who* now settled down in Bismarck's vacated seat . . .	**4.** . . . und mit erstaunlicher Unbefangenheit die Zügel der Regierung in die Hand nahmen . . .
4. . . . and with astonishing ease took the reins of government into their hands . . .	**5.** Die Nation lag tief unter dem Niveau, **welches** sie zwanzig Jahre vorher bereits erreicht hatte. (*which/whom*)
5. The nation lay far below the level *which* it had already achieved (attained) twenty years previously.	**6.** **regieren** = *to rule* **die Regierung** = ___________
6. *the government*	**7.** Die Zügel der Regierung, **welche** Bismarck nunmehr in die Hand nahm . . . (*whom/which*)
7. The reins of government *which* Bismarck now took in hand . . .	**8.** Alle Persönlichkeiten, **welche** Bismarck irgendwie als denkbare Nachfolger verdächtig waren . . . (*what/which/who*)
8. All the individuals *who* were in any way suspect to Bismarck as possible successors . . .	**9.** **die Firma** = *business, establishment, firm* **unter der Firma** = *under the style of, under the leadership of* Die Firma der „monarchischen Regierung", unter **welcher** die Nation nunmehr alles über sich ergehen läßt . . .
9. The leadership of the "monarchical government," under *which* the nation patiently bears everything . . .	**10.** **hegen** = *to cherish, to entertain (a feeling)* Als Folge der mißbräuchlichen Benutzung des Gefühls, **welches** die Nation für die Monarchie hegte . . . (*whom/which*)

10.	As a consequence of the misuse (improper use) of the sentiment *which* the nation felt toward the monarchy . . .	**11.**	**wirken** = *to effect, to influence* Das politische Erbe Bismarcks, **welches** weiter auf die deutsche Nation wirkte . . . (*which/who*)
11.	Bismarck's political heritage, *which* further influenced the German nation . . .	**12.**	Die politische Tradition, **welche** der große Staatsmann hinterließ . . . (*dative/accusative*)
12.	accusative The political tradition *which* the great statesman left behind (bequeathed) . . .	**13.**	Die politische Qualifikation, mit **welcher** er das Land irgendwie regieren wollte . . . (*nominative/dative*)
13.	dative The political qualifications with *which* he somehow wanted to govern the country . . . (Note plural meaning)	**14.**	Der große Staatsmann, von **welchem** das Volk alles erwartete . . . (*dative/nominative*)
14.	dative The great statesman, from *whom* the people expected everything . . .	**15.**	Neben seinem rasenden Argwohn auf alle Persönlichkeiten, **welche** ihm irgendwie als denkbare Nachfolger verdächtig waren . . . (*which/who*)
15.	Besides his uncontrollable distrust of all individuals whom he in any way suspected of being possible successors . . . (lit.: w*ho* were to him in any way suspect as possible successors . . .)	**16.**	**Welchen** Staatsmann meinen Sie? (*interrogative/relative*)
16.	interrogative *Which* statesman do you mean?	**17.**	**meinen** = *to mean, to think, to be of the opinion* Meint Weber, daß Bismarck ein Unstern ist?
17.	Does Weber think that Bismarck is an unlucky star?	**18.**	Das monarchische Gefühl, **welches** der Diktator irgendwie mißbrauchte . . . (*relative/interrogative*)
18.	relative The monarchical sentiment, *which* the dictator somehow misused . . .	**19.**	**Welches** Gefühl mißbraucht jeder Diktator? (*relative/interrogative*)
19.	interrogative *What* feeling does every dictator misuse?	**20.**	Die Nation, **welche** Weber meint, ist Deutschland. (*relative/interrogative*)
20.	relative The nation to *which* Weber is referring is Germany.	**21.**	**Welche** politische Tradition herrscht nunmehr in den Vereinigten Staaten? (*interrogative/relative*)

21. interrogative *What* political tradition prevails at the present time in the United States?	**22.** Die Firma der monarchischen Regierung, unter **welcher** die Nation leidet . . . (*whom/which*)
22. The leadership of the monarchical government under *which* the nation suffers . . .	**23.** Der große Staatsmann, von **welchem** das Volk alles erwartete . . . (*dative/nominative*)
23. dative The great statesman, from *whom* the people expected everything . . .	

PROGRESS TEST

A. Give the meaning of the indicated word.

1. Bismarck, *dessen* Parlament völlig machtlos war . . .
(a) who (b) of that (c) which (d) whose

2. Die Nation, an *deren* Spitze ein Diktator saß . . .
(a) which (b) whose (c) that (d) whom

3. Dagegen hinterließ er ein Parlament, mit *welchem* man unzufrieden war.
(a) which (b) what (c) who (d) that

4. Der schwerste Schaden, *welchen* der große Staatsmann hinterließ . . .
(a) whom (b) what (c) to which (d) that

B. Choose all the answers that describe the italicized word.

1. Innerlich selbständige Köpfe und vollends Charaktere, *welche* Bismarck weder herangezogen noch auch nur ertragen hatte . . .
(a) feminine (b) plural (c) singular (d) nominative (e) accusative

2. Die Firma der monarchischen Regierung, unter *welcher* die Nation fatalistisch über sich ergehen ließ . . .
(a) feminine (b) singular (c) plural (d) nominative (e) dative

3. Der politische Wille einer Nation, ohne *welchen* ein Volk völlig machtlos ist . . .
(a) singular (b) plural (c) dative (d) accusative

4. Alle Persönlichkeiten, *welchen* er verdächtig war . . .
(a) singular (b) plural (c) dative (d) accusative

Answer key: A. **1.** (d); **2.** (b); **3.** (a); **4.** (d).
B. **1.** (b, e); **2.** (a, b, e); **3.** (a, d); **4.** (b, c).

43. Wer, was, *and* wo *used as relatives*

1. Wer appears in indefinite relative clauses and is translated *he who, those who,* or *whoever* (see also chapter 8). It does not have an antecedent:

***Wer* kein Geld hat, darf nicht mit.**	***Those who*** *have no money may not go along.*

2. Was is used similarly when no antecedent exists and is translated *whatever*:

***Was* nicht gut ist, ist schlecht.**	***Whatever*** *is not good is bad.*

3. After the following neuter antecedents **was** may be translated as *that,* or it may be left untranslated:

***Alles, was* er sagt . . .**	***All*** (***that***) *he says . . .*
***Nichts, was* er sagt . . .**	***Nothing*** (***that***) *he says . . .*
***Vieles, was* er sagt . . .**	***Much*** (***that***) *he says . . .*
***Etwas, was* er sagt . . .**	***Something*** (***that***) *he says . . .*
***Manches, was* er sagt . . .**	***Much, many a thing*** (***that***) *he says . . .*
***Einiges, was* er sagt . . .**	***Some things*** (***that***) *he says . . .*
Ich gab ihm *das Beste, was* ich hatte.	*I gave him* ***the best*** (***that***) *I had.*

4. When **was** sums up or derives a conclusion from another clause, translate it as *which is something that*:

Er hielt es aus, *was* ich eigentlich nicht verstehen kann.	*He endured it,* ***which is something that*** *I really cannot understand.*

5. Was when referring to the thought of a previous clause is best translated *which*:

Wir fahren morgen nach München, *was* uns sehr erfreut.	*We are going to Munich tomorrow,* ***which*** *makes us very happy.*

6. Wo used as a relative is translated *in which, where,* or *when*:

Ich kannte die Straße nicht, *wo* wir uns trafen.	*I did not know the street* ***where*** *we met.*
Zu der Zeit, *wo* ich in Berlin wohnte . . .	*At the time* ***when*** *I lived in Berlin . . .*

As you read the following sentences give the meanings of the indicated words.

	1. **hinnehmen** = *to accept* **Wer** das Böse ohne Widerspruch hinnimmt, arbeitet in Wirklichkeit mit ihm zusammen. (Martin Luther King, Jr.) (*who/where/those who*)
1. *Those who* accept evil without protest in reality are working together with it.	**2.** **Wer** seine Zeit recht sehen will, soll sie von Ferne betrachten. (Ortega y Gasset) (*those who/who/where*)
2. *Those who* want to see their age accurately should look at it from a distance.	**3.** **Was** er immer sagt, ich kann es nicht glauben. (*what/whatever*)
3. *No matter what* (*whatever*) he says, I cannot believe it. (**Immer** is used as an intensifier.)	**4.** **Was** das Gefühl der Macht erhöht, ist gut. (*what/whatever*)
4. *Whatever* heightens the feeling of power is good.	**5.** **hatte gemacht** = *had made* Und Gott sah an alles, **was** er gemacht hatte: und siehe da, es war sehr gut. (Bibel) (*what/that*)
5. And God looked at everything *that* he had made and behold, it was very good.	**6.** **die Erfüllung** = *fulfillment* Einiges, **was** der Unstern der Nation gewollt hatte, ging in Erfüllung. (*whatever/that*)
6. Some of the things *that* the unlucky star of the nation had willed were fulfilled.	**7.** **beschließen** = *to decide, to resolve* Die Nation ließ fatalistisch über sich ergehen, **was** man über sie beschloß. (*that/what*)
7. The nation fatalistically accepted *what* was decided (*what* one decided) for it.	**8.** Bismarck hinterließ ein völlig machtloses Parlament, **was** Max Weber richtig verstand. (*what/which is something that*)
8. Bismarck left behind a completely powerless parliament, *which is something that* Max Weber accurately understood.	**9.** **das Glück** = *happiness, luck* Bismarcks politisches Erbe war eine Nation ohne alle und jede politische Erziehung, **was** für Deutschland ein Unglück war.
9. Bismarck's political heritage was a nation without any kind of political education, *something that* was a calamity for Germany.	**10.** **der Sinn** = *meaning, sense* **Sinn haben** = *to make sense* Zwei Soldaten kamen und ergriffen den Zivilisten, **was** für Kafka keinen Sinn hatte.
10. Two soldiers came and seized the civilian, *which* to Kafka did not make sense.	**11.** Nietzsche nach sollen die Schwachen und Mißratenen zugrunde gehen, **was** heute undenkbar ist. (*which/what*)

11. According to Nietzsche the weaklings and misfits ought to perish, *which* today is unthinkable.	**12.** Ich kenne das Haus nicht mehr, **wo** wir uns zum erstenmal sahen. (*where/who*)
12. I no longer know the house *where* we saw each other for the first time.	**13.** Das ist die Stadt, **wo** er immer noch wohnt. (*where/who*)
13. That is the city *where* he is still living.	

PROGRESS TEST

Now test yourself with the following exercises.

1. **die Wolke** = *cloud*
   Wer viel verspricht, und hält nicht, der ist wie Wolken und Wind ohne Regen. (Die Sprüche Salomos 25, 14)
   (a) where (b) he who (c) when (d) which
2. *Was* das Gefühl der Macht erhöht, ist gut.
   (a) that (b) where (c) whatever (d) who
3. Nichts, *was* Gott machte, war böse.
   (a) that (b) whatever (c) who (d) where
4. Bismarcks Sohn hatte nur bescheidene staatsmännische Qualitäten, *was* Bismarck nicht wußte.
   (a) what (b) that (c) whom (d) which was something that
5. Ich kenne das Haus nicht mehr, *wo* wir uns zum erstenmal sahen.
   (a) where (b) why (c) who (d) which
6. Einiges, *was* der Unstern gewollt hatte . . .
   (a) who (b) which (c) what (d) whom

Answer key: **1.** (b); **2.** (c); **3.** (a); **4.** (d); **5.** (a); **6.** (b).

44. Da- *and* wo- *compounds*

1. Wo- (**wor-** before a vowel) compounds are contractions of **wo** (*where*) and a preposition. They refer only to things and may be used as interrogatives in direct questions or as relatives:

***Womit* schreiben Sie?**	***What*** *are you writing* ***with****?*
Der Bleistift, *womit* (*mit dem, mit welchem*) ich schreibe, ist meiner.	*The pencil* ***with which*** *I am writing is mine.* (*Less literally: The pencil I am writing* ***with*** *is mine.*)

2. When used interrogatively **wo**(**r**)- is best translated *what.* When used as a relative it means *which* and should then follow the preposition when you are translating:

Wovon **spricht er?**	***What*** *is he talking* ***about?***
Das Buch, ***wovon*** **er spricht, ist schon ausverkauft.**	*The book* ***of which*** *he speaks is already sold out. (Less literally: The book he is* ***speaking about*** *is already sold out.)*

3. Da- (**dar-** before a vowel) compounds are contractions of **da** (*there*) and a preposition. These contractions refer to prepositions plus nouns or pronouns of any gender as long as they are things or ideas:

Der Mensch besteht aus Fleisch und Bein. Er besteht ***daraus.***	*Human beings consist of flesh and bone. They consist* ***of that.***
Karl-Heinz steht vor dem Haus. Er steht ***davor.***	*Karl-Heinz is standing in front of the house. He is standing* ***in front of it.***
Sehen Sie meine Bücher? Was halten Sie ***davon?***	*Do you see my books? What do you think* ***of them****?*

Note: **da**(**r**)- can be translated as *it, that, this,* or *them.*

4. A **da**(**r**)- compound may refer to a dependent clause which follows it. In this case the **da**(**r**)- compound may or may not be translated:

Er glaubt fest ***daran,*** **daß der Mensch auch einen Geist besitzt.**	*He believes firmly (**in the fact, in the following**) that human beings also possess a spirit.*

5. Damit may be either a subordinating conjunction (*so that*) or a **da-** compound (*with that, with this, with it, with them*):

Geben Sie mir den Ball, ***damit*** **ich ihn werfen kann!**	*Give me the ball* ***so that*** *I can throw it!*
Damit **kann ich spielen.**	*I can play* ***with that.***

Give the meaning of the indicated words.

	1. Woran war die Nation gewöhnt? (*to what/to whom*)
1. *What* was the nation accustomed *to*?	**2.** Eine Nation, **daran** gewöhnt, unter der Firma der „monarchischen Regierung“ fatalistisch über sich ergehen zu lassen . . . (*to that*/need not be translated)

2. need not be translated A nation, accustomed to letting everything happen fatalistically under the leadership of the "monarchical government" . . .	**3.** Eine politische Tradition **dagegen** hinterließ Bismarck überhaupt nicht. (*on the other hand/against it*)
3. *On the other hand,* Bismarck did not leave behind any political tradition at all.	**4.** **Woraus** besteht eine politische Tradition? (*of whom/of what*)
4. *What* does a political tradition consist *of*?	**5.** Die Firma der „monarchischen Regierung", **worunter** die Nation damals litt . . . (*under whom/under which*)
5. The leadership of the "monarchichal government" *under which* the nation suffered at that time . . .	**6.** **Darunter** darf man nicht mehr leiden. (*from that/under that*)
6. One must not suffer *from that* anymore. (Remember that **nicht dürfen** means *must not.*)	**7.** Die erstaunliche Unbefangenheit, **womit** Bismarcks Nachfolger die Zügel der Regierung in die Hand nahmen . . . (*with what/with which*)
7. The astonishing ease *with which* Bismarck's successors took the reins of government into their hands . . .	**8.** Das Volk hatte nichts **dagegen**, daß man über es beschloß, was man wollte. (*on the other hand/against the fact that*)
8. The people had nothing *against the fact that* others decided for them whatever they wished.	**9.** Wollen wir **damit** anfangen? (*with that/so that*)
9. Do we want to begin *with that*?	**10.** **entfernen** = *to remove* Bismarck entfernte alle innerlich selbständigen Köpfe, **damit** er allein regieren konnte. (*with that/so that*)
10. Bismarck removed all the spiritually independent minds *so that* he could govern alone.	**11.** **die Gewalt** = *power, force, might* **gewaltig** = *enormous, powerful, mighty* **das gewaltige Prestige** = __________
11. *the enormous prestige*	**12.** **das Ergebnis** = *result* **Was** war das Ergebnis Bismarcks gewaltigen Prestiges? (*whatever/that/what*)

12. *What* was the result of Bismarck's enormous prestige?	**13. gegenüber** = *opposite (to), in relation to, opposed (to)* **demgegenüber** = *as opposed to that, on the other hand* **Demgegenüber** hinterließ Bismarck ein völlig machtloses Parlament.
13. *On the other hand,* Bismarck left behind a completely powerless parliament.	**14. rein** = *purely (pure)* Ein völlig machtloses Parlament war das rein negative Ergebnis **seines** gewaltigen Prestiges. (*of his/of its*)
14. A completely powerless parliament was the purely negative result *of his* enormous prestige.	**15. nun** = *well!, then* (also: *now*) (**nun**, an interjection, need not be translated in this example) Demgegenüber nun als ein rein negatives Ergebnis seines gewaltigen Prestiges hinterließ Bismarck ein völlig machtloses Parlament.
15. On the other hand, Bismarck left behind, as a purely negative result of his enormous prestige, a completely powerless parliament.	

PROGRESS TEST

Choose the correct meaning of the italicized words. If you miss any, review the grammar point in question before going on.

1. *Womit* regiert ein Diktator?
(a) to whom (b) to where (c) with what (d) who

2. Die Regierung, *worunter* die Nation damals litt . . .
(a) under them (b) under that (c) under this (d) under which

3. Wollen wir *damit* anfangen?
(a) so that (b) with which (c) with whom (d) with that (or with this)

4. *Daran* kann man sehen, daß er ein innerlich selbständiger Kopf ist.
(a) in the following (b) by that (c) toward what (d) to that

5. Sie tun das, *damit* sie ihm nicht irgendwie als denkbare Nachfolger verdächtig werden.
(a) with that (b) so that (c) therewith (d) in the following

6. Er besteht *darauf,* daß sein Sohn die Regierung übernehmen wird.
(**bestehen auf** = *to insist*)
(a) on top of it (b) thereupon (c) need not be translated (d) thereby

Answer key: **1.** (c); **2.** (d); **3.** (d); **4.** (b); **5.** (b); **6.** (c).

Max Weber: „Die Erbschaft Bismarcks" in: *Gesammelte Politische Schriften*.
Verlag J. C. B. Mohr (Paul Siebeck), Tübingen, 1958.

Max Weber: Die Erbschaft Bismarcks

Was war infolgedessen ... BISMARCKS politisches Erbe? Er hinterließ eine Nation ohne alle und jede politische Erziehung, tief unter dem Niveau, welches sie in dieser Hinsicht zwanzig Jahre vorher bereits erreicht hatte. Und vor allem [hinterließ er] eine Nation ohne allen und jeden politischen Willen, gewohnt, daß der große Staatsmann an ihre Spitze für sie die Politik schon besorgen werde. Und ferner, als Folge der mißbräuchlichen Benutzung des monarchischen Gefühls ... [hinterließ er] eine Nation, [die] daran gewöhnt [war], unter der Firma der „monarchischen Regierung" fatalistische [alles] über sich ergehen zu lassen, was man über sie beschloß, ohne Kritik an der politischen Qualifikation derjenigen, welche sich nunmehr auf BISMARCKS leergelassenen Sessel niederließen und mit erstaunlicher Unbefangenheit die Zügel der Regierung in die Hand nahmen. An diesem Punkt lag der bei weitem schwerste Schaden. Eine politische Tradition dagegen hinterließ der große Staatsmann überhaupt nicht. Innerlich selbständige Köpfe und vollends Charaktere hatte er weder herangezogen, noch auch nur ertragen. Und der Unstern der Nation hatte überdies gewollt, daß er [Bismarck] neben seinem rasenden Argwohn auf alle Persönlichkeiten, die ihm irgendwie als denkbare Nachfolger verdächtig waren, auch noch einen Sohn besaß, dessen wahrlich bescheidene staattsmännische Qualitäten er erstaunlich überschätzte. Demgegenüber nun als ein rein negatives Ergebnis seines gewaltigen Prestiges [hinterließ er]: ein völlig machtloses Parlament.

Chapter Thirteen

Reading: From Oswald Spengler:
Jahre der Entscheidung
Gedanken

45. *Past participles—recognition*

1. The past participle is generally recognized by a **ge-** prefix and an **-(e)t** or **-en** suffix attached to the stem. Weak verb past participles end in **-(e)t:**

antworten — **geantwort*et*** *to answer — answered*
rauchen — **geraucht*t*** *to smoke — smoked*

Strong verb past participles end in **-en.** In addition, the stem vowel will generally change:

singen — **ges*u*ng*en*** *to sing — sung*
sterben — **gest*o*rb*en*** *to die — died*
schlafen — **geschl*afen*** *to sleep — slept*

2. **Haben, sein,** and **werden** have the following past participles:

gehabt (*had*), **gewesen** (*been*), **geworden** (*become*)

3. Irregular weak verb past participles are recognized by a **ge-** prefix, a **-t** suffix, and also a stem vowel change:

brennen — **gebr*a*nn*t*** *to burn — burned*
kennen — **gek*a*nn*t*** *to know — known*

4. The **ge-** prefix of separable prefix verbs is found between the separable prefix and the stem:

aussehen — **aus*ge*sehen** *to appear — appeared*
einsetzen — **ein*ge*setzt** *to put in — put in*

5. Inseparable prefix verbs take no **ge-** prefix; however, they do take an **-(e)t** or **-en** suffix:

verbinden — **verbund*en*** *to unite* — *united*
zerstören — **zerstör*t*** *to destroy* — *destroyed*

6. Verbs ending in **-ieren** also take no **ge-** prefix. The suffix will always be **-t:**

studieren — **studier*t*** *to study* — *studied*
organisieren — **organisier*t*** *to organize* — *organized*

7. Remember that **ge-** may also be an inseparable prefix. Therefore, not all verbs with a **ge-** prefix will be past participles:

gehören — **gehört** *to belong* — *belonged*
gelingen — **gelungen** *to succeed* — *succeeded*
geschehen — **geschehen** *to happen* — *happened*

The purpose of this exercise is to familiarize you with the forms of the past participle.

	1. **wagen** = *to dare* **gewagt** = ________
1. *dared*	**2.** **zweifeln** = *to doubt* **gezweifelt** = ________
2. *doubted*	**3.** **schreien** = *to cry* **geschrien** = ________
3. *cried*	**4.** **ziehen** = *to pull* **gezogen** = ________
4. *pulled*	**5.** **wenden** = *to turn* **gewandt (gewendet)** = ________
5. *turned*	**6.** **denken** = *to think* **gedacht** = ________
6. *thought*	**7.** **schwanken** = *to sway* **geschwankt** = ________
7. *swayed*	**8.** **bringen** = *to bring* **gebracht** = ________
8. *brought*	**9.** **schaffen** = *to create* **geschaffen** = ________
9. *created*	**10.** **rasieren** = *to shave* **rasiert** = ________
10. *shaved*	**11.** **telefonieren** = *to telephone* **telefoniert** = ________
11. *telephoned*	**12.** **ausbrechen** = *to break out* **ausgebrochen** = ________

12. *broken out*	**13. ausrotten** = *to exterminate* **ausgerottet** = ________
13. *exterminated*	**14. genießen** = *to enjoy* **genossen** = ________
14. *enjoyed*	**15. sich entscheiden** = *to decide* **entschieden** = ________
15. *decided*	**16. telegrafieren** = *to send a telegram* **telegrafiert** = ________
16. *sent a telegram*	**17. beleidigen** = *to insult* **beleidigt** = ________
17. *insulted*	**18. abändern** = *to alter* **abgeändert** = ________
18. *altered*	

46. *The present perfect tense—recognition, meaning, and word order*

1. The present tense of **haben** or **sein** plus the past participle identifies the present perfect tense:

Ich *habe* das gestern *gesagt*. — *I* ***said*** *that yesterday.*
Georg *ist* bei uns *geblieben*. — *Georg* (**has**) ***stayed*** *with us.*

2. The meaning of the present perfect tense may be expressed in one of two ways, depending on the context:

Ich *habe* vier Jahre lang *studiert*. — I ***attended the university*** *for four years.*
(***studieren*** = *to be a student at a college or university*) (event ended in the past)
Ihr *seid* aber groß *geworden!* — *You* ***have gotten*** *tall!*
(action began in the past and its effects are related to the present)
Sie *haben* mich schon oft *besucht*. — *You* ***have*** *often* ***visited*** *me.*
(intermittent action in the past continuing up to the present)

However, if the past continues *unchanged* into the present, with the prospect of continuing into the future, then the present tense is required in German, usually adding **seit** (*since*), **schon,** (*already*), **erst** (*only*), a combination thereof, or similar expressions:

Er *raucht* schon lange. — *He* ***has been smoking*** (***has smoked***) *for a long time* (with the prospect of continuing).
Er *raucht* erst seit letzten Sonntag. — *He* ***has*** *only* ***been smoking*** *since last Sunday.*

3. Whereas English uses only the verb *to have* as an auxiliary, German calls for the verb **sein** when the verb is intransitive (that is, not accompanied by a direct object) and shows a change of place or condition. The verbs **sein** and **bleiben** also take **sein** as an auxiliary:

Wie weit *ist* er *gefahren?*	*How far **did** he **drive**?*
Marie *ist* gestern in die Stadt *geritten*.	*Marie **rode** into town yesterday.*
Er *ist* vor einer Woche *gestorben*.	*He **died** a week ago.*
Wie lange *sind* Sie da *geblieben?*	*How long **did** you **stay** there?*
***Sind* Sie gestern im Büro *gewesen*?**	***Were** you in the office yesterday?*

4. The past participle is either the last or the penultimate word in the clause. If the word order is normal or inverted, the past participle will be the final word of the clause:

Der Mann mit dem schwarzen Bart *hat* sein Brot *gegessen*.	*The man with the black beard **ate** his bread.*
Bist* du gestern in die Stadt *gegangen?	***Did** you **go** to town yesterday?*

If the word order is dependent, **haben** or **sein** will be the final element in the clause, and the past participle will immediately precede the auxiliary:

Ich weiß, wie lange du *geschlafen hast*.	*I know how long you **slept**.*
Daß ihr groß *geworden seid*, sehe ich schon.	*I can see that you **have gotten** tall.*

A past participle may, however, be the first word of a clause for purposes of emphasis:

Er *hat* das nicht *gesagt*.	*He **did** not **say** that.*
***Gesagt hat* er das nicht, aber *gedacht hat* er es bestimmt.**	*He **did** not **say** that, but he certainly **thought** it.*

5. Occasionally the past participle of the inseparable prefix verb will be the same as a form from another tense:

Past:	
Wir waren traurig, als wir unsere Bücher *verloren*.	We were sad when we ***lost*** our books.
Present perfect:	
Wir *haben* unsere Bücher *verloren*.	We ***lost*** (***have lost***) *our books.*
Present:	
Günter, der die Frage *beantwortet*, ist mein Freund.	*Günter, who **is answering** the question, is my friend.*
Present perfect:	
Hat* Heidi die Frage *beantwortet?	***Has** Heidi **answered** the question?*

6. The inseparable prefix **ge-** may be mistaken for the **ge-** of the past participle if word order is forgotten or the auxiliary is overlooked:

Present:

Ich weiß, daß das Buch mir *gehört.*	*I know that the book* ***belongs*** *to me.*

Present perfect:

Er *hat* das Auto auf der Straße *gehört.*	*He* ***heard*** *the car in the street.*

7. The past participle of a verb ending in **-ieren** may be mistaken for a similar present-tense form. The presence or absence of an auxiliary will indicate the tense:

Was *hat* er auf der Universität *studiert?*	*What* ***did*** *he* ***study*** *at the university?*
Wissen Sie, ob er Deutsch *studiert?*	*Do you know if he* ***is studying*** *German?*

The purpose of these frames is to help you to recognize the present perfect tense as well as to introduce you to the reading passage.

	1. Im letzten Kapitel **haben** wir **gelesen,** was Weber über Bismarck sagte. (*read/have read*)
1. In the last chapter we *read* what Weber said about Bismarck.	**2.** Sie **haben** sicher einmal von Oswald Spengler **gehört.** (*have heard/heard*)
2. You *have* certainly *heard* of Oswald Spengler at some time or another.	**3.** Oswald Spengler **hat** von 1880 bis 1936 **gelebt.** (*has lived/lived*)
3. Oswald Spengler *lived* from 1880 to 1936.	**4.** **das Land** = *country* **der Morgen** = *morning* **das Morgenland** = *the orient, the East* **der Abend** = *evening* **das Abendland** = ________
4. *the occident, the West*	**5.** **der Untergang** = *(down) fall, decline* Das größte Werk, das er **geschrieben hat,** heißt *Der Untergang des Abendlandes.* (*wrote/has written*)
5. The major (greatest) work that he *wrote* is called *The Decline of the West.*	**6.** **behaupten** = *to claim* Was **behauptet** Spengler in diesem Werk?
6. What *does* Spengler *claim* in this work?	**7.** **erleben** = *to experience* Unsere westliche Zivilisation erlebt jetzt einen Untergang.
7. Our western civilization is now experiencing a decline.	**8.** In diesem Werk **hat** Spengler **behauptet,** daß unsere westliche Zivilisation jetzt den Untergang erlebt. (*claimed/claims*)

8. In this work Spengler *claimed* that our western civilization is now experiencing its decline.	**9.** **erreichen** = *to reach* Unsere Kultur, unsere Zivilisation **hat** jetzt ihren Winter **erreicht.** (*reaches/has reached*)
9. Our culture, our civilization *has* now *reached* its winter.	**10.** **erscheinen** = *to appear* *Der Untergang des Abendlandes* **ist** zwischen den Jahren 1918 und 1922 **erschienen.**
10. *The Decline of the West appeared* between 1918 and 1922.	**11.** Spengler **hat** andere Bücher **geschrieben.**
11. Spengler *wrote* other books.	**12.** **die Entscheidung** = *decision* Eins heißt *Jahre der Entscheidung.*
12. One is called *Years of Decision.*	**13.** **der Gedanke** = *thought* Hier sind einige Gedanken **daraus.** (*of that/from it*)
13. Here are some ideas *from it.*	**14.** **das Tier** = *animal* **rauben** = *to rob* **das Raubtier** = ___________
14. *beast of prey, predator*	**15.** **der Abschnitt** = *section* In einem Abschnitt seines Buches behauptet Spengler, daß der Mensch ein Raubtier ist.
15. In one section of his book Spengler claims that man is a predator.	**16.** **ob** = *if* Er fragt nicht, ob der Mensch immer ein Raubtier **gewesen ist.**
16. He does not ask if man *has* always *been* a predator.	**17.** **geschehen** = *to happen* Wenn ein Unglück **geschieht,** sagt Spengler . . .
17. Whenever an accident *happens*, says Spengler . . .	**18.** **die Tugend** = *virtue* **der Tugendbold** = *paragon of virtue* (ironical) . . . so laufen alle Tugendbolde und Sozialethiker auf der Straße zusammen.
18. . . . then all the paragons of virtue and social moralists congregate in the street.	**19.** **genießen** = *to enjoy* Sie **genießen** etwas auf der Straße, meint Spengler.
19. Spengler feels that they *enjoy* something in the street.	**20.** Die Tugendbolde und Sozialethiker genießen **dasselbe** auf der Straße . . . (*the same thing/themselves*)
20. The paragons of virtue and the social moralists enjoy *the same thing* in the street . . .	**21.** **das Blatt** = *leaf, leaflet, paper, magazine* . . . was sie im Film und in den illustrierten Blättern **genossen haben.**

21. . . . that they *have enjoyed* in the movies and in the magazines.	**22.** **zusammen** = *together* **laufen** = *to run* **zusammenlaufen** = *to congregate, to gather* Warum laufen sie auf der Straße zusammen, wenn ein Unglück **geschehen ist?**
22. Why do they congregate in the street when an accident *has happened*?	**23.** **erregen** = *to excite, stir up, to stimulate* Weiß man, was ihre Nerven **erregt hat?**
23. Do we know what *stirred* them up (lit.: *excited* their nerves)?	**24.** Spengler will sagen, daß diese Tugendbolde und Sozialethiker nur Raubtiere sind . . .
24. Spengler wishes to say that these paragons of virtue and social moralists are simply predators . . .	**25.** **sich erregen** = *are stirred up* . . . und nur **darum** erregen sich ihre Nerven. (*around that/for that reason*)
25. . . . and it is only *for that reason* that they are stirred up.	**26.** **beleidigen** = *to offend, to insult* Spengler fragt: Wenn ich den Menschen ein Raubtier nenne, wen **habe** ich damit **beleidigt,** den Menschen—oder das Tier?
26. Spengler asks: When I call man a predator whom *have* I *insulted* by doing so, human beings or animals?	**27.** **die Schlacht** = *battle* **die Schlächterei** = *slaughter* Er meint, daß die Tugendbolde und Sozialethiker nichts gegen die Schlächtereien der Bolschewisten **gehabt haben.**
27. He feels that the paragons of virtue and the social moralists *had* nothing against the Bolshevist slaughters.	**28.** **die Tatsache** = *fact* **Ur-** (prefix) = *original, primeval, basic* **die Urtatsache** = ____________________
28. *original fact, basic fact*	**29.** **kämpfen** = *to fight, to struggle, to battle* Er behauptet auch, daß der **Kampf** die Urtatsache des Lebens ist.
29. He also claims that *struggle* is the original fact of life.	**30.** **die Lust** = *joy, pleasure* Er sagt, daß der Pazifist die Lust daran nicht ganz **ausgerottet hat.** (*has rotted out/has extinguished*)
30. He says that the pacifist *has* not quite *extinguished* his enjoyment of it.	**31.** **gelingen** = *to succeed* Das **gelingt** den Pazifisten nicht.
31. The pacifists *do* not *succeed* (in doing that). (Note the use of the dative with the impersonal verb **gelingen**.)	**32.** **der Jammer** = *misery* **jämmerlich** = *miserable, wretched* Es gelingt dem jämmerlichsten Pazifisten nicht . . .

32. The most wretched pacifist does not succeed . . .	**33.** Es **ist** auch dem jämmerlichsten Pazifisten nicht **gelungen,** die Lust an dem Kampf in seiner Seele ganz auszurotten, sagt Spengler.
33. Spengler says, not even the most wretched pacifist *has succeeded* in completely extinguishing the enjoyment of fighting from his soul.	

PROGRESS TEST

Give the meaning of the italicized verbs.

1. Weiß Helene, wie das Buch heißt, das Spengler *geschrieben hat?*
(a) has scribbled (b) wrote (c) writes (d) is writing

2. Das Werk *ist* im Jahre 1922 *erschienen.*
(a) had appeared (b) is shining (c) appeared (d) is appearing

3. Wissen Sie, wie lange sie schon auf der Straße *laufen?*
(a) have laughed (b) have been running (c) are running (d) are laughing

4. Wem *hat* Klaus das Buch *gebracht?*
(a) did bring (b) has broken (c) needed (d) did break

5. Vor wie langer Zeit *ist* Spengler *gestorben?*
(a) is dying (b) did die (c) is dead (d) has died

Answer key: **1.** (b); **2.** (c); **3.** (b); **4.** (a); **5.** (b).

47. *The past perfect tense—recognition and meaning*

1. The past perfect tense is formed by the past tense of **haben** or **sein** plus the past participle. As in English, it expresses an action or describes a situation which took place before another given or implied action or situation in the past:

Ich *hatte* fünf Jahre lang *studiert*, als . . .	*I* ***had attended*** *the university for five years when . . .*
Sie *hatte* schon lange Zigarren *geraucht*.	*She* ***had smoked*** *cigars for a long time.*
Wir *waren* noch nie in Österreich *gewesen*.	*We* ***had*** *never been in Austria.* (**noch** intensifies **nie**)
Wart* ihr aber groß *geworden!	***Had*** *you ever* ***gotten*** *tall!*
Hatten* sie es *gehabt?	***Had*** *they* ***had*** *it?*
Waren* Sie vorher mit dem Zug *gefahren?	***Had*** *you* ***traveled*** *by train before?*

2. Uses of the auxiliary and word order are the same as for the present perfect tense.

3. The German past tense used with **seit**, **schon**, **erst**, or a combination thereof is translated by the English past perfect progressive:

Er *rauchte schon seit* zwei Jahren, als er plötzlich Krebs bekam.	*He **had been smoking for** two years when he suddenly got cancer.*

These frames will help you recognize the past perfect tense.

	1. Die Tugendbolde und Sozialethiker **haben** alle anderen **gehaßt.**
1. The paragons of virtue and social moralists *hated* all others.	**2.** **der Angriff** = *attack* Die Tugendbolde und Sozialethiker **hatten** andere wegen der Angriffe **gehaßt.**
2. The paragons of virtue and social moralists *had hated* others because of the attacks.	**3.** **vermeiden** = *to avoid* Sie **hatten** selbst die Angriffe weislich **vermieden.**
3. They themselves *had* prudently *avoided* attacks.	**4.** Sie **können** es nicht **vermeiden,** ein Buch über Kriege zu lesen.
4. They *can*not *avoid* reading a book about wars.	**5.** **schwach** = *weak* Sie **waren** zu schwach **gewesen,** um ein Buch über Kriege zu lesen.
5. They *had been* too weak to read a book about wars.	**6.** **wagen** = *to dare* Sie **hatten** es nicht mehr **gewagt,** auf der Straße zusammenzulaufen.
6. They *had* no longer *dared* to congregate in the street.	**7.** Was **war** er immer wieder **geworden?**
7. What *had* he *become* over and over again?	**8.** **die Trümmer** = *fragments, ruins* Die Städte liegen in Trümmern.
8. The cities are (lie) in ruins.	**9.** **altgeworden** = *become old, ancient* Die Städte altgewordener Kulturen **waren** in Trümmer **gesunken.**
9. The cities of ancient cultures *had sunk* into ruins.	**10.** **edel** = *noble* Ist der Mensch schon immer edel **gewesen?** (*was/has been*)
10. *Has* the human being always *been* noble?	**11.** **das Geschöpf** = *creature* **Waren** die großen Raubtiere edle Geschöpfe **gewesen?**
11. *Had* the great predators *been* noble creatures?	**12.** **entrüsten** = *to provoke* **sich entrüsten** = *to become indignant* **entrüstet** = __________

12. *indignant*	**13.** Die Tugendbolde und Sozialethiker **sind entrüstet**. (*are indignant/have grown indignant*)
13. The paragons of virtue and social moralists *are indignant*.	**14.** **morden** = *to murder* Ein Lustmörder ist jemand, **der** aus sexueller Lust mordet. (*the/who*)
14. A *Lustmörder* is someone *who* murders because of sexual desire.	**15.** **hinrichten** = *to execute* Die Sozialethiker **hatten sich** immer **entrüstet**, wenn der Staat einen Lustmörder **hingerichtet hatte.**
15. The social moralists *had* always *grown indignant* whenever the state *had executed* a sex murderer.	**16.** Die Sozialethiker **waren** immer entrüstet **gewesen**, wenn der Staat einen Lustmörder **hingerichtet hatte**.
16. The social moralists *had* always *been* indignant whenever the state *had executed* a sex murderer.	**17.** **fahren** = *to drive, to travel* **erfahren** = *to experience, to find out about, to hear about* Was **haben** sie **erfahren**?
17. What *did* they *find out*?	**18.** **heimlich** = *secretly* Was **haben** sie heimlich **genossen**?
18. What *did* they secretly *enjoy*?	**19.** **gegen** = *against, toward* **der Gegner** = *opponent* Aber sie **hatten es** heimlich **genossen,** wenn sie den Mord an einem politischen Gegner erfuhren.
19. But they *had* secretly *enjoyed* it whenever they found out about the murder of a political opponent. (Lit.: to a political opponent; note the use of the dative **einem**.)	**20.** Auch dem jämmerlichsten Pazifisten **war** es nicht **gelungen**, die Lust daran in seiner Seele ganz auszurotten.
20. Even the most pitiable pacifist *had* not *succeeded* in completely extinguishing the enjoyment of it in his soul.	

PROGRESS TEST

A. Choose the correct meaning of the italicized words.

1. Der Mensch *ist* immer ein Raubtier *gewesen*.
(a) has been (b) had been (c) is becoming (d) is

2. Was *war* aus Karl *geworden?*
(a) had become (b) was becoming (c) did become (d) became

3. Seine ganze Familie *ist* nach Europa *gefahren.*
(a) is traveling (b) traveled (c) had traveled (d) is to travel

4. Alle Pazifisten *sind entrüstet.*
(a) have run away (b) are arming (c) are indignant (d) have prepared

B. And now choose the infinitive for the indicated verb.

1. Sie haben alle anderen *gehaßt.*
(a) haben (b) heißen (c) haßten (d) hassen

2. Es war ihnen nicht *gelungen.*
(a) gelangen (b) gelungen (c) gelingen (d) geliehen

3. Vor wie langer Zeit ist er *gestorben?*
(a) sterben (b) starben (c) streben (d) gestorben

4. Wann ist Spenglers Buch *erschienen?*
(a) erschienen (b) erschien (c) erscheinen (d) scheinen

Answer key: A. **1.** (a); **2.** (a); **3.** (b); **4.** (c);
B. **1.** (d); **2.** (c); **3.** (a); **4.** (c).

48. *Modals—past participle, conjugation in the present perfect and past perfect tenses*

1. The past participles of the modals are as follows:

dürfen — **gedurft**
können — **gekonnt**
mögen — **gemocht**
müssen — **gemußt**
sollen — **gesollt**
wollen — **gewollt**

Note the disappearance of the umlauts and also the change of the **-g** of **mögen** to the **-ch** of **gemocht.**

2. All modals are conjugated with the auxiliary **haben** in the present perfect and past perfect tenses. They follow the same rules of word order as previously outlined:

Er *hat* das *gedurft.*	*He **was permitted** to do that.*
Vater wußte, daß er das immer *gewollt hatte.*	*Father knew that he **had** always **wanted** (to do) that.*

3. More often modals are used with another verb, resulting in the so-called *double infinitive construction,* which will be explained in chapter 14:

Georg ***hat*** **sein Auto** ***verkaufen müssen***. — *Georg* ***had to sell*** *his car.* (Lit.: ***has had to sell*** . . .)

The purpose of these exercises is to familiarize you with the past participle forms of the modal auxiliaries. **Sollen** *and* **müssen** *are not represented as they are rarely used in this manner.*

	1. **Haben** sie das wirklich **gewollt**? (*did want/had wanted*)
1. *Did* they really *want* that?	**2.** Alle Sozialethiker **hatten** das **gewollt**. (*have wanted/had wanted*)
2. All the social moralists *had wanted* that.	**3.** Ihr **habt** es nicht mehr **gekonnt**. (*could do/had been able to do*)
3. You *could* not *do* it anymore.	**4.** Daß ihr es **gekonnt hattet**, wußte ich gar nicht. (*were able to do/had been able to do*)
4. I didn't know that you *had been able to do* that.	**5.** Er **hatte** alle Gegner des Pazifismus nicht **gemocht**, aber . . . (*has . . . liked/had . . . liked*)
5. He *had* not *liked* all the opponents of pacifism, but . . .	**6.** **Hat** er das immer noch **gemocht**? (*does like/did like*)
6. *Did* he still *like* that?	**7.** Ich **hatte** das nicht **gedurft**, aber du **hast** es doch **gedurft.**
7. I *had* not *been allowed* (to do) that, but you *were allowed to.*	

READING PREPARATION

Give the meaning of the following sentences.

	1. **zurückkehren** = *to return* Wir werden **jetzt** zu dem zurückkehren, was Spengler über Tugendbolde und Sozialethiker schrieb. (*now/never*)
1. We will *now* return to what Spengler wrote about paragons of virtue and social moralists.	**2.** Spengler **wird** es immer wieder **sagen**: Der Mensch ist ein Raubtier. (*will/become*)
2. Spengler *will say* it again and again: Man is a predator.	**3.** **gelangen** = *to reach, to attain* Aber der Sozialethiker **will** zur Macht **gelangen**.

3. But the social moralist *wants to attain* power.	**4. darüber hinaus** = *above and beyond that* Der Mensch ist ein Raubtier. Der Sozialethiker **will** darüber hinaus **gelangen**.
4. Man is a predator. The social moralist *wants to rise* above and beyond that.	**5. der Zahn** = *tooth* All die Tugendbolde und Sozialethiker haben Zähne.
5. All paragons of virtue and social moralists have teeth.	**6. ausbrechen** = *to break out* All die Tugendbolde und Sozialethiker haben **ausgebrochene** Zähne. (*broken/break out*)
6. All paragons of virtue and social moralists have *broken* teeth.	**7.** All die Tugendbolde und Sozialethiker, **die** darüber hinaus sein oder gelangen wollen . . .
7. All the paragons of virtue and social moralists *who* want to be above or get beyond that . . .	**8.** . . . sind nur Raubtiere mit **ausgebrochenen** Zähnen.
8. . . . are merely predators with *broken* teeth.	**9.** Welche Leute sind nur Raubtiere mit ausgebrochenen Zähnen?
9. What people are merely predators with broken teeth?	**10.** All die Tugendbolde und Sozialethiker, **die** darüber hinaus sein oder gelangen wollen, sind nur Raubtiere mit ausgebrochenen Zähnen.
10. All the paragons of virtue and social moralists *who* claim to be beyond that or want to rise above it are simply predators with broken teeth.	**11. ansehen** = *to look at* Seht **sie** doch an! (*she/them*)
11. Look at *them*! (**Seht . . . an!** is the imperative form of **ihr** [you].)	**12.** Warum laufen die Tugendbolde und Sozialethiker auf der Straße zusammen, wenn ein Unglück **geschehen ist**?
12. Why do the paragons of virtue and social moralists congregate on the street when an accident *has occurred*?	**13. das Geschrei** = *shouting, screams* Sie laufen auf der Straße zusammen, **um ihre Nerven** an dem Blut und Geschrei **zu erregen**.
13. They congregate in the street *in order to be excited* by the blood and the screams. (Lit.: in order to arouse/excite their nerves.)	**14.** Was werden sie tun, wenn sie auch das **nicht** mehr **wagen können**?
14. What will they do when they *cannot dare to do* that anymore?	**15. vollkommen** = *perfect* Die großen Raubtiere sind vollkommene Geschöpfe.

15. The great predators are perfect creatures.	**16.** **die Art** = *kind, sort, type* Die großen Raubtiere sind edle Geschöpfe in **vollkommenster** Art.
16. The great predators are noble creatures of the *most perfect* sort.	**17.** **schwach** = *weak* **die Schwäche** = __________
17. *weakness*	**18.** Ist der Mensch nur aus Schwäche moralisch?
18. Is the human being moral only out of weakness?	**19.** **lügen** = *to lie* **verlogen** = *lying, mendacious, false, hypocritical* **die Verlogenheit** = __________
19. *mendacity, falseness, hypocrisy*	**20.** Sind die großen Raubtiere ohne die Verlogenheit menschlicher Moral aus Schwäche?
20. Are the great predators without the hypocrisy of human morality that results from weakness?	**21.** Die Sozialethiker und Tugendbolde sind entrüstet, wenn ein Lustmörder **hingerichtet wird**. (*will exectue/is executed*)
21. The social moralists and paragons of virtue are indignant when a sex murderer *is executed*.	**22.** **Was für ein** politischer Gegner ist er?
22. *What kind of* a political opponent is he?	**23.** Sind sie entrüstet, wenn sie den Mord an einem politischen Gegner erfahren?
23. Are they indignant when they hear about the murder of a political opponent?	**24.** Sie sind nicht entrüstet, sie genießen es heimlich, wenn sie den Mord an einem politischen Gegner erfahren.
24. They are not indignant, they secretly enjoy it when they hear about the murder of a political opponent.	**25.** **mögen** = *to like* **möchten** = *would like* Was möchte theoretisch auch der jämmerlichste Pazifist?
25. What would even the most pitiable pacifist theoretically like?	**26.** **der Kampf** = *battle* **kämpfen** = *to fight* **bekämpfen** = __________
26. *to combat, to fight against*	**27.** **vernichten** = *to annihilate, to exterminate* Möchte er alle Gegner **des** Pazifismus bekämpfen und vernichten? (*the/of*)
27. Would he like to fight against and exterminate all the opponents *of* pacifism?	**28.** **wenig** = *little* **minder** = *less* **mindest** = *least* **zum mindesten** = __________

28. *at least*	**29.** Zum mindesten möchte der Pazifist alle Gegner des Pazifismus bekämpfen und vernichten.
29. The pacifist would at least like to fight against and exterminate all the opponents of pacifism.	**30.** *Vom **Sinn** der Geschichte* (*sin/meaning*)
30. *Of the Meaning of History*	**31.** **das Ereignis** = *event* Man weiß wenig von den **Ereignissen** der Zukunft.
31. One knows little of the *events* of the future.	**32.** Deshalb kann man nur glauben.
32. Therefore one can only believe.	**33.** Man weiß wenig von der **Zukunt**. Und von der **Vergangenheit**?
33. One knows little of the *future.* And of the *past*?	**34.** **bewegen** = *to move* Was sind die **bewegenden** Mächte der Zukunft und der Vergangenheit?
34. What are the *moving* forces of the future and the past?	**35.** **so wenig . . . so sicher** = *as little as . . . nonetheless certain* **So wenig** man von den Ereignissen der Zukunft weiß, **so sicher** ist es, daß . . .
35. *As little* as one knows of the events of the future, it is *nonetheless certain* that . . .	**36.** . . . die bewegenden Mächte der Zukunft keine anderen sind **als die** der Vergangenheit. (*as the/than those*)
36. . . . the moving forces of the future are none other *than those* of the past.	**37.** **besitzen** = *to possess, to own* **der Besitz** = *possession* Die bewegenden Mächte sind **die**: der Wille des Stärkeren, die gesunden Instinkte, die Rasse, der Wille zu Besitz. (*the/these*)
37. The moving forces are *these:* the will of the stronger individual, healthy instincts, race, the will to possession (to possess).	**38.** **wirken** = *to work, to effect, to act* **die Wirkung** = *action, effect* **wirkungslos** = __________
38. *ineffectual, futile*	**39.** **darüber hin** = *above them* **schwanken** = *to sway, to waver* Und darüber hin **schwanken** wirkungslos die Träume . . .
39. And above them [i.e., above these moving forces] dreams *waver* ineffectually . . .	**40.** Und darüber hin schwanken wirkungslos die Träume, die immer Träume bleiben **werden**. (*will/become*)

40. And above them waver ineffectually those dreams which *will* always remain dreams.	**41.** Und darüber hin schwanken wirkungslos die Träume, die immer Träume bleiben **werden**: Gerechtigkeit, Glück, Friede.
41. And above them waver ineffectually those dreams which *will* always remain dreams: justice, happiness, peace.	**42.** *Vom Schicksal*
42. *Of Fate*	**43.** Nur wenige Genies **haben** die Welt **bewegt**.
43. Only a few geniuses *have moved* the world. (Note: Spengler uses **Genies** as the plural of **Genie** [genius]. The standard plural is **Genien**.)	**44.** **der Zufall** = *fate, chance* Der Zufall **hat** sie an ihren Platz **gestellt**.
44. Chance *assigned* them their place in the world. (Chance *put* them into their place.)	**45.** **gering** = *small, low, unimportant* Meist waren es viel **geringere** Personen, die der Zufall an ihren Platz stellte.
45. Usually it was much *less important* people whom chance assigned to their place.	**46.** *Von der* ***Seele*** *des Menschen* (*soul/seal*)
46. *Of the Soul of Man*	**47.** **zweifeln an** + dative = *to doubt* Die Seele des Menschen zweifelt an allem.
47. The soul of man doubts everything.	**48.** Der **Jüngling** weiß alles. (*teacher/youth*)
48. The *youth* knows everything.	**49.** **der Greis** = *der alte Mann* Der Greis weiß nichts.
49. The old man knows nothing.	**50.** **wissen** = *to know* **die Gewißheit** = *certainty* **Erst** der Greis kommt zur Gewißheit, daß er nichts weiß. (*first/only*)
50. It is *only* the old man who comes to the certainty that he knows nothing.	**51.** **die Ehe** = *marriage* *Von der Ehe*
51. *Of Marriage*	**52.** Dieser Mann und diese Frau **haben** eine glückliche Ehe **gehabt**.
52. This man and this woman *have had* a happy marriage.	**53.** **wünschen** = *to wish, to desire, to long for* Was ist eine Ehe, in der Kinder nicht **gewünscht** oder nicht **vermißt werden**?

53. What is a marriage in which children *are* not *desired* or *missed*?	**54.** **der Junggeselle** = *bachelor* **Sie** ist ein Konkubinat eines männlichen und weiblichen Junggesellen. (*she/it*)
54. *It* is a concubinage of a male and a female bachelor.	**55.** **das Ziel** = *goal* *Von dem Ziel*
55. *Of Goals*	**56.** Ein Ziel ist ein Ende.
56. A goal is an end.	**57.** **die Leere** = *emptiness* **der Schöpfer** = *creator, Creator (God)* Der **schöpferische** Mensch kennt und fürchtet die Leere.
57. The *creative* individual knows and fears emptiness.	**58.** **vollenden** = *to complete* **die Vollendung** = *completion* Die Leere **folgt** auf die Vollendung eines Werkes.
58. Emptiness *follows* the completion of a work.	**59.** **deshalb** = *therefore* **Soll** deshalb jeder wirklich schöpferische Mensch **fürchten**, ein Ziel zu haben?
59. *Should* every really creative person therefore *be afraid* of having (to have) a goal?	

PROGRESS TEST

Choose the correct meaning. Before continuing, review the points you miss.

1. Sie laufen auf der Straße zusammen, *denn sie sind zu schwach,* Raubtiere mit ausgebrochenen Zähnen zu sehen.
(a) For they are too weak.
(b) Because they want to watch.
(c) Then they are to attack.
(d) Than those that are clean.

2. Denn die großen Tiere sind edle Geschöpfe *in vollkommenster Art* und ohne die Verlogenheit menschlicher Moral aus Schwäche.
(a) Perfectly artful.
(b) In a welcome form.
(c) In the most popular manner.
(d) Of the most perfect sort.

3. Die jämmerlichsten Pazifisten haben nichts gegen die Schlächtereien der Bolschewisten, denn *sie genießen es heimlich,* wenn sie den Mord an einem politischen Gegner erfahren.
(a) They soon learn of it.
(b) They reject it openly.
(c) They secretly enjoy it.
(d) They find it intolerable.

4. Man beleidigt den Menschen, wenn man die Raubtiere Menschen nennt.
(a) To call man an animal is an insult to all.
(b) To call predators humans is an insult to the animal.
(c) To call predators humans is an insult to humans.
(d) To call animals predators is an insult to them.

5. Die Urtatsache des Lebens ist, daß man die Angriffe anderer weislich vermeiden soll.
(a) The life of a hermit is what one should always avoid.
(b) It is a wise person who avoids the attacks of others.
(c) The basic fact of life is that one should defend oneself wisely against another's fury.
(d) The attacks of others should not deter one from seeking the basic facts about life.

6. Die bewegenden Mächte der Zukunft sind genau wie die der Vergangenheit.
(a) Past and future governments will be the same.
(b) The past and the present determine the future.
(c) The moving forces of the past are the same as those of the present.
(d) The future and the past are governed by the same powers.

Answer key: **1.** (a); **2.** (d); **3.** (c); **4.** (c); **5.** (b); **6.** (d).

From *Jahre der Entscheidung. Erster Teil. Deutschland und die weltgeschichtliche Entwicklung.* C. H. Beck'sche Verlagsbuchhandlung, München, 1933.

Oswald Spengler: Jahre der Entscheidung

Der Mensch ist ein Raubtier. Ich werde es immer wieder sagen. All die Tugendbolde und Sozialethiker, die darüber hinaus sein oder gelangen wollen, sind nur Raubtiere mit ausgebrochenen Zähnen, die andere wegen der Angriffe hassen, die sie selbst weislich vermeiden. Seht sie doch an: sie sind zu schwach, um ein Buch über Kriege zu lesen, aber sie laufen auf der Straße zusammen, wenn ein Unglück geschehen ist, um ihre Nerven an dem Blut und Geschrei zu erregen, und wenn sie auch das nicht mehr wagen können, dann genießen sie es im Film und in den illustrierten Blättern. Wenn ich den Menschen ein Raubtier nenne, wen habe ich damit beleidigt, den Menschen—oder das Tier? Denn die großen Raubtiere sind edle Geschöpfe vollkommenster Art und ohne die Verlogenheit menschlicher Moral aus Schwäche.

Sie schreien: Nie wieder Krieg!—aber sie wollen den Klassenkampf. Sie sind entrüstet, wenn ein Lustmörder hingerichtet wird, aber sie genießen es heimlich, wenn sie den Mord an einem politischen Gegner erfahren. Was haben sie je gegen die Schlächtereien der Bolschewisten einzuwenden gehabt? Nein, der Kampf ist die Urtatsache des Lebens, ist das Leben selbst, und es gelingt auch dem jämmerlichsten Pazifisten nicht, die Lust daran in seiner Seele ganz auszurotten. Zum mindesten theoretisch möchte er alle Gegner des Pazifismus bekämpfen und vernichten.

From *Gedanken*. C. H. Beck'sche Verlagsbuchhandlung,
München, 1941.

Gedanken

Vom Sinn der Geschichte

So wenig man von den Ereignissen der Zukunft weiß . . . so sicher ist es, daß die bewegenden Mächte der Zukunft keine anderen sind als die der Vergangenheit: der Wille des Stärkeren, die gesunden Instinkte, die Rasse, der Wille zu Besitz und Macht. Und darüber hin schwanken wirkungslos die Träume, die immer Träume bleiben werden: Gerechtigkeit, Glück und Friede.

Vom Schicksal

Unter den weltbewegenden Personen sind nur sehr wenige Genies, und nur wenige der Genies haben die Welt bewegt: meist waren es viel geringere Personen, die der Zufall an ihren Platz stellte.

Von der Seele des Menschen

Der Jüngling weiß alles. Der Mann zweifelt an allem. Erst der Greis kommt zur Gewißheit, daß er nichts weiß.

Von der Ehe

Eine Ehe, in der Kinder nicht gewünscht oder nicht vermißt werden, ist ein Konkubinat eines männlichen und weiblichen Junggesellen.

Von dem Ziel

Ein Ziel ist ein Ende . . . Jeder wirklich schöpferische Mensch kennt und fürchtet die Leere, die auf die Vollendung eines Werkes folgt.

Chapter Fourteen

49. *Double infinitive construction*

1. The double infinitive construction consists of the infinitive of a modal or other helping verb plus an infinitive of another verb. It occurs in the present perfect, past perfect, or future tense. It occurs when another verb is dependent upon a modal in one of these tenses:

Ihr *habt* es *tun können.*	*You* **have been able to do** *it.*
Hatte* er in die Stadt *fahren dürfen?	***Had*** *he* **been allowed to drive** *to the city?*
Wer *wird* morgen *gehen müssen?*	*Who* **will have to go** *tomorrow?*

2. In the present perfect and past perfect tenses the meaning of the second infinitive is usually expressed in English by the simple past or a past participle:

Er *hat* den Film *sehen wollen.*	*He* **wanted** (**has wanted**) **to see** *the movie.*

Remember that the present perfect tense is often translated by the English past tense:

Er hat tanzen wollen.	*He* **wanted to dance**.

In this example the **hat wollen** was translated as *wanted,* to which the dependent infinitive was appended.

3. The double infinitive construction is usually the last element in the sentence, no matter what the word order:

Normal word order:

Ihr *habt* das *sagen dürfen.*	*You* **were allowed** (**have been allowed**) **to say** *that.*

Inverted word order:

Haben **sie das** ***singen können?***	***Were*** *they* ***able*** *(**have . . . been able**)* ***to sing*** *that?*

Dependent word order:

Karin weiß, daß Jörg das ***wird tun müssen.***	*Karin knows that Jörg* ***will have to do*** *that.*

4. The verb **lassen** is also commonly used in double infinitive constructions. It has the following meanings:

(a) *to let, to permit, to allow* (a second action to take place)

Blaubart ***hat*** **seine Bräute nicht** ***weglaufen lassen.***	*Bluebeard* ***did*** *not* ***let*** *his brides* ***run away****.*

(b) *to have something done, to cause, to make* (a second action to take place)

Der König ***wird*** **den Koch die Suppe** ***bringen lassen.***	*The king* ***will have*** *the cook* ***bring*** *the soup.*

(c) *to leave*

Helmut ***hatte*** **seinen Mantel bei mir** ***hängen lassen.***	*Helmut* ***had left*** *his coat* ***hanging*** *at my house.*

5. Several other verbs appear in double infinitive constructions, among which are:

brauchen	*to need*
heißen	*to order, to bid*
helfen	*to help*
hören	*to hear*
sehen	*to see*

Er ***hatte*** **nicht** ***zu gehen brauchen.***	*He* ***had*** *not* ***needed to go****.*

(Note that **brauchen** requires the use of **zu** except in colloquial German.)

Er ***hat*** **seine Sekretärin ins Büro** ***kommen heißen.***	*He* ***had*** *his secretary* ***come*** *into his office.*
Sie ***hatte*** **ihn** ***kommen hören.***	*She* ***had heard*** *him* ***come*** (or ***coming***).
Hat **der Alte die fliegende Untertasse wirklich** ***vorbeisausen sehen?***	***Did*** *the old man really* ***see*** *the flying saucer* ***whiz by****?*
Der Vater ***wird*** **seinem Sohn** ***radfahren helfen.***	*The father* ***will help*** *his son* ***to ride a bicycle.***

The purpose of the following exercises is to give you practice in distinguishing the various tenses of the double infinitive construction. Give the meaning of the underlined verbs.

	1. **die Brücke** = *bridge* Sie **hat** ihn über die Brücke **kommen sehen.**
1. She *saw* him *come* over the bridge.	2. Sie **hatte** ihn über die Brücke **kommen sehen.**
2. She *had seen* him *come* over the bridge.	3. Sie wird ihn über die Brücke **kommen sehen.**
3. She *will see* him *come* over the bridge.	4. **Hat** Hans Sauerkraut nicht mehr **essen wollen?**
4. *Did*n't Hans *want to eat* sauerkraut anymore?	5. **Hatte** er Sauerkraut nicht mehr **essen wollen?**
5. *Had*n't he *wanted to eat* sauerkraut anymore?	6. **Wird** er Sauerkraut nicht mehr **essen wollen?**
6. *Won't* he *want to eat* sauerkraut anymore?	7. **Hat** Heidi den Brief **lesen dürfen?**
7. *Was* Heidi *allowed to read* the letter?	8. **Hatte** er den Brief nicht **zu lesen brauchen?**
8. *Had* he not *needed to read* the letter?	9. **Wird** er den Brief nicht **zu lesen brauchen?**
9. *Will* he not *need to read* the letter?	10. Ich weiß, daß Bärbel **hat schwimmen können.**
10. I know that Bärbel *was able to swim.*	11. Ich weiß, daß Bernd damals **hatte schwimmen dürfen.**
11. I know that at the time Bernd *had been allowed to swim.*	12. Ich weiß, daß Katarina am Montag wird **schwimmen wollen.**
12. I know that on Monday Katarina *will want to swim.*	13. Der Polizist **hat** mich **gehen heißen.**
13. The policeman *ordered* me *to go.*	14. Ich **werde** den Soldaten nicht **gehen heißen.**
14. I *will* not *order* the soldier *to go.*	15. **der Anzug** = *suit* Er **hat** sich einen neuen Anzug **machen lassen**.
15. He *had* a new suit *made.*	16. Rudi **hat** das Mädchen **warten lassen.**
16. Rudi *made* the girl *wait* (*kept* the girl *waiting*).	17. **eilig** = *in a hurry* Sie hatte es eilig, darum **hat** sie alles **stehen- und liegenlassen.**

17. She was in a hurry; therefore she *left* everything just as it was (*standing* and *lying*). (Note that here the two infinitives are joined together.)	**18.** Sie **hat** den Jungen nicht näher **kommen lassen.**
18. She *did* not *let* the boy *come* any closer.	

PROGRESS TEST

Choose the correct meaning.

1. Was hatte sie den Mann essen sehen?
(a) What did she see eating the man?
(b) What had seen it eating the man?
(c) What had she seen the man eating?
(d) What had seen the man eating it?

2. Wird Ingeborg Franz das wirklich sagen hören?
(a) Is Ingeborg really heard saying that to Franz?
(b) Will Ingeborg truly hear Franz say that?
(c) Will Franz truly say that Ingeborg should hear that?
(d) Is Franz really heard by Ingeborg to say that?

3. Peter hatte nicht dafür zu sorgen brauchen.
(a) Peter has no need to trouble himself about that.
(b) Peter didn't care about that.
(c) Peter needed to care not only for that.
(d) Peter had not needed to take care of that.

Answer key: **1.** (c); **2.** (b); **3.** (d).

50. *Reflexive verbs and pronouns*

1. A verb is said to be reflexive when its subject and object are the same person(s) or thing(s). You have previously met a few reflexive verbs and have become aware of some of their functions. The specific meanings which may be expressed by the reflexive are:

(a) an action done by the subject to itself

Ich wasche *mich*.	*I wash* ***myself****. (I am washing.)*
Hast du *dich* gleich angezogen?	*Did you get dressed immediately? (Did you dress* ***yourself*** *immediately?)*

(b) a reciprocal action

Wir werden *uns* wiedersehen.	*We will see **one another** again.*
Sie geben *sich* die Hände.	*They shake hands.* (Lit.: *They give the hands **to one another**.*)

(c) a passive sense, often translated by the English passive

Das Problem *hat sich gelöst.*	*The problem **was solved**.*
Das Buch *liest sich* leicht.	*The book **is** easily **read**.*

Note that the reflexive pronoun may often be omitted in translation.

2. **Sich lassen** plus infinitive has the passive meaning *can be* plus past participle:

Es *läßt sich* nicht *machen.*	*It **can**not **be done**.*
Das Buch *ließ sich* nicht gleich *finden.*	*The book **could** not **be found** immediately.*

3. The reflexive pronoun can also be used in an infinitival clause to refer to a preceding object:

Er rät mir, *mich* zu beeilen.	*He is advising me to hurry up.*
Ich bat ihn, *sich* daran zu erinnern.	*I asked him to remember it.*

4. German uses the personal pronouns as reflexives in the first and second person singular and plural. The third person form as well as that of the formal **Sie** is **sich.** The genitive forms will be covered later:

	Singular		**Plural**	
Dative	**mir**	*myself*	**uns**	*ourselves*
Accusative	**mich**		**uns**	
Dative	**dir**	*yourself*	**euch**	*yourselves*
Accusative	**dich**		**euch**	
Dative	**sich**	*himself, herself, itself, oneself*	**uns**	*themselves, each other, one another*
Accusative	**sich**		**uns**	

	Formal	
Dative	**sich**	*yourself, yourselves*
Accusative	**sich**	

5. Occasionally the addition of the reflexive pronoun changes the meaning of a verb:

denken	*to think*
sich denken (dative)	*to imagine*
erinnern	*to remind*
sich erinnern	*to remember*
setzen	*to set* (something)
sich setzen	*to sit down*

6. The reciprocal pronoun **einander** is translated *one another* or *each other:*

Wir sehen *einander* später. — *We will see* ***each other*** *later.*

Give the meanings of the underlined reflexive verbs and pronouns.

	1. **sich beugen** = *to bend, to bow* Der Einzelne muß **sich** der Zukunft gegenüber **beugen.**
1. The individual must *bow* to the future.	**2.** **sich unterhalten** = *to talk, to discuss* Wir **haben uns** über dieses und jenes **unterhalten.**
2. We *talked* about this and that.	**3.** Das **machte sich** leicht.
3. That *was* easy.	**4.** Das Lied **läßt sich** nicht gleich **singen.**
4. The song *cannot be sung* immediately.	**5.** **Setzen Sie sich hin!**
5. *Sit down.*	**6.** **der Wald** = *forest, woods* **Sahen** sie **sich** im Wald?
6. *Did* they *see each other* in the woods?	**7.** Die Lösung dieses Problems **wird sich** nicht gleich **finden.**
7. The solution of this problem *will* not *be found* immediately.	**8.** **durchsetzen** = *to enforce* Dieses Gesetz **wird sich** einfach nicht **durchsetzen lassen.**
8. This law *will* simply not *be able to be enforced.*	**9.** Haben sie **einander** sehen dürfen?
9. Were they allowed to see *each other?*	**10.** Wir werden **einander** wohl wiedersehen, nicht wahr?
10. We will see *each other* again, won't we? ("isn't that true?")	

51. *The intensive pronouns* selbst *and* selber

1. The intensive pronouns **selbst** and **selber** are often used with reflexive pronouns to emphasize their meanings. When they follow immediately after a noun or personal pronoun they are translated:

Er wäscht sich *selbst* (*selber*).	*He washes* ***himself****.*
Er *selbst* (*selber*) fliegt nach Deutschland.	*He* ***himself*** *will fly to Germany.*
Sie ist die Güte *selbst*.	*She is goodness* ***itself****.*

2. When **selbst** precedes the object, it is translated *even:*

Selbst **Einstein hatte seine Fehler.**	***Even*** *Einstein had his weaknesses.*
Selbst **er konnte das nicht erklären.**	***Even*** *he could not explain that.*

Select the correct answer or else give the meaning of the indicated words.

	1. Wir haben **uns selber** nicht mehr daran erinnern können. (*ourselves/themselves*)
1. We *ourselves* were not able to remember it.	2. Sie **selber** hat dem Mann helfen wollen. (*herself/themselves*)
2. She *herself* wanted to help the man.	3. Er hat **sich selbst** ausziehen sollen. (*itself/himself*)
3. He was supposed to get undressed by *himself.*	4. **Selbst** er interessiert sich dafür. (*himself/even*)
4. *Even* he is interested in it.	5. Könnt ihr **euch selbst** hinlegen? (*herself/yourselves*)
5. Can you lie down by *yourselves?*	6. Schämst du **dich selber** nicht? (*yourself/yourselves*)
6. Aren't you ashamed of *yourself*?	7. **Selbst** ihr habt euch schämen müssen. (*yourselves/even*)
7. *Even* you had to be ashamed.	8. Sie freuen **sich selbst** über die Nachricht. (*herself/themselves*)
8. They *themselves* are happy about the news.	

PROGRESS TEST

Choose the correct meaning of the indicated words.

1. Schämt ihr **euch** darüber nicht!
   (a) their (b) his (c) your (d) none
2. Das läßt **sich** nicht mehr machen.
   (a) himself (b) yourself (c) herself (d) none
3. **Selbst** der Mensch ist ein Raubtier.
   (a) even (b) himself (c) itself (d) none
4. Wolfgang **setzte sich hin.**
   (a) set it down (b) is sitting down (c) sat down (d) none
5. Ich **erinnerte mich** an Liese.
   (a) remembered (b) reminded (c) reminded myself (d) none
6. Wir waschen **einander** die Hände.
   (a) our own (b) another's (c) one another's (d) none
7. Das Kind will **sich selber** waschen.
   (a) itself (b) yourself (c) themselves (d) none

Answer key: **1.** (d); **2.** (d); **3.** (a); **4.** (c); **5.** (a); **6.** (c); **7.** (a).

52. *Special uses of the dative*

1. Certain verbs take only the dative case where one might expect the accusative.

Bitte, *helfen* Sie mir!	*Please, **help** me!*
Helga *dankte* ihm dafür.	*Helga **thanked** him for it.*
Er *antwortete* dem jungen Mann.	*He **answered** the young man.*

2. Certain adjectives call for the dative case and generally follow the word they govern:

Meine Schwester ist mir *böse*.	*My sister is **mad** at me.*
Ich blieb ihm *treu*.	*I remained **true** to him.*
Das Buch ist mir zu *schwer*.	*The book is too **difficult** for me.*

Choose the correct answer, or give the meaning of the following.

	1. Der Polizist folgte **dem Dieb.** (*dative singular/accusative singular*)
1. dative singular: **folgen** requires a dative object. The policeman followed *the thief.*	**2.** **angenehm** = *pleasing, pleasant* Es ist **ihm** angenehm, die deutsche Sprache zu hören. (*for him/to him*)
2. It pleases *him* (it is pleasing *to him*) to hear the German language.	**3.** **der Inhalt** = *contents* **der Gedicht** = *poem* Jetzt **besprechen** wir den Inhalt eines Gedichtes von Erich Kästner.
3. Now we *will discuss* the contents of a poem by Erich Kästner. (Lit.: *are discussing*)	**4.** **der Gedanke** = *thought* **Machen** Sie **sich** nachher Ihre eigenen Gedanken darüber.
4. Draw your own conclusions (*make to yourself* your own thoughts) about it afterwards.	**5.** **betrachten** = *to look at* Der **Dichter** Erich Kästner betrachtet das Führerproblem genetisch.
5. The poet Erich Kästner looks at the "leader problem" genetically.	**6.** Gott **schuf** die Welt in sechs Tagen.
6. God *created* the world in six days.	**7.** **fehlen** = *to lack* Am ersten Wochenende meinte Gott, **der Welt** fehlte nichts. (*nominative/dative*)
7. dative: **fehlen** requires a dative object. On the first weekend, God thought the world lacked nothing (nothing was lacking *to the world*).	**8.** **reiben** = *to rub* Da **rieb** er **sich** die Hände. (*present/past*)
8. past Then he *rubbed* his hands together.	**9.** **sich vergnügen** = *to enjoy oneself* **vergnügt** = *pleased* Gott war vergnügt, als er die Welt **besah.** (*inspected/had inspected*)
9. God was pleased when he *inspected* the world.	**10.** **gefallen** = *to please* Die Welt, wie er sie schuf, gefiel **ihm** sehr gut. (**Ihm** tells that **gefallen** takes a ________ object.)
10. dative The world, as he created it, pleased *him* very well.	**11.** Er rieb sich vergnügt die Hände. Er war **stolz darauf**. (*proud of it/unhappy with it*)

11. Pleased, he rubbed his hands together. He was *proud of it.*	**12.** **der Mut** = *courage* **der Übermut** = *pride, excessive pride* Hatte Gott eine **Art** von Übermut, nachdem er die Welt schuf? (*art/kind*)
12. Did God have a *kind* of excessive pride after he created the world?	**13.** Eine Art von Übermut **packte** ihn. (*packed/seized*)
13. A sort of excessive pride *seized* him.	**14.** **die Liebe** = *love* **lieb** = *lovable, dear* Die Welt war **ihm** sehr lieb, und er blickte stolz darauf. (**Lieb** appears to govern the _______ case.)
14. dative The world was very dear *to him,* and he looked at it with pride.	**15.** Was sah er denn **überhaupt**? (*overhead/anyway*)
15. What did he see *anyway*? (**Denn** here serves as an intensifier.)	**16.** **die Tuberkulose** = *tuberculosis* **die Tuberkel** (pl. **Tuberkeln**) = *tubercle* (small granular tumor formed in the lungs or other organs in consumption) Er sah Tuberkeln, Standard Oil und **Waffen.** (*weapons/waffles*)
16. He saw tuberculosis (tubercles), Standard Oil, and *weapons.*	**17.** **schwer** = *hard, difficult* **die Beschwerde** = *complaint* (also: *hardship*) Was **aber** jetzt aus Deutschland kam, war eine Beschwerde. (*but/however*)
17. What now came out of Germany, *however,* was a complaint.	**18.** Es fehlte **den Deutschen** etwas. (*masculine accusative/dative plural*)
18. dative plural The Germans lacked something (something was lacking *to the Germans*).	**19.** **schaffen** = *to create, to provide* **erschaffen** = *to create* Die Beschwerde lautete so: „Du hast vergessen, uns einen Führer zu erschaffen."
19. The complaint ran thus: "You forgot to create a leader for us."	**20.** **versäumen** = *to neglect* Gott versäumte, **ihnen** einen Führer zu erschaffen.
20. God neglected to create a leader *for them.*	**21.** **bestürzen** = *to dismay* **bestürzt =** _________
21. *dismayed* (past participle)	**22.** Gott war bestürzt, als er hörte, daß er versäumt hatte, **den Deutschen** einen Führer zu erschaffen.

22. God was dismayed when he heard that he had forgotten to create a leader *for the Germans.*	**23.** **halt** = *just* (dialect) Er schrieb **ihnen** zurück: „Mein liebes deutsches Volk, es muß halt ohne Führer gehen.“
23. He wrote back *to them:* “My dear German people, you will just have to do without a leader.”	**24.** **mit Ohne** = *without a leader* Nun standen die Deutschen mit Ohne da. (**mit Ohne** [lit.: *with without*] is a humorous manipulation of normal German; **mit nichts** [lit.: *with nothing*])
24. Now the Germans stood there without a leader.	**25.** **der Freund** = *friend* **freundlich** = *friendly, kind* **freundlichst** = ________
25. *most friendly, most kindly*	**26.** **überlassen** = *to leave to, to relinquish to* Die Deutschen waren **der Weltgeschichte** freundlichst überlassen. (*nominative/dative*)
26. dative God was so kind as to leave the Germans *to world history*. (Lit.: The Germans were most kindly left *to world history.*)	**27.** Nun **standen** sie mit Ohne da, der Weltgeschichte freundlichst überlassen. (*stand/stood*)
27. There they now *stood* leaderless; God had been so kind as to leave them at the mercy of world history (most kindly left to world history).	**28.** **fassen** = *to grasp, to comprehend* Das kann man **überhaupt nicht** fassen!
28. That is *impossible* to comprehend!	**29.** **geschehen** = *to happen* Was seitdem **geschah**, ist nicht zu fassen.
29. What *has happened* since then is incomprehensible (is not to be grasped).	**30.** **weisen** = *to show* **hinweisen** = *to point to, to point out* **der Hinweis** = ________
30. *reference, hint*	**31.** Können Sie mir einen Hinweis geben?
31. Can you give me a hint?	**32.** Das ist **aber** ein wertvoller Hinweis!
32. That is *really* a valuable reference!	**33.** Alles, was seitdem geschah, ist ohne diesen Hinweis nicht zu fassen.
33. Everything that has happened since then is incomprehensible without this reference.	**34.** Grüß Gott! Viel Glück!
34. Good day! Best of luck!	

READING PREPARATION

Select the correct answer or else give the meaning of the sentence. This section is to prepare you for the reading selection.

	1. **wohl** = *probably* (used as an intensifier) Sie alle kennen wohl den Namen Adolf Hitler.
1. You probably all know the name Adolf Hitler.	**2.** **der Herr** = *gentleman, lord, master* **herrschen** = *to rule* Er ist nur einer von denen, die über Deutschland **geherrscht haben**.
2. He is only one of those who *have ruled* Germany.	**3.** **hervorbringen** = *to produce, to bring forth* Deutschland hat viele verschiedene **Führer** hervorgebracht. (*singular/plural*)
3. plural Germany has produced many different *leaders.*	**4.** Aber **keiner** war wie Hitler, und wahrscheinlich wird es **keinen mehr** wie ihn geben. (*none/no/not a/not another*)
4. But *none* of them was like Hitler, and there probably will *not* be *another* one like him.	**5.** Wir werden es **wenigstens** hoffen.
5. We *at least* hope so. (Or: Let us *at least* hope so.)	**6.** Alan Bullock, der eine Biographie über Hitler schrieb, **hat** Hitler den größten Demagogen der Weltgeschichte **genannt.** (*has called/had called*)
6. Alan Bullock, who wrote a biography about Hitler, *has called* Hitler the greatest demagogue in world history.	**7.** **der Auszug** = *excerpt* In diesem Kapitel werden wir einen Auszug aus Hitlers *Mein Kampf* lesen.
7. In this chapter we will read an excerpt from Hitler's *Mein Kampf.*	**8.** **mischen** = *to mix* **die Mischung =** *mixture* **die Rasse =** *race* **die Rassenmischung =** ________
8. *racial mixture, miscegenation*	**9.** **zunächst** = *first of all* Zunächst werden Sie von **den Gefahren** der Rassenmischung lesen. (singular/plural)
9. plural First of all, you will read about *the dangers* of miscegenation.	**10.** **das Volk** = *people, nation* **völkisch** = _______

10. *national, having to do with the people, proceeding from the people* (The Nazi use of the word implied "racial").	**11.** Der nächste Auszug **handelt** von dem völkischen Staat und der Rassenhygiene. (*handles/deals*)
11. The next excerpt *deals* with the national state and with eugenics.	**12.** **das heißt** = *that is* Das heißt, wer darf und wer soll Kinder haben, und **welche** Rolle spielt der Staat dabei? (*that/what*)
12. That is, who may and who should have children, and *what* role does the state play in this?	**13.** **der Mensch** = *man* **das Recht** = *right, justice, law* **das Menschenrecht** = ________
13. *human rights, human law*	**14.** **verletzen** = *to injure, to violate* Wir **werden** das heilige Menschenrecht nie **verletzen.**
14. We *will* never *violate* sacred human rights.	**15.** Wir **haben** das heilige Menschenrecht nicht **verletzen können.**
15. We *have* not *been able to violate* sacred human rights.	**16.** Wir **hatten** das heiligste Menschenrecht nicht zu **verletzen brauchen.**
16. We *had* not *needed to violate* the most sacred human right.	**17.** **die Verpflichtung** = *obligation, duty* Hitler **hat** auch **sagen lassen**, daß das heiligste Menschenrecht zugleich die heiligste Verpflichtung ist.
17. Hitler also *let* it *be said* that the most sacred human right is at the same time the most sacred obligation.	**18.** **erhalten** = *to preserve* (also: *to keep; to receive*) Er behauptete, daß das Blut rein **erhalten bleiben soll.**
18. He claimed that blood *is to be kept* pure.	**19.** **zeugen** = *to produce* (also: *to procreate*) Was **soll** jeder gesunde Mensch **zeugen**?
19. What is every healthy person *supposed to produce*?	**20.** **berufen** = *to call upon, to appoint* Der Staat **hat** jeden gesunden Menschen **berufen lassen** . . .
20. The state *caused* every healthy person *to be called upon* . . .	**21.** **das Ebenbild** = *image* Der Staat **hat** jeden gesunden Menschen **berufen lassen,** Ebenbilder des Herrn zu zeugen.
21. The state *had* every healthy person *called upon* to produce children in the image of God (to produce images of God).	**22.** **heißen** = *to order, to command* Der völkische Staat **hieß** alle gesunden Menschen Ebenbilder des Herrn **zeugen.**

22. The national state *ordered* all healthy people *to produce* children in the image of God.	**23.** **die Geburt** = *birth* **die Mißgeburt** = *deformed person, animal, monstrosity* Mißgeburten zwischen Mensch und Affe **soll** der Staat nicht **leben lassen.**
23. The state *is* not to *permit* monstrosities *to live* which are halfway between man and ape.	**24.** **die Rasse** = *race* **die Schande** = *defilement* (also: *disgrace, shame*) **die Rassenschande** = __________
24. *racial defilement*	**25.** **die Ehe** = *marriage* Der völkische Staat sah die Ehe **anders** als wir sie sehen.
25. The national state saw marriage *differently* than we do.	**26.** **dauernd** = *constant, continuous* **heben** = *to lift* **herausheben** = *to raise from* Der völkische Staat **wird** die Ehe aus einer dauernden Rassenschande **herausheben müssen.**
26. The national state *will have to raise* marriage above the level of a continuous racial defilement. (Or: out of a continuous racial defilement.)	**27.** Der Staat **hat** die Ehe aus dem Niveau einer dauernden Rassenschande **herauszuheben.**
27. The state *has* (the duty) *to raise* marriage above the level of a continuous racial defilement. (Or: *needs to raise*)	**28.** **Dürfen** wir Mißgeburten zwischen Mensch und Affe **leben lassen**?
28. *Ought* we *to let* monstrosities *live* which are halfway between man and ape?	**29.** **die Linie** = *the line* **in erster Linie** = *above all, first of all* Dürfen sie in erster Linie Mißgeburten leben lassen?
29. Above all, ought they to let monstrosities live?	**30.** **erreichen** = *to accomplish* Was hoffte Hitler zu erreichen?
30. What did Hitler hope to accomplish?	**31.** **bewahren** = *to preserve, to keep* **die Bewahrung** = __________
31. *preservation*	**32.** Was sollte man immer bewahren?
32. What should one always to preserve?	**33.** **das Wesen** = *nature, essence, being* Das Wesen des Menschen ist immer noch **unerklärt.** (*explained/unexplained*)
33. Man's nature is still *unexplained.*	**34.** **das Menschentum** = *mankind* Was hoffte Hitler durch die Bewahrung **des** besten Menschentums zu erreichen?

34. What did Hitler hope to accomplish by preserving the best in mankind? (Lit.: through the preservation *of the* best mankind.)	**35.** Was **erhalten** wir durch die Bewahrung des besten Menschentums?
35. What *do* we *gain* by the preserving the best in mankind?	**36.** **entwickeln** = *to develop, to unfold, to evolve* **die Entwicklung** = __________
36. *development, evolution*	**37.** Hoffte Hitler, uns eine **edlere** Entwicklung zu geben?
37. Did Hitler hope to give us a *more noble* development?	**38.** **möglich** = *possible* **die Möglichkeit** = __________
38. *possibility*	**39.** Hoffte er, uns die Möglichkeit **einer edleren** Entwicklung zu geben?
39. Did he hope to give us the possibility *of a more noble* development?	**40.** Durch die Bewahrung des besten Menschentums will Hitler die Möglichkeit einer edleren Entwicklung **dieser** Wesen geben. (*of these/to these*)
40. By preserving the best in mankind Hitler wants to make possible a more noble development *of these* beings.	**41.** Was will der völkische Staat **der Ehe** geben? (*of marriage/to marriage*)
41. What does the national state want to give *to marriage*?	**42.** **die Weihe** = *sanctification, consecration, ordination* Der Staat will der Ehe die Weihe **dieser** Institution geben. (*of this/to this*)
42. The state wants to give marriage the sanctification *of this* institution.	**43.** Die Ehe ist berufen, Ebenbilder des Herrn zu zeugen und nicht Mißgeburten zwischen Mensch und Affe.
43. Marriage is called upon to produce children who are images of God and not misbegotten crosses between man and ape.	**44.** Ein völkischer Staat wird die Ehe aus dem Niveau **einer** dauernden Rassenschande herauszuheben haben. . . . (*of a/to a*)
44. A national state will have to raise marriage above the level *of a* continuous racial defilement. . . .	**45.** . . . um **ihr** (der Ehe) die Weihe einer Institution zu geben, die berufen ist, Ebenbilder des Herrn zu zeugen. (*to her/to it*)
45. . . . in order to give *it* (marriage) the sanctification of an institution which is intended to produce images of God.	**46.** **allgemein** = *all, general, everyday* Die Rasse ist der Mittelpunkt **des allgemeinen Lebens**.

46. Race is the center *of all life.*	**47.** Der völkische Staat hat die Rasse **in den Mittelpunkt** des allgemeinen Lebens zu setzen.
47. The national state needs to put race *into the center* of everyday life.	**48.** Das Kind ist das **kostbarste** Gut eines Volkes. (*precious/most precious*)
48. The child is the *most precious* treasure of a nation.	**49.** Was ist eine Schande?
49. What is a disgrace?	**50.** Es gibt nur eine Schande: bei eigener Krankheit und eignen **Mängeln** Kinder in die Welt zu setzen. (*mangelers/defects*)
50. There is only one disgrace: being sick and having *defects* one brings children into the world.	**51.** Wie wird der Mensch **sich schänden**?
51. How will human beings *defile themselves*?	**52.** **eigen** = *own* **bei eigener, bei eigenen** = *with one's own* Man schändet sich, wenn man bei eigener Krankheit und eigenen Mängeln **dennoch** Kinder in die Welt setzt. (*nevertheless/in spite of*)
52. People defile themselves when, being sick and having defects, *nevertheless* bring children into the world.	**53.** Was ist die höchste Ehre?
53. What is the highest honor?	**54.** Darauf zu verzichten, bei eigener Krankheit und eigenen Mängeln Kinder in die Welt zu setzen.
54. Being afflicted with sickness and defects, to give up bringing children into the world.	**55.** **werfen** = *to throw* **verwerfen** = *to reject* (i.e., *to throw out*) Was müssen wir immer verwerfen?
55. What must we always reject?	**56.** **verwerflich** = *reprehensible* Was ist verwerflich?
56. What is reprehensible (i.e., to be rejected)?	**57.** **gelten** = *to be considered, to be valued* Was muß als verwerflich gelten?
57. What must be considered (to be) reprehensible?	**58.** **vorenthalten** = *to withhold* Es gilt als verwerflich, gesunde Kinder **der** Nation vorzuenthalten. (*of the/from the*)
58. It is considered reprehensible to withhold healthy children *from the* state.	**59.** Man **hat** dem Staat gesunde Kinder nicht **vorenthalten dürfen.**

59. One *was* not *allowed to withhold* healthy children from the state.	**60.** **auftreten** = *to act, to appear* Wie muß der Staat auftreten?
60. How must the state act?	**61.** **bewahren** = *to preserve* **der Wahrer** = *guardian* (*protector*) Der Staat muß **dabei** als Wahrer einer tausendjährigen Zukunft auftreten. (*with that/at the same time*)
61. *At the same time* the state must act as the guardian of a millennial (thousand-year) future.	**62.** **eigen** = *own* **suchen** = *to seek* **die Eigensucht** = *selfishness, self-centeredness* Die Eigensucht des einzelnen gilt **als nichts.**
62. The self-centeredness of the individual is considered *worthless* (*as nothing*).	**63.** **Der Zukunft gegenüber** darf der Wunsch und die Eigensucht des einzelnen als nichts gelten.
63. *With regard to the future*, the wishes and the selfishness of the individual must be considered worthless.	**64.** Der Zukunft gegenüber **erscheinen** der Wunsch und die Eigensucht des einzelnen als nichts.
64. With regard to the future, the desire and the self-centeredness of the individual *appear* to be worthless.	**65.** **beugen** = *to bend* Der Zukunft gegenüber **haben** sie **sich zu beugen.**
65. They *need to submit themselves* to the future.	**66.** **Fassen wir** jetzt **zusammen**, was Hitler schreibt.
66. *Let us* now *sum up* what Hitler writes.	**67.** Die Ehe ist berufen, Ebenbilder des Herrn zu zeugen, und nicht Mißgeburten zwischen Mensch und Affe.
67. Marriage is called upon (i.e., it is the calling of marriage) to produce children in the image of God, and not misbegotten crosses between man and ape.	**68.** Es gibt nur eine Schande: bei eigener Krankheit und eigenen Mängeln dennoch Kinder in die Welt zu setzen.
68. There is only one disgrace: being afflicted with sickness and defects and nevertheless bringing children into the world.	**69.** Gesunde Kinder darf man **aber** der Nation nicht vorenthalten.
69. One must, *however*, not withhold healthy children from the nation.	

PROGRESS TEST

Choose the closest approximation to the given sentences.

1. Die Zeugung von Mißgeburten zwischen Mensch und Affe ist die Aufgabe jedes völkischen Staates.
(a) The state should promote the production of monstrosities.
(b) Crosses between men and apes appear as monstrosities to the state.
(c) The state should do away with monstrosities which are a cross between men and apes.
(d) none

2. Gesunde Kinder der Nation vorzuenthalten, ist wie der Versuch, ein Auto zu fahren mit zu wenig Benzin.
(a) The healthy children of the nation are like a car without fuel.
(b) Not to educate healthy children of the nation is like driving a car without fuel.
(c) Withholding healthy children from the state is like trying to drive a vehicle with too little gasoline.
(d) none

3. Durch die Bewahrung des besten Menschentums wird die Möglichkeit einer edleren Entwicklung aller Wesen gegeben.
(a) One furthers the best in mankind by giving all beings a noble birthright.
(b) For the noble development of all beings one will first need to make such a dream possible.
(c) All beings need help in becoming more noble specimens of the human race.
(d) The possibility of a more noble development is given to all beings by preserving the best of mankind.

4. Dem Staat gegenüber erscheinen der Wunsch und die Eigensucht des einzelnen als nichts.
(a) There is no future when one opposes the state.
(b) The state appears to respect the wishes and desires of none other than its own people.
(c) The state does not respect the wishes and desires of the individual.
(d) The wishes and desires of the people do not oppose the state.

Answer key: **1.** (a); **2.** (c); **3.** (d); **4.** (c).

Adolf Hitler: Mein Kampf

Gefahren der Rassenmischung

Es gibt nur ein heiligstes Menschenrecht, und dieses Recht ist zugleich die heiligste Verpflichtung, nämlich: dafür zu sorgen, daß das Blut rein erhalten bleibt, um durch die Bewahrung des besten Menschentums die Möglichkeit einer edleren Entwicklung dieser Wesen zu geben.

Ein völkischer Staat wird damit in erster Linie die Ehe aus dem Niveau einer dauernden Rassenschande herauszuheben haben, um ihr die Weihe jener Institution zu geben, die berufen ist, Ebenbilder des Herrn zu zeugen und nicht Mißgeburten zwischen Mensch und Affe.

VÖLKISCHER STAAT UND RASSENHYGIENE

Er [der völkische Staat] hat die Rasse in den Mittelpunkt des allgemeinen Lebens zu setzen. Er hat für ihre Reinerhaltung zu sorgen. Er hat das Kind zum kostbarsten Gut eines Volkes zu erklären. Er muß dafür Sorge tragen, daß nur, wer gesund ist, Kinder zeugt; daß es nur eine Schande gibt: bei eigener Krankheit und eigenen Mängeln dennoch Kinder in die Welt zu setzen, doch eine höchste Ehre: darauf zu verzichten. Umgekehrt aber muß es als verwerflich gelten: gesunde Kinder der Nation vorzuenthalten. Der Staat muß dabei als Wahrer einer tausendjährigen Zukunft auftreten, der gegenüber der Wunsch und die Eigensucht des einzelnen als nichts erscheinen und sich zu beugen haben.

From *Bei Durchsicht meiner Bücher.* Atrium Verlag, Zürich.

Erich Kästner: Das Führerproblem, genetisch betrachtet

Als Gott am ersten Wochenende
die Welt besah, und siehe, sie war gut,
da rieb er sich vergnügt die Hände.
Ihn packte eine Art von Übermut.

Er blickte stolz auf seine Erde
und sah Tuberkeln, Standard Oil und Waffen.
Da kam aus Deutschland die Beschwerde:
„Du hast versäumt, uns Führer zu erschaffen!"

Gott war bestürzt. Man kann's verstehn.
„Mein liebes deutsches Volk," schrieb er zurück,
„es muß halt ohne Führer gehn.
Die Schöpfung ist vorbei. Grüß Gott. Viel Glück."

Nun standen wir mit Ohne da,
der Weltgeschichte freundlichst überlassen.
Und: Alles, was seitdem geschah,
ist ohne diesen Hinweis nicht zu fassen.

Chapter Fifteen

53. Der *words*

1. The following words are declined according to the pattern of the definite article and are therefore called **der** words:

dieser	*this*
jener	*that*
jeder (**pl.: alle**)	*each, every* (pl.: *all, everyone*)
mancher	*many a* (pl.: *some*)
solcher	*such (a), like that*
welcher	*which, what*

Be sure to distinguish between **jeder** and **jener:**

***Jeder* Mensch will so etwas tun.**	***Every*** *person wants to do something like that.*
***Jener* Mensch wird das aber nicht tun.**	***That*** *person, however, will not do that.*

2. Using **dieser** as an example, the **der** words are declined as follows:

	M	F	N	Pl
N	**dies*er***	**dies*e***	**dies*es*** (**dies**)	**dies*e***
G	**dies*es***	**dies*er***	**dies*es***	**dies*er***
D	**dies*em***	**dies*er***	**dies*em***	**dies*en***
A	**dies*en***	**dies*e***	**dies*es*** (**dies**)	**dies*e***

3. These endings identify gender, number, and case of the nouns which follow:

Dies*er* Mann und jen*e* Frau sind verheiratet.	*This man and that woman are married.*
Welch*es* Kind sahst du auf dem Tisch?	*Which child did you see on the table?*

4. These words may be used as pronouns. The endings will be the same as the **der** words:

***Welche* gehen heute?**	***Which ones** are going today?*
***Jeder* kennt das Lied.**	***Everyone** knows the song.*
***Dieser* kommt nicht.**	***This person** is not coming.*

Dieser and **jener** as pronouns are often used to express *the latter* (**dieser**) and *the former* (**jener**):

Herr Lehner hat einen Volkswagen und einen Mercedes; *jener* ist billig, *dieser* ist teuer.	*Mr. Lehner has a Volkswagen and a Mercedes; **the former** is inexpensive, the **latter** is expensive.*

The following exercises will introduce you to Albert Schweitzer as well as drill the meanings of the **der** *words.*

	1. Sicher kennen Sie alle den Namen Albert Schweitzer.
1. Surely you all know the name Albert Schweitzer.	**2.** **Manche** Menschen kennen den Namen Albert Schweitzer. (*those/some*)
2. *Some* people know the name Albert Schweitzer.	**3.** **Solch** ein Name ist der ganzen Welt bekannt. (*like that/which*)
3. A name *like that* is known to the whole world.	**4.** Jeder sollte **diesen** Mann und sein Leben kennen. (*this/those*)
4. Everyone should know *this* man and his life.	**5.** Nicht **jeder** kennt den Theologen, Musiker und Missionsarzt.
5. Not *everyone* knows the theologian, musician, and missionary doctor.	**6.** **Jener** Mensch ist der ganzen Welt bekannt. (*every/that*)
6. *That* man is known to the whole world.	**7.** **die Vorstellung** = *idea, conception* (also: *performance*) **Welche** Vorstellung hat man von ihm? (*what/whose*)
7. *What* idea does one have of him?	**8.** **Jeder,** der den Namen kennt, hat irgendeine Vorstellung von ihm. (*that person/every person*)
8. *Every person* who knows the name has some idea of him.	**9.** **Dieser** Mensch hat jahrelang als Missionsarzt gearbeitet.
9. *This* man worked for years as a missionary doctor.	**10.** **das Gebiet** = *area, field* Auf **welchen** anderen Gebieten hat er gearbeitet? (*that/what*)

10. In *what* other areas did he work?	**11.** **tätig sein** = *to be active* Er war ein Meister auf **jedem** Gebiet, auf welchem er tätig war. (*that/every*)
11. He was a master in *every* area in which he was active.	**12.** **Manche** können das nicht. (*some/which*)
12. *Some* people are unable to do that.	**13.** Im französischen Kongogebiet, **nämlich** in Lambarene, war er Missionsarzt.
13. In the French Congo, namely in Lambarene, he was a missionary doctor.	**14.** **der Urwald** = *jungle* In **jenem** Urwald arbeitete er als Missionsarzt. (*every/that*)
14. In *that* jungle he worked as a missionary doctor.	**15.** Sind **solche** Menschen wie Schweitzer sehr leicht auf der Welt zu finden? (*such/which*)
15. Are people *such* as Schweitzer very easy to find in the world?	**16.** Wieviele findet man heute in den Urwäldern?
16. How many does one find in the jungles today?	

PROGRESS TEST

Give the meaning and/or use of the italicized der *words.*

1. *Solche* Menschen wollen wir überhaupt nicht fressen!
(a) so many (b) like that (c) nominative (d) accusative

2. Dort ist ein Mann zusammen mit seiner Tante. *Diese* ist jünger als *jener.*
(a) the latter, the former (b) this, that (c) nominative, nominative (d) accusative, genitive

3. *Die Kinder mancher Mütter* sind nicht zu ertragen.
(a) some children's mothers (b) some mothers' children (c) children and mothers (d) the child of many a mother

4. *Jeder* Mensch hat seinen Vogel!
(a) that (b) every (c) nominative (d) genitive plural

5. Mit *welchem* Elefanten will Hannibal die Alpen überschreiten?
(a) which (b) whose (c) singular (d) plural (e) dative (f) accusative

Answer key: **1.** (b, d); **2.** (b, c); **3.** (b); **4.** (b, c); **5.** (a, c, e).

54. Der *as a demonstrative pronoun*

1. Der, die, das when used with nouns are definite articles and mean *the.* As demonstrative pronouns they are used to replace a noun or a personal pronoun and are then best translated *he, she, it, that, they,* or one of their objective forms:

Der **hat kein Geld.**	***He*** *has no money.*
Der **verschenkte ich mein Herz.**	*I gave* ***her*** *my heart.*

The use of the demonstrative pronoun may indicate special emphasis (like the emphasis indicated by stressed pronunciation in English), or it may, in colloquial German, be used as a substitute for a personal pronoun.

2. Der, die, das are declined as follows when used as demonstrative pronouns:

	M	F	N
N	**der** (*he, it*)	**die** (*she, it*)	**das** (*it, that*)
G	**dessen** (*his, its*)	**deren** (*hers, its*)	**dessen** (*its, of it*)
D	**dem** (*to him, him, it*)	**der** (*to her, her, it*)	**dem** (*to it, it*)
A	**den** (*him, it*)	**die** (*her, it*)	**das** (*it, that*)

Plural	
N	**die** (*they, those*)
G	**deren** (*their*) or: **derer** (*of those*)
D	**denen** (*to them, them, to those, those*)
A	**die** (*them, those*)

3. With the exception of the second genitive plural form **derer**, the demonstrative **der** has the same forms as those of the relative **der**:

Die Frau, *die* eben hier war . . .	*The woman* ***who*** *was just here . . .*
Diese Frau, *die* hat nie Geld!	*This woman,* ***she*** *never has any money!*
Der Mann, *den* Sie gesehen hatten . . .	*The man* ***whom*** *you had seen . . .*
Den **haben Sie nicht sehen können!**	*You could not have seen* ***him!***
Die Frauen, *deren* Kinder gestern hier waren . . .	*The women* ***whose*** *children were here yesterday . . .*
Er ist ein Freund *derer,* die ihm helfen.	*He is a friend* ***of those*** *who help him.*

4. Generally, the demonstratives **dessen** and **deren** are used as a substitute for the possessive adjectives **sein** (*his*) and **ihr** (*her, their*) to avoid ambiguity and are then translated *the latter:*

Jasmin, Liesl und *deren* Freund gehen ins Kino.	*Jasmin, Liesl, and* ***the latter's*** *friend are going to the movies.*
Er schickte seinen Freund und *dessen* Frau in die Kirche.	*He sent his friend and* ***the latter's*** *wife to church.*

Derer always precedes a relative clause:

Die Frauen *derer, die* nicht hier sind . . .	*The wives **of those who** are not here . . .*

5. Unlike the definite article, the demonstrative pronoun **der** does not generally modify a noun:

***Der Mann* sah mich nicht.**	***The man** did not see me.*
***Der* sah mich nicht.**	***He** did not see me.*

6. Unlike the relative pronoun, the demonstrative pronoun **der** does not affect word order:

Das Mädchen, mit *dem* du heute sprachst, ist meine Freundin.	*The girl with **whom** you spoke today is my girlfriend.*
Es war einmal ein Bauer, *der* hatte einen Sohn.	*There was once a farmer; **he** had a son.*

Respond to the following sentences by choosing the correct alternative or by giving the correct meaning.

	1. Wir werden jetzt lesen, was Schweitzer in dem Urwald erlebte.
1. We are now going to read what Schweitzer experienced in the jungle.	**2.** **berichten** = *to report, to tell* In welchem Buch, **das** er damals schrieb, berichtet Schweitzer uns davon?
2. In which book *that* he wrote at that time does Schweitzer tell us about it?	**3.** **der Erlebnisbericht** = *report of experiences* Der Erlebnisbericht, **der** damals sehr bekannt wurde . . . (*he/which*)
3. The report of his experiences, *which* became very well known at that time . . .	**4.** Der Erlebnisbericht, **den** er damals schrieb, heißt *Zwischen Wasser and Urwald.* (*that/him/it*)
4. The report of his experiences *that* he wrote at the time is called *Between Water and Jungle.*	**5.** **der Auszug** = *excerpt* In diesem Kapitel **werden** Sie einen Auszug davon lesen. (*become/will*)
5. In this chapter you *will* read an excerpt from it.	**6.** **beschreiben** = *to describe* Was beschreibt Schweitzer in diesem Auszug?
6. What does Schweitzer describe in this excerpt?	**7.** Er berichtet uns von einer Operation im Urwald.
7. He tells us about an operation in the jungle.	**8.** Was für Operationen sind **es**? (*it/they*)
8. What kind of operations are *they*?	**9.** **häufig** = *frequent* **Am häufigsten** hat er es mit Brüchen (Hernien) zu tun.

9. *Most frequently* he needs to deal with. hernias. (Or: is faced with)	**10.** **dringlich** = *urgent* Diese Operationen sind sehr dringlich.
10. These operations are very urgent.	**11.** **unternehmen** = *to undertake* An Operationen unternimmt man im Urwald nur **die, die** dringlich sind. (*which, those/those, which*)
11. In the jungle one undertakes only *those* operations *which* are urgent.	**12.** Nur die, die dringlich sind und sicheren **Erfolg** versprechen, unternimmt man im Urwald. (*success/failure*)
12. In the jungle one undertakes only those which are urgent and promise certain *success.*	**13.** **behaftet mit** = *afflicted with, subject to* Die Neger Zentralafrikas sind oft **mit** Brüchen **behaftet**.
13. The Negroes of Central Africa are often *afflicted with* hernias.	**14.** Die Neger Zentralafrikas, mit **deren** Brüchen Schweitzer zu tun hat . . . (*whose/those*)
14. The Negroes of Central Africa, with *whose* hernias Schweitzer needs to deal . . .	**15.** Im Gegensatz zu den Weißen sind die Neger Zentralafrikas öfter **damit** behaftet. (*to them/so that*)
15. In contrast to the whites, the Negroes of Central Africa are subject *to them* more frequently.	**16.** **Diese** haben sehr viele, **jene** haben wenige. (*these . . . those/the latter . . . the former*)
16. *The latter* have very many, *the former have* few.	**17.** **eingeklemmt** = *strangulated* (also *pinched*) Die Neger Zentralafrikas sind öfter mit eingeklemmten Brüchen behaftet als die Weißen.
17. The Negroes of Central Africa are more often afflicted with strangulated hernias than the whites.	**18.** Eingeklemmte Brüche (inkarzerierte Hernien) sind bei **jenen** viel häufiger als bei **diesen**. (*the former . . . the latter/those . . . these*)
18. Strangulated (incarcerated) hernias are much more frequent with *the former* than with *the latter.*	**19.** **durch** = *through* **der Gang** = *passage* **der Durchgang** = __________
19. *passageway*	**20.** **der Darm** = *intestines* Der Darm ist **undurchgänglich**. (Note: *Darm* has plural meaning here.)
20. The intestines are *impassable* (blocked).	**21.** In dem eingeklemmten Bruch wird der Darm undurchgänglich.
21. In strangulated hernias the intestines become impassable. (Note here the plural meaning of **Bruch**.)	**22.** **leer** = *empty* **entleeren** = *to empty* Ein undurchgänglicher Darm kann sich nicht mehr entleeren.

22. A blocked intestine is not able to empty itself anymore.	**23.** Ein Mann, **dessen** Darm undurchgängiglich ist, und **der** sich also nicht mehr entleeren kann . . . (*whose . . . which/which . . . he*)
23. A man *whose* intestines are blocked, and *which* therefore can no longer empty themselves . . .	**24.** **treiben** = *to drive, to push* **auftreiben** = *to distend, to cause to swell up* Die Gase treiben den Darm auf.
24. The gases distend the intestines.	**25.** **wird aufgetrieben** = *is distended, is bloated* Was wird durch die Gase aufgetrieben?
25. What is distended by the gases?	**26.** **bilden** = *to form* **sich bilden** = *to form (itself)* Er (der Darm) wird durch die sich bildenden Gase aufgetrieben.
26. They (the intestines) are bloated by the gases forming in them.	**27.** Ein Darm, **der** sich nicht mehr entleeren kann, wird durch **die** sich bildenden Gase aufgetrieben. (*which . . . the/the . . . who*)
27. Intestines *which* cannot discharge themselves anymore are bloated by *the* gases forming in them.	**28.** **der Schmerz** = *pain* Jene **Auftreibung** führt zu furchtbaren Schmerzen. (*swelling/deflation*)
28. That *swelling* leads to terrible pains.	**29.** **herrühren** = *to come from, to originate* Von dieser Auftreibung rühren die furchtbaren Schmerzen her.
29. The terrible pains come from this swelling.	**30.** **grausig** = *gruesome* Der Tod ist grausig.
30. Death is gruesome.	**31.** In Afrika ist dieses grausige Sterben **etwas Gewöhnliches.** (*something unusual/something quite usual*)
31. In Africa this gruesome death is *something quite usual.*	**32.** Von einer inkarzerierten Hernie zu sterben ist doch etwas Grausiges.
32. To die of a strangulated hernia is truly something gruesome.	**33.** **sich wälzen** = *to roll around, to writhe* Ein Mann **wälzt** sich im Sande. (*present/past*)
33. present A man *is writhing* in the sand.	**34.** **heulen** = *to cry, to howl* **heulend** = *howling* Der Mann **wälzte** sich heulend im Sande. (*present/past*)

34. past The man *was writhing* in the sand howling.	**35.** **die Hütte** = *hut* **Tagelang** wälzte sich der Mann heulend im Sande der Hütte. (*for days/long days*)
35. *For days* the man writhed howling in the sand of the hut.	**36.** Schon als Knabe war der Neger **dabei**, wenn ein Mann sich tagelang heulend im Sand der Hütte wälzte. (*present/next to that*)
36. Already as a boy the Negro was *present* whenever for days a man was writhing and howling in the sand of the hut.	**37.** **erlösen** = *to save* Er heulte, bis der Tod als **Erlöser** kam.
37. He howled until death came as a *savior.*	**38.** **Der** wälzte sich tagelang heulend im Sande der Hütte. (*he/who/the*)
38. *He* writhed for days, howling in the sand of the hut.	**39.** **So etwas** ist grausig zu hören und zu sehen.
39. *Such a thing* is gruesome to hear and to see.	**40.** **flehen** = *to plead* **anflehen** = *to implore, to beg* (for help) Ein Mann, **dessen** Bruch eingeklemmt ist, fleht jemand an, ihm zu helfen. (*whose/those*)
40. A man *whose* hernia is strangulated begs someone to help him.	**41.** **sein** = *his* **die Seinen** = *his loved ones, his family* Er fleht die Seinen an.
41. He begs his loved ones.	**42.** **Um was** fleht er die Seinen an?
42. *What* does he beg of his loved ones? (Lit.: *for what*)	**43.** Die Seinen fleht er an, ihn ins Kanoe zu legen und zu mir zu **führen**.
43. He begs his loved ones to lay him in the canoe and to *bring* him to me.	**44.** **kaum** = *scarcely, hardly* Kaum fühlt **also** ein Mann, daß sein Bruch eingeklemmt ist . . .
44. *Therefore*, scarcely does a man feel that his hernia is strangulated . . .	**45.** . . . so fleht er die Seinen an, ihn zu Schweitzer zu **führen**.
45. . . . when he begs his loved ones to *take* him to Schweitzer.	**46.** Bei Frauen sind Hernien **viel seltener** als bei Männern. (*much more frequent/much less frequent*)
46. Hernias are *much less frequent* in women than in men.	

PROGRESS TEST

Choose the correct meaning for the italicized words.

1. *Der* gibt er das Buch bestimmt nicht!
(a) he (b) who (c) to her (d) to those

2. *Der* kommt heute bestimmt nicht mehr!
(a) he (b) who (c) her (d) to them

3. *Die* wollen wir überhaupt nicht mehr sehen.
(a) whom (b) they (c) her (d) she

4. *Die* hat überhaupt kein Geld mehr.
(a) who (b) they (c) her (d) she

5. Es war einmal ein Kind, *das* hatte keinen Vater und keine Mutter mehr.
(a) who (b) whom (c) it (d) the

6. *Denen* werde ich nicht helfen!
(a) whom (b) them (c) whose (d) these

7. *Dessen* Sohn ist ein Lump!
(a) his (b) her (c) of it (d) the

8. *Dem* verschenke ich nicht meine Tochter.
(a) them (b) to him (c) whom (d) who

9. Hugo, Fritz und *dessen* Freundin gehen ins Kino.
(a) the former's (b) the latter's (c) whose (d) those

10. Der Mann, mit *dessen* Frau du bekannt bist, ist kein ehrlicher Kerl.
(a) his (b) those (c) whose (d) the latter's

Answer key: **1.** (c); **2.** (a); **3.** (c); **4.** (d); **5.** (c); **6.** (b); **7.** (a); **8.** (b); **9.** (b); **10.** (c).

55. *Other demonstratives*

1. Dies, das, and **es** are translated as *this, that,* and *it* when introducing singular predicate subjects, and *these, those,* and *they* when introducing plural predicate subjects:

***Dies* ist mein Freund!**	***This*** *is my friend!*
***Das* ist mein Auto.**	***That*** *is my car.*
***Es* ist kein großes Haus.**	***It*** *is not a large house.*
***Dies* sind meine Kinder.**	***These*** *are my children.*
***Das* sind nicht meine Freunde.**	***Those*** *are not my friends.*
***Es* sind seine Kinder, nicht meine.**	***They*** *are his children, not mine.*

2. Derselbe (*the same*) and **derjenige** (*that, the one;* pl. *those*) decline both components; **der-** is declined like the definite article, **selb-** and **jenig-** like weak adjectives:

Er hat *denselben* Professor wie ich. — *He has **the same** professor as I do.*
***Diejenigen*, die dies nicht verstehen, müssen mehr arbeiten.** — ***Those** who do not understand this must study more.*

This section continues to introduce new reading vocabulary and gives you practice in recognizing the demonstratives. Respond to the exercises as indicated.

	1. Schweitzer fragt, wie er seine Gefühle **beschreiben** kann . . . (*write/describe*)
1. Schweitzer asks, how he can *describe* his feelings . . .	**2.** **arm** = *poor* **ein Armer** = *a poor* (*an unfortunate*) *person* . . . wenn ihm solch ein Armer **gebracht wird.** (*is brought/will bring*)
2. . . . when such an unfortunate person *is brought* to him.	**3.** Schweitzer ist ja **der einzige** . . . (*the only one/one of many*)
3. Schweitzer is *the only one* . . . (**ja** is an intensifier)	**4.** Er ist ja der einzige, der hier helfen kann, auf hunderte von Kilometern. (*he/who*)
4. He is the only one, for hundreds of kilometers, *who* can help here.	**5.** **retten** = *to save* Schweitzer **redet nicht davon**, daß er den Armen retten kann.
5. Schweitzer *does not mention* (lit.: does not speak/talk about) that he can save the poor man.	**6.** **der Fall** = *condition* (also: *case*) Wenn es **derselbe** Fall ist, können wir ihn retten.
6. If it is *the same* condition, we can save him.	**7.** **Dasselbe** kann er auch sagen. (*himself/the same*)
7. He also can say *the same* thing.	**8.** **Der** kann das auch sagen. (*he/that*)
8. *He* can say that, too.	**9.** **Diejenigen, die** nach ihm kommen, sind zu retten. (*those who/all who*)
9. *Those who* come after him can be saved.	**10.** **Denjenigen, die** krank sind, soll man helfen. (*those who/him who*)
10. We are to help *those who* are sick.	**11.** **quälen** = *to torture, to worry* **qualvoll, qualenreich** = *painful, excruciating, agonizing* **die Qual** = ________

11. *pain, torment, agony*	**12.** **die Gnade** = *privilege* (also: *mercy, grace*) Was **empfindet** Schweitzer als die große, immer neue Gnade?
12. What does Schweitzer *feel* the great, ever-new privilege to be?	**13.** Er darf die Tage **der Qual** von einem nehmen.
13. He can save someone from days *of pain.*	**14.** Das ist es, was er als die große, immer neue Gnade empfindet.
14. That is what he feels the great, ever-new privilege to be.	**15.** Aber **sterben** müssen wir alle. (*strive/die*)
15. But we must all *die.*	**16.** **furchtbar** = *terrible* Der Schmerz ist ein **furchtbarerer** Herr als der Tod.
16. Pain is a *more terrible* ruler than death is.	**17.** **jammern** = *to lament, to moan* **jammernd** = *moaning* Er sieht einen **jammernden** Menschen vor sich.
17. In front of him he sees a person *moaning.*	**18.** **die Stirne** = *forehead* Schweitzer legt dem jammernden Menschen die Hand auf die Stirne.
18. Schweitzer puts his hand on the forehead of the person moaning.	**19.** **sei ruhig** = *don't be afraid* (lit.: *be calm, quiet, still*) Er sagt ihm: „Sei ruhig."
19. He tells him: "Don't be afraid." (**Sei** is an imperative form of **sein.**)	**20.** In einer Stunde **wirst** du **schlafen** . . .
20. In one hour you *will be asleep* . . .	**21.** **wachen** = *to wake, to watch over* . . . und wenn du wieder **erwachst,** ist kein Schmerz mehr.
21. . . . and when you *wake up* again, the pain will be gone.	**22.** Die Operation ist **vorüber.** (*begun/over*)
22. The operation is *over.*	**23.** **aufwachen** = *to wake up* **das Aufwachen** = __________
23. *the waking up*	**24.** **überwachen** = *to supervise, to look after* Schweitzer **überwacht** das Aufwachen des Patienten.
24. Schweitzer *supervises* the waking up of the patient.	**25.** **dunkel** = *dark* Unter der dunklen **Schlafbaracke** überwacht er das Aufwachen des Patienten.

25. *In the dark sleeping quarters* he supervises the awakening of the patient. (Lit.: under the dark sleeping hut.) (Notice that the **e** of **dunkel** was dropped when the **-en** was added.)	**26.** **sich besinnen** = *to think of, to recollect* **die Besinnung** = *reflection, consciousness* **bei Besinnung** = __________
26. *conscious*	**27.** Der Patient ist jetzt bei Besinnung.
27. The patient is now conscious.	**28.** Kaum ist er bei Besinnung, so **schaut** er erstaunt **umher**.
28. Hardly is he conscious when he *looks around* with astonishment.	**29.** **holen** = *to fetch, get* **wieder** = *again* Der Patient **wiederholt fort und fort** . . .
29. The patient *repeats over and over* . . . (**fort** is a false cognate meaning *gone, away*).	**30.** Er ist der Freund **derer, die** fort und fort wiederholen . . . (*they who/of those who*)
30. He is the friend *of those who* repeat over and over . . .	**31.** **weh** = *hurt, pain* **weh haben** = *to hurt* Ich habe ja nicht mehr weh!
31. It doesn't hurt anymore! (Lit.: I no longer have pain!)	**32.** **die meine** = *mine* (singular) Da der Patient nicht mehr weh hat, **sucht** seine Hand **die meine**.
32. Since the patient doesn't have any more pain, his hand *searches for mine*.	**33.** Seine Hand will die meine nicht mehr **loslassen**. (*to let loose/to let go*)
33. His hand does not want *to let go* of mine.	**34.** Schweitzer **fängt an** zu erzählen.
34. Schweitzer *begins* to tell a story.	**35.** **sitzen** = *to sit* **dabei** = *there, nearby* **dabeisitzen** = ________
35. *to sit there, to sit nearby*	**36.** Dann fängt Schweitzer an, dem Patienten und **denen, die** dabeisitzen, zu erzählen . . . (*they who/those who*)
36. Then Schweitzer begins to tell the patient and *those who* are sitting nearby . . .	**37.** **gebieten** = *to command* . . . daß es der Herr Jesus ist, **der** dem Doktor und seiner Frau geboten hat . . .
37. . . . that it is the Lord Jesus *who* has commanded the doctor and his wife . . .	**38.** . . . hier an den Ogowe zu kommen.
38. . . . to come here to the Ogowe (a river in equatorial Africa).	**39.** **Diejenigen,** die dabeisitzen, sind Freunde des Patienten.

39. *Those* who are sitting nearby are friends of the patient.	**40.** Wer sind jene Menschen, die uns **Mittel** geben, unsere Krankheiten zu heilen? (**Mittel** probably means: *middle/means*)
40. *means* Who are those people who give us the means to heal our illnesses?	**41.** **geboren** = *born* **eingeboren** = *inherent, innate* **die Eingeborenen** = *natives* Die Eingeborenen leiden viel unter **Krankheiten**.
41. The natives suffer a lot from *diseases*.	**42.** **Woher** wissen die Europäer, daß die Eingeborenen so viel unter Krankheiten leiden?
42. *How is it that* the Europeans know that the natives suffer so much from diseases?	**43.** **der Kaffee** = *coffee* **der Strauch** = *bush, shrub* **der Kaffeestrauch** = ________
43. *the coffee bush*	**44.** Durch die Kaffeesträucher hindurch scheint die afrikanische Sonne in die dunkle Hütte.
44. The African sun shines through the coffee bushes into the dark hut.	**45.** **Dies** sind meine Kaffeesträucher, jene sind deine. (*this/these*)
45. *These* are my coffee bushes, those are yours.	**46.** **Das** sind seine Freunde. (*that/those*)
46. *Those* are his friends.	**47.** Wer gibt uns die Mittel, um hier für die Kranken zu leben?
47. Who gives us the means to live here to cure the sick (in order to live for the sick)?	**48.** Wer sind **jene** Menschen, wo wohnen sie? (*that/those*)
48. Who are *those* people, where do they live?	**49.** **geben** = *to give* **gebend** = *giving, generous* Die gebenden Freunde sind in Europa.
49. The generous friends are in Europe.	**50.** Wenn nur die gebenden Freunde in Europa dabei sein **könnten!** (**könnten** probably means: *can/could*)
50. If only the generous friends in Europe *could* be here with us! (*könnten* is subjunctive; see chapter 21.)	**51.** Wir aber, Schwarz und Weiß, sitzen **untereinander** und erleben es: „Ihr aber seid alle Brüder." (*under one another/side by side*)
51. But we, black and white, sit *side by side* and experience the meaning of the words: "And all ye are brethren."	**52.** Ach, könnten die gebenden Freunde in Europa in einer solchen Stunde dabei sein!

52.	Oh, if only the generous friends in Europe could be here at such a moment! (Lit.: in such an hour)	**53.**	**verdienen** = *to earn, to deserve* **Der** verdient Macht.
53.	*He* deserves power.	**54.**	**rechtfertigen** = *to justify* Der rechtfertigt seine Macht.
54.	*He* justifies his power.	**55.**	**der Tag** = *day* **Täglich** rechtfertigt er seine Macht.
55.	He justifies his power *daily.*	**56.**	Nur **der** verdient Macht, **der** sie täglich rechtfertigt. (Dag Hammarsjköld)
56.	Only *he* deserves power *who* justifies it daily.		

PROGRESS TEST

A. Give the meaning of the italicized words.

1. *Es sind* seine zwei Freunde.
(a) there are (b) he is (c) they are (d) that is

2. Er ist der Held *derselben* Frauen wie ich.
(a) of the same (b) the same (c) to the same (d) those

3. *Diejenigen,* die das nicht glauben, können zum Teufel gehen.
(a) she (b) they (c) the same (d) those

4. *Das sind* dumme Esel.
(a) that is (b) those are (c) it is (d) who are

B. Choose the answers describing the italicized words.

1. Er hilft *denselben* Professoren wie ich.
(a) dative (b) accusative (c) singular (d) plural

2. *Derjenige,* der nicht helfen kann, ist kein Freund von uns.
(a) nominative (b) dative (c) genitive (d) singular (e) plural

C. Choose the closest approximate meaning for the given sentence or phrase.

1. Am häufigsten unternimmt man Operationen, die nicht dringlich sind und sicheren Erfolg versprechen.
(a) All operations are pressing and those which promise certain success are most frequently unsuccessful.
(b) Operations which are not urgent and which promise certain success are most frequently performed.
(c) The most frequent operations are those which are both urgent and promise the most success.
(d) Most frequently one undertakes only urgent operations and does not promise certain success.

2. Ein undurchgänglicher Darm verspricht furchtbare Schmerzen *und den Tod als Erlöser.*
(a) and deadly sickness
(b) and previous to death
(c) and the fate of the losers
(d) and death as a savior

3. Daß eingeklemmte Brüche bei Frauen viel seltener sind als bei Männern, zeigt, daß die Gleichheit der Geschlechter nur ein Mythus ist.
(a) Men and women are not equal.
(b) Men and women are equal.
(c) Men never have the advantage over women.
(d) It is seldom that men and women suffer from the myth of equality.

4. Die Eingeborenen leiden unter Krankheiten.
(a) Those born into this society carry burdens.
(b) The laborers clean the hospital.
(c) The natives suffer from illnesses.
(d) The firstborn are susceptible to illnesses.

5. Die große, immer neue Gnade ist, daß man die Qual von einem nehmen darf.
(a) One is permitted to undertake new sufferings.
(b) All suffering is by the grace of God.
(c) One receives ever-new grace by taking away one's pain.
(d) Removing one's pain is the great, ever-new privilege.

Answer key: A. **1.** (c); **2.** (a); **3.** (d); **4.** (b).
B. **1.** (a, d); **2.** (a, d).
C. **1.** (b); **2.** (d); **3.** (a); **4.** (c); **5.** (d).

From *Zwischen Wasser und Urwald.* Paul Haupt Verlag, Bern, 1922.

Albert Schweitzer: Zwischen Wasser und Urwald

An Operationen unternimmt man im Urwald natürlich nur die, die dringlich sind und sicheren Erfolg versprechen. Am häufigsten habe ich es mit Brüchen (Hernien) zu tun. Die Neger Zentralafrikas sind viel mehr mit Brüchen behaftet als die Weißen. Woher dies kommt, wissen wir nicht. Eingeklemmte Brüche (Inkarzerierte Hernien) sind bei ihnen also auch viel häufiger als bei den Weißen. In dem eingeklemmten Bruch wird der Darm undurchgänglich. Er kann sich also nicht mehr entleeren und wird durch die sich bildenden Gase aufgetrieben. Von dieser Auftreibung rühren die furchtbaren Schmerzen her. . . . In Afrika ist dieses grausige Sterben . . . etwas Gewöhnliches. Schon als Knabe war der Neger dabei, wenn ein Mann sich tagelang heulend im Sande der Hütte wälzte, bis der Tod als Erlöser kam. Kaum fühlt also ein Mann, daß sein Bruch eingeklemmt ist—Hernien bei Frauen sind viel seltener als bei Männern—so fleht er die Seinen an, ihn ins Kanoe zu legen und zu mir zu führen.

Wie meine Gefühle beschreiben, wenn solch ein Armer gebracht wird! Ich bin ja der einzige, der hier helfen kann, auf hunderte von Kilometern ... Ich rede nicht davon, daß ich ihm das Leben retten kann. Sterben müssen wir alle. Aber daß ich die Tage der Qual von ihm nehmen darf, das ist es, was ich als die große, immer neue Gnade empfinde. Der Schmerz ist ein furchtbarerer Herr als der Tod.

So lege ich dem jammernden Menschen die Hand auf die Stirne und sage ihm: „Sei ruhig. In einer Stunde wirst du schlafen, und wenn du wieder erwachst, ist kein Schmerz mehr ..."

Die Operation ist vorüber. Unter der dunklen Schlafbaracke überwache ich das Aufwachen des Patienten. Kaum ist er bei Besinnung, so schaut er erstaunt umher und wiederholt fort und fort; „Ich habe ja nicht mehr weh, ich habe ja nicht mehr weh!" ... Seine Hand sucht die meine und will sie nicht mehr loslassen. Dann fange ich an, ihm und denen, die dabeisitzen, zu erzählen, daß es der Herr Jesus ist, der dem Doktor und seiner Frau geboten hat, hier an den Ogowe zu kommen und daß weiße Menschen in Europa uns die Mittel geben, um hier für die Kranken zu leben. Nun muß ich auf die Fragen, wer jene Menschen sind, wo sie wohnen, woher sie wissen, daß die Eingeborenen so viel unter Krankheiten leiden, Antwort geben. Durch die Kaffeesträucher hindurch scheint die afrikanische Sonne in die dunkle Hütte. Wir aber, Schwarz und Weiß, sitzen untereinander und erleben es: „Ihr aber seid alle Brüder." Ach, könnten die gebenden Freunde in Europa in einer solchen Stunde dabei sein! ...

Chapter Sixteen

56. *Possessive adjectives*

1. The following words function as possessive adjectives when they qualify a noun. Their endings follow the **ein/kein** pattern (see chapter 4) and thus indicate gender, number, and case of the noun which follows:

	SINGULAR	FORMAL	PLURAL
1st person:	**mein** (*my*)		**unser** (*our*)
2nd person:	**dein** (*your*)	**Ihr** (*your:* sing. and plur.)	**euer** (*your*)
3rd person:	(M) **sein** (*his, its*) (F) **ihr** (*her, its*) (N) **sein** (*its*)		**ihr** (*their*)

***Meine* Eltern sind nicht zu Hause.** — ***My** parents are not at home.*
Das ist *ihr* Buch. — *That is **her** (their) book.*
***Eu(e)re* Freunde kommen heute nicht wieder.** — ***Your** friends are not coming back today.*
***Ihre* Bücher liegen auf dem Tisch.** — ***Her** (**your**: sing, or plur., **their**) books are lying on the table.*

2. **Ihr** when beginning a sentence may have one of six different meanings. As a personal pronoun it could mean *you* or (*to*) *her*; as a possessive adjective it could mean *her, its, your,* or *their.* **Ihr** when capitalized within a sentence will always mean *your* (formal), but it may be either singular or plural. In all of these instances the context (e.g., verb ending) will give a clue to the correct meaning:

***Ihr* seid aber nicht nett zu mir.** — ***You** are not nice to me.*
***Ihr* werde ich gar nicht helfen.** — *I will not help **her** at all.*
Sind das *Ihre* Bücher? — *Are they **your** books?*
***Ihr* Buch liegt auf dem Tisch.** — ***Her** (**your, their**) book is lying on the table.*
Läuft denn die Maschine noch? Nein! *Ihr* Motor ist kaputt! — *Does the machine still run? No! **Its** motor isn't working.*

Within the sentence uncapitalized **ihr** may have one of five different meanings. As a personal pronoun it could mean *you* or *(to) her*; as a possessive adjective it could mean *her, their, its*:

Habt *ihr* kein Deutsch studiert?	*Haven't **you** studied German?*
Ich werde *ihr* gar nicht helfen.	*I will not help **her** at all.*
Ist *ihr* Deutsch gräßlich?	*Is **her** (**their**) German horrible?*
Die Maschine läuft nicht. Wissen Sie, ob *ihr* Motor kaputt ist?	*The machine doesn't run. Do you know if **its** motor is working or not?*

3. The possessive adjective **sein** generally has one of two meanings, *his* or *its*. However, it is also possible to translate it as *her*. Context will indicate the correct equivalent:

Günter hat *seine* Schuhe verloren.	*Günter lost **his** shoes.*
Der Stuhl steht in der Ecke. *Seine* Beine wurden neulich renoviert.	*The chair is standing in the corner. **Its** legs were recently refinished.*
Das Mädchen verlor *seine* Schuhe.	*The girl lost **her** shoes.*

4. **Unser** and **euer** may drop the **-e** of the stem or the **-e** of the inflectional ending: **unsre, eures, unsrem** (or **unserm**).

5. The idea *of mine, of yours,* etc., is expressed in German by the preposition **von** plus the personal pronoun:

Er ist ein guter Freund *von mir*.	*He is a good friend **of mine**.*

6. When ownership is clear, the definite article is often substituted for the possessive adjective, particularly when referring to clothing or parts of the body. Frequently, a dative of the appropriate reflexive pronoun is added:

Manfred steckt *sich die* Hand in *die* Tasche.	*Manfred puts **his** hand in **his** pocket.*
Du ziehst *dir die* Schuhe an.	*You are putting on **your** shoes.*

In this section you are introduced to the vocabulary of the reading passage as well as drilled on the uses of the possessive adjectives. Continue to circle words that you do not know and review them before going on to the next section.

	1. **der Abschnitt** = *section* In diesem Abschnitt lesen wir das letzte Kapitel aus Erich Maria Remarques *Im Westen nichts Neues.*
1. In this section we will read the last chapter of Erich Maria Remarque's *All Quiet on the Western Front.*	**2.** Das Buch war **sein** erstes Werk und machte Remarque weltberühmt. *(his/to be)*

2. The book was *his* first work and made Remarque world famous.	**3.** **erscheinen** = *to appear* Das Buch erschien zum ersten Male im Jahre 1929 und machte **dessen** Autor weltberühmt. (*his/its*)
3. The book appeared for the first time in 1929 and made *its* author world famous.	**4.** **die Auflage** = *edition* Damals **erreichte** das Buch eine Auflage von sechs Millionen.
4. At that time the book *reached* an edition of six million copies.	**5.** Das Werk des 32 jährigen Autors **wurde** 1930 verfilmt. (*was/became*)
5. The work of the 32-year-old author *was* made into a movie in 1930.	**6.** Bei der Berliner Premiere **ließ** Goebbels Mäuse laufen. (past of: *lesen/lassen*)
6. *lassen* At the premiere in Berlin Goebbels *had* mice released.	**7.** **treiben** = *to drive* Er tat das, **um** das „pazifistische" Publikum auf die Stühle **zu** treiben.
7. He did that *in order to* make the pacifistic audience get up on their chairs (drive the pacifistic audience onto their chairs).	**8.** **heroisieren** = *to glamorize* **entheroisieren** = *to deglamorize* Das Buch entheroisiert den Krieg: **deshalb** ließ Goebbels Mäuse laufen. (*therefore/that is why*)
8. The book deglamorizes war (takes heroism out of war): *that is why* the mice were released by Goebbels.	**9.** **die Seite** = *side* **einseitig** = *one-sided* **die Einseitigkeit** = ____________
9. *one-sidedness*	**10.** Remarque schreibt mit bitterem Sarkasmus und Zynismus, aber auch mit **bewußter** Einseitigkeit. (*conscious/unconscious*)
10. Remarque writes with bitter sarcasm and cynicism, but also with *conscious* one-sidedness.	**11.** **zeigen** = *to demonstrate* Er will die **Sinnlosigkeit** des Krieges zeigen. (*sinlessness/senselessness*)
11. He wants to demonstrate the *senselessness* of war.	**12.** **schildern** = *to describe* Das Buch schildert die **Erlebnisse** eines jungen Mannes in dem Großen Krieg. (*experiences/memories*)
12. The book describes the *experiences* of a young man in the Great War. (i.e., World War I)	**13.** Was er erlebt und gedacht hat, **wird** uns **geschildert**. (*is described/will describe*)

13. What he experienced and thought *is described* to us.	**14.** **die Ruhe** = *rest* In dem letzten Kapitel des Buches hat er **vierzehn Tage Ruhe** . . .
14. In the last chapter of the book he has *a fourteen-day leave* . . .	**15.** **schlucken** = *to swallow* . . . weil er etwas Gas **geschluckt hat**.
15. . . . because he *swallowed* some gas.	**16.** **enttäuschen** = *to disappoint* **die Enttäuschung** = __________
16. *disappointment*	**17.** Hier spricht er von den Hoffnungen und Enttäuschungen der Soldaten.
17. Here he speaks of the hopes and disappointments of the soldiers.	**18.** Er ist der letzte von den sieben Mann aus **seiner** Klasse hier. (*its/his*)
18. He is the last of the seven of *his* class here.	**19.** **die Waffe** = *weapon* **die Stille** = *quiet, stillness* **der Stand** = *position, condition, state* **der Waffenstillstand** = __________
19. *armistice*	**20.** **Jeder** spricht von Frieden und Waffenstillstand. (*that one/everyone*)
20. *Everyone* speaks of peace and armistice.	**21.** Da sind unsere Feinde. **Ihr** Waffenstillstand bedeutet eigentlich nichts. (*your/its/their*)
21. There are our enemies. *Their* armistice actually means nothing.	**22.** **Das** ist wirklich eine Enttäuschung! (*the/that*)
22. *That* is really a disappointment!	**23.** **Ihre** Enttäuschung ist groß, denn sie haben keine Zeit mehr. (*your/their*)
23. *Their* disappointment is great for they don't have any more time.	**24.** **zusammenbrechen** = *to break down* Wenn Friede und Waffenstillstand wieder eine Enttäuschung sind, dann **werden** die Soldaten **zusammenbrechen**. (*will break down/become broken down*)
24. If peace and armistice are again a disappointment, then the soldiers *will break down*.	**25.** **stark** = *strong, large, great* Sie werden zusammenbrechen, denn **Ihre** Hoffnungen sind zu stark. (*her/their/your*)
25. You will break down, for *your* hopes are too high.	**26.** **fortschaffen** = *to get rid of, to dismiss, to take away* Die Hoffnungen **lassen sich** nicht mehr **fortschaffen**.

26. The hopes *can* no longer *be dismissed* (lit.: no longer *let themselves be dismissed*).	**27.** Die Hoffnungen **haben** sich nicht mehr **fortschaffen lassen**.
27. The hopes *could* no longer *be dismissed.*	**28.** Gibt es wieder eine Enttäuschung, werdet **ihr** zusammenbrechen. (*her/you/its*)
28. If there is a disappointment again, *you* will break down.	**29.** Die Hoffnungen **haben** sich nicht mehr **fortschaffen lassen**, ohne zu explodieren.
29. Hope *could* no longer *be taken away* without exploding.	**30.** **stocken** = *to stop, falter, to come to a standstill* Hier stocken **seine** Gedanken. (*his/her/its*)
30. Here *his* thoughts falter.	**31.** **weiter** = *further* **bringen** = *to bring* **weiterbringen** = __________
31. *to carry further, to help along*	**32.** Hier stocken meine Gedanken und sind nicht weiterzubringen.
32. Here my thoughts falter and cannot be carried further.	**33.** **warten** = *to wait* **erwarten** = *to wait, to expect* **Selbst** er hat so etwas nicht erwartet. (*himself/even*)
33. *Even* he did not expect such a thing.	**34.** Was erwartet **ihr**? (*you/her/their*)
34. What do *you* expect?	**35.** Was erwartet **mich**?
35. What awaits *me?*	**36.** Was erwartet **euch**?
36. What awaits *you*?	**37.** Was erwartet **sie**? (*she/they*)
37. What does *she* expect? (Also: What awaits *her*? What awaits *them*?)	**38.** Wo stocken **Ihre** Gedanken? (*her/your*)
38. Where do *your* thoughts falter?	**39.** **das Leben** = *life* **die Gier** = *greed, inordinate desire* **die Lebensgier** = __________
39. *desire for life*	**40.** Der Soldat, **der** Lebensgier hat—ist er ein guter oder ein schlechter Soldat? (*the/who/he*)
40. The soldier *who* has a desire for life—is he a good or a bad soldier?	**41.** **das Ziel** = *goal* Was für Ziele hat **jener** Mensch? (*this/that/every*)

41. What goals does *that* person have?	**42.** Aber **es sind** keine Ziele. (*it is/those are*)
42. But *those are* no goals.	**43.** **sich retten** = *to save oneself* Er **hat sich** im letzten Moment **gerettet**.
43. He *saved himself* at the last minute.	**44.** **retten** = *to save* **die Rettung** = *rescue* **der Rausch** = *intoxication, ecstasy* Der Rausch der Rettung, **den** jeder Soldat hat . . . (*whom/which/the*)
44. The intoxication of being rescued (from death) *which* every soldier has . . .	**45.** **hinziehen** = *to attract* Der Rausch der Rettung **zieht** ihn **hin**.
45. The intoxication of being rescued *attracts* him.	**46.** **die Übermacht** = *superior force* Der Rausch der Rettung zieht ihn **mit Übermacht** hin.
46. He is *overwhelmingly* drawn towards the intoxicating idea of rescue.	**47.** **fühlen** = *to feel* **das Gefühl** = *feeling* Was mich mit Übermacht hinzieht und erwartet, sind Gefühle.
47. *Feelings* are what overwhelmingly draw me and await me.	**48.** **die Heimat** = *native place, native country, homeland, home* **das Heimatgefühl =**____________
48. *feeling (of love) for one's home*	**49.** Es ist Lebensgier, es ist Heimatgefühl, was mich mit Übermacht hinzieht.
49. It is lust for life, it is the love for my home, which overwhelmingly attracts me.	**50.** Lebensgier und der Rausch der Rettung sind keine Ziele, **selbst** das Heimatgefühl ist kein Ziel. (*himself/itself/even*)
50. Desire for life and the ecstasy of rescue are not goals; *even* the love for one's home isn't really a goal.	**51.** **fesseln** = *to fetter* **entfesseln =** *to unfetter, to unleash, to release* Unsere Erlebnisse **hatten** einen Sturm **entfesselt.** (*have unleashed/had unleashed*)
51. Our experiences *had unleashed* a storm.	**52.** **die Stärke** = *strength* **der Schmerz** = *pain* Die Stärke und der Schmerz unserer Erlebnisse, **die** haben einen Sturm entfesselt! (*they/who/which*)

52. The strength and pain of our experiences, *they* have unleashed a storm!	**53.** **zurecht** = *in the right place, in good order* **finden** = *to find* **sich zurechtfinden** =__________
53. *to find one's way*	**54.** Wir **finden uns** nicht mehr auf dieser Welt **zurecht**.
54. We *can* no longer *find our way* in this world.	**55.** Die Stärke und der Schmerz unserer Erlebnisse haben einen Sturm entfesselt, und wir **werden** uns nicht mehr **zurechtfinden können.**
55. The strength and pain of our experiences have unleashed a storm, and we *will* not *be able to find our way* any longer.	**56.** **die Wurzel** = *root* **wurzellos** = *rootless, without a root* Wenn wir jetzt zurückkehren, sind wir müde, **zerfallen,** ausgebrannt, wurzellos und ohne Hoffnung. (*in ruins/in good spirits*)
56. If we return now, we will be tired, *in ruins,* burnt out, rootless and without hope.	**57.** **das Geschlecht** = *generation* Das neue Geschlecht kann den Krieg nicht verstehen.
57. The new generation cannot understand the war.	**58.** Das alte Geschlecht kann **ihn** nicht vergessen. (*it/them*)
58. The old generation cannot forget *it*.	**59.** **verbringen** = *to spend, to pass (time)* Er **wird** das Jahr mit uns **verbringen**.
59. He *will spend* the year with us.	**60.** **gemein** = *common* **gemeinsam** = *in common, together* Er hat das Jahr gemeinsam mit uns verbracht.
60. He spent the year together with us.	**61.** **zwar** = *indeed, I admit* Das neue Geschlecht, **das** zwar die Jahre hier gemeinsam mit uns verbrachte . . . (*the/which/it*)
61. The new generation *which* indeed spent years here together with us . . .	**62.** **der Beruf** = *profession* **Was für einen** Beruf hat der Mann?
62. *What kind of a* profession does the man have?	**63.** Selbst **der** weiß es nicht! (*he/who/the*)
63. Even *he* doesn't know it!	**64.** Vor uns wächst ein Geschlecht, **das** Bett und Beruf hatte . . . (*the/which/it*)
64. In front of us a generation is growing up *which* had a bed and a profession . . .	**65.** . . . und jetzt **zurückgeht** in seine alten Positionen.

65. . . . and now *returns* to its old positions.	**66.** Es geht in seine alten Positionen zurück, in **denen** es den Krieg vergessen wird. (*which/whose/those*)
66. It will go back into its old positions, where (lit.: in *which*) it will forget the war.	**67.** **ähnlich** = *similar to* Hinter uns wächst ein Geschlecht, ähnlich uns **früher** . . . (*early/earlier/earliest*)
67. A generation is growing up after us, similar to the way we used to be . . . (lit.: similar to us *earlier*)	**68.** Es wächst hinter uns ein Geschlecht, ähnlich uns früher, **das** wird uns fremd sein. (*relative pronoun/demonstrative pronoun*)
68. demonstrative: the word order tells you so, i.e., **wird** follows immediately after **das** which is the subject. A generation is growing up after us, similar to the way we used to be, and *they* will be strangers to us. (Note: **das** is singular = *it*, but the context demands *they*.)	**69.** Ein Geschlecht, **das** uns fremd sein wird, wächst hinter uns. (*relative/demonstrative*)
69. relative: **wird** is at the end of the clause. A generation *which* will be like strangers to us is growing up after us.	**70.** **bei** = *by, at* **die Seite** = *side* **schieben** = *to push* **beiseiteschieben** = __________
70. *to push aside*	**71.** **Das** Geschlecht wird uns beiseiteschieben.
71. *That* generation will push us aside. (**Das** when stressed is translated *that*.)	**72.** Ein Geschlecht wächst hinter uns, ähnlich uns früher, **das** wird uns fremd sein und uns beiseiteschieben.
72. A generation is growing up after us, similar to us as we used to be; and *they* will be strangers to us and push us aside.	**73.** **überflüssig**= *superfluous* Wir sind überflüssig **für uns selbst**.
73. We are superfluous *to ourselves.*	**74.** Er wurde **ihr** überflüssig. (*you/to her/their*)
74. He became superfluous *to her.*	**75.** **sich anpassen** = *to adapt oneself* **Einige** passen sich an. (*own/some*)
75. *Some* adapt themselves.	**76.** Einige **haben** sich **angepaßt.**
76. Some *have adapted* themselves.	**77.** **sich fügen** = *to submit, to subordinate oneself* Einige werden sich anpassen, andere sich fügen, aber wir werden **wachsen.**

77. Some will adapt themselves, others will subordinate themselves, but we will *grow.*	**78.** **Rat** = *advice, counsel* Andere werden sich fügen, und viele werden **ratlos** sein. (*ruthless/helpless*)
78. Others will subordinate themselves, and many will be *helpless* (baffled, at a loss to know what to do).	**79.** **zerrinnen** = *to pass by, to melt away, to vanish* Die Jahre werden zerrinnen.
79. The years will pass by.	**80.** **schließlich** = *finally* Die Jahre werden zerrinnen, und schließlich werden wir zugrunde gehen.
80. The years will pass by, and finally we will perish.	**81.** Ist es das Los der Menschen, daß die Jahre zerrinnen werden, und daß **sie** schließlich zugrunde gehen werden? (*she/they*)
81. Is it the fate of human beings that the years will pass by and that *they* will finally perish?	

PROGRESS TEST

Choose the correct answer for the italicized word.

1. Gibt es wieder eine Enttäuschung, werdet *ihr* zusammenbrechen.
(a) you (b) her (c) its (d) your

2. Das Mädchen bleibt stehen, *seine* Gedanken stocken.
(a) their (b) her (c) its (d) to be

3. Ich weiß nicht, ob *Ihre* Probleme sich lösen werden.
(a) you (b) her (c) their (d) your

4. Ich hatte einen Wagen, aber schließlich lief *sein* Motor nicht mehr.
(a) its (b) his (c) to be (d) her

5. Kehrt ihr zu *ihr* zurück?
(a) you (b) your (c) her (d) their

6. Ich bin der letzte Mann aus __________ (*my*) Klasse.
(a) meiner (b) unserer (c) seiner (d) ihrer

7. _____ (*our*) Hoffnungen sind zu stark.
(a) eure (b) ihre (c) Ihre (d) unsere

8. In _____ (*your*) kleinen Garten sitze ich den ganzen Tag in der Sonne.
(a) ihrem (b) unsrem (c) deinem (d) seinem

Answer key: **1.** (a); **2.** (b); **3.** (d); **4.** (a); **5.** (c); **6.** (a); **7.** (d); **8.** (c).

57. Possessives used as predicate adjectives or as pronouns

1. When possessives appear in the predicate (i.e., after the verb) they may either be adjectives or pronouns:

Das Buch ist *mein.*	*That book is* ***mine.*** (adj.)
Sein Haus ist größer als *unsres* (*das unsere, das unsrige*).	*His house is larger than* ***ours.*** (pronoun)

2. If the possessive is used *adjectivally*, it will have no ending; **ihr** and **Ihr,** however, are always inflected: (i.e., take an ending).

Dieses alte Auto ist *sein.*	*This old automobile is* ***his.***
Das Auto ist *Ihres.*	*That automobile is* ***yours.***
Das Buch ist ihres.	*That book is* ***hers.***

3. The possessive used *as a pronoun* will take an ending. Note the possibilities when the definite article is added to the possessive pronouns. Though rare, these variants do occur from time to time:

Ich schicke meiner Schwester einen Ring. Was schickst du *deiner* (*der deinen, der deinigen*)?	*I am sending my sister a ring. What are you sending* ***yours?***
Mein Vater ist in Deutschland. *Eurer* (*der eure, der eurige*) ist in der Schweiz.	*My father is in Germany.* ***Yours*** *is in Switzerland.*

The following frames test your knowledge of possessives used as adjectives and as pronouns. You will continue to be introduced to the vocabulary of the reading passage.

	1. **schmecken** = *to taste* Unser Bier schmeckt nicht so gut wie **deins.** (*your/ yours*)
1. Our beer doesn't taste as good as *yours.*	**2.** **das Fahrrad** = *bicycle* Das Fahrrad ist **ihres.** (*her/ hers*)
2. The bicycle is *hers.*	**3.** **Das meinige** steht auf der Straße. (*mine/ my*)
3. *Mine* is standing on the street.	**4.** **Das seinige** ist kaputt.
4. *His* is broken.	**5.** **Die ihre** habe ich nicht mehr.
5. I do not have *hers* (*theirs*) anymore.	**6.** Das Messer gehört Macki, die Pistole ist **mein.**
6. The knife belongs to Macki; the pistol is *mine.*	**7.** Es ist **unseres.** (*our/ ours*)

7. It is *ours.*	**8.** Es ist **das unsere.** (*our/ ours*)
8. It is *ours.*	**9.** **Die Meinen** werden mich lieben. (*mine/those who belong to me*)
9. *Those who belong to me* will love me.	**10.** Er lief auf **die Seinen** zu. (*his/his loved ones*)
10. He ran towards *his loved ones.*	**11.** Im Frühling summen die Bienen im Garten.
11. In Spring the bees *hum* in the garden.	**12.** Die Bienen, die im Garten summen, sind doch **eure.** (*your/ yours*)
12. The bees that are humming in the garden are *yours.*	**13.** **Eure** Bienen habe ich lange nicht mehr gesehen. (*your/ yours*)
13. I haven't seen *your* bees for a long time.	**14.** **Ihre** Bienen wohnen in **Bienenstöcken.**
14. *Your* (*her, their*) bees live in *beehives.*	**15.** Und jetzt **kehren wir zurück** zu *Im Westen nichts Neues.*
15. And now *let us return* (lit.: *turn we back*) to *All Quiet on the Western Front.*	**16.** **schwer** = *heavy* **der Mut** = *courage, spirit, heart* **die Schwermut** = *melancholy, depression, sadness* Ihm **liegt** eine große Schwermut auf dem Herzen.
16. His heart *is filled* with great sadness. (Great sadness *lies* on his heart.)	**17.** **stürzen** = *to fall* **bestürzen** = *to confound, to dismay* **die Bestürzung** = __________
17. *dismay, consternation, confusion*	**18.** Alles, was er denkt, ist nur Schwermut und Bestürzung.
18. His thoughts are full of melancholy and dismay. (Lit.: Everything that he is thinking is nothing but [only] melancholy and confusion.)	**19.** **der Staub** = *dust* **stäuben** = *to fly off or about like dust* **fort** = *away, gone* **fortstäuben** = *to fly away like dust* Schwermut und Bestürzung stäuben fort.
19. Melancholy and confusion fly away like dust.	**20.** Schwermut und Bestürzung stäuben fort, wenn ich unter den **Pappeln** stehe. (*poplars/poppies*)
20. Melancholy and confusion fly away like dust when I stand under the *poplars.*	**21.** Aber vielleicht ist auch alles dieses, was ich denke, nur Schwermut und Bestürzung, **die** fortstäubt . . . (*which/ they*)

21. *which:* the word order of **fortstäubt** tells you that *die* is a relative pronoun; were it a demonstrative, the verb would be **stäubt fort.** But perhaps everything that (all this) I am thinking is only melancholy and confusion *which* will fly away like dust . . .	**22.** **lauschen** = *to listen* . . . wenn ich wieder unter den Pappeln stehe und dem Rauschen **ihrer** Blätter lausche. (*of their/of her/of its*)
22. . . . when I again stand under the poplars and listen to the rustle *of their* leaves.	**23.** **der Vogel** = *bird* Lauscht er auch dem Singen **der** Vögel? (*the/of the*)
23. *of the*, as **der Vögel** can only be genitive plural. Is he also listening to the singing *of the* birds?	**24.** **weich** = *soft* Das Weiche macht unser Blut unruhig.
24. The softness makes our blood restless.	**25.** Das Weiche, das unser Blut unruhig machte, kann nicht fort sein.
25. The softness that made our blood restless cannot be gone.	**26.** **bestürzen** = *to dismay, to confound* **bestürzend** = *dismaying, confounding* **das Bestürzende** = __________
26. *the dismaying thing* (*the thing that fills us with dismay*)	**27.** **das Kommende** = __________
27. *the coming thing* (*the thing that is coming*)	**28.** Das Bestürzende, das Kommende macht unser Blut weich.
28. The dismaying thing, the coming thing makes our blood soft. (Or: weakens our blood)	**29.** **das Gesicht** = *face* Das Ungewisse, die tausend Gesichter der Zukunft, **das** kann nicht untergehen. (*which/that*)
29. What is uncertain, the thousand faces of the future, (*that*) cannot perish.	**30.** **die Ahnung** = *idea, notion, thought, presentiment* Die Ahnung der Frauen hat sein Blut unruhig **gemacht.**
30. The thought of women *made* his blood restless.	**31.** Es kann nicht sein, daß es fort ist, die Melodie aus Träumen und Büchern, das Rauschen der Pappeln und die Ahnung der Frauen.
31. It cannot be that it is gone, the melody from dreams and books, the rustling of the poplars and the presentiment of women.	**32.** **die Trommel** = *drum* **das Feuer** = *fire* **das Trommelfeuer** = *ceaseless bombardment* **Ist** das alles im Trommelfeuer **untergegangen**?

32. *Has* all that *perished* in the ceaseless bombardment?	**33.** **der Zweifel** = *doubt* **verzweifeln** = *to despair* **die Verzweiflung** = __________
33. *despair*	**34.** **die Mannschaft** = *troops* Es kann nicht sein, daß all das untergegangen ist im Trommelfeuer, Verzweiflung und **Mannschaftsbordells.** (**Mannschaftsbordells** probably means = __________)
34. *troop brothels* It can't be that all that has perished in the ceaseless bombardment, despair, and *troop brothels*.	**35.** **leuchten** = *to shine* Wie leuchten die Bäume!
35. Look how the trees are shining!	**36.** **bunt** = *multicolored, colorful* Es ist **Herbst**, die Bäume leuchten bunt und golden. (*harvest/autumn*)
36. It is *autumn*, the trees are shining with varied colors and gold.	**37.** **die Eberesche** = *mountain ash, rowan* Die Ebereschen tragen jetzt rote **Beeren.** (*beer/berries*)
37. The mountain ash now have red *berries.*	**38.** **das Laub** = *foliage* Die Beeren der Ebereschen **stehen rot** im Laub.
38. The berries of the mountain ash *are red* among the foliage.	**39.** **laufen** = *to run* **zulaufen** = *to run towards* Die Beeren stehen rot im Laub. Landstraßen laufen weiß auf den Horizont zu.
39. The berries are red among the foliage, the highways run, white, towards the horizon.	**40.** **der Friede** = *peace* **das Gerücht** = *rumor* Die Kantinen summen wie Bienenstöcke von **Friedensgerüchten.**
40. The canteens are humming like beehives with *rumors of peace.*	**41.** Friedensgerüchte, **wie Bienen**, summen überall.
41. Rumors of peace are humming everywhere, *like bees.*	**42.** Ich stehe auf und bin sehr **ruhig.** (*calm/restless*)
42. I get up and am very *calm.*	**43.** **mögen** = *let,* implying concession **Mögen** die Monate und Jahre kommen, sie können mir nichts mehr nehmen.

43.	*Let* the months and years come. They cannot take anything more from me.	**44.**	**gegen** = *against, toward* **entgegen** = *against, toward* **sehen** = *to see* **entgegensehen** = ___________
44.	*to look forward to, to await*	**45.**	Ich kann **den Monaten** und **Jahren** ohne Furcht entgegensehen. (*dative plural/masculine singular*)
45.	dative plural: the verb takes a dative object. I can look forward *to the months* and *years* without fear.	**46.**	Ich bin so allein und so ohne **Erwartung**, daß ich ihnen entgegensehen kann ohne Furcht. (*expectation/surprise*)
46.	I am so alone and so without *expectation* that I can look forward to them without fear.	**47.**	**tragen** = *to carry* Das Leben **trägt** mich durch diese Jahre. (*carries/will carry*)
47.	Life *will carry* me through these years.	**48.**	**das Auge** = *eye* Das Leben, das mich durch diese Jahre **trug**, ist noch in meinen Händen und Augen.
48.	Life, which *carried* me through these years, is still in my hands and eyes.	**49.**	**überwinden** = *to overcome* Ob ich das Leben **überwunden habe**, weiß ich selbst nicht.
49.	I don't know myself whether I *have overcome* life.	**50.**	Aber **so lange** das Leben da ist, wird es sich seinen Weg suchen . . .
50.	But *as long as* life is there, it will seek its own way . . . (lit.: it will itself seek its way)	**51.**	**mag dieses** = *whether that* **wollen** = *to wish, to want . . .* **mag dieses**, das in mir „Ich" sagt, **wollen** oder nicht.
51.	. . . *whether that* which in me says "I" *wishes* it or not. (Note: Here is an example of a modal, **wollen**, dependent on another modal **mag**.)	**52.**	Er fiel im Oktober 1918: der Tag war ruhig und still.
52.	He *fell* in October 1918. The day was calm and peaceful.	**53.**	**das Heer** = *army* **der Bericht** = *report* **der Heeresbericht** = ___________
53.	*army communiqué*	**54.**	**melden** = *to report* Der Heeresbericht lautet: Im Westen ist nichts Neues zu melden.
54.	The army communiqué reads: There is nothing new to report from the West (i.e., Western front).	**55.**	**sich beschränken** = *to restrict oneself* Der Heeresbericht beschränkt sich nur auf den Satz, im Westen **sei** nichts Neues zu melden.

55. The army communiqué is restricted to the sentence that there *is* nothing new to report from the Western front. (**sei** = subjunctive form of **sein**, §76)	**56.** **vornübergesunken** = *sunk forward* Er war vornübergesunken und lag **wie schlafend** an der Erde.
56. He had fallen forward and was lying on the ground *as if sleeping.*	**57.** **drehen** = *to turn* **umdrehen** = *to turn over, to turn around* Man **drehte** ihn **um.**
57. They *turned* him *over.*	**58.** **die Qual** = *pain, torment, suffering* **sich quälen** = *to suffer* Er **hat sich** nicht lange **gequält.**
58. He *did* not *suffer* long.	**59.** Als man ihn umdrehte, sah man, daß er **sich** nicht lange **gequält haben konnte.**
59. When they turned him over, they saw that he *could* not *have suffered* for long.	**60.** Von seinem **Gesicht** sah man, daß er sich nicht lange gequält haben konnte.
60. From his *face* they saw that he could not have suffered for long.	**61.** **gefaßt** = *calm, composed* Sein Gesicht hatte einen so gefaßten **Ausdruck** . . . (*expression/impression*)
61. His face had such a calm *expression* . . .	**62.** Er war zufrieden **damit.** (*so that/with that*)
62. He was satisfied *with that.*	**63.** **als wäre** = *as if . . . were* Sein Gesicht hatte einen so gefaßten Ausdruck, als wäre er beinahe zufrieden damit, daß es so **gekommen war.** (*was happening/had happened*)
63. His face had such a calm expression, as if he were almost satisfied that it *had happened* that way. (**Wäre** = subjunctive form of **sein,** §73; **damit** refers to the clause that follows.)	

PROGRESS TEST

A. Check your knowledge of the meaning of the possessives used as predicate adjectives or as pronouns.

1. Die Bienenstöcke sind doch nicht *deine!*
(a) your (b) yours (c) your loved ones

2. Die Pappeln, worunter wir jetzt so ruhig und allein stehen, sind *die deinen.*
(a) your (b) yours (c) your loved ones

3. *Das eurige* läßt sich nicht sehen.
   (a) our (b) your (c) yours (d) ours
4. Mit *dem ihren* können wir nicht ins Kino fahren.
   (a) it (b) your family (c) his family (d) hers
5. *Die Ihren* werden mich lieben.
   (a) your (b) your loved ones (c) she (d) they

B. And now which choice conveys the meaning or sense of the German original?

1. Gemeinsam verbrachten wir die Jahre, überflüßig für uns selbst, bis wir ratlos wurden.
   (a) Through the years we had only the best of feelings for one another.
   (b) Once we were separated, our lives lost their meaning.
   (c) We became restless with the years because we had seen the futility of our lives.
   (d) We eventually became helpless because of long years of feeling superfluous.
2. Wenn der Waffenstillstand nicht kommt, werde ich zusammenbrechen.
   (a) The armistice brings to many a desire to go home.
   (b) One of the disappointments which must be accepted is that of the armistice.
   (c) The lack of an armistice breeds disappointment.
   (d) Armistice and disappointment are inevitable.
3. Wenn unsere Erlebnisse eine Revolution entfesseln, werden wir hinfallen und sterben.
   (a) All revolutions come from those dissatisfied with life.
   (b) Whenever we had a revolution we likewise buoyed up our spirits.
   (c) If a revolution takes place, we will not live through it.
   (d) A revolution would not have taken place, had it not been for our decadence.
4. Hinter uns ist ein Geschlecht, das uns überholen wird.
   (a) The new generation will fail.
   (b) Soon there will be a generation to replace us.
   (c) Another species will soon overtake the human race.
   (d) Behind us is a decadent generation.
5. Den Jahren und Monaten sehen sie entgegen, nicht ohne Furcht und Verzweiflung.
   (a) Despair and fear will gradually be dispelled.
   (b) Months and years will pass away without fear and despair.
   (c) You see fear and despair not only in the here and now but also in the years and months to follow.
   (d) They look to the future with fear and despair.

Answer key: A. **1.** (b); **2.** (b); **3.** (c); **4.** (d); **5.** (b).
B. **1.** (d); **2.** (c); **3.** (c); **4.** (b); **5.** (d).

From *Im Westen nichts Neues,* Verlag Kiepenheuer & Witsch, Köln, 1964.

Erich Maria Remarque: Im Westen nichts Neues

Es ist Herbst. Von den alten Leuten sind nicht mehr viele da. Ich bin der letzte von den sieben Mann aus unserer Klasse hier.

Jeder spricht von Frieden und Waffenstillstand. Alle warten. Wenn es wieder eine Enttäuschung wird, dann werden sie zusammenbrechen, die Hoffnungen sind zu stark, sie lassen sich nicht mehr fortschaffen, ohne zu explodieren. Gibt es keinen Frieden, dann gibt es Revolution.

Ich habe vierzehn Tage Ruhe, weil ich etwas Gas geschluckt habe. In einem kleinen Garten sitze ich den ganzen Tag in der Sonne. Der Waffenstillstand kommt bald, ich glaube es jetzt auch. Dann werden wir nach Hause fahren.

Hier stocken meine Gedanken und sind nicht weiterzubringen. Was mich mit Übermacht hinzieht und erwartet, sind Gefühle. Es ist Lebensgier, es ist Heimatgefühl, es ist das Blut, es ist der Rausch der Rettung. Aber es sind keine Ziele.

Wären[1] wir 1916 heimgekommen, wir hätten[2] aus dem Schmerz und der Stärke unserer Erlebnisse einen Sturm entfesselt. Wenn wir jetzt zurückkehren, sind wir müde, zerfallen, ausgebrannt, wurzellos und ohne Hoffnung. Wir werden uns nicht mehr zurechtfinden können.

Man wird uns auch nicht verstehen—denn vor uns wächst ein Geschlecht, das zwar die Jahre hier gemeinsam mit uns verbrachte, das aber Bett und Beruf hatte und jetzt zurückgeht in seine alten Positionen, in denen es den Krieg vergessen wird,—und hinter uns wächst ein Geschlecht, ähnlich uns früher, das wird uns fremd sein und uns beiseiteschieben. Wir sind überflüssig für uns selbst, wir werden wachsen, einige werden sich anpassen, andere sich fügen, und viele werden ratlos sein:—die Jahre werden zerrinnen, und schließlich werden wir zugrunde gehen.

Aber vielleicht ist auch alles dieses, was ich denke, nur Schwermut und Bestürzung, die fortstäubt, wenn ich wieder unter den Pappeln stehe und dem Rauschen ihrer Blätter lausche. Es kann nicht sein, daß es fort ist, das Weiche, das unser Blut unruhig machte, das Ungewisse, Bestürzende, Kommende, die tausend Gesichter der Zukunft, die Melodie aus Träumen und Büchern, das Rauschen und die Ahnung der Frauen, es kann nicht sein, daß es untergegangen ist in Trommelfeuer, Verzweiflung und Mannschaftsbordells.

Die Bäume hier leuchten bunt und golden, die Beeren der Ebereschen[3] stehen rot im Laub. Landstraßen laufen weiß auf den Horizont zu, und die Kantinen summen wie Bienenstöcke von Friedensgerüchten.

Ich stehe auf.

Ich bin sehr ruhig. Mögen die Monate und Jahre kommen, sie nehmen mir nichts mehr, sie können mir nichts mehr nehmen. Ich bin so allein und so ohne Erwartung, daß ich ihnen entgegensehen kann ohne Furcht. Das Leben, das mich durch diese Jahre trug, ist noch in meinen Händen und Augen. Ob ich es überwunden habe, weiß ich nicht. Aber so lange es da ist, wird es sich seinen Weg suchen, mag dieses, das in mir „Ich" sagt, wollen oder nicht.

* * *

1 wären (*subjunctive form*) = *had*

2 hätte (*subjunctive form*) = *would have*

3 *mountain ash, rowan* (*tree*)

Er fiel im Oktober 1918, an einem Tage, der so ruhig und still war an der ganzen Front, daß der Heeresbericht sich nur auf den Satz beschränkte, im Westen sei nichts Neues zu melden.

Er war vornübergesunken und lag wie schlafend an der Erde. Als man ihn umdrehte, sah man, daß er sich nicht lange gequält haben konnte;—sein Gesicht hatte einen so gefaßten Ausdruck, als wäre er beinahe zufrieden damit, daß es so gekommen war.

Chapter Seventeen

58. *Indefinite pronouns and adjectives*

1. The most common indefinite pronouns and adjectives are as follows:

man	*one, you, they, we, people, a person, someone*
einer	*one, someone*
keiner	*nobody, no one, none*
jemand	*somebody, someone, anybody, anyone*
irgend jemand	*anyone*
jemand anders	*someone else, anyone else*
sonst jemand	*someone else, anyone else*
niemand	*nobody, no one*
niemand anders	*no one else*
sonst niemand	*no one else*
jedermann	*everybody, everyone*
jeder	*everybody, everyone*
all(**e**)	*all, everyone*
alles	*everything*
alles mögliche	*everything possible*
alles übrige	*all the rest*
alles andere	*all else*
viel	*much, a lot*
viele	*many, lots of*
vieles	*many things, lots of things*
wenig	*little* (in quantity)
wenige	*few*
nichts	*nothing*
irgend	*any, some (or other)* [rarely used alone]
irgendein (adj.)	*some (or other), any*
irgendeiner	*someone* (emphatic)
etwas	*something, some* (meaning: *just a little*)

irgend etwas	*something (or other), anything*
etwas anderes	*something else, anything other, anything else*
nichts anderes	*nothing else*
ein paar	*a few, several*
ein Paar (**n.**)	*a pair, two, a couple*
mehrere	*several* (in the sense of *more*)
verschiedene	*several* (in the sense of *different*), *various*
einige	*some, a few*
etliche	*some, several, a few*
ander-	*other*
mancher	*many a* (person)
manches	*some things*
manche	*some* (people)
allerlei	*all sorts of*
ein bißchen	*a little*
beides	*both things*
beide	*both*

Give the meanings of the bold words.

	1. Vielleicht kennen Sie den Namen Karl Jaspers.
1. Perhaps you are acquainted with the name Karl Jaspers.	**2.** Er ist **einer** von den großen deutschen Philosophen des zwanzigsten Jahrhunderts.
2. He is *one* of the great German philosophers of the twentieth century.	**3.** **versäumen** = *to neglect, to fail, to miss* **Keiner** soll die Gelegenheit versäumen, **etwas** aus seinen Schriften zu lesen.
3. *No one* should neglect the opportunity to read *something* from his writings.	**4.** In diesem Kapitel werden Sie einen Auszug lesen aus seinem Werk: *Die Atombombe und die Zukunft des Menschen.*
4. In this chapter you will read an extract from his *The Atom Bomb and the Future of Man.*	**5.** **besprechen** = *to discuss* Wir werden jetzt **einige** Gedanken daraus besprechen.
5. We will now discuss *some* ideas from it.	**6.** **abschaffen** = *to abolish, to scrap* Jaspers schreibt daß **jeder** will, daß die Atombomben abgeschafft werden.
6. Jaspers writes that *everybody* wants atom bombs to be abolished.	**7.** Oder ist **irgend jemand** dagegen?
7. Or is *anyone* (*someone*) against that?	**8.** **erklären** = *to declare* **bereit** = *ready* Will **jedermann** sich dazu bereit erklären?
8. Is *everyone* willing to declare himself ready to do that?	**9.** **Alle** Denkenden wollen es, und **alle** Staaten erklären sich bereit.

9. *All* thinking people desire it, and *all* states declare themselves ready.	**10.** **wagen** = *to dare* **anwenden** = *to use, to employ* **Niemand** wird es wagen, die Atombomben anzuwenden.
10. *No one* will dare to use atom bombs.	**11.** **die Waffe** = *weapon* Wird **jemand anders** es wagen, diese Atomwaffen anzuwenden?
11. Will *anyone else* dare to employ these atomic weapons?	**12.** Darf **sonst jemand** außer den Russen und den Amerikanern Atomwaffen besitzen?
12. Is *anyone else* except the Russians and the Americans allowed to possess atomic weapons?	**13.** **Niemand anders** wird so verrückt sein. Atomwaffen besitzen zu wollen, **oder**?
13. *No one else* will be so mad as to want to possess atomic weapons, *will they*?	**14.** **treffen** = *to strike* Wenn eine Waffe **beide Gegner** trifft . . . (If **gegen** means *against,* **Gegner** must mean ________)
14. *opponent* If a weapon strikes *both opponents* . . . (Note: **Gegner** may be singular or plural depending on context.)	**15.** . . . wird **jemand** diese Waffe anwenden wollen?
15. . . . will *anyone* want to employ this weapon?	**16.** **Viele** glauben, daß ein Atomkrieg unmöglich geworden ist.
16. *Many* believe that an atomic war has become impossible.	**17.** Gibt es **irgendeinen,** der nicht glaubt, daß ein Atomkrieg stattfinden wird?
17. Is there *anyone* who does not believe that an atomic war will take place?	**18.** **verhältnismäßig** = *relatively* Wollen Sie sagen, daß nur verhältnismäßig **wenige** einen Krieg wollen?
18. Do you mean to say that only a relatively *few* want there to be a war?	**19.** **Etliche** glauben, daß jeder Krieg unmöglich geworden ist.
19. *A few* believe that any (every) war has become impossible.	**20.** **Manche** glauben, daß keine Großmacht mehr wagen wird, einen Krieg zu beginnen.
20. *Some* believe that no major power will dare anymore to begin a war.	**21.** **vernichten** = *to destroy, to annihilate* **die Vernichtung** = ________
21. *annihilation, destruction*	**22.** **könnte** = *could* Heute will **mancher** nicht glauben, daß es je einen Vernichtungskrieg geben könnte.
22. *Many a person* today does not want to believe that there could ever be a war of annihilation.	**23.** **das Zeitalter** = *age* Ist unser Zeitalter **irgend etwas anderes** als das Zeitalter der Kriege?
23. Is our age *anything other* than the age of war?	**24.** **Beides** können wir nicht auf einmal haben: Krieg und Frieden.

24. War and peace: we cannot have *both* at the same time.	**25.** **Vieles** wird gesagt.
25. *Much* is (*many things* are) said.	**26.** Es wird **viel** gesagt.
26. *Much* is said. (Many things are said.) (Note the "dummy" subject **es**.)	**27.** **Manches** wird gesagt, aber nichts wird getan.
27. *A great deal* is said, but nothing is done.	**28.** **herstellen** = *to manufacture* Kann man **nichts anderes** tun, als nur zuschauen, wie Atomwaffen hergestellt werden?
28. Can one do *nothing but* watch atomic weapons being manufactured?	**29.** **Alles** können die großen Nationen nicht tun.
29. The major nations cannot do *everything.*	**30.** Wir müssen **alles mögliche** tun.
30. We must do *everything possible.*	**31.** Es kann **nur wenig** gesagt werden.
31. There's *not much* one can say (that can be said).	**32.** **Alles übrige** muß man eben erfahren.
32. One will just have to experience *all the rest.*	**33.** **fortlaufen** = *to run away, to continue on* **fortlaufend** = *continuous* Wir müssen **irgendeine** Kontrolle für die fortlaufende Produktion der Atombomben finden.
33. We must find *some kind of* control for the continuous production of atomic bombs.	**34.** **Verschiedene** Nationen wollen keinen Krieg, **verschiedene** scheinen doch den Krieg zu wollen.
34. *Some* nations do not want war; *some,* however, do seem to want war.	**35.** **Mehrere** haben sich neutrale Länder genannt.
35. *Several* have proclaimed themselves neutral countries.	**36.** **Ein paar** scheinen überhaupt kein Interesse daran zu haben.
36. *A few* seem to have no interest at all in the issue.	**37.** **reden** = *to talk* **Allerlei** wird geredet.
37. *All sorts of things* are said.	**38.** Ist **ein bißchen** Krieg besser als gar keiner?
38. Is *a little* war better than none at all?	**39.** Muß man **alles andere** einfach in die Hände Gottes legen?
39. Must one simply place *everything else* into God's hands?	**40.** **entstehen** = *to originate, to arise, to break out* Für **andere** ist es unmöglich, daß je ein Vernichtungskrieg wird entstehen können.
40. For *others* it is impossible that a war of annihilation will ever be able to break out.	

PROGRESS TEST

Choose the correct meaning for the indicated word.

1. Ist *jemand* gegen die Abschaffung der Atomwaffen?
(a) all the rest (b) everyone (c) anyone (d) someone else

2. *Jeder* will, daß die Großmächte nicht in einen Krieg geraten.
(a) many (b) everyone (c) several (d) some

3. *Irgendeiner* muß doch eingreifen!
(a) a considerable number (b) several (c) a few (d) someone

4. *Alles übrige* müssen Sie tun.
(a) all the rest (b) everything possible (c) all sorts of things (d) anything

5. *Allerlei* wird geglaubt.
(a) all the rest (b) everything (c) all sorts of things (d) anything

6. *Etliche* wollen nicht, daß sie denken sollen.
(a) some (b) many (c) all the rest (d) something

7. Es ist *sonst niemand* da.
(a) something (b) no one else (c) nothing (d) someone

8. *Verschiedene* können das nicht verstehen.
(a) all of them (b) someone else (c) many (d) various people

Answer key: **1.** (c); **2.** (b); **3.** (d); **4.** (a); **5.** (c); **6.** (a); **7.** (b); **8.** (d).

59. *Special uses of the genitive*

1. The genitive is used to express indefinite time:

eines Tages	*one day, some day*
eines Morgens	*one morning, some morning*
eines Abends	*one evening, some evening*
morgens	*in the morning*
abends	*in the evening*
nachts	*at night*
etc.	

2. *On my* (*your, his,* etc.) *account* is expressed by the possessive adjectives in combination with the preposition **wegen:**

meinetwegen, deinetwegen, seinetwegen, etc.

Note the **-et-** insertion between the possessive adjective and **wegen.**

3. Similarly *for my* (*your, his,* etc.) *sake* is expressed by a combination of the possessive adjective with **um . . . willen:**

um meinetwillen, um deinetwillen, um seinetwillen, etc.

Give the meaning of the indicated phrases.

	1. **einkaufen** = *to shop* **Vormittags** gehen wir immer einkaufen. (*in the morning/in the afternoon*)
1. We always go shopping *in the morning.*	**2.** **Eines Tages** müssen wir aufhören, Kriege zu führen. (*for one day/one of these days*)
2. *One of these days* we must stop having (conducting) wars.	**3.** **Euretwegen** ist er nicht gekommen.
3. He did not come *because of you.*	**4.** **Ihretwegen** dürfen wir nicht ins Kino gehen.
4. *Because of them* (*her, you*) we cannot go to the movies.	**5.** **Um ihretwillen** müssen sie das Rauchen aufgeben.
5. They have to give up smoking *for their* (*her*) *sake.*	**6.** **Meinetwegen** können Sie nach Hause gehen.
6. *As far as I'm concerned* you can go home.	

READING PREPARATION

Since Jaspers wrote these thoughts in 1957 the relations between the superpowers have undergone many changes. In which of his predictions for the future was he right, and in which was he wide of the mark? Look also for his underlying view of human nature as it is revealed in relationships between nations when war is not renounced.

	1. **gültig** = *valid* **die Gültigkeit** = *validity* Was Karl Jaspers damals in den fünfziger Jahren über die Atombombe zu sagen hatte, hat immer noch Gültigkeit.
1. What Karl Jaspers had to say in the fifties about the atomic bomb is still valid (today).	**2.** Alle Denkenden wollen, daß die Atomwaffen **abgeschafft werden.** (*will abolish/to be abolished*)
2. All thinking people want atomic weapons *to be abolished.*	**3.** Alle Staaten erklären sich bereit.
3. All countries declare themselves ready.	**4.** **abschaffen** = *to abolish* **die Abschaffung** = __________

4. *the abolition*	**5. zuverlässig** = *reliable* Wir wollen **aber** eine zuverlässige Abschaffung. (*but/however*)
5. We want, *however,* a reliable abolition.	**6.** Aber die Abschaffung ist nur zuverlässig, wenn **zugleich** eine Kontrolle stattfindet.
6. But abolition is only reliable if *at the same time* a control is established.	**7. die Gegenseite** = *opposite side, reverse* **die Gegenseitigkeit** = *reciprocity* **gegenseitig** = *mutual, reciprocal* Eine Abschaffung ist nur zuverlässig, wenn zugleich **eine gegenseitige Kontrolle** stattfindet.
7. An abolition is only reliable if at the same time *mutual surveillance* is established.	**8.** Ein zweiter Gedanke ist . . .
8. A second thought is . . .	**9.** . . . **auch wenn** die Atombomben nicht abgeschafft sind . . . (*also when/even if*)
9. . . . *even if* atom bombs are not abolished . . .	**10.** . . . wird niemand es wagen, **sie** anzuwenden. (*they/them*)
10. . . . no one will dare to use *them.*	**11. herstellen** = *to produce* **die Herstellung** = __________
11. *production*	**12. das Gift** = *poison* **das Gas** = *gas* die Herstellung der Giftgase
12. the production of poisonous gases	**13. die Masse** = *mass, bulk* **massenhaft** = *wholesale, enormous* **Trotz** massenhafter Herstellung der Giftgase . . . (*because of/in spite of*)
13. *In spite of* wholesale production of poisonous gases . . .	**14. setzen** = *to set* **einsetzen** = *to employ* Hitler **hat** die Giftgase in seiner Katastrophe nicht **eingesetzt.**
14. Hitler *did* not *employ* poisonous gases in his catastrophe.	**15.** Trotz massenhafter Herstellung der Giftgase hat Hitler diese **auch** in seiner Katastrophe nicht eingesetzt. (*also/even*)
15. In spite of wholesale production of poisonous gases Hitler did not employ these *even* in his catastrophe.	**16. anwenden** = *to use, employ* **anwendbar** = *usable, employable* Die Waffe ist **unanwendbar** geworden.

16. The weapon has become *unusable.*	**17.** Wenn eine Waffe **notwendig** beide Gegner vernichtend trifft . . . (*necessarily/unnecessarily*)
17. If a weapon *necessarily* annihilates both opponents . . .	**18.** . . . ist **sie** unanwendbar geworden.
18. . . . *it* becomes (has become) unusable.	**19.** **Weil** der Atomkrieg unmöglich geworden ist, ist jeder Krieg unmöglich geworden? (*because/while*)
19. *Because* atomic war has become impossible, has every war become impossible?	**20.** **einsetzen** = *to employ* **der Einsatz** = __________
20. *the employment, use*	**21.** **drohen** = *to threaten* . . . der Einsatz **der** Atombombe droht . . .
21. . . . the use *of the* atomic bomb threatens . . .	**22.** **irgend** = *any, some* (*or other*) **wann** = *when* **irgendwann** = *at some time* (*or other*) In einem Weltkrieg droht **irgendwann** der Einsatz der Atombombe.
22. In a world war the use of the atomic bomb will be a threat *at some time or other.* (Lit.: threatens)	**23.** **der Staat** = *state* **die Ordnung** = *order* **die Staatsordnung** = __________
23. *political system, political order*	**24.** **der Sinn** = *meaning* der Sinn der Staatsordnung
24. the meaning of political order	**25.** **um** = *over, about* ein Weltkrieg um **den Sinn der Staatsordnung**
25. a world war over *political ideology* (i.e., *the meaning of political order*)	**26.** In einem Weltkrieg um den Sinn der Staatsordnung **droht** irgendwann **doch** der Einsatz der Atombombe.
26. In a world war over political ideology the use of the atomic bomb *will be a threat* at some time or other. (**Doch** is used here as an intensifier and is not translated.)	**27.** **auf Leben und Tod** = *to the death* **Denn da** in einem Weltkrieg um den Sinn der Staatsordnung auf Leben und Tod . . .
27. *For since* in a world war to the death over political ideology . . .	**28.** Denn da in einem Weltkrieg um den Sinn der Staatsordnung auf Leben und Tod irgendwann **doch** der Einsatz der Atombombe **droht** . . .
28. For since in a world war to the death over political ideology the use of the atomic bomb *does threaten* at some time or other . . .	**29.** . . . wird **keine** Großmacht **mehr** wagen, den Krieg zu beginnen.

29. . . . no major power will *any longer* dare to start a war.	**30.** **würde** = *would become* **Weil** der Krieg für alle der Vernichtungs-krieg würde, kann er nicht mehr entstehen.
30. *Because* the war would become a war of annihilation for all, it can no longer happen.	**31.** **retten** = *to deliver, to save, to rescue* **der Retter** = *deliverer, rescuer, savior* **die totale Rettung** = __________
31. *the total deliverance*	**32.** **bedrohen** = *to threaten* **die totale Bedrohung** = __________
32. *the total threat*	**33.** **zeugen** = *to beget, to produce* **erzeugen** = *to breed, to generate, to produce* Die totale Bedrohung erzeugt die totale Rettung.
33. Total threat produces total deliverance.	**34.** Der Vernichtungskrieg kann nicht mehr **entstehen**, denn die totale Bedrohung erzeugt die totale Rettung.
34. A war of annihilation can no longer *happen*, since total threat produces total deliverance.	**35.** **die Not** = *distress (need, necessity)* **die Notsituation** = __________
35. *the state of distress or emergency*	**36.** **das Dasein** = *life, presence, existence* **gestalten** = *to shape, form* **die Gestaltung** = *the shaping, the form* **die Daseinsgestaltung** = __________
36. *the shaping of life, the form of existence*	**37.** **zwingen** = *to force, to compel* **erzwingen** = *to determine necessarily, to force* Die Notsituation erzwingt die Daseinsgestaltung.
37. The state of distress necessarily determines the shaping of existence.	**38.** **äußerst** = *utmost, most extreme, extremely* Die äußerste Notsituation erzwingt die Formen **politischer** Daseinsgestaltung.
38. The most extreme state of distress necessarily determines the shaping *of political* forms of existence.	**39.** Diese Formen, zusammen mit der Atom-bombe, machen auch den Krieg **überhaupt** unmöglich.
39. These forms, together with the atom bomb, also make war *completely* impossible.	**40.** Die äußerste Notsituation erzwingt die Formen politischer Daseinsgestaltung, die mit der Atombombe auch den Krieg überhaupt unmöglich machen.
40. The most extreme state of distress produces forms of political existence which, together with the atomic bomb, also make war completely impossible.	**41.** **entwickeln** = *to develop, to unfold* **die Entwicklung** = __________

41. *the development*	**42.** **wäre** = *would be* (subjunctive form of **sein**; cf. chapter 21) Es wäre die **glücklichste** Entwicklung.
42. It would be the *most fortunate* development.	**43.** **liegen** = *to lie* **läge** (subjunctive) = *would lie* Das Zeitalter der Kriege läge hinter uns.
43. The age of war would lie behind us.	**44.** **bewegen** = *to stir, to set in motion* Neue, ganz andere Probleme **würden** uns bewegen.
44. New, completely different problems *would* stir us. (Or: *would* set us in motion.)	**45.** **bleiben** = *to remain* **ausbleiben** = *to stay away, to be absent* **das Ausbleiben** = __________
45. *absence, failure (to appear)*	**46.** Was **würde** durch das Ausbleiben der Kriege **entstehen**?
46. In the absence of wars, what would come into being? (Lit.: What *would begin* because of the absence of wars?)	**47.** Neue, ganz andere schwere Probleme, **die** durch das Ausbleiben der Kriege entstehen, würden uns bewegen. (*who/which*)
47. New, completely different, and difficult problems *which* arise in the absence of war would stir us.	**48.** **geschehen** = *to happen* Was **aber** geschieht wirklich?
48. What, *however,* really happens?	**49.** **gestehen** = *to confess* **zugestehen** = *to concede, admit* **zugestanden** = *conceded, admitted* Was **wird** nicht **zugestanden?**
49. What *is* not *conceded?*	**50.** Was aber geschieht wirklich, **da** die gegenseitige Kontrolle nicht zugestanden wird?
50. What, however, really happens, *since* mutual control is not conceded?	**51.** Weil die gegenseitige Kontrolle nicht zugestanden wird, findet eine fortlaufende Produktion der Atombomben statt.
51. Because mutual control is not conceded, a *continual* production of atom bombs takes place.	**52.** **ständig** = *continually* Und trotz der Atombombe gibt es ständig Kriege.
52. And in spite of the atom bomb there are wars continually.	**53.** **die Wüste** = *desert* **verwüsten** = *to devastate* Sie sind aber **verwüstende** Kriege.
53. They are, however, *devastating* wars.	**54.** **messen** = *to measure* **gemessen** = *measured* **Gemessen** am Weltkrieg . . .
54. *Compared* to a world war . . .	**55.** **zwar** = *it is true, indeed* Gemessen am Weltkrieg sind es **zwar** kleine lokale Kriege . . .

55. Compared to a world war they are small local wars, *it is true* . . .	**56.** **jedoch** = *yet, however* . . . hier jedoch sind sie furchtbar verwüstende Kriege.
56. . . . here, however, they are terribly devastating wars.	**57.** Gemessen am Weltkrieg sind es **zwar** kleine lokale Kriege, hier jedoch furchtbar verwüstende Kriege.
57. Compared to a world war they are *indeed* small local wars; here, however, they are terribly devastating wars.	**58.** **der Satz** = *proposition, tenet* (also: *sentence*) **Statt des Satzes**: es wird keine Kriege geben . . .
58. *Instead of the proposition*: there will be no wars . . .	**59.** **vielmehr** = *rather* . . . **muß es vielmehr heißen**: es kann heute Kriege geben ohne Atombombe.
59. . . . *it really ought to read:* today there can be wars without the atomic bomb. (Lit.: *it must rather state*)	**60.** **das Vorrecht** = *privilege* Ist es nur ein Vorrecht der kleinen Nationen, Krieg zu **führen?** (*lead/wage*)
60. Is it only a privilege of the small nations to *wage* war?	**61.** **der Schreck(en)** = *terror, fright* **schrecklich** = *terrible, frightful, dreadful* **Sollte** es ein schreckliches Vorrecht der Kleinen **werden,** Krieg zu führen?
61. *Should* it *become* a terrible privilege of the small nations to wage war?	**62.** **die Gewalt** = *power, force* **der Akt** = *act* **der Gewaltakt** = __________
62. *the act of violence*	**63.** **vollziehen** = *to execute, to accomplish* Sie vollziehen schreckliche Gewaltakte.
63. They execute terrible acts of violence.	**64.** **der Zustand** = *state, condition* Sie vollziehen Gewaltakte, **um** ihren Zustand **zu ändern.**
64. They carry out acts of violence *in order to change* their condition.	**65.** **ob** = *over, above* **siegen** = *to win, to be victorious* **obsiegen** = *to triumph over, to conquer* Sie wollen mit schrecklicher Gewalt obsiegen.
65. They want to conquer with terrible force.	**66.** **das Verfahren** = *procedure, method, system* Es ist ein altes Verfahren.
66. It is an old procedure.	**67.** Sie bedrohen ihre kleinen Gegner, **um nach** alten Verfahren ob**zu**siegen.
67. *According to* old procedures they threaten their small opponents *in order to* conquer them.	**68.** **die Gefahr** = *danger* **irgendeine** Gefahr des Weltkrieges

68. *any* danger of world war	**69.** **wirken auf** = *to have an effect on* Irgendeine Gefahr des Weltkrieges wirkt auf uns.
69. Any danger of world war has an effect on us.	**70.** **schüchtern** = *shy* **einschüchtern** = *to intimidate* **einschüchternd** = *intimidating* Die Gefahr des Weltkrieges wirkt **einschüchternd** auf die Großen.
70. The danger of world war has an *intimidating* effect on the great nations.	**71.** **der Vertrag** = *treaty (agreement, contract)* Die Kleinen brechen Verträge.
71. The small nations break treaties.	**72.** **die Gewalt** = *power, force* **gewaltsam** = *forcible, violent* **Verschiedene** kleine Nationen brechen gewaltsam Verträge.
72. *Various* small nations forcibly break treaties.	**73.** Wenn **die Kleinen** gewaltsam Verträge brechen, wagen die Großen nicht . . .
73. Whenever *the small nations* forcibly break treaties, the great nations do not dare . . .	**74.** **achten** = *to respect, to pay attention* **die Achtung** = __________
74. *respect, attention*	**75.** **schaffen** = *to create, to make, to do* **verschaffen** = *to gain, to promote* **Irgendetwas** muß Achtung verschaffen.
75. *Something* must promote respect.	**76.** Kann man durch Gewalt Achtung verschaffen?
76. Can one promote respect through force?	**77.** **das Recht** = *privilege, right* **brechen** = *to break* Das Recht, durch Gewalt **gebrochen** . . .
77. Rights *violated* by force . . . (lit.: *broken*)	**78.** Das durch Gewalt gebrochene Recht . . .
78. Rights violated by force . . .	**79.** Die Großen wagen nicht, **dem gebrochenen Recht** Achtung zu verschaffen.
79. The great nations do not dare to promote respect *for violated rights.*	**80.** Die Großen wagen nicht, **dem durch Gewalt gebrochenen Recht** durch Gewalt Achtung zu verschaffen.
80. The great nations do not dare to promote respect by force *for rights violated by force.* (This is an example of a modified participial construction to be dealt with in §60.)	**81.** **Wenn** die Kleinen gewaltsam Verträge brechen, wagen die Großen nicht, dem durch Gewalt gebrochenen Recht durch Gewalt Achtung zu verschaffen.

81. *When* (*whenever*) small nations break treaties forcibly, great nations do not dare to promote respect by force for rights broken by force.	**82.** **eins** = *one* **einig** = *in agreement, agreed* Unter den großen Staaten ist **keiner** einig.
82. Among the great nations *no one* is in agreement.	**83.** **verteidigen** = *to defend* **die Verteidigung** = ________
83. *defense*	**84.** Die Großen sind nicht einig in der Verteidigung **des** Rechts und **der** Verträge.
84. The great nations are not in agreement about the defense *of* rights and treaties.	**85.** Aber dies Vorrecht **der souveränen Kleinen**, Kriege zu führen, ist nur möglich, weil die Großen nicht einig sind in der Verteidigung des Rechts und der Verträge.
85. But this privilege *of the small sovereign nations* to wage wars is possible only because the great nations are not in agreement concerning the defense of rights and treaties.	**86.** **nutzen** = *to make use of, to utilize* **ausnutzen** = *to exploit* Die großen Mächte **nutzen** die Kleinen **aus**.
86. The great powers *exploit* the small ones.	**87.** Die Großen nutzen **vielmehr** die Akte der Kleinen aus. (*rather/much more*)
87. *Rather* the great powers exploit the acts of the small.	**88.** **behaupten** = *to maintain, to hold* Die Großmächte wollen ihre **eigenen** Machtpositionen behaupten.
88. The major powers want to maintain their *own* positions of power.	**89.** **weiter** = *farther* **erweitern** = *to enlarge, to extend* Die Großen wollen ihre eigenen Machtpositionen **gegeneinander** erweitern oder behaupten.
89. The great nations want to extend or to maintain their own positions of power *with respect to one another.*	**90.** Sie nutzen vielmehr die Akte der Kleinen aus, **um** die eigenen Machtpositionen gegeneinander **zu** erweitern oder **zu** behaupten.
90. They exploit rather the acts of the small nations *in order to* extend or *to* maintain their own positions of power with respect to one another.	**91.** **lähmen** = *to paralyze* **gelähmt** = *paralyzed* **Je mächtiger** die Staaten, **desto mehr** scheinen sie gelähmt.
91. *The more powerful* the nations, *the more* they seem paralyzed.	**92.** **vorläufig** = *for the present, for the time being* Die mächtigen Staaten **scheinen** vorläufig gelähmt.
92. The powerful nations *appear* for the time being to be paralyzed.	**93.** Je mächtiger die Staaten **durch** die Bombe sind, desto mehr scheinen sie vorläufig gelähmt . . .

93. The more powerful the nations are *because of* the bomb, the more they appear for the time being to be paralyzed . . .	**94.** . . . **während** die Kleinen ihre Gewaltakte vollziehen.
94. . . . *while* the small nations carry out their acts of aggression.	**95.** Was ist **nun** weiter möglich?
95. *Now* what else is (further) possible?	**96.** **die Mühe** = *trouble, pains* **sich die Mühe geben** = *to take pains* **sich bemühen** = ________
96. *to take trouble, to take pains, to strive*	**97.** Die großen Staaten bemühen sich . . .
97. The large nations strive . . .	**98.** **der Kampf** = *the fight, struggle* **kämpfen** = *fight, struggle* **kämpfend** = ________
98. *fighting, struggling*	**99.** Die Großen bemühen sich, die kämpfenden Kleinen zum **Frieden** zu bringen. (*freedom/peace*)
99. The great nations strive to bring the little nations who are fighting to *a peaceful settlement* (i.e., to *peace*).	**100.** **hinter** = *behind* **der Gedanke** = *thought* **der Hintergedanke** = ________
100. *ulterior motive*	**101.** Die Großen bemühen sich, die kämpfenden Kleinen zum Frieden zu bringen, **aber nicht ohne** Hintergedanken.
101. The great nations strive to bring the small nations who are fighting to a peaceful settlement, *but not without* ulterior motives.	**102.** **dulden** = *to endure, to tolerate, to put up with* **die Duldung** = ________
102. *endurance, tolerance*	**103.** **der Schutz** = *protection, defense* Die kleinen Staaten kämpfen unter der Duldung und dem Schutz der Großen.
103. The small countries fight under the toleration and protection of the large.	**104.** **teilweis**(**e**) = *in part* Unter **ihrem** teilweisen Schutz kämpfen die kleinen Nationen.
104. The small nations fight under *their* partial protection.	**105.** Während die Kleinen unter der Duldung und unter dem teilweisen Schutz der Großen kämpfen . . .
105. While the small nations fight under the toleration and under the partial protection of the great nations . . .	**106.** **geraten** = *to get into* . . . so geraten die Großen in die **Gefahr** des Weltkrieges. (*safety/danger*)

106.	. . . the large nations are in *danger* of getting into a world war.	**107.**	**tragen** = *to carry* **austragen** = *to have it out with, to wage* Die Gefahr des Weltkrieges, der **zwischen** den Großmächten auszutragen ist . . .
107.	The danger of a world war which is to be waged *between* the great powers . . .	**108.**	Die Gefahr des zwischen ihnen **aus-zutragenden** Weltkriegs . . .
108.	The danger of a world war *to be waged* between them . . .	**109.**	So geraten **sie ständig selber** in die Gefahr des zwischen ihnen auszutragen-den Weltkriegs.
109.	So *they themselves* are *continuously* in danger of getting into a world war to be waged between themselves.	**110.**	So geraten die Großen, während die Kleinen unter ihrer Duldung und ihrem teilweisen Schutz kämpfen, ständig selber **in die Gefahr des zwischen ihnen auszutragenden Weltkriegs**.
110.	Thus the large nations themselves are continually *in danger of (getting into) a world war to be waged against each other (between themselves)* while the small nations fight under the tol-eration and the partial protection of the large ones. (Another example of a modified participial construction; see §60.)	**111.**	**gemein** = *common* **gemeinsam** = *(in) common* Keine gemeinsame Ordnung hält die Großen zusammen.
111.	No common order holds the large nations together.	**112.**	**bewußt** = *known* **sein** = *to be* **das Bewußtsein** = *consciousness* Kein Bewußtsein **gemeinsamer** Ord-nung hält sie zusammen.
112.	No consciousness *of a common* order holds them together. (Notice the genitive use of **gemeinsamer.**)	**113.**	**hinaus** = *out, away from* **schieben** = *to shove, to push* **hinausschieben** = *to postpone, to put off* **das Hinausschieben** = ________
113.	*postponement*	**114.**	Es ist **wie** ein Hinausschieben des Weltkriegs.
114.	It is *like* a postponement of world war.	**115.**	Es ist, da kein Bewußtsein gemeinsamer Ordnung zusammenhält, **immer nur** wie ein Hinausschieben des Weltkriegs.
115.	It is *always* like a postponement of world war, since no common order holds (them) together.	**116.**	**die Welt** = *world* **der Brand** = *burning, conflagration* **der Weltbrand** = ________

116. *world conflagration*	**117.** **bergen** = *to conceal, to harbor* Jeder Krieg birgt in sich die Gefahr des **Weltbrandes.**
117. Every war harbors in itself the danger of *world conflagration.*	**118.** **der Schleier** = *veil, (smoke) screen* **verschleiern** = *to veil, to disguise* **verschleiert** = *veiled, disguised, in disguise* Jeder kleine Krieg ist verschleiert ein Krieg zwischen den Großmächten.
118. Every small war is a war between the great powers in disguise.	**119.** Da jeder kleine Krieg verschleiert schon ein Krieg zwischen den Großmächten ist . . .
119. Since every small war is already a disguised war between the great powers . . .	**120.** . . . birgt jeder in sich die Gefahr des Weltbrandes.
120. . . . each harbors in itself the danger of world conflagration.	

PROGRESS TEST

Choose the correct meaning for the following sentences.

1. Trotz massenhafter Herstellung der Atomwaffen wird der Krieg unmöglich gemacht, denn jeder Staat hat Angst, Kriege zu führen.
(a) War will exist in spite of the massive production of atomic weapons.
(b) Because of the production of atomic weapons all nations fear war.
(c) War is impossible because of the tremendous production of atomic weapons.
(d) War is impossible in spite of the massive production of atomic weapons, because every nation is afraid to make war.

2. Es gibt ständig Kriege, die furchtbar verwüstend sind, denn das ist das Vorrecht der Kleinen.
(a) No one has the right to wage war.
(b) Standing wars are the most devastating because little people will always win.
(c) It is the privilege of small nations to wage war continually.
(d) The privilege of war should only be given to small countries.

3. So geraten die Großen, während die Kleinen unter ihrer Duldung und ihrem Schutz kämpfen, ständig selber in die Gefahr des zwischen ihnen auszutragenden Weltkriegs.
(a) Great nations cause small nations to become embroiled in fighting wars.
(b) The danger of having small nations fight wars is that the large nations who support them may become caught up.
(c) Large and small nations are continually fighting a war which may bring them both to their knees if they are not careful.
(d) World war is only a possibility if the large nations do not get caught up in the affairs of the small.

4. Wenn die äußerste Notsituation die Formen politischer Daseinsgestaltung erzwingt, ist es die glücklichste Entwicklung.
   (a) Forms of political success are a rare achievement.
   (b) If forms of political distress bring about extreme forms of government, it is a most unlucky development.
   (c) We are most fortunate if the extreme state of distress determines the forms of political existence.
   (d) Forms of political existence luckily develop from extremely small situations.

Answer key: **1.** (d); **2.** (c); **3.** (b); **4.** (c).

Before proceeding to the reading passage, review the vocabulary you have circled. Repetition in learning a language is not a vice.

From *Die Atombombe und die Zukunft des Menschen:* R. Piper & Co. Verlag. München. 1957.

Karl Jaspers: Was soll politisch geschehen?

Alle Denkenden wollen, daß die Atomwaffen abgeschafft werden. Alle Staaten erklären sich bereit. Aber die Abschaffung ist nur zuverlässig, wenn zugleich die gegenseitige Kontrolle stattfindet.

Der zweite Gedanke ist: Auch wenn die Atombomben nicht abgeschafft sind, wird niemand es wagen, sie anzuwenden. Hitler hat trotz massenhafter Herstellung der Giftgase diese auch in seiner Katastrophe nicht eingesetzt. Wenn eine Waffe notwendig beide Gegner vernichtend trifft, ist sie unanwendbar geworden.

Der dritte Gedanke ist: Weil der Atomkrieg unmöglich geworden ist, ist jeder Krieg unmöglich geworden. Denn da in einem Weltkrieg um den Sinn der Staatsordnung auf Leben und Tod irgendwann doch der Einsatz der Atombombe droht, wird keine Großmacht mehr wagen, überhaupt den Krieg zu beginnen. Weil es für alle der Vernichtungskrieg würde, kann er nicht mehr entstehen. Die totale Bedrohung erzeugt die totale Rettung. Die äußerste Notsituation erzwingt die Formen politischer Daseinsgestaltung, die mit der Atombombe auch den Krieg überhaupt unmöglich machen. Es wäre die glücklichste Entwicklung. Das Zeitalter der Kriege läge hinter uns. Neue, ganz andere schwere Probleme, die durch das Ausbleiben der Kriege entstehen, würden uns bewegen.

Was aber geschieht wirklich?

Weil die gegenseitige Kontrolle nicht zugestanden wird, findet eine fortlaufende Produktion der Atombomben statt.

Und trotz der Atombombe gibt es ständig Kriege. Gemessen am Weltkrieg sind es zwar kleine lokale, hier jedoch furchtbar verwüstende Kriege. Statt des Satzes: es wird keine Kriege geben, weil es Atombomben gibt, muß es vielmehr heißen: es kann heute Kriege geben ohne Atombombe. Sollte es ein schreckliches Vorrecht der Kleinen werden, Krieg zu führen? Sie vollziehen Gewaltakte, um ihren Zustand zu ändern. Sie bedrohen ihre kleinen Gegner, um nach alten Verfahren mit Gewalt obzusiegen. Sie bedrohen die Großen durch die Gefahr des Weltkrieges. Diese Gefahr wirkt einschüchternd. Wenn die Kleinen gewaltsam Verträge brechen, wagen die Großen nicht, dem durch Gewalt gebrochenen Recht durch Gewalt Achtung zu verschaffen. Aber dies Vorrecht der souveränen Kleinen ist nur möglich, weil die Großen nicht einig sind in der Verteidigung des Rechts und der Verträge. Sie nutzen vielmehr die Akte der Kleinen aus, um die eigenen Machtpositionen gegeneinander zu erweitern oder zu behaupten . . . Je mächtiger die Staaten durch die Bombe sind, desto mehr scheinen sie vorläufig gelähmt, während die Kleinen ihre Gewaltakte vollziehen.

Was ist nun weiter möglich? Die Großen bemühen sich, die kämpfenden Kleinen zum Frieden zu bringen, aber nicht ohne Hintergedanken. Sie ergreifen Partei und sind fast immer Partei gegeneinander. So geraten sie, während die Kleinen unter ihrer Duldung und unter ihrem teilweisen Schutz kämpfen, ständig selber in die Gefahr des zwischen ihnen auszutragenden Weltkriegs. Es ist, da kein Bewußtsein gemeinsamer Ordnung zusammenhält, immer nur wie ein Hinausschieben des Weltkriegs. Da jeder kleine Krieg verschleiert schon ein Krieg zwischen den Großmächten ist, birgt jeder in sich die Gefahr des Weltbrandes.

Chapter Eighteen

60. *Modified participial constructions*
61. *Absolute participial constructions*

**Reading: From Albert Schweitzer:
Die Ehrfurcht vor dem Leben**

60. *Modified participial constructions*

1. In German as well as in English, present and past participles may be used as adjectives. They will take the appropriate adjective ending:

der *singende* Mann	*the **singing** man*
der *entsetzte* Mann	*the **horrified** man*

Remember that the present participle in German is formed by adding a **-d** (cf. English *-ing*) to the infinitive.

2. Participial constructions may be modified by

(a) an adverb:

der *laut* singende Mann	*the **loudly** singing man*

(b) a prepositional phrase:

der *zum Tode* entsetzte Mann	*the man (who is/was) terrified **to death***

(c) another prepositional phrase modifying the participle:

Der *von dem Hund* zum Tode entsetzte Mann . . .	*The man (who was) terrified to death **by the dog** . . .*

(d) another present participle:

Der von dem *heranlaufenden* Hund zum Tode entsetzte Mann . . .	*The man (who was) terrified to death by the dog **running toward** him . . .*

(e) another adverb modifying the present participle:

Der von dem *blitzschnell* heranlaufenden Hund zum Tode entsetzte Mann . . . — *The man (who was) terrified to death by the dog that was **very rapidly** running toward him ("as fast as lightning") . . .*

3. The steps taken below outline a general formula for getting to the meaning of these constructions:

(a) Notice the two words that warn of such a construction: **Der von . . .**
(b) Find the noun with which the initial article or other **der** or **ein** word agrees in gender, number, and case:

Der . . . *Mann*

(c) Translate the adjective which is in front of the noun, in this case a past participle, and then any modifiers of the adjective, such as an adverb or a prepositional phrase:

Der . . . *zum Tode entsetzte* Mann

It will sometimes be necessary to break down the modified participial construction into a series of participial constructions as has been done here.

(d) Translate the next prepositional phrase and its modifiers:

Der *von dem blitzschnell heranlaufenden Hund* zum Tode entsetzte Mann

4. To summarize: Go from the beginning of the phrase to the end and work backward, using relative clauses, where feasible, to reduce the extended modifiers:

	5			
Der /	**von dem blitzschnell heranlaufenden Hund /**	**zum Tode /**	**entsetzte Mann**	
1	4	3	2	

(5 = **blitzschnell**)

The /	*man was terrified /*	*to death /*	*by the dog that was very rapidly running toward him*
1	2	3	4

(5 = *very rapidly*)

5. If a genitive object follows a noun ending a modified participial construction, the genitive object should be translated first before working back:

Die /	**von so vielen Wissenschaftlern /**	**beachtete /**	**Arbeit /**	***Einsteins . . .***
1	5	4	2	3

The /	*work /*	*of Einstein /*	*held in high esteem /*	*by so many scientists . . .*
1	2	3	4	5

6. One or more unmodified adjectives may precede the main noun. If so, they should be translated before working back:

Der von Ford erfundene und von den Deutschen weiterentwickelte *billige* Wagen des Volkes . . .	*The **inexpensive** car of the people, invented by Ford and further developed by the Germans . . .*

Note that with this sentence **von Ford erfundene und von den Deutschen weiterentwickelte** is one phrase. The double use of **von** indicates this as well as the time sequence in the phrase itself: *Ford invents, Germans develop further.*

Translate the following phrases into English, using natural English word order.

	1. **das Auto**
1. *the car*	**2.** **treffen** = *to hit, strike* **getroffen** = *struck* das **getroffene** Auto
2. the car *which has been struck*	**3.** **der Blitz** = *lightning* das **von dem Blitz** getroffene Auto
3. the car struck *by lightning*	**4.** **aussuchen** = *to search out, to select* **ausgesucht** = *sought out* das von dem Blitz **ausgesuchte und** getroffene Auto
4. the car *sought out and* struck by lightning	**5.** das **schnell** von dem Blitz ausgesuchte und getroffene Auto
5. the car which was *quickly* sought out and struck by lightning	**6.** das schnell von dem Blitz ausgesuchte und getroffene Auto **des jungen Studenten**
6. the car *of the young student* which was quickly sought out and struck by lightning	**7.** **die Hexe**
7. *the witch*	**8.** die **tanzende** Hexe
8. the *dancing* witch	**9.** die **zu der Musik** tanzende Hexe
9. the witch dancing *to the music*	**10.** **schlecht** = *badly* die **schlecht** zu der Musik tanzende Hexe
10. the witch (who is) dancing *badly* to the music	**11.** **abscheulich** = *abominable* die schlecht zu der Musik tanzende, **abscheu-liche** Hexe
11. the *abominable* witch (who is) dancing badly to the music	**12.** die schlecht zu der Musik tanzende, abscheuliche Hexe **des 15. Jahrhunderts**

12. the abominable witch *of the 15th century* who is not dancing in time to the music (who is dancing badly)	**13.** **eine Sprache**
13. *a language*	**14.** **bestehen** = *to exist, to last* **bestehend** = *existing* eine **bestehende** Sprache
14. an *existing* language	**15.** eine **über den Dialekten** bestehende Sprache
15. a language which exists *over and above dialects*	**16.** eine **von Luther gebrauchte**, und über den Dialekten bestehende Sprache
16. A language *which Luther used* and which exists over and above the dialects	**17.** **alle Anstrengungen**
17. *all efforts*	**18.** **unternehmen** = *to undertake* **unternommen** = *undertaken* alle **unternommenen** Anstrengungen
18. all efforts *which were made (undertaken)*	**19.** alle **von der Philosophie** unternommenen Anstrengungen
19. all efforts which were made *by philosophy*	**20.** **die Zone zwischen dem Norden und dem Süden**
20. *the zone between the North and the South*	**21.** **begrenzen** = *to limit, to bound, to restrict* **begrenzt** = *limited, bounded, restricted* die Zone zwischen dem Norden und dem **begrenzten** Süden
21. the zone between the North and the South *which is bounded*	**22.** die Zone zwischen dem **skandinavischen** Norden und dem **vom Mittelmeer** begrenzten Süden . . .
22. the zone between the *Scandinavian* North and the South which is bounded *by the Mediterranean Sea . . .*	**23.** . . . zwischen dem kontinentalen Osten und dem Westen . . .
23. . . . between the continental East and the West . . .	**24.** **reichen** = *to extend* **reichend** = *extending* . . . zwischen dem kontinentalen Osten und dem daran **reichenden** Westen . . .
24. . . . between the continental East and the West *extending (to)*	**25.** . . . zwischen dem kontinentalen Osten und dem **an den Atlantischen Ozean** reichenden Westen . . .
25. . . . between the continental East and the West which extends *to the Atlantic Ocean . . .*	**26.** Die Zone liegt zwischen dem skandinavischen Norden und dem vom Mittelmeer begrenzten Süden, dem kontinentalen Osten und dem an den Atlantischen Ozean reichenden Westen.

26. The zone lies between the Scandinavian North and the South which is bounded by the Mediterranean Sea; between the continental East and the West which extends to the Atlantic Ocean.	**27.** **triefen** = *to drip, to trickle* **triefend** = *dripping, trickling* **der Triefende** = __________
27. *the dripping man* (Note that the subject is a present participle used as an adjectival noun.)	**28.** der **von Schweiß** Triefende
28. the man dripping *with sweat*	**29.** der **wegen der Sonne** von Schweiß Triefende
29. the man who is dripping with sweat *because of the sun*	**30.** **untergehen** = *to go down, to go under* **untergehend** = *going down, going under* der wegen der **untergehenden** Sonne von Schweiß Triefende
30. the man who is dripping with sweat because of the sun *which is going down*	**31.** der wegen der **heißen** untergehenden Sonne von Schweiß Triefende
31. the man who is dripping with sweat because of the *hot* sun which is going down	**32.** **fürchten** = *to fear* **gefürchtet** = *feared* **die Gefürchtete** = ________
32. *the woman who is feared* (Here the subject is a past participle used as an adjectival noun.)	**33.** die **von den Kindern** Gefürchtete
33. the woman feared *by the children*	**34.** die von den Kindern und **Eltern** Gefürchtete (*friends/parents*)
34. the woman feared by the children and *parents*	**35.** die von den Kindern und **deren** Eltern Gefürchtete (*their/those*)
35. the woman feared by the children and *their* parents	**36.** **zugleich** = *at the same time, together with* die von den Kindern und deren Eltern **zugleich** Gefürchtete
36. the woman feared by the children *together with* their parents (Note that **zugleich** is tied to **Eltern,** not to **Gefürchtete.**)	

PROGRESS TEST

Choose the correct meaning of the following noun phrases and sentences.

1. Der schnell vom Realisten zum Idealisten umgewandelte Mensch . . .

(a) The man changed from an idealist to a realist.

(b) The realist quickly changed into an idealist.

(c) The man was both a realist and an idealist.

(d) To change from a realist to an idealist is no great trick.

2. Der wegen des Wetters etwas verspätete, mit Schifahrern überfüllte Zug aus Garmisch . . .

(a) Because the weather was fair the train to Garmisch was somewhat ahead of schedule.

(b) The train from Garmisch was full of skiers because the weather was bad.

(c) The train from Garmisch, which was bursting with skiers, arrived somewhat late because of the weather.

(d) The train to Garmisch was full of skiers because the weather promised to be great for skiing.

3. Die durch die Luft von Sibirien zum Mittelmeer dahergeflogene Maschine der reichen Dame stürzte in Italien ab.

(a) The airplane which belonged to the rich woman from Italy flew from Siberia to the Mediterranean.

(b) An airplane which flies from the Mediterranean to Siberia can be expected to cause air pollution in Italy.

(c) The rich woman's airplane which had flown from Siberia to the Mediterranean crashed in Italy.

(d) The rich woman flies machines produced in Italy to Siberia.

4. Der von Max und Moritz durch ein lautes „Meck, meck, meck!!" herbeigerufen, zur Tür heraussausende und ins Wasser stürzende Schneider, der sich Böck benannte, schrie, daß er ertrinke.

(a) The tailor raced out the door to save the teasing boys who had fallen into the water and were crying for help.

(b) The boys cried out that they were drowning in order to tease Böck, the tailor, which in turn caused him to throw them into the water.

(c) Max and Moritz gave the tailor the name of Böck, meaning goat, because he continually bleated at them, but then they threw him into the water.

(d) The tailor raced out the door and fell into the water because Max and Moritz intimated that he was an old goat.

Answer key: **1.** (b); **2.** (c); **3.** (c); **4.** (d).

61. *Absolute participial constructions*

1. The present participle may be used as follows in literary German:

Leise vor sich *hinpfeifend,* sah er den neuen Mercedes an. *Whistling softly to himself, he looked at the new Mercedes.*

2. Past participles are similarly used:

Zum Tode *betrübt,* ging er die Straße entlang. ***Grieved*** *to death, he walked along the street.*

Notice that in German the participles end the phrase, while in English they begin it.

Give the meanings of the participial phrases.

	1. Laut **singend**, saß er inmitten der Straße.
1. *Singing* loudly he sat in the middle of the street.	2. **stoßen** = *to bump* Vor Freude **tanzend**, stieß er gegen den Elefanten.
2. *Dancing* for joy he bumped into the elephant.	3. **zurück** = *back(wards)* **ziehen** = *to pull, to draw, to drag* **sich zurückziehen = ________**
3. *to withdraw*	4. **das Gespenst** = *ghost, specter* Vor dem Gespenst **sich fürchtend,** zog er sich schnell zurück.
4. *Frightened* of the specter he quickly withdrew.	5. **begnadigt** = *pardoned, allowed (mercy)* Zum Leben **begnadigt**, mußte er ein neues Leben anfangen.
5. *Allowed* to live, he had to begin a new life.	6. Von allen **gehaßt**, ging sie allein durch die Stadt.
6. *Hated* by all she went alone through the city.	7. In Salzburg **geboren**, als Wunderkind von ganz Europa **gefeiert** und in Armut und Vergessenheit **gestorben:** Mozart.
7. *Born* in Salzburg, *celebrated* as a child prodigy by all of Europe, and *deceased* in poverty and oblivion: Mozart.	8. **hinüberführen auf** = *to lead into* Das andere ist Donauland, hügelig oder flach, auf Ungarns Ebenen **hinüberführend.**
8. The other is Danube country, hilly or flat, *leading into* Hungary's plains.	9. Aus dem Elsaß **stammend:** Albert Schweitzer.
9. *Originating* from Alsace: Albert Schweitzer.	

PROGRESS TEST

1. Zum Tode betrübt, saß der junge Mann auf der Bank und dachte an seine Geliebte.
The word which means *grieved* is
(a) dachte (b) betrübt (c) saß (d) Geliebte

2. Von Maikäfern geplagt, sauste Onkel Fritz aus dem Bett und haute und trampelte alles tot.
The word which means *tormented* is
(a) geplagt (b) sauste (c) trampelte (d) haute

3. Wieder aus dem Auto steigend, mußte der Autofahrer noch einmal die Scheinwerfer putzen, da es soviel Schnee darauf gab.
The word which means *getting* is
(a) putzen (b) wieder (c) Scheinwerfer (d) steigend

Answer key: **1.** (b); **2.** (a); **3.** (d).

READING PREPARATION

In this section all of the structures and vocabulary for the reading passage are introduced and drilled. Continue to circle all words that you do not immediately recognize. Review them thoroughly before going on to the passage itself.

	1. Sie wissen **schon** etwas über Albert Schweitzer. (*already/beautiful*)
1. You *already* know something about Albert Schweitzer.	**2.** Über seine Arbeit als Arzt im Urwald **haben** Sie schon etwas **gelesen.** (*have read/had read*)
2. You *have* already *read* something about his work as a doctor in the jungle.	**3.** Jetzt **werden** Sie etwas aus seinen philosophischen Schriften **lesen.** (*will read/is read*)
3. Now you *will read* something from his philosophical writings.	**4.** **die Ansprache** = *speech* Er hat einmal eine Ansprache gehalten über das „Thema“ Das Problem **des** Ethischen. (*before/of the*)
4. He once gave a speech on the topic “The Problem *of the* Ethical.”	**5.** **der Begriff** = *concept* In dieser Ansprache **bespricht** er den Begriff . . . (*speaks/discusses*)
5. In this speech he *discusses* the concept . . .	**6.** **die Ehre** = *honor* **die Furcht** = *fear* **die Ehrfurcht** = *awe, deep respect, reverence* Ehrfurcht **vor** dem Leben (*from/for*)

6. reverence *for* life (Note: This phrase connotes also deep respect when confronting life itself.)	**7.** Von Schweitzers Begriff „Ehrfurcht vor dem Leben“ **haben** Sie vielleicht schon **gehört.** (*have belonged/have heard*)
7. Perhaps you *have* already *heard* of Schweitzer's concept "reverence for life."	**8.** **Folgendes** ist unsere Situation in der Welt, sagt Schweitzer:
8. Schweitzer says that our situation in the world is *as follows:*	**9.** „Ich bin Leben, das leben will, inmitten von Leben, das leben will.“
9. "I am life which wants to live, in the midst of life which wants to live."	**10.** **der Friede** = *peace* **befriedigen** = *to satisfy* **befriedigend** = ______
10. *gratifying, satisfying*	**11.** **Ist** uns eine befriedigende Erkenntnis der Welt **gegeben?** (*is given/has given*)
11. *Is* a satisfying knowledge of the world *given* to us?	**12.** Eine vollständige und befriedigende Erkenntnis der Welt ist **uns** nicht gegeben. (*us/ourselves*)
12. A complete and satisfying knowledge of the world is not given to *us.*	**13.** **feststellen** = *to establish, to observe, to determine* **die Feststellung** = *observation,* Wir haben die **Feststellung** gemacht, daß das Leben sehr schwer ist.
13. We made the *observation* that life is very difficult.	**14.** **beschränken** = *to limit* Wir müssen **uns** auf die Feststellung beschränken . . . (*them/ourselves*)
14. We must limit *ourselves* to the observation . . .	**15.** Wir müssen uns auf die **einfache** Feststellung beschränken . . . (*simple/complex*)
15. We must limit ourselves to the *simple* observation . . .	**16.** Was ist diese einfache Feststellung, **worauf** wir uns beschränken müssen? (*on which/to which*)
16. What is this simple observation *to which* we must limit ourselves?	**17.** **gleich** = *like, equal, similar* Diese Feststellung ist, daß alles Leben in der Welt uns gleich ist.
17. This observation is that all life in the world is similar to ourselves.	**18.** **geheim** = *secret, private* **das Geheimnis** = *secret, mystery* Alles Leben ist **Geheimnis.**
18. All life is a *mystery.*	**19.** Alles in der Welt ist Leben gleich **uns selber** und alles ist Geheimnis.
19. Everything in the world is life similar *to ourselves* and everything is a mystery.	**20.** **das Bewußtsein** = *consciousness* Verstehen wir, was das Bewußtsein **eines** Menschen ist?

20. Do we understand what the consciousness *of an* individual is?	**21.** **die Gegebenheit** = *reality, (given) fact, factor* **der Grund** = *ground, basis, reason* **die Grundgegebenheit** = *fundamental factor* Die Grundgegebenheit **unseres** Bewußtseins ist . . .
21. The fundamental factor *of our* consciousness is . . .	**22.** **unmittelbar** = *immediate, direct* Die unmittelbare Grundgegebenheit unseres Bewußtseins ist: Ich bin Leben, das leben will, inmitten von Leben, das leben will.
22. The immediate fundamental factor of our consciousness is: I am life that wants to live, in the midst of life that wants to live.	**23.** **zurück** = *back* **leiten** = *to lead, to direct* **zurückleiten** = ______
23. *to lead back*	**24.** **jedesmal** = *every time* Was ist die unmittelbare Grundgegebenheit unseres Bewußtseins, auf die wir jedesmal wieder **zurückgeleitet werden**? (*will lead back/are led back*)
24. What is the immediate fundamental factor of our consciousness to which we *are led back* again every time?	**25.** **verstehen** = *to understand* **das Verständnis** = *understanding, comprehension, appreciation* Das Verständnis **unserer selbst** . . . (*of themselves/of ourselves*)
25. The understanding *of ourselves* . . .	**26.** **dringen** = *to press, penetrate* **vordringen** = *to advance, to press forward, to make headway* Wollen wir zu einem Verständnis unserer selbst und **unserer** Situation in der Welt vordringen? (*dative/genitive*)
26. *genitive* Do we want to press forward to an understanding of ourselves and *of our* situation in the world?	**27.** Ist die unmittelbare Grundgegebenheit unseres Bewußtseins, auf die wir jedesmal wieder zurückgeleitet werden, wenn wir zu einem Verständnis unserer selbst und unserer Situation in der Welt vordringen wollen . . .
27. Is the immediate fundamental factor of our consciousness, to which we are led back again every time when we want to press forward to an understanding of ourselves and our situation in the world. . .	**28.** . . . daß ich Leben bin, **das** leben will, inmitten von Leben, **das** leben will? (*which/the*)

28.	. . . that I am life, *which* wants to live, in the midst of life, *which* wants to live?	**29.**	**ja** = *yes* **bejahen** = *to affirm, to say yes to* **Da** Schweitzer „Wille zum Leben" ist, bejaht er sein Leben. (*there/since*)
29.	*Since* Schweitzer is "will-to-live" (will to life), he affirms his life.	**30.**	**sagen** = *to say* **besagen** = *to mean, to say* Was will er **damit** besagen? (*with that/by that*)
30.	What does he mean *by that*?	**31.**	Das will nicht **einfach** besagen . . . (*simple/simply*)
31.	That does not *simply* mean . . .	**32.**	**fortsetzen** = *to continue* . . . daß Schweitzer sein Leben **einfach nur** fortsetzen will, oder?
32.	. . . that Schweitzer wants *merely* to continue his life, or does it?	**33.**	**das Sein** = *being* **das Dasein** = *existence* Will er sein Dasein einfach nur fortsetzen?
33.	Does he merely want to continue his existence?	**34.**	**Wert legen auf** = *to attach importance to, to set great store by* Legt er Wert darauf, sein Dasein **nur fortzusetzen**?
34.	Does he attach importance *just to continuing* his existence? (Note: **darauf** anticipates the following phrase.)	**35.**	**empfinden** = *to feel* Was empfindet Schweitzer als **höchstes** Geheimnis?
35.	What does Schweitzer feel is the *greatest* mystery? (Lit.: highest)	**36.**	**die Pflicht** = *duty* **verpflichten** = *to oblige, to obligate* **die Verpflichtung** = __________
36.	*obligation, duty*	**37.**	**Welche** Verpflichtung empfindet Schweitzer?
37.	*What* obligation does Schweitzer feel?	**38.**	**gleich** = *alike, equal(ly)* **achten** = *to esteem* **gleichachten** = *to esteem alike* Welchen Willen zum Leben **achtet** Schweitzer **gleich**?
38.	Which will-to-live does Schweitzer *esteem to be equal to his own*?	**39.**	**jeglich** = *every* Jeglichen Willen zum Leben achtet er **dem seinen** gleich. (*to his/to its*)

39. He esteems every will-to-live to be equal *to his* own.	**40.** **um** = *around* **die Welt** = *the world* **die Umwelt** = *environment, the world around us* Schweitzer empfindet die Verpflichtung, jeglichen Willen zum Leben in **seiner** Umwelt **dem seinen** gleichzuachten.
40. Schweitzer feels the obligation to esteem every will-to-live in *his* environment as equal *to his own.*	**41.** **gebieten** = *to tell, to order, to command* Was **gebietet** uns die Grundidee des Guten? (*present/past*)
41. present What *does* the fundamental idea of the good *command* us to do?	**42.** **erhalten** = *to preserve, to maintain* Man soll das Leben erhalten und **fördern**. (*promote/negate*)
42. One is to preserve and *promote* life.	**43.** Die Grundidee des Guten gebietet uns, das Leben zu erhalten und zu fördern.
43. The fundamental idea of the good commands us to preserve and to promote life.	**44.** **steigern** = *to raise, to heighten* Man soll das Leben **nicht nur** erhalten und fördern, **sondern auch** zu seinem höchsten Wert steigern.
44. One is *not only* to preserve and promote life, *but also* raise it to its highest value.	**45.** **Das Böse** steigert das Leben nicht zu seinem höchsten Wert.
45. *Evil* does not raise life to its highest value.	**46.** Die Grundidee des Guten **besteht** also **darin**, daß sie uns gebietet . . . (*consists of/stands in*)
46. Therefore the fundamental idea of the good *consists of* commanding us . . .	**47.** . . . das Leben zu erhalten, zu fördern und zu seinem höchsten Wert zu steigern.
47. . . . to preserve life, to promote it, and to raise it to its highest value.	**48.** **bedeuten** = *to mean, to signify* Was bedeutet das Böse für Schweitzer?
48. What does evil signify for Schweitzer?	**49.** **entwickeln** = *to develop* **die Entwicklung** = *development* Das Böse bedeutet: Leben vernichten, **schädigen**, an seiner Entwicklung hindern. (*to make whole/to injure*)
49. Evil means to destroy, *injure*, and to hinder life in its development.	**50.** Das Böse **hat** das Leben **vernichten**, **schädigen**, an seiner Entwicklung **hindern wollen.**
50. Evil (*has*) *wanted to destroy, injure,* and *hinder* life in its development.	**51.** **entdecken** = *to discover* Religion und Philosophie **haben** das Prinzip der Liebe **entdeckt**.

51.	Religion and philosophy (*have*) *discovered* the principle of love.	**52.**	**ist entdeckt worden** = *has been discovered, was discovered* Das Prinzip der Liebe ist **durch** Religion und Philosophie entdeckt worden.
52.	The principle of love was discovered *by* religion and philosophy. (**ist entdeckt worden** is a passive form. See §64.)	**53.**	Das Prinzip dieser *veneratio vitae* entspricht **dem** der Liebe. (*to that/to which/the*)
53.	The principle of this *veneratio vitae* (veneration of life) corresponds *to that* of love.	**54.**	**forschen** = *to search* Wonach **forschten** Religion und Philosophie? (*present/past*)
54.	past What *did* religion and philosophy *search* for?	**55.**	Religion und Philosophie forschten **nach** dem Grundbegriff des Guten. (*for/without*)
55.	Religion and philosophy searched *for* the fundamental idea of the good.	**56.**	Das Prinzip der Liebe **ist** durch Religion und Philosophie **entdeckt worden,** als sie nach dem Grundbegriff des Guten forschten.
56.	The principle of love *was discovered* by religion and philosophy as they searched for the fundamental concept of the good.	**57.**	Ist der Begriff Ehrfurcht vor dem Leben **lebendiger oder weniger lebendig** als der Begriff Liebe?
57.	Is the concept "reverence for life" *more alive or less alive* than the concept "love"?	**58.**	Schweitzer meint, der Begriff Ehrfurcht vor dem Leben sei allgemeiner und **deshalb** weniger lebendig als der Begriff Liebe.
58.	Schweitzer feels that the concept "reverence for life" is more general and *therefore* less alive than the concept "love." (**Sei** is a subjunctive form. See §76.)	**59.**	**bergen** = *to contain* (also: *to shelter, to conceal, to rescue*) Birgt der Begriff Ehrfurcht vor dem Leben die gleichen Kräfte in **sich** wie der Begriff Liebe? (*himself/themselves/itself*)
59.	Does the concept "reverence for life" contain the same powers (in *itself*) as the concept "love" does?	**60.**	Obwohl der Begriff Ehrfurcht vor dem Leben allgemeiner und deshalb weniger lebendig als der Begriff Liebe ist, schreibt Schweitzer . . .
60.	Although the concept "reverence for life" is more general and therefore less vital than the concept "love," Schweitzer writes . . .	**61.**	. . . so birgt **er** doch die gleichen Kräfte in sich. (*he/it*)
61.	. . . *it* still contains the same powers.	**62.**	**ziehen** = *to draw, to pull, to drag* **sich beziehen** = *to relate, to refer* **die Beziehung** =
62.	*relation, reference, relationship*	**63.**	**treten** = *to step, to enter* Wie können wir mit der Welt in **geistige Beziehung** treten?

63. How can we enter into a *spiritual relationship* with the world?	**64.** Schweitzer antwortet: „Durch die Ehrfurcht vor dem Leben treten wir mit der Welt in geistige Beziehung.“
64. Schweitzer answers: “Through reverence for life we enter into a spiritual relationship with the world.”	**65.** Bonhoeffer spricht von einer anderen geistigen Beziehung zur Welt.
65. Bonhoeffer speaks of a different spiritual relationship with the world.	**66.** Diesseitigkeit ist für ihn, in der Fülle der Aufgaben, Fragen, Erfolge und Mißerfolge, Erfahrungen und Ratlosigkeiten leben.
66. For him life in this world is to live in the fullness of tasks, questions, successes and failures, experiences and perplexities.	**67.** **bauen** = *to build* **erbauen** = *to erect, to edify* Die Philosophie **hat** großartige Systeme **erbaut**. (*has erected/had erected*)
67. Philosophy *has erected* magnificent systems.	**68.** **vergeblich** = (*in*) *vain, futile* All die großartigen Systeme, die die Philosophie erbaut hat, **sind** vergeblich **geblieben.** (*have remained/are remaining*)
68. All the magnificent systems which philosophy has erected *have remained* futile.	**69.** **Um** uns in Beziehung mit dem Absoluten **zu** setzen, hat die Philosophie großartige Systeme erbaut, die vergeblich geblieben sind.
69. *In order to* relate us to (place us into a relationship with) the absolute, philosophy has erected magnificent systems, which have remained futile.	**70.** **vorstellen** = *to represent* **die Vorstellung** = __________
70. *representation, conception, idea*	**71.** **bezeichnen** = *to denote, to stand for* Das Absolute bezeichnet eine abstrakte Vorstellung.
71. The absolute stands for an abstract idea.	**72.** **greifen** = *to grasp* **begreifen** = *understand* **das Begreifen** = ________
72. *the understanding*	**73.** **entziehen** = *to take away, to withdraw* **sich entziehen** = *to avoid, to escape* Das Absolute entzieht sich dem lebendigen Begreifen.
73. The absolute escapes human (living) understanding. (Note that **entziehen** takes a dative object.)	**74.** Kann das Absolute **eine so** abstrakte Vorstellung bezeichnen, daß es sich dem lebendigen Begreifen entzieht? (*a so/such a*)

74. Can the absolute stand for *such an* abstract idea that it escapes human understanding?	**75.** **bescheiden** = *to grant, to give* **beschieden** = *granted, given* Was ist uns nicht **beschieden**? (*is granted/has granted*)
75. What *is* not *granted* to us?	**76.** **der Schöpfer** = *Creator* **der Wille** = *will* **der Schöpferwille** = __________
76. *the will of the Creator*	**77.** Es ist uns nicht beschieden, dem Schöpferwillen zu **dienen**. (**dienen** takes the *dative/accusative*)
77. dative It is not given to us to *serve* the Creator's will.	**78.** **gründen** = *to found, to ground* **ergründen** = *to fathom, to explore* Der Schöpferwille ist **unendlich** und **unergründlich**.
78. The will of the Creator is *infinite* and *unfathomable.*	**79.** **ruhen** = *to rest, to repose* **beruhen**= *to rest, to be based on* Alles **Sein** beruht auf dem unendlichen und unergründlichen Schöpferwillen. (*being/to be*)
79. All *being* rests upon the unending and unfathomable will of the Creator.	**80.** **die Absicht** = *intention* Was sind die **Absichten** des unendlichen und unergründlichen Schöpferwillens?
80. What are the *intentions* of the infinite and unfathomable will of the Creator?	**81.** **um** = *of, about* (with *Wissen*) Ein klares **Wissen um** sein Wesen und seine Absichten ist uns nicht beschieden.
81. A clear *knowledge of* its nature and intentions is not given to us.	**82.** **Müssen** wir, um dem Schöpferwillen zu dienen, im klaren Wissen um sein Wesen und seine Absichten **sein**?
82. In order to serve the Creator's will, *do* we *have to have* clear knowledge (*or:* a clear understanding) of its essence and intentions?	**83.** Dem Schopferwillen, auf dem alles Sein beruht, kann man nicht im klaren Wissen um sein Wesen und seine Absichten dienen.
83. We cannot serve the Creator's will, on which all being rests, with a clear knowledge of its nature and its intentions.	**84.** **das Verhältnis** = *relationship* Wie treten wir in ein geistiges Verhältnis **zu** dem Schöpferwillen? (*to/with*)
84. How do we enter into a spiritual relationship *with* the Creator's will?	**85.** **wirken** = *to work, to effect, to act* **einwirken** = *to influence, to act upon* **die Einwirkung** = __________

85.	*influence*	**86.**	**Wenn** wir uns bewußt bleiben, unter der Einwirkung des Lebensgeheimnisses zu stehen . . . (*if/whenever/when*)
86.	*If* we remain conscious of being under the influence of the mystery of life. . .	**87.**	. . . treten wir in ein geistiges Verhältnis zu dem Schöpferwillen.
87.	. . . we enter into a spiritual relationship with the Creator's will.	**88.**	**hingeben** = *to give to, to sacrifice, to devote* **Wenn** wir uns an alle lebendigen Wesen hingeben . . .
88.	*If* we devote ourselves to all living creatures . . .	**89.**	. . . haben wir die Gelegenheit und die Möglichkeit, **ihnen** zu helfen. (*them/you*)
89.	. . . we have the opportunity and the possibility of helping *them.*	**90.**	**die Tat** = *deed* **tätig** = *active(ly)* Wenn wir uns tätig hingeben an alle lebendigen Wesen, **denen** zu helfen wir die Gelegenheit und die Möglichkeit haben . . . (*whom/those*)
90.	If we devote ourselves actively to all living creatures *whom* we have the opportunity and the possibility of helping . . .	**91.**	**bedeuten** = *to mean, to signify* **die Bedeutung** = *meaning, significance* **Was für eine** Bedeutung kann diese Ethik haben? (*what a/what kind of*)
91.	*What kind of* significance can this ethic have?	**92.**	Wozu **verpflichtet** uns diese Ethik?
92.	What *does* this ethic *obligate* us to (do)?	**93.**	**die Gesellschaft** = *society* Diese Ethik verpflichtet uns **zum Dienst an der** menschlichen Gesellschaft.
93.	This ethic obligates us *to serve* human society. (Lit.: *to the service to the*)	**94.**	**einzig** = *nur* Eine Ethik, **die** uns einzig zum Dienst am Menschen und der menschlichen Gesellschaft verpflichtet, kann diese Bedeutung nicht haben.
94.	An ethic *which* only obligates us to serve mankind and human society cannot have this meaning.	**95.**	**fassen** = *to grasp, to hold* **umfassen** = *to embrace, to comprise* **umfassend** = __________
95.	*extensive, comprehensive*	**96.**	**aufmerken** = *to note, to give heed to* **aufmerksam** = *attentive* **die Aufmerksamkeit** = __________

96. *attention, attentiveness*	**97.** **wahrhaft** = *truly* Nur eine umfassende Ethik setzt uns wahrhaft in ein inneres Verhältnis zum Universum und dem Willen **dessen, der** sich in ihm manifestiert. (*of him who/those which*)
97. Only a comprehensive ethic puts us truly into an inner relationship with the universe and the will *of him who* manifests himself in it.	**98.** **legen** = *to lay* **auferlegen** = *to impose upon* Was **wird** eine umfassende Ethik uns **auferlegen**?
98. What *will* a comprehensive ethic *impose* upon us?	**99.** **zuwenden** = *to turn to* Wir sollen unsere tätige Aufmerksamkeit allen **Lebewesen** zuwenden. (*singular/plural*)
99. plural We are to turn our active attention to all *living beings.*	**100.** Nur eine umfassende Ethik, die uns auferlegt, unsere tätige Aufmerksamkeit allen Lebewesen **zuzuwenden** . . .
100. Only a comprehensive ethic which requires us *to turn* our active attention *to* all living beings . . .	**101.** . . . setzt uns wahrhaft in ein inneres Verhältnis zum Universum und dem Willen, **der** sich in ihm manifestiert. (*who/which*)
101. . . . truly places us in an inner relationship to the universe and the will *which* manifests itself therein.	

PROGRESS TEST

Choose the correct meaning of the indicated words.

1. Wir müssen uns auf die **Feststellung** beschränken, daß alles in der Welt gleich uns selber und alles Leben Geheimnis ist.
(a) indication (b) observation (c) understanding (d) knowledge

2. Ich lege nicht Wert darauf, mein Dasein **fortzusetzen.**
(a) to continue (b) to progress (c) to follow through (d) to examine

3. Ich bejahe mein Leben, was nicht einfach **besagen** will, daß ich Wert darauf lege, mein Dasein fortzusetzen.
(a) to be said (b) mean (c) approve (d) feel

4. Was **gebietet** die Grundidee des Guten?
(a) does command (b) does demand (c) does offer (d) does try

5. Sie gebietet, das Leben **zu erhalten.**
(a) to receive (b) to get (c) to hold (d) to preserve

6. Sie gebietet, das Leben zu erhalten, zu fördern und zu seinem höchsten Wert **zu steigern.**
(a) to stagger (b) to climb (c) to raise (d) to push

7. Wir treten in ein geistiges Verhältnis zu dem Schöpferwillen, wenn wir uns **bewußt** bleiben, unter der Einwirkung des Lebensgeheimnisses zu stehen.
(a) thoroughly (b) unaware (c) apparent (d) conscious

8. Eine Ethik, die uns einzig zum Dienst am Menschen und der menschlichen Gesellschaft verpflichtet, kann diese **Bedeutung** nicht haben.
(a) revelation (b) difference (c) meaning (d) understanding

9. Nur eine umfassende Ethik setzt uns **wahrhaft** in ein inneres Verhältnis zum Universum.
(a) firmly (b) finally (c) thoroughly (d) truly

10. Alle von der Philosophie unternommenen **Anstrengungen** sind vergeblich geblieben.
(a) efforts (b) findings (c) struggles (d) duties

11. Das Absolute **bezeichnet** eine so abstrakte Vorstellung . . .
(a) explains (b) stands for (c) draws (d) follows

12. Das Absolute bezeichnet eine so abstrakte Vorstellung, daß es sich dem lebendigen Begreifen **entzieht.**
(a) explains (b) despairs (c) escapes (d) develops

Answer key: **1.** (b); **2.** (a); **3.** (b); **4.** (a); **5.** (d); **6.** (c); **7.** (d); **8.** (c); **9.** (d); **10.** (a); **11.** (b); **12.** (c).

Albert Schweitzer: Die Ehrfurcht vor dem Leben

Eine vollständige und befriedigende Erkenntnis der Welt ist uns nicht gegeben. Wir müssen uns auf die einfache Feststellung beschränken, daß alles in ihr [der Welt] Leben gleich uns selber und alles Leben Geheimnis ist . . .

Die unmittelbare Grundgegebenheit unseres Bewußtseins, auf die wir jedesmal wieder zurückgeleitet werden, wenn wir zu einem Verständnis unserer selbst und unserer Situation in der Welt vordringen wollen, ist: *Ich bin Leben, das leben will, inmitten von Leben, das leben will.*

Da ich Wille zum Leben bin, bejahe ich mein Leben—was nicht einfach besagen will, daß ich Wert darauf lege, mein Dasein fortzusetzen, sondern daß ich es als höchstes Geheimnis empfinde.

Wenn ich über das Leben nachdenke, empfinde ich die Verpflichtung, jeglichen Willen zum Leben in meiner Umwelt dem meinen gleichzuachten.

Die Grundidee des Guten besteht also darin, daß sie gebietet, das Leben zu erhalten, zu fördern und zu seinem höchsten Wert zu steigern; und das Böse bedeutet: Leben vernichten, schädigen, an seiner Entwicklung hindern.

Das Prinzip dieser *veneratio vitae* [*reverence for life*] entspricht dem der Liebe, wie es durch Religion und Philosophie entdeckt worden ist, als sie nach dem Grundbegriff des Guten forschten.

Der Begriff *Ehrfurcht vor dem Leben* ist allgemeiner und deshalb weniger lebendig als der Begriff Liebe. Aber er birgt die gleichen Kräfte in sich.

⋆ ⋆ ⋆

Durch die Ehrfurcht vor dem Leben treten wir mit der Welt in geistige Beziehung. Alle von der Philosophie unternommenen Anstrengungen, all die großartigen Systeme, die sie erbaut hat, um uns in Beziehung mit dem Absoluten zu setzen, sind vergeblich geblieben.

Das Absolute bezeichnet eine so abstrakte Vorstellung, daß es sich dem lebendigen Begreifen entzieht. Es ist uns nicht beschieden, dem unendlichen und unergründlichen Schöpferwillen, auf dem alles Sein beruht, im klaren Wissen um sein Wesen und seine Absichten zu dienen. Aber wir treten in ein geistiges Verhältnis zu ihm, wenn wir uns bewußt bleiben, unter der Einwirkung des Lebensgeheimnisses zu stehen, und uns tätig hingeben an alle lebendigen Wesen, denen zu helfen wir die Gelegenheit und die Möglichkeit haben.

Eine Ethik, die uns einzig zum Dienst am Menschen und der menschlichen Gesellschaft verpflichtet, kann diese Bedeutung nicht haben. Nur eine umfassende Ethik, die uns auferlegt, unsere tätige Aufmerksamkeit allen Lebewesen zuzuwenden, setzt uns wahrhaft in ein inneres Verhältnis zum Universum und dem Willen, der sich in ihm manifestiert.

Chapter Nineteen

62. *The future tense—conjugation, word order, modals*

1. As you have already learned, the future tense in German is formed by the present tense of **werden** plus an infinitive:

ich werde gehen	*I will go*
du wirst gehen	*you will go*
er, sie, es wird gehen	*he, she, it will go*
wir werden gehen	*we will go*
ihr werdet gehen	*you will go*
sie werden gehen	*they will go*
Sie werden gehen	*you will go*

Note that the verb **wollen** is not used to form the future tense:

Ich will gehen means *I want to go.*

2. The infinitive will be the last word in the clause in normal and inverted word order. Dependent word order requires some form of **werden** to be last with the infinitive immediately preceding:

Du *wirst* ihn *besuchen*.	*You* ***will visit*** *him.*
Wann *werdet* ihr nach Frankreich *fliegen*?	*When* ***will*** *you* ***fly*** *to France?*
Ich weiß nicht, ob er mir einen Brief *schreiben wird*.	*I don't know whether he* ***will write*** *me a letter.*

3. Modals used with another verb in the future tense will appear in infinitive form at the end of the clause (even in dependent clauses) in the so-called double infinitive construction. When deciphering the meaning of the double infinitive, go to the modal first, then to the preceding verb:

Du *wirst* ihn *besuchen müssen*.	*You* **will have to visit** *him.*
Wann *werdet* ihr nach Frankreich *fliegen wollen*?	*When* **will** *you* **want to fly** *to France?*
Ich weiß nicht, ob er mir einen Brief *wird schreiben dürfen*.	*I don't know whether he* **will be allowed to write** *me a letter.*

4. The future tense in German is used in essentially the same way as in English. If an adverb is used which expresses futurity, German prefers the present tense:

Morgen fährt er nach Rußland.	*Tomorrow he* **will travel** *to Russia.*

Used with an adverb like **schon** or **wohl**, meaning *probably,* the future may express probability in the present:

Sie *wird* das *wohl verstehen*.	*She* **probably** (**doubtless**) **understands** *that.*

In the following sentences, give the meanings of the indicated verbs.

	1. Sie **werden** bald nach Österreich **fliegen**.
1. They *will* soon *fly* to Austria.	**2.** Ich glaube nicht, daß du bald nach Österreich **fliegen wirst**.
2. I do not believe that you *will* soon *fly* to Austria.	**3.** Wissen Sie, daß sie bald nach Österreich **wird fliegen dürfen**?
3. Do you know that she *will* soon *be permitted to fly* to Austria?	**4.** **das Zeug** = *the* (often "*that*") *stuff* Ihr **werdet** das Zeug nicht **essen**.
4. You *will* not *eat* that stuff.	**5.** Du weißt, daß er das Zeug nicht **essen wird**.
5. You know that he *will* not *eat* that stuff.	**6.** Ich weiß nicht, ob ich das Zeug **werde essen können**.
6. I do not know whether I *will be able to eat* that stuff.	**7.** Wann **werdet** ihr nach Österreich **fliegen dürfen**?
7. When *will* you *be permitted to fly* to Austria?	**8.** Wie **wirst** du das Zeug **essen können**?
8. How *will* you *be able to eat* that stuff?	**9.** Alle Menschen **werden** immer älter.
9. All people *get* (*are getting*) older and older.	**10.** Wir **werden** alle nicht **kommen**.
10. None of us *will come*.	**11.** Er **will** überhaupt nicht **kommen**.

11. He *does* not *want to come* at all.	**12.** Er **wird** das wohl **tun können**.
12. He *can* probably *do* that. (*is* probably *able to do*)	**13.** Er **wird** dick, denn er trinkt zuviel deutsches Bier.
13. He *is getting* fat, for he drinks too much German beer.	**14. Wird** Frieda nächstes Jahr einen Mercedes **kaufen**?
14. *Will* Frieda *buy* a Mercedes next year?	**15.** Herbert **will** nicht zuviel deutsches Bier **trinken**, sonst **wird** er dick.
15. Herbert *does* not *want to drink* too much German beer, otherwise he *will get* fat.	**16.** Heike **wird** wohl den Mercedes nicht **kaufen wollen**.
16. Heike probably *doesn't want to buy* the Mercedes.	**17.** Was **wird** aus dem kleinen Jungen?
17. What *will become* of the little boy?	

63. *The future perfect tense—conjugation, word order*

1. The future perfect, as rare in German as it is in English, is conjugated with the present tense of **werden** plus the perfect infinitive. (The perfect infinitive consists of a past participle and the infinitive **haben** or **sein**.)

Like the past perfect, future perfect is normally used with another tense to show a sequencing of events.

2. The future perfect is conjugated as follows:

ich werde gegangen sein	*I will have gone*
du wirst gegangen sein	etc.
er, sie, es wird gegangen sein	
wir werden gegangen sein	
ihr werdet gegangen sein	
sie werden gegangen sein	
Sie werden gegangen sein	
ich werde gesagt haben	*I will have said*
du wirst gesagt haben	etc.
er, sie, es wird gesagt haben	

wir werden gesagt haben
ihr werdet gesagt haben
sie werden gesagt haben

Sie werden gesagt haben

3. The perfect infinitive will be found at the end of the clause or immediately preceding **werden** in dependent word order:

normal

Er *wird* bis übermorgen das Buch *gelesen haben.*	*He **will have read** the book by the day after tomorrow.*

inverted

Wird* er mit ihr darüber *gesprochen haben?	***Will** he **have spoken** with her about it?*

dependent

Ich weiß, daß du ihm bis dann einen Brief *geschrieben haben wirst.*	*I know that you **will have written** him a letter by then.*

4. Used with **schon**, **wohl**, **doch**, or **wahrscheinlich**, the future perfect may express probability of a completed action in the past:

Max *wird wohl* seine Arbeit *beendet haben.*	*Max **probably has finished** his work.*

The following sentence variations are based on lines taken from German children's rhymes. Give the meanings of the indicated verbs.

	1. **holen** = *to fetch, to get* Der Storch **hat** sich drei Brote **geholt**.
1. The stork *got* (*has got*) itself three loaves of bread.	**2.** Der Storch **hatte** sich drei Brote **geholt**.
2. The stork *had gotten* itself three loaves of bread.	**3.** Der Storch **wird** sich drei Brote **holen**.
3. The stork *will get* itself three loaves of bread.	**4.** Der Storch **wird** sich drei Brote geholt **haben**.
4. The stork *will have gotten* itself three loaves of bread.	**5.** **der Henker** = *the hangman* **ausschicken** = *to send out* Der Herr **hat** den Henker **ausgeschickt**.
5. The lord (master) *sent out* (*has sent out*) the hangman.	**6.** Der Herr **hatte** den Henker **ausgeschickt**.
6. The lord *had sent out* the hangman.	**7.** Der Herr **wird** den Henker **ausschicken**.

7. The lord *will send out* the hangman.	**8.** Der Herr **wird** den Henker wohl **ausge-schickt haben**.
8. The master probably *sent out* the hangman.	**9.** Alle Vögel **sind** schon da **gewesen**.
9. All the birds *were* (*have been*) already there.	**10.** Alle Vögel **waren** schon da **gewesen**.
10. All the birds *had* already *been* there.	**11.** Alle Vögel **werden** schon da **sein**.
11. All the birds *are* probably already there.	**12.** Alle Vögel **werden** schon da **gewesen sein**.
12. All the birds *were* probably already there.	**13.** So **sind** die Reiter auf ihren stolzen Pferden **geritten**.
13. That is the way the riders *rode* (*have ridden*) on their proud horses. (**so** = *this way, in this manner*)	**14.** So **waren** die Reiter auf ihren stolzen Pferden **geritten**.
14. That is the way the riders *had ridden* on their proud horses.	**15.** So **werden** die Reiter auf ihren stolzen Pferden **reiten**.
15. This is the way the riders *will ride* on their proud horses.	**16.** So **werden** die Reiter auf ihren stolzen Pferden **geritten sein**.
16. This is the way the riders *will have ridden* on their proud horses.	

PROGRESS TEST

Choose the future form of the verb from the following possibilities.

1. _______ Marianne dieses Jahr nach Marienbad _______?
(a) will . . . fliegen (b) wird . . . getragen worden sein (c) würde . . . gehen (d) wird . . . fahren

2. Ob Erich die Zeitung _______?
(a) wird gelesen worden sein (b) darf gelesen werden (c) wird lesen dürfen (d) will lesen

3. Glauben Sie, daß es heute Regen _______?
(a) geben wird (b) gegeben wird (c) muß gegeben werden (d) gegeben haben will

4. _______ ihr bestimmt nach Ungarn _______?
(a) Werdet . . . gereist (b) Will . . . reisen (c) Werdet . . . reisen wollen (d) Wird . . . gereist worden sein

5. Berlin _______ wohl die größte Stadt Deutschlands _______.
(a) wird . . . gewesen sein (b) wird . . . gesungen müssen (c) wird . . . sein (d) will . . . sein

Answer key: **1.** (d); **2.** (c); **3.** (a); **4.** (c); **5.** (c).

READING PREPARATION

The following frames are to prepare you for the reading passage.

	1. Sie **haben** wohl von Wernher von Braun **gehört**.
1. You *have* surely *heard* of Wernher von Braun.	**2.** **die Fahrt** = *trip, journey, voyage* Vielleicht wissen manche von Ihnen, daß er ein Buch schrieb, welches betitelt ist: *Erste Fahrt zum Mond.*
2. Perhaps some of you know that he wrote a book which is titled: *First Men to the Moon* (*First Trip to the Moon*).	**3.** **das Lesestück** = *reading passage* Aus dem **Vorwort** nehmen wir das Lesestück für dieses Kapitel.
3. From the *foreword* we are taking the reading passage for this chapter.	**4.** **etliche** = *some* Im Vorwort beantwortet von Braun etliche Fragen, die an ihn **gestellt werden**. (*are put/will put*)
4. In the foreword von Braun answers some questions which *are put* to him.	**5.** **laut** = *loud* **lauten** = *to read, to state* E i n e Frage lautet: „Warum glauben Sie, daß andere Welten **bewohnt** sind?" (*inhabitable/inhabited*)
5. One question reads: "Why do you believe that other worlds are *inhabited*?"	**6.** **der Beweis** = *proof, evidence* **Was für** Beweise hat man, daß andere Welten bewohnt sind? (*what/what for*)
6. *What* proof do we have that other worlds are inhabited? (Note the use of the singular to translate the plural **Beweise**.)	**7.** **sparen** = *to save, to spare, to be sparing* **spärlich** = *scanty, frugal* Beweise sind **noch etwas** spärlich. (*still somewhat/something else*)
7. Proof is *still somewhat* scanty.	**8.** **vorhanden** = *at hand, existing* **das Vorhandensein** = ________
8. *existence, presence*	**9.** Beweise für das Vorhandensein von **Leben** auf anderen Welten sind noch etwas spärlich. (*love/life*)
9. Proof for the existence of *life* on other worlds is still somewhat scanty.	**10.** **annehmen** = *to assume, to accept* **die Annahme** = ________
10. *assumption, acceptance*	**11.** **die Ruhe** = *rest* **beruhen** = *to rest* Worauf beruht denn die Annahme **seiner** Existenz? (*of his/of its*)

11. Upon what then does the assumption *of its* existence rest?	**12.** Die Annahme beruht **entweder** auf Glauben **oder** auf wissenschaftlicher Extrapolation. (*either. . . or/neither . . . nor*)
12. The assumption rests *either* on belief *or* on scientific extrapolation.	**13.** **verbinden** = *to tie, to unite, to join, to bind up* **die Verbindung** = __________
13. *union, binding up, combination*	**14.** Diese Annahme kann auch auf einer Verbindung von beiden beruhen.
14. This assumption can also rest on a combination of both.	**15.** **Deshalb** beruht die Annahme seiner Existenz entweder auf Glauben oder auf wissenschaftlicher Extrapolation oder auf einer Verbindung von beiden.
15. *Therefore* the assumption of its existence rests either on faith or on scientific extrapolation or on a combination of both.	**16.** **fassen** = *to hold, to grasp, to take* **auffassen** = *to understand, comprehend* **die Auffassung** = ________
16. *comprehension, interpretation, conception*	**17.** Welche Auffassung von dem Vorhandensein von Leben . . .
17. What conception of the presence of life . . .	**18.** Welche Auffassung von dem Vorhandensein von Leben auf anderen Welten hatten die meisten Physiker gegen Ende des 19. Jahrhunderts?
18. What conception of the presence of life on other worlds did most physicists have toward the end of the 19th century?	**19.** Es war eine materialistische Auffassung.
19. It was a materialistic conception.	**20.** **die Gewalt** = *power, force* **gewaltig =** ___________
20. *powerful, mighty, gigantic*	**21.** **die Uhr** = *clock* Das Universum war ein gewaltiges **Uhrwerk**. (*clock that works/clockwork*)
21. The universe was a gigantic *clockwork*.	**22.** **betrachten** = *to consider* Die meisten Physiker betrachteten das Universum als eine Art **gewaltigen Uhrwerks**. (The case is __________)
22. genitive Most of the physicists considered the universe to be a sort *of gigantic clockwork*.	**23.** **ziemlich** = *pretty, moderate(ly), fairly* Die Physiker glaubten den Mechanismus ziemlich gut zu verstehen. (The gender of **Mechanismus** is _______)

23. masculine: **den** tells you the word is *masculine singular accusative.* The physicists believed they could understand the mechanism fairly well.	**24.** Das Uhrwerk, **dessen** Mechanismus sie ziemlich gut zu verstehen glaubten . . .
24. The clockwork *whose* mechanism they believed they could understand fairly well . . .	**25.** **gestehen** = *to confess* **zugestehen** = *to concede, to admit* Sie **wollten** dem Schöpfer nur zugestehen . . .
25. They *were* only *willing* to concede to the creator . . . (Note that **zugestehen** takes a dative object.)	**26.** **die Aufgabe** = *task* Dem Schöpfer wollten sie als einzige Aufgabe **nur noch** zugestehen . . .
26. The only task that they were *still* willing to concede to the Creator . . .	**27.** **aufziehen** = *to wind up* Der Schöpfer **hat** das Urwerk **gebaut** und **aufgezogen**.
27. The Creator *constructed* and *wound up* the clockwork.	**28.** **konnte** = *could* (indicative mood) **könnte** = *could* (subjunctive mood) Der Schöpfer **könnte** dieses Uhrwerk **gebaut** und **aufgezogen haben**.
28. The Creator *could have constructed* and *wound up* this clockwork (or: "might have").	**29.** **wandeln** = *to change* Die Physik hat sich **gründlich** gewandelt. (*finally/thoroughly*)
29. Physics has changed *thoroughly.* (The reflexive **sich** often remains untranslated.)	**30.** **die Strecke** = *stretch, distance, section* **auf der Strecke bleiben** = *to remain by the* ________
30. *wayside*	**31.** **die Ehre** = *honor* **würdig** = *worthy* Manch **ehrwürdiges** Prinzip blieb auf der Strecke. (*respectable/early*)
31. Many a *respectable* principle remained by the wayside.	**32.** Manch ehrwürdiges Prinzip blieb auf der Strecke, als die Relativitätstheorie **zeigte** . . .
32. Many a respectable principle remained by the wayside when the theory of relativity *showed* . . .	**33.** **besitzen** = *to possess, to have* **Raum** und Zeit besitzen keinen absoluten Wert. (*room/space*)
33. *Space* and time do not have an absolute value.	**34.** **das Maß** = *dimension, measure* Die **Maße** von Raum und Zeit besitzen keinen absoluten Wert.
34. The *dimensions* of space and time have no absolute value.	**35.** **die Grundlage** = *foundation* Die Grundlagen unserer physikalischen **Vorstellungen**, die Maße von Raum und Zeit, besitzen keinen absoluten Wert. (*illusions/ideas*)

35.	The foundations of our *ideas* about the physical world, the dimensions of space and time, have no absolute value.	**36.**	**nachweisen** = *to point out, to prove* Manch ehrwürdiges Prinzip blieb auf der Strecke, als die Relativitätstheorie **nachwies** . . .
36.	Many a respectable principle remained by the wayside, when the theory of relativity *proved* . . .	**37.**	. . . daß die Grundlagen unserer physikalischen Vorstellungen, die Maße von Raum und Zeit, keinen absoluten Wert besitzen.
37.	. . . that the foundations of our ideas about the physical world, the dimensions of space and time, have no absolute value.	**38.**	**bauen** = *to build* **der Stein** = *stone* die **Bausteine** der Welt
38.	the *building blocks* of the world	**39.**	**winzig** = *tiny* die **winzigen** Bausteine der Welt
39.	the *tiny* building blocks of the world	**40.**	**sich bewegen** = *to move, to agitate* **Wie bewegen sich** die winzigen Bausteine der Welt?
40.	*How do* the tiny building blocks of the world *move*?	**41.**	**gleichmäßig** = *uniform, similar, equal* Die winzigen Bausteine bewegen sich nicht **gleichmäßig** . . .
41.	The tiny building blocks do not move *uniformly* . . .	**42.**	**springen** = *to jump, to leap* Sie bewegen sich nicht gleichmäßig, sondern sie machen **Sprünge**. (*sounds/leaps*)
42.	They do not move uniformly, rather they move erratically (make *leaps*).	**43.**	**führen** = *to lead, to conduct, to guide* **vollführen** = *to execute, to carry out* Sie vollführen Sprünge.
43.	They move erratically ("execute leaps").	**44.**	Als die Quantentheorie **nachwies**, daß die winzigen Bausteine der Welt Sprünge vollführen . . .
44.	When the quantum theory *showed* that the tiny building blocks of the world move erratically . . .	**45.**	Man **spaltet** das Atom. (*splits/fuses*)
45.	We *split* the atom.	**46.**	**wurde gespalten** = *was split* Als das Atom **gespalten wurde** . . .
46.	When the atom *was split* . . . (Passive voice, see §64.)	**47.**	Das **unteilbare** Atom wurde gespalten. (*divisible/indivisible*)
47.	The *indivisible* atom was split.	**48.**	**angeblich** = *alleged(ly)* das **angeblich** unteilbare Atom
48.	the *allegedly* indivisible atom	**49.**	Manch ehrwürdiges Prinzip blieb auf der Strecke, als das angeblich unteilbare Atom **doch** gespalten wurde.

49. Many a venerable principle remained by the wayside when the allegedly indivisible atom was *indeed* split.	**50.** **bevorzugen** = *to favor* **der Bevorzugte** = ________
50. *the favored individual*	**51.** Nur **wenige** Bevorzugte können mathematische Erklärungen verstehen.
51. Only *a few* favored individuals can understand mathematical explanations.	**52.** Die **schwerverständlichen** mathematischen Erklärungen, die nur wenige Bevorzugte verstehen können . . .
52. The mathematical explanations *which are difficult to understand* and which only a few favored individuals can understand . . .	**53.** Die schwerverständlichen mathematischen Erklärungen, **deren** innere Schönheit nur wenige Bevorzugte verstehen können . . .
53. The mathematical explanations which are hard to understand, *whose* inner beauty only a few favored individuals can comprehend . . .	**54.** **weichen** = *to give way, to yield* Die schönen mechanischen Modelle **wichen** . . . (*present/past*)
54. past The beautiful mechanical models *gave way to* . . .	**55.** **allmählich** = *gradual(ly)* Die schönen mechanischen Modelle **wichen allmählich** schwerverständlichen mathematischen Erklärungen.
55. The beautiful mechanical models *gradually gave way to* mathematical explanations which were hard to understand. (Notice that the verb **weichen** takes a dative object.)	**56.** **vereinfachen** = *to simplify* **vereinfacht** = *simplified* Die schönen vereinfachten mechanischen Modelle . . .
56. The beautiful simplified mechanical models . . .	**57.** **allzusehr** = *all too much, much too* Die schönen, allzusehr vereinfachten mechanischen Modelle . . .
57. The beautiful, much too simplified mechanical models . . .	**58.** Die schönen, allzusehr vereinfachten mechanischen Modelle wichen allmählich schwerverständlichen mathematischen Erklärungen.
58. The beautiful, much too simplified mechanical models gradually gave way to mathematical explanations which are difficult to understand.	**59.** **darstellen** = *to represent* Diese Modelle **sollten** das Uhrwerk des Universums **darstellen**.
59. These models *were meant to represent* the clockwork of the universe.	**60.** Die schönen, allzusehr vereinfachten mechanischen Modelle, **die** das Uhrwerk des Universums darstellen sollten . . .

60.	The beautiful, much too simplified mechanical models *which* were meant to represent the clockwork of the universe . . .	**61.**	**die Zeit** = *time* **der Genosse** = *comrade, companion* (m) **die Genossin** = *comrade, companion* (f) **zeitgenössisch** = *contemporary* Wie **sahen** die zeitgenössischen Physiker das Universum **an**?
61.	How did the contemporary physicists *look at* the universe?	**62.**	Die zeitgenössischen Physiker sahen das Universum nicht mehr als gigantisches Uhrwerk an, sondern **eher** als einen großen Gedanken, eine göttliche Idee. (*rather/before*)
62.	The contemporary physicists no longer looked at the universe as a gigantic clockwork but *rather* as a great thought, a divine (godly) idea.	**63.**	**d.h.** = **das heißt** = *that is* = *i.e.* Für Wernher von Braun ist Leben das Element des göttlichen Genius in dieser göttlichen Idee, **d.h.** in dem Universum.
63.	For Wernher von Braun life is the element of divine genius in this divine idea, i.e., in the universe.	**64.**	**das Haupt** = *chief, main* **das Ziel** = *objective, goal* **das Hauptziel** = ___________
64.	*main objective*	**65.**	Das Leben ist Gottes Hauptziel im Kosmos.
65.	Life is God's main objective in the cosmos.	**66.**	**weit** = *far* (also: *extensive, far, far-reaching, broad*) **weitest** = *broadest* Das Leben ist im weitesten **Sinne** Gottes Hauptziel im Kosmos. (*sin/sense*)
66.	Life in its broadest *sense* is God's main objective in the cosmos.	**67.**	**der Tropfen** = *drop* Kein Tropfen Wasser ist **völlig** steril auf der Erde.
67.	No drop of water on earth is *completely* sterile.	**68.**	**die Krume** = *crumb, speck* Keine Krume Boden **enthält** keine lebenden Organismen. (*holds out/does contain*)
68.	There is no speck of ground which *does* not *contain* living organisms.	**69.**	**waren** = *were* (indicative) **wären** = *were, would be* (subjunctive) **enthielten** = *contained* (indicative) **enthielten** = *would contain* (subjunctive) Man findet auf der Erde keinen Tropfen Wasser und keine Krume Boden, die völlig steril **wären** und keine lebenden Organismen **enthielten.**

69. On earth one does not find one drop of water and not one speck of ground which *would be* completely sterile and which *would* not *contain* any living organisms.	**70.** Von Braun weiß auch, daß **es** viele Millionen von Welten **gibt**, worauf es Leben geben könnte.
70. Von Braun knows also that *there are* many millions of worlds on which there could be life.	**71.** **unbelebt** = *lifeless* Andere Welten sind unbelebt.
71. Other worlds are lifeless.	**72.** **offen** = *open* **die Sicht** = *view, sight* **offensichtlich** = *evident, obvious* **Es sind** aber noch mehr Planeten, die offensichtlich unbelebt sind.
72. *There are,* however, still more planets which are evidently lifeless.	**73.** Das Leben ist das Hauptziel Gottes im Kosmos.
73. Life is God's main objective in the cosmos. (the main objective of God.)	**74.** **die Öde** = *wasteland* (also: *bleakness, dreariness*) Hier ist eine Öde.
74. Here is a wasteland.	**75.** **scheinbar** = *apparent, seeming* Wir haben **aber** eine scheinbare Öde. (*but/however*)
75. We have, *however,* an apparent wasteland.	**76.** **vertragen** = *to bear, to tolerate* **sich vertragen** = *to agree* Wie verträgt sich diese scheinbare Öde mit dem Glauben, daß das Leben das Hauptziel Gottes im Kosmos ist?
76. How does this apparent wasteland agree with the belief that life is God's main objective in the cosmos?	**77.** **das Fach** = *line (of study), subject, specialty* **der Fachmann** = *specialist* **die Rationalisierung** = *rationalizing* **der Rationalisierungsfachmann** = ________________
77. *the rationalizing specialist*	**78.** Von Braun will den Kosmos nicht mit den Augen eines Rationalisierungsfachmannes betrachten.
78. Von Braun does not want to consider the cosmos with the eyes of a rationalizing specialist.	**79.** **der Überfluß** = *superabundance, excess* (also: *abundance, plenty*) Der Überfluß **gehört** zum Wesen der Natur. (*belongs/belonged*)
79. Superabundance *belongs* to the essence of nature.	**80.** **verschwenden** = *to squander, to waste* **verschwenderisch** = *wasteful* **Verschwenderischer** Überfluß gehört zum Wesen der Natur.

80. *Wasteful* excess belongs to the essence of nature.	**81.** **seit jeher** = *from time immemorial* Von Braun antwortet: „Verschwenderischer Überfluß gehört seit jeher zum Wesen der Natur.“
81. Von Braun answers: “From time immemorial wasteful excess *has belonged* to the essence of nature.” (Lit.: *belongs*)	**82.** **der Samen** = *seed* **das Korn** = *seed, grain* **das Samenkorn** = *seed* Man braucht nur die Samenkörner zu betrachten.
82. One needs only to consider the seed.	**83.** **herum** = *around* **liegen** = *to lie* **liegend** = *lying* **herumliegend** = ________
83. *lying around*	**84.** Man braucht nur **die herumliegenden Samenkörner** zu betrachten.
84. One needs only to consider *the seeds which are lying around.*	**85.** Man braucht **sich** nur **umzusehen**.
85. One needs only *to look around.*	**86.** **nutzen** = *to make use of, to utilize* **genutzt** = *used, utilized* **ungenutzt** = ________
86. *unused, unutilized*	**87.** Man braucht sich nur umzusehen und die Millionen ungenutzt herumliegenden Samenkörner zu betrachten.
87. One only needs to look around and to observe the millions of seeds which are lying around unutilized.	**88.** Seit jeher gehören diese ungenutzt herumliegenden Samenkörner zum Wesen der Natur.
88. Since time immemorial these unused seeds which are lying around have belonged to the essence of nature.	**89.** **wachsen** = *to grow* **heranwachsen** = *to grow up* Alle Samenkörner können zu einer **Blume** oder einem **Baum** heranwachsen.
89. All seeds can grow up into a *flower* or a *tree.*	**90.** **fähig** = *capable, qualified, able* **die Fähigkeit** = ______________
90. *capacity, ability*	**91.** Alle Samenkörner besitzen die Fähigkeit, zu einer schönen Blume oder einem gewaltigen Baum **heranzuwachsen**.
91. All seeds possess the capacity *to grow up* into a beautiful flower or a mighty tree.	**92.** Wieviele Samenkörner **werden** dieses Potential **nutzen**?

92. How many seeds *will use* this potential?	**93.** **der Bruchteil** = *fraction* **der Bruch** = *break* **der Teil** = *part, piece, section, portion* Nur ein winziger Bruchteil erhält die **Gelegenheit**, dieses Potential zu nutzen. (*necessity/opportunity*)
93. Only a tiny fraction gets the *opportunity* to use this potential.	**94.** **jemals** = *ever* Nur ein winziger Bruchteil der Samenkörner erhält **jemals** die Gelegenheit, dieses Potential zu nutzen.
94. Only a tiny fraction of seeds *ever* gets the opportunity to utilize this potential.	**95.** Für von Braun ist Leben eine göttliche, universale Idee.
95. For von Braun, life is a divine universal idea.	**96.** **teilen** = *to share, to divide* **verteilen** = *to distribute* Was verteilt Gott über das ganze Universum?
96. What does God distribute throughout the whole universe?	**97.** **die Saat** = *seed* Gott verteilt seine Saat über das ganze Weltall. (**Weltall** probably means ___________)
97. *universe* God distributes his seed throughout the whole universe.	**98.** Von Braun ist sicher, daß Gott seine Saat über das ganze Weltall **verteilt hat**.
98. Von Braun is positive that God *has distributed* his seed throughout the entire universe.	**99.** **Worauf** aber fällt die Saat?
99. *Upon what,* however, does the seed fall?	**100.** **der Boden** = *ground* Viel Saat fällt auf **unfruchtbaren** Boden. (*fruitful/barren*)
100. Much of the seed falls on *barren* ground.	**101.** Aber Gott weiß, daß viel Saat auf unfruchtbaren Boden fällt.
101. But God knows that much of the seed falls on barren ground.	**102.** **genug** = *enough* **genügend** = *sufficient* Gott hat genügend Zeit.
102. God has sufficient time.	**103.** Er hat genügend Zeit, **auf die Ergebnisse** zu warten.
103. He has sufficient time to wait *for the results.*	

PROGRESS TEST

After reviewing the items you have circled, choose the meaning of the indicated words.

1. Die **Annahme,** daß andere Welten bewohnt sind, beruht entweder auf Glauben oder auf wissenschaftlicher Extrapolation.
(a) judgment (b) accusation (c) assumption (d) investigation

2. Sie wollten nur **zugestehen,** daß der Schöpfer dieses Uhrwerk gebaut und aufgezogen hatte.
(a) to stand (b) to envision (c) to deny (d) to concede

3. Manch ehrwürdiges Prinzip blieb auf der Strecke, da in den letzten fünfzig Jahren die Physik sich gründlich **wandelte.**
(a) wandered (b) changed (c) started over (d) passed itself

4. Die **Grundlagen unserer physikalischen Vorstellungen** besitzen keinen absoluten Wert.
(a) conceptions of the physical world (b) foundations of our ideas about the physical world (c) beginnings of our physical worlds (d) furthering of our physical nature

5. Die winzigen Bausteine der Welt bewegen sich nicht gleichmäßig, sondern **vollführen Sprünge.**
(a) spring up (b) full of springs (c) move erratically (d) spring fully

6. Die vereinfachten mechanischen Modelle **wichen** allmählich schwerverständlichen mathematischen Erklärungen.
(a) gave way (b) followed (c) weakened (d) caused

7. Nur wenige **Bevorzugte** können diese innere Schönheit verstehen.
(a) undisputed individuals (b) favored individuals (c) extraordinary individuals (d) predestined individuals

8. Was **enthielt** jede Krume Boden?
(a) did hold out (b) did contain (c) did discover (d) did uncover

Answer key: **1.** (c); **2.** (d); **3.** (b); **4.** (b); **5.** (c); **6.** (a); **7.** (b); **8.** (b).

And now to the thoughts of Wernher von Braun as to the nature of the universe in which we find ourselves:

Wernher von Braun: Erste Fahrt zum Mond

Frage: Warum glauben Sie, daß andere Welten bewohnt sind?

Antwort: Beweise für das Vorhandensein von Leben auf anderen Welten sind noch etwas spärlich. Deshalb beruht die Annahme seiner Existenz entweder auf Glauben oder auf wissenschaftlicher Extrapolation oder auf einer Verbindung von beiden.

Gegen Ende des 19. Jahrhunderts hatten die meisten Physiker eine materialistische Auffassung: sie betrachteten das Universum als eine Art gewaltigen Uhrwerks, dessen Mechanismus sie ziemlich gut zu verstehen glaubten. Dem Schöpfer wollten sie als einzige Aufgabe nur noch zugestehen, daß er dieses Uhrwerk gebaut und aufgezogen haben könnte.

In den letzten fünfzig Jahren hat sich die Physik gründlich gewandelt. Manch ehrwürdiges Prinzip blieb auf der Strecke, als die Relativitätstheorie zeigte, daß die Grundlagen unserer physikalischen Vorstellungen, die Maße von Raum und Zeit, keinen absoluten Wert besitzen; als die Quantentheorie nachwies, daß die winzigen Bausteine der Welt sich nicht gleichmäßig bewegen, sondern Sprünge vollführen; und als das angeblich unteilbare Atom doch gespalten wurde. Die schönen, allzusehr vereinfachten mechanischen Modelle, die das Uhrwerk des Universums darstellen sollten, wichen allmählich schwerverständlichen mathematischen Erklärungen, deren innere Schönheit nur wenige Bevorzugte verstehen können. Aber die Folge war, daß die zeitgenössischen Physiker das Universum nicht mehr als gigantisches Uhrwerk ansahen, sondern eher als einen großen Gedanken, eine göttliche Idee.

Für mich ist Leben das Element des göttlichen Genius in dieser göttlichen Idee. Es ist im weitesten Sinne Gottes Hauptziel im Kosmos. Man findet auf der Erde keinen Tropfen Wasser und keine Krume Boden, die völlig steril wären und keine lebenden Organismen enthielten.

Von Braun goes on to say that the universe with its many millions of suns is made up of the same elements as our own earth. Those suns probably also have planetary systems as does our own in which at least one planet could support life. Then von Braun asks how one can reconcile this apparent absence of life, comparatively speaking, with the belief that life in the cosmos is God's chief objective. He answers his own question by pointing out that from the beginning of time an excess of waste is part of the essence of nature. Only a tiny fraction of the seeds on this earth have the opportunity to make use of their potential.

Verträgt sich diese scheinbare Öde mit dem Glauben, daß das Leben das Hauptziel Gottes im Kosmos ist?

Ich denke, wir sollten den Kosmos nicht mit den Augen eines Rationalisierungsfachmannes betrachten. Verschwenderischer Überfluß gehört seit jeher zum Wesen der Natur. Man braucht sich nur umzusehen und die Millionen ungenutzt herumliegenden Samenkörner zu betrachten. Alle besitzen die Fähigkeit, zu einer schönen Blume oder einem gewaltigen Baum heranzuwachsen, aber nur ein winziger Bruchteil erhält jemals die Gelegenheit, dieses Potential zu nutzen.

Leben ist eine göttliche, universale Idee. Ich bin sicher, daß Gott seine Saat über das ganze Weltall verteilt hat. Aber er weiß, daß viel auf unfruchtbaren Boden fällt, und er hat genügend Zeit, auf die Ergebnisse zu warten.

Chapter Twenty

64. *Passive voice*

1. You were briefly introduced to the passive voice in chapter 3 and have met it periodically in your reading. In the active voice, the subject performs the action, i.e., it does something; in the passive voice, it receives the action, i.e., it has something done to it.

active:	*I hit the ball.*
passive:	*The ball was hit by me.*

2. The present tense of the passive in German is formed by the present tense of **werden** plus the past participle of the main verb:

ich werde gesehen	*I am (being) seen*
du wirst gesehen	*you are (being) seen*
er, sie, es wird gesehen	*he, she, it is (being) seen*
wir werden gesehen	*we will be seen*
ihr werdet gesehen	*you will be seen*
sie werden gesehen	*they will be seen*
Sie werden gesehen	*you will be seen*

Note: Remember that the future tense of the active voice is formed by **werden** plus the infinitive while the passive must always use the past participle. Do not confuse the two verb forms:

Future active:

Ich *werde* es *reparieren*.	*I **will fix** it.*

Passive present:

Es *wird* von mir *repariert*.	*It's **being** (**getting**) **fixed** by me.*

3. A synopsis of the passive for **sehen** in the six tenses is as follows (note that **gesehen** appears in each tense):

Present:	
ich werde gesehen	*I am (being) seen*
Past:	
ich wurde gesehen	*I was (being) seen*
Pres. perf.:	
ich bin gesehen worden	*I have been seen, was seen*
Past perf.:	
ich war gesehen worden	*I had been seen*
Future:	
ich werde gesehen werden	*I will be seen*
Fut. perf.:	
ich werde gesehen worden sein	*I will have been seen*

Note:

1. **Worden** (translated *been*) is a shortened form of the past participle **geworden**.

2. Some form of the verb **sein**, the auxiliary of **werden**, appears in the perfect tenses. **Sein** is translated by a form of *have.*

3. The infinitive form of **werden** in the future passive is translated *be.*

4. **Von** (*by*), **durch** (*by means of*), and **mit** (*with, by*) are the prepositions which express agency or instrument:

Das Buch wurde *von* Hemingway geschrieben. (past)	*The book was written* ***by*** *Hemingway.*
Die Stadt ist *von* den Russen *durch* die Armee geschützt worden. (present perfect)	*The city was protected* ***by*** *the Russians* ***by means of*** *the army.*
War das Brot *mit* einem Messer geschnitten worden? (past perfect)	*Had the bread been cut* ***with*** *a knife?*

5. As usual, the participles and infinitives will occupy the final position in the clause except in dependent word order:

Das Lied wird *gesungen werden.*	*The song will* ***be sung****.*
Sie weiß, daß das Lied *gesungen werden* wird.	*She knows that the song will* ***be sung****.*

(Note that the agent performing the action need not appear in either German or English.)

These exercises are based on phrases and vocabulary drawn from a passage by Jung concerning flying saucers. Give the meaning expressed by the verbs in these sentences.

	1. **beobachten** = *to observe* Tag und Nacht **werden** Objekte von uns **beobachtet.**
1. Night and day objects *are observed* by us. (Lit.: day and night)	**2.** Tag und Nacht **werden** wir Objekte **beobachten.**
2. Night and day we *will observe* objects.	**3.** Tag und Nacht **wurden** Objekte von uns **beobachtet.**
3. Night and day objects *were observed* by us.	**4.** Tag und Nacht **sind** Objekte **beobachtet worden.**
4. Night and day objects *have been observed* (*were observed*).	**5.** Tag und Nacht **waren** Objekte **beobachtet worden.**
5. Night and day objects *had been observed.*	**6.** Tag und Nacht **werden** Objekte **beobachtet werden.**
6. Night and day objects *will be observed.*	**7.** Tag und Nacht **werden** wir Objekte **beobachten.**
7. Night and day we *will observe* objects.	**8.** Tag und Nacht **werden** Objekte **beobachtet werden.**
8. Night and day objects *will be observed.*	**9.** Tag und Nacht **werden** Objekte **beobachtet worden sein**.
9. Night and day objects *will have been observed.*	**10.** **feurig** = fiery **strahlend** = *shining* Feurig strahlende Körper **werden** von ihnen **gesehen.**
10. Fiery shining bodies *are seen* by them.	**11.** Sie **werden** feurig strahlende Körper **sehen.**
11. They *will see* fiery shining bodies. (or: you *will see* . . .)	**12.** Feurig strahlende Körper **wurden gesehen.**
12. Fiery shining bodies *were seen.*	**13.** Feurig strahlende Körper **sind** von ihnen **gesehen worden.**
13. Fiery shining bodies *have been seen* (*were seen*) by them.	**14.** Feurig strahlende Körper **waren gesehen worden.**
14. Fiery shining bodies *had been seen.*	**15.** Feurig strahlende Körper **werden gesehen werden.**
15. Fiery shining bodies *will be seen.*	**16.** Feurig strahlende Körper **werden gesehen worden sein.**

16. Fiery shining bodies *will have been seen.*	**17.** **der Gedanke** = *thought* **bewußt** = *conscious* Der Gedanke **wird** nicht bewußt **gedacht.**
17. The thought *is* not consciously *thought.*	**18.** Man **wird** den Gedanken nicht bewußt **denken.**
18. One *will* not consciously *think* the thought.	**19.** Der Gedanke **wurde** nicht bewußt **gedacht.**
19. The thought *was* not consciously *thought.*	**20.** Der Gedanke **ist** nicht bewußt **gedacht worden.**
20. The thought *has* not *been* consciously *thought* (*was . . . thought*).	**21.** Der Gedanke **war** nicht bewußt **gedacht worden.**
21. The thought *had* not *been* consciously *thought.*	**22.** Der Gedanke **wird** nicht bewußt **gedacht werden.**
22. The thought *will* not *be* consciously *thought.*	**23.** Man **wird** den Gedanken nicht bewußt **denken.**
23. One *will* not consciously *think* the *thought.*	**24.** Der Gedanke **wird** nicht bewußt **gedacht werden.**
24. The thought *will* not *be* consciously *thought.*	**25.** Der Gedanke **wird** nicht bewußt **gedacht worden sein.**
25. The thought *will* not *have been* consciously *thought.*	

A reminder: The German present perfect is often equivalent to the English past tense. See examples 4, 13, and 20 above and 4 below.

PROGRESS TEST

Choose the correct verb form for the indicated verb.

1. The book *will have been read.*
(a) wird gelesen
(b) wird gelesen worden sein
(c) wird gelesen werden
(d) wird gelesen sein müssen

2. The test *was passed.*
(a) wird bestanden
(b) war bestanden worden
(c) wurde bestanden
(d) hatte bestanden

3. The orchestra *is being conducted* by Toscanini.
(a) ist geleitet worden
(b) wird geleitet werden
(c) hat geleitet werden müssen
(d) wird geleitet

4. Stravinsky's violin concerto *was played* by Jascha Heifitz.*
(a) war gespielt worden (b) mußte gespielt werden
(c) wird gespielt werden (d) ist gespielt worden

5. Letters *have been sent* every day.
(a) sind geschickt (b) waren geschickt worden
(c) sind geschickt worden (d) werden geschickt werden

6. Dinner *will be served.*
(a) will serviert werden (b) wird servieren
(c) wird serviert werden (d) wird serviert worden sein

Answer key: **1.** (b); **2.** (c); **3.** (d); **4.** (d); **5.** (c); **6.** (c).

*Reminder: The German present perfect is often equivalent to English past tense.

65. *Use of modals in the passive*

1. There are no passive forms of the modals themselves, but modals may be used in the passive voice:

Present:
Der Brief muß geschrieben werden. *The letter must be written.*
Past:
Der Brief mußte geschrieben werden. *The letter had to be written.*
Pres. perf.:
Der Brief hat geschrieben werden müssen. *The letter has had to be written, had to be written.*
Past perf.:
Der Brief hatte geschrieben werden müssen. *The letter had had to be written.*
Future:
Der Brief wird geschrieben werden müssen. *The letter will have to be written.*

Note that the verb **werden** in its infinitive form is again translated *be.*

The future perfect passive with a modal is for all practical purposes non-existent. It is replaced by the active voice:
Man *wird* den Brief *haben schreiben müssen.* One ***will have to have written*** *the letter.*

But here is an example of the future perfect passive:

> **Der Brief** ***wird haben geschrieben werden müssen.*** *The letter* ***will have to have been written****.* (Here **werden** is translated *been.*)

Now you can see why it is replaced by the active voice.

2. Look to the end of the clause to find the modal verb:

> **Das Lied hatte gesungen werden** ***müssen.*** *The song had* ***had*** *to be sung.*

3. Because of the double infinitives in the present perfect, past perfect, and future tenses, the inflected form of the verb will precede the participial construction in dependent word order:

> **Er glaubt, daß der Wagen von den Pferden** ***hat*** **gezogen werden können.** *He believes that the wagon could have been pulled* (lit.: ***has*** *been able to be pulled*) *by the horses.*

Give the meaning of the following verb tenses.

	1. Das Brot **wird** mit einem Messer **geschnitten.**
1. The (loaf of *or* piece of) bread *is cut* with a knife.	**2.** Das Brot **soll** mit einem Messer **geschnitten werden.**
2. The bread *is supposed to be cut* with a knife.	**3.** Das Brot **sollte** mit einem Messer **geschnitten werden.**
3. The bread *was supposed to be cut* with a knife.	**4.** Das Brot **mußte** mit einem Messer **geschnitten werden.**
4. The bread *had to be cut* with a knife.	**5.** **Hat** das Brot mit einem Messer **geschnitten werden müssen?**
5. *Did* the bread *have to be cut* with a knife?	**6.** Das Brot **ist** mit einem Messer **geschnitten worden.**
6. The bread *has been cut* (*was cut*) with a knife.	**7.** Ich weiß, daß das Brot mit einem Messer **hatte geschnitten werden müssen.**
7. I know that the bread *had had to be cut* with a knife.	**8.** **Kann** das Brot mit einem Messer **geschnitten werden?**
8. *Can* the bread *be cut* with a knife?	**9.** **Wird** das Brot mit einem Messer **geschnitten werden müssen?**
9. *Will* the bread *have to be cut* with a knife?	**10.** Das Buch **muß** von ihm **gefunden werden.**
10. The book *must be found* by him.	**11.** Das Buch **mußte** von ihm **gefunden werden.**
11. The book *had to be found* by him.	**12.** Das Buch **wurde** von ihm **gefunden.**

12. The book *was found* by him.	**13.** Ich weiß, daß das Buch von ihm **hat gefunden werden können.**
13. I know that the book *could have been found* by him.	**14.** Das Buch **war** von ihm **gefunden worden.**
14. The book *had been found by* him.	**15.** **Wird** das Buch von ihm **gefunden werden können?**
15. *Will* the book *be able to be found* by him? (i.e., Will he be able to find the book?)	**16.** **Darf** das Buch von ihm **gefunden werden?**
16. *May* the book *be found* by him?	**17.** Charlotte weiß, daß das Buch von ihm nicht **hat gefunden werden sollen.**
17. Charlotte knows that the book *was* not *supposed to be found* by him.	

Note again that the German present perfect is often equivalent to the English past tense. See examples 5, 13, and 17.

PROGRESS TEST

Choose the correct form for the indicated verb.

1. The chair *was supposed to be brought* yesterday.
(a) wird gebracht werden sollen
(b) sollte gebracht worden sein
(c) sollte gebracht werden
(d) ist gebracht worden

2. The book *will have to be begun.*
(a) wird begonnen worden sein
(b) will begonnen werden müssen
(c) wird begonnen werden müssen
(d) soll begonnen werden müssen

3. The door *had not been able to be closed.*
(a) hatte nicht geschlossen werden können
(b) hat nicht geschlossen werden können
(c) konnte nicht geschlossen werden
(d) hatte nicht schließen können

4. That *must not be sung.*
(a) durfte nicht gesungen werden
(b) darf nicht gesungen werden
(c) hat nicht gesungen werden dürfen
(d) mußte nicht gesungen werden

5. The hotel *had to be sold.*
(a) hatte verkauft werden müssen
(b) wird verkauft haben
(c) hat verkauft werden müssen
(d) muß verkauft werden

Answer key: **1.** (c); **2.** (c); **3.** (a); **4.** (b); **5.** (c).

66. *The impersonal passive*

1. Constructions such as the following, formed from intransitive verbs, are examples of the impersonal passive. The pronoun **es** is either used in first position or understood:

Es wurde gesungen.	*There was singing.*
Mir wird gesagt . . .	*I am told . . .* [lit.: (*It*) *is said to me.*]
Heute abend wird getanzt.	*There is a dance this evening. There will be dancing this evening.* (Note the future meaning of the passive present in this example.)
Ihm wurde nicht geantwortet.	*He was not answered.*

Give the meaning of the following passive constructions.

	1. **wider** = *against* **sprechen** = *to speak* Dem Professor **wurde** nie **widersprochen.**
1. The professor *was* never *contradicted.*	**2.** **bestimmt** = *certainly* Dir **wird** bestimmt nicht **geglaubt!**
2. You *will* certainly not *be believed* (*are . . . believed*). (Note here the future meaning of the present passive tense.)	**3.** Es **ist** bis spät in die Nacht **getanzt** und **gesungen worden.**
3. *Singing* and *dancing went on* until late into the night (there *was singing* and *dancing . . .*)	**4.** Ihm **war** zu seinem Geburtstag **gratu-liert worden.**
4. He *had been congratulated* on his birthday. (Or: He *had been wished* a happy birthday. **Ich gratuliere zum Geburtstag** means *Happy Birthday.*)	**5.** Es **wird** dem alten Mann bestimmt **geholfen werden müssen.**
5. The old man *will* certainly *have to be helped.*	**6.** Meine Herren, es **wird** hier nicht **geraucht!**
6. Gentlemen, there *is* no *smoking* here.	

67. *Constructions translated by an English passive*

1. The passive is rather cumbersome in German and is often replaced by the following substitutes:

(a) **man** plus the active voice:

Hier trinkt man kein Wasser.	*Water is not drunk here.*
Man spricht Deutsch.	*German is spoken here.*

(b) a form of the verb **sein**, followed by **zu** or **nicht zu:**

Wie ist das zu machen?	*How can that be done?* (or: *How is that to be done?*)
Er ist nicht zu verstehen.	*He cannot be understood.*

(c) **sich lassen** plus a dependent infinitive:

Das läßt sich machen.	*That can be done.*
Die große dicke Zigarre läßt sich bestimmt nicht rauchen.	*That big, fat cigar certainly cannot be smoked.*

Note that in (b) and (c) the English equivalent is *can* + *be* + past participle.

Give the meaning of the following sentences.

	1. Man **hat** ihm nicht **geantwortet.**
1. He *was* not *answered.*	**2.** Man **kann** ihn nicht **sehen.**
2. He *cannot be seen.*	**3.** Wo **ist** das Buch **zu finden?**
3. Where *can* the book *be found?*	**4.** **überzeugen** = *to convince* Ich sehe, daß du nicht **zu überzeugen bist.**
4. I see that you *cannot be convinced.*	**5.** **das Lied** = *song* Können Sie mir zeigen, wie dieses Lied **zu singen ist?**
5. Can you show me how this song *is to be sung?*	**6.** Das **läßt sich** einfach nicht **glauben!**
6. That simply *cannot be believed!*	**7.** Das **ließ sich** überhaupt nicht **verstehen.**
7. That *could not be understood* at all.	**8.** Sein neues Lied **läßt sich** bestimmt **singen.**
8. *It is* certainly *possible to sing* his new song. (His new song *can* certainly *be sung.*)	

68. *The apparent or statal passive*

1. The apparent passive is conjugated with a form of **sein** plus a past participle. The participle acts only as an adjective, not as a verb.

2. Contrast the apparent passive with the true passive, which you have just learned:

PRESENT:

Die Tür ist geschlossen.	*The door is closed.*
Die Tür wird geschlossen.	*The door is being closed.*

PAST:

Die Tür war geschlossen.	*The door was closed.*
Die Tür wurde geschlossen.	*The door was being closed.*

FUTURE:

Die Tür wird geschlossen sein.	*The door will be closed.*
Die Tür wird geschlossen werden.	*The door will be closed.* (*One will be closing the door.*)

The apparent passive describes the result of a previous action. The true passive describes an action taking place at the time the verb indicates.

3. The true passive is often used to describe a customary occurrence:

Die Tür *wird* um acht Uhr *geöffnet*. — *The door* ***is opened*** (regularly) *at eight o'clock.*

The apparent passive only tells that the door is open:

Die Tür *ist* um acht Uhr *geöffnet*. — *The door* ***is open*** *at eight o'clock.*

Give the meaning of the following sentences.

	1. Das Licht **ist** um 10 Uhr **ausgemacht**.
1. The light *is off* at 10 o'clock.	**2.** Das Licht **wird** immer um 10 Uhr **ausgemacht.**
2. The light *is* always *turned off* at 10 o'clock.	**3.** **beenden** = *to finish* Die Arbeit **war beendet.**
3. The work *was finished.*	**4.** Die Arbeit **wurde** um 10 Uhr **beendet.**

4. The work *was finished* at 10 o'clock.	**5.** **übermorgen** = *the day after tomorrow* Das Hotel **wird** übermorgen bestimmt **verkauft sein.**
5. The hotel *will* certainly *be sold* by the day after tomorrow (i.e., the transaction will have been completed or have taken place).	**6.** Das Hotel **wird** übermorgen bestimmt **verkauft werden.**
6. The hotel *will* certainly *be sold* the day after tomorrow (i.e., the transaction will be taking place on that day).	

PROGRESS TEST

Give the meaning of the sentence.

1. Dem Lehrer wird nicht gehorcht.
(a) The teacher does not obey.
(b) The teacher will not obey.
(c) The teacher will not be obeyed.
(d) The teacher is not obeyed.

2. Es wurde bis spät in die Nacht geplaudert.
(a) We talked late into the night.
(b) We often talk late in the night.
(c) We will talk late into the night.
(d) Late that night we talked.

3. Man tut das eigentlich nicht.
(a) That just is not done.
(b) The man just does not do it.
(c) We will just not do it.
(d) He really had not done it.

4. Else hat sich ihr Haar machen lassen.
(a) Else let her hair fall out.
(b) Else has made her own hair.
(c) Else herself did her hair.
(d) Else had her hair done.

5. Das Haus war aus Steinen gebaut.
(a) The house was being built of stones.
(b) The house had been built of stones.
(c) The house was built of stones.
(d) The house had to be built of stone.

Answer key: **1.** (d); **2.** (a); **3.** (a); **4.** (d); **5.** (c).

READING PREPARATION

Continue to circle all new or unfamiliar words. Review them two or three times before going on to the reading passage.

	1. **veröffentlichen** = *to publish* Im Jahre 1958 **wurde** ein Buch von dem berühmten Psychologen und Psychiater C. G. Jung (1875–1961) **veröffentlicht.**
1. In 1958 a book by the famous psychologist and psychiatrist C. G. Jung (1875–1961) *was published.*	**2.** Der Titel lautet: *Ein moderner Mythus, von Dingen, die am Himmel gesehen werden.*
2. The title reads: *A Modern Myth, of Things Which Are Seen in the Sky.* (The English title is: *Flying Saucers, A Modern Myth of Things Seen in the Skies.*)	**3.** **untersuchen** = *to investigate* In diesem Buch **will** er die Ufos nicht als physikalische Realität **untersuchen**.
3. In this book he *does* not *want* to *investigate* UFOs as physical realities.	**4.** **sich zuwenden** = *to turn to* Er will sich **lieber** der Frage nach der psychischen Natur des Phänomens zuwenden.
4. He wants *rather* to turn to the question of the psychic aspects of the phenomenon.	**5.** **zugeben** = *to admit* Er gibt zu, daß etwas **gesehen wird.**
5. He admits that something *is seen* (*is being seen*).	**6.** Einige Fragen **können gestellt werden.**
6. Some questions *can be asked.*	**7.** Zum Beispiel, „Was **wird** am Himmel **gesehen**?"
7. For example, "What *is seen* in the sky?"	**8.** **Wenn** nichts da ist, warum wird etwas gesehen?
8. *If* nothing is there, why is something seen?	**9.** **deuten** = *to signify, to interpret, to indicate* Deutet dies auf eine **Änderung** in der menschlichen Psyche?
9. Does this signify a *change* in the human psyche?	**10.** **die Folge** = *consequence* Was sind die psychischen Folgen davon, die möglich sind?
10. What are psychic consequences which are possible?	**11.** Und jetzt **wenden wir uns** dem Text zu.
11. And now *let us turn* to the text.	**12.** **beobachten** = *to observe* **die Beobachtung** = __________
12. *the observation*	**13.** **deuten** = *to mean, to interpret* **die Deutung** = __________
13. *meaning, explanation, interpretation*	**14.** die Beobachtung und Deutung der Ufos

14. the observation and interpretation of UFOs	**15.** **Anlaß geben** = *to give rise to* Wozu **haben** die Beobachtung und Deutung der Ufos **Anlaß gegeben?**
15. What *have* the observation and interpretation of UFOs *given rise to?*	**16.** **bilden** = *to form* Sie haben zu einer richtigen **Legendenbildung** Anlaß gegeben.
16. They have given rise to a veritable *formation of a legend.*	**17.** **all-** = *all* **bereit** = *ready* **allbereits** = ___________
17. *already*	**18.** Die Beobachtung und Deutung der Ufos haben allbereits zu einer richtigen Legendenbildung Anlaß gegeben.
18. The observation and interpretation of UFOs have already led to a veritable formation of a legend.	**19.** **die Reihe** = *the series* Es gibt heute eine Reihe von Büchern **darüber.**
19. Today there is a series of books *about it.*	**20.** Es gibt **heute auch schon** eine Reihe von Büchern über diesen Gegenstand. (*already/beautiful*)
20. There is *already* a series of books on this subject.	**21.** **ganz abgesehen** = *quite apart* Ganz abgesehen von den Tausenden von **Zeitungs**notizen und -artikeln. (**Zeitung** = *newspaper*)
21. Quite apart from the thousands of *newspaper* reports and articles.	**22.** **der Schwindel** = *humbug, swindle* **Zum Teil** sind diese Bücher Schwindel.
22. *In part* these books are humbug.	**23.** **der Ernst** = *earnestness, severity* **ernsthaft** = *serious, grave* Zum Teil sind die Zeitungsnotizen und -artikel und Bücher ernsthaft.
23. In part the newspaper reports and articles and books are serious.	**24.** Es gibt heute auch schon eine Reihe von Büchern über diesen Gegenstand—pro et contra, zum Teil Schwindel, zum Teil ernsthaft.
24. There is now a whole literature on the subject—pro and con, some of it humbug, some of it serious.	**25.** **beeindrucken** = *to impress* Die Ufos selber **lassen sich** nicht **beeindrucken** von all den Büchern und den Tausenden von Zeitungsnotizen und -artikeln.
25. The UFOs themselves *are* not *impressed* by all the books and the thousands of newspaper reports and articles.	**26.** Das Phänomen selber **scheint sich** davon nicht beeindrucken zu lassen. (*appears/shines*)

26. The phenomenon itself *appears* not to be impressed by them.	**27.** **dartun** = *to show, to prove* Wie die neuesten Beobachtungen dartun . . .
27. As the latest observations show . . .	**28.** Wie die neuesten Beobachtungen dartun, scheint sich das Phänomen selber davon nicht beeindrucken zu lassen.
28. As the latest observations show, the phenomenon itself appears not to be impressed by them.	**29.** **vorderhand** = *for the time being, for the present* Das Phänomen scheint vorderhand weiter zu gehen.
29. The phenomenon appears for the time being to be going on its way.	**30.** **Was** es immer sein mag, eines steht fest.
30. *Whatever* it may be, one thing is certain.	**31.** Das Phänomen **ist** zu einem lebendigen Mythus **geworden.**
31. The phenomenon *has become* a living myth.	**32.** **die Sage** = *legend* Das Phänomen ist auch schon eine Sage.
32. The phenomenon is already a legend.	**33.** **stehen** = *to stand* **entstehen** = *to begin* (also: *to originate, to grow out of*) Eine Sage **ist entstanden.**
33. A legend *has begun.*	**34.** **bilden** = *to form* Eine Sage **ist gebildet worden.**
34. A legend *has been formed.*	**35.** **die Gelegenheit** = *opportunity* Wir haben hier eine Gelegenheit zu sehen, wie eine Sage entsteht.
35. We have here an opportunity to see how a legend begins.	**36.** **erzählen** = *to tell* **die Erzählung** = *tale* Eine **Wundererzählung** bildet sich.
36. A *miraculous tale* is taking shape.	**37.** **schwer** = *difficult* **schwierig** = *difficult* **dunkel** = *dark, somber* In einer schwierigen und dunkeln Zeit **der** Menschheit bildet sich eine Wundererzählung.
37. In a difficult and dark time *for* (*of*) humanity a miraculous tale is taking shape.	**38.** **eingreifen** = *to intervene* (also: *to interfere*) **der Eingriff** = ______
38. *the intervention*	**39.** **versuchsweise** = *by way of experiment* ein versuchsweiser Eingriff

39.	an experimental intervention (lit.: an intervention by way of experiment)	**40.**	Eine Wundererzählung bildet sich von einem versuchsweisen Eingriff „himmlischer" Mächte.
40.	A miraculous tale of an experimental intervention of "heavenly" powers is taking shape.	**41.**	**nah** = *near* **näher** = *nearer* **annähern** = *to approach* **die Annäherung** = __________
41.	*the approach*	**42.**	**die Erde** = *earth* **irdisch** = *terrestrial* **außer** = *outside of* **außerirdisch** = __________
42.	*extraterrestrial*	**43.**	eine Annäherung außerirdischer „himmlischer" Mächte
43.	an approach of extraterrestrial "heavenly" powers	**44.**	Eine Wundererzählung von einem versuchsweisen Eingriff oder wenigstens einer Annäherung außerirdischer „himmlischer" Mächte **wird gebildet werden.**
44.	A miraculous tale of an experimental intervention or at least an approach by extraterrestrial or "heavenly" powers *will be formed.*	**45.**	**sich anschicken** = *to prepare* (*to set about, to get ready*) Die menschliche **Phantasie** schickt sich an . . .
45.	Human *imagination* is preparing . . .	**46.**	**der Weltraum** = *space* **die Fahrt** = *journey, travel* **die Weltraumfahrt** = __________
46.	*space travel*	**47.**	Die menschliche Phantasie schickt sich an, die **Möglichkeit** der Weltraumfahrt zu diskutieren.
47.	Human imagination is getting ready to discuss the *possibility* of space travel.	**48.**	**das Gestirn** = *star, heavenly body* Die menschliche Phantasie schickt sich an, die Möglichkeit **der Invasion anderer Gestirne** zu diskutieren.
48.	Human imagination is preparing to discuss the possibility *of invasion of other heavenly bodies.*	**49.**	**zugleich** = *at the same time* Zugleich leben wir in einer Zeit, **da** die menschliche Phantasie sich anschickt. . . . (*because/in which*)
49.	At the same time we live in a time *in which* human imagination is preparing . . .	**50.**	. . . die Möglichkeit der Weltraumfahrt und des Besuches oder sogar der Invasion anderer Gestirne **allen Ernstes** zu diskutieren.

50.	. . . to discuss *seriously* (*in all earnestness*) the possibility of space travel and of visiting or even invading other heavenly bodies.	**51.**	**diesseits** = *this side of* **jenseits** = *that side of* **unsererseits** = *for our part, as for us* Wir unsererseits wollen zum Mond oder Mars.
51.	We for our part want to visit the moon or Mars.	**52.**	**ihrerseits** = *for their part, for her part* Und **ihrerseits** wollen die Bewohner anderer Planeten zu uns. (*for their part/for her part*)
52.	And *for their part* the inhabitants of other planets want to visit us.	**53.**	**der Stern** = *star* **der Fixstern** = *fixed star* Wollen ihrerseits die Bewohner anderer Planeten unseres Systems **oder sogar** von Planeten der Fixsternsphäre zu uns?
53.	For their part, do the inhabitants of other planets of our system *or even* of planets of fixed stars (of the fixed star sphere) wish to visit us?	**54.**	**bewußt** = *conscious* Unsere **Weltraumaspiration** ist uns bewußt.
54.	We are conscious of our *space aspirations.*	**55.**	Die außerirdische **Tendenz** ist mythologische Konjektur. (*tendency/intention*)
55.	The extraterrestrial *intention* is mythological conjecture.	**56.**	**entsprechen** = *to correspond to* **entsprechend** = *corresponding* Die entsprechende außerirdische Tendenz aber ist mythologische Konjektur, d.h. Projektion.
56.	The corresponding extraterrestrial intention, however, is mythological conjecture, i.e., projection.	**57.**	Unsere Weltraumaspiration ist uns bewußt, die entsprechende außerirdische Tendenz aber ist mythologische Konjektur, d.h. Projektion.
57.	We are conscious of our space aspiration; the corresponding extraterrestrial intention, however, is mythological conjecture, i.e., projection.	**58.**	**schwer** = *difficult, hard* **unschwer** = *not difficult* **vermuten** = *to suppose, to suspect* Was **könnte** man **unschwer vermuten**?
58.	What *could* one *easily suppose*?	**59.**	Was **wird** unschwer **vermutet worden sein?**
59.	What *will have been* easily *supposed?*	**60.**	Weiß er, was unschwer **hätte vermutet werden können**?
60.	Does he know what *could have* easily *been supposed*? (See subjunctive, §74)	**61.**	**eng** = *small, narrow* Man könnte unschwer vermuten, daß es der Menschheit auf der Erde zu eng **wird.**

61. One could easily suppose that the earth *is becoming* too small for mankind.	**62.** **fangen** = *to catch* **hat gefangen** = *has caught* **das Gefängnis** = *prison* Ist die Erde ein Gefängnis für die Menschheit?
62. Is the earth a prison for mankind?	**63.** **mögen** = *to like* **möchte** = *would like* (subjunctive) Möchte die Menschheit **ihrem Gefängnis** entfliehen? (**Entfliehen** takes a __________ object.)
63. dative Would mankind like to flee *from its prison?*	**64.** **drohen** = *to threaten* Was droht **der Menschheit**, daß sie der Erde, ihrem Gefängnis, entfliehen möchte? (**Drohen** takes a __________ object.)
64. dative What threatens *mankind* that it would like to escape from the earth, its prison?	**65.** Nicht **bloß** die Wasserstoffbombe droht. (*blossom/only*)
65. Not *only* does the hydrogen bomb threaten.	**66.** **die Zahl** = *number* **die Bevölkerung** = *population* **die Bevölkerungszahl** = *the (total) population* Was **geben** uns die Bevölkerungszahlen?
66. What do the world's population figures *tell* us?	**67.** Was **ist** uns durch die Bevölkerungs-zahlen **gegeben worden?**
67. What *has* the total population of the world *been telling* us?	**68.** **schwellen** = *to swell* **anschwellen** = *to swell (up)* **das Anschwellen** = *the swelling up* Was gibt uns das Anschwellen der Bevölkerungszahlen?
68. What does the increase in the world's population tell us?	**69.** **die Lawine** = *avalanche* **-artig** = *like, resembling* (suffix) **lawinenartig** = __________
69. *like an avalanche, prodigious*	**70.** Was gibt uns das lawinenartige Anschwellen der Bevölkerungszahlen?
70. What does the prodigious (avalanche-like) increase in the world's population tell us?	**71.** **sorgen** = *to worry, take care* **besorgen** = *to take care of, look after* **besorgt** = *anxious, solicitous* **die Besorgnis** = __________

71. *anxiety, fear, concern*	**72.** **der Anlaß** = *cause* Das lawinenartige Anschwellen der Bevölkerungszahlen **gibt Anlaß zu** ernstlicher Besorgnis.
72. The prodigious increase in the world's population *gives cause for* serious concern.	**73.** **tief** = *deep, profound* Nicht bloß die Wasserstoffbombe droht, sondern—**tiefer noch**—das lawinenartige Anschwellen der Bevölkerungszahlen, **das** Anlaß zu ernstlicher Besorgnis gibt. (**das** = *the* or *which*?)
73. Not only the hydrogen bomb threatens, but, what is even *more profound*, the prodigious increase in the world's population threatens, *which* gives cause for serious concern.	**74.** **eng** = *narrow, small* **verengern** = *to narrow, to shrink* **der Wohnraum** = *dwelling space* **der Lebensraum** = *living space* Der Wohn- und Lebensraum verengert sich.
74. The dwelling and living space is shrinking.	**75.** **tatsächlich** = *in fact, as a matter of fact* Tatsächlich verengert sich **der Wohn- und Lebensraum der Menschheit.**
75. *Man's dwelling and living space* is, in fact, shrinking.	**76.** **das Maß** = *degree, extent* **In welchem Maße** verengert sich tatsächlich der Wohn- und Lebensraum der Menschheit?
76. *To what degree* is man's living space, in fact, shrinking?	**77.** **nehmen** = *to take* **zunehmen** = *to increase, to grow* **zunehmend** = *increasing, growing* In zunehmendem Maße verengert sich tatsächlich der Wohn- und Lebensraum der Menschheit.
77. Man's living space, in fact, is shrinking to an ever-increasing degree.	**78.** **überschreiten** = *to overstep, to exceed* **Ist** das Optimum für eine Reihe von Völkern schon **überschritten?**
78. *Is* the optimum for many nations (a series of peoples) already *exceeded?*	**79.** **geraum** = *considerable* **vor geraumer Zeit** = *some time ago* **für geraume Zeit** = __________
79. *for some time*	**80.** Für eine Reihe von Völkern **ist** das Optimum **schon** für geraume Zeit **überschritten.**

80. For many nations the optimum *has already been exceeded* for some time. (Note: English uses the present perfect for an action or state of being beginning in the past and extending into the present. German uses the present tense.)	**81.** Tatsächlich verengert sich der Wohn- und Lebensraum der Menschheit in zunehmendem Maße, und für eine Reihe von Völkern ist das Optimum schon für geraume Zeit überschritten.
81. Man's dwelling and living space, in fact, is shrinking to an ever-increasing extent, and for many nations the optimum has long been exceeded.	**82.** **rücken** = *to move* **zusammenrücken** = *to move close together* das Zusammenrücken wachsender Bevölkerungen
82. the coming together of growing populations	**83.** Die Katastrophengefahr wächst **proportional** dem Zusammenrücken wachsender Bevölkerungen.
83. The danger of catastrophe grows *in proportion* to the degree that the expanding populations come in closer contact.	**84.** **eng** = *narrow, tight, close, confined* **die Enge** = __________
84. *closeness, narrowness, tightness, crampedness*	**85.** **zeugen** = *to generate, to give rise to* **erzeugen** = *to procreate, to breed, to generate, to produce* Enge erzeugt **Angst**.
85. Closeness breeds *fear*. (or: Cramped conditions produce *fear*.)	**86.** **der Bereich** = *sphere* (also: *scope, range, province*) Angst sucht Hilfe im außerirdischen Bereich.
86. Fear seeks help from extraterrestrial sources (in the extraterrestrial sphere).	**87.** Erzeugt Enge Angst, **welche** Hilfe im außerirdischen Bereich sucht?
87. Do cramped conditions produce fear *which* (in turn) seeks help from extraterrestrial sources.	**88.** **gewähren** = *to grant, to provide* Die Erde **gewährt** Hilfe nicht.
88. The earth *provides* no help.	**89.** **anderswo** = *elsewhere* **Da** die Erde Hilfe nicht gewährt, suchen wir sie anderswo? (*there/since*)
89. *Since* the earth does not provide help, do we look for it elsewhere?	**90.** **meinen** = *to think* Jung meint: Enge erzeugt Angst, welche Hilfe im außerirdischen Bereich sucht, da die Erde sie nicht gewährt.
90. Jung thinks: Cramped conditions produce fear, which seeks help from extraterrestrial sources, since the earth does not provide it.	

PROGRESS TEST

Choose the approximate meaning of the following items.

1. Die Beobachtung und Deutung der Ufos hat allbereits zu Tausenden von Zeitungsnotizen und -artikeln Anlaß gegeben.
(a) Thousands of articles in newspapers give rise to a rash of UFO sightings.
(b) The meaning of UFOs has been thoroughly explained in the newspapers.
(c) Thousands of newspaper articles help give the public an understanding of UFOs.
(d) The observation of UFOs has already led to thousands of newspaper articles.

2. Eine Legende von einem versuchsweisen Eingriff oder wenigstens einer Annäherung außerirdischer „himmlischer Mächte" wird sich bilden.
(a) Experimental intervention of heavenly powers gives rise to the legend that they are at least trying to invade the earth.
(b) No heavenly powers are invading the earth, just observing it.
(c) A legend about supernatural powers invading or at least experimenting with the earth is being developed right now.
(d) Experimental intervention or at least an approach by extraterrestrial powers will be part of a miraculous tale to be formed.

3. *Schickt sich* die menschliche Phantasie *an,* die Möglichkeit einer Weltraumfahrt zu diskutieren?
(a) is sending itself (b) is getting ready (c) is imagining (d) is finding itself

4. Die Erde gewährt keine Hilfe vor der Katastrophenangst.
(a) Fear of catastrophe is not relieved by the earth.
(b) Fear is a product of the earth's inability to give help.
(c) The earth grants help only to those who are not afraid of catastrophic danger.
(d) Danger and fear thereof are all that the earth can grant an individual.

5. Das Zusammenrücken wachsender Bevölkerungen wird zu einer Katastrophe führen.
(a) The expanding population leads to row upon row of people.
(b) The pressing together of people makes stringent sanitation measures necessary.
(c) Overpopulation of the earth could lead to increased anxiety.
(d) Population pressures will lead to disaster.

6. Unsere Weltraumaspiration ist uns bewußt: man könnte unschwer vermuten, daß die entsprechende außerirdische Tendenz genau so bewußt ist.
(a) Our space aspirations may well be the same as those of extraterrestrial beings.
(b) One could easily feel that all space travel will come to naught.
(c) The tendency to ascribe our space aspirations to those of other planets is unconscious speculation.
(d) Conscious speculation about inhabitants of other worlds and their space aspirations leads to a greater desire on our part to travel in space.

Answer key: **1.** (d): **2.** (d): **3.** (b): **4.** (a): **5.**(d): **6.** (a).

Carl Gustav Jung: Ein moderner Mythus

Die Beobachtung und Deutung der Ufos [haben] allbereits zu einer richtigen Legendenbildung Anlaß gegeben. Ganz abgesehen von den Tausenden von Zeitungsnotizen und -artikeln gibt es heute auch schon eine Reihe von Büchern über diesen Gegenstand—pro et contra, zum Teil Schwindel, zum Teil ernsthaft. Das Phänomen selber scheint sich, wie die neuesten Beobachtungen dartun, davon nicht beeindrucken zu lassen. Es scheint vorderhand weiter zu gehen. Was es immer sein mag, eines steht fest: es ist zu einem *lebendigen Mythus* geworden. Wir haben hier eine Gelegenheit zu sehen, wie eine Sage entsteht, und wie in einer schwierigen und dunkeln Zeit der Menschheit eine Wundererzählung von einem versuchsweisen Eingriff oder wenigstens einer Annäherung außerirdischer „himmlischer" Mächte sich bildet: in einer Zeit zugleich, da die menschliche Phantasie sich anschickt, die Möglichkeit der Weltraumfahrt und des Besuches oder sogar der Invasion anderer Gestirne allen Ernstes zu diskutieren. Wir unsererseits wollen zum Mond oder Mars, und ihrerseits wollen die Bewohner anderer Planeten unseres Systems oder sogar von Planeten der Fixsternsphäre zu uns. Unsere Weltraumaspiration ist uns bewußt, die entsprechende außerirdische Tendenz aber ist mythologische Konjektur, d.h. Projektion ... Man könnte unschwer vermuten, daß es der Menschheit auf der Erde zu eng wird, und daß sie ihrem Gefängnis entfliehen möchte, wo nicht bloß die Wasserstoffbombe droht, sondern—tiefer noch—das lawinenartige Anschwellen der Bevölkerungszahlen, das Anlaß zu ernstlicher Besorgnis gibt.

* * *

Tatsächlich verengert sich der Wohn- und Lebensraum der Menschheit in zunehmendem Maße, und für eine Reihe von Völkern ist das Optimum schon für geraume Zeit überschritten. Die Katastrophengefahr wächst proportional dem Zusammenrücken wachsender Bevölkerungen. Enge erzeugt Angst, welche Hilfe im außerirdischen Bereich sucht, da die Erde sie nicht gewährt.

Chapter Twenty-One

69. *The subjunctive—definition of the subjunctive mood and the formation of the present tense verb form*

1. The mood of the verb shows the perception of the speaker with regard to the action. All verb forms which have been presented up to this time have been in the indicative mood, that is, the mood of actuality, in which the speaker perceives the action as a fact.

ACTIVE VOICE:

Ich *habe* ihn *gesehen*.	*I* ***have seen*** *him.* *I* ***saw*** *him.*

PASSIVE VOICE:

Er *ist* von mir *gesehen worden*.	*He* ***has been seen*** *by me.* *He* ***was seen*** *by me.*

2. The subjunctive mood is the mood of uncertainty, doubt, conjecture based on a condition, possibility, wishes. It is also used to signal indirect discourse (vs. direct quotations) and politeness. You will find subjunctive forms of German in:

(a) expressions contrary to fact based on a condition (see chapter 22):

Wenn ich Zeit *hätte*, *würde* ich nach Berlin *fliegen*.	*If I* ***had*** *time, I* ***would fly*** *to Berlin.* (Condition: having time.)

(b) wishes, expressions of doubt or conjecture, and polite requests (see chapters 22 through 24):

Wenn ich nur in Wien *wäre!*	*If I **were** only in Vienna!*
Könnten* Sie mir bitte ein Glas Wasser *bringen?	***Could** you please **bring** me a glass of water?*

Note: Wishes are contrary to fact. Here the fact is: You are not in Vienna.
Politeness is indicated by being less direct. Not: *Bring me a glass of water,* or even *Can you bring me a glass of water?*

(c) certain commands and suggestions that may not be followed:

***Sei* brav Sigurd!**	***Be** good, Sigurd!*

(d) indirect discourse

Sie sagte ihrem Freund, er *solle* nach Hause *gehen.*	*She told her friend that he **should go** home.*

(vs. the direct quotation, *She said to her friend, "Go home."*)

3. Most subjunctive forms have disappeared from English. Therefore, when English lacks the equivalent subjunctive forms, the German subjunctive is translated by the English indicative or by verb forms with *would* as the auxiliary.

Sie *wäre* verrückt, wenn sie mit ihm *ausginge.*	*She **would be** crazy, if she **went out** with him.*

4. The present tense forms of the subjunctive are identical with the indicative for **ich**, **wir**, **sie** and **Sie**, except for the modals and the verbs **sein** and **wissen**. The subjunctive is distinguished from the indicative in the other persons by the following endings or marks using as a base the infinitive minus the final **-n**.

WEAK VERBS		STRONG VERBS	
Personal pronouns for which indicative and subjunctive forms are the same:			
INDICATIVE	SUBJUNCTIVE	INDICATIVE	SUBJUNCTIVE
ich sage	**ich sage**	**ich gebe**	**ich gebe**
wir sagen	**wir sagen**	**wir geben**	**wir geben**
sie sagen	**sie sagen**	**sie geben**	**sie geben**
Sie sagen	**Sie sagen**	**Sie geben**	**Sie geben**
Personal pronouns for which indicative and subjunctive forms are different:			
INDICATIVE	SUBJUNCTIVE	INDICATIVE	SUBJUNCTIVE
du sagst	**du sag*est***	**du gibst**	**du *gebest***
er sagt	**er sag*e***	**er gibt**	**er geb*e***
ihr sagt	**ihr sag*et***	**ihr gebt**	**ihr geb*et***

IRREGULAR WEAK VERBS

Personal pronouns for which indicative and subjunctive forms are the same:

INDICATIVE	SUBJUNCTIVE
ich kenne	**ich kenne**
wir kennen	**wir kennen**
sie kennen	**sie kennen**
Sie kennen	**Sie kennen**

Personal pronouns for which indicative and subjunctive forms are different:

INDICATIVE	SUBJUNCTIVE
du kennst	**du kenn*est***
er kennt	**er kenn*e***
ihr kennt	**ihr kenn*et***

Decide whether the verb is in the indicative or subjunctive form. Do not worry about the meaning of the verb. It will be explained in the subsequent chapter.

	1. Er **glaubt** mir nicht.
1. indicative He *doesn't believe* me.	**2.** Er sagte, er **glaube** mir nicht.
2. subjunctive He said he *didn't believe* me.	**3.** Der König **lebe** lange!
3. subjunctive Long *live* the king! (*May* the king *live* long!)	**4.** Der König **lebt** immer noch.
4. indicative The king *is* still *living*.	**5.** Luzie fragte Charlie noch einmal, ob er einen Dummkopf **kenne**.
5. subjunctive Lucy asked Charlie once again whether he *knew* a blockhead.	**6.** Sie **kennt** einen Dummkopf.
6. indicative She *knows* a blockhead.	**7.** **Seht** ihr Wendelin **an**?
7. indicative *Are* you *looking* at Wendelin?	**8.** Er **sagte,** daß Liesl ihn nicht mehr **ansehe.**
8. subjunctive He said that Liesl *was* not *looking at* him anymore.	**9.** Was **sprichst** du da?
9. indicative What *are* you *saying*?	**10.** Bianca glaubte, du **sprechest** mit Max.
10. subjunctive Bianca thought you *were speaking* with Max.	

70. *The subjunctive—the formation of the past tense verb forms of strong, weak, and irregular verbs*

1. In the past tense of strong verbs and irregular weak verbs, the subjunctive is distinguished from the indicative by the verb endings, vowel change, and when possible by an umlaut. If the vowel of a strong verb is **a**, **o**, or **u**, it will take the umlaut. The past subjunctive stem vowel of irregular weak verbs does not change from that of the present:

STRONG VERBS

	INDICATIVE	SUBJUNCTIVE
ich	**g*a*b**	**g*ä*b*e***
du	**g*a*bst**	**g*ä*b*est***
er, sie, es	**g*a*b**	**g*ä*b*e***
wir	**g*a*ben**	**g*ä*ben**
ihr	**g*a*bt**	**g*ä*b*et***
sie	**g*a*ben**	**g*ä*ben**
Sie	**g*a*ben**	**g*ä*ben**

IRREGULAR WEAK VERBS

	INDICATIVE	SUBJUNCTIVE
ich	**kannt*e***	**kennt*e***
du	**kannt*est***	**kennt*est***
er, sie, es	**kannt*e***	**kennt*e***
wir	**kannt*en***	**kennt*en***
ihr	**kannt*et***	**kennt*et***
sie	**kannt*en***	**kennt*en***
Sie	**kannt*en***	**kennt*en***

2. In the past tense of regular weak verbs, the forms of the two moods are identical. Since the forms are identical, only the context tells which meaning is meant:

WEAK VERBS

	INDICATIVE	SUBJUNCTIVE
ich	**sag*te***	**sag*te***
du	**sag*test***	**sag*test***
er, sie, es	**sag*te***	**sag*te***
wir	**sag*ten***	**sag*ten***
ihr	**sag*tet***	**sag*tet***
sie	**sag*ten***	**sag*ten***
Sie	**sag*ten***	**sag*ten***

Decide whether the verb is in the indicative or subjunctive form. Reread point 3 on p. 362, and observe the translation, but do not fret about the meaning of the verb.

	1. Er sagte, wir **sähen** ihn später.
1. subjunctive He said we *would see* him later.	**2.** Wir **sahen** ihn später.
2. indicative We *saw* him later.	**3.** Wenn er mir nur einen Brief **schriebe!**
3. subjunctive If he would only *write* me a letter!	**4.** Er **schrieb** ihr einen Brief.
4. indicative He *wrote* her a letter.	**5.** Du **sprachst** nicht mehr darüber.
5. indicative You *did not say* any more about it.	**6.** Wenn du nur zu mir **sprächest**!
6. subjunctive If you *would* only *speak* to me!	**7.** Ihr **nanntet** ihn einen Dummkopf? Armer Charlie!
7. indicative You *called* him a blockhead? Poor Charlie!	**8.** Linus sagte, ihr **nenntet** Charlie immer einen Dummkopf.
8. subjunctive Linus said you always *called* Charlie a blockhead.	**9.** Ich **empfand** nur Sympathie für ihn.
9. indicative I *felt* only sympathy for him.	**10.** Wenn ich nur Sympathie für ihn **empfände!**
10. subjunctive If only I *felt* sympathy for him!	

71. *The present and past tense verb forms of the modals and the verbs* wissen, haben, sein, *and* werden

1. The subjunctive present and past tense verb forms of the modals and **wissen** follow patterns similar to the strong verbs and the irregular weak verbs of the indicative. Notice that the present tense forms of the subjunctive are identical with the indicative forms for **wir**, **sie**, and **Sie**:

PRESENT TENSE FORMS

	INDICATIVE	SUBJUNCTIVE	INDICATIVE	SUBJUNCTIVE	INDICATIVE	SUBJUNCTIVE
ich	**darf**	***dürfe***	**kann**	***könne***	**mag**	***möge***
du	**darfst**	***dürfest***	**kannst**	***könnest***	**magst**	***mögest***
er	**darf**	***dürfe***	**kann**	***könne***	**mag**	***möge***
wir	**dürfen**	**dürfen**	**können**	**können**	**mögen**	**mögen**
ihr	**dürft**	***dürfet***	**könnt**	***könnet***	**mögt**	***möget***
sie	**dürfen**	**dürfen**	**können**	**können**	**mögen**	**mögen**
Sie	**dürfen**	**dürfen**	**können**	**können**	**mögen**	**mögen**
ich	**muß**	***müsse***	**soll**	***solle***	**will**	***wolle***
du	**mußt**	***müssest***	**sollst**	***sollest***	**willst**	***wollest***
er	**muß**	***müsse***	**soll**	***solle***	**will**	***wolle***
wir	**müssen**	**müssen**	**sollen**	**sollen**	**wollen**	**wollen**
ihr	**müßt**	***müsset***	**sollt**	***sollet***	**wollt**	***wollet***
sie	**müssen**	**müssen**	**sollen**	**sollen**	**wollen**	**wollen**
Sie	**müssen**	**müssen**	**sollen**	**sollen**	**wollen**	**wollen**
ich	**weiß**	***wisse***				
du	**weißt**	***wissest***				
er	**weiß**	***wisse***				
wir	**wissen**	**wissen**				
ihr	**wißt**	***wisset***				
sie	**wissen**	**wissen**				
Sie	**wissen**	**wissen**				

PAST TENSE FORMS

	INDICATIVE	SUBJUNCTIVE	INDICATIVE	SUBJUNCTIVE	INDICATIVE	SUBJUNCTIVE
ich	**durfte**	**dürfte**	**konnte**	**könnte**	**mochte**	**möchte**
du	**durftest**	**dürftest**	**konntest**	**könntest**	**mochtest**	**möchtest**
er	**durfte**	**dürfte**	**konnte**	**könnte**	**mochte**	**möchte**
wir	**durften**	**dürften**	**konnten**	**könnten**	**mochten**	**möchten**
ihr	**durftet**	**dürftet**	**konntet**	**könntet**	**mochtet**	**möchtet**
sie	**durften**	**dürften**	**konnten**	**könnten**	**mochten**	**möchten**
Sie	**durften**	**dürften**	**konnten**	**könnten**	**mochten**	**möchten**
ich	**mußte**	**müßte**	**sollte**	**sollte**	**wollte**	**wollte**
du	**mußtest**	**müßtest**	**solltest**	**solltest**	**wolltest**	**wolltest**
er	**mußte**	**müßte**	**sollte**	**sollte**	**wollte**	**wollte**
wir	**mußten**	**müßten**	**sollten**	**sollten**	**wollten**	**wollten**

ihr	**mußtet**	**müßtet**	**solltet**	**solltet**	**wolltet**	**wolltet**
sie	**mußten**	**müßten**	**sollten**	**sollten**	**wollten**	**wollten**
Sie	**mußten**	**müßten**	**sollten**	**sollten**	**wollten**	**wollten**
ich	**wußte**	**wüßte**				
du	**wußtest**	**wüßtest**				
er	**wußte**	**wüßte**				
wir	**wußten**	**wüßten**				
ihr	**wußtet**	**wüßtet**				
sie	**wußten**	**wüßten**				
Sie	**wußten**	**wüßten**				

Notice that except for sollen and wollen the subjunctive forms differ from the indicative forms by the addition of an umlaut. The past subjunctive forms of **sollen** and **wollen** take no umlaut.

2. The present and past tense subjunctive forms of **haben** and **sein** are irregular:

	PRESENT		**PAST**		**PRESENT**		**PAST**	
	INDICATIVE	SUBJUNCT.	INDICATIVE	SUBJUNCT.	INDICATIVE	SUBJUNCT.	INDICATIVE	SUBJUNCT.
ich	habe	habe	hatte	hätte	bin	sei	war	wäre
du	hast	habest	hattest	hättest	bist	sei(e)st	warst	wär(e)st
er	hat	habe	hatte	hätte	ist	sei	war	wäre
wir	haben	haben	hatten	hätten	sind	seien	waren	wären
ihr	habt	habet	hattet	hättet	seid	sei(e)t	wart	wär(e)t
sie	haben	haben	hatten	hätten	sind	seien	waren	wären
Sie	haben	haben	hatten	hätten	sind	seien	waren	wären

3. The present and past tense subjunctive forms of **werden** follow a pattern similar to strong verbs:

	PRESENT		**PAST**	
	INDICATIVE	SUBJUNCTIVE	INDICATIVE	SUBJUNCTIVE
ich	**werde**	**werde**	**wurde**	**würde**
du	**wirst**	**werdest**	**wurdest**	**würdest**
er	**wird**	**werde**	**wurde**	**würde**
wir	**werden**	**werden**	**wurden**	**würden**
ihr	**werdet**	**werdet**	**wurdet**	**würdet**
sie	**werden**	**werden**	**wurden**	**würden**
Sie	**werden**	**werden**	**wurden**	**würden**

Give both the mood and the form of the indicated verbs.

	1. ihr **könnet**
1. present subjunctive form	2. ihr **könnt**
2. present indicative	3. ihr **könntet**
3. past subjunctive form	4. ihr **konntet**
4. past indicative	5. wir **möchten**
5. past subjunctive form	6. wir **mögen**
6. present indicative or present subjunctive (the latter is rare)	7. ihr **sollt**
7. present indicative	8. er **solle**
8. present subjunctive form	9. er **sollte**
9. past indicative or past subjunctive form (Both are common!)	10. er **müßte**
10. past subjunctive form	11. er **mußte**
11. past indicative	12. er **muß**
12. present indicative	13. er **müsse**
13. present subjunctive form	14. er **habe**
14. present subjunctive form	15. du **habest**
15. present subjunctive form	16. du **hast**
16. present indicative	17. ihr **seid**
17. present indicative	18. ihr **seiet**
18. present subjunctive form	19. er **wäre**

19. past subjunctive form	**20.** sie **wüßte**
20. past subjunctive form	**21.** sie **wußte**
21. past indicative	**22.** sie **weiß**
22. present indicative	**23.** sie **wisse**
23. present subjunctive form	**24.** ihr **wißt**
24. present indicative	**25.** ihr **wisset**
25. present subjunctive form	**26.** ihr **wußtet**
26. past indicative	**27.** ihr **wüßtet**
27. past subjunctive form	

72. *The subjunctive—formation of the compound tenses*

1. The compound tenses of the subjunctive mood are formed by changing the auxiliary verbs to the corresponding subjunctive forms.

PRESENT PERFECT TENSE FORMS

INDICATIVE	SUBJUNCTIVE
ich *habe* gesagt etc.	**ich *habe* gesagt etc.**
ich *bin* gegangen etc.	**ich *sei* gegangen etc.**

PAST PERFECT TENSE FORMS

INDICATIVE	SUBJUNCTIVE
ich *hatte* gesagt etc.	**ich *hätte* gesagt etc.**
ich *war* gegangen etc.	**ich *wäre* gegangen etc.**

FUTURE TENSE FORMS

INDICATIVE	SUBJUNCTIVE
ich *werde* sagen (gehen) etc.	**ich *werde* sagen (gehen) etc.**

FUTURE PERFECT TENSE FORMS

INDICATIVE	SUBJUNCTIVE
ich *werde* gesagt haben etc.	**ich *werde* gesagt haben etc.**
ich *werde* gegangen sein etc.	**ich *werde* gegangen sein etc.**

Give the tense and mood of the following. Do not disquiet yourself about the meaning of the sentences. For the moment, concentrate on the verb forms.

	1. Caruso gab zu, er **habe** das Lied **gesungen.**
1. present perfect subjunctive Caruso admitted he *had sung* the song.	**2.** Er sagte, er **hätte** das Lied **gesungen.**
2. past perfect subjunctive He said he *had sung* the song.	**3.** Caruso erklärte, daß er das Lied **singen werde.**
3. future subjunctive Caruso stated that he *would sing* the song.	**4.** Er erklärte, er **werde** morgen in der Oper die schönste Arie schon **gesungen haben,** bevor der König **ankäme** (**ankomme**).
4. future perfect subjunctive He explained that he *would* already *have sung* the most beautiful aria in the opera tomorrow by the time (before) the king *arrived.*	**5.** Ich **bin** in die Stadt **gegangen.**
5. present perfect indicative I *went* to town.	**6.** Ich **wäre** in die Stadt **gegangen,** wenn . . .
6. past perfect subjunctive I *would have gone* to town if . . .	**7.** Hilde sagte, daß sie in die Stadt **gehen werde.**
7. future subjunctive Hilde said she *would go* to town.	**8.** Sie **wird** wohl in die Stadt **gegangen sein,** nicht wahr?
8. future perfect indicative She probably *went* to town, didn't she? (Note here the future perfect is expressing past probability.)	**9.** Er fragte, ob sie es **gewesen wäre.**
9. past perfect subjunctive He asked if it *had been* she.	**10.** Sie fragte, ob er das Buch **gehabt hätte.**
10. past perfect subjunctive She asked whether he *had had* the book.	**11.** Ob sie krank **geworden wäre,** wenn . . . ?
11. past perfect subjunctive I wonder whether she *would have gotten* sick if . . .	**12.** Ob es morgen **regnen wird.**
12. future indicative I wonder whether it *is going to rain* tomorrow.	

PROGRESS TEST

Choose the subjunctive form from the given possibilities. See if you can give the tense of the form as well.

1. glauben
(a) er glaubt (b) du glaubst (c) sie glaube (d) ihr glaubt

2. wissen
(a) er wüßte (b) ich wußte (c) ihr wißt (d) sie wußten

3. sprechen
(a) ich sprach (b) wir sprächen (c) ihr sprecht (d) sie spricht

4. wollen
(a) er will (b) du willst (c) ihr wollt (d) ihr wolltet

5. mögen
(a) ich mag (b) er mochte (c) ihr mögt (d) wir möchten

6. sein
(a) ich war (b) er wird gewesen sein (c) wir seien gewesen (d) ihr seid gewesen

7. haben
(a) du hättest gehabt (b) er hat gehabt (c) sie hatte (d) ihr hattet gehabt

8. werden
(a) du bist geworden (b) ich wurde (c) er werde (d) ihr wart geworden

9. grüßen
(a) du grüßt (b) er wird grüßen (c) sie werde grüßen (d) ihr habt gegrüßt

10. lieben
(a) er liebt (b) sie hatte geliebt (c) sie liebten (d) du wirst geliebt haben

Answer key: **1.** (c, present); **2.** (a, past); **3.** (b, past); **4.** (d, past); **5.** (d, past); **6.** (c, present perfect); **7.** (a, past perfect); **8.** (c, present); **9.** (c, future); **10.** (c, past).

READING PREPARATION

Remember that vocabulary building requires frequent review of new words in context. When you finish this set of exercises, go back over the words you have circled, and then go to the next section.

	1. Wir lesen jetzt, was Heinrich Heine über Immanuel Kant zu sagen hat.
1. We are now going to read what Heinrich Heine has to say about Immanuel Kant.	**2.** Heine schreibt, daß die Lebensgeschichte des Immanuel Kant schwer zu **beschreiben** ist . . . (*write/describe*)
2. Heine writes that the life history of Immanuel Kant is difficult to *describe* . . .	**3.** . . . denn Kant hatte **weder** Leben **noch** Geschichte.
3. . . . for Kant had *neither* a life *nor* a history.	**4.** **der Hagestolz** = *bachelor* **das Hagestolzenleben** = __________

4. *life of a bachelor*	**5.** **geordnet** = *ordered* Er lebte ein mechanisch geordnetes, **fast** abstraktes Hagestolzenleben.
5. He lived a mechanically ordered, *almost* abstract bachelor's life.	**6.** **die Gasse** = *lane, street* **das Gäßchen** = *alley(way), narrow (little) street* Er lebte in einem Gäßchen in Königsberg.
6. He lived on a narrow street in Königsberg.	**7.** **abgelegen** = *remote* In einem stillen, abgelegenen Gäßchen zu Königsberg lebte der große Philosoph.
7. The great philosopher lived on a quiet, remote little street in Königsberg.	**8.** **Damals** war Königsberg eine alte Stadt an der nordöstlichen Grenze Deutschlands.
8. *At the time* Königsberg was an old city on the northeast border of Germany.	**9.** **ziemlich** = *fairly* Heute ist Königsberg eine ziemlich abgelegene Stadt in Rußland. Jetzt heißt es Kaliningrad.
9. Today Königsberg is a fairly remote city in Russia. Now it is called Kaliningrad.	**10.** Der Teil Preußens, in dem Königsberg lag, **gehört** jetzt Rußland.
10. The part of Prussia in which Königsberg was located now *belongs* to Russia.	**11.** **dort** = *there* **dortig** = *in that town, of that place* Die Uhr **der** dortigen Kathedrale ist sehr groß. (*of the/whose*)
11. The clock *of the* cathedral in that city is very large.	**12.** **die Leidenschaft** = *passion* **leidenschaftlich** = *full of passion* **leidenschaftslos** = __________
12. *dispassionate*	**13.** **die Regel** = *rule* **regelmäßig** = *regular(ly)* Kants Leben war **genau so** leidenschaftslos und regelmäßig **wie** das Leben dieser Uhr.
13. Kant's life was *just as* dispassionate and regular *as* the life of this clock.	**14.** **vollbringen** = *to accomplish* Die große Uhr der dortigen Kathedrale **voll-brachte** ihr Tagewerk leidenschaftslos und regelmäßig.
14. The large clock of the cathedral there *accomplished* its daily work dispassionately and regularly.	**15.** **äußeres** = *exterior* **Leidenschaftsloser** und **regelmäßiger** wie ihr Landsmann Immanuel Kant vollbrachte diese Uhr ihr äußeres Tagewerk nicht.
15. This clock did not accomplish its exterior daily work *more dispassionately* and *more regularly* than its compatriot Immanuel Kant. (Normally one would expect **als** rather than **wie** in the above sentence.)	**16.** Was mußte Kant **immer** tun?

16. What did Kant *always* have to do?	**17.** **spazieren** = *to take a walk* **gehen** = *to go* **spazierengehen** = __________
17. *to go for a walk*	**18.** **das Kolleg** = *course of lectures* **Kollegien lesen** = *to give lectures* Kant hat schwierige Kollegien gelesen.
18. Kant gave difficult lectures.	**19.** Aufstehen, Kaffeetrinken, Schreiben, Kollegienlesen, Essen, Spazierengehen, alles hatte seine **bestimmte** Zeit.
19. Getting up, drinking coffee, writing, giving lectures, eating, going for a walk, everything had its *definite* time.	**20.** Es war immer **halb vier,** wenn Kant aus seinem Haus trat. (*3:30/4:30*)
20. It was always *3:30* (lit.: half of four) when Kant stepped out of his house.	**21.** Die Nachbarn wußten **genau,** daß es halb vier war. (*for sure/probably*)
21. The neighbors knew *for sure* that it was 3:30.	**22.** **die Glocke** = *bell* Die Nachbarn sie wußten genau, daß die Glocke halb vier **sei,** wenn Kant aus seiner Haustüre trat. (*was/had*)
22. The neighbors knew for sure that it *was* 3:30 when Kant stepped out of the door of his house.	**23.** **der Leib** = *body* **der Rock** = *coat* (for men), *skirt* (for women) **der Leibrock** = *dress coat* Er trug **fast immer** einen grauen Leibrock . . .
23. He *almost always* wore a gray dress coat . . .	**24.** **das Rohr** = *cane* (also: *reed, tube, pipe*) **das Röhrchen** = (small) *cane* . . . in der Hand das spanische Röhrchen.
24. . . . in his hand (was) the Spanish cane.	**25.** Wenn Kant in seinem grauen Leibrock, das spanische Röhrchen in der Hand, aus seiner Haustüre trat . . .
25. Whenever Kant stepped from the door of his house in his gray dress coat with the Spanish cane in his hand . . .	**26.** **die Linde** = *linden tree* **die Allee** = *drive, avenue* **die Lindenallee** = __________
26. *linden drive, linden avenue*	**27.** **wandeln** = *to walk* . . . und **nach** der kleinen Lindenallee wandelte . . . (*after/toward*)
27. . . . and walked *toward* the small Linden Drive . . .	**28.** Die Nachbarn wußten genau, daß die Glocke halb vier sei, wenn Kant nach der kleinen Lindenallee wandelte.

28.	The neighbors knew for certain that it was 3:30 when Kant walked to the small Linden Avenue.	**29.**	**der Gang** = *walk* **Seinetwegen** nennt man die Lindenallee den Philosophengang.
29.	*Because of him* one calls Linden Avenue the Philosopher's Walk.	**30.**	**Noch jetzt** nennt man seinetwegen die Lindenallee den Philosophengang.
30.	*Even now* Linden Drive is called Philosopher's Walk because of him.	**31.**	**auf und ab** = *back and forth* **Achtmal** spazierte Kant auf dem Philosophengang auf und ab. (*eight times/slowly*)
31.	Kant walked back and forth on the Philosopher's Walk *eight times.*	**32.**	In jeder **Jahreszeit** spazierte er achtmal dort auf und ab.
32.	In every *season* he walked back and forth there eight times.	**33.**	**trübe** = *gloomy* **dienen** = *to serve* Wenn das Wetter trübe war, wandelte sein Diener hinter ihm. (**Diener** probably means ________.)
33.	*servant* When the weather was gloomy, his servant walked behind him.	**34.**	**verkündigen** = *to forecast* Wenn das Wetter trübe war oder die grauen Wolken einen Regen verkündigten . . . (**Wolken** probably means ___________)
34.	*clouds* When the weather was gloomy or the gray *clouds* forecast rain . . .	**35.**	**drein** = **darein** = *along* . . . sah man seinen Diener **immer** hinter ihm drein wandeln.
35.	. . . one *always* saw his servant walking along behind him.	**36.**	**die Angst** = *anxiety, dread* **ängstlich** = ___________
36.	*anxious, uneasy, distressed, nervous, timid*	**37.**	**besorgt** = *anxious* Der Diener, der Lampe hieß, wandelte **ängstlich besorgt** hinter ihm drein.
37.	The servant, whose name was Lampe, walked *anxiously* (lit.: *anxiously concerned*) along behind him.	**38.**	Der Diener trug einen langen **Regenschirm** unter dem Arm, wenn das Wetter trübe war . . .
38.	The servant carried a long *umbrella* under his arm, when the weather was gloomy . . .	**39.**	. . . oder wenn die grauen Wolken einen Regen **verkündigten**.
39.	. . . or whenever the gray clouds *forecast* rain.	**40.**	**vorsehen** = *to provide for* **die Vorsehung** = ___________
40.	*providence*	**41.**	Wenn der Diener ängstlich besorgt hinter ihm drein wandelte, **sah** er **aus** wie ein Bild der Vorsehung.

41. When the servant walked anxiously along behind him, he *looked like* a picture of providence.	**42.** Der Diener, mit einem langen Regenschirm unter dem Arm, sah aus wie ein Bild der Vorsehung.
42. The servant, with a long umbrella under his arm, looked like a picture of providence.	**43.** **zermalmen** = *to crush* **zermalmend** = *crushing* Kant hatte **weltzermalmende** Gedanken.
43. Kant had *world-crushing* ideas (thoughts).	**44.** **sonderbar** = *strange, singular* **Sonderbarer** Kontrast zwischen dem äußeren Leben des Mannes . . . (*a strange/a stranger*)
44. *A strange* contrast between the external life of the man . . .	**45.** **zerstören** = *to destroy, to demolish* **zerstörend** = *destructive* . . . und seinen zerstörenden, weltzermalmenden Gedanken!
45. . . . and his destructive, world-crushing thoughts!	**46.** **grauenhaft** = *dreadful* **die Scheu** = *awe, shyness* Die Bürger **haben** eine grauenhafte Scheu **empfunden**. (*felt/found*)
46. The citizens *felt* a dreadful awe.	**47.** **ahnen** = *to sense* Wahrlich, **hätten** die Bürger von Königsberg die ganze Bedeutung dieser Gedanken **geahnt** . . . (*have sensed/had sensed*)
47. Truly, *had* the citizens of Königsberg *sensed* the full meaning of these thoughts . . .	**48.** . . . **hätten** sie vor jenem Manne eine weit grauenhaftere Scheu **empfunden** . . . (*would have felt/will feel*)
48. . . . they *would have felt* a far more dreadful awe in the presence of that man (before that man). . . .	**49.** **der Scharfrichter** = *executioner* . . . als vor einem Scharfrichter, der nur Menschen **hinrichtet.** (*saves/executes*)
49. . . . than in the presence of an executioner, who only *executes* people.	**50.** **die Tasche** = *pocket* **die Uhr** = *clock* **die Taschenuhr** = ________________
50. *pocket watch*	**51.** Wenn Kant zur **bestimmten** Stunde vorbeiwandelte . . . (*appointed/unappointed*)
51. Whenever Kant walked by at the *appointed* hour . . .	**52.** **grüßen** = *to greet* . . . grüßten sie freundlich . . .

52. . . . they gave him a friendly greeting (greeted him in a friendly way) . . .	**53.** **richten** = *to set* . . . und richteten **etwa** nach ihm ihre Taschenuhr. (*perhaps/never*)
53. . . . and *perhaps* set their pocket watches by him. (Note: Die Bürger richteten ihre **Taschenuhr**. [Each citizen has *one pocket watch*.] Die Bürger richteten ihre **Taschenuhren**. [Each citizen has *two or more pocket watches*.])	

PROGRESS TEST

Choose the sentence which most closely approximates the meaning of the given sentence.

1. Ein fast abstraktes Hagestolzenleben in einer stillen, abgelegenen Uhr lebte leidenschaftslos und regelmäßig Kants alter Diener.
(a) Kant, together with his servant, lived on a small quiet street. His life was less passionate than it was monotonous.
(b) Old philosophers and their servants always live dispassionate and monotonous lives.
(c) Kant's servant lived a quiet life in a remote clock.
(d) A clock could not be more dispassionate and monotonous than that old bachelor Kant.

2. Seinetwegen nennt man die kleine Lindenallee den Philosophengang.
(a) Groups of philosophers wandered through the linden alley.
(b) He is responsible for the fact that philosophers live on Linden Street.
(c) The Linden Avenue and the Philosopher's Walk are one and the same.
(d) Linden Street is now called Kant Street.

3. Ein Scharfrichter hat weniger Bedeutung als die zerstörenden, weltzermalmenden Gedanken, die Kants Nachbarn damals nicht ahnten.
(a) Kant and his neighbors thought devastating thoughts.
(b) Kant's thoughts meant nothing to his neighbors nor to the judge.
(c) An executioner has more importance than the thoughts which Kant's neighbors thought.
(d) The destructive thoughts which Kant's neighbors did not suspect have more meaning than an executioner.

4. In jeder Jahreszeit wandelte der alte, ängstliche Lampe hinter dem mit einem langen Regenschirm unter dem Arm spazierenden Philosophen.
(a) Old Lampe was afraid to offer an umbrella to the philosopher.
(b) The walking philosopher was followed by a man named Lampe.
(c) In every season of the year an umbrella accompanied by a frightened servant followed the philosopher.
(d) The philosopher took an umbrella and an old lamp with him whenever he took a walk.

Answer key: **1.** (c); **2.** (c): **3.** (d); **4.** (b).

READING PREPARATION

Kant's most influential work was his lengthy **Kritik der reinen Vernunft** *(Critique of Pure Reason). The spirit of his life and work is expressed in a short work,* **Beantwortung der Frage: Was ist Aufklärung?** *from which the following vocabulary is extracted.*

	1. **die Aufklärung** = *enlightenment, the (Age of) Enlightenment* Was ist Aufklärung?
1. What is enlightenment?	**2.** Diese Frage hat Kant **einmal** versucht zu beantworten.
2. Kant *once* tried to answer this question.	**3.** **der Wahlspruch** = *motto* Für Kant ist der Wahlspruch der Aufklärung: *Sapere aude!*
3. For Kant the motto of the Age of Enlightenment is: *Sapere aude* (Dare to know)!	**4.** **verstehen** = *to understand* **der Verstand** = *reason, mind, intellect, (common) sense, understanding* Hast du den **Verstand** verloren?
4. Have you lost your *senses* (i.e., the *ability to reason, to think, to understand*)?	**5.** **sich bedienen** = *to make use of* Man sollte sich seines **eigenen Verstandes** bedienen. *(others' thinking/own reason)*
5. One should make use of one's *own reason.* (Notice that **sich bedienen** takes a genitive object.)	**6.** **der Mut** = *courage* Habe Mut, sagt Kant, dich deines eigenen Verstandes zu bedienen!
6. Kant says to have the courage to use your own faculty of reason.	**7.** Das ist **also** der Wahlspruch der Aufklärung.
7. That is *therefore* the motto of the (Age of) Enlightenment.	**8.** **unmündig** = *immature* **die Unmündigkeit** = __________
8. *immaturity*	**9.** **verschulden** = *to be the cause of, to blame for* **selbstverschuldet** = *self-imposed* Die Unmündigkeit ist oft selbstverschuldet.
9. Immaturity is often self-imposed.	**10.** Die Unmündigkeit eines Menschen kann **entweder** selbstverschuldet sein **oder** nicht.
10. The immaturity of a person can be *either* self-imposed *or* not.	**11.** **der Eingang** = *entrance* **der Ausgang** = __________
11. *exit*	**12.** Aufklärung ist der Ausgang des Menschen aus seiner **selbstverschuldeten** Unmündigkeit.
12. Enlightenment is the exit of a person out of his own *self-imposed* immaturity.	**13.** **das Vermögen** = *ability* **das Unvermögen** = __________

13. *inability*	**14.** Unmündigkeit ist das Unvermögen, mich **meines eigenen** Verstandes zu bedienen.
14. Immaturity is the inability to make use *of my own* faculty of reason.	**15.** **die Leitung** = *guidance, direction* Unmündigkeit ist **das Unvermögen eines Menschen**, sich seines Verstandes ohne die Leitung eines anderen zu bedienen.
15. Immaturity is *the inability of a person* to make use of his powers of reasoning without the guidance of another.	**16.** Warum ist diese Unmündigkeit selbstverschuldet?
16. Why is this immaturity self-imposed?	**17.** **die Ursache** = *cause, reason* Die Ursache der Unmündigkeit liegt nicht am **Mangel** des Verstandes . . . (*mangle/lack*)
17. The reason for this immaturity lies not in the *lack* of understanding . . .	**18.** **sich entschließen** = *to decide, to resolve* **die Entschließung** = *resolution, resolve, determination* . . . sondern die Ursache liegt am Mangel **der Entschließung** und **des Mutes** . . .
18. . . . rather the cause lies in the lack *of determination* and *courage* . . .	**19.** . . . sich **des Verstandes** ohne Leitung eines andern zu bedienen.
19. . . . to make use of *one's powers of reasoning* without the direction of another.	**20.** **derselben** = *of the same* Selbstverschuldet ist diese Unmündigkeit, **wenn** die Ursache derselben . . .
20. This immaturity is self-imposed *whenever* the reason for it . . . (Note: Here **derselben** is the genitive singular of **dieselbe**, *the same*, and refers back to **Unmündigkeit**.)	**21.** . . . nicht am Mangel des Verstandes, sondern **der Entschließung** und **des Mutes** liegt.
21. . . . lies not in the lack of the faculty of reason but rather in the lack *of resolve* and *courage.*	**22.** **seiner** = *of it* **sich seiner zu bedienen** = *to make use of it* Die Ursache der Unmündigkeit liegt nicht am Mangel des Verstandes, sondern der Entschließung und des Mutes, **sich seiner** ohne Leitung eines andern **zu bedienen**.
22. The cause of immaturity lies not in the lack of the faculty of reason but rather in the lack of resolution and courage *to use it* without the direction of another.	**23.** **faul** = *lazy* **feige** = *cowardly* **Faulheit und Feigheit** = __________

23. *laziness and cowardice*	**24.** Faulheit und Feigheit sind Ursachen . . .
24. Laziness and cowardice are the causes (reasons) . . .	**25. zeitlebens** = *for life* . . . warum **ein so großer Teil der Menschen** gerne zeitlebens unmündig bleiben.
25. . . . why such *a large number of people* like to remain immature all their lives.	**26. de Mund** = *mouth* **der Vormund** = *guardian* Andere **werden** ihre Vormünder.
26. Others *become* their guardians.	**27. werfen** = *to throw* **sich aufwerfen** = *to set oneself up* Es wird Anderen **leicht,** sich zu Vormündern aufzuwerfen. (*light/easy*)
27. It becomes *easy* for others to set themselves up as guardians. (Note that **leicht** requires a dative object.)	**28.** Faulheit und Feigheit sind die Ursachen, warum es Anderen so leicht wird, sich zu **deren** Vormündern aufzuwerfen. (*their/her*)
28. Laziness and cowardice are the reasons why it becomes so easy for others to set themselves up as *their* guardians.	**29.** Faulheit und Feigheit sind die Ursachen, warum ein so großer Teil der Menschen **gerne** zeitlebens unmündig bleiben . . .
29. Laziness and cowardice are the reasons why such a great number of people *like* to remain immature for life . . .	**30.** . . . und warum es Anderen so leicht wird, sich zu **deren** Vormündern aufzuwerfen.
30. . . . and why it becomes so easy for others to set themselves up as *their* guardians.	**31.** Es ist so **bequem,** unmündig zu sein. (*comfortable/uncomfortable*)
31. It is so *comfortable* to be immature.	**32.** Habe ich ein Buch, das für mich Verstand hat . . .
32. If I have a book which supplies me with a faculty of reason . . . (Note that **wenn** is understood in the sentence and that its place is taken by the verb.)	**33. die Seele** = *soul* **sorgen für** = *to care for, to look after* **der Seelsorger** = __________
33. *the pastor*	**34.** Habe ich einen Seelsorger, der für mich **Gewissen** hat . . . (*knowledge/conscience*)
34. If I have a pastor who supplies me with a *conscience* . . .	**35. beurteilen** = *to judge, assess* Habe ich einen Arzt, **der** für mich die Diät beurteilt . . . (*who/which/the*)

35. If I have a doctor *who* assesses a diet for me . . .	**36.** Habe ich ein Buch, das für mich Verstand hat, einen Seelsorger, der für mich Gewissen hat, einen Arzt, der für mich die Diät beurteilt, usw. . . .
36. If I have a book which supplies me with a faculty of reason, a pastor who supplies me with conscience, a doctor who assesses a diet for me, etc. . . .	**37.** **die Mühe** = *trouble, pains* **sich bemühen** = ________
37. *to take trouble, to take pains*	**38.** . . . **so** brauche ich mich ja nicht selbst zu bemühen. (*so then*)
38. . . . *then* I do not need to take the trouble myself.	**39.** **nötig** = *necessary* Ich habe **nicht** nötig zu denken.
39. It is not *necessary* for me to think.	**40.** **bezahlen** = *to pay* Wenn ich nur bezahlen kann, habe ich nicht nötig zu denken.
40. When I can simply pay, it is not necessary for me to think.	**41.** **verdrießlich** = *annoying, vexing* Das Denken ist mir **verdrießlich**.
41. Thinking is *annoying* for me. (Note that **verdrießlich** calls for a dative object.)	**42.** **das Geschäft** = *business* Andere werden das verdrießliche Geschäft **übernehmen.** (*overcome/take over*)
42. Others will *take over* this (the) vexing business.	**43.** **schon** = *no doubt, surely* Andere werden das verdrießliche Geschäft **schon** für mich übernehmen.
43. Others will *surely* take over this vexing business for me.	**44.** Was ist die **Gefahr**, wenn andere das verdrießliche Geschäft für mich übernehmen?
44. What is the *danger* of others taking over (if others take over) this vexing business for me?	

PROGRESS TEST

Choose the correct meaning for the indicated words.

1. Aufklärung ist der **Ausgang** des Menschen aus seiner selbstverschuldeten Unmündigkeit.
(a) beginning (b) end (c) exit (d) entrance

2. Das **Unvermögen,** sich seines eigenen Verstandes zu bedienen, ist Unmündigkeit.
(a) inability (b) possibility (c) capability (d) misapplication

3. Dieser **Mangel** des Verstandes ist selbstverschuldet.
(a) mangling (b) achievement (c) wretchedness (d) lack

4. Die Ursache liegt am Mangel der **Entschließung** und des Mutes.
(a) opening (b) resolve (c) unlocking (d) disentanglement

5. Der **Wahlspruch** der Aufklärung ist *sapere aude*!
(a) motto (b) findings (c) decision (d) resolution

6. Faulheit und **Feigheit** sind die Ursachen, warum so viele Menschen unmündig sind.
(a) laziness (b) anxiety (c) fear (d) cowardice

7. Ist es wirklich **bequem,** unmündig zu sein?
(a) worthwhile (b) comfortable (c) easy (d) difficult

8. Ein **Seelsorger** hat Gewissen für mich.
(a) pastor (b) seeker of souls (c) doctor (d) seeker of truth

9. Die meisten Menschen wollen **zeitlebens** unmündig bleiben.
(a) lively (b) all their lives (c) live and let live (d) time to live

10. Er ist der **Vormund** dessen, der seine Diät nicht selbst beurteilen will.
(a) finder (b) helper (c) guardian (d) preserver

Answer key: **1.** (c); **2.** (a); **3.** (d); **4.** (b); **5.** (a); **6.** (d); **7.** (b); **8.** (a); **9.** (b); **10.** (c).

Before proceeding to the reading passage review all the words which you circled.

Heinrich Heine: Zur Geschichte der Religion und Philosophie in Deutschland

Die Lebensgeschichte des Immanuel Kant ist schwer zu beschreiben. Denn er hatte weder Leben noch Geschichte. Er lebte ein mechanisch geordnetes, fast abstraktes Hagestolzenleben in einem stillen, abgelegenen Gäßchen zu Königsberg, einer alten Stadt an der nordöstlichen Grenze Deutschlands. Ich glaube nicht, daß die große Uhr der dortigen Kathedrale leidenschaftsloser und regelmäßiger ihr äußeres Tagewerk vollbrachte wie ihr Landsmann Immanuel Kant. Aufstehen, Kaffeetrinken, Schreiben, Kollegienlesen, Essen, Spazierengehn, alles hatte seine bestimmte Zeit, und die Nachbarn wußten ganz genau, daß die Glocke halb vier sei, wenn Immanuel Kant in seinem grauen Leibrock, das spanische Röhrchen in der Hand, aus seiner Haustüre trat und nach der kleinen Lindenallee wandelte, die man seinetwegen noch jetzt den Philosophengang nennt. Achtmal spazierte er dort auf und ab, in jeder Jahreszeit, und wenn das Wetter trübe war oder die grauen Wolken einen Regen verkündigten, sah man seinen Diener, den alten Lampe, ängstlich besorgt hinter ihm drein wandeln, mit einem langen Regenschirm unter dem Arm, wie ein Bild der Vorsehung.

Sonderbarer Kontrast zwischen dem äußeren Leben des Mannes und seinen zerstörenden, weltzermalmenden Gedanken! Wahrlich, hätten die Bürger von Königsberg die ganze Bedeutung dieses Gedankens geahnt, sie würden vor jenem Manne eine weit grauenhaftere Scheu empfunden haben als vor einem Scharfrichter, vor einem Scharfrichter, der nur Menschen hinrichtet—aber die guten Leute sahen in ihm nichts anderes als einen Professor der Philosophie, und wenn er zur bestimmten Stunde vorbeiwandelte, grüßten sie freundlich und richteten etwa nach ihm ihre Taschenuhr.

Immanuel Kant: Was ist Aufklärung?

Aufklärung ist der Ausgang des Menschen aus seiner selbstverschuldeten Unmündigkeit. Unmündigkeit ist das Unvermögen, sich seines Verstandes ohne Leitung eines anderen zu bedienen. *Selbstverschuldet* ist diese Unmündigkeit, wenn die Ursache derselben nicht am Mangel des Verstandes, sondern der Entschließung und des Mutes liegt, sich seiner ohne Leitung eines andern zu bedienen. *Sapere aude* [*Dare to know*]*!* Habe Mut, dich deines *eigenen* Verstandes zu bedienen! ist also der Wahlspruch der Aufklärung.

Faulheit und Feigheit sind die Ursachen, warum ein so großer Teil der Menschen . . . gerne zeitlebens unmündig bleiben; und warum es Anderen so leicht wird, sich zu deren Vormündern aufzuwerfen. Es ist so bequem, unmündig zu sein. Habe ich ein Buch, das für mich Verstand hat, einen Seelsorger, der für mich Gewissen hat, einen Arzt, der für mich die Diät beurteilt, u.s.w., so brauche ich mich ja nicht selbst zu bemühen. Ich habe nicht nötig zu denken, wenn ich nur bezahlen kann; andere werden das verdrießliche Geschäft schon für mich übernehmen.

Chapter Twenty-Two

73. *The subjunctive—present time*

1. The following subjunctive forms express a wish, a request, or a contrary-to-fact condition with reference to present time:

(a) past tense verb form

Wenn ich nur ein Vogel *wäre!*	*If I only **were** a bird!*
***Hätten* Sie vielleicht ein Zimmer mit Bad?**	***Would** you perhaps **have** a room with bath?*
Wenn ich Geld *hätte,* so *flöge* ich nach Deutschland.	*If **I had** the money **I would fly** to Germany.*
Wäre* er nicht so dumm, so *würde* er ein neues Leben *anfangen.	*If he **were** not so stupid, he **would begin** a new life.*

Note that **wenn** (*if*) may be omitted in German. The verb then takes its position in the sentence.

Würde* er doch *bestraft! *If he **were** only **punished!***

The above is in the passive subjunctive. It is rarely used.

(b) past tense verb form of **werden** plus infinitive

Sie *würde singen,* wenn sie eine Stimme hätte.	*She **would sing** if she had a voice.*
Würdest* du gerne eine Tasse Kaffee *trinken?	***Would** you like **to drink** a cup of coffee?*
Ich *würde* gerne zusammen mit Ihnen *gehen.*	*I **would** gladly **go** with you.*

Do not confuse this subjunctive form with the future, which is formed by the present indicative of **werden** plus the infinitive:

Ich *werde singen,* wenn ich meine Stimme wieder habe. — *I **will sing** when I have my voice back again.*

Give the meaning of the indicated verbs.

	1. Wenn Sie das Buch nur **schreiben würden!** (*will write/would write/are writing*)
1. If you *would* only *write* the book!	**2.** Ich **werde** ein Buch **schreiben.** (*will write/would write/am writing*)
2. I *will write* a book.	**3.** Das Buch **wird** von mir **geschrieben.** (*will write/would write/is being written*)
3. The book *is being written* by me.	**4.** Wenn das doch besser **erklärt würde!**
4. If that *were* only *explained* better!	**5. das Lied** = *song* Ich wußte, daß Fischer-Dieskau das Lied **singen würde.**
5. I knew that Fischer-Dieskau *would sing* the song.	**6.** Ich weiß, daß er das Lied **singen wird.**
6. I know that he *will sing* the song.	**7.** Das Lied **wurde** von ihm **gesungen.**
7. The song *was sung* by him.	**8.** Wenn das Lied nur von Fischer-Dieskau **gesungen würde!**
8. If only that song *were being sung* by Fischer-Dieskau. (Also: *would be sung*)	**9. Ginget** ihr gerne nach Rußland?
9. *Would* you like *to go* to Russia?	**10.** Wenn er nur Zeit **hätte!** (*did have/had/would have*)
10. If he only *had* time!	**11.** Wann **hatte** er Zeit? (*had/did have/would have*)
11. When *did* he *have* time?	**12. Hätten** Sie noch etwas für mich? (*have/had/would have*)
12. *Would* you still *have* something else for me?	**13.** Wenn Brigitte nur nicht so hübsch **wäre!** (*was/were*)
13. If only Brigitte *were* not so pretty!	**14.** Wann **war** Lisa zu Hause? (*were/was*)
14. When *was* Lisa at home?	**15.** Wenn sie das Lied **sänge, wäre** es eine Katastrophe. (*sang . . . were/were to sing . . .would be*)
15. If she *were to sing* the song, it *would be* a catastrophe.	**16. gescheit** = *clever, shrewd* Wenn er Philosophie **studierte,** so **wäre** er ein gescheiter Mensch. (*studied . . . were/were to study . . . would be*)

16.	If he *were to study* philosophy, he *would be* a clever man.	**17.**	**verrückt** = *crazy* Wenn wir dieser Musik länger **zuhören, werden** wir verrückt. (*listen to . . . will go/were to listen . . . would become*)
17.	If we *listen to* this music any longer, we *will go* crazy.	**18.**	Dieses Buch **wird geschrieben**, wenn wir Zeit **haben.** (*will write . . . would have/will be written . . . have*)
18.	This book *will be written* if we *have* time.	**19.**	**Sängen** Sie das Lied, wenn Sie **wüßten,** daß es dafür kein Geld gibt? (*sing . . . know/sang . . . knew/would sing . . . knew*)
19.	*Would* you *sing* that song if you *knew* that you would not receive any money? (Lit: that there is no money for that)	**20.**	**als ob, als wenn** = *as if* Er sieht aus, als ob er Hunger **hätte.**
20.	He looks as if he *were* hungry. (**Als ob** and **als wenn** are subordinating conjunctions and are used primarily with the subjunctive.)	**21.**	**die Nachtigall** = *nightingale* Sie singt, als **wäre** sie eine Nachtigall.
21.	She sings as if she *were* a nightingale. (**Als ob** and **als wenn** frequently drop the **ob** or **wenn.** The verb then moves into the place of the missing **ob** or **wenn.**)	**22.**	Wenn es nur **regnen würde!**
22.	If it *would* only *rain!*	**23.**	Wenn es morgen nur **regnete!**
23.	If it *would* only *rain* tomorrow!	**24.**	Wenn das Bild nur von Van Gogh **gemalt wäre!**
24.	If that picture *were* only *painted* by Van Gogh!	**25.**	Sie spricht, als **wäre** sie aus Deutschland.
25.	She speaks as if she *were* from Germany.		

PROGRESS TEST

Choose the equivalent of the indicated words.

1. Albrecht erzählt diese Geschichte, als **wäre** er betrunken.
(a) would have (b) were (c) was (d) would be

2. Sie sah ihn an, als **würde** sie ihn gleich zerreißen.
(a) was (b) would (c) will (d) became

3. Franzel **wird** bestimmt von Michael **geschlagen werden.**
   (a) will be hit (b) becomes hit (c) would be hit (d) is being hit
4. Wenn ich Geld **hätte,** so **kaufte** ich mir einen ganz neuen Mercedes.
   (a) would have . . . bought (b) had . . . buy (c) will have . . . bought (d) had . . . would buy
5. Ach, **wärest** du nur hier!
   (a) was (b) were (c) would be (d) could be
6. Wenn wir nur einen neuen Mercedes **hätten.**
   (a) have (b) have had (c) will have (d) had

Answer key: **1.** (b); **2.** (b); **3.** (a); **4.** (d); **5.** (b); **6.** (d).

74. *The subjunctive—past time*

The following subjunctive forms express a wish, a condition, or a contrary-to-fact statement with reference to past time:

(a) past perfect tense verb form

Wenn sie nur Deutsch *gesprochen hätten!*	*If only they **had spoken** German!*
Sie *wären* damals nach Berlin *geflogen*, wenn sie das nötige Geld dazu *gehabt hätten.*	*They **would have flown** to Berlin at the time, if they **had had** the necessary money.*
Heinz sieht aus, als ob er *getadelt worden wäre.**	*Heinz looks as if he **had been scolded.***

* Note again the passive subjunctive in the last example.

(b) past tense verb form of **werden** plus the perfect infinitive

Wenn ich die Antwort gewußt hätte, dann *würde* ich sie *gegeben haben.*	*If I had known the answer, I **would have given** it.*
Hättest du Zeit gehabt, *würdest* du bestimmt zu mir *gekommen sein.*	*If you had had time, you certainly **would have come** to my house.*

These are rarely used because the shorter past perfect tense forms mean the same thing:

hätte gegeben	***would have given***
wäre gekommen	***would have come***

Give the meaning of the indicated phrases.

	1. Er **würde** das **gesagt haben . . .** (*will have said/would have said/would be said*)
1. He *would have said* that . . .	**2.** **wahrscheinlich** = *probably* Er **wird** das wahrscheinlich **gesagt haben.**
2. He probably *said* that. (Remember that future perfect used with **schon, wohl, doch,** or **wahrscheinlich** indicates past probability.)	**3.** Das **wurde** bestimmt nicht **gesagt!** (*would say/would have said/was said*)
3. That certainly *was* not *said!*	**4.** Das **wäre** bestimmt nicht **gesagt worden!** (*would have been said/were to be said/was said*)
4. That *would* certainly not *have been said!*	**5.** Ich **würde** ein Buch **gekauft haben . . .** (*would have bought/would buy/will have bought*)
5. I *would have bought* a book . . .	**6.** Er **wird** wohl das Buch **gekauft haben.** (*would have bought/bought/would buy*)
6. He probably *bought* the book.	**7.** Das Buch **wurde** von ihm **gekauft.** (*would buy/would have bought/was bought*)
7. The book *was bought* by him.	**8.** **wünschen** = *to wish* Er wünscht, er **hätte** nicht so viel **getrunken.** (*had drunk/drunk/could have drunk*)
8. He wishes that he *had* not *drunk* so much.	**9.** Ich wußte, daß er zuviel **getrunken hatte.** (*had drunk/drunk/has drunk*)
9. I knew that he *had drunk* too much.	**10.** **Wäret** ihr nur zu Hause **geblieben!** (*had remained/were to remain*)
10. If you *had* only *remained* at home!	**11.** **Wäre** das Buch **gekauft worden** . . . (*had been bought/would have been bought/were to be bought*)
11. *Had* the book *been bought* . . .	**12.** Ihr **wart** noch nicht in die Stadt **gegangen,** als er anrief. (*had gone/were going/were gone*)
12. You *had* not yet *gone* into the city when he called.	**13.** **Hättest** du lieber in München **gewohnt?** (*would have lived/had lived*)
13. *Would* you rather *have lived* in Munich?	**14.** **Hatten** sie früher schon einmal in München **gewohnt?** (*would have lived/had lived*)
14. *Had* they ever *lived* in Munich before?	**15.** **Wären** Sie nur nach Skandinavien **gefahren!** (*were to travel/had traveled*)

15.	If you *had* only *traveled* to Scandinavia!	**16.**	**Waren** Sie schon jemals in Skandinavien **gewesen?** (*would have been/had been*)
16.	*Had* you ever *been* to Scandinavia before?	**17.**	Ich wünsche, ich **hätte** ihn nicht **kennengelernt.**
17.	I wish I *had* not *made* his *acquaintance.*	**18.**	**nett** = *nice* Es **wäre** nett **gewesen,** wenn du meinen Geburtstag nicht **vergessen hättest.**
18.	It *would have been* nice, if you *had* not *forgotten* my birthday.	**19.**	Wenn ich nur Arzt **gewesen wäre!**
19.	If I *had* only *been* a doctor!	**20.**	**Hätte** mein Freund ein Auto **gehabt**, so **hätte** er es mir **gegeben.**
20.	If my friend *had had* a car, he *would have given* it to me.	**21.**	**das Pferd** = *horse* **der Sumpf** = *swamp* **Wäre** er nicht auf dem Pferd **geritten,** so **wäre** er nicht in den Sumpf **gefallen.**
21.	If he *had* not *ridden* the horse, he *would* not *have fallen* into the swamp.	**22.**	Wenn du mir auch tausend Mark **gegeben hättest, hätte** ich die Arbeit nicht gemacht.
22.	Even if you *had given* me a thousand marks, I *would* not *have done* the work.	**23.**	Er sah aus, als **hätte** er ein Gespenst **gesehen.**
23.	He looked as if he *had seen* a ghost.	**24.**	Sie sprach, als wenn sie gerade vom Lande **gekommen wäre.**
24.	She spoke as if she *had* just *come* from the country.	**25.**	Wir **hätten** der Musik länger **zugehört** aber dann **wären** wir vielleicht verrückt **geworden.**
25.	We *would have listened to* the music longer but then we perhaps *would have gone* crazy.	**26.**	Es **wurde** immer an dem Buch fleißig **gearbeitet.**
26.	We always *worked* hard on the book.	**27.**	**Hätte** ich mich **gezeigt,** so **wäre** ich **gesehen worden.**
27.	*Had* I *shown* myself, I *would have been seen.*		

PROGRESS TEST

Choose the equivalent of the indicated verbs.

1. Er sagte, Maria hat an dem Abend gesungen, als ob sie verliebt **gewesen wäre.**
(a) was being (b) had been (c) would have been (d) were becoming

2. Penthesilea hatte Achilles angesehen, als **hätte** sie ihn am liebsten **zerrissen.**
(a) would have torn to pieces (b) would tear to pieces (c) were to tear to pieces (d) were to be torn to pieces

3. Wenn Klaus von Dieter **gesehen worden wäre . . .**
(a) was seen (b) had been seen (c) were to be seen (d) had seen

4. Wenn ich Geld **gehabt hätte,** so **hätte** ich das Schiff **gekauft.**
(a) have had . . . had bought (b) would have . . . would have bought (c) had . . . would buy (d) had had . . . would have bought

5. Liesl **wird** Gerd wohl **geheiratet haben.**
(a) would have married (b) married (c) had married (d) is to be married

Answer key: **1.** (b); **2.** (a): **3.** (b); **4.** (d); **5.** (b).

READING PREPARATION

The following frames will introduce you to the reading passage. Continue to circle all words you do not understand.

	1. **berühmt** = *famous* In diesem Kapitel **werden** Sie einen Auszug aus dem berühmtesten deutschen Werk **lesen.**
1. In this chapter you *will read* an extract from the most famous of all German works.	**2.** Das Werk heißt naturlich *Faust.*
2. Naturally, the title of the work is *Faust.*	**3.** Der Autor ist Johann Wolfgang von Goethe, 1749 geboren, 1832 gestorben.
3. Johann Wolfgang von Goethe is the author, born 1749, died 1832.	**4.** Ungefähr sechzig Jahre lang **hat** Goethe an diesem Werk **gearbeitet.**
4. Goethe *worked* on this book for approximately sixty years.	**5.** **der Gelehrte** = *scholar* Faust ist ein Gelehrter, der alles **verstehen will.**
5. Faust is a scholar who *wants to understand* everything.	**6.** Sie kennen solche Menschen, nicht wahr?
6. You know people like that, don't you?	**7.** **Ob** er alles gelernt hat, was zu wissen ist? Um das herauszufinden, müssen Sie das Werk selber lesen. (*up/whether*)
7. I wonder *whether* he learned everything there is to know. You must read the work for yourself to find that out.	**8.** In einem berühmten Monolog erfahren wir, was Faust schon erreicht hat und was er noch erreichen will.

8. In a famous monologue we learn what Faust has already achieved and what he still wants to achieve.	**9.** **die Juristerei** = *jurisprudence* Faust hat Philosophie, Juristerei und Medizin studiert.
9. Faust has studied philosophy, jurisprudence, and medicine.	**10.** **leider** = *unfortunately* Leider hatte er auch Theologie studiert.
10. Unfortunately he had even studied theology.	**11.** Er **hätte** Theologie lieber nicht **studiert.** (*would have studied/had studied*)
11. He *would* rather not *have studied* theology.	**12.** **durchaus** = *thoroughly* Am Anfang seines Monologs sagt er: „Habe **nun**, ach! Philosophie, Juristerei und Medizin, und leider auch Theologie durchaus studiert." (*now/none*)
12. At the beginning of his monologue he says, "Oh! I have *now* made a thorough study of philosophy, jurisprudence, medicine, and unfortunately even theology."	**13.** Faust hat Philosophie, Juristerei, Medizin und, wie er sagt, leider auch Theologie durchaus studiert.
13. Faust has made a thorough study of philosophy, jurisprudence, medicine, and, as he says, unfortunately even theology.	**14.** **sich bemühen** = *to take trouble, to take pains, to strive* **das Bemühen** = __________
14. *trouble, pains, effort*	**15.** Er hat sie durchaus studiert, mit **heißem** Bemühn (Bemühen).
15. He has studied them thoroughly with *passionate* effort. (Lit.: *hot*)	**16.** **obwohl** = *although* Obwohl er mit heißem Bemühn studiert hat . . .
16. Although he has taken great pains to study . . .	**17.** **das Tor** = *gate* **der Tor** = *fool* . . . steht er da und ist nur ein armer **Tor**.
17. . . . there he stands and is just a poor *fool*.	**18.** **zuvor** = *previously* Er ist nur so klug als wie zuvor. (*stupid/smart*)
18. He is only as smart as he was before.	**19.** Was er studiert hat, hat ihm nicht geholfen.
19. What he has studied has not helped him.	**20.** „Da steh' ich nun, ich armer Tor, und bin so klug als wie zuvor", sagt er.
20. "Here I stand now, a poor fool, and am only as smart as I was before," he says.	**21.** **der Magister** = *Master* (of Arts) Obwohl er Magister und **gar** Doktor heißt . . . (*even/therefore*)

21. Even though he is a Master and *even* a Doctor . . .	**22.** . . . und obwohl er schon zehn Jahre **unterrichtet hat** . . . (*has taught/has practiced*)
22. . . . and although he *has* already *taught* for ten years . . .	**23.** . . . sieht er, daß wir nichts wissen können.
23. . . . he sees that we cannot know anything.	**24.** **die Schule** = *school* **der Schüler** = __________ (*pupil/schools*)
24. *pupil*	**25.** **ziehen** = *to pull* **herumziehen** = *to pull around* die Schüler **an der Nase** herumziehen (*by the nose/on the nose*)
25. to pull the pupils around *by the nose* (to lead around by the nose)	**26.** Er zieht schon zehn Jahre seine Schüler an der Nase **herum.**
26. He *has* already *pulled* his pupils *around* by the nose for ten years.	**27.** **herauf** = *up* **herab** = *down* Nicht nur herum zieht er seine Schüler an der Nase, sondern auch herauf und herab.
27. Not only does he pull his pupils around by the nose but he also pulls them up and down.	**28.** **quer** = *across* **krumm** = *crooked, curved* **quer und krumm** = *to and fro, all around* Herauf, herab und quer und krumm, zieht er seine Schüler an der Nase herum.
28. Up and down, to and fro, he pulls his pupils around by the nose.	**29.** Man kann Magister oder gar Doktor heißen und **trotzdem** nichts wissen.
29. One can be called a Master or even a Doctor and *still* (*in spite of that*) know nothing.	**30.** **verbrennen** = *to consume by fire, to burn up* Das Nichts-wissen-können verbrennt Faust das Herz.
30. This being able to know nothing consumes Faust's heart.	**31.** **schier** = *nearly, almost, just about* Das will ihm **schier** das Herz verbrennen, daß er nichts wissen kann.
31. The fact that he is not able to know anything is *about to* consume his heart.	**32.** **Würde** es schier unser Herz verbrennen, wenn wir nichts wissen **könnten**?
32. *Would* it about consume our hearts if we *were* not *able* to know anything?	**33.** **schreiben** = *to write* **der Schreiber** = __________
33. *writer, scribe*	**34.** **der Pfarrer** = *parson, parish priest* **der Pfaffe** = *priest, member of the clergy* (now a contemptuous expression for **Pfarrer**) Faust ist klüger als alle die Schreiber und Pfaffen.

34. Faust is smarter than all the clerks (writers) and clergy.	**35.** **der Laffe** = *fop, dandy* Faust sagt, daß er zwar **gescheiter** sei als alle die Laffen, Doktoren, Magister, Schreiber und Pfaffen . . . (*clever/more clever*)
35. Faust says that he is indeed *more clever* than all the fops, doctors, masters, clerks, and clergy.	**36.** Die Laffen und Pfaffen, die Schreiber, Magister und Doktoren sind nicht zwar gescheiter als Faust, aber verdienen sie mehr Geld?
36. The fops and parsons, the scribes, masters and doctors are certainly not more clever than Faust, but do they earn more money?	**37.** **zweifeln** = *to doubt* **der Zweifel** = *doubt* Faust hat **weder** Skrupel **noch** Zweifel.
37. Faust has *neither* scruples *nor* doubts.	**38.** **plagen** = *to plague, to trouble* **Keine** Skrupel **noch** Zweifel plagen ihn.
38. He is plagued by *neither* scruples *nor* doubts.	**39.** Wenn Skrupel oder Zweifel ihn **geplagt hätten**, wie **hätte** er seine Schüler an der Nase **herumziehen können**?
39. If scruples or doubts *had plagued* him, how *could* he *have pulled* his pupils around by the nose?	**40.** Er fürchtet sich weder vor Hölle noch Teufel. (If **Hölle** means *hell* then **Teufel** must mean ___________)
40. *devil* He fears neither hell nor the devil.	**41.** **reißen** = *to tear* **entreißen** = *to wrest from, to tear from, to snatch away* Alle Freude **ist** ihm auch **entrissen**.
41. All joy *is* also *wrested* from him.	**42.** Dafür ist ihm auch alle Freud' entrissen.
42. In return (for that), all joy is also wrested from him.	**43.** **sich einbilden** = *to imagine* Faust bildet sich nicht ein, daß er etwas weiß.
43. Faust *does* not *imagine* that he knows anything.	**44.** **was Rechts = etwas Rechtes** = *something worthwhile, something to be proud of* Faust bildet sich nicht ein, **was Rechts** zu wissen.
44. Faust does not imagine that he knows *anything worthwhile.*	**45.** Er bildet sich nicht ein, er könnte **was** lehren . . .
45. He does not imagine that he could teach *anything* . . .	**46.** **bekehren** = *to convert* . . . die Menschen zu bessern und zu bekehren.
46. . . . to improve and to convert people.	**47.** Was **müßte** man **machen**, um die Menschen zu bessern und zu bekehren?

47. What *would* one *have to do* in order to improve and to convert people?	**48.** **Nicht nur** weiß Faust, daß wir nichts wissen können, **sondern** er hat **auch** kein Geld.
48. *Not only* does Faust know that we can know nothing, *but in addition* he has no money.	**49.** **das Gut** = *property, possessions, goods* Auch hat er **weder** Gut **noch** Geld.
49. He also has *neither* possessions *nor* money.	**50.** **ehren** = *to honor* **die Ehre** = __________
50. *honor*	**51.** **herrlich** = *splendid, glorious* **die Herrlichkeit** = __________
51. *splendor, glory*	**52.** Auch hab' ich weder Gut noch Geld, noch Ehr' und Herrlichkeit der Welt. (The apostrophe on **hab'** and **Ehr'** replaces the letter ___.)
52. *e* I have in addition neither possessions nor wealth, nor worldly honor and glory.	**53.** Es **möchte** kein Hund so länger leben, meint Faust. (*would like/may*)
53. Faust feels that not even a dog *would like* to live any longer (as he lives now).	**54.** **drum = darum** = *for that reason* Drum will Faust **Magie** studieren. (*magi/magic*)
54. For that reason Faust wants to study *magic.*	**55.** **sich ergeben** = *to take to, to surrender to* Drum **hat** er **sich** der Magie **ergeben**.
55. For that reason he *has taken* to magic.	**56.** **die Kraft** = *power* **der Mund** = *mouth* **Kraft und Mund** = *power and voice* Durch **Geistes** Kraft und Mund . . . (*spirit's/ghost's*)
56. By means of the power and voice of spirits . . . (lit.: Through the *spirit's* power and mouth . . .)	**57.** **erkennen** = *to discern* . . . will er erkennen, was die Welt **im Innersten** zusammenhält. (*in its innermost being/in its extremities*)
57. . . . he wants to discern what holds the world together *in its innermost being.*	**58.** **das Geheimnis** = *secret* Er will die **Geheimnisse** der Welt erkennen.
58. He wants to discern the *secrets* of the world.	**59.** **sauer** = *sour* Er will nicht mehr mit saurem **Schweiß** sagen, was er nicht weiß.
59. He no longer wants to say with sour *sweat* what he does not know.	**60.** **wirken** = *to have an effect* **die Wirkenskraft** = *actuating force* Er will die Wirkenskraft der Welt **schauen.** (*to know/to see*)

60. He wants *to see* the actuating force of the world.	**61.** Nicht nur die Wirkenskraft, sondern auch **die Samen** der Welt will er schauen. (*the same/the seeds*)
61. He wants to see not only the actuating force but also *the seeds* of the world.	**62.** **kramen** = *to rummage around* Faust will nicht mehr in Worten kramen.
62. Faust does not want to rummage around in words any longer.	**63.** **sich ausdrücken** = *to express oneself* So **drückt** er **sich aus**: „Drum hab' ich mich der Magie ergeben . . .
63. He *expresses himself* in this way: "For this reason I have turned to magic . . .	**64.** **kund** = *known, manifest* . . . ob mir durch Geistes Kraft und Mund nicht manch Geheimnis **würde kund** . . .
64. . . . to see if by means of the power and speech of spirits many a secret *would become manifest* to me . . .	**65.** . . . daß ich nicht mehr mit saurem Schweiß zu sagen brauche, was ich nicht weiß . . .
65. . . . so that I no longer need to say with sour sweat what I do not know . . .	**66.** . . . daß ich erkenne, was die Welt im Innersten zusammenhält . . .
66. . . . that I may discern what holds the world together in its innermost being . . .	**67.** . . . schau' alle Wirkenskraft und Samen . . .
67. . . . see all the actuating forces and seeds . . . (**schau'** = **schaue**, *see, look at, observe*)	**68.** **tu'** = **tue** = *do* . . . und tu' nicht mehr in Worten kramen."
68. . . . and no longer rummage around in words."	**69.** Durch Magie lernte Faust die Welt nicht kennen.
69. Faust did not come to know the world through magic.	**70.** **die Droge** = *drug* Ergeben sich heute manche nicht nur der Magie, um die Welt zu erkennen, sondern auch den Drogen?
70. Today do some turn not only to magic but also to drugs in order to understand the world?	**71.** **leicht** = *easy* Wenn es nur so leicht **wäre**, die Welt zu erkennen!
71. If it *were* only that easy to understand the world!	**72.** Die große Frage ist, ob durch Geistes Kraft und durch Magie manches Geheimnis kund **wird**. (*becomes/will become*)
72. The big question is whether by means of the power of the spirit and magic many a secret *will become* known.	**73.** **kundmachen** = *to make known* Oder **werden** alle Geheimnisse nur durch sauren Schweiß **kundgemacht?**

73. Or *are* all secrets only *made known* through bitter sweat?	**74.** In der Bibel **steht es geschrieben:** (*it stands written/it is written*)
74. *It is written* in the Bible:	**75.** **das Angesicht** = *face* Im Schweiße deines Angesichts sollst du dein Brot essen. (1. Mose 3.19)
75. *By the* sweat of thy brow shalt thou eat thy bread.	

PROGRESS TEST

Choose the sentence that comes closer to the meaning of the German than any of the others.

1. Es will mir schier das Herz verbrennen, wenn ich daran denke, daß ich mit heißem Bemühn studiert habe und doch nur so klug bin als wie zuvor.
(a) My heart is continually burning because I thought only of studying.
(b) No matter how hard one studies, one never becomes any smarter.
(c) If I thought I could become smarter, my heart would burn with joy.
(d) Because I studied industriously, I became even smarter.

2. Entrissen ist mir alle Freud', denn ich bin zwar gescheiter als die Laffen, Pfaffen und Teufel.
(a) Freud does not believe he is certainly smarter than fops, priests, and devils.
(b) In spite of my knowledge I don't experience any joy.
(c) I am bereft of joy because of devils, priests, and fops.
(d) I revel in my cleverness.

3. Die Ehre und Herrlichkeit der Welt werden nur durch die Magie kundgemacht.
(a) Honor and glory are revealed only to those who practice magic.
(b) Magic reveals only a loss of worldly honor and glory.
(c) Magic is the only true honor and glory of the world.
(d) Only magic can give honor and glory to the world.

4. „Leider erkenne ich", sagt Faust, „was die Welt im Innersten zusammenhält."
(a) Faust delights in his knowledge of the world's inner workings.
(b) Faust rues his knowledge of the natural world.
(c) Fortunately Faust knows what holds the world together.
(d) Unfortunately Faust is holding the world together.

5. Mich plagt weder Hölle noch Teufel, denn ich habe weder Skrupel noch Zweifel.
(a) The lack of scruples and doubts makes one a free man.
(b) One plays with neither scruples nor doubts, with neither hell nor the devils.
(c) Pursued by hell and the devils, I had neither doubts nor scruples.
(d) Doubts and scruples lack the immediacy of hell and the devil.

Answer key: **1.** (b); **2.** (b); **3.** (a); **4.** (b); **5.** (a).

Before going on to the reading passage, review the vocabulary items you have circled.

Johann Wolfgang von Goethe: Faust

FAUST. Habe nun, ach! Philosophie,
Juristerei und Medizin,
Und leider auch Theologie
Durchaus studiert, mit heißem Bemühn.
Da steh' ich nun, ich armer Tor,
Und bin so klug als wie zuvor!
Heiße Magister, heiße Doktor gar,
Und ziehe schon an die zehen Jahr'
Herauf, herab und quer und krumm
Meine Schüler an der Nase herum—
Und sehe, daß wir nichts wissen können!
Das will mir schier das Herz verbrennen.
Zwar bin ich gescheiter als alle die Laffen,
Doktoren, Magister, Schreiber und Pfaffen;
Mich plagen keine Skrupel noch Zweifel,
Fürchte mich weder vor Hölle noch Teufel—
Dafür ist mir auch alle Freud' entrissen,
Bilde mir nicht ein, was Rechts zu wissen,
Bilde mir nicht ein, ich könnte was lehren,
Die Menschen zu bessern und zu bekehren.
Auch hab' ich weder Gut noch Geld,
Noch Ehr' und Herrlichkeit der Welt;
Es möchte kein Hund so länger leben!
Drum hab' ich mich der Magie ergeben,
Ob mir durch Geistes Kraft und Mund
Nicht manch Geheimnis würde kund;
Daß ich nicht mehr mit sauerm Schweiß
Zu sagen brauche, was ich nicht weiß;
Daß ich erkenne, was die Welt
Im Innersten zusammenhält,
Schau' alle Wirkenskraft und Samen,
Und tu' nicht mehr in Worten kramen.

(354–385)

Chapter Twenty-Three

75. *Subjunctive statements with the modals*

1. The following forms incorporating modal auxiliaries express a wish, a request, or a conditional or contrary-to-fact meaning:

(a) The past subjunctive verb form of the modal and generally an additional infinitive is used to refer to present time:

Könnte **ich nur** ***schwimmen!***	*If I* ***could*** *only* ***swim!***
Dürfte **ich bitte da vorbei?**	***Might*** *I get past there, please?*
Wenn er ***wollte, könnte*** **er eine Fahrkarte** ***kaufen.***	*If he* ***wished****, he* ***could buy*** *a ticket.*
Möchten **Sie noch ein Stück Kuchen?**	***Would*** *you* ***like*** *another piece of cake?*
Wenn ihr nur das ***müßtet!***	*If you only* ***had to do*** *that! (or: If only you* ***had to do*** *it! It would be easier to get it done.)*
Wer ***sollte*** **das** ***tun*****, wenn wir es nicht** ***täten*****?**	*Who* ***would*** *(****ought to, should****)* ***do*** *it, if we* ***did*** *not* ***do*** *it?*

(b) The past perfect subjunctive verb form of the modal is used to express past time. Most often the double infinitive appears.

Hätte er **es** ***gedurft*****, so** ***hätte*** **er die Zigarre** ***geraucht.***	*If* ***he had been permitted to****, he* ***would have smoked*** *the cigar.*
Wenn ich nur ***hätte schwimmen können!***	*If only I* ***had been able to swim!***
Hans ***hätte*** **ihr Singen nicht** ***gemocht*****, wenn sie eine häßliche Stimme** ***gehabt hätte.***	*Hans* ***would*** *not* ***have liked*** *her singing if she* ***had had*** *an ugly voice.*
Hätten **sie mich nur nicht** ***besuchen müssen!***	*If only they* ***hadn't had to visit*** *me!*

2. The following table outlines an approach to knowing the approximate meanings of double infinitive constructions in the subjunctive. The pronoun and verb are used for illustrative purposes only. They could, of course, be replaced by any subject or verb with appropriate verb endings:

er hätte es tun dürfen	*he would have been allowed to do it,* or *he would have been permitted to do it*
er hätte es tun können	*he could have done it,* or *he would have been able to do it*
er hätte es tun mögen	*he would have liked to do it,* or *he would have wanted to do it*
er hätte es tun müssen	*he would have been obliged (forced) to do it,* or *he would have had to do it*
er hätte es tun sollen	*he should have done it,* or *he ought to have done it*
er hätte es tun wollen	*he would have wanted to do it*

The following frames will review the meanings of the modals in the present and past indicative and also give you examples of conditional statements in which modals are used. Give the meaning of the indicated verbs as well as the meaning of the sentence.

	1. Kalman **kann** gut **schwimmen**.
1. Kalman *can swim* well.	**2.** Egon **konnte** gut **schwimmen.**
2. Egon *was able to (could) swim* well.	**3.** **faul** = *lazy* **Könnte** Gustav gut **schwimmen**, wenn er nicht so faul wäre?
3. *Could* Gustav *swim* well, if he were not so lazy?	**4.** Oskar **hätte gut schwimmen können**, aber er war zu faul.
4. Oskar *could have swum* well, but he was too lazy.	**5.** Wenn Arthur es **gekonnt hätte**, **wäre** er nicht ertrunken.
5. If Arthur *had been able to* do it, he would not have drowned.	**6.** Hier **darfst** du nicht **rauchen.**
6. You *must* not *smoke* here.	**7.** Hier **durftest** du **rauchen**.
7. You *were permitted to smoke* here.	**8.** **Dürfte** ich hier **rauchen?**
8. *Might (may)* I *smoke* here?	**9.** Hier **hättest** du **rauchen dürfen.**
9. You *would have been permitted to smoke* here.	**10.** Hier **hättest** du nicht **rauchen dürfen.**
10. You would not *have been allowed to smoke* here.	**11.** Wenn wir das Buch **lesen müssen,** werden wir es tun.

11. If we *have to read* the book, we will do it.	**12.** **Mußten** wir das Buch **lesen?**
12. *Did* we *have to read* the book?	**13.** **Müßten** wir das Buch **lesen**, um die Vorlesung zu verstehen?
13. *Would* we *have to read* the book in order to understand the lecture?	**14.** Wenn wir das Buch **hätten lesen müssen, hätten** wir es **gemacht**.
14. If we *had had to read* the book, we *would have done* it.	**15.** Wenn wir es nicht **gemußt hätten, hätten** wir das Buch nicht **gelesen**.
15. We *would* not *have read* the book if we *hadn't had to.*	**16.** **Machen wir es!** = *Let's do it!* (imperative form) Wenn ihr in die **Berge fahren wollt,** dann machen wir es doch!
16. If you *wish to drive* to the mountains, then let's do it!	**17.** **Wolltet** ihr in die **Berge fahren?**
17. *Did* you *want to drive* to the mountains?	**18.** **Würdet** ihr in die **Berge fahren wollen**, wenn wir Zeit **hätten**?
18. *Would* you *want to drive* to the mountains if we *had* the time?	**19.** **Hättet** ihr in die **Berge fahren wollen,** dann **hätten** wir euch **mitgenommen**.
19. If you *had wanted to drive* to the mountains, we *would have taken* you *along*.	**20.** **Hättet** ihr es **gewollt,** so **wären** wir in die Berge **gefahren**.
20. If you *had wanted to,* we *would have driven* to the mountains.	**21.** Er **mag** dich.
21. He *likes* you.	**22.** Er **mochte** das nicht.
22. He *did* not *like* that.	**23.** Sobald sie da ist, **möchte** er **abfahren.**
23. As soon as she is there, he *would like to leave.*	**24.** Er **hätte** das **tun mögen,** wenn sie da **gewesen wäre**.
24. He *would have liked to do* that, *had* she *been* there.	**25.** Er **hätte** es **gemocht,** wenn sie da *gewesen wäre.*
25. He *would have liked* it if she *had been* there.	**26.** Wenn er das **hätte tun mögen, wäre** sie froh **gewesen**.
26. If he *had liked* (or *wanted*) *to do* that she *would have been* glad.	**27.** Ich **soll** jetzt nach Hause **gehen.**
27. I *am supposed to go* home now.	**28.** **müde** = *tired* Ich **sollte** vor einer Stunde nach Hause **gehen,** aber ich war zu müde.
28. I *was supposed to go* home an hour ago, but I was too tired.	**29.** Ich **sollte** jetzt eigentlich nach Hause **gehen**, aber ich **mag nicht**.

29. I really *ought to go* home now but I *don't feel like* it.	**30.** Ich weiß, ich **hätte** nach Hause **gehen sollen.**
30 I know I *should have gone* home.	

And now check yourself with the following frames. If you have trouble getting the meaning, review the previous chapter and the meanings of the modals.

	1. Ich **müßte** ein Fisch **sein**, um da schwimmen zu können.
1. I *would have to be* a fish to be able to swim there. (Lit.: in order to be able to swim there)	**2.** Wenn Sie Lust **hätten, könnten** wir ins Kino **gehen**.
2. If you wished (*had* the desire) we *could go* to the movies.	**3.** **Dürfte** ich noch ein Glas Wasser **haben**, bitte?
3. *Might* I (*Could* I) *have* another glass of water, please?	**4.** **wollte** = *wish* Ich **wollte**, es **regnete** morgen.
4. I *wish* it *would rain* tomorrow.	**5.** Wenn ich **schlafen könnte,** so **täte** ich es auch.
5. If I *could* sleep, I *would do* it (too).	**6.** Wenn wir **dürften, gingen** wir ins Kino.
6. If we *were permitted,* we *would go* to the movies.	**7.** Wir **würden** die ganze Stadt **sehen können,** wenn die Luft nicht so ver-pestet **wäre**.
7. We *would be able to see the* whole city if the air *were* not so polluted.	**8.** **verzweifeln** = *to despair* **der Narr** = *fool* Wenn weise Männer nicht **irrten, müßten** die Narren **verzweifeln**. (Goethe)
8. If wise men *did* not *err,* fools *would have to despair.*	**9.** **übertreten** = *to break* (a law) Wenn man alle Gesetze **studieren sollte,** so **hätte** man gar keine Zeit, sie **zu übertreten.** (Goethe)
9. If one *were to study* all the laws, one *would not have* any time *to break* them.	**10.** Ich **wünschte,** ich **hätte** Zeit, alle Gesetze **zu studieren**!
10. I *wish* I *had* time *to study* all the laws!	

PROGRESS TEST

Give the meaning of the indicated verbs.

1. Ich wünschte, ich **könnte** Wienerschnitzel statt Sauerkraut **essen.**
(a) can eat (b) could eat (c) would eat (d) would have been able to eat

2. Er **hätte** das schon **sagen dürfen,** denn wir haben hier Pressefreiheit.
(a) had to be permitted to say (b) must be permitted to say (c) was permitted to say (d) would have been permitted to say

3. Wenn ich ihn nicht nur **hätte singen hören müssen!**
(a) had not been obliged to hear . . . sing (b) would not have to hear . . . sing (c) had not been able to hear . . . sing (d) were not supposed to hear . . . sing

4. Wenn du **wolltest,** könnten wir spazierengehen.
(a) wish (b) wished (c) will (d) want

5. **Müßte** ich mit euch spazierengehen, wäre ich lieber tot.
(a) have to (b) must (c) had to (d) were to

6. **Möchten** Sie gerne spazierengehen?
(a) could (b) would like (c) may (d) can

Answer key: **1.** (b); **2.** (d); **3.** (a); **4.** (b); **5.** (c); **6.** (b).

76. *Indirect discourse—definition, meaning*

1. Indirect discourse reports what someone else has said or thought without using his or her exact words. Usually subjunctive verb forms are used:

Fritz sagte: „Ich habe keine Zeit."	*Fritz said, "I have no time."*
Fritz sagte, er *habe* (*hätte*) keine Zeit.	*Fritz said he **had** no time.*
Marion fragte: „Ist Jürgen zu Hause?"	*Marion asked, "Is Jürgen at home?"*
Marion fragte, ob Jürgen zu Hause *sei*(*wäre*).	*Marion asked if Jürgen **were** at home.*
Waltraud sagt, sie *kommt* morgen.	*Waltraud says, she **is coming** tomorrow.*
Otmar fragt, wann Mimi nach Graz *fährt*.	*Othmar asks, when Mimi **is traveling** to Graz.*

Note: Verbs of *saying*—especially in the present tense and particularly in the first person—are frequently followed by the indicative.

2. The following subjunctive forms express indirect discourse in the active voice:

Ilse antwortete, daß sie jetzt *gehe* (*ginge*).	*Ilse answered that she **was leaving** (**would leave**) **now.***
Norbert sagte, Ilse *sei* (*wäre*) schon *weggegangen*.	*Norbert said that Ilse **had** already **gone** away.*

Erich gab zu, er *habe* (*hätte*) gestern *geraucht*.	*Erich admitted he **had smoked** yesterday.*
Anna sagte, daß sie *singen werde* (*würde*).	*Anna said that she **would sing**.*
Christa glaubte, sie *werde* (*würde*) das Buch bis morgen *fertiggelesen haben*.	*Christa believed she **would have finished reading** the book by tomorrow.*

Notice that in indirect discourse the subjunctive is also used to express things the reporter will not vouch for, whereas the indicative is used to express what he considers to be indeed true:

Franz sagte, er *komme* [*käme*] morgen.	*Franz said he **would come** tomorrow.*
Franz sagte, er *kommt* morgen.	*Franz said he **is coming** tomorrow.*

3. The following subjunctive forms express indirect discourse in the passive voice:

Ludwig fragte, ob der Brief jetzt von Lotte *geschrieben werde* (*würde*).	*Ludwig asked whether the letter **were being written** by Lotte now.*
Du antwortetest, du *seiest* (*wärest*) von ihm *gesehen worden*.	*You answered that you **had been seen** by him.*
Sie glaubten, das Haus *werde* (*würde*) bald von Bomben *getroffen werden*.	*They believed the house **would** soon **be hit** by bombs.*

The following frames give you practice in translating indirect discourse. Choose the correct meaning of the indicated verb.

	1. Er meinte, der Rolls-Royce **sei** der beste Wagen. (*is/was*)
1. He felt the Rolls-Royce *was* the best car.	**2.** Er meinte, der Rolls-Royce **wäre** der beste Wagen. (*is/was*)
2. He felt the Rolls-Royce *was* the best car.	**3.** Er meinte, der Mercedes **sei** (**wäre**) vielleicht der beste Wagen für ihn. (*is/was/would be*)
3. He felt the Mercedes *would* perhaps *be* the best car for him. (Notice that **sei** and **wäre** can have future meaning depending on the context.)	**4.** Er meinte, der Rolls-Royce **sei der** beste Wagen **gewesen.** (*is being/has been/had been*)
4. He felt the Rolls-Royce *had been* the best car.	**5.** Er meinte, der Rolls-Royce **wäre** der beste Wagen **gewesen.** (*was being/would be/had been*)
5. He felt the Rolls-Royce *had been* the best car.	**6.** Er meinte, der Rolls-Royce **werde** der beste Wagen **sein.** (*will be/would be/is being*)
6. He felt the Rolls-Royce *would be* the best car.	**7.** Er meinte, der Rolls-Royce **würde** der beste Wagen **sein.** (*would be/will be/would have been*)

7. He felt the Rolls-Royce *would be* the best car.	**8.** Er meinte, der Rolls-Royce **werde** wohl der beste Wagen **gewesen sein.** (*would be/had been/would have been*)
8. He felt the Rolls-Royce *would* probably *have been* the best car (or: *would be*). (Remember the future perfect may express past meaning.)	**9.** Ich fragte ihn, ob er Zeit für mich **habe.** (*has/would have*)
9. I asked him if he *would have* time for me.	**10.** Ich fragte ihn, ob er Zeit für mich **hätte.**(*would have/has*)
10. I asked him whether he *would have* time for me.	**11.** Ich fragte ihn, ob er gestern Zeit für sie **gehabt habe.** (*would have/had had*)
11. I asked him whether he *had had* time for her yesterday.	**12.** Ich fragte ihn, ob er gestern Zeit für mich **gehabt hätte,** wenn ich **gekommen** wäre. (*would have had/has had*) (*had come/would come*)
12. I asked him whether he *would have had* time for me yesterday if I *had come.*	**13.** Ich fragte ihn, ob er morgen Zeit für mich **haben werde.** (*will have/would have*)
13. I asked him whether he *would have* time for me tomorrow.	**14.** Ich fragte ihn, ob er Zeit **haben würde.** (*would have/would have had*)
14. I asked him whether he *would have* time.	**15.** Ich fragte ihn, ob er bis morgen mittag genug Zeit **gehabt hätte,** um den Rolls-Royce zu putzen. (*would have had/would have to*)
15. I asked him whether he *would have had* enough time by tomorrow noon to clean the Rolls-Royce.	**16.** Sie sagte, das Haus **werde** eben **gebaut.** (*is being built/was built/was being built*)
16. She said the house *was* just *being built.*	**17.** Sie sagt, das Haus **würde** gerade **gebaut.** (*would be built/is being built/would have been built*)
17. She says the house *is* just *being built.* (Note: Subjunctive **werde** does not always mean *would* due to introductory verb [here **sagt**] being in the present tense. See nos. 21, 24, and 27 for further examples of tense matching.)	**18.** Sie sagte, das Haus **sei** letztes Jahr **gebaut worden.** (*is being built/has been built/had been built*)
18. She said the house *had been built* last year.	**19.** Sie sagte, das Haus **wäre** letztes Jahr **gebaut worden.** (*is being built/had been built/was being built*)

19.	She said the house *had been built* last year.	**20.**	Sie sagte, das Haus **werde** nächstes Jahr **gebaut werden.** (*will be built/will have built/would be built*)
20.	She said the house *would be built* next year.	**21.**	Sie sagt, das Haus **werde** nicht vor dem Frühjahr **fertiggebaut sein.** (*would have built/will be finished*)
21.	She says the house *will* not *be finished* (*be completely built*) before spring.	**22.**	**suchen** = *to look for* Sie schrieb, er **suche** den alten Hut. (*was looking for/looked for*)
22.	She wrote that he *was looking for* the old hat.	**23.**	Sie wünschte, er **fände** bald den alten Hut. (*would find/has found*)
23.	She wished he *would* soon *find* the old hat.	**24.**	Sie schreibt, er **habe** endlich seinen alten Hut **gefunden.** (*would have found/had found/has found*)
24.	She writes that he *has* finally *found* his old hat.	**25.**	Sie schrieb, er **hätte** endlich seinen alten Hut **gefunden.** (*had found/would have found*)
25.	She wrote that he *had* finally *found* his old hat.	**26.**	Sie schrieb, er **werde** den alten Hut wieder **verlieren.** (*would lose/is lost*)
26.	She wrote that he *would lose* the old hat again.	**27.**	Sie schreibt, er **werde** den alten Hut bestimmt wieder **verlieren.** (*would have lost/was lost/will lose*)
27.	She writes that he *will* surely *lose* the old hat again.	**28.**	Sie schrieb, er **werde** wahrscheinlich den Hut inzwischen schon wieder **verloren haben.** (*will have lost/would have lost/had lost*)
28.	She wrote that he *had* probably already *lost* the hat again in the meantime. (Notice the past meaning of the future perfect.)	**29.**	Sie schrieb, **er werde** (**würde**) wohl den Hut schon längst wieder **verloren haben.** (*would have lost/lost/will be lost*)
29.	She wrote that he probably *lost* the hat again a long time ago.		

PROGRESS TEST

Choose the correct meaning of the indicated verbs.

1. Das Kind meinte, der König **habe** keine Kleider **an.**
(a) did . . . have on (b) had . . . had on (c) has . . . on (d) would . . . have on

2. Der Wolf fragte Rotkäppchen, wohin sie **ginge.**
(a) will go (b) goes (c) did go (d) was going

3. Anna fragte, ob Großmutter und Rotkäppchen wirklich von dem Wolf **verschlungen worden seien.**
(a) have been devoured (b) would have been devoured (c) are being devoured (d) had been devoured

4. Klein-Bärchen schrie, jemand **habe** seine Suppe ganz **aufgegessen.**
(a) has eaten up (b) had eaten up (c) could have eaten up (d) has to eat up

5. Rotkäppchen versprach, sie **werde** nie wieder Blumen **pflücken.**
(a) will pick (b) are picked (c) would pick (d) were picked

6. Der Spiegel hatte der Königin gesagt, sie **sei** nicht die Schönste im ganzen Lande.
(a) is (b) was (c) had (d) has been

7. Der Erzähler las, Schneewittchen **wäre** von den Zwergen vor der Königin **gewarnt worden.**
(a) had been warned (b) was being warned (c) would have been warned (d) was warned

8. Aschenputtel sagte, sie **würde** so gerne zum großen Ball **hingehen.**
(a) was going (b) would go (c) would have gone (d) will go

9. Die böse Königin hoffte, Schneewittchen **werde** von dem Jäger **getötet werden.**
(a) was killed (b) will be killed (c) would be killed (d) would have been killed

Answer key: **1.** (a); **2.** (d); **3.** (d); **4.** (b); **5.** (c); **6.** (b); **7.** (a); **8.** (b); **9.** (c).

77. *Modals in indirect discourse—active and passive voice*

1. In active voice modals may be used as follows:

Margit sagte, daß sie jetzt *gehen müsse* (*müßte*).	*Margit said that she **had to go now.***
Die Studenten erzählten, sie *hätten* gestern *rauchen dürfen.*	*The students related that they **had been allowed to smoke** yesterday.*
Sie sagten, sie *haben* gestern *rauchen dürfen.*	*They said they **were allowed to smoke** yesterday (and I assure you it's true).*
Er behauptete, er *werde* (*würde*) dafür kein Geld *sparen können.*	*He claimed **he would** not **be able to save** any money for that.*

2. In passive voice modals may be used as follows:

Er fragte, ob das Buch *gelesen werden müsse* (*müßte*).	*He asked whether the book **would have to be read.***
Sie sagte, das Lied *habe* (*hätte*) von ihm *gesungen werden sollen.*	*She said that the song **should have been sung** by him.*

The following frames will give you practice with the use of modals in active and passive voice in indirect discourse.

	1. Die drei kleinen Schweinchen dachten, der böse Wolf **könne** (**könnte**) sie nicht **verschlingen.** (*could swallow/could have swallowed*)
1. The three little pigs thought the bad wolf *could* not *swallow* them up.	**2.** Sie sagten, der Wolf **habe** (**hätte**) sie nicht **verschlingen können.**
2. They said the wolf *had* not *been able to swallow* them up.	**3.** Sie glaubten, der Wolf **werde** (**würde**) sie nicht **verschlingen können.** (*will be able to swallow/would be able to swallow*)
3. They thought the wolf *would* not *be able to swallow* them up.	**4.** Ich dachte, die drei Schweinchen **müßten** von dem Wolf **verschlungen werden.** (*must be swallowed/would have to be swallowed*)
4. I thought the three little pigs *would have to be swallowed* by the wolf.	**5.** Ich sagte, die drei Schweinchen **hätten** von dem Wolf **verschlungen werden sollen.** (*should have been eaten/shall have eaten*)
5. I said the three little pigs *should* (*ought to*) *have been eaten* by the wolf.	**6.** Er schrieb, der Prinz **wolle** durch das ganze Land **reiten,** um Aschenputtel zu finden. (*wants to ride/wanted to ride*)
6. He wrote that the prince *wanted to ride* through the whole country in order to find Cinderella.	**7.** Er schrieb, der Prinz **habe** (**hätte**) sie nicht **finden können.**
7. He wrote that the prince *had* not *been able to find* her.	**8.** Er glaubte, der Prinz **werde** (**würde**) sie nicht **finden können.** (*would be able to find/could have found*)
8. He believed that the prince *would* not *be able to find* her.	**9.** Der Prinz wollte wissen, ob Aschenputtel von ihm **gefunden werden könnte.** (*can be found/could be found*)
9. The prince wanted to know whether Cinderella *could be found* by him.	**10.** Er dachte, sie **hätte** von ihm **gefunden werden sollen.** (*shall be found/should have been found*)
10. He thought she *should have been found* by him.	

PROGRESS TEST

Choose the correct meaning of the indicated verbs.

1. Peppo fragte, ob er wirklich in die Stadt **gehen müsse.**
(a) has to go (b) had to go (c) must go (d) would go

2. Ich dachte, das Buch **könnte** von ihm gelesen **werden.**
(a) had been read (b) has been able to read (c) could be read (d) is able to read

3. Sie wunderte sich, warum man hier **nicht rauchen dürfe.**
(a) may not smoke (b) cannot smoke (c) is not permitted to smoke (d) was not allowed to smoke

4. Er fragte, warum das Auto **habe** (**hätte**) **gewaschen werden müssen.**
(a) had had to be washed (b) has had to be washed (c) would have to be washed (d) has to be washed

5. Schneewittchen fürchtete, sie **werde** den Weg zu den sieben Zwergen nicht mehr **finden können.**
(a) has found (b) will be able to find (c) would be able to find (d) would have found

Answer key: **1.** (b); **2.** (c); **3.** (d); **4.** (a); **5.** (c).

READING PREPARATION

The following frames will introduce you to the vocabulary of the reading passage. Continue to circle all words you do not recognize and review them before going on to the reading passage. The passage consists of excerpts from Act I of **Der Rosenkavalier.** *All the excerpts deal with the nature and mystery of the passage of time. The characters mentioned in the excerpts are:* **die Marschallin** (*the field marshal's wife*), *a beautiful, mature woman whose physical beauty is just beginning to fade;* **Baron von Ochs,** *her "evil fellow" of a cousin, who is to wed a young pretty girl; and* **Quin-quin,** *her young lover and also a cousin, who eventually will wed the young woman.*

	1. **das Lesestück** = *reading passage* Das Lesestück am Ende dieses Kapitels **besteht aus** drei Auszügen aus dem ersten Akt des *Rosenkavaliers.*
1. The reading passage at the end of this chapter *consists of* three excerpts from the first act of *Der Rosenkavalier.*	**2.** **komponieren** = *to compose, to write music* Vielleicht wissen Sie schon, daß der *Rosenkavalier* eine Oper ist, die von Richard Strauss **komponiert wurde.**
2. Perhaps you already know that *Der Rosenkavalier* is an opera (which *was*) *composed* by Richard Strauss.	**3.** **hervorragend** = *outstanding* Das Libretto ist aber von einem der hervorragendsten osterreichschen Dichter des zwanzigsten Jahrhunderts, Hugo von Hofmannsthal.
3. The libretto, however, is by one of the most outstanding Austrian poets of the twentieth century, Hugo von Hofmannsthal.	**4.** Und jetzt zum Text!

4. And now on to the text!	**5.** **geheimnisvoll** = *mysterious* Das Thema ist „die Zeit" und was für ein geheimnisvolles Ding sie ist.
5. The theme is "time" and what a mysterious thing it is.	**6.** **besuchen** = *to visit* **der Besuch** = *visitor, visit* Als der Monolog beginnt, hat die Marschallin **eben** Besuch gehabt. (*even/just*)
6. As the monologue begins, the Marschallin has *just* had a visitor.	**7.** **der Ochs** = *ox* Es war der Baron von Ochs.
7. It was (the) Baron von Ochs.	**8.** Der Baron von Ochs, ein älterer, **schlechter** Kerl, will ein ganz junges und hübsches Mädchen heiraten. (*fine/evil*)
8. Baron von Ochs, an elderly *evil* fellow, wants to marry a very young and pretty girl.	**9.** **aufblasen** = *to blow up* **aufgeblasen** = *puffed up, inflated* Der Monolog fängt mit diesen Worten an: „Da geht er hin, der aufgeblasene, schlechte Kerl."
9. The monologue begins with these words: "There he goes, the puffed-up, evil fellow."	**10.** **kriegen** = *to get* Der aufgeblasene, schlechte Kerl kriegt das hübsche, junge Ding.
10. The puffed-up evil fellow is getting the pretty young thing (i.e., girl). ("Ding" is used at this point in the libretto for "Mädchen.")	**11.** **der Binkel** = *leather bag* **ein Binkel Geld** = *a leather bag full of money* Nicht nur das Mädchen kriegt er, sondern einen Binkel Geld dazu, als **müßte** es so **sein**. (*must/had*)
11. He is getting not only the girl but in addition a purse full of money, as if it *had to be* that way.	**12.** **müßts** = **müßte es** Der aufgeblasene, schlechte Kerl kriegt einen Binkel Geld dazu, als **müßts** so sein.
12. In addition, the puffed-up evil fellow is getting a purse full of money, as if *it had* to be so.	**13.** **sich einbilden** = *to pride oneself, to flatter oneself, to imagine* **sich etwas vergeben** = *to compromise oneself about something* Er bildet sich ein, daß er sich etwas vergibt.
13. He prides himself (in thinking) that he is compromising his dignity (compromising himself).	**14.** **noch** = *moreover* Er bildet sich noch ein, daß ers (= er es) ist, der sich was vergibt.

14.	Moreover, he prides himself in thinking that it is he who is lowering himself.	**15.**	**sich erzürnen** = *to get angry* Die Marschallin fragt, warum sie sich darüber **erzürnen solle.** (*should get angry/gets angry*)
15.	The Marschallin asks why she *should get angry* about it. (Note: **was erzürn' ich!** is an idiom like *what do I care!*)	**16.**	**der Lauf** = *the way* Es ist **doch** der Lauf der Welt. (*still/after all*)
16.	It is, *after all,* the way of the world.	**17.**	**das Kloster** = *convent* (nuns), *monastery* (monks) Sie kommt frisch aus dem Kloster.
17.	She comes fresh from the convent.	**18.**	**das Mädel** = *girl* Sie **kann sich** auch an ein Mädel **erinnern** . . .
18.	She *can* also *remember* a girl . . .	**19.**	**die Ehe** = *marriage* **der Ehestand** = *married state, wedlock* . . . die frisch aus dem Kloster in den heiligen Ehestand **kommandiert worden ist.** (*had been ordered/was ordered*)
19.	. . . who *was ordered,* fresh from the convent, into the holy state of matrimony.	**20.**	Es ist der Lauf der Welt, daß ein Mädel in den heiligen Ehestand **kommandiert wordn** (**worden**) **ist.**
20.	It is the way of the world that a girl *was ordered* into the holy state of matrimony.	**21.**	Die Marschallin fragt, wo dieses Mädchen jetzt **sei**.
21.	The Marschallin asks, where this girl *is* now. (When the introductory verb of an indirect statement is in the present tense, you can translate the present tense subjunctive with the present indicative.)	**22.**	**der Spiegel** = *mirror* Die Marschallin nimmt einen Handspiegel und fragt, wo sie (d.h. das Mädchen) jetzt sei.
22.	The Marschallin takes a hand mirror and asks where she (i.e., that girl) is now. (Note that here the feminine personal pronoun **sie** is used instead of the neuter **es** which would agree in gender with **das Mädchen**.)	**23.**	**vergehen** = *to pass away* **vergangen** = *past* Sie **solle** den Schnee vom vergangenen Jahr **suchen.** (*is to seek/should look for*)
23.	She *should look for* the snow from the previous year.	**24.**	**Resi** = *nickname for Theresa, the Marschallin's middle name* Wo ist die kleine Resi jetzt? Ja, **such dir** den Schnee vom vergangenen Jahr.

24. Where is little Resi now? Might as well *look for* the snow of the previous year. (Well, *seek for yourself* the snow of the previous year.)	**25.** Aber wie **kann** das **sein**, daß ich die kleine Resi war . . .
25. But how *can* that *be,* that I was little Resi . . .	**26.** . . . und daß ich auch einmal die alte Frau **sein werd** (= **werde**)! (*would be/will be*)
26. . . . and that I *will* also one day *be* the old woman.	**27.** **der Fürst** = *prince* **die Fürstin** = *princess* Siehst du es, da geht sie, die alte Fürstin Resi.
27. Do you see (that), there she goes, old Princess Resi.	**28.** **siehgst** = **siehst du** **s'** = **sie** Siehgst es, da geht s', die alte Fürstin Resi!
28. See that, there she goes, old Princess Resi!	**29.** Wie **könnte** denn das **geschehen?**
29. How *could* that *happen?*	**30.** Wie **macht** denn das der liebe Gott, wo sie doch immer die gleiche ist?
30. How *does* the dear God *do* that, when she is always the same person?	**31.** Und wenn ers (= er es) schon so machen muß . . .
31. And if He has to do it this way . . .	**32.** **dabei** = *at the same time* . . . warum **laßt** (= **läßt**) er mich denn zuschaun (zuschauen) dabei?
32. . . . why does He *let* me look on at the same time? (The Marschallin leaves out the umlaut from time to time. This omission is typical for southern German and Austrian dialects.)	**33.** **der Sinn** = *understanding* Sie fragte, warum **lasse** Gott sie denn zuschauen dabei mit gar so klarem Sinn.
33. She asked why God *let* her look on at the same time with such a clear understanding.	**34.** **verstecken** = *to hide* Warum *versteckt* ers (= er es) nicht vor mir? (*does hide/did hide*)
34. Why *does* He not *hide* it from me?	**35.** **geheim** = *mysterious* (also: *secret, clandestine*) Das alles ist geheim, so viel geheim.
35. All that is mysterious, so very mysterious.	**36.** **ertragen** = *to endure* Der Mensch soll das ertragen, **dazu** ist er hier. (*for that purpose/there to*)
36. We are to endure that, that is why we are here. (Lit.: Man is to endure that, *for that purpose* is he here.)	**37.** Und man ist dazu da, daß mans (= man es) ertragt (= erträgt).

37. And we are here to endure it. (Again the umlaut is missing in her speech.)	**38.** **der Unterschied** = *difference* Der ganze Unterschied liegt in dem „Wie" man das **Geheime** erträgt. (*mystery/mysterious*)
38. The whole difference lies in the "how" we endure the *mysterious*.	**39.** Und in dem „Wie" da liegt der ganze Unterschied.
39. And in the "how" there lies the whole difference.	**40.** In dem zweiten und dem dritten Auszug spricht die Marschallin mit Quin-quin.
40. In the second and the third excerpts the Marschallin is speaking with Quin-quin.	**41.** **winden** = *to wind, to twist* **sich entwinden** = *to wrest oneself* (*from*) Die Marschallin **entwindet sich** Quin-quin.
41. The Marschallin *wrests herself* from Quin-quin (from his embrace).	**42.** Die Marschallin, sich ihm entwindend, sagt, daß Quin-quin ihr gut sein **solle**. (*shall/should/is*)
42. The Marschallin, disentangling herself from him, says that Quin-quin *should* be good to her.	**43.** **Er** = *you* (a more formal form of *you* than the **Sie** form) O **sei** Er gut, Quin-quin. (Here **sei** is the imperative and means __________)
43. *be* O *be* good, Quin-quin.	**44.** **zeitlich** = *temporal* **das Zeitliche** = __________
44. *the temporal* (*things*)	**45.** **spüren** = *to feel, to sense* Die Marschallin spürt **das Zeitliche**.
45. The Marschallin feels the temporal aspect of things.	**46.** **recht** = *clear* Sie spürt die **Schwäche** von allem Zeitlichen recht bis in ihr Herz hinein. (*weakness/frailty*)
46. She feels the *frailty* of all temporal things right to the bottom of her heart.	**47.** **mir ist zumute** = *I have a feeling* Es ist **der Marschallin zumute** . . .
47. *The Marschallin has a feeling* . . . (Note that **zumute** governs the dative case.)	**48.** Es ist ihr zumut (= zumute), als ob sie die Schwäche von allem Zeitlichen recht **spüren müsse**, bis in ihr Herz hinein. (*must sense/ought to sense*)
48. She has a feeling as if she *must sense* the frailty of all temporal things right to the bottom of her heart.	**49.** Man **soll** nichts halten. (*should/is supposed to*)
49. One *is* not *supposed to* hold anything.	**50.** **packen** = *to grasp* Man kann nichts packen.

50. One can grasp nothing.	**51.** Man soll **weder** etwas halten **noch** etwas packen.
51. We are *neither* to hold anything *nor* to grasp anything.	**52.** **laufen** = *to run* **zerlaufen** = *to melt* Alles zerlauft (= zerläuft) zwischen den Fingern.
52. Everything melts between our fingers.	**53.** **greifen** = *to reach* Alles, **wonach** wir greifen . . . (*for which/afterward*)
53. Everything we reach *for* . . .	**54.** **lösen** = *to loosen* **sich auflösen** = *to dissolve* Alles **löst sich auf**, wonach wir greifen.
54. Everything we reach for *dissolves*.	**55.** **dunstig** = *vaporous, misty, hazy* **der Dunst** = __________
55. *mist, vapor, haze*	**56.** **zergehen** = *to vanish, to melt, to dissolve* Alles zergeht **wie** Dunst. (*how/like*)
56. Everything vanishes *like* mist.	**57.** Alles zergeht wie Dunst und Traum.
57. Everything vanishes like mist and dreams.	**58.** **die Sache** = *circumstance* Die Zeit **ändert nichts** an den Sachen. (*does not alter/does not suggest*)
58. Time *does not alter* the circumstances. (Note that **ändern** plus **an** takes the dative.)	**59.** **im Grund**(**e**) = *fundamentally* Im Grund ändert die Zeit **doch** nichts an den Sachen.
59. Fundamentally time *really* does not alter the circumstances.	**60.** **sonderbar** = *strange* Die Zeit, **die** ist ein sonderbares Ding. (*it/who/which*)
60. Time, *it* is a strange thing. (**die** is here a demonstrative, not a relative pronoun.)	**61.** Sie sagte, daß die Zeit sonderbar **sei**.
61. She said that time *was* strange.	**62.** **hinleben** = *to live from day to day* Wenn man **so** hinlebt . . . (*so/like this*)
62. If one lives *like this* from day to day . . .	**63.** **rein** = *purely* **rein gar nichts** = *nothing at all, a mere nothing* Wenn man so hinlebt, ist sie rein gar nichts.
63. If one lives like this from day to day, it (= time) is a mere nothing.	**64.** **auf einmal** = *all of a sudden* Dann auf einmal spürt man **nichts als** die Zeit. (*nothing more/nothing else but*)

64. Then all of a sudden one feels *nothing else but* time.	**65.** Aber dann auf einmal **würde** man nichts als sie **spüren**.
65. But then all of a sudden one *would feel* nothing else but that.	**66.** **drinnen** = *inside, within* Die Zeit ist **nicht nur** um uns herum, sie ist **auch** in uns drinnen.
66. Time is *not only* all around us, it is *also* within us.	**67.** **rieseln** = *to trickle down* Die Zeit rieselt in den Gesichtern.
67. Time trickles down in our faces.	**68.** Nicht nur in den Gesichtern rieselt die Zeit, sondern auch im Spiegel rieselt sie.
68. Time not only trickles down in our faces but also trickles down in the mirror.	**69.** **die Schläfe** = *temple* (of the head) Die Zeit **fließt** in unseren Schläfen. (*flows/stops*)
69. Time *flows* in our temples.	**70.** Zwischen der Marschallin und Quin-quin fließt die Zeit.
70. Time flows between the Marschallin and Quin-quin.	**71.** Und zwischen mir und dir da fließt sie **wieder.** (*against/again*)
71. And there it is *again*, flowing between me and you.	**72.** **lauten** = *to sound* **der Laut** = *sound* **laut** = *loud, noisy* **lautlos** = __________
72. *soundless, noiseless, silent*	**73.** Die Zeit ist so lautlos wie eine **Sanduhr.**
73. Time is as soundless as an *hourglass.*	**74.** **aufhalten** = *to stop, to detain* **unaufhaltsam** = *undetainable* Die Zeit ist unaufhaltsam.
74. Time cannot be stopped.	**75.** In den Schläfen fließt die Zeit unaufhaltsam.
75. Time flows incessantly in our temples.	**76.** **manchmal** = *sometimes, now and again* Manchmal, sagte die Marschallin, **habe** sie die Zeit unaufhaltsam **fließen hören.**
76. Sometimes, said the Marschallin, she *had heard* time *flowing* incessantly.	**77.** Manchmal **wäre** sie mitten in der Nacht **aufgestanden.**
77. Sometimes, she *had gotten up* in the middle of the night.	**78.** **stehenlassen** = *to stop* Sie läßt die Uhren alle stehen.
78. She stops all the clocks.	**79.** Manchmal hör (= höre) ich die Zeit unaufhaltsam fließen.
79. Sometimes I hear time flowing incessantly.	**80.** Manchmal steh (= stehe) ich auf und laß (= lasse) die Uhren alle stehen.

80. Sometimes I get up and stop all the clocks.	**81.** **allein** = *yet, but, however* Allein man muß sich auch vor der Zeit nicht fürchten.
81. However, one need not be afraid even of time. (Note: **allein** is a coordinating conjunction when used initially in a sentence with normal word order.)	**82.** **das Geschöpf** = *creature, creation* Die Zeit ist auch ein Geschöpf des Vaters.
82. Time is also a creation of the Father.	**83.** Allein die Zeit ist auch ein Geschöpf **dessen, der** uns alle geschaffen hat. (*whose, who/of him, who*)
83. But time is also a creation *of Him Who* (has) created us all.	

PROGRESS TEST

Choose the answer that most accurately reflects the sense of the original sentence.

1. Man soll sich nicht erzürnen, denn es ist der Lauf der Welt, wenn ein Mädchen einen Mann ins Kloster kommandiert.
(a) Men and women belong in either a monastery or a convent.
(b) Such is the world, when a girl orders a man to enter the monastery.
(c) A girl has been sent to the convent and I should not worry about it, as it is the way of the world.
(d) One should not get angry when girls are sent to the convent.

2. Warum versteckt er es vor mir und läßt mich zugleich zuschauen dabei?
(a) Why does he let me watch while hiding it from me?
(b) Why does he show me and at the same time place it before me?
(c) Why does he hide from me when I am not looking?
(d) Why does he let me hide from him while he looks on?

3. Alles außer Geld zerläuft, zergeht und löst sich auf bis in unser Herz hinein.
(a) Only the heart conquers all.
(b) Everything, even money, is conquered by the heart.
(c) Money is the only permanent thing on this earth.
(d) Our heart loves money above all else.

4. Das Zeitliche ist wie Dunst und Traum, und lebt in der Schwäche des Herzens fort.
(a) The frailty of the heart is a temporal thing.
(b) Temporal things can only exist in one's dreams.
(c) Temporal things pass away like mist and dreams.
(d) The frailty of the heart is a permanent home for temporal things like dreams and mist.

5. Die unaufhaltsame Zeit ändert doch alles an den Sachen, da sie so sonderbar ist.
 (a) Time is a strange thing because it is incessant.
 (b) Incessant time alters all things.
 (c) Time appears to move incessantly forward despite our wishes.
 (d) Incessant time is a product of circumstances.

6. In den Gesichtern und Schläfen rieselt die Zeit.
 (a) We experience time trickling down in our faces and our sleep.
 (b) Time trickles through the history of our daily sleep.
 (c) Time makes itself known in our faces and temples.
 (d) History rustles through our temples.

Answer key: **1.** (b); **2.** (a); **3.** (c); **4.** (d); **5.** (b); **6.** (c).

Review the vocabulary items you circled before going on to the reading passage.

Hugo von Hofmannsthal: Der Rosenkavalier

MARSCHALLIN

allein

Da geht er hin, der aufgeblasene, schlechte Kerl,
und kriegt das hübsche, junge Ding und einen Binkel Geld dazu,
als müßts so sein.
Und bildet sich noch ein, daß ers ist, der sich was vergibt.
Was erzürn ich mich denn? ist doch der Lauf der Welt.
Kann mich auch an ein Mädel erinnern,
die frisch aus dem Kloster ist in den heiligen Ehestand kommandiert wordn.

Nimmt den Handspiegel

Wo ist die jetzt? Ja, such dir den Schnee vom vergangenen Jahr.
Das sag ich so:
Aber wie kann das wirklich sein,
daß ich die kleine Resi war
und daß ich auch einmal die alte Frau sein werd! . . .
Die alte Frau, die alte Marschallin!
„Siehgst es, da geht's, die alte Fürstin Resi!"
Wie kann denn das geschehen?
Wie macht denn das der liebe Gott?
Wo ich doch immer die gleiche bin.
Und wenn ers schon so machen muß,

warum laßt er mich denn zuschaun dabei
mit gar so klarem Sinn? Warum versteckt ers nicht vor mir?
Das alles ist geheim, so viel geheim.
Und man ist dazu da, daß mans ertragt.
Und in dem „Wie“ da liegt der ganze Unterschied—

* * *

MARSCHALLIN

sich ihm entwindend

O sei Er gut, Quin-quin. Mir ist zumut,
daß ich die Schwäche von allem Zeitlichen recht spüren muß,
bis in mein Herz hinein:
wie man nichts halten soll,
wie man nichts packen kann,
wie alles zerlauft zwischen den Fingern,
alles sich auflöst, wonach wir greifen,
alles zergeht, wie Dunst und Traum.

* * *

Die Zeit im Grund, Quin-quin, die Zeit,
die ändert doch nichts an den Sachen.
Die Zeit, die ist ein sonderbares Ding.
Wenn man so hinlebt, ist sie rein gar nichts.
Aber dann auf einmal,
da spürt man nichts als sie:
sie ist um uns herum, sie ist auch in uns drinnen.
In den Gesichtern rieselt sie, im Spiegel da rieselt sie,
in meinen Schläfen fließt sie.
Und zwischen mir und dir da fließt sie wieder.
Lautlos, wie eine Sanduhr.
O Quin-quin!

Manchmal hör ich sie fließen unaufhaltsam.
Manchmal steh ich auf, mitten in der Nacht,
und laß die Uhren alle stehen.
. . .
Allein man muß sich auch vor ihr nicht fürchten.
Auch sie ist ein Geschöpf des Vaters,
der uns alle geschaffen hat.

Chapter Twenty-Four

78. *Additional uses of the subjunctive*

The subjunctive is used to express:

(a) possibility

Das *könnte* (*dürfte*) wahr sein.	*That* **could** *(***might***) be true.*

(b) uncertainty

Wie *wäre* es denn, wenn wir einen Spaziergang machten?	*How* **would** *it* **be** *if we were to take a walk (if we took a walk)?*

(c) conjecture

Er kommt morgen bestimmt, *es sei denn*, es *gäbe* kein schönes Wetter.	*He will certainly come tomorrow* **unless** *the weather* **were** *not good (***is** *not good).*
Ob sie *geblieben wäre*?	*I wonder if she* **would have stayed***?*

(d) anticipation, purpose

Alma gab ihm ihre Telefonnummer, damit er sie *anrufe*.	*Alma gave him her telephone number so that he* **would call** *her* **up***.*

(e) doubt

Ich glaube nicht, daß sie Zeit *hätte*.	*I do not believe that she* **would have** *time.*

(f) concession

***Wäre* das Wetter noch so schön, ich gehe doch nicht schwimmen.**	*No matter how good the weather **is** (**might be**), I will still not go swimming.*

Note that some of these uses are interrelated.

The following frames will give you additional examples for the above grammar explanation. Give the correct meaning of the indicated verbs as well as the meaning of the entire frame. Continue to circle all words you do not recognize and review them before going to the next section.

	1. **Wäre** es möglich, daß wir die letzten Menschen auf Erden sind? (*is/was*)
1. *Is* it (*could* it *be*) possible that we are the last people on earth?	**2.** **allerlei** = *all (sorts of)* Denn wie der Mensch allerlei lebendige Tiere **nennen würde**, so **sollten** sie **heißen**. (Bibel)
2. For whatever man *would name* all living creatures, that is what they *should be called*. (More literally: For however man *would name* all living animals, thus *should* they *be called*.)	**3.** **bitten** = *to ask* **ums = um das** = *for the* Wo bittet unter euch ein Sohn den Vater ums Brot, der ihm einen Stein dafür **biete**? (Bibel) (*offer/would offer*)
3. Where among you is there a father who, when asked for bread by his son, *would offer* him a stone?	**4.** **dahin** = *to that place* Denn wer will ihn [den Menschen] dahin bringen, daß er **sehe**, was nach ihm geschehen wird? (Bibel) (*see/may see/saw*)
4. For who will bring him [man] to that place, that he *may see* what will take place after him?	**5.** **gewiß** = *certain* **der Verfasser** = *writer, author* Gewisse Bücher scheinen geschrieben zu sein, nicht damit man daraus **lerne,** sondern damit man **wisse**, daß der Verfasser etwas gewußt hat. (Goethe) (*may learn . . . may know/learned . . . knew*)
5. Certain books appear to be written not so that one *may learn* from them but so that one *may know* that the writer knew something.	**6.** Welche Regierung die beste **sei**? Diejenige, die uns lehrt, uns selbst zu regieren. (Goethe) (*is/was*)
6. Which government *is* the best? The one which teaches us to govern ourselves. (In such rhetorical questions, indirect discourse is often inferred: You ask(ed) which government is . . . ? Therefore the subjunctive is used in German.)	**7.** **der Odem** = *spirit* **das Vieh** = *animal* Wer weiß, ob der Odem der Menschen aufwärts **fahre**, und der Odem des Viehes unterwärts unter die Erde **fahre**? (Bibel) (*goes/went*)

7.	Who knows whether the spirit of man *goes* upwards and the spirit of animals *goes* downwards beneath the earth?	**8.**	Es ist nicht gut, daß der Mensch allein **sei**. (Bibel) (*should be/would be*)
8.	It is not good that man *should be* alone.	**9.**	Er kommt bestimmt, **es sei denn**, er hat keine Zeit. (*there is/unless*)
9.	He will certainly come, *unless* he has no time.	**10.**	Ob das Hotel wohl **gebaut werden würde?** (*is being built/would be built*)
10.	I wondered whether the hotel *would be built?*	**11.**	Ob er ein kluger Mann **sei?** (*is/was*)
11.	I wonder if he *is* an intelligent man?	**12.**	**das Erbe** = *legacy, inheritance* **erben** = *to inherit* **der Erbe, die Erbin** = *heir, heiress* Sie wird kein Geld haben, **es sei denn**, sie hat es geerbt.
12.	She will not have any money, *unless* she has inherited it.	**13.**	**die Gehilfin** = (female) *helpmate* Aber für den Menschen ward (wurde) keine Gehilfin gefunden, die um ihn **wäre**. (Bibel)
13.	But for man no helpmate was found who *would be* with him.	**14.**	Er brachte allerlei Tiere und allerlei Vögel zu dem Menschen, daß er **sähe**, wie er sie **nennte.** (Bibel)
14.	He brought all kinds of animals and all kinds of birds to man, so that He *could see* how he *would name* them.	**15.**	Sie glaubt nicht, daß er ins Kino **dürfe.** (*could/might/may*)
15.	She does not think that he *may* (*can*) go to the movies.	**16.**	Lene glaubt nicht, daß Elsie Sauerkraut **äße**. (*eats/would eat*)
16.	Lene does not think that Elsie *would eat* sauerkraut.	**17.**	**füttern** = *to feed* **Wäre** der Wolf **noch so** gefährlich, ich werde ihn doch füttern. (*no matter how . . . is/no matter how . . . was*)
17.	*No matter how* dangerous the wolf *is* (*might be*), I will still feed it.	**18.**	**Hätte** er noch so viel Geld, ich werde ihn doch nicht heiraten.
18.	No matter how much money he *has* (*might have*), I will not marry him.		

PROGRESS TEST

Choose the correct meaning for the indicated verbs.

1. **Wäre** es möglich, daß es heutzutage noch Menschenfresser gibt?
   (a) is (b) were (c) was (d) would have
2. Das **hätte** er **tun können!**
   (a) had done (b) could have done (c) has been able to do (d) could do
3. Sie können das nicht tun, **es sei denn,** sie fragen zuerst ihren Vater darüber.
   (a) but (b) it is for that reason (c) unless (d) because
4. Er liest das Buch, damit er etwas daraus **lerne.**
   (a) taught (b) will teach (c) learned (d) may learn
5. **Bliebe** er noch so lange da, sie will ihn doch nicht sehen.
   (a) stays (b) stayed (c) would stay (d) was staying

Answer key: **1.** (a); **2.** (b); **3.** (c); **4.** (d); **5.** (a).

79. *Imperative forms*

The following forms express requests, commands, or wishes:

(a) the familiar singular (the **du** form)

Christa, *sing*(*e*) das Lied!	*Christa,* ***sing*** *the song!*
***Sei* ruhig, Sigurd!**	***Be*** *quiet, Sigurd!*
Sieh* mich *an!	***Look*** *at me!*

(b) the familiar plural (the **ihr** form)

***Sprecht* nicht so schnell, Kinder!**	***Don't speak*** *so quickly, children!*
***Seid* ruhig, Helga und Monika!**	*Helga and Monika,* ***be*** *quiet!*
Hört* doch *auf!	***Stop*** *it!*

(c) the formal singular and plural (the **Sie** form)

***Fahren Sie* nicht zu schnell!**	***Don't drive*** *too fast!*
***Seien Sie* ruhig, bitte!**	***Be quiet,*** *please!*
Halten Sie* es *fest!	***Hold*** *it* ***tight!***

Note that in the imperative forms the **du**, **ihr**, and **Sie** are left out, just as the "you" is omitted in English.

(d) a first- or third-person imperative in the subjunctive present tense

***Es lebe* die Freiheit!**	***May** freedom **live! Long live** freedom!*
Gehen wir!	***Let's go!***
***Besuchen wir* ihn morgen!**	***Let's visit** him tomorrow!*

(e) the present infinitive (for the general public, not addressed to a specific person)

***Einsteigen* bitte!**	***Get in (on)**, please!*
Ruhig *bleiben!*	***Keep** quiet!*
Nicht *rauchen* bitte!	*No **smoking**, please.*

(f) the past participle (for a quick response; a stronger emphasis common to the military)

***Aufgepaßt*!**	***Watch out!***
***Stillgestanden*!**	***Stand still!***

Give the meaning of the indicated verbs as well as the sentence.

	1. Du **liest** das Buch nicht.
1. You *are* not *reading* the book.	**2.** **Lies** das Buch!
2. *Read* the book!	**3.** **schauen** = *to look* **anschauen** = *to look at* Du **schaust** Roswitha **an.**
3. You *are looking at* Roswitha.	**4.** **Schau** Irene nicht so **an!**
4. *Don't look at* Irene that way.	**5.** Ihr **schlaft** zuviel.
5. You *sleep* too much.	**6.** **Schlaft** nicht soviel!
6. *Don't sleep* so much!	**7.** Warum **fahrt** ihr nicht morgen nach Hamburg **zurück**?
7. Why *don't* you *go back* (*are . . . going back*) to Hamburg tomorrow?	**8.** Ja, **fahrt** morgen nach Hamburg zurück!
8. Yes, *go back* to Hamburg tomorrow!	**9.** **Verstehen** Sie mich?
9. *Do* you *understand* me?	**10.** **Verstehen** Sie mich, bitte!
10. Please, *understand* me!	**11.** Sie **sind** ein dummer Kerl!

11. You *are* a stupid fellow!	**12.** **Seien** Sie nicht so dumm!
12. *Don't be* so stupid!	**13.** **umsteigen** = *to transfer, to change* Sie **müssen** hier **umsteigen.**
13. You *must transfer* here (from one streetcar, bus, train, etc., to another).	**14.** **Umsteigen!**
14. *Transfer* (cars, trains, buses, etc.)!	**15.** **aussteigen** = *to climb out, to get out* **Wollen** wir hier **aussteigen?**
15. Do we *want to get out* here?	**16.** **Aussteigen**, bitte!
16. *Get out,* please!	**17.** Hilda **ist** um sechs Uhr **aufgestanden.**
17. Hilda *got up* at six o'clock.	**18.** **Aufgestanden!**
18. *Get up!*	**19.** **stillhalten** = *to keep quiet, to hold still* **den Mund halten** = *to hold one's tongue* **Kann** er den Mund überhaupt nicht **halten?**
19. *Can*'t he *hold* his tongue at all?	**20.** Jetzt aber **stillgehalten!**
20. Now *hold still!*	**21.** Der König **lebt** sehr lange, nicht wahr?
21. The king *is living* a very long time, isn't he?	**22.** **Es lebe** der König!
22. *Long live* the king!	**23.** Gott **ist** mit uns.
23. God *is* with us.	**24.** Gott **sei** mit euch!
24. God *be* with you!	**25.** **der Heiland** = *savior* **Denke** nur niemand, daß man auf ihn als den Heiland **gewartet habe.** (Goethe)
25. *Let* no one *think* that one *has waited* for him as the savior!	**26.** Niemand **sage,** wenn er versucht wird, daß er von Gott **versucht werde.** (Bibel)
26. *Let* no one *say,* if he is tempted, that he *is tempted* by God.	**27.** Und Gott sprach: **Lasset** uns Menschen machen, ein Bild, das uns gleich **sei.** (Bibel)
27. And God spoke, *let* us make man in our own image (an image that *is* like [unto] ourselves).	**28.** **fruchtbar** = *fruitful* **sich mehren** = *to multiply, to increase* **Seid** fruchtbar und **mehret euch** und **füllet** die Erde. (Bibel)

28. *Be* fruitful and *multiply* and *fill* the earth.	**29.** **die Ameise** = *ant* **faul** = *lazy* **Gehe** hin zur Ameise, du Fauler; **siehe** ihre Weise **an** und **lerne**. (Bibel)
29. *Go* to the ant, thou sluggard; *watch* the way it does things and *learn* from it.	

PROGRESS TEST

Choose the correct meaning for the indicated verb.

1. **Sei** Er doch gut zu mir!
(a) is (b) be

2. **Seid** ihr alle hier?
(a) are (b) be

3. **Empfange** ihn mit offenen Armen!
(a) receives (b) receive

4. Bitte, die Fenster **schließen!**
(a) shut (b) are shutting

5. Jetzt aber langsam **gefahren!**
(a) go (b) gone

Answer key: **1.** (b); **2.** (a); **3.** (b); **4.** (a); **5.** (a).

80. *The uses of* werden

1. The general uses and meanings of the verb **werden** in both the active and passive voice in the indicative mood may be summarized as follows:

(a) **werden** + adjective or noun = *to become, to get*

Er *wird* Arzt.	*He is **becoming** (**is going to be**) a doctor.*
Sie *wurden* alt.	*They (you) **were getting** old.* *They (you) **got** old.*
Wie groß *ist* er *geworden*?	*How tall **has** he **gotten** (**did** he **get**)?*

(b) **werden** + infinitive(s) = future, or probability in the present

Wir *werden* ihn nächste Woche *sehen*.	*We **will see** him next week.*
Du *wirst* ihn nicht *kommen hören*.	*You **will** not **hear** him **come**.*
Er *wird* wohl jetzt *schlafen*.	*He **is** probably **sleeping** now.*

(c) **werden** + perfect participle (perfect infinitive) = future perfect, or probability in the past

Bis morgen *werde* ich zehn Seiten *gelesen haben*.	*I **will have read** ten pages by tomorrow.*
Sie *wird* das Buch wahrscheinlich schon *gelesen haben*.	*She **has** probably **read** the book already.*

(d) **werden** + past participle = passive: present or past

Was *wird gesagt?*	*What is **being said?***
Das Buch *wurde* 1960 *geschrieben*.	*The book **was written** in 1960.*

(e) **werden** + passive infinitive(s) = future passive

Das Auto *wird repariert werden*.	*The car **will be repaired**.*
Das Auto *wird repariert werden müssen*.	*The car **will have to be repaired**.*

(f) **worden** (*been*) = passive; in the perfect tenses

Das Schiff *ist gesehen worden*.	*The ship **has been seen** (**was seen**).*
Das Schiff *war gesehen worden*.	*The ship **had been seen**.*
Das Schiff *muß gesehen worden sein*.	*The ship **must have been seen**.*

2. The general uses and meanings of the verb **werden** in the active and passive voice of the subjunctive mood may be summarized as follows:

(a) Subjunctive of **werden** + adjective or noun = *would become, would get, would have become, was getting,* etc.

Er sagte, er *werde* dick.	*He said he **was getting** fat.*
Er *würde* Arzt, wenn er genug Geld hätte.	*He **would become** a doctor if he had enough money.*
Er *wäre* dick *geworden*, wenn er immer Kartoffeln mit Butter gegessen hätte.	*He **would have gotten** fat if he had always eaten potatoes with butter.*

(b) **würden** + infinitive(s) = subjunctive: present or future meaning

Wir *würden gehen*, wenn wir Zeit hätten.	*We **would go** if we had the time.*
Evelyn sagte, sie *würde* es mir morgen *geben können*.	*Evelyn said she **would be able to give** it to me tomorrow.*

(c) **würden** + perfect participle (perfect infinitive) = subjunctive past meaning

Alban *würde* den Mantel (wohl) *gekauft* hätte er das nötige Geld gehabt.	*Alban (probably) **would have boughthaben,** the coat, if he had had the necessary money.*

(d) subjunctive of **werden** + past participle = passive subjunctive: present meaning

Arnold fragte, was für ein Unsinn hier *getrieben werde*.	*Arnold asked what nonsense **was going on** here. (. . . what kind of nonsense **was being done** here.)*

(e) **worden** = passive subjunctive: past meaning

Agnes fragte, wann das Haus *zerstört worden sei*.	*Agnes asked when the house **had been destroyed.***
Wenn das Hotel nur *gebaut worden wäre!*	*If the hotel **had** only **been built!***

The following frames review only the general uses and meaning of **werden.** *If more detailed study is needed or desired, review those grammar sections which discuss the conjugation and meaning of verbs.*

	1. **schlank** = *thin* Er **wird** schlank, wenn er Zigaretten raucht.
1. He *will get* thin if he smokes cigarettes. (Or: He gets thin when he smokes cigarettes.)	**2.** Er **wurde** wieder jung, als er das hübsche Mädchen sah.
2. When he saw the pretty girl he *became* young again.	**3.** **Wird** man schlank **bleiben,** wenn man immer Zigaretten raucht?
3. *Will* you *stay* thin if you always smoke cigarettes?	**4.** Ich **werde** d e m Dummkopf immer **helfen müssen.**
4. I *will* always *have to help* that blockhead.	**5.** Wie klug er **geworden ist!**
5. How smart he *has become!*	**6.** Gretel **wird** wohl zu Hause **geblieben sein.**
6. Gretel probably *stayed* at home.	**7.** **Wird** sie das Auto schon **gekauft haben,** bevor ich sie warnen kann?

7. *Will* she already *have bought* the car before I am able to warn her?	**8.** Der alten Frau **wurde geholfen.**
8. The old woman *was helped.*	**9.** **heute abend** = *this evening* Es **wird** heute abend **gesungen.**
9. There *will be singing* this evening.	**10.** Das Fenster **wird geöffnet werden müssen.**
10. The window *will have to be opened.*	**11.** Der Brief **hat geschrieben werden müssen.**
11. The letter *has had to be written* (*had to be written*).	**12.** Hier **ist** viel **getrunken worden.**
12. A lot of *drinking went on* here.	**13.** Man konnte sehen, daß hier viel **getrunken worden war.**
13. One could see that people had done a lot of *drinking* here.	**14.** Mein Freund **würde** mir gerne **helfen**, wenn er nur wüßte, wie.
14. My friend *would* like *to help* me if he only knew how.	**15.** Sie wollte wissen, ob Berlin von Bomben **zerstört worden sei.**
15. She wanted to know if Berlin *had been destroyed* by bombs.	**16.** **längst** = *long ago* Das Haus **hätte** längst **zerstört werden sollen.**
16. The house *should have been destroyed* long ago.	**17.** **genügen** = *to suffice* Spengler **würde** es immer wieder **sagen**, daß der Mensch ein Raubtier sei, aber einmal genügt.
17. Spengler *would say* over and over again that man is a predator, but once is enough.	**18.** **fehlen** = *to lack* **mir fehlt etwas** = *I am lacking something* Ich **würde** meinen Freund **besuchen können,** fehlte mir nicht die Zeit und das Geld dazu.
18. I *would be able to visit* my friend if I did not lack the time and the money. (Note: **könnte besuchen** has the same meaning as **würde besuchen können**.)	**19.** Wenn unser Haus nur nicht durch Feuer **zerstört worden wäre!**
19. If only our house *had* not *been destroyed* by fire!	

READING PREPARATION

Rudolf Walter Leonhardt was a longtime German journalist and commentator of the German scene. In this passage he gives not only his assessment of some Germans as they were in the 1960s but also an insight into how an intelligent, observant German can both see the foibles of his countrymen and still possibly love his people and his country.

	1. **x-mal** = *any number of times, at any moment* Unser letztes Lesestück stammt aus Rudolf Walter Leonhardts *X-mal Deutschland.*
1. Our final reading passage comes from Rudolf Walter Leonhardt's book *X-mal Deutschland.* (The English title is *This Germany.*)	**2.** In seinem Buch versuchte Leonhardt das Deutschland der sechziger Jahren zu beschreiben.
2. Leonhardt tried to describe the Germany of the sixties in his book.	**3.** Leonhardt ist ein bekannter deutscher Journalist, der schon **einige** Bücher über andere Länder geschrieben hat. (*a few/own*)
3. Leonhardt is a well-known German journalist who has already written *a few* books about other countries.	**4.** Jetzt versucht er, als Deutscher über sein **eigenes** Land zu schreiben. (*several/own*)
4. Now, as a German, he is trying to write about his *own* country.	**5.** **unter anderem** = *among other things* Unter anderem beschreibt er seine **Unterhaltungen** mit Studenten aus anderen Ländern. (*conversations/fights*)
5. Among other things he describes his *conversations* with students from other countries.	**6.** **Eine** von ihnen fragte, ob er es eigentlich schön finde, Deutscher zu sein. (*a girl/a boy*)
6. *a girl:* the **-e** shows this. One of them, a girl, asked whether he really liked being a German.	**7.** Unser Lesestück ist ein Teil **seiner** Antwort auf diese Frage. (*his/of his*)
7. Our reading passage is a part *of his* answer to this question.	**8.** **gestehen** = *to confess* Leonhardt gesteht, daß er Deutschland und die Deutschen liebt, aber nicht nur **die** im Westen, sondern auch **die** im Osten. (*whom/the/those*)
8. Leonhardt confesses that he loves Germany and the Germans, but not only *those* in the West but also *those* in the East.	**9.** **zuweilen** = *at times, now and then, occasionally* Leonhardt schreibt, diese Liebe **sei** zuweilen eine schmerzliche Liebe.
9. Leonhardt writes that this love *is* occasionally a painful love.	**10.** **trotz** = *in spite of* **der Trotz** = *defiance, obstinacy* Zuweilen ist sie eine schmerzliche Liebe, und es ist viel Trotz **dabei.** (*thereby/along with it*)
10. Now and then it is a painful love, and there is a lot of defiance *along with it.*	**11.** Warum ist diese Liebe zuweilen schmerzlich, und warum ist viel Trotz dabei?

11. Why is this love at times painful, and why is there a lot of defiance along with it?	**12.** **richten** = *to judge* **der Richter** = _______
12. *the judge*	**13.** Trotz den deutschen Politikern, Richtern und Parteifunktionären in der DDR . . .
13. In spite of the German politicians, judges, and party functionaries in the GDR (German Democratic Republic) . . . (Note that Leonhardt uses the dative case with **trotz**, instead of the normal genitive.)	**14.** Trotz den Parteifunktionären in der DDR, **deren** Haß gegen die Deutsche Bundesrepublik ein deutscher Haß ist . . .
14. In spite of the party functionaries in the GDR *whose* hate towards the German Federal Republic is a German hate . . .	**15.** Und trotz manchem, was in der Bundesrepublik hassenswert **sein möge** . . . (*may be/could be*)
15. And in spite of much in the Federal Republic that *may be* worthy of hate . . .	**16.** **verleugnen** = *to deny* Die deutsche **Vergangenheit** kann man nicht verleugnen. (*past/present/future*)
16. We cannot deny Germany's *past.*	**17.** Trotz der deutschen Vergangenheit, die wir ja nicht **einfach** verleugnen können . . . (*simple/simply*)
17. In spite of Germany's past, which we *simply* cannot deny . . .	**18.** **offenbar** = *obviously, evidently* Offenbar haben **manche** Deutsche nichts aus der Vergangenheit gelernt. (*many a/some*)
18. Evidently *some* Germans have learned nothing from the past.	**19.** Und trotz **den** Leuten, die aus der Vergangenheit offenbar nichts gelernt haben . . . (*the/those*)
19. And in spite of *those* people who evidently have learned nothing from the past . . .	**20.** Zuweilen gibt es Deutsche, die offenbar nichts aus der Vergangenheit gelernt haben.
20. Occasionally there are Germans who evidently have learned nothing from the past.	**21.** **gering** = *small, petty, inferior* **schätzen** = *to value, to esteem* **die Geringschätzung** = *contempt, disdain, scorn* **geringschätzen** = __________
21. *to despise, to scorn*	**22.** Manche können das **gar nicht** geringschätzen. (*not often/not at all*)
22. Some can*not* despise that *at all.*	**23.** Manche könnten das **gar nicht geringer schätzen.**

23. Some could *not despise* that *more.*	**24.** Es gibt Deutsche, die alles Deutsche **gar nicht geringer schätzen könnten . . .**
24. There are Germans who *could not despise* all that is German *more . . .*	**25.** **allgemein** = *general* **schön allgemein** = *nice and general* . . . solange die **Geringschätzung** nur schön allgemein und abstrakt bleibt. (*contempt/appreciation*)
25. . . . as long as the *contempt* remains nice and general and abstract.	**26.** Ihr fragt, ob die Geringschätzung irgendeinen Wert **habe**?
26. You ask whether that contempt *has* any value?	**27.** Wie wollen die gleichen Deutschen ihre **eigene** kleine Welt sehen?
27. How do the same Germans want to see their *own* small world?	**28.** Rot, braun, grün, blau, orange, gelb und purpur sind Farben. (**Die Farbe** probably means __________)
28. *color* Red, brown, green, blue, orange, yellow, and purple are colors.	**29.** Wollen die gleichen Deutschen ihre eigene kleine Welt nicht anders als in den **allerfreundlichsten** Farben sehen? (*most hateful/most friendly*)
29. Do the same Germans want to see their own small world in nothing but (not other than) the *friendliest* (*most friendly*) colors?	**30.** Ihre eigene kleine Welt, die sie in den allerfreundlichsten Farben **sehen wollen**, . . .
30. Their own small world which they *want to see* in the friendliest colors . . .	**31.** . . . ist ihre Stadt, ihr **Beruf**, ihre Partei, sie selber. (*occupation/church*)
31. . . . is their city, their *occupation,* their party, and themselves.	**32.** **der Kalte Krieg** = *the Cold War* **der Krieger** = *warrior* Wir Soldaten des Zweiten Weltkrieges haben **die Kalten Krieger** vermißt. (*the cold warriors/the Cold War warriors*)
32. We soldiers of the Second World War have missed *the Cold War warriors.* (Note: **die kalten Krieger** = *the cold warriors*)	**33.** Wir haben die Kalten Krieger vermißt, als der Krieg heiß **wurde**.
33. We missed the Cold War warriors when the war *became* hot.	**34.** Schon beim letzten Male haben wir sie vermißt, als der Krieg heiß wurde.
34. We missed them the last time when the war became hot.	**35.** **preisen** = *to praise, to extol, to glorify* Was preisen uns die deutschen Pseudo-Patrioten?
35. What do Germany's pseudo-patriots extol to us?	**36.** **äußerst** = *extreme* Sie preisen uns „äußerste Härte." (*severity/softness*)

36. They extol extreme frugality (*severity* in economic matters).	**37.** **wieder einmal** = *once again* Die deutschen Pseudo-Patrioten, die uns öffentlich wieder einmal „äußerste Härte" preisen . . .
37. Germany's pseudo-patriots who once again *openly* praise extreme frugality to us . . .	**38.** **der Grund** = *ground, soil* **der Besitz** = *possession* **der Grundbesitz** = *real estate* . . . haben *privatissime* Grundbesitz in Irland. (*openly/secretively*)
38. . . . *secretly* have real estate in Ireland.	**39.** **das Bankkonto** = *bank account* **Die** haben *privatissime* Grundbesitz in Irland und ein Bankkonto in der Schweiz. (*who/they/she*)
39. *They* secretly have real estate in Ireland and a bank account in Switzerland.	**40.** Trotz den deutschen Pseudo-Patrioten, die uns öffentlich wieder einmal „äußerste Härte" preisen . . .
40. In spite of Germany's pseudo-patriots, who once again extol extreme frugality to us in public . . .	**41.** . . . **während** sie *privatissime* Grundbesitz in Irland und ein Bankkonto in der Schweiz haben. (*while/during*)
41. . . . *while* they secretly have real estate in Ireland and a bank account in Switzerland.	**42.** **die Vernunft** = *reason, common sense* **der Grund** = *argument, reason* **der Vernunftgrund** = __________
42. *argument based on reason, sensible reason*	**43.** **dennoch** = *yet* Für so viel Trotz und dennoch Liebe **gebe es** keine Vernunftgründe, meint Leonhardt.
43. Leonhardt feels that *there are* no sensible reasons for so much defiance and yet love.	**44.** Sind die Provinz-Europäer und die **Halbgroß-**Industriellen wirklich liebenswert? (*half-big/pseudo-big*)
44. Are the provincial Europeans and the *pseudo-big* industrialists really likable?	**45.** Die Halbgroß-Industriellen sitzen in **irgendeinem** Schweizer Hotel.
45. The pseudo-big industrialists sit in *some* Swiss hotel.	**46.** **brüllen** = *to bellow, to roar* In irgendeinem Schweizer Hotel **brüllen** sie „das Personal" **an**.
46. In some Swiss hotel they *bellow at* the personnel.	**47.** **greifen** = *to grasp, to catch* **begreifen** = *to understand, to comprehend* Sie können sich selber nur als Mittelpunkt begreifen und brüllen „das Personal" an.
47. They can only understand themselves as the center of attention and they roar at the personnel.	**48.** Sie können „das Personal" nur als **etwas Anzubrüllendes** begreifen.

48. They can see the personnel only as *something to bellow at.*	**49.** If **Nachteil** = *disadvantage* then **Vorteil** = __________
49. *advantage*	**50.** **wahrnehmen** = *to perceive, to notice, to observe* **einen Vorteil wahrnehmen** = __________
50. *to look after one's own interests*	**51.** **der Held** = *hero, champion* Die **Auto-Helden** nehmen jeden Vorteil wahr.
51. The *car supermen* look after their own interests every time.	**52.** **fahren** = *to drive* **die Bahn** = *the road, path* **wechseln** = *to change* **fahrbahnwechselnd** = __________
52. *changing lanes*	**53.** **der Rücken** = *back* **die Sicht** = *view* **die Rücksicht** = *consideration, respect, regard* **rücksichtslos** = __________
53. *inconsiderate, without regard*	**54.** **dauernd** = *continually* Die Auto-Helden, die dauernd fahrbahnwechselnd rücksichtslos jeden Vorteil wahrnehmen . . .
54. The car supermen, who continually change lanes and who inconsiderately look out for their own interests . . .	**55.** **großartig** = *great* Diese rücksichtslosen Auto-Helden **kommen sich dabei** großartig **vor.**
55. These inconsiderate car supermen *think they are* great (*think themselves* great).	**56.** **der Mut** = *courage, boldness* **mutig** = *courageous, brave* Sind die **Pseudo-Mutigen** wirklich liebenswert?
56. Are people who are *pseudo-brave* really likable?	**57.** **empor** = *up, upwards* **wachsen** = *to grow* **emporwachsen** = *to grow upwards* Die Pseudo-Mutigen wachsen empor.
57. People who are pseudo-brave grow upwards.	**58.** **überhöht** = *excessive* Sie wachsen zu überhöhter Arroganz empor.
58. They grow upwards to excessive heights of arrogance.	**59.** **ducken** = *to cringe, to cower, to duck* **geduckt** = *cringing, cowering* Aus geducker **Haltung** wachsen sie zu überhöhter Arroganz empor.
59. From a cringing *position* they grow to excessive heights of arrogance.	**60.** Sie wachsen zu überhöhter Arroganz empor, wo sie sicher sind . . .

60. They grow to excessive heights of arrogance where they are sure . . .	**61.** . . . daß ihnen niemand auf die Finger **klopfen** wird. (*rap/clop*)
61. . . . that nobody is going to *rap* their knuckles.	**62.** Die Freiheitsapostel halten sich für **unfehlbar**. (*fallible/infallible*)
62. The apostles of freedom consider themselves *infallible.*	**63.** Die **selbstgerechten** Freiheitsapostel, die sich für unfehlbar halten . . . (*self-deprecating/self-righteous*)
63. The *self-righteous* apostles of freedom, who consider themselves infallible . . .	**64.** **gönnen** = *to grant* Wollen die selbstgerechten Freiheitsapostel niemandem Freiheit gönnen?
64. Don't the self-righteous apostles of freedom want to grant anyone freedom?	**65.** Sie wollen niemandem die wichtigste **aller** menschlichen Freiheiten gönnen.
65. They do not want to grant anyone the most important *of all* human freedoms.	**66.** **sich irren** = *to err, to go astray* Die wichtigste Freiheit, die sie niemandem gönnen wollen, ist die Freiheit, sich zu irren.
66. The most important freedom, which they do not want to grant to anyone, is the freedom to err.	**67.** Sind denn diese Provinz-Europäer und Halbgroß-Industriellen, diese Auto-Helden, Pseudo-Mutigen und Freiheitsapostel wirklich alle liebenswert?
67. Are all these provincial Europeans and pseudo-big industrialists, these car supermen, pseudo-brave people and apostles of freedom really likable?	**68.** Sind denn diese Politiker, Richter, Parteifunktionäre, Kalten Krieger und Pseudo-Patrioten wirklich alle liebenswert?
68. Are all these politicians, judges, party functionaries, Cold War warriors, and pseudo-patriots really likable?	**69.** **je nun** = *well now, well really, well* Je nun . . .
69. Well now . . .	

PROGRESS TEST

Choose the sentence that comes closer to the meaning of the German than any of the others.

1. Zuweilen wollen wir unsere Vergangenheit einfach verleugnen: offenbar liegt noch viel Trotz in unserer Seele.
   (a) We always want to lie about the past because we are rebellious souls at heart.
   (b) Defiant souls occasionally like to stir up the past.
   (c) There is apparently no defiance in our souls, only questions about the present state of affairs.
   (d) When we deny the past it is probably because we have rebellious souls.

2. Einige Deutsche schätzen alles Deutsche gering, solange die Geringschätzung schön allgemein und abstrakt bleibt.
(a) Some Germans practice contempt only in generalities.
(b) Germans are their own best critics.
(c) All things German do not deserve our contempt.
(d) Most Germans are very outspoken about those things they do not like.

3. Leute, die *privatissime* ein Bankkonto in der Schweiz und Grundbesitz in Irland haben, preisen immer noch „äußerste Härte".
(a) One should still praise people for their extreme frugality even though they secretly have a bank account in Switzerland and real estate in Ireland.
(b) Extreme frugality is a virtue which is still praised by those who secretly have a bank account and real estate.
(c) Extreme frugality leads us to have secret bank accounts in Switzerland and secret real estate in Ireland.
(d) People who secretly have a bank account in Switzerland and real estate in Ireland still consider themselves good examples of extreme frugality.

4. Geringer schätzen könnten wir diese schmerzliche Liebe, wenn Barbara hassenswert wäre.
(a) Painful love causes despair.
(b) We could despise Barbara more if only she were not so hateful.
(c) We could look on this love with greater contempt if Barbara were a less likable person.
(d) Love and hate may coexist in the same individual.

5. Fahrbahnwechselnd brüllte der Auto-Held rücksichtslos alle anderen Fahrer an.
(a) The car-superman bellows at other drivers because they are inconsiderate.
(b) Inconsiderate drivers are those who bellow at others because they continuously weave back and forth.
(c) All other drivers were inconsiderately yelled at by the car-superman as he continually switched lanes.
(d) Changing lanes, the car-superman bellowed at the other inconsiderate drivers.

6. Wir sollten den Pseudo-Mutigen ihre überhöhte Arroganz gönnen, denn sie irren sich genauso wie alle anderen Menschen.
(a) The pseudo-brave are in danger of becoming arrogant.
(b) The pseudo-courageous err just like everyone else and therefore we should grant them their excessive arrogance.
(c) Although the pseudo-brave err as do all others, we will not grant them excessive arrogance.
(d) Excessive arrogance is a virtue possessed only by those who do not grant the right to err.

Answer key: **1.** (d); **2.** (a); **3.** (b); **4.** (c); **5.** (c); **6.** (b).

Before proceeding to the reading passage, review those items which you have circled in the reading preparation frames.

R. Piper & Co.Verlag, Munchen, 1964.

Rudolf Walter Leonhardt: X-mal Deutschland

Ja, ich liebe dieses Deutschland, das ganze Deutschland, und ich liebe die Deutschen, die in Dresden wie die in Hamburg. Das ist eine zuweilen schmerzliche Liebe, und es ist viel Trotz dabei: trotz den deutschen Politikern, Richtern, Parteifunktionären in der DDR, deren Haß gegen die Deutsche Bundesrepublik ein deutscher Haß ist—und trotz manchem, was in der Bundesrepublik hassenswert sein mag: trotz der deutschen Vergangenheit, die wir ja nicht einfach verleugnen können—und trotz den Leuten, die aus dieser Vergangenheit offenbar nichts gelernt haben: trotz den Deutschen, die alles Deutsche gar nicht geringer schätzen könnten, solange die Geringschätzung nur schön allgemein und abstrakt bleibt, und trotz den gleichen Deutschen, die ihre eigene kleine Welt (ihre Stadt, ihren Beruf, ihre Partei, sich selber) nicht anders als in den allerfreundlichsten Farben sehen wollen: trotz den Kalten Kriegern, die wir Soldaten des Zweiten Weltkrieges schon beim letzten Male vermißt haben, als der Krieg heiß wurde; trotz den deutschen Pseudo-Patrioten, die uns öffentlich wieder einmal „äußerste Härte" preisen, während sie *privatissime* Grundbesitz in Irland und ein Bankkonto in der Schweiz haben. . . .

Und warum so viel Trotz? Und warum dennoch Liebe? Dafür gibt es keine Vernunftgründe. . . .

Sind sie denn wirklich liebenswert: die Provinz-Europäer und Halbgroß-Industriellen, die in irgendeinem Schweizer Hotel sich selber nur als Mittelpunkt und „das Personal" nur als etwas Anzubrüllendes begreifen können? die Auto-Helden, die dauernd fahrbahnwechselnd rücksichtslos jeden Vorteil wahrnehmen und sich dabei großartig vorkommen? die Pseudo-Mutigen, die aus geduckter Haltung zu überhöhter Arroganz emporwachsen, wo sie sicher sind, daß ihnen niemand auf die Finger klopft? die selbstgerechten Freiheitsapostel, die sich selber für unfehlbar halten und die wichtigste aller menschlichen Freiheiten niemandem gönnen wollen: die Freiheit sich zu irren? Sind sie denn wirklich alle, alle liebenswert? Je nun . . .

Appendices

1. *Glossary of grammatical terms*
2. *Pronunciation guide*
3. *Numerals*

1. GLOSSARY OF GRAMMATICAL TERMS

Accusative case The form of the noun, pronoun, article, or adjective when used as a direct object, or when used with certain prepositions:

Sie ißt *den roten Apfel*.	She eats *the red apple*.
Sie geht ohne *ihn*.	She goes without *him*.

Active voice *see* Voice.

Adjective A word that typically limits, qualifies, or describes a noun:

Das Wetter wird *schlecht*.	The weather's getting *bad*.
ein *großer* Hund	a *big* dog

Sometimes the definite and indefinite articles, the **der** and **ein** words and **alle** are grouped under the term "limiting adjective." The term "descriptive adjective" would then necessarily encompass all other adjectives.

Adverb A word that modifies a verb, an adjective, or another adverb:

Sie spricht *sehr schnell*.	She speaks *very quickly*.

Antecedent The word, phrase, or clause to which a pronoun refers:

Ich sah den *Mann*. Er war alt.	I saw the *man*. He was old.
Das ist der *Mann*, den ich kenne.	That's the *man* I know.

Auxiliary verb A verb that helps form a compound tense (**haben, sein,** and **werden**):

Er *hatte* es getrunken.	He *had* drunk it.
Ich *bin* in die Stadt gegangen.	I *have* gone to town.
Sie *wird* bestimmt kommen.	She *will* certainly come.

Also, a verb accompanied by a dependent infinitive: the model auxiliaries:

Ich *mag* nicht kochen. — I *don't like* to cook.

Case The form of the noun, pronoun, article, or adjective that indicates its function or its relationship to other words in a given phrase or clause. There are four cases in German: the nominative, the genitive, the dative, and the accusative.

Clause A group of words that contains both a subject and predicate (i.e., verb).

Conjugate To give the various tenses, numbers, persons, voices, moods of a verb. The present tense conjugation of the indicative mood of the verb *to see* is: *I see; you see; he, she, it sees; we see; you see; they see.*

Conjunction A word used to link together words or phrases:

Hans *und* Sigrid gingen in die Oper, *aber* sie hatten ihre Karten vergessen. — *Hans* ***and*** *Sigrid went to the opera,* ***but*** *they had forgotten their tickets.*

Dative case The form of the noun, pronoun, or adjective when used as an indirect object and with certain prepositions, verbs, adjectives, and expressions:

Gehst du mit *ihm*? — Are you going with *him*?
Das ist *mir* schwer. — That is difficult for *me.*
Sie gibt *ihnen* das Buch. — She is giving *them* the book.

Decline To give the various forms of nouns, articles, pronouns, and adjectives indicating gender, number, and case. The noun **Mann** is declined:

der Mann, des Mannes, dem Manne, den Mann
die Männer, der Männer, den Männern, die Männer

Definite articles In German, the forms of **der, die, das:** in English, *the.*

Dependent word order The word order used in dependent (subordinate) clauses. The verb with the personal ending is generally the last element:

Sie blieb zu Hause, weil sie eine kranke Mutter *hatte*. — She remained at home, because her mother was sick (because she *had* a sick mother).

Der words Words declined like the definite article: **dieser, jeder, jener, mancher, solcher, welcher.**

Gender Any set of categories into which words are divided and which determine agreement with modifiers, referents, or grammatical forms. In German a noun may be masculine, feminine, or neuter:

***der* Mann** (m.), ***die* Frau** (f.), ***das* Kind** (n.)	the man, the woman, the child

Genitive case The form of a noun, pronoun, article, or adjective that indicates possession or relationship. Certain prepositions, verbs, adjectives, and expressions that do not necessarily indicate possession also take the genitive case.

der Bruder *des Mädchens*	the brother *of the girl*
Wegen *des schlechten Wetters*, blieb er zu Hause.	He stayed at home *on account of the bad weather.*
Ich fahre *zweiter Klasse*.	I travel *second class.*

Imperative A form of the verb expressing a command or request:

***Sprich* langsamer!**	*Speak* more slowly!

Indefinite article In German, the forms of **ein, eine, ein;** in English, *a* and *an*.

Indicative mood The mode of expression which deals with reality or fact:

Deutsch *ist* eine schwere Sprache.	German *is* a difficult language.

Infinitive The base form of the verb that expresses the general meaning but does not identify the time or the performer of the action. In German the infinitive is identified by the endings **-en** or **-n**:

singen	*to sing*
erinnern	*to remind*

This is the form used to list a verb in the dictionary, and it is hence also called the citation form.

Infinitive stem That part of an infinitive that remains after it has been shorn of its endings: **leben** (*to live*), **leb-**.

Irregular weak verb A verb that in the past tense and the past participle takes the vowel change of the strong verb and the endings of the weak verb:

bringen, brachte, gebracht	to bring, brought, brought

Modal auxiliaries Verbs that express attitudes of permission, ability, possibility, necessity, obligation, intention. The modals in German are: **dürfen, können, mögen, müssen, sollen, wollen.**

Mood The point of view from which the action is seen: statements of actuality or fact (indicative); statements of conditional actuality, of possibility, of doubt (subjunctive); statements of necessity (imperative).

Nominative case The case of nouns, pronouns, articles, adjectives, and predicate nouns that are the subject of the verb:

Der Student* da drüben ist *mein bester Freund.	*That student* over there is *my best friend.*
Sie* ist *meine beste Freundin.	*She* is *my best friend.*

Number The form of the noun, pronoun, adjective, or verb which indicates how many persons or things are referred to:

Die alte Katze bleibt hier.	The old cat remains here.
Die alten Katzen bleiben hier.	The old cats remain here.
Sie hat kein Geld.	She has no money.

Object The word that receives the action of a verb, either directly or indirectly:

Hans sieht seine *Frau.*	Hans sees his *wife* (direct object).
Nachher gibt er *ihr* einen Kuß.	Afterwards he gives *her* a kiss (indirect object).

The noun or pronoun that is governed by the preposition:

Ich gehe mit *ihm.*	I am going with *him.*
Er geht ohne *sie.*	He is going without *her.*

See also Genitive case, Dative case, and Accusative case.

Participle A form of the verb that may be used as a verb, as part of a compound tense, as an adjective or adverb. There are two, the present and the past:

(**past**) ***Gesagt, getan.***	No sooner *said* than *done.*
(**past**) **Hat Maria ihn schon *gesehen*?**	Has Maria *seen* him already?
(**present**) ***Singend* stand er da.**	He stood there *singing.*
(**present**) **Der *herlaufende* Mensch . . .**	The man *running* towards us . . .
(**past**) **Er kam *gelaufen.***	He came *running.*

Passive voice *See* Voice.

Person The form of the pronoun or verb that indicates whether the subject is the speaker (first person), the person spoken to (second person), or the person of whom one is speaking (third person). All nouns are third person:

ich **bin;** ***wir*** **sind**—*I* am, *we* are (first person)
du **bist;** ***ihr*** **seid;** ***Sie*** **sind**—*you* are (second person)
er, sie, es **ist;** ***sie*** **sind**—*he, she, it* is; *they* are (third person).
Der ***Vater*** **sucht seinen** ***Sohn.***—The *father* is looking for his *son.* (Both nouns are third person.)

Preposition A word that relates a noun or pronoun in time, position, manner, or direction to other elements in a clause:

Er geht ***vor*** **die Klasse.** He goes *to the front of* the class.

Pronoun A word that stands in place of a noun:

Klaus hat seine Uhr vergessen. ***Er*** **hat** ***sie*** **vergessen.** Klaus forgot his watch. *He* forgot *it.*

Relative pronoun A pronoun that joins two clauses and has its noun antecedent in the preceding clause:

Das Mädchen, mit ***dem*** **er befreundet ist, ist hübsch.** The girl with *whom* he is friends is pretty.

Strong verb or irregular verb A verb that changes its stem vowel when going from the present tense to the past tense:

er ***findet,*** **er** ***fand*** he *finds,* he *found*

The past participle ends in **-(e)n: gefunden**—*found.*

Subjunctive mood The mode of expression that deals with conditions contrary to fact, unlikely, uncertain, hypothetical, wishes, doubts, possibilities, indirect discourse:

Wenn ich sie geliebt ***hätte, hätte*** **ich sie geheiratet.** If I *had* loved her, I *would have* married her.
Möchten **Sie ins Kino gehen?** *Would* you like to go to the movies?

Tense The form of the verb that indicates the time of the action or state of being, such as past, present, or future.

Verb A word that expresses action or state of being:

Das Wetter ***war*** **elend.** The weather *was* wretched.
Sie ***haben*** **sich** ***erkältet.*** They *caught* (*have caught*) cold.

Voice The form of the verb that indicates whether the subject acts (active voice) or is acted upon (passive voice):

Active: **Wolfgang *fängt* den Ball.**	Wolfgang *catches* the ball.
Passive: **Der Ball *wird* von Wolfgang *gefangen*.**	The ball *is (being) caught* by Wolfgang.

Weak verb or regular verb A verb that shows the change from present to past tense by its ending, rather than by a vowel change. In German a **-t-** or **-et-** is added to the stem:

er *sagt*, er *sag-t-e*	he *says*, he *said*
er beantwortet, er beantwort-et-e	he *answers*, he *aswered*

The past participle ends in **-t** or **-et: gesagt** = *said*; **beantwortet** = *answered*.

2. PRONUNCIATION GUIDE

The following guide to the pronunciation of German can only give you the approximate sounds of the language. Pronunciation of German will vary among different areas of Germany, Austria, and Switzerland, even as the pronunciation of English will vary within Great Britain, the United States,, and Australia, for example. Oral instruction in pronunciation should supplement what is presented here. In general, German is pronounced as it is spelled with no silent letters except *h* when it indicates that the preceding vowel is long. The accented syllable is generally the first syllable or the stem syllable: **Deútschland**, **Váter**, **beántworten**.

Vowels—general rules of pronunciation

1. Vowels may be either long or short.
2. They are long
   a. when doubled or followed by *h*:
      Haar Ohr
   b. when either final in the word or at the end of an accented syllable:
      du há-ben
   c. and generally when followed by a single consonant:
      rot grün
3. They are short
   a. when followed by a double consonant:
      küssen Mann
   b. when followed by two or more consonants:
      sitzen Fenster

Specific rules of pronunciation:

a	Long as in *father*	Vater, Saat, Bahn
	Short as in *ton*	Mann, Hand, Ball

e	Long as in *gate* but without the final *ee* sound	Schnee, stehen, geben
	Short as in *bed*	Bett, nennen, Fenster
	Unaccented as in *eh*	Tage, Pflaume, gebe
i	Long as in *spleen*	Klima, Tiger, ihnen
	Short as in *fist*	ist, Mitte, Liste
ie	Generally as the long *i*	fliegen, sieben, die
o	Long as in *no* but without the final *u* sound	Boot, Rose, Lohn
	Short as in *omit, obey*	oft, Gold, Gott
u	Long as in *fool*	Schuh, du, Hut
	Short as in *push*	und, Mutter, mußte

The umlauted vowels (modified vowels)

ä	Long as in either *gate* or as in *their* (some German speakers make no distinction)	Väter, Mädchen, wähne
	Short as in *bed* (i.e., it is identical to the short *e*)	Männer, Säckchen, Kämme
ö	There is no sound in English for either the long or short *ö*.	
	Long: Say the long German *a* as in *gate*, then round your lips and say it again.	Öfen, Söhne, schön
	Short: Say the German short *e* as in *bed,* then round your lips and say it again.	östlich. können, Hölle
ü	There is no corresponding sound for either the long or short *ü*.	
	Long: round lips to pronounce the *oo* in *fool* but instead articulate the *ee* as in *spleen.*	kühl, Füßen, Bücher
	Short: round lips to pronounce the *oo* in *fool* but instead articulate the short *i as* in *fist.*	küssen, Mütter, müßte

ä, ö, ü, are occasionally written **ae, oe, ue**: **spaet, oeffnen, ueber** instead of **spät, öffnen, über**. In modern printed German this is seen mainly in names: Mueller, Schaeffer, Goethe.

The diphthongs

ei, ai, ey, ay are like the *i* in *mine*	mein, Mai, Speyer, Mayer
au is like the *ou* in *mouse*	Maus, Haus, Laus
eu, äu are like the *oi* in *foil*	neun, Feuer, Häuser, Fräulein

The consonants—general rules of pronunciation

The following consonants and combinations of consonants are pronounced as they are in English: **f, h, k, m, n, p, t, ck, nk, ph.**

Special rules of pronunciation

b	when beginning a word or syllable is like the English *b*	**B**all, ent**b**inden
	when ending a word or syllable is like the English *p*	Gra**b**, a**b**fallen, gi**b**t, ge**b**t
c	when preceding **ä, e, i, y** is like *ts*	**C**äsar, **C**ent, **C**i**c**ero, **C**yrenius
	when preceding **a, o, u** is like the English *k*	**C**afe, **C**ousine, **C**uxhaven
ch	There are four different sounds:	
	a. the back **ch** or **ach** sound used after **a, o, u** and **au**. This sound is produced by arching the tongue against the rear part of the palate. The tip of the tongue rests below the teeth of the lower jaw.	a**ch**, do**ch**, Bu**ch**, Bau**ch**
	b. The front **ch** or **ich** sound follows all other vowels. It is pronounced like the *h* in *hew.*	i**ch**, Bü**ch**er, Be**ch**er, Ei**ch**e
	c. When beginning words of Greek origin or preceding the vowels **a** and **u** or consonants, it is pronounced like the English *k*.	**Ch**rist, **Ch**or, **Ch**arakter
	When preceding **i** or **e** however it takes the front **ch** sound.	**Ch**ina, **Ch**emie, **Ch**irurg
	d. When beginning words of French origin it is pronounced like the English *sh*.	**Ch**ef, **Ch**auffeur, **Ch**auvinist
chs	is like the English *ks* when *s* is part of the stem	se**chs**, O**chs**, wa**chs**en

	When s is an ending the **ch** is pronounced according to the rules already given, and the **s** is pronounced separately.	versu**chs**t, verflu**chs**t
d	when beginning a word or syllable is like the English *d*	**d**umm, Bru**d**er
	when ending a word or syllable is like the English *t*	Han**d**, Mä**d**chen
dt	is like the English *t*	Sta**dt**, wan**dt**e
g	when beginning a word or syllable is like the English *g* in *girl*	**G**arten, le**g**en, Mor**g**en
	when ending a word or syllable is like the English *k*	Ta**g**, le**g**st
	The ending **-ig** is pronounced like the German **ich**.	Küni**g**, fleißi**g**, weni**g**
	However, when an ending is added, **g** becomes as the *g* in *go.*	fleißi**g**er, weni**g**er
	Initial **g** in words of French origin keeps its French pronunciation.	**G**enre, **g**enie
gn	Both letters are pronounced.	**Gn**om, **Gn**ostizismus
h	is silent when used to lengthen a vowel.	ste**h**en, i**h**nen
	When beginning a word or syllable, it is like the English *h*.	**h**aben, zu**h**ören, a**h**a
j	is like the English *y* in *yellow*	**j**a, **J**ahr, **j**ung
j	is like the final consonant sound in *garage* when it introduces words of French origin.	**J**ournalist
kn	Both letters are pronounced.	**Kn**ie, **kn**oten
l	Pronounce this letter by placing the tip of the tongue against the upper teeth or the front edge of the upper gums.	so**ll**en, **l**ang, Ba**ll**, ba**l**d, Stuh**l**
ng	is like the English *ng* in *singer* (and not like the *ng* in *finger*)	Si**ng**er, Fi**ng**er, E**ng**land
pf	Both letters are pronounced.	**Pf**effer, A**pf**el

ps	Both letters are pronounced.	**Ps**ychologie, **Ps**eudonym
qu	is like the English *kv*	**Qu**alität, **qu**alifizieren
r	is produced either by vibrating the tip of the tongue against the upper gum (the apical **r**) or by vibrating the uvula (the gutteral **r**). In other words the gutteral **r** is a dry gargle.	**r**ennen, g**r**aben, studie**r**en, füh**r**t Pfa**rr**er
	A final **r** has the following pronunciations:	
	There is a faint remnant of the apical or gutteral **r** in the ending **-r** following **ah** or **a**:	Jah**r**, kla**r**
	After the other vowels, **-är, -er, -ir, -or, -ör, -ur, -ür,** it is a vowel glide ending in the sound *uh*. So *ihr* sounds something like ee‿uh; *Uhr* something like oo‿uh, etc.	Bä**r**, Finge**r**, di**r**, To**r**, stö**r**, Flu**r**, Tü**r**
s	when beginning a word or syllable before a vowel is like the English *z* in *zoo*.	**s**ieben, E**s**el, Kä**s**e, al**s**o
	In all other cases it is like the English *s* in *some*.	Hau**s**, Po**s**t, ha**s**t
	Before **p** and **t**, **s** is pronounced like the English *sh* when it begins a word or syllable.	**St**ein, ab**st**eigen, **Sp**iegel
ss, ß	are like the *ss* in the English *miss* (**ss** is only used between two short vowels whenever a differentiation is made between **ss** and **ß**).	mü**ss**en, grü**ß**en, flie**ß**en, be**ss**er
th	is like the English *t*	**Th**ron, **Th**eater, **Th**eorie
-tion	**t** is pronounced *ts,* the vowels are long	na**tion**al, Rota**tion**
tz	is like the English *ts* in *cats*	Pla**tz**, se**tz**en
v	is like the English *f* in words of Germanic origin	**v**on, **V**ater, bra**v**
	In words of foreign origin it is pronounced like the English *v*.	No**v**ember, E**v**angelium, **V**ase, Uni**v**ersität

w	is like the English *v*	**W**ind, **w**ann, ge**w**esen
x	is pronounced like the English *ks* or final *x*	Ma**x**, A**x**t, He**x**e
z	is pronounced like the English *ts* in *cats*	**Z**eit, tan**z**en, kur**z**

The Glottal Stop

In addition to the sounds listed above the pronunciation of German words is characterized by an **explosive quality**. This results from closing the glottis (the space between the vocal cords) an instant before pronouncing a word or syllable which begins with an accented vowel.

áuf, Óhr, beéinflussen, íst, ǘberáus

Accent

Rules for stressing the word already briefly mentioned above are as follows:

1. Simple German words are accented on the first syllable:

háben, Mútter, Kínder, lángsam

2. Compound nouns usually receive the accent on the first element:

Kránkenhaus, Ráumkapsel, Úntertasse

3. Separable prefixes are accented:

éinsteigen, ánfangen, vórgehen, wíedersehen

4. The inseparable prefixes **be-, emp-, ent-, er-, ge-, miß-, ver-, zer-** are unaccented:

bekómmen, entstéhen, empfínden, erréichen, gemácht, mißhándeln, verstéhen, zerbréchen

5. Words of non-Germanic origin usually receive the accent on the last syllable:

Studént, Universitǟt, Revolutión

6. The suffix **-ei** receives the accent:

Metzgeréi, Schlachteréi, Schweineréi

3. NUMERALS

Cardinal numbers

0	null				
1	eins (ein-)	11	elf	21	einundzwanzig*
2	zwei	12	zwölf	22	zweiundzwanzig
3	drei	13	dreizehn	30	dreißig
4	vier	14	vierzehn	40	vierzig
5	fünf	15	fünfzehn	50	fünfzig
6	sechs	16	sechzehn	60	sechzig
7	sieben	17	siebzehn	70	siebzig
8	acht	18	achtzehn	80	achtzig
9	neun	19	neunzehn	90	neunzig
10	zehn	20	zwanzig	100	hundert

101	hunderteins
200	zweihundert
333	dreihundertdreiunddreißig
1000	tausend
2000	zweitausend
4444	viertausendvierhundertvierundvierzig
10 000	zehntausend
100 000	hunderttausend
1 000 000	eine Million
1 000 000 000	eine Milliarde
1 000 000 000 000	eine Billion

Ordinal numbers

The endings **-t** or **-st** added to cardinal numbers signify ordinal numbers.

first	**erst-**	ninth	**neunt-**
second	**zweit-**	tenth	**zehnt-**
third	**dritt-**	twentieth	**zwanzigst-**
fourth	**viert-**	twenty-first	**einundzwanzigst-***
fifth	**fünft-**	thirtieth	**dreißigst-**
sixth	**sechst-**	hundredth	**hundertst-**
seventh	**siebent-, siebt-**	thousandth	**tausendst-**
eighth	**acht-**	*etc.*	**usw.**

These ordinal numbers are used adjectivally and will take some kind of ending, generally an **-e** or **-en**:

das zweit**e** Kind mit dem dritt**en** Bruder

---

*Note that the unit digit precedes the tens digit, as in "Four and twenty blackbirds / Baked in a pie."

Fractions

The endings **-tel** or **-stel** indicate a fraction:

½ halb, die Hälfte	$^4/_{25}$ vier Fünfundzwanzigstel
$^3/_{10}$ drei Zehntel	1½ anderthalb, eineinhalb
$^{15}/_{17}$ fünfzehn Siebzehntel	2½ zweieinhalb

General rules concerning numerals

1. Decimals are indicated by commas, not periods:

33,33 (German) = 33.33 (English)

2. A thin space is used where English uses the comma:

1 333 333 (German) = 1,333,333 (English)

3. Several numeral suffixes are:

German		English			
-ens	=	-ly	**erstens**	=	firstly
			zweitens	=	secondly
			drittens	=	thirdly
-erlei	=	of different kind	**einerlei**	=	one of a kind
			zweierlei	=	two different kinds
			dreierlei	=	three different kinds
-fach	=	-fold (same kind)	**einfach**	=	simple, simply (one-fold)
			zweifach	=	two-fold
			dreifach	=	three-fold
-mal	=	-ce, times	**einmal**	=	once
			zweimal	=	twice
			dreimal	=	thrice
			viermal	=	four times
			fünfundzwanzigmal	=	twenty-five times

Vocabulary

General guidelines for use of the vocabulary.

1. When two endings follow a noun, the first ending is genitive, the second is plural:
der **Mann**, **-es**, **¨er** = der **Mann**, des **Mannes**, die **Männer**

2. One ending following a masculine or neuter noun indicates the genitive form:
das **Leben**, **-s** = das **Leben**, des **Lebens**

3. After feminine nouns the ending given indicates the plural form:
die **Frau**, **-en** = die **Frau**, der **Frau** (genitive), die **Frauen** (plural)

4. **-** given as the plural form indicates that the nominative singular and plural are identical:
der **Wagen**, **-s**, **-** = der **Wagen**, des **Wagens**, die **Wagen**

5. Generally no endings will be given for adjectives and verbs used as nouns:
der **Kranke**, das **Rauschen**
However, (**-r**) indicates the singular change on the adjective with *ein*: **ein Kranker**

6. No endings following certain feminine nouns will indicate that there is no plural:
die **Zufriedenheit**

7. The principal parts of verbs with a stem vowel shift are given along with the auxiliary **sein** or **haben**
gehen (**geht**), **ging, ist gegangen**
können (**kann**), **konnte, hat gekonnt**

8. Verbs with separable prefixes are indicated with a centered period:
ab·weisen

9. Intransitive verbs are indicated by the auxiliary **sein**:
ist gefahren

A

abends in the evening
aber but, however
abgelegen remote
abgesehen von apart from, without regard to
ab·halten (**hält ab**), **hielt ab, hat abgehalten** to hold, to give
der **Ablösungstermin, -s, -e** (work)shift
ablösungsweise in relays
ab·magern to grow thin
ab·schaffen to abolish, to scrap
die **Abschaffung, -en** abolition, doing away with
ab·schneiden (**schneidet ab**), **schnitt ab, hat abgeschnitten** to cut off

die **Absicht, -en** intention
der **Abtritt, -(e)s, -e** lavatory
ab·weisen (weist ab), wies ab, hat abgewiesen to reject
achtmal eight times
achten to respect, to think highly of
die **Achtung** respect
der **Affe, -n, -n** ape
afrikanisch African
ahnen to sense, to have a presentiment of
ähnlich similar to
die **Ahnung, -en** idea, presentiment
allbereits already
alle und jede all and every, any kind of
die **Allee, -n** drive, avenue
allein alone
aller, alle, alles all, everything
allerfreundlich most friendly
allgemein general
allmählich gradual(ly)
allzuoft all too often
allzusehr all too much, much too
die **Alpen** the Alps
als as, than, when
also thus, so, therefore, hence, consequently
alt old
das **Alter, -s, -** age
im Alter von at the age of
an at, on, from
in **Anbetracht** considering, in view of, in consideration of
ander different, other, else
der **Andere (-r), -n, -n** other person
ändern to change
anderswo elsewhere
an·fangen (fängt an), fing an, hat angefangen to begin
an·flehen to implore
angeblich alleged
sich an·gewöhnen to get accustomed
der **Angriff, -(e)s, -e** attack
die **Angst, ⸚e** fear, anxiety
ängstlich anxious, uneasy, distressed, nervous, timid
der **Anlaß, -sses, Anlässe** cause, motive, reason
Anlaß geben to give rise to
die **Annäherung, -en** approach
die **Annahme, -n** assumption, acceptance
sich an·passen to adapt oneself
an·schauen to look at
sich an·schicken to prepare, to get ready
das **Anschwellen** the swelling up
an·sehen (sieht an), sah an, hat angesehen to look at
das **Ansehen, -s** esteem
der **Anspruch, (e)s, ⸚e** claim
die **Anstrengung, -en** exertion, struggle, effort
die **Antwort, -en** answer
antworten to answer
an·weisen (weist an), wies an, hat angewiesen to direct, to order
an·wenden (wendet an), wandte or **wendete an, hat angewandt** or **angewendet** to use, to employ
an·ziehen (zieht an), zog an, hat angezogen to attract
arbeiten to work
arbeitend working
der **Arbeiter, -s, -** worker
der **Arbeitstag, -(e)s, -e** workday
der **Argwohn, -s** suspicion
der **Arm, -es, -e** arm
arm poor, needy, miserable
ärmlich shabby
der **Arme (-r)** poor man, unfortunate person
die **Armenbüchse, -n** poor box
die **Armut** poverty
die **Art, -en** kind, sort, type, manner
der **Arzt, -es, ⸚e** doctor
der **Astronom, -en, -en** astronomer
der **Atomkrieg, -(e)s, -e** atomic war
die **Atomwaffe, -n** atomic weapon
auch even, also
auch wenn even if
auf on, in, at, over
auf und ab back and forth
auf·bauen to build up
auf·blasen (bläst auf), blies auf, hat aufgeblasen to inflate
auf·erlegen to impose
die **Auferstehung** resurrection
auf·fassen to regard
die **Auffassung, -en** conception, comprehension, interpretation
auf·fordern to ask, to challenge
die **Aufgabe, -n** task, duty
der **Aufgeklärte (-r)** enlightened person
auf·hängen (hängt auf), hing auf, hat aufgehangen to hang

die **Aufklärung, -en** explanation, enlightenment, the Age of Enlightenment
sich auf·lösen to dissolve
die **Aufmerksamkeit,** attention, attentiveness
auf·reißen (reißt auf), riß auf, hat aufgerissen to tear open
auf·stehen (steht auf), stand auf, ist aufgestanden to stand up, to get up
das **Aufstehen** getting up
auf·treiben (treibt auf), trieb auf, hat aufgetrieben to distend
die **Auftreibung, -en** swelling, distention
auf·treten (tritt auf), trat auf, ist aufgetreten to appear, come forward
auf·wachen (aux. **sein**) to awake
das **Aufwachen** the waking up
sich auf·werfen (wirft sich auf), warf sich auf, hat sich aufgeworfen to set up
die **Aufzeichnung, -en** note, noting down
auf·ziehen (zieht auf), zog auf, hat aufgezogen to wind up (a watch)
das **Auge, -s, -n** eye
der **Augenblick, -(e)s, -e** moment
aus from, out of
das **Ausbleiben** absence, failure (to appear)
aus·brennen (brennt aus), brannte aus, hat or **ist ausgebrannt** to burn out
der **Ausdruck, -(e)s, ¨-e** expression
der **Ausgang, -(e)s, ¨-e** exit
ausgebrochen broken out
ausgerottet exterminated, wiped out, destroyed
die **Ausnahme, -n** exception
aus·rotten to exterminate, to wipe out, to destroy
außer except, besides
äußeres exterior
außerirdisch extraterrestial
sich äußern to express oneself
äußerst most extreme, extremely
aus·tragen (trägt aus), trug aus, hat ausgetragen to carry out, to carry on, to fight out
aus·üben to wield, to exercise

B

bald soon
das **Bankkonto, -s, -ten** or **-s** bank account
das **Bankwesen, -s, -** banking system
die **Baracke, -n** hut, shack
bauen to build
der **Bauernstand, -(e)s, ¨-e** peasantry
der **Baum, -(e)s, ¨-e** tree
der **Baustein, -s, -e** building stone, component
der **Bayer, -n, -n** Bavarian
die **Bayerischen Alpen** the Bavarian Alps
das **Bayern** Bavaria
die **Beantwortung, -en** answer
bedecken to cover
bedeckt covered
das **Bedenken, -s, -** scruple, doubt
bedeuten to mean, to signify
die **Bedeutung, -en** meaning, significance
sich bedienen to make use of
bedingen to stipulate, to be conditioned by, to be conditional (dependent) on
die **Bedrohung, -en** threat
beeindrucken to impress
die **Beere, -n** berry
beeinflussen to influence
befangen self-conscious, awkward
sich befinden (befindet sich), befand sich, hat sich befunden to be
befriedigen to satisfy
befriedigend gratifying, satisfying
beginnen (beginnt), begann, hat begonnen to begin, to start
begreifen (begreift), begriff, hat begriffen to understand, to comprehend
das **Begreifen** understanding
der **Begriff, -(e)s, -e** concept
die **Begründung, -en** reason
behaften to burden
behaftet afflicted with, subject to
behaupten to maintain
bei on, at, by, in case of
beide both
beinahe almost
beiseite·schieben (schiebt beiseite), schob beiseite, hat beiseitegeschoben to push aside
das **Beispiel, -(e)s, -e** example
zum Beispiel for example
bei·tragen (trägt bei), trug bei, hat beigetragen to contribute
bejahen to affirm, to say yes to
bekämpfen to fight against
bekannt known

bekehren to convert
bekennen (**bekennt**), **bekannte, hat bekannt** to confess
bekommen (**bekommt**), **bekam, hat bekommen** to receive
beleidigen to insult
das **Belgien, -s** Belgium
sich bemühen to take trouble, to take pains, to strive
das **Bemühen** striving
benutzen to use, to utilize
benutzt utilized
die **Benutzung, -en** use
die **Beobachtung, -en** observation
bequem comfortable
der **Bequeme** (**-r**) comfortable one
der **Bereich, -**(**e**)**s, -e** sphere, scope, range, province, area
bereit ready
bereits already
der **Berg, -**(**e**)**s, -e** mountain
bergen (**birgt**), **barg, hat geborgen** to contain, to shelter, to conceal, to harbor
der **Beruf, -**(**e**)**s, -e** profession
berufen (**beruft**), **berief, hat berufen** to call forth
beruhen to rest, to be based on
berühmt famous
besagen to mean
bescheiden modest (adj.)
bescheiden, beschied, ist beschieden to grant, to give
beschließen (**beschließt**), **beschloß, hat beschlossen** to decide, to resolve
beschränken to limit, to restrict
die **Beschränkung, -en** limitation, restriction
beschreiben (**beschreibt**), **beschrieb, hat beschrieben** to describe
die **Beschwerde, -n** complaint
besehen (**besieht**), **besah, hat besehen** to inspect
die **Besinnung, -en** reflection, consciousness
der **Besitz, -es, -e** possession
besitzen (**besitzt**), **besaß, hat besessen** to possess
besorgen to manage
die **Besorgnis, -se** anxiety, fear
besorgt anxious
besser better
bessern to better
bestehen (**besteht**), **bestand, hat bestanden** to consist, to exist, to withstand
bestimmt specific, definite, certain
bestürzen to dismay, to bewilder, to amaze
das **Bestürzende** dismaying thing
bestürzt dismayed, bewildered, confused
die **Bestürzung, -en** dismay, bewilderment, confusion
der **Besuch, -**(**e**)**s, -e** visit
besuchen to visit
betrachten to regard, to look upon, to consider
beträchtlich considerable
der **Betriebsame** (**-r**) busy person
die **Bettstelle, -n** bedstead
das **Bett**(**t**)**uch, -**(**e**)**s, ¨-er** sheet
das **Bettzeug, -**(**e**)**s** bedding
sich beugen to submit oneself, to bow
beurteilen to judge, to criticize, to assess
die **Bevölkerung, -en** population
die **Bevölkerungszahl, -en** population figure
bevor before
der **Bevorzugte** (**-r**) the favored one
die **Bewahrung, -en** preservation
bewegen to move, to stir, to agitate
bewegend moving
die **Bewegungsfreiheit** freedom of movement
der **Beweis, -es, -e** proof, evidence
bewirtschaften to cultivate
bewohnen to live or reside in, to occupy
der **Bewohner, -s, -** inhabitant
bewohnt inhabited
bewußt conscious, self-aware, deliberate
das **Bewußtsein, -s** consciousness
bezahlen to pay
bezeichnen to denote, to stand for
bezeigen to show
die **Beziehung, -en** relationship, reference, connection
die **Bibel, -n** Bible
die **Bibelübersetzung, -en** Bible translation
der **Bienenstock, -**(**e**)**s, ¨-e** beehive
bieten (**bietet**), **bot, hat geboten** to bid, to offer
das **Bild, -es, -er** picture
bilden to form
bildend forming
bis until, as far as, up to
das **Blatt, -es, ¨-er** leaf, page

bleiben (**bleibt**)**, blieb, ist geblieben** to stay, to remain
blicken to glance
bloß simply, only
die **Blume, -n** flower
das **Blut, -es** blood
der **Boden, -s, ¨** territory, ground, floor
der **Bodensee, -s** Lake Constance
der **Bolschewist, -en, -en** Bolshevist
das **Böse** evil
brauchen to need
brav good
brechen (**bricht**)**, brach, gebrochen** to break
der **Brief, -s, -e** letter
bringen (**bringt**)**, brachte, hat gebracht** to bring
das **Brot, -**(**e**)**s, -e** bread
der **Bruch, -s, ¨e** hernia
der **Bruchteil, -**(**e**)**s, -e** fraction
der **Bruder, -s, ¨** the brother
das **Bruttosozialprodukt, -**(**e**)**s, -e** gross national product
der **Buchstabe, -s, ¨e** letter (alphabet)
buchstäblich literally
das **Bundesland, -es, ¨er** state, Land of the Federal Republic of Germany

C

der **Chemiker, -s, -** chemist
der **Christ, -en, -en** Christian
das **Christentum, -s** Christianity
christlich Christian
der **Christus** Christ
Credo quia absurdum (Latin) I believe it because it is absurd

D

da here, there, since, then, because, in which, when, while, thereupon
dabei at the same time, thereby, close to it (them)
dabei sein to be present, to take part
dabei·sitzen (**sitzt dabei**)**, saß dabei, hat dabeigesessen** to sit next to, close by
dadurch through it (that), in this way, by this means
dagegen on the other hand, against
daher thus
dahingegen on the other hand
damals at that time
damit with that
das **Dänemark, -s** Denmark
dann then
daran thereon, on it, at it
darauf on that, thereupon
darin in it, within
der **Darm, -**(**e**)**s, ¨e** intestine
dar·stellen to represent
dar·tun (**tut dar**)**, tat dar, hat dargetan** to show, to prove
darüber hinaus beyond it (that), in addition
darum therefore
das which, that, the, who, it, those, etc.
das **Dasein, -s** existence
die **Daseinsgestaltung** shaping, forming, fashioning of existence
daß that
dauern to last
dauernd constant, continuous
davon by it, of it, from it
die **Decke, -n** cover
der **Deckschild, -**(**e**)**s, -e** cover
demgegenüber opposed to which, in relation to which
denkbar conceivable, possible
denken (**denkt**)**, dachte, hat gedacht** to think
der **Denkende** (**-r**) the thinking person
denn for, because, then
dennoch nevertheless
der which, who, that, the, he, those, etc.
derjenige, diejenige, dasjenige the one, he, she, that, that one, those, who, they
derselbe, dieselbe, dasselbe the same
deshalb therefore
deutsch German (adj)
das **Deutsch** the German language
der **Deutsche** (**-r**)**, -n, -n** the German
das **Deutschland, -s** Germany
deutschsprachig German speaking (land, area)
die **Deutung, -en** meaning, signification, interpretation
d.h. = **das heißt** i.e., that is
die **Diät, -en** diet
der **Dichter, -s, -** poet
die which, who, that, the, she, those, etc.

dienen to serve
der **Diener, -s, -** servant
der **Dienst, -es, -e** service
der **Dienstag, -(e)s, -e** Tuesday
dies, dieser, diese, dieses this, this one, the latter
diesseitig temporal
die **Diesseitigkeit** temporality, secular life, worldliness
diesseits this side
das **Ding, -(e)s, -e** thing
doch after all, since, but, nevertheless, though, still, yet, indeed
die **Donau** Danube
dort there
dortig in that town, of that place
drei three
drein = darein along, into that (it)
der **Dreißigjährige Krieg, -es** Thirty Years' War
dreizehn thirteen
dringlich urgent(ly), pressing(ly)
dritte third
drohen to threaten, to menace
die **Duldung** toleration
dunkel dark, somber
der **Dunst, -(e)s, ⸚e** vapor
durch through, by
durchaus absolutely
das **Durchgangsland, -(e)s, ⸚er** country through which others travel, land corridor
dürfen (darf), durfte, hat gedurft to be allowed

E

eben simply
das **Ebenbild, -(e)s, -er** image
ebenfalls likewise
die **Eberesche, -n** mountain ash, rowan (tree)
die **Ecke, -n** corner
edel noble
die **Ehe, -n** marriage
ehemalig former
eher rather, before
der **Ehestand, -(e)s** married state
die **Ehre, -n** honor
ehrenwert honorable, respectable
die **Ehrfurcht** awe, deep respect, reverence
ehrlich honest(ly)
ehrwürdig respectable
eigen own
die **Eigensucht** selfishness
eigentlich actual(ly)
einander another
sich ein·bilden to imagine
der **Eine** one (person)
einer, eine, eines one (thing, person)
einfach simple, simply
der **Einfall, -(e)s, ⸚e** notion
ein·fallen (fällt ein), fiel ein, ist eingefallen to occur, to have an idea
ein·flößen to instill, to strike
der **Einfluß, -sses, ⸚sse** influence
eingeboren innate, inherent, native
der **Eingeborene (-r)** native
eingeklemmt strangulated, pinched
der **Eingriff, -(e)s, -e** intervention
die **Einheit, -en** unity
einig united
einige some
einmal once
einmalig unique
der **Einsatz, -es, ⸚e** employment, use
ein·setzen to employ, to put in
einstig former
ein·wenden (wendet ein), wandte ein or **wendete ein, hat eingewandt** or **eingewendet** to object
die **Einwirkung, -en** influence
der **Einwurf, -(e)s, ⸚e** objection
einzeln single, individual
einzig only, single, sole
das **Eisen, -s, -** iron
die **Eisenbahn, -en** railway
die **Eisengießerei, -en** iron foundry
eisern iron (adj.)
der **Eiserne Vorhang** Iron Curtain
das **Elend, -(e)s** misery
das **Elsaß** Alsace
empfinden (empfindet), empfand, hat empfunden to feel
enden to finish
eng narrow, tight, close, cramped
engagiert employed
die **Enge, -n** closeness, narrowness, tightness, crampedness
der **Engländer, -s, -** Englishman
entdecken to discover
entfesseln to release, to unleash

entfliehen (entflieht), entfloh, ist entflohen to flee from, to escape
entgegen·sehen (sieht entgegen), sah entgegen, hat entgegengesehen to look forward to
enthalten (enthält), enthielt, hat enthalten to contain
entleeren to empty out
entreißen (entreißt), entriß, hat entrissen to tear away
entrüstet indignant, angry
entscheiden (entscheidet), entschied, hat entschieden to decide
die **Entscheidung, -en** decision
die **Entschließung, -en** resolution, determination, resolve
entsprechen (entspricht), entsprach, hat entsprochen to correspond to
entsprechend corresponding
entstehen (entsteht), entstand, ist entstanden to begin, to originate, to grow out of, to break out of
die **Enttäuschung, -en** disappointment
entweder . . . oder either . . . or
die **Entwicklung, -en** development
sich entwinden (entwindet sich), entwand sich, hat sich entwunden to wrest oneself
sich entziehen (entzieht sich), entzog sich, hat sich entzogen to avoid, to shun
das **Erbe, -s** legacy, heritage, inheritance
die **Erbschaft, -en** legacy, inheritance
die **Erde, -n** earth, ground
das **Ereignis, -ses, -se** event
erfahren (erfährt), erfuhr, hat erfahren to find out, to discover, to hear about
die **Erfahrung, -en** experience
der **Erfolg, -(e)s, -e** success, result
sich ergeben (ergibt sich), ergab sich, hat sich ergeben to submit
das **Ergebnis, -ses, -se** result
die **Ergebung, -en** submission
ergehen (ergeht), erging, ist ergangen to happen, to fare, to go
ergreifen (ergreift), ergriff, hat ergriffen to catch (seize, get, lay) hold of
erhalten (erhält), erhielt, hat erhalten to preserve, to maintain, to obtain, to receive
erhöhen to increase, to heighten
sich erinnern to remember
erkennen (erkennt), erkannte, hat erkannt to recognize
die **Erkenntnis, -se** knowledge (of the truth), comprehension, perception
erklären to declare, to explain
die **Erklärung, -en** explanation, interpretation
erleben to experience
das **Erlebnis, -ses, -se** experience
der **Erlöser, -s, -** redeemer, deliverer
der **Erlöser, -s** (bib.) Savior, Redeemer
ernst serious
ernsthaft serious, grave
ernstlich serious
erregen to excite
erreichen to reach
erschaffen (erschafft), erschuf, hat erschaffen to create
erscheinen (erscheint), erschien, ist erschienen to appear
erst only, first, for the first time
erstaunen to astonish, to amaze
erstaunlich astonishing
erstaunt astonished
ertragen (erträgt), ertrug, hat ertragen to tolerate, to bear
erwachen (aux. **sein**) to awake
der **Erwachsene (-r)** adult
erwarten to await
die **Erwartung, -en** expectation
erzählen to tell, to relate
erzeugen to procreate, to breed, to generate, to produce
die **Erziehung** education
erzürnen to get angry
erzwingen (erzwingt), erzwang, hat erzwungen to determine, to force
das **Essen, -s,** food, eating, meal, dinner, supper
das **Ethische** the ethical
etwa perhaps
etwas something, somewhat

F

fahren (fährt), fuhr, ist gefahren to drive, to go, to ride
die **Fahrt, -en** trip, journey, voyage, drive, ride
der **Fall, -(e)s, ¨-e** case
fallen (fällt), fiel, ist gefallen to fall
die **Farbe, -n** color

faßbar tangible, concrete
fassen to lay hold of, to comprehend, to understand
fast almost, all but
faul lazy
die **Faulheit** laziness
die **Feder, -n** feather
der **Fehler, -s, -** mistake
feiern to celebrate
feige cowardly
die **Feigheit** cowardliness
der **Feind, -(e)s, -e** enemy
die **Feindseligkeit, -en** hostility
das **Fenster, -s, -** window
fern far
ferner furthermore, farther
fest firm, fast, strong, firmly
fest·halten (hält fest), hielt fest, hat festgehalten to hold fast
fest·stehen (steht fest), stand fest, hat festgestanden to stand firm, to be certain
die **Feststellung, -en** ascertainment, observation
das **Feuer, -s, -** fire
finden (findet), fand, hat gefunden to find
die **Firma, -men** (pl.) firm, business
unter der Firma under the style (leadership) of
die **Fixsternsphäre, -n** fixed star (sphere)
fleißig industrious
flehen to plead
fliehen (flieht), floh, ist geflohen to flee
fließen (fließt), floß, ist geflossen to flow
die **Flur, -en** field
die **Folge, -n** succession, consequence, series, continuation
als Folge as a consequence
folgen (aux. **sein**) to follow; (aux. **haben**) to obey
folgend following
fördern to promote
die **Forderung** demand, challenge, standard
forschen to search
fort gone, away
fort und fort over and over
fort·laufen (läuft fort), lief fort, ist fortgelaufen to run away, to continue on
fortlaufend continuous
fort·schaffen to carry off, to take away, to remove
fort·setzen to continue
fort·stäuben to fly away like dust
fortwährend incessantly
die **Frage, -n** question, problem
auf die Fragen Antwort geben to answer the questions
das **Frankreich, -s** France
der **Franzose, -n, -n** Frenchman
französisch French (adj.)
die **Frau, -en** woman, wife
die **Freiheit** freedom
der **Freitag, -(e)s, -e** Friday
fremd strange, unfamiliar
der **Fremde (-r), -n, -n** stranger
die **Freude, -n** joy
der **Freund, -(e)s, -e** friend
freundlich friendly, in a friendly way
der **Friede, -ns** peace
das **Friedensgerücht, -(e)s, -e** rumor of peace
friedlich peaceable
der **Friese, -n, -n** Frisian
frisch fresh
früh early
sich fügen to subordinate oneself
fühlen to feel, to perceive
führen to lead, to carry, to bring, to wage
führend leading
der **Führer, -s, -** leader
die **Fülle** fullness
fünf five
der **Fünfte (-r)** fifth one (male person)
fünfundvierzig forty-five
fünfzig fifty
der **Funke, -n, -n** spark
für for
die **Furcht** fear
furchtbar terrible, fearful, awful, frightful
fürchten to fear
sich fürchten vor (+dative) to be afraid of
die **Fürstin, -nen** princess
der **Fußboden, -s, ¨-** floor

G

der **Gang, -(e)s, ¨-e** walk
ganz complete, completely, whole, entire, entirely, totally, very, all
ganz und gar entirely

das **Ganze** the whole (**ein Ganzes:** a whole), the whole thing
gar even
das **Gäßchen, -s** alley(way), narrow street
die **Gasse, -n** alley(way), street, lane
gebären (**gebiert**), **gebar, hat geboren** to give birth to, to produce
geben (**gibt**), **gab, hat gegeben** to give
es gibt there is (are)
es gab there was (were)
gebend giving
das **Gebiet, -(e)s, -e** field, area
gebieten (**gebietet**), **gebot, hat geboten** to tell, to order, to command
das **Gebirgsland, -(e)s, ¨-er** mountainous country
geboren born
das **Gebot, -(e)s, -e** commandment
die **Geburt, -en** birth
der **Gedanke, -ns, -n** thought, idea
das **Gedicht, -(e)s, -e** poem
die **Gefahr, -en** danger
das **Gefängnis, -ses, -se** prison
gefaßt composed
das **Gefühl, -(e)s, -e** sentiment, feeling
gegen toward(s), against
gegeneinander contrary to, opposing one another, against
der **Gegensatz, -es, ¨-e** contrast
gegenseitig mutual, reciprocal
der **Gegenstand, -(e)s, ¨-e** subject, object
gegenüber towards
die **Gegenüberstellung, -en** confrontation
gegenwärtig present
der **Gegner, -s, -** opponent
geheim secret
das **Geheimnis, -ses, -se** secret, mystery
gehen (**geht**), **ging, ist gegangen** to go, to walk
gehören to belong
der **Geist, -es, -er** spirit
geistig spiritual
gelangen (aux. **sein**) to reach
das **Geld, -es, -er** money
die **Gelegenheit, -en** opportunity, occasion
bei Gelegenheit on the occasion of
gelingen (**gelingt**), **gelang, ist gelungen** to succeed
gelten (**gilt**), **galt, hat gegolten** to be considered
gemeinsam common, together
gemessen measured
gemessen am Weltkrieg compared to a world war
genau precisely, exactly, definite, for sure, for certain
das **Genie, -s, -s** genius
genießen (**genießt**), **genoß, hat genossen** to enjoy
der **Genosse, -n, -n** comrade, companion
die **Genossin -, -nen** comrade, companion
genügend sufficient
geordnet ordered
geraten (**gerät**), **geriet, ist geraten** to fall into, get into
geraum some (considerable)
für geraume Zeit for a long time, for some time
vor geraumer Zeit some time ago
der **Gerechte** (**-r**), **-n, -n** the just individual, righteous man
die **Gerechtigkeit, -en** justice
gering slight, little
die **Geringschätzung, -en** disdain
der **Germane, -n, -n** Teuton
gern with pleasure, gladly, readily, willingly
gerührt full of emotion
gesamt entire, total
das **Geschäft, -(e)s, -e** business
geschehen (**geschieht**), **geschah, ist geschehen** to happen, to occur
gescheit shrewd, clever, intelligent
die **Geschichte, -n** history, story
geschickt skilled
das **Geschlecht, -(e)s, -er** generation
das **Geschöpf, -(e)s, -e** creature
das **Geschrei, -s** cry, cries, shouting, shouts
die **Gesellschaft, -en** society, company
das **Gesetz, -es, -e** law
das **Gesicht, -(e)s, -er** face
die **Gesinnung, -en** disposition, characteristic way of thinking, mental attitude
das **Gespenst, -es, -er** ghost, apparition, phantom, specter
die **Gestalt, -en** shape, figure
gestern yesterday
das **Gestirn, -(e)s, -e** star, heavenly body
gesund healthy
der **Gesunde** (**-r**), **-n, -n** the healthy man
die **Gesundheit** health
gewähren to grant, to allow
die **Gewalt, -en** power

der **Gewaltakt, -(e)s, -e** act of violence
gewaltig gigantic, powerful
gewinnen (gewinnt), gewann, hat gewonnen to acquire, to gain
gewiß certainly
die **Gewißheit, -en** certainty
sich gewöhnen to accustom, to familiarize
gewöhnlich usual, ordinary
etwas Gewöhnliches something quite usual
gewohnt accustomed
gewünscht desired, wished
das **Giftgas, -es, -e** poison gas
die **Gier** greed, inordinate desire, avarice
gießen to pour, to cast
die **Gießerei** foundry
der **Glaube, -ns** religious faith
glauben to believe, to think, to suppose
gleich like, equal, similar, same
gleich·achten to esteem alike
gleichmäßig uniform, similar, equal
gleich·stellen to place on the same level
die **Glocke, -n** bell
das **Glück, -(e)s** luck, happiness
glücklich happy
glücklichst luckiest, happiest, most advantageous, most fortunate
die **Gnade, -n** privilege, mercy
der **Gott, -es, ¨-er** god, deity, God
göttlich divine, godly
grau gray
grauenhaft horrible, dreadful, ghastly, hideous
grausam cruel, brutal, fierce
grausig gruesome, grisly, lurid, weird
greifen (greift), griff, hat gegriffen to grasp, to touch
der **Greis, -es, -e** old man
die **Grenze, -n** border
groß great, large, big, major
großartig splendid, magnificent, wonderful
das **Großbritannien, -s** Great Britain
die **Großen** the nations, the large nations
die **Großmacht, ¨-e** major power
der **Grund, -(e)s, ¨-e** basis
der **Grundbegriff, -(e)s, -e** fundamental concept
der **Grundbesitz, -es** landed property, real estate
die **Grundgegebenheit, -en** fundamental factor
die **Grundidee, -n** fundamental idea
die **Grundlage, -n** foundation, basis
gründlich thoroughly
das **Grundstück, -(e)s, -e** plot (of land), real property *or* estate
grüßen to greet
Grüß Gott! Good day (to you)!
günstig favorable
gut good, well
das **Gut, -(e)s, ¨-er** treasure, property, goods
das **Gute** the good

H

haben (hat), hatte, hat gehabt to have
die **Haft** arrest
das **Hagestolzenleben, -s** life of a bachelor
halb half
halt just
halten (hält), hielt, hat gehalten to hold
das **Hammerwerk, -(e)s, -e** iron works
die **Hand, ¨-e** hand
der **Handspiegel, -s, -** hand mirror
hängen (hängt), hing, hat gehangen to hang
die **Hansestadt, ¨-e** Hanseatic city
die **Härte** hardness
der **Haß, -sses** hatred
hassen to hate
hassenswert hateful
der **Haufen, -s, -** pile
häufig frequent
am häufigsten most frequently
das **Haupt, -(e)s, ¨-er** head
die **Hauptstadt, ¨-e** capital city
das **Hauptziel, -(e)s, -e** main objective
das **Haus, -es, ¨-er** home, house
die **Haustür(e), -en** front door
der **Heeresbericht, -s, -e** army communiqué
heilig holy
der **Heilige (-r), -n, -n** saint
das **Heimatgefühl, -(e)s, -e** love for one's home
heim·kommen (kommt heim), kam heim, ist heimgekommen to come or return home
heimlich (adj.) secret, concealed, hidden; (adv.) secretly, furtively, stealthily
heiß hot
heißen (heißt), hieß, hat geheißen to name, to be called, to mean, to command

helfen (**hilft**), **half, hat geholfen** to help
herab down
heran·ziehen (**zieht heran**), **zog heran, hat herangezogen** to draw upon, to enlist, to bring in
herauf up
heraus·heben (**hebt heraus**), **hob heraus, hat herausgehoben** to lift out
der **Herbst, -es, -e** autumn
der **Herd, -(e)s, -e** stove
der **Herr, -n, -en** master, lord, ruler, God, Mr.
herrlich marvelous, glorious, magnificent
die **Herrlichkeit, -en** grandeur, glory, splendor
her·rühren to originate, to come from
die **Herstellung, -en** production, establishment, making, bringing about
herum about, on this account
das **Herz, -ens, -en** heart
heulen to howl, to cry, to scream
heulend howling
heute today
heutig present-day
hier here
hierhin here, this way
hierin herein, in this
hiervon out of this, from this
die **Hilfe, -n** help
der **Himmel, -s, -** sky, heaven, the heavens
himmlisch heavenly
hinaus·langen to reach out (beyond)
darüber hinaus·langen to reach beyond that (this)
das **Hinausschieben** postponement
hindern to hinder
hindurch through, over, throughout, all through
hin·geben (**gibt hin**), **gab hin, hat hingegeben** to give away
sich hin·geben (**gibt sich hin**), **gab sich hin, hat sich hingegeben** to devote, to submit, to execute
die **Hinsicht, -en** respect, view
hinter behind
der **Hintergedanke, -ns, -n** ulterior motive
hinterlassen (**hinterläßt**), **hinterließ, hat hinterlassen** to leave behind
das **Hinterstübchen, -s, -** small back room
der **Hinweis, -es, -e** reference, allusion, hint
hin·ziehen (**zieht bin**), **zog hin, hat hingezogen** to attract, to be drawn to
hinzu·fügen to add, to append, to join
historisch historic, historically
die **Hitze** heat
der **Hochofen, -s, ¨** blast furnace
höchst highest, greatest
hoffen to hope
die **Hoffnung, -en** hope
die **Hölle** hell
hören to hear
hübsch pretty
die **Humanität** humanity
der **Hund, -(e)s, -e** dog
hundert hundred
die **Hütte, -n** cottage, hut

I

die **Idealforderung, -en** ideal standard
die **Idee, -n** idea
ihm (to) him
ihnen (to) them
ihr (to) her, you, her
ihre her, their, its
ihrerseits for their part, for her part
im in (the)
immer always, ever
immer noch **still**
immer wieder always, again and again
in into, in
indem in that, while, as, since
indulgieren to indulge, to cater to
inmitten in the middle of, in the midst of
inner inner
innerlich within, inwardly, spiritually
das **Interesse, -s, -n** interest
irgend some, any
irgendein some, any, someone, anyone
irgendwann at some time or other
irgendwie in any way, somehow
irre·werden (**wird irre**), **wurde irre, ist irregeworden** to become disconcerted, confused, perplexed, lost
das **Italien,** Italy
italienisch Italian (adj.)

J

ja yes, truly, even, of course
die **Jacke, -n** jacket
das **Jahr, -es, -e** year

die **Jahreszeit, -en** season
das **Jahrhundert, -s, -e** century
-jährig -year-old
jämmerlich wretched, deplorable, piteous, woeful
jammern to lament, to moan, to yammer, to whine, to mourn
jammernd moaning, lamenting
je ever
je nun why!, well (now)!
je . . . desto the . . . the
jeder, jede, jedes each, every
jedesmal every time, each time, always
jedoch however, yet, still
jeglich every, each
jemand someone, somebody
jener, jene, jenes that, the former
jetzt now, at present
Johannes der Täufer John the Baptist
das **Journal, -(e)s, -e** newspaper, magazine, journal, diary
jüdisch Jewish (adj)
das **Jugoslawien -s** Yugoslavia
jung young
der **Junge, -n, -n** youth (boy)
der **Junggeselle, -n, -n** bachelor
der **Jüngling, -s, -e** youth, young man, lad, adolescent, youngster
die **Juristerei** law

K

der **Kaffeestrauch, -(e)s, ⸚er** coffee bush
das **Kaffeetrinken** drinking of coffee
der **Kaiser, -s, -** emperor
die **Kaiserstadt, ⸚e** imperial city
der **Kalte Krieg** Cold War
der **Kampf, -(e)s, ⸚e** struggle, fight, battle, warfare
kämpfen to fight, to struggle
kämpfend fighting, struggling
die **Kantine, -n** canteen
der **Käse, -s, -** cheese
die **Katastrophengefahr, -en** danger of catastrophe
kaum scarcely, hardly
kein, keine, kein no (one), none, no
kennen (**kennt**)**, kannte, hat gekannt** to know
kennen·lernen to get to know
der **Kerl, -s, -e** fellow, chap, character
das **Kind, -(e)s, -er** child
die **Kindheit** childhood
der **Kirchenmann, -es, ⸚er** churchman
kirchlich ecclesiastical, churchly, clerical
klar clear
der **Klassenkampf, -(e)s, ⸚e** class struggle
klassisch classic(al)
kleben to stick, to paste, to glue
die **Kleidung** clothes, clothing, dress
klein small
im kleinen on a small scale
das **Kloster, -s, ⸚** monastery, convent
klug smart, intelligent, bright, clever
der **Knabe, -n, -n** boy, youth, lad
das **Kollegienlesen** giving of lectures
kommandieren to command, to order
die **Kommassation** reallocation of land
kommen (**kommt**)**, kam, ist gekommen** to come
das **Kommende** (the) coming thing
der **Komponist, -en, -en** composer
der **König, -(e)s, -e** king
das **Königreich, -s, -e** kingdom
das **Konkubinat, -(e)s, -e** concubinage
können (**kann**)**, konnte, hat gekonnt** to be able to, can
der **Kopf, -(e)s, ⸚e** head
das **Korn** corn, grain
der **Körper, -s, -** body
kostbar precious
die **Kraft, ⸚e** power, force, strength
kramen to rummage
krank sick
der **Kranke -n** (**-r**) invalid, sick person
die **Krankheit, -en** illness, disease
unter Krankheiten from diseases
der **Krieg, -(e)s, -e** war
kriegen to get
die **Kritik, -en** criticism
die **Krume, -n** crumb, speck
krumm crooked, bent, curved, twisted
der **Kuhfuß, -es, ⸚e** cow's foot
der **Kulturbereich, -(e)s, -e** cultural sphere
die **Kulturgesellschaft, -en** civilized society
der **Künstler, -s, -** artist, performer

L

lächeln to smile
der **Laden, -s, ⸚** shop, store
der **Laffe, -n, -n** fop

die **Lage, -n** position, condition, situation
die **Lampe, -n** lamp
das **Land, -(e)s, ¨-er** state, countryside, country, land
die **Landkarte, -n** map
die **Landschaft, -en** scenery
die **Landstraße, -n** highway
lang long
langen to reach, to be sufficient
lassen (läßt), ließ, hat gelassen to let, to leave, to cause
das **Laster, -s, -** vice, depravity, viciousness
der **Laszive (-r)** lascivious person, sensualist
das **Laub, -(e)s** foliage, leaves
der **Lauf, -(e)s, ¨-e** course, path
laufen (läuft), lief, ist gelaufen to run
lauschen to listen
laut loud
lauten to be, to read, to state
lautlos soundless
lawinenartig resembling an avalanche, prodigious
leben to live
das **Leben, -s** life, lifetime
auf Leben und Tod to the death
lebend living
lebendig living, alive, lively
das **Lebensgeheimnis, -ses, -se** mystery of life
die **Lebensgeschichte, -n** life history (story)
die **Lebensgier** desire to live
die **Lebensmittel** food (stuffs), groceries
der **Lebensraum, -s** living space, sphere of existence
das **Lebewesen, -s, -** living being, living creature
leer empty, void
die **Leere, -n** emptiness, void(ness)
leergelassen left empty
legen to lay, to place
die **Legendenbildung, -en** formation of a legend
die **Lehre, -n** teaching
lehren to teach
der **Leib, -(e)s, -er** body
die **Leiche, -n** corpse, dead body
leicht easy
leiden (leidet), litt, hat gelitten to suffer
das **Leiden, -s, -** the suffering
die **Leidenschaft, -en** passion
leidenschaftslos apathetic, dispassionate, calm
leider unfortunately
leisten to accomplish
die **Leitung, -en** guidance, direction, control, leadership
lernen to learn
lesen (liest), las, hat gelesen to read
letzt last
leuchten to shine
die **Leute** (pl.) people
der **Liberalismus** liberalism
lieb dear, beloved
die **Liebe** love
lieben to love
liebenswert worthy of love
liegen (liegt), lag, hat gelegen to lie, to be situated, to be located
die **Lindenallee, -n** linden drive, linden avenue *or* Linden Drive, Linden Avenue
die **Linie, -n** line
in erster Linie above all
das **Loch, -(e)s, ¨-er** hole
lokal local
los·lassen (läßt los), ließ los, hat losgelassen to let loose
der **Lumpen, -s, -** rag, tatter
die **Lust, ¨-e** enjoyment, desire, wish, lust
der **Lustmörder, -s, -** sex murderer

M

machen to make, to do
die **Macht, ¨-e** power, force, command, control
das **Machtinteresse, -s, -n** interest in power, desire for power
machtlos powerless
das **Mädchen, -s, -** girl
das **Mädel, -s, -** girl
mager thin, skinny
die **Magie** magic
der **Magister** master (degree)
magyarisch Magyar (adj.)
der **Majoritätsbeschluß, -sses, ¨-sse** resolution carried by a majority
das **Mal, -(e)s, -e** time, occasion
einige Male several times
man one, they, we, you, people, men
mancher, manche, manches many, many a; (pl.) some
manchmal sometimes
der **Mangel, -s, ¨-** lack, defect, shortage

der **Mann, -es, ¨-er** man, male, husband
mannigfaltig diverse, varied
männlich male, masculine
das **Mannschaftsbordell, -s, -e** troop's brothel
das **Märchen, -s, -** fairy tale
das **Maß, -es, -e** degree, extent, measure, moderation, dimension
massenhaft abundant, numerous, wholesale
die **Maßnahme, -n** arrangement, measure
Maßnahmen treffen to take measures
die **Maßregel, -n** measure
der **Mathematiker, -s, -** mathematician
die **Mauer, -n** the wall
die **Medizin, -en** medicine
mehr more
mehrere several
die **Meile, -n** mile
meinen to be of the opinion, to mean, to suppose
meist most, mostly
melden to report
der **Mensch, -en, -en** human being, man, person
die **Menschenliebe** love of one's fellow man, philanthropy
das **Menschenrecht, -(e)s, -e** human right
das **Menschentum, -s** mankind
die **Menschheit** humanity, mankind, human race
menschlich human
messen (mißt), maß, hat gemessen to measure
die **Messestadt, ¨-e** trade fair city
mich me
die **Milch** milk
das **Militär, -s** military
minder less
der **Mißbrauch, -s, ¨-e** abuse, misuse
mißbräuchlich improper, wrong
der **Mißerfolg, -(e)s, -e** failure
die **Mißgeburt, -en** badly deformed person/animal, monstrosity, misbegotten cross
der **Mißratene, -n, -n** misfit
mit with
das **Mitleid, -(e)s** compassion, pity
mit·leiden (leidet mit), litt mit, hat mitgelitten to suffer with
mittags in the afternoon
die **Mitte** the middle
das **Mittel, -s, -** means
das **Mitteleuropa, -s** central Europe
der **Mittelpunkt, -(e)s, -e** center
das **Möbel, -s, -** (piece of) furniture
möchten would like (subjunctive)
das **Modell, -(e)s, -e** model
mögen (mag), mochte, hat gemocht to like to
möglich possible
die **Möglichkeit, -en** possibility, opportunity
der **Monat, -(e)s, -e** month
der **Mond, -(e)s, -e** moon
der **Montag, -(e)s, -e** Monday
die **Moral** morality, morals
moralinfrei free of moral hypocrisy
der **Mord, -(e)s, -e** murder
morgen tomorrow
der **Morgen, -s** morning
morgens in the morning
müde tired, weary, drowsy
die **Mühe, -n** trouble, pains, toil
München Munich
der **Mund, -(e)s, ¨-er** mouth
die **Mundart, -en** dialect
der **Musiker, -s, -** musician
müssen (muß), mußte, hat gemußt must, to have to
der **Mut, -(e)s** courage
die **Mutter, ¨-** mother
die **Muttersprache** mother tongue
der **Mythos, Mythus, -, Mythen** (pl.) myth

N

nach for, after, from, according to, toward
der **Nachbar, -s, -n** neighbor
das **Nachbarland, -(e)s, ¨-er** neighboring country
nach·denken (denkt nach), dachte nach, hat nachgedacht to reflect, ponder
der **Nachfolger, -s, -** successor, follower
nach·forschen to investigate
nachmittags in the afternoon
nächst next
der **Nächste (-r), -n, -n** neighbor, the next (person)
die **Nacht, ¨-e** night
die **Nachtarbeit, -en** night work
die **Nachtmannschaft, -en** night shift
das **Nachtpersonal, -(e)s** night staff

die **Nachtzeit** nighttime
nach·weisen (weist nach), wies nach, hat nachgewiesen to point out, to prove
nackt naked
nah near, closely
die **Nahrung** food
der **Name, -ns, -n** name
nämlich namely, that is (to say), because
die **Nase, -n** nose
natürlich naturally
neben beside, next to
der **Neger, -s, -** negro
nehmen (nimmt), nahm, hat genommen to take
nennen (nennt), nannte, hat genannt to call, to name
neu new, recent, modern
neun nine
neunjährig nine-year-old
neunzehnjährig nineteen-year-old
nicht not
nichts nothing
nichts anderes nothing else
nie never
die **Niederlage** defeat
die **Niederlande** the Netherlands
sich niederlassen (läßt sich nieder), ließ sich nieder, hat sich niedergelassen to settle down
niemand nobody, no one
das **Niveau, -s, -s** level
noch still, yet; nor (see **weder**)
noch etwas one thing more, something else, anything else
das **Nomadenvolk, -(e)s, ̈-er** nomadic people
nominell nominal
der **Norden, -s** north
nordöstlich northeastern
die **Nordsee** the North Sea
nötig necessary
die **Notsituation, -en** state of distress, state of emergency
notwendig necessary, necessarily, urgent
die **Nummer, -n** number
nun now, at present
nunmehr now, by this time
nur only, merely, but, just
nur noch still, only just, barely
der **Nutzen, -s** advantage, profit, benefit

O

die **Oberfläche, -n** surface
obig above (mentioned), former
obwohl although
der **Odem, -s,** *no pl.* (poetical) breath
oder or
offen open, unclosed, not shut
offenbar obvious, evident, apparent
öffentlich open(ly), (in) public
der **Offizier, -s, -e** officer
oft often, frequently, many times
der **Ogowe** a river in Africa
ohne without
ohne alle und jede politische Erziehung without any kind of political education
ohne allen und jeden politischen Willen without any kind of political will
ökonomisch economic(al)
ordnen to arrange, to order, to organize
die **Ordnung, -en** order, putting in order, tidiness
der **Ostdeutsche (-r), -n, -n** East German (person), inhabitant of East Germany
das **Ostdeutschland, -s** East Germany
der **Osten, -s** east
das **Österreich, -s** Austria
osteuropäisch East European
die **Ostsee** the Baltic Sea

P

packen to seize, to pack
die **Pappel, -n** poplar
die **Partei, -en** party, faction
Partei ergreifen to espouse a cause
der **Parteifunktionär, -s, -e** party official
der **Parteikampf, -(e)s, ̈-e** party struggle
der **Pazifismus** pacifism
die **Persönlichkeit, -en** individual
der **Pfaffe, -n, -n** parson, priest (pejorative)
der **Pfarrer, -s, -** pastor, clergyman, parson
das **Phänomen, -s, -e** phenomenon
die **Phantasie, -n** imagination, fancy, tale, fiction
der **Philosophengang, -es, ̈-e** philosopher's walk
plagen to plague, to pester, to bother, to worry, to torment

platt shallow, level, flat, even
der **Platz, -es, ⸚e** place, locality
das **Polen, -s** Poland
die **Politik** politics
der **Politiker, -s, -** politician
politisch political, politic
der **Polizeidiener, -s, -** policeman
das **Polizeigericht, -(e)s, -e** police court
der **Polizeirichter, -s, -** police magistrate
praktisch practical, pragmatic, practically
preisen (preist), pries, hat gepriesen to praise, to glorify
das **Preußen, -s** Prussia
preußisch Prussian
das **Prinzip, -s, -ien** principle
privatissime (Latin) most private
die **Produktionskosten** (pl.) costs of production
der **Professor, -s, -en** professor
die **Projektion, -en** projection
der **Proletarier, -s, -** proletarian
proportional in proportion, proportionately
die **Provinz, -en** province
das **Prozent, -(e)s, -e** percent
der **Punkt, -(e)s, -e** point

Q

die **Qual, -en** pain, torment, pang, agony
sich quälen to work oneself to death, to agonize
quer across

R

rasend furious, mad
die **Rasse, -n** race, breed, stock
die **Rassenhygiene** eugenics
die **Rassenmischung, -en** miscegenation
die **Rassenschande, -n** racial defilement
der **Rat, -(e)s, ⸚e** advice, counsel
ratlos baffled, at a loss, helpless
die **Ratlosigkeit** perplexity
das **Raubtier, -(e)s, -e** beast of prey
der **Raum, -(e)s, ⸚e** space, area, expanse, room
der **Rausch, -es, -e** intoxication, inebriation, ecstasy
das **Rauschen** rustle
recht right
das **Recht, -(e)s, -e** right
die **Rede, -n** speech, address, oration
reden to speak
regelmäßig regular, regularly, well regulated, orderly
der **Regen, -s** rain
die **Regierung, -en** government
das **Register, -s, -** record, register, list
reiben (reibt), rieb, hat gerieben to rub
das **Reich, -(e)s, -e** empire
der **Reiche (-r), -n, -n** rich person
reichen (bis/an) to extend (to)
die **Reichsgesetzgebung, -en** legislation of the Reich
der **Reichstag, -(e)s** Parliament (1871–1945)
die **Reichstagsrede, -n** speech made before the Reichstag
die **Reihe, -n** series, row
rein pure, purely, clean
die **Reinerhaltung** preservation of purity
reinigen to cleanse
die **Relativitätstheorie** theory of relativity
der **Religionsphilosoph, -en, -en** religious philosopher
der **Renaissance-Stil, -(e)s** Renaissance style
retten to save, to rescue, to preserve, to deliver
die **Rettung, -en** deliverance, rescue, saving
richten to judge, to try, to sentence, to arrange, to set (right)
der **Richter, -s, -** judge
richtig true, right, real
rieseln to ripple, to murmur
der **Rock, -(e)s, ⸚e** coat, skirt
das **Rohr, -(e)s, -e** cane, pipe, reed, tube
die **Rolle, -n** role
die **Romanen** Neo-Latin people (Romance nations)
romanisch neo-Latin
Romaunsch Romansh, Romansch
der **Römer, -s, -** Roman (person)
die **Römerzeit** the time of the Romans
die **Rücksicht, -en** consideration, regard, respect
die **Ruhe** rest, quiet, peace, calm
die **Ruheperiode, -n** period of rest, lull, pause
ruhig calm, quiet, peaceful
rühren to move, to stir, to affect, to touch
das **Rumänien, -s** Rumania

das **Rußland, -s** Russia
die **Rüstung, -en** armor, armament, (military) equipment

S

die **Saat, -en** seed
die **Sache, -n** thing
das **Sachsen, -s** Saxony
die **Sage, -n** legend, fable, myth
sagen to tell, to say, to express
der **Samen, -s, -** seed
das **Samenkorn, -(e)s, ¨-er** seed
sammeln to collect
der **Samstag, -(e)s, -e** Saturday
sämtlich all
die **Sanduhr, -en** hourglass
Sapere aude! (Latin) Dare to know!
der **Satz, -es, ¨-e** sentence, tenet
sauer sour
der **Schade(n), -ns, ¨-n** damage, harm, injury
schädigen to wrong, to prejudice
schädlich damaging, injurious, detrimental
schaffen (schafft), schuf, hat geschaffen to bring, to pass, to create
die **Schande, -n** disgrace, defilement, shame
der **Scharfrichter, -s, -** executioner, hangman
schätzen to value, to estimate, to esteem
schauen to look, to see, to observe
scheinen (scheint), schien, hat geschienen to shine, to appear, to seem
die **Scheu** shyness, awe
das **Schicksal, -(e)s, -e** fate, destiny, fortune
schier nearly, almost, just about
die **Schlächterei, -en** slaughter, butchery
die **Schlafbaracke, -n** sleeping quarters, dormitory
die **Schläfe, -n** temple
schlafen (schläft), schlief, hat geschlafen to sleep, to be asleep
schlecht bad, badly, poor, poorly
schlechthin simply
schließlich finally, in conclusion
schlucken to swallow, to gulp, to drink (down)
schlummern to slumber, to lie dormant
schmal narrow, slim, thin
der **Schmerz, -e(n)s, -en** pain, ache, sorrow, grief, anguish
schmerzlich painful, aching
die **Schmiede, -n** forge
der **Schnee, -s** snow
die **Schokolade, -n** chocolate
schon no doubt, surely, already, as early as
schön beautiful
die **Schönheit, -en** beauty
der **Schöpfer, -s, -** creator, Creator (God)
schöpferisch creative, inventive, original
der **Schöpferwille, -ns** creative will
die **Schöpfung, -en** creation
der **Schrecken, -s, -** terror, fright, alarm, shock
schrecklich frightful, dreadful, terrible, awful
das **Schreiben, -s** writing, letter
der **Schreiber, -s, -** scribe, writer (of a letter), clerk
die **Schuld, -en** guilt, fault, blame
der **Schüler, -s, -** pupil, schoolboy, student, disciple
die **Schürze, -n** apron
das **Schurzfell, -(e)s, -e** leather apron
der **Schutz, -es** (no pl.) protection, defense
schwach weak, feeble, frail
der **Schwache (-r), -n, -n** weakling
die **Schwäche, -n** weakness, feebleness, frailty, infirmity
schwanken to waver, to wave to and fro, to totter
schwarz black, dark
der **Schwarze (-r), -n, -n** negro, black man
der **Schweiß, -es** sweat, perspiration
die **Schweiz** Switzerland
schwer serious, difficult, hard, heavy
die **Schwermut, -(e)s** melancholy, sadness, dejection
der **Schwerpunkt, -(e)s, -e** emphasis, stress, focal point, center of gravity
schwerverständlich difficult to understand
schwierig difficult, hard, delicate, tough
die **Schwierigkeit, -en** difficulty
der **Schwindel, -s** humbug, swindle, fraud
sechs six
die **Seele, -n** soul
der **Seelsorger, -s, -** pastor
sehen (sieht), sah, hat gesehen to look, to view, to see
sehr very
sei es be it
sein (ist), war, ist gewesen to be
sein his, its
das **Sein, -s** being, existence, essence, true nature

die **Seinen** (pl.) his loved ones, his family
seinetwegen because of him
seit since
seitdem since then, from that time, ever after
selber myself, himself, yourself, themselves, etc.
selbst oneself, myself, yourself, etc.; even (adv.)
selbständig independent, self-reliant
selbstverschuldet self-imposed
selten seldom, rare, unusual
der **Sessel, -s, -** armchair, seat
setzen to place, to set, to put
sich himself, herself, itself, themselves, yourself, yourselves, oneself, each other
sicher sure, certain, secure, safe
sicherlich surely
sichern to secure, to steady, to fortify, to safeguard, to protect, to guarantee
sie she, her, it, they, them
sieben seven
der **Sinn, -es, -e** meaning, mind, sense, intellect
sitzen (**sitzt**)**, saß, hat gesessen** to sit
der **Skandinavier, -s, -** Scandinavian (person)
der **Slawe, -n, -n** Slav (person)
slawisch Slavic
die **Slowakei,** Slovakia
das **Slowenien, -s** Slovenia
so so, thus, therefore, then
so ein, so eine such a
sogar even
sogenannt so-called, as it is called
sogleich immediately
der **Sohn, -(e)s, ⸚e** son
solange as long as
solch ein such a
der **Soldat, -en, -en** soldier
sollen (**soll**)**, sollte, hat gesollt** to be obliged, to be supposed to
sonderbar strange, singular, peculiar, odd
sondern but
die **Sonne, -n** sun
sonstig other, former
die **Sorge, -n** care, grief, sorrow, anxiety
sorgen to care for, to take care of, to look after
soviel so much
der **Sozialethiker, -s, -** social moralist
der **Sozialismus** socialism
spalten to split, to divide
spärlich scanty, frugal, meager
spät late
spazieren (aux. **sein**) to walk (leisurely), to stroll
das **Spazierengehen** going for a walk
der **Spiegel, -s, -** mirror, reflector
spielen to play
die **Spitze, -n** head, point, top
die **Sprache, -n** language
sprachlich linguistic(ally)
sprechen (**spricht**)**, sprach, hat gesprochen** to speak, to talk
springen to jump, to leap
der **Sprung, -(e)s, ⸚e** jump, leap
spüren to feel, to notice
der **Staat, -(e)s, -en** the state, government
das **Staatsleben, -s** life of a state, political life
der **Staatsmann, -es, ⸚er** statesmen
staatsmännisch statesmanlike
die **Staatsordnung, -en** political system, political order
die **Stadt, ⸚e** town, city
der **Stahlfabrikant, -en, -en** steel manufacturer
der **Stamm, -(e)s, ⸚e** tribe, race, family
stammen to come from, to stem from, to be descended from
ständig constant, continuously
der **Standpunkt, -(e)s, -e** point of view
stark strong, stout, large, great
die **Stärke** strength, force, robustness
der **Stärkere** (**-r**)**, -n, -n** stronger one (person)
statt instead of
statt·finden (**findet statt**)**, fand statt, hat stattgefunden** to take place
stehen (**steht**)**, stand, hat gestanden** to stand, to remain standing, to be, to stop
stehlen (**stiehlt**)**, stahl, hat gestohlen** to steal
steigern to raise, to heighten
stellen to put, to place
sterben (**stirbt**)**, starb, ist gestorben** to die
das **Sterben, -s** (no pl.) death, dying
der **Stern, -(e)s, -e** star
still quiet, calm, motionless, peaceful
das **Stillschweigen, -s** silence
die **Stirne, -n** forehead

stocken to come to a standstill, to falter, to stop
stolz proud, haughty, disdainful
die **Straße, -n** street
die **Strecke, -n** way, distance, stretch, route
auf der Strecke by the wayside
streuen to strew
das **Strohdach, -(e)s, ¨-er** thatched roof
das **Stück, -(e)s, -e** piece, part, portion, fragment, play
die **Stunde, -n** hour
der **Sturm, ¨-(e)s, -e** storm
der **Sturz, -es, ¨-e** fall
suchen to search for, to look for, to seek
der **Süden, -s** south
südeuropäisch South European
südlich southern (to the south)
der **Südosten, -s** southeast
summen to buzz, to hum
der **Sünder, -s, -** sinner

T

der **Tag, -(e)s, -e** day
tagelang for days
die **Tagesarbeit, -en** day's work
die **Tageszeit, -en** time of day
das **Tagewerk, -(e)s** day's work
das **Tal, -(e)s, ¨-er** valley
die **Taschenuhr, -en** pocket watch
die **Tat, -en** act, action, deed, achievement
tätig active, actively
tatsächlich in fact, as a matter of fact
das **Tausend, -s, -e** thousand
tausendjährig millennial
der **Teil, -(e)s, -e** part, piece, portion, section
zum Teil in part, partly
teilbar divisible
teilen to divide
teilweise in part, partial, partially
die **Tendenz, -en** tendency, inclination
der **Teufel, -s, -** devil
der **Theolog(e), -en, -en** theologian
theoretisch theoretical, theoretically
die **These, -n** thesis
tief deep, profound
die **Tiefe, -n** depth, deep, deep place, profoundness, profundity
tief unter dem Niveau far below the level
das **Tier, -(e)s, -e** animal, (dumb) creature, beast, brute
der **Tod, -(e)s, -e** death
das **Tor, -(e)s, -e** gate, gateway, archway, door, goal
der **Tor, -en, -en** fool, simpleton
tot dead
die **Totenschau, -en** coroner's inquest
tragen (trägt), trug, hat getragen to wear, to carry, to bear
der **Traum, -(e)s, ¨-e** dream
treffen (trifft), traf, hat getroffen to strike, to hit, to meet
trennen to divide
treten (tritt), trat, ist (hat) getreten to enter, to step, to walk, to tread, to kick
das **Trommelfeuer, -s** ceaseless bombardment
der **Tropfen, -s, -** drop
trotz in spite of
der **Trotz, -es** spite, defiance, obstinacy
trotzdem nevertheless
trübe gloomy, dejected, sad, downcast, cloudy, overcast
das **Tschechien, -s** the Czech Republic
die **Tschechoslowakei** Czechoslovakia
die **Tuberkel, -n** tubercle
die **Tuberkulose, -n** tuberculosis
die **Tüchtigkeit** efficiency, ability, proficiency
die **Tugend, -en** virtue, good quality
der **Tugendbold,-(e)s,-e** paragon of virtue
tun (tut), tat, hat getan to do, to perform
die **Tür(e), -en** door

U

über over
überdies besides, moreover
überflüssig superfluous
übergehen (übergeht), überging, hat übergangen to overlook, to omit, to skip, to ignore
überhaupt in general, on the whole, altogether, at all
überhaupt nicht not at all
überlassen (überläßt), überließ, hat überlassen to give *or* to yield up, to leave, to abandon
die **Übermacht** supreme power, superiority, superior numbers

der **Übermut, -(e)s** pride, presumption, haughtiness, arrogance
übermütig presumptuous, haughty
übernehmen (übernimmt), übernahm, hat übernommen to take over, to take possession of
überschätzen to overestimate, to overrate
überschreiten (überschreitet), überschritt, hat überschritten to exceed, to overstep
übersehen (übersieht), übersah, hat übersehen to overlook
die **Übertreibung, -en** exaggeration, overstatement
überwachen to watch over, to supervise
überwinden (überwindet), überwand, hat überwunden to overcome
die **Überwindung, -en** overcoming, conquest
die **Uhr, -en** clock, watch, o'clock
das **Uhrwerk, -(e)s, -e** clockwork
um in order to, at, around, about
um·drehen to turn (around), to twist
umfassend extensive, comprehensive
umgeben (umgibt), umgab, hat umgeben to surround, to wall *or* fence in
umgekehrt vice versa, reversed
umgrenzt enclosed
umher·schauen to look around
umringen (umringt), umrang, hat umrungen to surround, to encircle, to enclose
umschließen (umschließt), umschloß, hat umschlossen to surround, to enclose
die **Umwelt** environment, the world around us, milieu
unanwendbar inapplicable, unusable
unaufhaltsam irresistible, unavoidable, unflagging
unbefangen uninhibited, without inhibition
die **Unbefangenheit** ease, simplicity, naiveté
das **Unbehagen, -s** discomfort, uneasiness, qualm
die **Unbill, -bilden** injustice, injury, insult, wrongs
und and
undurchgänglich impassable, blocked
unendlich infinite, endless, boundless
unergründlich unfathomable, inscrutable
unfähig incapable, unfit
unfaßbar inconceivable, incomprehensible
unfruchtbar unfruitful, barren, sterile, unproductive
das **Ungarn, -s** Hungary
ungefähr approximately, roughly, almost, about
der **Ungerechte, -n, -n** unjust *or* unfair person
das **Ungewisse** uncertainty, doubt
das **Ungeziefer, -s** vermin
unglaublich incredible, unbelievable
das **Unglück, -(e)s** accident, misfortune, ill luck, calamity
das **Universum, -s** universe
unmittelbar immediate, direct
unmöglich impossible
unmündig immature
die **Unmündigkeit** immaturity
das **Unrecht, -(e)s** injustice, wrong
unruhig restless, troubled
uns ourselves, us
unschwer (adv). easily, without difficulty; (adj.) easy, not difficult
unser our
unsererseits for our part, as for us
der **Unstern, -(e)s** unlucky *or* evil star, misfortune, disaster, adverse fate
unteilbar indivisible
unter under, among
untereinander together, one (with) another, among one another, each other
unter·gehen (geht unter), ging unter, ist untergegangen to perish, to go down, to become extinct
unterhalten (unterhält), unterhielt, hat unterhalten to entertain, to amuse
unternehmen (unternimmt), unternahm, hat unternommen to undertake, to venture
das **Unterpfand, -(e)s** pledge, pawn, security
der **Unterschied, -(e)s, -e** difference, distinction
untersuchen to examine, to investigate
unteilbar indivisible
das **Unvermögen, -s** inability, incapacity
unwiderruflich irrevocable, irreversible, beyond recall
unwürdig unworthy
die **Ursache, -n** cause, reason, motive, occasion
die **Urtatsache, -n** original fact

der **Urwald, -(e)s, ¨-er** jungle, primeval *or* virgin forest
u.s.w. = und so weiter etc., and so forth

V

der **Vater, -s, ¨-** father
veneratio vitae (Latin) reverence for life
veranlassen to cause, to bring about, to induce
die **Verbindung, -en** union, combination, connection
verbrennen (verbrennt), verbrannte, hat verbrannt to burn up
verbringen (verbringt), verbrachte, hat verbracht to spend, to pass (one's time)
verdächtig suspect, suspicious
verdienen to earn
verdrießlich annoying, vexing, tiresome, troublesome
vereinfacht simplified
vereinigen to unite, to combine
sich verengern to narrow, to shrink
vergangen past, gone
die **Vergangenheit** past, past times
vergeben (vergibt), vergab, hat vergeben to award, to allocate, to give away; to forgive, to pardon
sich vergeben (vergibt sich), vergab sich, hat sich vergeben to compromise oneself
vergeblich (in) vain
vergessen (vergißt), vergaß, hat vergessen to forget
die **Vergessenheit** oblivion
der **Vergleich, -(e)s, -e** comparison, parallel
vergnügt pleased, delighted
das **Verhältnis, -ses, -se** relationship
verheerend devastating
verkaufen to sell
verkündigen to announce, to prophesy, to make known
die **Verlängerung, -en** prolongation, extension, lengthening
verleugnen to deny, to disavow, to renounce
die **Verlogenheit, -en** untruthfulness, mendacity
die **Vermehrung, -en** increase, multiplication
vermeiden (vermeidet), vermied, hat vermieden to avoid, to shun, to evade
vermissen to miss
das **Vermögen, -s, -** ability, power, means
vermuten to suppose, to suspect
vernichten to destroy, to annihilate
der **Vernichtungskrieg, -(e)s, -e** war of extermination
die **Vernunftgründe** (pl.) reasonable grounds
verpassen to miss, to lose by delay, to let slip
verpflichten to obligate, to oblige
die **Verpflichtung, -en** obligation, duty
versäumen to neglect, to miss, to leave undone
sich verschieben (verschiebt sich), verschob sich, hat sich verschoben to change, to shift
verschieden different, various, distinct
verschleiern to veil, to gloss over, to disguise
verschulden to be the cause of, to be guilty of, to blame for
die **Versöhnung, -en** reconciliation
versprechen (verspricht), versprach, hat versprochen to promise
der **Verstand, -es** the faculty of reason, understanding, comprehension, discernment, intelligence
das **Verständnis, -ses** understanding, comprehension, appreciation, perception
verstecken to hide, to conceal
verstehen (versteht), verstand, hat verstanden to understand
die **Verstorbene** deceased one (fem.)
versuchen to try, to attempt, to tempt, to entice
versuchsweise by way of experiment, experimental
verteilen to distribute, to divide, to assign
der **Vertrag, -(e)s, ¨-e** treaty
das **Vertrauen, -s** confidence, trust
vervollständigen to complete, to supplement, to complement
verwerflich reprehensible, objectionable
verwüsten to devastate, to wreck, to ravage
verzehren to consume
verzeihen (verzeiht), verzieh, hat verziehen to forgive
verzichten to renounce, to abandon, to give up, to do without
die **Verzweiflung, -en** despair
das **Vieh, -(e)s** livestock, cattle, animal

viel much, many, a great deal
vielleicht perhaps
vielmehr rather
viert fourth
der **Vierte** (**-r**) fourth one (male person)
das **Vierundzwanzig-Stundensystem, -**(**e**)**s** twenty-four hour system
vierzehn fourteen
der **Viktualienhändler, -s, -** grocer
das **Volk, -**(**e**)**s, ¨-er** people, nation
völkisch national, popular, racial, ethnic, folkish
voll full, full of
vollbringen (**vollbringt**)**, vollbrachte, hat vollbracht** to accomplish
vollends quite, altogether, entirely, wholly
die **Vollendung, -en** completion
vollführen to execute, to carry out
völlig fully
vollkommen perfect
vollständig complete
von of, from, about, by
vor before, in front of, for, from, in the presence of, ago
vor allem above all
vorbei over, completed
vorbei·wandeln to walk past
vorderhand for the time being, for the present
vor·dringen (**dringt vor**)**, drang vor, ist vorgedrungen** to advance, to press forward, to make headway
vor·enthalten (**enthält vor**)**, enthielt vor, hat vorenthalten** to withhold
vorhanden at hand, on hand, ready
das **Vorhandensein, -s** existence, presence
der **Vorhang, -**(**e**)**s, ¨-e** curtain
vorher beforehand, before, in advance
vorig last, previous
sich vorkommen to seem
die **Vorliebe, -n** preference, liking
der **Vormund, -**(**e**)**s, -e & ¨-er** guardian
vornüber·sinken (**sinkt vornüber**)**, sank vornüber, ist vornübergesunken** to sink forwards
das **Vorrecht, -**(**e**)**s, -e** privilege, prerogative, priority
der **Vorschuß, -sses, ¨-sse** (cash) advance
vor·sehen (**sieht vor**)**, sah vor, hat vorgesehen** to provide for
die **Vorsehung** providence
die **Vorstellung, -en** presentation, performance, representation, notion, idea
vorüber over, past
vor·weisen (**weist vor**)**, wies vor, hat vorgewiesen** to display, to show
vorwiegend predominantly, mainly, chiefly

W

wachen to be awake, to watch (over), to care (for)
wachsen (**wächst**)**, wuchs, ist gewachsen** to grow, to expand
die **Waffe, -n** weapon
der **Waffenstillstand, -**(**e**)**s, ¨-e** armistice, ceasefire
wagen to dare
der **Wahlspruch, -**(**e**)**s, ¨-e** motto
wahr true, real, genuine
während during, while
der **Wahrer, -s, -** guardian (of peace)
wahrhaft true, veracious; (adv.) really
wahrlich truly, certainly
wahrscheinlich probable, probably
die **Währung, -en** currency
der **Wald,** (**e**)**s, ¨-er** woods, forest
sich wälzen to roll around, to wallow
das **Walzwerk, -**(**e**)**s, -e** rolling mill
wandeln (vt w/**haben**) to change
wandeln (vi w/**sein**) to walk, to stroll
warten to wait
warum why
was what, whatever
was für what kind of
das **Wasser, -s, -** water
die **Wasserstoffbombe, -n** hydrogen bomb
der **Wechsel, -s, -** alternation, change, rotation
wechseln to vary
weder . . . noch neither . . . nor
der **Weg, -**(**e**)**s, -e** way, path, route
das **Weh, -**(**e**)**s** misery, woe, pain
sich wehren to resist, to defend oneself
weiblich female, womanly, feminine
die **Weiche** softness
weichen (**weicht**)**, wich, ist gewichen** to give way, to yield

die **Weihe, -n** consecration, ordination, inauguration
weil because, since
weislich wisely, prudently
weiß white
die **Weißen** (pl.) the white races
weit wide, immense, far-reaching, distant, far
bei weitem by far
noch weiter still further
weiter·bringen (bringt weiter), brachte weiter, hat weitergebracht to bring further
weiter·gehen (geht weiter), ging weiter, ist weitergegangen to continue, to go on
welcher, welche, welches which, what, that
die **Welt, -en** world
das **Weltall, -s** universe
weltberühmt world-famous
weltbewegend earth-shaking
der **Weltbrand, -es, ¨-e** universal conflagration
die **Weltgeschichte** world history
der **Weltkrieg, -(e)s, -e** world war
die **Weltliteratur** world literature
die **Weltraumaspiration, -en** space aspiration
die **Weltraumfahrt, -en** space travel
weltzermalmend world-crushing
wenig few, little
wenigstens at least
wenn when(ever), if
wer who, he who, whoever
werden (wird), wurde, ist geworden to become
werfen (wirft), warf, hat geworfen to throw
das **Werk, -(e)s, -e** to work, literary work, factory work
der **Wert, -(e)s, -e** worth, value
wertvoll valuable, precious
das **Wesen, -s, -** essence, creature
der **Western, -s, -** western
westlich western, to the west
das **Wetter, -s, -** weather
wichtig important
die **Wichtigkeit** importance
widersprechen (widerspricht), widersprach, hat widersprochen to disagree, to contradict
der **Widerstand,-(e)s, ¨-e** resistance, obstacle
der **Widerstandskämpfer, -s, -** resistance fighter
wie as, like, such, how
wieder again
die **Wiederherstellung** restoration, reestablishment, recovery
wiederholen to repeat
die **Wiedervereinigung** reunification
die **Wiedervereinigungsfrage, -n** question of reunification
Wien Vienna
der **Wiener Vertrag** Vienna Treaty
der **Wille(n), -ns** will
der **Wille zum Leben** the "will-to-live"
winzig tiny
wirken to have an effect
die **Wirkenskraft** actuating force
wirklich real, really, true, truly
wirtschaftlich economic
wissen (weiß), wußte, hat gewußt to know
das **Wissen, -s** knowledge, learning
die **Wissenschaft, -en** science, learning, knowledge
der **Wissenschaftler, -s, -** scientist, man of science *or* learning
wissenschaftlich scientific, learned, scholarly
die **Witwe, -n** widow
wo where
die **Woche, -n** week
das **Wochenende, -s, -n** weekend
woher from where, how
wohl indeed, well, fit
wohnen to live, to dwell
der **Wohnraum, -s, ¨-e** dwelling space, living room
die **Wohnung, -en** apartment
die **Wolke, -n** cloud
wollen (will), wollte, hat gewollt to want, to will, to intend, to be about to
worin wherein, in which
das **Wort, -es, ¨-er** *or* **-e** word
die **Wundererzählung, -en** miraculous tale, legend
das **Wunderkind, -(e)s, -er** child wonder, prodigy
wunderschön beautiful

der **Wunsch, -es, ⸚e** wish
wünschen to wish, to desire, to long for
würdig worthy, suitable
wurzellos without roots

X

x-mal ever so many times, over and over again, umpteen times

Z

der **Zahn, -(e)s, ⸚e** tooth
zehn ten
zeigen to show
die **Zeit, -en** time
das **Zeitalter, -s, -** age, era
zeitgenössisch contemporary
zeitlebens for life
zeitlich temporal, transient, secular
der **Zeitungsartikel -s, -** newspaper article
die **Zeitungsnotiz, -en** newspaper item
das **Zentrum, -s, -tren** center
zerbeißen (zerbeißt), zerbiß, hat zerbissen to bite (to pieces)
zerfallen (zerfällt), zerfiel, ist zerfallen to fall to pieces
zergehen (zergeht), zerging, ist zergangen to disperse, to dissolve
zerlaufen (zerläuft), zerlief, ist zerlaufen to flow, to melt away
zermalmen to crush, to bruise, to crunch
zerrinnen (zerrinnt), zerrann, ist zerronnen to melt away, to dissolve, to pass by
zerschlagen, (zerschlägt), zerschlug, hat zerschlagen to smash (up), crush, break up
zerschneiden (zerschneidet), zerschnitt, hat zerschnitten to cut to pieces *or* through
zerstören to destroy, to demolish
zeugen to generate, to give rise to
ziehen (zieht), zog, hat gezogen to pull, to draw, to tug
das **Ziel, -(e)s, -e** goal, objective
ziemlich pretty, moderate, moderately, fairly, rather
das **Zimmer, -s, -** room
zitieren to summon, to call *or* conjure up, to quote
die **Zivilisation, -en** the civilization
der **Zivilist, -en, -en** civilian
zu too, to, into, at
die **Zucht** discipline, decency, manners, propriety
zueinander towards each other
der **Zufall, -(e)s, ⸚e** chance, accident, coincidence
zufrieden satisfied, content
die **Zufriedenheit** satisfaction, contentment
zu·fügen to add to
der **Zügel, -s, -** rein, bridle
zu·gestehen (gesteht zu), gestand zu, hat zugestanden to concede, to admit, to confess
zugleich simultaneously, also, at the same time
zugrunde gehen (geht zugrunde), ging zugrunde, ist zugrunde gegangen to go to destruction, to perish
zugunsten in favor of, for the benefit of
die **Zukunft** future
zumute sein to feel
zu·nehmen (nimmt zu), nahm zu, hat zugenommen to increase, to grow
zunehmend increasing, growing
sich zurecht·finden (findet sich zurecht), fand sich zurecht, hat sich zurechtgefunden to find one's way about
zurück·kehren to return
zurück·leiten to lead back
zurück·schreiben (schreibt zurück), schrieb zurück, hat zurückgeschrieben to write back
zusammen together
zusammen·brechen (bricht zusammen), brach zusammen, ist zusammengebrochen to break down, to collapse (under), to succumb
zusammen·fassen to concentrate, to summarize, to include
zusammen·halten (hält zusammen), hielt zusammen, hat zusammengehalten to hold together, to keep together

zusammen·hängen (hängt zusammen), hing zusammen, hat zusammengehangen to be connected with
zusammen·laufen (läuft zusammen), lief zusammen, ist zusammengelaufen to run together, to blend
die **Zusammenlegung, -en** the combining of
das **Zusammenrücken** the moving nearer, the coming together
zu·schauen to watch, to look on
zu·sehen (sieht zu), sah zu, hat zugesehen to look on, to watch
der **Zustand, -es, ⸚e** condition, state, position, situation
zustande bringen (bringt zustande), brachte zustande, hat zustande gebracht to bring about
zuverlässig reliable, certain, trustworthy
zuvor before, formerly
zuweilen at times, now and then, occasionally
zu·wenden (wendet zu), wandte zu *or* **wendete zu, hat zugewandt** *or* **zugewendet** to turn towards
zwanzig twenty
zwanzig Jahre vorher twenty years previously
zwar indeed, certainly
zwar . . . jedoch it is true . . . yet
und zwar namely
zwei two
der **Zweifel, -s, -** doubt, disbelief, hesitation
zweifeln to doubt, to have one's doubts about (a thing)
zweit second
der **Zweite Weltkrieg** the Second World War
zwingen (zwingt), zwang, gezwungen to force, to compel
zwischen between, among
zwölf twelve
zwölfstündig twelve hours long

Index

Index prepared by Virginia M. Coombs.